The Psychosocial Interior of the Family

09011 155 704

# The Psychosocial Interior of the Family

*A Sourcebook for the Study of Whole Families*

EDITED BY GERALD HANDEL

*London*
GEORGE ALLEN AND UNWIN LTD

Copyright © 1967 by Gerald Handel

SBN 04 301012 1

PRINTED IN GREAT BRITAIN BY PHOTOLITHOGRAPHY
UNWIN BROTHERS LIMITED, WOKING AND LONDON

"The whole business of science does not lie in getting into realms which are unfamiliar in normal experience. There is an enormous work of analyzing, of recognizing similarities and analogies, of getting the feel of the landscape, an enormous qualitative sense of family relations, of taxonomy. It is not always tactful to try to quantify; it is not always clear that by measuring one has found something very much worth measuring. It is true that for the Babylonians it was worth measuring—noting— the first appearances of the moon because it had a practical value. Their predictions, their prophecies, and their magic would not work without it; and I know that many psychologists have the same kind of reason for wanting to measure. It is a real property of the real world that you are measuring, but it is not necessarily the best way to advance true understanding of what is going on; and I would make this very strong plea for pluralism with regard to methods that, in the necessarily early stages of sorting out an immensely vast experience, may be fruitful and may be helpful."

—ROBERT OPPENHEIMER

# Preface

This book is offered both as a conceptual contribution to the study of the family and as a textbook for a variety of theoretical and applied fields. To research workers—in social, clinical, personality, and developmental psychology; family sociology; psychiatry; and culture and personality and perhaps other fields of anthropology—the book provides a body of materials and a framework that will, I hope, serve to advance their own investigations. At the same time, it is not a monograph, but rather a collection of varied writings organized to present a wide and systematic view of a rapidly developing field. It should therefore prove suitable as a textbook, not only for academic courses in the social sciences but also for several fields of practice—psychiatry, social work, marriage and family counseling, and the rapidly growing field of family therapy.

The book is organized to show that a great diversity of work carried on in an apparently unrelated fashion constitutes in fact the nucleus of a potentially coherent though far-reaching field of family study. Part I presents a general framework for analysis of whole families that draws upon several streams of thought in social science (including psychology) and psychoanalysis. Part II illustrates and discusses methods by which the psychosocial interior of the family can be and is studied. This section on method is placed early in the book so that the reader can quickly see the research tools that are increasingly making this a manageable field of study rather than merely a vaguely idealized goal.

Part III presents what I believe is a rather novel view of the relationship of the family to culture and society. It shows the family as active rather than passive in relation to society and culture, or, more precisely, as a selective agent that screens and adapts what the culture and society make broadly available. Part IV continues this emphasis on the family's selectivity in its relations with the extrafamilial world. Specifically, it deals with the ways in which families create boundaries to their own worlds, and it demonstrates that the kinds of boundaries a family creates for itself are highly significant for the life course of its members. Next, Part V shows something of the ways in which families constitute worlds of perception, belief, and communication.

Part VI focuses upon patterns of separateness and connectedness in the family. This term is not simply a cumbersome substitute for the more familiar term, "patterns of interpersonal relations." In contrast, the term I use is intended to call attention to the fact that what a person is to and for himself is intertwined with what he is to and for others. Part VI shows how some separateness-connectedness patterns develop and some of the diverse forms they take. Finally, Part VII analyzes and evaluates what has been accomplished thus far in studying the psychosocial interior of the family from a holistic standpoint, as well as suggesting some future directions.

The writings included in this book are reprinted without alteration, except for obvious typographical errors in the originals. My aim has been to provide the reader with as full an acquaintance with this field as can be accomplished within the confines of an anthology. For this reason, not only have the footnotes been retained but also the cross references, so that the reader who is stimulated to pursue a topic in the context of its original publication will find his way facilitated. This is particularly pertinent, of course, for those writings taken from previously published books.

Originally, the book was to include a section on family therapy. Unfortunately, the excessive length of the first draft necessitated some drastic cutting, and I decided to delete this section on the ground that while books and articles on family therapy are now appearing in some profusion, a presentation of a general social psychology of the family has not yet been made elsewhere.

# Contents

Introduction ................................................................ 1

PART I: A FRAMEWORK FOR ANALYSIS

1. The Family as a Psychosocial Organization
   *Robert D. Hess* and *Gerald Handel* ................................ 10

PART II: RESEARCH METHODS

2. My Life with the Families of Psychotic Children
   *Jules Henry* .......................................................... 30
3. Some Comments on Method
   *Robert D. Hess* and *Gerald Handel* ................................ 46
4. Family Experiments: A New Type of Experimentation
   *Jay Haley* ............................................................ 54
5. The Family as a Three-Person Group
   *Fred L. Strodtbeck* .................................................. 80
6. Prediction of Family Interaction from a Battery of
   Projective Techniques
   *Dorothy Terry Sohler, Jules D. Holzberg, Stephen
   Fleck, Alice R. Cornelison, Eleanor Kay,* and
   *Theodore Lidz* ....................................................... 90
7. Analysis of Correlative Meaning: The TAT in the Study
   of Whole Families
   *Gerald Handel* ....................................................... 104

A*  ix

PART III: THE FAMILY AS MEDIATOR OF THE CULTURE

8. An Anthropological Approach to Family Studies
   *Oscar Lewis* .................................................................. 131
9. Urban Families: The Norms of Conjugal Roles
   *Elizabeth Bott* ............................................................. 141
10. Neurotic Patterns in the Family
    *E. J. Cleveland* and *W. D. Longaker* .................................. 159

PART IV: THE MEANINGS OF FAMILY BOUNDARIES

11. Extended Family Relations of Disturbed and Well
    Families
    *Norman W. Bell* ........................................................... 189
12. The Closed Circuit: The Study of a Delinquent Family
    *G. W. Elles* ................................................................. 206
13. The Family and the Idea of a Cardinal Role
    *Harold Fallding* .......................................................... 220

PART V: THE FAMILY AS A UNIVERSE OF COGNITION AND
        COMMUNICATION

14. The Family of the Schizophrenic: A Model System
    *Jay Haley* .................................................................. 251
15. Intrafamilial Environment of the Schizophrenic Patient:
    The Transmission of Irrationality
    *Theodore Lidz, Alice Cornelison, Dorothy Terry
    Carlson,* and *Stephen Fleck* ......................................... 276
16. Differential Patterns of Social Outlook and
    Personality in Family and Children
    *Else Frenkel-Brunswik* ................................................. 292

PART VI: PATTERNING SEPARATENESS AND
         CONNECTEDNESS

17. New Light on the Honeymoon
    *Rhona Rapoport* and *Robert N. Rapoport* ....................... 332
18. Crucible of Identity: The Negro Lower-Class Family
    *Lee Rainwater* ............................................................ 362
19. The Family in Psychosomatic Process
    *James L. Titchener, Jules Riskin,* and *Richard
    Emerson* .................................................................... 401
20. The Emotionally Disturbed Child as the Family
    Scapegoat
    *Ezra F. Vogel* and *Norman W. Bell* .............................. 424

21. Pseudo-Mutuality in the Family Relations of
Schizophrenics
*Lyman C. Wynne, Irving M. Ryckoff, Juliana Day,*
and *Stanley I. Hirsch* ............................................................ 443

PART VII: RETROSPECT AND PROSPECT

22. Family Interaction Processes and Schizophrenia:
A Review of Current Theories
*Elliot G. Mishler* and *Nancy E. Waxler* ............................. 469
23. Psychological Study of Whole Families
*Gerald Handel* ........................................................................ 517

Index ................................................................................. 551

The Psychosocial Interior of the Family

# Introduction

This book is an effort to delineate, by way of diverse writings, a social psychology of the family that seeks to capture and comprehend the interplay of self and collectivity in family life. The family is at once a significant source of individuality and the expression of the most binding ties in social life. It is thereby doubly—and conflictfully—imperative to its members. The book tries to mark out some ideas, concepts, data, and research methods that can get us under way in the study of these intricate phenomena.

By its very nature as an anthology, this book cannot pretend to offer a comprehensive—or even a limited and unified—theory. Indeed, neither the data nor the concepts from which such a theory could be built are as yet available. But the book does propose a view of what must some day be encompassed. It envisages a social psychology that integrates data now scattered over a range of disciplines—biology, sociology, anthropology, psychology, psychiatry—and numerous specialties within them. The section headings are themselves a first array of rudimentary concepts for identifying subfields within this newly developing field. And the variegated writings indicate some of the ways these topics can be thought about, investigated, and utilized in practical applications. The book includes work from such diverse fields as psychosomatic medicine and experimental social psychology, to cite just two indicators of the range.

The province of the book is the psychosocial interior of the family. This means that attention is most fully given to what the family is to and for itself and its members rather than what it is to and for the larger society. The psychosocial interior is that region of the universe where the members of a family meet and make a life together. It is a region of the mind, that "place" where there is a meeting of minds primarily in the sense of individual selves confronting, engaging, and being struck off from

1

one another, rather than in the usual sense of reaching agreement through rational discussion.

It is no less a region where there is a meeting of bodies and of body and mind. For in no other human group does the body play such a decisive role in both the formation and the outcome of relationships. The family is not only the primary locus of sexuality; it is also the group where the body and its functions are given their first meanings, where touch has its freest rein and serves to unite or alienate, where eating becomes social and elimination is trained, where tension and relaxation take on their initial character. Respiration, digestion, endocrine secretion, and muscle tone become responsive to the moods and communications of other family members. Hearing and sight acquire their first power as well as their first subject matter in the family. Here too the child first tries out his reach, his gait, his pace, and his rhythm, and he learns how these are received. Details of physiognomy are given a lineage in efforts to determine which side of his family a child "favors," and relationships are structured by judgments that a daughter is more beautiful or less beautiful than her mother or sisters. Height, weight, and girth are given meaning in terms of lineage, beauty, strength, and developmental course. In the family, more pervasively than in other social groups, bodies enter into the formation of relationships and of the self. The child learns what his body means to others, and from these meanings and his own experiencings of it, he develops his own bodily meanings.

The psychosocial interior of the family is not an isolated realm. It is a region of a larger social world. But whereas a purely sociological concern directs attention to what the society in its various forms does to the family, this book directs attention in the opposite direction. It focuses upon families in their own formative powers. Families do not merely reflect the larger culture and social structure; they create meanings and relationships and individualities, not all of them welcomed by the larger society. Families utilize the broader culture in differential ways, sometimes to their own detriment. And, as some selections in this book show, families can be more or less involved with the larger society. They have their own ways of defining themselves and their boundaries.

Thus, this book is concerned not with the family as an institution but with families as living groups, within which the members create relationships even as each proceeds on his individual life course. The themes of individuality and collectivity are pervasive in the selections, and, broadly speaking, illuminate the reciprocal problems of individuality as a product of group life and the family's corporate character as a product of its members' individuality. The book brings together various efforts to define and understand the corporate character of families, the ways by which they create worlds of their own, with particular kinds of boundaries separating them from the larger world and particular kinds of climates for their members. The nature of family cohesion or integration is thus a central topic, and the reader will not take long to discover that no simple unidimensional scale or index is adequate to tell us what we need to know to understand such phenomena. The data reported in these writings make manifest that there is no such simple thing as family integration that exists only in degrees of more or less. The phenomena push us, at least at this necessarily early stage, toward the conceiving of *kinds* of integration. Before we shall ever arrive at any useful index, we shall have to grapple with the question: "What are the different ways in which a family can be a family, even within the same segment of society?" There are surely many ways of being a middle-class American family, but what are they? We now presume that some ways are schizophrenic, some are neurotic, and some are pathological in other directions, even though we are not yet sure why they are. Even after we turn our attention from these deviant ways, we shall want to know the different ways of being a normal or nonclinical middle-class or working-class American or English family. In short, within any major social category or aggregate—tribe, ethnic group, social class, or whatever—there is family diversity that we must presume is not random but responsive to organizing principles whose nature is only now becoming dimly apparent to us.

Any family thus has its own corporate character, and this book points to the tasks facing us in our efforts to discern diverse characters and comprehend the processes by which they are established and maintained. It also presents a variety of efforts that have been made to deal with these tasks. The first task is often finding families to study, particularly nonclinic families in Western societies. Studies that seek to probe into the interior of family life require extended cooperation over a period of time. It can be time-consuming simply to locate cooperative families meeting certain criteria of composition. This problem is less difficult for clinical investigators since they ordinarily study families who have sought help and who have therefore made themselves available, at least in some degree.

Another task is finding ways to make observations of families. In this work we are still trying to decide what observations are worth making, what situations seem promising of useful data. Not enough work has gone on to assess the relative value of different vantage points and procedures, partly because not enough conceptual work has yet been accomplished. As soon as we cite the problem of making useful observations, straightway we face the problem of what criteria enable us to judge whether observations are useful. At this point in the development of this field, we must recognize that we are not yet in a position to sustain rigid criteria of inclusion and exclusion. Yet we must and can have a sense of direction. We must press toward making observations that will enable us to understand how a family creates, maintains, and evolves its own corporate character and how it utilizes the individuality of its members as it does so. The goal of such a program must be to discover principles for intrafamilial organization, principles that account both for the structure and developmental course of the family and for the several developmental courses of its members, insofar as these are family-determined.

Methodologically, the book focuses on efforts to study families as wholes. This does not mean that I believe it is not worthwhile to study less-than-whole-family relationships. The exclusion of such segmental studies would be absurd. Obviously, much has been learned, and more can be, by studying husband-wife, mother-child, and father-child relationships. And the greatest immediate proportionate advance perhaps await us if we study sibling relationships, for it seems to me that we know next to nothing about these. Such massive handbooks as those edited by Mussen[1] and Christensen[2] have very little to say on this subject.

The study of families as wholes in many ways goes against the traditions of psychiatry and the prevailing modes of thought of psychology. It is perhaps more congenial to the thoughtways of sociology and anthropology, although even in anthropology the study of groups as wholes is evidently sometimes felt to conflict with what are considered the imperatives of science. In introducing his book on the little community, Robert Redfield writes:

"The point of departure is a certain strain or struggle, so to speak, between the claims of the human whole—person or village or civilization—to communicate to us its nature as a whole, a convincing complex entity, on the one hand, and the disposition of science to take things apart and move toward the precise description of relationships between parts and parts, on the other. Human wholes persist through time, each one preserving, for years or centuries, a certain unique character which one may come to know through personal experience or reading. Each person, each stable human settlement with an organized way of life, each historical people, even each art or body of literature associated with such a people, has a sort of integrity which is recognized both by common sense and by much scholarship, humanistic or anthropological. Yet each of these entities arouses the disposition to make acquaintance with such things into more strictly controlled knowledge about them. We want, also, to compare one community or one personality with another. What shall be the forms of thought that will help us toward this more strictly controlled knowledge, a knowledge that will preserve some of the holistic qualities of the things compared?"[3]

The need to maintain a hold on the holistic qualities of families is obvious to me, and I believe most, if not all, of the writers whose work is included in this book would concur. To be sure, the understanding of segmental relationships within the family is a difficult enough task,[4] but this is no reason to assume that we cannot embark on the study of families as wholes until we have definitively understood the nature of the one-to-one relationships within the family. In the first place, that day of ultimate understanding will never come. In the second, there are no adequate grounds for believing that the understanding of more complex units is a simple additive process of understanding its component parts.[5]

Third, and perhaps most important, families exist as wholes. Prototypically, they consist of a group of people inhabiting a common household over an extended period of time. A family is, therefore, a naturally occurring unit, and it has at least this much in common with a molecule or the solar system, however significant may be its differences in other respects. As a unit that occurs in nature, which expresses the social nature of man, the family invites our interest at its own level of organization and in its own complexity. Just as it is of interest to inquire into the nature of the marital bond or the mother-child relationship, it is equally of interest and equally pertinent to want to know what the bonds are that obtain in a family as a group. Many clinical investigators are coming to believe, or at least to adopt as a working assumption, that mental illness is a function of the bonds operative in a family as a whole. While this view may thus far be no more than an article of faith, it is an article of faith whose tenability merits extended scrutiny through research, for it cannot be said that any competing view of the origins of mental illness has established itself beyond reasonable doubt.

The concept of studying families as wholes has two different, though related, meanings. On the one hand, it refers to the developing of concepts and theories about families as entities. Of course, at the level of ordinary discourse we already make use of such concepts when we speak of the Bachs as a musical family or the Kennedys as an energetic or hard-driving family. We recognize such corporate characteristics among our neighbors as well as among the celebrated. We know sports-minded families and intellectual families, flamboyant families and secretive families, orderly families and disorderly ones, lively families and dispirited, money-minded, affectionate, conflictful, and so on. Such characterizations may not take us very far, but at least they enable us to form some initial impressions about families as corporate entities. Perhaps it would be premature to dismiss surface characteristics as starting points for more searching inquiries, and, in the case of families whose life style appears to be dominated by a particular quality or commitment, we could do worse than take those qualities as starting points. Within the realm of normal families, such visible characteristics can serve as the equivalent of what the psychiatrist or the physician calls presenting symptoms, an introductory function on the way to investigating more hidden qualities.

One meaning of the study of whole families is, then, the analysis of families as wholes. A different but related meaning of the term is obtaining data from each member of the family. If we intend to study how families are organized, I do not see how we can do so without data from all the family members. I think this is particularly true for studies of the nuclear family, where the task is not impossible, even though it may be difficult. The study of extended families is obviously somewhat different in character since their very extension makes it unlikely that data from all members would be relevant, even if it were possible to obtain them, which it is ordinarily not. Thus, in the study of extended families the definition of the problem will determine the selection of persons from whom data are to be obtained.

An understanding of the nuclear family can be fully developed, however, only if we learn from each member what he is like. Intrafamilial relationships are interlocking and contingent upon one another. The relationship of husband and wife both affects and is affected by the relationship of each to each child. Further, I think we need to study the individuality of each member as a component of intrafamilial functioning. It is a common observation that two children in a family can resemble their parents in personality yet be different from each other. Would it not be useful to have in mind the genetic principle that explains biological differences among offspring in terms of the independent assortment and combination of genes from the parents? Something analogous seems to occur in psychosocial development. Each child in a family may draw upon or identify with different aspects of each parent; a parent may make different aspects of himself available to each child. Although we have here a statement of a problem, I do not believe that we yet have very much idea of the principles accounting for such psychosocial assortment within the family, nor do I see how we may acquire firm knowledge about such matters without obtaining data from each family member.

The concepts of the psychosocial interior of the family and the study of whole families are, then, related. The first refers to the kinds of phenomena to be studied, and the second designates both the kinds of concepts that are aimed at and the sources of the data that will provide material for fashioning these concepts. The articles in this book exemplify one or the other or both of these two overarching concepts. They were selected because they were thought to contribute toward answering such questions as:

—What is the nature of a family's collective life?
—How is the family's character as a collectivity fashioned from the several individualities of its members?
—How does each family member relate to and express the family's collective character?
—How does each member take his "family-ness" and use it in the larger world?

—How do family processes contribute to good or poor mental health?
—By what methods and techniques can family processes be studied?

The readings are grouped together in sections that are intended to point toward a set of dimensions that would be useful in studying any particular kind of family. Thus the writings are not divided according to prevailing clinical or sociological categories. My aim has been, rather, to utilize papers built around such specific categories to suggest certain generic dimensions of family organization.

The papers reveal certain predilections. They represent, first, my views of what ought to be encompassed in this new field of whole family study—what its subject matter and scope ought to be—insofar as these are exemplified in extant writings known to me.

The selections represent also my view of where this field of study stands today. Most of the papers included do not express research findings in quantitative form. Although I certainly do not rule out quantitative or experimental work in a newly emerging field of study, as this one is, I believe that beginning work needs to be predominantly qualitative.[6] To hold, as I think many do, that one has no science until one can quantify is to commit what I would call the fallacy of misplaced exactness. It is first necessary to locate and identify the phenomena to be studied and to discriminate what is worth measuring, as well as what is important but cannot be measured. There seems to be an increasingly prevalent view in the social sciences that the only proper form for a scientific question is: "How does the amount of something vary with the amounts of other things?" But the first question that must be asked is: *"What* is there?" This may be followed by a question no less scientific in form than the quantitative variation question: "What kinds are there?" Then: "What is the pattern or structure of each kind?" Understandably, I was pleased to come upon the words of Robert Oppenheimer that serve as the epigraph, for we are in the "necessarily early stages of sorting out an immensely vast experience."[7] That sorting will have to make use of a variety of types of observation obtained under a variety of conditions. I think that we do not yet know very fully, much less very exactly, what we should be looking for when we try to study whole families, although I think the readings in this volume provide a substantial number of very good beginnings. Consequently, I believe that our contemporary emphasis should be upon making as wide a range of observations as possible, in line with the tasks I have tried to define, and upon developing fruitful and adequate concepts for what we observe. Let measurement and experimentation play their part—and no doubt they will play a growing part as time goes on— but let us not suppose that they will suffice in this field in our time.

The psychosocial interior of the family is still "a far country." Enough exploration has been done to let us know that it is rocky ground, not easily explored. Yet enough has been done to let us know also that it can be explored. The problems of such research are formidable but not insoluble. The results obtained to date suggest that we shall be working in a province that still contains many mysteries. The study of whole families holds out the promise of fascinating discoveries of how people become what they are and how their lives are anchored in one another.

## NOTES

1. Paul H. Mussen, ed., *Handbook of Research Methods in Child Development* (New York: John Wiley and Sons, 1960).
2. Harold T. Christensen, ed., *Handbook of Marriage and the Family* (Chicago: Rand McNally and Company, 1964). Two contributors to this handbook discuss sibling relationships, but both restrict their discussion to an analysis of the effects of position in the birth order. See the chapters by Jesse R. Pitts, "The Structural-Functional Approach," and Edward Z. Dager, "Socialization and Personality Development in the Child." It seems unnecessarily restrictive to limit the study of sibling relationships by studying only birth-order effects, as now appears to be the case. Other questions seem pertinent, for example, does the type of parental discipline influence sibling relationships? Do parental personality and parental values influence sibling relationships? Why do some siblings become friends and others not? If a physician has three sons of whom two become physicians and the third follows some career not at all related, how is this phenomenon—and others like it—to be understood? Questions such as these undoubtedly do not admit of easy answers, but it is not apparent that they will prove less fruitful for the understanding of human development than questions about the effects of birth order.
3. Robert Redfield, *The Little Community; Viewpoints for the Study of a Human Whole* (Chicago: University of Chicago Press, 1955), pp. 1–2.
4. For a searching discussion of the complexities of the mother-child relationship, see John Bowlby, "The Nature of the Child's Tie to His Mother, *International Journal of Psychoanalysis,* Vol. 39 (1958), pp. 350–73.
5. Some aspects of this issue are discussed by Robert S. Weiss in "Alternative Approaches in the study of Complex Situations," *Human Organization,* Autumn 1966.
6. I also believe that much advanced work needs to be qualitative. It is not helpful to equate measurement with scientific advancement. Applying sophisticated techniques of measurement to data that are cognized in a superficial way is a dubious road to advancement. Knowledge advances by better and fuller observation and by more adequate conceptualizing as well as by more discriminating measurement.
7. Robert Oppenheimer, "Analogy in Science," *The American Psychologist,* Vol. 11, No. 3 (March 1956), p. 135.

# Part I

# A FRAMEWORK FOR ANALYSIS

The opening selection in this volume is an effort to provide a general set of concepts useful in guiding observation of families as wholes. Unlike most work devoted to the psychosocial interior of the family, this selection is an effort to create a dynamic framework applicable to ordinary or non-clinical families as well as those that produce clinically disordered individuals. The framework is dynamic in that it seeks to encompass the interplay—both supportive and conflictful—between fantasy and overt action, between person and person, between family member and family group, and between family group and the extrafamilial world.

# 1:

# The Family as a Psychosocial Organization

*Robert D. Hess* and *Gerald Handel*

However its life spreads into the wider community, there is a sense in which a family is a bounded universe. The members of a family—parents and their young children—inhabit a world of their own making, a community of feeling and fantasy, action and precept. Even before their infant's birth, the expectant couple make plans for his family membership, and they prepare not only a bassinet but a prospect of what he will be to them. He brings his own surprises, but in time there is acquaintance, then familiarity, as daily the family members compose their interconnection through the touch and tone by which they learn to know one another. Each one comes to have a private transcript of their common life, recorded through his own emotions and individual experiences.

In their mutual interaction, the family members develop more or less adequate understanding of one another, collaborating in the effort to establish consensus and to negotiate uncertainty. The family's life together is an endless process of movement in and around consensual understanding, from attachment to conflict to withdrawal—and over again. Separateness and connectedness are the underlying conditions of a family's life, and its common task is to give form to both.

This volume describes how five families have each, in distinctive ways, dealt with this and other tasks. The ways in which a family is a unit and the ways it provides for being a separate person are, in one sense, what every family's life is about. The psychosocial portraits which we have sketched are intended to convey something of the particularity of American family worlds. These are American families, but the wider

Reprinted from *Family Worlds* by Robert D. Hess and Gerald Handel by permission of the University of Chicago Press. © 1959 by the University of Chicago. Robert D. Hess is professor of human development and education, Committee on Human Development and Graduate School of Education, University of Chicago. Gerald Handel, while editing this book, was vice-president, Social Research, Inc., an independent research organization in Chicago; he is now senior research associate, Center for Urban Education, New York. At the time of writing, the authors were, respectively, assistant professor of human development and research associate (instructor) in human development, University of Chicago.

culture was not our primary interest. Rather, we tried first to find the family's boundaries, then to explore its psychosocial dimensions. When we looked at the culture, it was in order to take the point of view of a family looking out at it. The reader will recognize in these analytic sketches versions of middle and lower class cultural themes; again, our aim has been to illustrate what this feels like to actual individuals who shape a life in an intimate group. The case study is the method of choice for this purpose, and its aim is to amplify the richness of perception of American family life.

Depiction is not our sole aim, however. We are concerned with developing a framework for understanding the nuclear family as a group. Within the family, events occur in far from random fashion; even uncertainty is given a customary place in a family's scheme of things. While illustrating distinctness, we work toward a systematic view of the family as a psychosocial organization. How may one describe a family, taking account of all its members? The multiplicity of household events takes place in a round robin of interaction which is a shapeless swirl only to the casual observer. There are nodes of connection, points at which feeling is concentrated and significance declared. There are tracks to which the interaction returns again and again. A family has discernible pattern and form.

We set ourselves the task of searching out the elements that give shape to a family's life. In so doing, we examined the personalities of the individual members, the relationships between pairs and in triangles, and the integration of these individual psychodynamic features and multiple relationships in the psychosocial structure of the group. We tried to comprehend in one view the supporting convergences and the intrinsic disruptions of a family, seen as a set of individual personalities, a system of interpersonal relations, and a local culture.

It is imperative to relate the nature of individuality to the form of the particular family group in which it occurs and to examine the participation of family psychological modes of interaction in the personalities of individual members. As a guiding principle we are proposing that the intrapsychic organization of each member is part of the psychosocial structure of his family; the structure of a family includes the intrapsychic organization of its individual members. For example, if separateness and connectedness constitute one of the most fundamental problems which a family must solve, then it is necessary first to adopt a standpoint from which one can see both tendencies as parts of the same solution and second to view this solution both as an extension of individual needs into the group interaction and as a significant determinant of individual personality.

An understanding of the relationship between individual dynamics and family interactional matrix may be furthered by a second principle: in his relationships in the family an individual member strives toward predictability of preferred experience, attempting to discover or create circumstances which fit his image of what the world around him should be—how it should respond to him and provide opportunity for expression of his own preferences. This principle indicates how one might examine the fashion in which individual uniqueness is transformed into family uniqueness as a result of his own and others' experience. It attends also to the impact upon the individual member of his success, or lack of it, in obtaining the emotional atmosphere he desires. Neither the ties that bind the members to one another nor the barriers that separate them are adequately indicated by overt social behavior alone. Connection to others is outward and inward in infinite variety. In the study of ordinary people, as in this book, the inner connections and the inner enclaves must command attention no less than the external encounters and the occasions for social privacy. Taking for granted, then, that the members of a nuclear family have personalities of their own, that each has a psychobiological individuality, and that each is guided by cultural role expectations, how shall we understand how they fashion a life together?

It is the purpose of this introductory chapter to indicate some concepts which are useful in understanding and describing in non-pathological terms the complexities of ordinary family interaction. The major processes described here give shape to the flux of family life, coherence to the extended array of events, perceptions, emotions, actions, learnings, and changes which the members experience or undertake. The essential processes discussed below are these:

1. Establishing a pattern of separateness and connectedness.

2. Establishing a satisfactory congruence of images through the exchange of suitable testimony.

3. Evolving modes of interaction into central family concerns or themes.

4. Establishing the boundaries of the family's world of experience.

5. Dealing with significant biosocial issues of family life, as in the family's disposition to evolve definitions of male and female and of older and younger.

## THE EFFORT TO ACHIEVE A SATISFACTORY PATTERN OF SEPARATENESS AND CONNECTEDNESS

Two conditions characterize the nuclear family. Its members are connected to one another, and they are also separate from one another. Every family gives shape to these conditions in its own way. Its life may show greater emphasis on the one or the other; yet both are constitutive of family life. The infant is born from the womb into the limits of his own skin, with individual properties of sensitivity and activity. He possesses an irreducible psychobiological individuality that no amount or kind of intense socialization can abolish. His parents, too, remain individual persons no matter how deep their love, how passionate their desire for one another or how diffuse their individual identities. Through the wishes and capacities of its members, the family defines and gives shape to separateness so that it looms large or small in family affairs, gives rise to pleasure or unhappiness. The range of possibilities is wide. The autistic child or the psychotic parent represents the pathological extreme of separateness. The benign extremes are more diverse—emotional richness, ego autonomy, individual creativity. Perhaps Erikson's concept of a clearly delineated ego identity best conveys the benign meaning of separateness.[1]

Yet connectedness of family members is equally basic. No human infant survives without ties. Connectedness can range from physical proximity and rudimentary child care to an intensity of mutual involvement which all but excludes all other interests. Separateness remains always, yet it can be transcended. Love and passion do unite family members and can make separateness seem infinitesimal—or comfortable. The signs of being connected to one another that the members of a family seek differ greatly even within the middle range. In one family intense emotional exchange is sought; the members need to relax defenses and public façade, and they respond freely. In other families such confrontation is threatening, though the wish to feel themselves together in binding ties may be great. A family of this kind may be able to approach its desire only through much formalized or ritualized action, such as giving gifts, celebrating birthdays and holidays, making joint excursions.

This fundamental duality of family life is of considerable significance, for the individual's efforts to take his own kind of interest in the world, to become his own kind of person, proceed apace with his efforts to find gratifying connection to the other members. At the same time, the other members are engaged in taking their kinds of interest in him, and in themselves. This is the matrix of interaction in which a family develops its life. The family tries to cast itself in a form that satisfies the ways in which its members want to be together and apart. The pattern it reaches is a resultant of these diverse contributions. This dual condition of inevitable individuality and inescapable psychosocial connection is a dynamic condition; it requires a family to make some kind of life together, lest the family dissolve. The family and its members must meet these two conditions in *some* way. The investigator's effort to understand family life is facilitated insofar as he asks constantly, In what way does this event or tendency or action bring the members together or keep them apart?

## CONGRUENCE OF IMAGES

It is useful to regard life in a family as the family's effort to attain a satisfactory congruence of individual and family images through the exchange of suitable testimony. This view initially directs attention to the family as a group of members. Family research must somehow face up to this very obvious fact. All the members of the nuclear household must be taken into account if we are to understand the family's life. Data must be obtained from each member. We do not understand a family if we know the spouses' roles as mates and as parents but nothing of their children, nor is our foundation adequate if we have firsthand materials from a mother and child in therapy but see the father and other children only through their eyes. Thus, this first implication is methodological. It says something of the range of data to be collected.

Living together, the individuals in a family each develop an image of what the other members are like. This image comprises the emotional meaning and significance which the other has for the member holding it. The concept of image is a mediating concept. Its reference extends into the personality and out into the interpersonal relationship. Referring to one person's emotionalized conception of another, an image is shaped by the personality both of the holder and of the object. The image emerges from the holder's past and bears the imprint of his experience, delimiting what versions of others are possible for him. It says something about him as a person. But it is also a cast into the future, providing the holder with direction in relating to and interacting with the object. While it represents the holder's needs and wishes, it also represents the object as a source of fulfilment.

Each family member has some kind of image of every other member and of himself in relation to them. This image is compounded of realistic and idealized components in various proportions, and it may derive from the personalities of its holder and its object also in various proportions. It draws from cultural values, role expectations, and the residue of the parents' experiences in their families of origin. One's image of another is the product of one's direct experience with the other and of evaluations of the other by third parties. From this experience, from evaluations of it and elaborations on it in fantasy, a conception of another person is developed, a conception which serves to direct and shape one's action to the other and which becomes a defining element of the interpersonal relationship. *An image of a person is one's definition of him as an object of one's own action or potential action.*

In studying a family, then, it is necessary to investigate both the images which the members hold of one another and the ways in which these images are interrelated. It is necessary to understand how the interaction of the members derives from and contributes to this interrelation of images. The implication of this stance is that interaction cannot be fully understood in its own terms, that, instead, it must be viewed in the context of how the participants define one another as relevant objects.

From his experience with the other members of his family and from experiences outside the family, an individual comes to have another kind of image—an image of his family which expresses his mode of relationship to the unit and which defines the kind of impact the family has on him. A woman may gratifyingly conceive of her family as dependents who need and reward her, or she may see them primarily as the group that enslaves her and for whom she wears herself out. A man may feel proud of his family as a demonstration of his masculinity, or his image may be of a group of perplexing people with emotions and reactions he doesn't understand, or his family may mean to him primarily a welcome retreat from and contrast with his workaday world. For a child, too, the family may have diverse meanings. To one it is the group he is happy to belong to. For another it consists of those he lives with because he has no place else to go. A person's image of his family embodies what he expects from it and what he gives to it, how important it is and what kind of importance it has.

The images held of one member by the others diverge in varying ways from one another and from his image of himself. The intimate and constant exchange that characterizes the nuclear family makes such divergence far from a matter of indifference. The members of a family want to and have to deal with one another; from the beginning they are engaged in evolving and mutually adjusting their images of one another. This mutual adjustment takes place in interaction, and it is, in part, the aim of interaction. Since complete consensus is most improbable, life in a family—as elsewhere—is a process ongoing in a situation of actual or potential instability. Pattern is reached, but it can never be complete, since action is always unfolding and the status of the family members is undergoing change.[2]

If a family system of interpersonal relations is to have any continuity, the images which members have of the family and of one another must in some sense tend toward compatibility. This is only to say that they strive toward some sort of stability or predictability of preferred behavior. When a child is born, the parents entertain an image of the child—which will be altered and elaborated with time, to be sure—which the child cannot share. The concept of socialization refers to the parents' efforts to get the child to regard himself in substantially the same way they regard him. From birth, also, the child is engaged in acquiring conceptions of his parents, striving to form a view of them which accords with their self-images. In an absolute sense, neither goal can be attained, but the efforts to reach satisfactory approximations—or congruence—constitute one of the springs of interaction.

It seems useful to draw an analytic distinction between the actual image which a person holds of another and his desired image. Not only does an individual have an ideal for his own behavior, an ego ideal, but he also forms conceptions of what he wants others to be. In some families the greatest discrepancies may occur among these ideal versions of each other. Such a discrepancy may be described as the discrepancy between a person's ego ideal (his own image of what he strives toward in himself) and another's desired image of him (what the other strives to realize in him). This type of situation appears in fairly clear outline in our discussion of the Littleton family (chap. iv).

In other families there may be relatively little strain of this order. Such a family's inter-involvement may be characterized as its effort to live as a satisfactory example of what is accepted as desirable. The "problems" of living in systems of this type are more likely to arise from "falling short" of what is consensually desirable and from the difficulties of living up to all desirable claims simultaneously rather than from disagreement about what is desirable.

Families also differ in their tolerance of incongruence of images. In some there is pressure toward closeness of fit in minute particulars. In others a looser relationship is accepted as satisfactory, or the system can deal with incongruence strains short of disruption.

The issue involved here is not one of how similar the members must be to each other, that is, whether a neat housekeeper requires her husband and children to be equally neat, or whether a serious man requires the other members of his family to be likewise. Rather, the issue is whether the differences and similarities among the members are mutually acceptable. Child guidance clinics echo with parents complaining that the offending child does as they do rather than as they say. The personalities of the parent and the child may be quite similar; yet they may hold images of each other which are discrepant and unsatisfactorily so. But personality dissimilarity—at whatever level—may provide a firm basis for a satisfactory congruence of images. If a serious man finds himself responsible but his gay wife frivolous, and if she feels that he is dull but she is sparkling, an incongruent set of images characterizes their relationship. Where the serious husband relishes his wife's gaiety as lively and stimulating, where she welcomes his sobriety as a form of strength and stability, and where both concur in what each should be, the images they hold of each other are satisfactorily congruent.

The commonality of experience in a family will conduce to some congruence of family images among the family members. The intrinsic distinctions of age, sex, birth order, and role in society conduce to divergence of images. The overlap and the divergences are expressed and acted out in family life, each member participating in terms of the definition incorporated in his image.

Even when the congruence of images is satisfactory, interaction still has reference to it. If exploration and testing diminish in importance, affirmation and reiteration of what has been established become the content of interaction. The family members demonstrate their agreement with the group and strive toward validation of personal worth in family terms. The positive features of the family image provide the criteria for evaluating individual behavior. The audience toward which testimony is directed may be primarily composed of the family itself, or it may be extended to non-family persons. Whatever its audience, validation is pursued through those dimensions of behavior that the family regards as significant.

A stable human relationship is one in which the members have reached a high degree of consensus about one another; the terms in which personal worth may be demonstrated are clear and are shared. Their interaction is an exchange of testimony of what the members are to one another. The action of each person in his family testifies to his image of it, of himself, and of the others. The members realize or seek out in interpersonal encounters those kinds of experiences which seem meaningful to them and with which they are comfortable. Feelings and actions are responded to in terms of their felt suitability. *Responsive judgments and feelings are responsive first to the inward images of self, other, and family. They then become responses to and for others, so that family life is shaped within the participants as well as between them.*

We have tried to sum up in a general statement how a family's life may be understood in terms of the images family members have of one another and themselves; the inevitable divergences and fluctuations of these images; the psychosocial task of relating to others and attaining viable stability amid this potential fluctuation; the image members develop of the family as a unit—its meaning to family members, the character of its emotional and social exchange; and the utilization of the positive features of the family image in affirming to each member and to the group their personal worth and their right to emotional acceptance and participation.

## THE FAMILY THEME

Individual images and responses are interrelated. In any particular family the kinds of action we have called testing, exploring, and affirming take place in terms of a particular content which may be termed a "family theme." A family theme is a pattern of feelings, motives, fantasies, and conventionalized understandings grouped about some locus of concern which has a particular form in the personalities of the individual members. The pattern comprises some fundamental view of reality and some way or ways for dealing with it. In the family themes are to be found the family's implicit direction, its notion of "who we are" and "what we do about it." In delineating a particular family theme, we may bring several criteria to bear.

First, the theme affects behavior in several important family areas and activities. It is a postulated mold which exerts a variable impress on the observable events and ascertainable consequences of a family life. Thus, a family's feelings about most of its activities can be construed as particular manifestations of a more inclusive organizing principle, which for one type of family might be stated in this way: The family feels itself to be essentially alone in the world. Individual members endeavor to communicate with one another. They strive to foster any symbol or semblance of communication. The process of communication itself is important to all family members, and attempts to achieve contact with one another must be pursued whenever possible. Failure or disruption in communication is a failure in meeting the family objective.

The theme is an implicit point of departure and point of orientation for this family's behavior. Father's return to the family at the end of the day stimulates a flurry of greeting and excitement; the family dinner becomes one of the most important events of the day. Chores around the home are seen as opportunities for conversation. Members are expected to be "considerate" of one another, avoiding the conflict and disharmony that might threaten communication. Independence or solitude is discouraged; the individual family member should keep himself ready and available for interaction; activities that take a member out of the group are discouraged.

This is a brief illustration of a theme. A fuller statement would take greater account of the forces that have to be contended with in holding to the direction of solution and integration actually followed.

Second, a theme is a significant issue in the life of the family, expressing basic forms of relating to the external world and of interpersonal involvement.

Third, all members of the family are involved in the psychosocial definitions and processes which enter into the theme, though each may be involved in a different way. Thus the theme arises from and has consequences for the personalities of all the members.

The theme, then, is a particularly useful unit for analysis of family life, for it provides a way of characterizing the family group in terms of broad and significant psychosocial and psychocultural dimensions. At the same time, it permits flexibility, since it is not an arbitrary unit and does not require that a family be understood in terms of a set of a priori categories. The investigator can assess the family in its own terms, responding to and following the saliences that center its life.[3]

The concept of the theme is advantageous in two other important ways. Since it is a characterization of the family in terms of a significant issue in its life, the concept provides a point of reference for understanding the individual members and particular interpersonal relationships as specific versions and expressions of the theme. The individual's place in the family—what he does and what happens to him there—can be understood as the way in which he participates in these broader currents which help to determine the quality of his family membership. If we understand a theme as consisting of some significant issue and the general direction of attempted solution or resolution of that issue, each member has some part to play in this larger configuration. His part is complexly determined, as is every role—in some measure assigned by others, in some measure self-created. By determining the salient themes in a family's life, we are able to see more clearly how any individual's fate is shaped, what opportunities he has for interlocking his life with others, and what pressures he must contend with.

The concept of the theme also makes it possible to compare one family with another. It provides a way of characterizing a whole group in a fashion that is relevant to the group's individual members; yet since it is a group-summary statement, it can be arrayed with other such characterizations.

## ESTABLISHING BOUNDARIES OF THE FAMILY'S WORLD OF EXPERIENCE

The concepts we have suggested are oriented toward revealing not only the family's internal functioning but its stance, the position it has taken up vis-à-vis the outer, non-family world. The significant themes consequently not only subsume the psychic content of the family's life but also indicate something of the breadth of its world. A family constitutes its own world, which is not to say that it closes itself off from everything else but that it determines what parts of the external world are admissible and how freely. The family maps its domain of acceptable and desirable experience, its life space. The outer limits of life space for any family are fairly definite and reasonably well marked. There are signposts for goals and signals for danger. But these metaphors fail because the boundaries lie within persons, and however firm they may be, there are always areas

B

of inexperience not adequately charted. As new experiences occur, as new feelings arise, new actions are taken and are brought to the internal limits of the person taking them and to the limits which others help to set. In this back-and-forth of interaction is to be found the family members' mutual regulation. Each directs himself toward others by virtue of the representation they have in his mind; the others respond to him in terms of the way he is represented in theirs. Limits to experience—broad or narrow—are established in a variety of ways and along several dimensions. Some of the more important are these:

1. *The differentiation of individual personality.*—How elaborated individual personalities of the family members are; how self-directing individuals are and are expected to become. From the gross categories of infantile experience, comfort and distress, incorporation and expulsion, personality develops to encompass a range of emotional experience and more mature ego mechanisms. The complexity and differentiation of personality can proceed further in some families than in others.

2. *The intensity of experience.*—How deep or how shallow experience is; how detached or how involved family members are in their activities and one another; how controlled or how spontaneous their behavior is. The question involved here is how much of the self is made available to experience—the fulness of intimacy or the enthusiasm of commitment to something.

3. *The extensity of experience.*—The literal geographical scope— the range and variety of actions; the importance of neighborhood and locality as compared with communities of more abstract definition—"democratic society," "the legal profession"; how much of the world it is important to know about and be interested in; how far actual acquaintance extends. Thus, less literally, how many kinds of life and action are conceived of, known of, or understood.

4. *The tendency to evaluate experience.*—Families differ in their inclination to permit members to make unique personal evaluations of and responses to stimuli. The constraints of evaluation—the internalization of criteria—modify and translate stimuli and experience. Values create in the individual member emotional positions on definable categories of experience—jazz, sports, "classical" art and music, comic books, politicians, science and scientists, literature—the broad range of stimuli available in our culture. The family also evaluates experience initiated by the individual member and evokes from him modes of responsiveness to his own behavior and the behavior of others. A prominent element of this dimension is the tendency toward moral evaluation of experience. The freedom from or constraint by guilt and the freedom to range inwardly in thought, impulse, and fantasy, to entertain unaccustomed possibilities, are involved here. Moral evaluation also affects the freedom to range

outwardly, to be at home in new circumstances, to find out for ones&.
The central issue is the need, or lack of it, to condemn and repudiate or
even simply to shun what is traditionally not one's own.

These are at least some of the most important dimensions which
describe the boundaries of a family's world and the kind of life that can
be lived within it. The characteristics of this arena help determine for each
member how multiplex his life is, how close to himself, how close to
others, how close to home. Establishing the boundaries of experience, in
the terms just enumerated, is one of the principal processes of family life.
It continues not only while the members live together but even after
they disperse—even influencing how far and in what direction they will go.

In a final sense, the predicated states are never reached. What turns
a life may take cannot be known, so that the pattern-establishing processes
do not result in changeless solutions. While it may be possible to predict
how a family of a given type will weather economic privation, if it should
occur, the predicted kind of change will not take place unless the financial
stress does. Similarly, in greater or lesser degree, the "establishing"
processes are always in play, responding to the new elements introduced
into the family's life. However, it is necessary to recognize that while in
a literal, concrete sense, the boundaries of experience are never definitively
established, it is possible to ascertain with high probability what they are
likely to be for a given family. If the life of a family never reaches a
final, unchangeable form—even for a delimited period of the family
cycle, such as the child-rearing stage—it nonetheless gains a recognizably
firm structure, as any human association must.

## DEALING WITH SIGNIFICANT GIVEN BIOSOCIAL ISSUES OF FAMILY LIFE

The most essential structural characteristics of the nuclear family are
well known and need not be extensively elaborated here. The fact that a
family, unlike other voluntary groups, must be established by one member
from each sex means that sex membership is a basic point of reference.
In the study of any particular family it is necessary to investigate what
it interprets male and female to be. What qualities are attributed to each
sex? What is demanded of each? What is accorded to each? How important is the distinction felt to be? Is the sex difference minimized, or does
it serve as a basis for proliferation of emotions and activities? Are the two
sexes differentially evaluated so that rewards and penalties are distributed
on the basis of sex membership? All of these questions have, of course,
certain conventionalized answers provided by the larger social units to

belongs—social class, ethnic group, community. Yet each ~~rovides answers of its own; each family makes use of sex ~~ structuring its own world.

parents choose each other voluntarily in marriage, their chil-~~me family members without exercise of choice. This fact, to-ge~~ ~~ith the fact that they are helpless at birth and hence born into the care and authority of their parents, sets the question of how the differences between the two generations will be construed and handled. How much of family life is to be regulated by considerations of authority becomes an important dimension. Parental authority—its scope, the manner in which it is exercised—is one of the forces shaping the pattern of separateness-connectedness. Its potential is realized in such consequences for the child as self-direction, submissiveness, a sense of injustice, or a readiness to learn from those of greater experience.

In dealing with this gulf in power and capacity between themselves and their children, parents have to make a decision (not a conscious decision, in its essentials, but one arising from their own personalities) about how insistently they will impose their images upon their children. Families differ in how far parents interact with their children, amending or reshaping their own aims as their children become increasingly formed. Where they expect the children to do all the adapting, there is little room for negotiating, so that the process of self- and mutual discovery is compressed within narrow limits.

Families differ also in how the parents pace their children through childhood—whether they push, encourage, or restrain. Parents seek to shape their children in keeping with their own desire to achieve preferred experience. They stimulate the children in accordance with what they feel children should be, as a part of their activity in defining their own world. The nature of parental stimulation—its intensity, frequency, and diversity —expresses the aims of their care and authority. When we observe that one parent is eager for his child to behave as much like an adult as quickly as possible, whereas another regrets his child's loss of babyish ways, it is clear that different personal wishes or aims are operating in the two cases. But it would appear that different concepts of growth and different time perspectives also operate here. In some families there is an urgency to growing up, sometimes motivated by the parent's wish to be quickly relieved or what are conceived as the taxing aspects of child rearing, or by an anxiety that each "delay" or concession to impulsivity is threatening to ultimate development. This idea seems to include a notion of a fixed termination point, a time when development has reached its goal and is then essentially over. The happenings beyond this point are construed not as growth but simply as events, important or not, in the passing of time. In other families a sense of a long, indefinite time span prevails, together with a belief that growth cannot be compressed. Children are seen as moving slowly toward maturity, and it is felt that they have time enough to do so. Growth is intricate, not readily mechanized, and the forces of childhood are tamed rather than broken.

Implicit in these several aspects of parental feeling and action vis-à-vis their offspring is another decision: *how much of the child's world does not belong to his parents?* In part, this is a matter of authority. In exercising authority, parents not only choose among techniques of reward and punishment. They also may or may not restrict themselves from incursions into the child's domain. Whether a child is granted privacy in any sense—privacy of quarters, of possessions, of thoughts and emotions, of responses to others—or whether these are all felt to be subject to his elders' inspection and manipulation is a question decided according to how parents define themselves and children. Bound up in the decision is a conception of integrity, for the terms on which people have access to one another, while communicated earlier in the infant-care context, become increasingly defined and actualized during childhood.

The relationships which develop among the various members of a family do not follow simply the intrinsic lines of sex and age. They are shaped as well by the underlying family themes and images which impart meanings to sex and age and also to various other personal characteristics. On the basis of the meanings which the members have for one another. particular interpersonal ties evolve. The closeness between any two members, for example, or the distance between a group of three closely joined members and a fourth who is apart, derives from the interlocking meanings which obtain among them. Each family tends to have a characteristic distribution of ties or pattern of alignment (which may be negative or positive in emotional tone) among members. How these patterns are developed and sustained is, then, a matter of considerable significance in understanding life within families as well as the course of any one member's life.

In these concepts we have attempted to provide a framework for understanding the family as an intimate group of members which functions in systematic ways. We have focused on the interior of the family, so that the framework is somewhat less useful for analyzing the relationship between the family and society. The case studies in this volume have been prepared in terms of the point of view advanced in the present chapter, though the concepts identified here are not reiterated with each detail of family life. At various points where it has seemed necessary, we have elaborated on some idea that seemed to us to illuminate the family being discussed. The frame of reference is intended to serve as just that— marking out the range of phenomena encompassed and the terms in which they are considered.

## NOTES

1. Erik Erikson, *Childhood and Society* (New York: W. W. Norton, 1950).
2. George Herbert Mead gave theoretical significance to this uncertainty of future action in his concept of the "I." "It is because of the 'I' that we say that we are never fully aware of what we are, that we surprise ourselves by our own action. It is as we act that we are aware of ourselves. . . . I want to call attention to the fact that this response of the 'I' is something that is more or less uncertain. . . . The 'I' gives the sense of freedom, of initiative" (*Mind, Self, and Society* [Chicago: University of Chicago Press, 1934], pp. 174, 176, 177).
3. The concept of the theme has been introduced into social science by Henry Murray in psychology and by Morris Opler in anthropology. See Henry A. Murray *et al., Explorations in Personality* (New York: Oxford University Press, 1938), and Morris Opler, "Themes as Dynamic Forces in Culture," *American Journal of Sociology*, LI, 198–206. Though he does not use the word, Fritz Redl's approach to group structure makes use of similar logic. See his "Group Emotion and Leadership," *Psychiatry*, V (1942), 573–96.

# Part II

# RESEARCH METHODS

Research methods can undoubtedly be classified in many ways: the several logics that underlie them; the types of data they yield; where the data are obtained; the goals they have in view; the relative prestige they enjoy; the scope of phenomena they can deal with; the precision with which their results can be stated; the significance of the conclusions that can be drawn from them; the costs of obtaining data; the professional training of those who practice them. Some of these allow fairly ready discrimination among research methods, others do not. It is, for example, relatively easy to describe types of data yielded by different methods. The significance of the conclusions drawn from these different types of data is more elusive and quickly leads into questions of philosophy of science and sociology of knowledge.

At the present time, four main types of research method appear to be used for the twofold objective of studying the psychosocial interior of families and studying them as wholes. Part II provides discussions of methodological issues and illustrations of three methods now in use. The fourth method, clinical psychiatric research, is omitted in Part II mainly because the writings that discuss and illustrate psychiatric research seemed more suitably placed elsewhere in this book, since they are also rich in their exploration of substantive topics.

Before commenting briefly on the three methods discussed in Part II, I should say that one conceivable method, which I am not aware of being widely practiced, I believe will perhaps come into greater use. This is the psychometric method, which involves giving psychological tests or other types of objectively scored instruments to all members of a family and analyzing the results by such statistical methods as factor analysis and multiple correlation.

The first general method presented is *field work*. The singular characteristic of field work is that it involves going where the people are, rather than having them come to where the researcher is, which ordinarily occurs in experimental or clinical methods. Field work affords the great advantage of seeing people in their own environment or habitat. Although it is sometimes objected that people being observed do not behave naturally, field workers generally discover that most people cannot sustain without relaxation a presentation of self that is entirely alien or uncharacteristic. People observed with consent undoubtedly often engage in maneuvers intended to hide some conception of themselves or their situation, but they do not do so invariably or completely. Indeed, the manner and extent of their doing so are in themselves data about them, for people fundamentally cannot help being themselves. This does not mean that a field worker cannot be misled—undoubtedly he can—but this does not make the method invalid. Rather, it means that the field worker faces a problem common to all research workers: he must find ways of checking his observations, estimating the scope, and judging the significance of what he observes. The laboratory scientist does not escape this problem. In fact, in the study of whole families, the experimental worker faces the added problem of discovering how to extrapolate from findings obtained under experimenter-determined conditions to the family's ordinary mode of behavior.

In addition to allowing observation of people in their natural setting, field work has two other important scientific advantages. One, the people being studied do what they want to do rather than what the research worker tells them to do. Fewer constraints are imposed upon them by requirements of the research process than by more structured methods. They can be more expressive and less rule-bound. Second, and related to this, field work is a flexible procedure. The research worker can follow up leads furnished by the people he is studying as they occur and adapt his observation and inquiry to them. In both respects, field work has much in common with clinical psychiatric research. An important difference, however, is that clinical interviewing may not be feasible for studying families who do not voluntarily present themselves to clinics. Field work thus has a pragmatic virtue: ordinary families may be willing to participate in research if the research worker comes to them but unwilling to do so if they must go to his office.

Field work is not a standardized or unitary procedure, especially for the study of whole families. Indeed, the term covers interviewing, which can be the dominant activity, as well as observation and, on occasion, psychological testing. It is carried out in many ways, depending on the workers' purposes, skills, and available facilities.

The two selections that discuss field work are quite different. Jules Henry lived in the homes of families who had a psychotic child in a residential treatment institution. As far as I know, he is the only research worker to succeed in such a thoroughgoing application of traditional anthropological method to the study of the psychosocial interior of families in our society. Whether this kind of entree into ordinary families in our society is possible remains to be seen, but perhaps Henry has at least shown the way to gain more comprehensive knowledge of other types of clinical families. He has included some of his data in a book[1] and plans additional publications based on this material. In the article presented here, he discusses the rationale for his method and how he carried out his work, as well as brief examples of the type of material he obtains.

The selection by Robert D. Hess and Gerald Handel discusses field work relying heavily on interviewing. The interviewing was primarily conversational, that is, the interviewer raises general topics, inviting the informant to talk about them in his own words rather than respond to choices preselected by the research worker. Their selection deals with what the authors term nonclinical families. Hess and Handel began with a rather vague goal of making an intensive study of ordinary families to learn more about the internal organization of family life. They chose relatively unstructured research methods in the belief that such methods would afford the greatest opportunity for discovery of phenomena of which they were unaware.

Two selections on *experimental methods* follow those on field methods. The great advantage of experiment is that it allows the investigator to control the research situation in such a way that he can systematically and precisely discern the relationships between variables. However, many things we wish to know about human behavior do not lend themselves to experimental study either because the variables in the situation cannot be controlled or because the range of people to be studied cannot be brought to a laboratory. It is well known that the majority of psychological experiments with humans use college students as subjects, and this is a shaky base to rely on for generalized laws. Equally important is that experiment in the social sciences may often be beside the point, since our goal is to know how people actually live as well as to understand the relationships between variables.

Although the subject matter of the social sciences precludes their becoming exclusively experimental, the advantages of experimental method in the natural sciences have attracted social psychologists for quite some time. Experimental study of whole families, however, is relatively new. Jay Haley delineates the goals that prompt family experiments and the logic that underlies them. He argues that a basis of classifying families is necessary, that the classification must be based on differences in communication patterns in families, and that only experimental methods can verify any classification that is proposed. Yet he also candidly acknowledges that it remains to be determined how well a family's behavior in an experi-

B*

mental situation accurately represents the family's typical pattern. To solve this problem he proposes studying the family repeatedly in several trials of the same experiment and studying the family in a variety of related experiments. In addition to his theoretical discussion, Haley reports on two experiments that he carried out with families with a schizophrenic member.

The following article, by Fred L. Strodtbeck, is one of the earliest, if not in fact the first, published experiments with families of more than two members. Unlike Haley's work, which emerges from psychiatric concerns, Strodtbeck works in one of the dominant streams of sociological small group study. The experiment he reports is an effort to discover whether certain results obtained from the study of ad hoc groups are also true of families. He finds both similarities and differences between these two groups, interpreting the differences as due to the fact that a family has a history of interpersonal relations where an ad hoc group, by definition, does not.

Both Haley and Strodtbeck study coalitions among family members. One may question whether it is adequate to regard such phenomena under the rubric of "communication patterns" and, further, whether communication patterns afford a sufficient basis for classifying families. Suggesting a negative answer to both questions is the fact that family members value each other in particular ways; while it is true that these valuations are expressed in behavior and thereby communicated, it does not follow that the terms that describe the communication of valuations describe the valuations themselves. Describing and measuring the strength or consistency of support that some family members give to others tells little or nothing of the terms on which support is offered. Our scientific curiosity leads us to ask: "When family members give or fail to give support to other members, what do they imagine they are doing? What are the conceptions of self, other, and situation that lie behind the giving or withholding of support?"

Such conceptions are revealed by *projective techniques,* among other methods. When a person is presented with a relatively ambiguous and unstructured stimulus, such as an inkblot or a picture of an undefined situation, and is asked to interpret it, he must utilize his own resources, his own perceptions, ideas, and imaginings to do so. Inevitably he reveals something about himself. That he reveals important things, including many he is unaware of, is quite certain, but it is also true that the amount and character of revelation vary from person to person and also, to some extent, for the same person at different times. A great deal of work is conducted that attempts to establish more precise relationships between the data yielded by projective techniques and data yielded by other procedures, such as direct observations, psychiatric interviews, objectively scored tasks, and systematically rated samples of behavior. While all of the work with projective techniques—including their clinical use as well as research designed to estimate their validity and reliability—establishes that all techniques are not helpful for all uses to which they have been put, it also establishes that they are useful for understanding a great many things about human behavior. Using them to understand the functioning of whole families is a relatively recent undertaking, and two ways of doing this are presented here.

The article by Dorothy Terry Sohler and her colleagues takes the form of a relatively traditional test of validity, although it reports on only one family. A battery of projective tests was administered individually to each member of a four-person family. The psychologists first wrote a report on each member and then on the family as a whole, including predictions of what the family interaction would be like. The report on the family was divided into 333 discrete interpretive statements in order to measure the extent to which the interpretations derived from projective data agreed with interpretations made by the psychiatrists who had conducted extensive therapeutic interviews with all four members of the family. This predictive effort was not highly successful, since predictions of overt family interaction were quite erroneous, although psychologist-psychiatrist agreement about the family was high in other respects. Whether further experience with predictions of family interaction from projective methods will yield greater success remains to be seen. At this point there is some question whether prediction of overt family interaction is the most important contribution to be sought from projective techniques. They may be more useful now for revealing the inner structure of family relationships rather than the overt behavior in which this structure will manifest itself.

The concluding paper in the section, by Gerald Handel, proposes a systematic procedure for the analysis of TAT data individually obtained from the several members of a family. In order to base the method on a sound theoretical foundation, the article begins by analyzing the basic character of family life, the creation of meaning. The task of TAT analysis in studying whole families is to discover the individual, interpersonal, and collective meanings in the family. The method avoids dependence on unusualness or similarity of projective responses, since commonplace responses and responses that are dissimilar from member to member also require interpretation.

The writings collected in Part II provide a focused look at methods for the study of whole families. Needless to say, they do not exhaust the topic, and selections in other parts of the book provide additional insight into research methods.

## NOTE

1. Jules Henry, *Culture against Man* (New York: Random House, 1963).

# 2:

# My Life with the Families of Psychotic Children

*Jules Henry*

In 1957, under a grant from the Ford Foundation, Bruno Bettelheim[1] asked me to study the families of some psychotic children by living in their homes. Since I had long wished to do this,[2] I was happy to accept the invitation. For many years it had been my conviction that the etiology of emotional illness required more profound study than had heretofore been possible and that the best way to new discoveries in the field was through study of the disease-bearing vector, the family, in its natural habitat, pursuing its usual life routines—eating, loving, fighting, talking, taking amusements, treating sickness, and so on—in other words, following the usual course of its life.

It had been clear to me that by confining the search for causes to the prestigeful instruments of psychiatry and psychology—that is to say, to the interview and therapy sessions and psychological tests, we were shutting out, rather than revealing, important causal factors. A moment's reflection indicates why this is so. Human social life is made up of innumerable events initiated at birth and continued through life, and when they are not seen they sink into forgetfulness, for they are too many to remember; and always repression lets us forget what it is necessary for us to forget.

It is difficult to communicate concretely what is meant by events so numerous as to be uncountable and unremembered, but if you try to recall all that you experienced between eating your dinner and arriving here tonight you will get some idea of what I mean. Who among you can recall *all* of the following: how often at dinner you and your wife picked up and set down your knife and fork; how much water or wine you drank; how many pieces of bread you ate; how fast you ate and how much you left on your plate; what you said to your wife and children and they to you and in what tone of voice; how much sugar you put in your coffee; whether or not you or your children stained the table cloth or dropped food on the table and what happened then, and so on? Who can tell with certainty whether he kissed his wife and children goodbye and whether on the cheek or on the lips; what he said when he departed and what they said in return? And granted the improbability that you remember *all* these things today, would you remember them tomorrow, next week, or a year hence? Yet it is clear to you, I am sure, that many of the incidents I have mentioned are significantly related to your inner state and to the relationship between you and your family; and some, indeed, may leave an indelible mark on the relationship even though the event itself may be forgotten. Naturalistic observation of the families of psychotic children is not concerned with *all* such details; I presented them simply in order to give at the very beginning a rough idea of what is meant by an uncountable and unremembered series of events.

Since the Greeks it has been clear to Man-in-the-West that science advances by reflection on experience[3]; and it is clear also that the universe is endless and potent with new revelations that can constantly provide material on which reflection can operate to produce new insights. We know that the telescope, the microscope, and free association, revealing as they did, new dimensions of the universe, made new theory possible. Direct observation of families functioning in their native habitats should be the microscope that reveals new phenomena of family existence and so provides the possibilities of new theory.[4]

Given this reasonable assumption, the problem for me was to live with these families. Before describing *something* of my life in these households and *more* of my findings, it is necessary to answer in advance questions that have been raised wherever I have spoken of naturalistic observation. The question in everyone's mind have been: (1) What was your entree into the family? (2) Didn't your presence distort the family way of life? (3) What did you do? (4) How did you stand it? (5) What did you record?

(1) *Entree into the family* was obtained by explaining to husband and wife that science was of the opinion that their child's illness was somehow related to family life, and that the best way to discover the relationship was by having a scientist study their family. It was further explained that it was our hope that my findings might contribute to the treatment of their child; and if not to their child, surely to future generations of children.

(2) *The problem of the distorting effects of the observer* may be treated under several headings.

(a) *The family as a culture.* Your experience as social beings and as therapists tells you that every family is different, and that this individuality maintains itself even in the presence of the determined efforts of the therapist to change it. Such stability, such resistance to change develops as a direct consequence of the social interaction of the members of the family with one another and of their mutual adaptation and conflict. Interaction, adaptation, and conflict, meanwhile, occur in relation to a set of values adapted by the family from the values of the culture. That is to say, if in one family the values of struggle, male dominance, female subordination, permissiveness, and so on have become frames of reference in terms of which all interaction takes place, these can arise only because they are present in the culture as a whole. If we put together the pattern of interaction and the value system we have the family culture.

The interaction that takes place in a family can be described accurately; it can be shown that the interaction may be examined in terms of specific interactional constellations, and it is possible to count the number of possible interactional constellations in terms of the equation

$$I = 2^n - n - 1.$$

This equation tells us that in a family of two parents and three children there is a total of 26 interactional constellations. Each system is relatively stable in its structure. That is to say, mother and father have a relatively fixed type of interaction, mother and child-one have another, father and child-one another, and so on. Since these patterns of interaction become standardized they change with great difficulty. All the features I have discussed contribute to an exceedingly stable social environment—however pathologic it may be—and we therefore accept with scepticism the hypothesis of ready modification in the presence of an observer.

Finally it is useful to point out that since all bio-social systems tend to low entropy, and since an interactional constellation in a family is a biosocial system, the bio-socially determined tendency is not easily disturbed.

(b) *The factors of custom and strain.* When an observer is in the home playing the role of a benign relative who, while making no demands and getting involved in no family disputes, at the same time makes himself useful, the family becomes accustomed to him. This factor of custom cannot, however, be considered apart from the problem of strain. Though a family may wish to protect itself from the eyes of the observer, its members cannot remain on guard constantly and everywhere, for the strain is too great. The problem of strain, however, is related to the pressure of impulses and fixed patterns of behavior, to be discussed in the next section.

(c) *Impulses and fixed behavior patterns.* Since behavior deriving from unconscious impulses cannot readily be controlled, often the members of a family cannot hide crucial dimensions of their behavior and feeling for the simple reason that they are unaware of them. In addition, we must take account of conscious impulses which, though conceivably socially unacceptable, are not hidden because they are too violent to be controlled. There are, furthermore, many forms of overt behavior which, though deemed socially acceptable by the subjects, have critical dimensions which, if known to the subject, might make him think twice before behaving as he does in the presence of an observer. For example, in one family studied in this research, the father detached himself completely from the family every evening, slumped in a corner of the sofa watching TV or reading the paper. Such behavior, though belonging to the natural order of things in the father's eyes, may in the long run, be disturbing to his family. As an example of a conscious, overt, though socially deplored attitude, I give the following: In one family the fat, balding, middle-aged father, when showing me photographs, handed me one of himself when he was young, slender and wavy-haired. I remarked, "You were a handsome dog in those days," at which his wife rasped sarcastically, "Lord Byron!" Thus, conscious and unconscious impulses and fixed action patterns of long standing in families reveal to an observer crucial dimensions of the family culture.

(d) *The position of the observer and the situation of the subject.* As scientists we are prone to imaginatively project our own learning and understanding into our subjects' minds. In my experience, persons skilled in dynamic psychology are particularly apt to do this, thinking that my subjects understand the implications of their own behavior as well as a trained observer does. Since this is not so, it follows that much of the time the subjects do not even know what one should inhibit or conceal.

(e) *Participation of the subject in the research.* In the families studied so far, the mother and father were interested in participating in the research in the hope of helping emotionally disturbed children. Guilt because of their role in their own child's illness also played a role in helping them believe that what was discovered about their own family might help other children. Hence, we start in some cases with a reduced tendency to conceal.

(f) *The pressures toward habitual behavior exerted by children in the home.* The inner needs of children, especially young and disturbed ones, are so powerful that they tend to come out even when "company" is around, and when "company" is around the strong impulses of the young may become an embarrassment even in so-called normal families. Since, however, I soon cease to be "company" the children's needs dominate them, and the expression of these needs *pushes the parents into habitual modes of conduct* even though they might choose to avoid them. An example is the rage of a 13-year-old boy which forced his parents into a characteristic pattern of anxious, hostile response and culminated before my eyes in an incipient asthmatic attack in the boy.

(g) *Inflexibility of personality structure.* Since under ordinary circumstances personality integration cannot readily change, this fact makes a massive contribution to the validity of naturalistic studies in the home. For example, a rough-and-ready extroverted individualist cannot suddenly become a passive, clinging conformist; nor can an unintelligent, ineffectual man be miraculously transformed into the opposite because an observer is in his home. Yet these personality integrations are precisely the target of observation in naturalistic observation, prevent distortion of the normal situation, and hence inexorably make their contribution to family life at all times.

Finally, with respect to validity, in the cases of the families of emotionally disturbed children it is usually possible to compare the naturalistic observations with different kinds of data obtained independently by other investigators: case work records, psychiatric treatment records, psychological tests, etc.

(3) *What did I do?* When I had a room in the home I got up when the family did, or maybe before, and retired when they did. If I was living outside I would get to the home around breakfast time and remain until the family went to bed. During the day I hung around the house. Since during the week the husband was away at work I naturally spent my time with the wife and children. Most of the time I talked to the wife about whatever happened to come up: about her neighbors, about her concerns for her children, about food and how to cook it, about her husband and herself, and so on. When the mother was doing household chores or taking care of the children I watched. If she went shopping, took a child for a haircut, went to pick him up at school, etc., I went along. If the family went out of an evening I went too. I went on picnics, to church, to Bible study, to a meeting of the chamber of commerce, and so on. With the husband I could talk about business, the state of the nation, politics, jobs, and so on. Always I was in the role of a visiting friend or relative. If the children wished to come up on my lap, take me out to play, show me what they had done, and so on, they were welcome. I remained, on the whole, passive and compliant.

I intervened rarely in any activity, but I tended to follow one rule, which was to intervene when some accident seemed to have happened to a child, or when the parent asked me to hold a child. Thus one day Pete Portman, age 16 months, uttered a loud shriek, and going into the bedroom I discovered he had knocked against something and made his lip bleed. When Georgie Ross was about to receive a shot from the doctor his mother asked me to hold him on my lap because, she said, she did not want him to undergo pain when in contact with her.

(4) *How did you stand it?* If one makes a commitment to a scientific enterprise he thereby binds himself not to destroy the subject matter of his investigation. It would therefore have been preposterous to have hurled myself upon the parents every time I felt they were doing something pathogenic; and it would have been absurd also if I had become so over-

whelmed by the pathogenic behavior I witnessed that I had to run screaming from the house. Having studied the Kaingang Indians of Brazil and
the Pilaga Indians of Argentina, and having spent months and years studying psychiatric institutions, I am long accustomed to the bizarre and the
destructive. This being the case, I maintained calm at all times but one, and
my sleep and my dreams were not unusually troubled. The one time I almost became angry was at the Browns when, while one of the boys was
having an asthmatic attack brought on in part by the parents' hostility and
stupidity, the father suggested we go for a walk. Case-hardened as I am,
I am not proof against everything. My notes on this occasion read as
follows:

Mr. Brown asked me to go for a walk. This irritated me a great deal and I
asked him, "Why am I here?" At first he didn't understand and I repeated it,
implying that my purpose in being here was to be present at such situations,
and that this was no time to leave. Mr. Brown dropped the subject.

I would say that for me this event represented the peak of strain, and that
no other event approached its emotional impact in this sense, although, as
you will see, living in the homes of these families, one constantly encounters situations that might be unsettling to an untrained observer. Experience and training, however, impose automatic restraints. I imagine it must
be remotely akin to the experience of an officer watching his men die on
the battlefield.

(5) *What did I record?* I recorded everything I could remember.
Whatever it was, whether a discussion with the mother on how to broil
chicken, an observation of how the mother fed the baby, or what the father told me about his job, everything I could recall went indiscriminately
into the record. The scientific study of human emotions has been ham-
pered by decisions made long ago about what was important for the vicissitudes of the emotional life. Obviously if I was to start naturalistic observation with a preconception of what is important, no advance would be possible. I therefore took the position that everything was important and as I
dictated from memory I made no attempt to arrange the data in sequence
or in categories. I felt it was scientifically unsound to "pre-think" the data,
and I felt sure that when the record was finished I would be able to make
sense out of it. After all, I have behind me a great history of a science that
made the confusing variety of the universe appear orderly. Why not profit
by the tradition and its brilliant successes?

## THE OBSERVATIONS

Since the title of this paper is "My Life with the Families of Psychotic
Children" I want to find a way of communicating to you something of my

*life* with them and something of my *observations*. This can be done only in part, for were I to limit myself only to data that gives you an idea of what *my* life was like the distortion would be too great, and the relatively *insignificant* datum (the observer) might tend to loom larger than the centrally *important* data, the families. In presenting this material to you I shall emphasize data rather than theory—although the latter will by no means be missing—because I want you to get a good idea of what can be seen in direct observation. Therefore I shall try to "let the data speak for itself," and to restrict interpretation.

The first selection is from the study of a family of father, mother, and three children living in a small town. Tommy, the fourth child, had just been admitted to the Sonia Shankman Orthogenic School as autistic. He was the first born and was nine years old on admission. His brothers, Bobby and Jackie, are six and three respectively, and Harriet is a year and a half old. Dr. Jones, the father, is a very bright, vainglorious, ambiguous, distrustful, and violent man. Much of his thought is cast in terms of survival, competition, and defeat, and he scoffs at golf and praises tennis because in the latter you can feel the shock of the contending bodies. Dr. Jones is also disorderly, in the sense of lacking firm orientations in the fundamental categories of time, space, and objects. It is not that he is psychotically disoriented in the clinical sense, but rather that he has no feeling for time schedules, certain serious obligations, evident danger signals in the environment, and the usual notions of material order. He leaves his car door open in the pouring rain and is careless about his dress. His consultation rooms look as if they had been orderly a week ago. In the intake interviews Dr. Jones and his wife gave me a history of violent strife between them, and while I *witnessed* nothing as bad as they recounted, their behavior during my week's visit with them was witness to the probable truth of the case history. Dr. Jones' relationship to the two boys, however, seemed good. They were visibly fond of him and their relationship was rough-and-tumble, hypermasculine.

Superficially Mrs. Jones was gentle. She seemed to dissociate strong affect quickly, to push things out of her mind, so to speak, and to be fundamentally gentle and passive. Actually she could fight back with biting sarcasms, and her behavior not infrequently was provocative. She was also strikingly pretty. Thus superficially the family seemed polarized between the vicious, slashing extroversion of the father, and the quiet, cutting, deep introversion of the mother. Bobby was much like his father, except that where the father's depression had to be inferred, Bobby's was visible in his face. Yet he was bright, agile, and physically self-confident. He constantly, and even dangerously, tormented Jackie, however, and avoided his mother except to ask her for specific objects and to insult and provoke her. Jackie was a rather immature three-year-old of garbled speech and fantasy. He constantly sucked his thumb and made weeping, screaming demands on his mother. Caught between his fierce brother, his athletic father, and his displacement by the new baby, Harriet, Jackie seemed to have nowhere to go but backward. Harriet was her mother's refuge, for it was there that Mrs. Jones was able to find surcease from the battering of Bobby and her husband, and it was there that what tendencies to gentleness and tranquility yet remained to her could be fully expressed. Hence the relationship between Mrs. Jones and Harriet was unruffled and rather underprotective.

I turn now to an arrowhead hunting expedition, an event of the first day of my visit with the Joneses. Naturally, on the first day of my visit, Dr. Jones felt he had to entertain me, and therefore, in line with his stereotypic model of an anthropologist, he suggested an arrowhead hunt. The account follows:

## A SAMPLE OF INTERACTION WITHIN THE JONES FAMILY

Dr. Jones, Bobby, Jackie and I drove out into the country to find an Indian mound and search it for arrowheads. We came to a little stream and we all began to wade along it because Dr. Jones said that this was the way to the mound. There was broken glass in the stream and Dr. Jones said there was danger from snakes. Jackie, the three-year-old, got frightened and complained of the cold. He was also afraid that the water was too deep for him. Dr. Jones paid little attention to Jackie's fear. Occasionally Dr. Jones stopped and picked some broken glass out of the bed of the stream. We wandered along the stream, up on the bank, down into the stream, up on the bank again, and so on, as the stream became impassible from time to time. Several times I carried Jackie, but finally Dr. Jones carried him for a long distance as he continued to complain of the cold, and it really was quite chilly for that time of the year. At last we reached a point where it was no longer possible to go on in the stream because it was too deep. We climbed up the bank through poison ivy and encountered a barbed wire fence over which we climbed as Jackie whimpered. No one was scratched on the wire. Over the wire we found ourselves at the far edge of a wide field covered with weeds, brambles, berry bushes, and so on, and we had to walk across it, barefooted, of course, in order to reach the road that bordered its far side. I carried Bobby across the field and Dr. Jones carried Jackie. Dr. Jones was surprised when I offered to carry Bobby and he tried to dissuade me, saying that Bobby was too huge and heavy. I found him neither huge nor heavy; as a matter of fact, I scarcely felt his weight even though the going was difficult. In the Jones case history Dr. and Mrs. Jones, but especially the former, frequently refer to Bobby as "huge," "strong," and so on. Because of this I was all prepared for a giant, but I found him an ordinary, rather good-looking kid. Throughout the entire "expedition" Bobby took matters very well and it was only Jackie who complained. At last we reached the road and walked back to the car. We got in and drove about a quarter of a mile to an old house where Dr. Jones spoke to the woman of the house about our desire to explore the mound which was just behind her house, and which we could have reached simply by driving that quarter of a mile instead of trying to wade to it along the stream. We climbed up a little on the mound and found no arrowheads or anything at all that looked as if it had ever belonged to an Indian. Actually, moderate scratching around in the mound showed that it was not an archeological mound at all but a natural geological formation of rotten shale.

*Analysis*

[Figure 1] may contribute to a clear understanding of this incident.

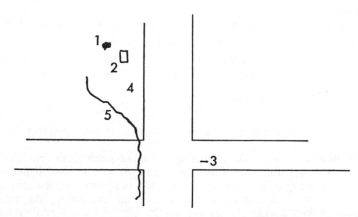

FIGURE 1: Probable relations of road, stream, field, house, and mound: (1) mound; (2) house; (3) car; (4) field; (5) stream.

It is not, of course, always necessary, especially when on a holiday, to take the shortest pathway between two points. Getting to a place by using a stream as the pathway can be fun: the pathway is defined by fun, which is the goal sought. The stream, however, was unknown, unsafe, and ultimately impassable, and turned out not to be fun. As a matter of fact, Dr. Jones had misstated the case even in regard to the direction, for the stream was not *the* way to the mound, but *a* way, a piece of information Dr. Jones withheld from us. In the presence of accumulating inconvenience and even of danger Dr. Jones did not for a long time turn back. Thus his misperception of the nature of the pathway was accompanied by an *inability to reverse himself;* and the entire venture was carried out *as if* the pathway were clear. We might say that Dr. Jones "forced the issue." It is well to bear these characteristics of the venture in mind: misperception, concealment of information, pathological as-ifness, and inability to reverse.

While wading in a stream can be fun, nobody was asked whether he wanted this kind of fun; and the enterprise was presented *as if* there was no alternative pathway. The result was that Dr. Jones endangered everybody. Such massive error of judgment, accompanied by the hiding of the alternative and an inability to reverse, suggests an obsessive process at work.

This brings us to the problem of depth. Obviously I perceive depth both in reference to myself and in reference to others; and if water is too deep, it can be too deep for me, for my child, or for both of us. Normally one reacts with anxiety to water that is too deep for one's child; and in a stream with unknown depth pockets the normal inclination would be to get out of the stream. Dr. Jones acted *as if* the danger from depth was minimal; yet he was at last *compelled* to abandon the stream because it really became too deep: *it thus took an acute and present danger, intruding upon him with overwhelming insistence,* to compel him to abandon the enterprise. Such *extreme persistence* raises the question of how *acute* and *present* a danger must be for a person to perceive it as dangerous. We have been told repeatedly about the "over anxious" parent who sees danger where there is none. We need to know more about the "under anxious" parent, who fails to see clear and present dangers. We need to know more about such *inappropriate composure.*

I have just described an event involving Dr. Jones and his two boys. Although I was part of the event I did not experience it as a member of the family did, yet since I was literally in it, I was acutely aware of all its objective features. Thus, in close proximity to the members of the family living in their native habitat, I was able to observe their actual life and arrive at some reasonably probable inferences. Because of the lack of space I do not, of course, give a complete theoretical analysis of the event. I believe it reasonably certain that the circumstances and spirit of this expedition could never be recovered from an interview. Thus naturalistic observation, by placing the observer in the midst of real family life, provides insights impossible to attain in any other way. Fundamentally, what it does is give *crucial behavior correlates of personality.*

## RELATIONSHIP TO THE OUTSIDE WORLD

I turn now to another significant aspect of family life revealed by naturalistic observation: the family's relation to the outside world. This is important to us not only because the outside world reacts to the family and so conditions its existence, but also because observations of transactions between the family and the outer world enable us to test the validity of our formulations about the family and to explore more completely its potentialities for health and illness. Meanwhile it is evident that an observer can give a better account of the family's transactions with the environment than a single member. It is also important that what seems critically significant to an observer might be withheld in an interview with a member of the family.

With these points in mind let us turn to my record of the Jones' evening at a Bible study group. The Joneses, particularly Dr. Jones, consider themselves very religious; they feel close to God; they pray; Dr. Jones reads Martin Buber and on Sunday not only goes to church but also to men's Sunday school. The account follows:

The Bible study group was made up of earnest and intelligent men who were searching for answers to questions like, What is faith? Can you trust people? Can you trust God if you don't trust people? What is the origin of faith? What makes a good religious leader? Can a religion be strong if leadership is weak? One of Dr. Jones' first acts was to attack St. Paul for what he considered Paul's pretentiousness—his pretense at humility while at the same time holding himself above everybody else. Nobody agreed with Dr. Jones. This reminds me of the violent attack he made on a couple that left before the rest of us. Dr. Jones attacked them for being rigid and unwilling to look at themselves. Meanwhile Mrs. Jones kept saying, gently, "Oh, oh" as if she was not agreeing with her husband. But that is all she said. During the course of the discussion Dr. Jones argued that faith in man is impossible, and that faith in man is entirely different from faith in God. In this he opposed almost the entire group. In the course of the discussion Dr. Jones developed the following ideas: (1) It is completely impossible for man to become one with God because man can never achieve perfection. (2) It is totally impossible for man to be unified with man, because all men are basically individuals. (3) All men are weak and full of error and evil. It seemed to me that, though always logical, Dr. Jones was sometimes very pedantic. For example, he insisted on reading the authoritative interpretation of the word "faith"; and as he read he attempted to pronounce all the foreign words with a proper foreign pronunciation. For example, he attempted to pronounce the Hebrew word with the proper Hebrew pronunciation. The limelight was focused on Dr. Jones because he was in complete opposition to everybody and was really very threatening to them, because he said he didn't trust anybody; and one woman, passionately religious, apparently, said that if his position were correct it would DESTROY HER REASON FOR LIVING. When Dr. Jones said he had no faith in anybody his wife said, "You mean to say you wouldn't even trust me not to be unfaithful?" and right out in front of everybody, he said, "No." When Dr. Jones said he had no faith that his wife would not betray him, and when he later said people are weak and may change completely from one day to the next, Mrs. Jones said this was a signal for her to go out and have a good time. As we left the meeting, one of the women asked him to repeat his position. He then mentioned a series of persons who had tried to trick him. It is interesting that he mentioned nobody who had ever been loyal. There is no doubt that his wife took all this declaration of no faith, distrust, and so on, in a very personal way. During the meeting Mrs. Jones took an active part in the discussion. It was a very different kind of Mrs. Jones from the one I encounter in trying to get her to talk about personal matters. It is interesting that right out in public she challenged her husband to tell her whether he believed she would never betray him. As we emerged from the meeting Dr. Jones at once lit into his wife for not having told the baby-sitter where he was, and the two wrangled about this all the way home. The argument was about who was to take responsibility for telling the baby-sitter where he can be reached. He said Mrs.

Jones should do the telling because she has the dealings with the baby-sitter; and she said they should both take the responsibility. However, he kept on insisting that she should do it; if two people took responsibility, nobody took responsibility. She responded that she's all concerned with telling the baby-sitter what to do with the children and is liable to forget the importance of his being in contact with his office and patients. She didn't give an inch in the argument. He was characteristically crude and she was characteristically resistant but not crude. His attack is very destructive, even when he doesn't use destructive words. His attitude is very brusque, as if talking to an inferior.

Eager to hear something about the aftermath of last night, I asked Mrs. Jones whether she and her husband had talked about it, and she said, "We only talked about it a little bit." I said, "It was quite a business," and in her usual way she made some comment which was off the main issue. So I brought the subject around directly to her husband's lack of faith in people, and she remarked that she believes this goes back to the fact that he spent a year in the hospital when he was an infant and got no real mothering. She says she believes this made it impossible for him to develop a relationship to people or any trust in them. When I raised the subject of his having said he couldn't trust her she said she *doesn't know* what it means.

As Dr. Jones and I were driving along, I brought up the subject of his lack of faith in people, and he said he raised the issue at the Bible study meeting yesterday primarily in order to test the people there, because he wants to know whether they will have faith in him should he make any mistakes in surgery. He said also that he is worried that if he gets too close to people he will become vulnerable, and this is somehow related to people's faith in him, and to his faith in them. When I reminded him of how concerned Ida was last night when he made statements about not trusting her, he laughed and affirmed that of course you can't absolutely trust anybody. After he had gone on for some time about all the people he couldn't trust and why, I asked, "Well, aren't there any people in your life who have been loyal?" and he said, "Yes, and one of them is Ida"; and then he mentioned one or two others. He said, however, that the cost of finding people you can trust is enormous; meaning that you use up a great many people trying to find a few you can trust. He said the people at the meeting were all confused—they talk about having faith in people but he doesn't believe that any of them really do.

We began to talk about the people at the Bible study meeting the other night, and Dr. and Mrs. Jones agreed that those people were entirely unrealistic about their own ability to have faith in others. Either Dr. or Mrs. Jones remarked that the husband of Sarah, one of the most active in protesting her faith in people, was a very hostile man. Dr. Jones said that Sarah's husband is the kind of man who will develop a coronary or a perforated ulcer later in life.

The Bible study group came together in order to examine the issue of faith in the light of the life and epistles of St. Paul. They hoped that in these they might, perhaps, find some basis for believing that faith of itself gives hope. However, the first thing they hear from Dr. Jones is a violent— a killing—personal attack on a sacred symbol of their religion. This is followed by an attempt by Dr. Jones to demolish by logic what hope remained: while the group hoped to come away with renewed hope, Dr. Jones tried to show there was none. Christianity rests on its sacred figures, on Jesus, Mary, and the Apostles. If the Apostles are degraded, much of Christianity becomes null, for their utterances become the mutterings of degraded men. What was threatening in what Dr. Jones had to say was not so much that St. Paul was "only a man," but that he was a pretentious one; and though pretense may lead, it can only betray. Dr. Jones' denials of the possibility of positive relations among human beings are clear from the record. Whoever does not agree with him is exposed to personal affront, like the couple that left before the meeting was over. Thus Dr. Jones attacked the group first by attacking the sacred foundations of its religion and then by attacking the premise of the meeting: that faith in man is possible. In this way he undermined the very possibility of a meeting. What became visible to the observer was the group's resentment and the anxiety and depression of one woman. It is reasonable to suppose that others felt anxiety and depression also.

In these various ways Dr. Jones turned the group, including his wife, against him and thus confirmed his underlying feeling that he could have faith in no one, and that he was therefore indeed a "lonely" man. If the intention of Dr. Jones had been to use the group to prove to himself once again that he stood alone, if it had been his intention to use it to *legitimize* his basic distrust, he could not have planned his strategy better.

Turning now to the last excerpt from the record, one finds Dr. and Mrs. Jones agreeing that the members of the group were "unrealistic about their own ability to have faith in others," as if "realism" had anything to do with the religiously motivated quest. When people in our culture engage in religious activity the real world is intuitively "suspended"[5] and one commits one's self to intercourse with the ideal. A sincere person does not go to church, to Sunday school, or to Bible study groups to learn about reality, but to have spiritual intercourse with the ideal, in the hope that it will become part of him. When, therefore, Dr. and Mrs. Jones agree that the people at the group were unrealistic they render an *inappropriate* judgment based on an inappropriate perception of what was going on. I have called this kind of error lack of circumspection. The function of this evaluation of the group as unrealistic is to legitimize—even to glorify, in a way—Dr. Jones' attack. By this time—two days later—Mrs. Jones no longer counts herself among the unrealistic ones, but has joined the "enemy," her husband, in the interest of maintaining domestic tranquility. Thus the *aftermath* of the quarrel with the group has been resolved.

Dr. Jones seems to have felt a certain expansiveness and pleasure, as the group centered its attention on him. Thus his pleasure was gained at the expense of the group. The fact that even as the group was breaking up a woman asked him to explain his position again is one sign of the dismay Dr. Jones left behind him.

As a direct aftermath of *their* quarrel during the meeting, Dr. and Mrs. Jones had an angry encounter over the baby-sitter; but as an aftermath of *Dr. Jones'* quarrel with the *group,* husband and wife had reached an *entente*: through the doctrine of "realism" his position at the meeting was *legitimized* and *his* status raised while the group's was lowered. *Family respect* was stabilized by viewing the *group* with *contempt.* Thus Dr. and Mrs. Jones *worked through* his tensions with the *group* as a *substitute* for working through their tensions with *each other:* the fundamental issue was *displaced* in favor of permitting the *domestic ambiguity* to continue.

For my last example I have chosen to describe a home visit of a 16-year-old schizophrenic boy, hospitalized in a prison-like state institution. We know that the reception a disturbed person receives on his return home often determines the outcome of his case, but all too often we can only guess what happens when he goes home. We will continue to know very little about the causes of recurrence of psychotic disturbance until we have a wide range of naturalistic observations of patients returned to their natural habitat.

Mrs. Burns is a histrionic woman who requires "oceans of love." It seems probable that because of a number of serious ailments she had in Eddie's early childhood he could not respond to his mother with anything approaching the flamboyant demonstrativeness she requires, with the result that she turned against him. On top of this Mrs. Burns is somewhat disoriented—just enough to complete the necessary pathogenesis. In contrast to Eddie, Mr. and Mrs. Burns are deeply involved in his sister, Trudy, now thirteen. The following announcement of the birth of Trudy gives the idea:

BURNS, INC.

*Proudly Presents*

GERTRUDE BURNS

*in*

HELLO WORLD

An original story of life based on Mother Nature

\*     \*     \*

Executive Producer ............................................................ John Burns
Associate Producer ......................................................... Evelyn Burns
Directed by ............................................................... Dr. J. Commons

*Assisted by the Cast of the*
*Mountain Hospital*

*Copywrited on April 6, 19—*
By Burns, Inc.

Special Costumes ............................ Triangular Panties, all subject to change.
Musical Arrangements by Evelyn's Sighs, accompanied by Gertrude's Cries.

C O M M E N T S

This production was nine months in the making. It is our prediction that
this is a 4-Star Masterpiece, and all who see this production will recognize the
exceptional performance of Gertrude Burns, and unanimously agree that she
receive the coveted award.

Don't miss our 2nd great attraction! Premiere to be held at 1205 Mercer
Street, Mansfield, Idaho. Admission—your very best wishes.

If there was such an announcement for Eddie, it was not shown me.
The following extracts of my observations show the attitude of the mother
toward Eddie on his home visit. I start with some of the preparations for
his return.

After we had been in the five-and-ten for about twenty minutes Mrs. Burns
came along and showed us immediately what she had bought. She had two
very unattractive shirts for Eddie but she said they were beautiful, one was
reduced from $3.99 to $1. At this time I am reminded that as we were going
around the five-and-ten looking for something for Eddie she said as we looked
at the candy, "I want to buy some junk for Eddie." I can't remember what
she ended up with. . . . Today in the supermarket the meat Mrs. Burns bought
for Eddie's lunch tomorrow was the cheapest hamburger she could find.

*Next day*

Almost from the moment Eddie came into the house Mrs. Burns interfered
with practically everything the boy did, in a yelling and very irritated way. As
a matter of fact, it seemed to me that her whole pattern of behavior with the
boy was so destructive and irritating that I constantly looked for effects of it
in him, and by the end of the day I think that Eddie was in pretty bad shape
for he was depressed. His facial tics had increased and he started biting his
fists. It is difficult to remember the many occasions upon which Mrs. Burns
blocked and attacked the boy. I shall try to enumerate the ones I can remember. When Eddie came into the house, you could see from his behavior
and from what he said that he wanted to soak up the house. He wanted to go
around and look at all the rooms. He wanted to sit on the porch and relax.
He wanted to go into his sister's room. Mrs. Burns would not let any of these
things happen but insisted that he sit down and eat breakfast because everybody was hungry. She dragged him off the porch by scolding him when he
was sitting out there just soaking the place up. He wanted to try on the new
pants and she said no he must eat his breakfast. . . . As a matter of fact
Mrs. Burns was a completely transformed person the minute this boy set foot
in this house. She became an irritated, nagging, destructive woman.

*At the Beach*

She was sitting on a raised platform at the back of the beach, this platform being the top of the staircase leading to the beach. Eddie, in order to
reach her, could either have gone up the steps or climbed up. Only a boy, a
young boy, would think of climbing up, so he climbed up and he was bawled

out by Mrs. Burns; and when he tried to go down the same way she bawled him out. Mr. Burns blocked him too. On the platform there were seated with Eddie quite a number of people including Mr. and Mrs. Burns; three girls, one of them his sister, who had come along with us to go swimming, and also a couple of strangers, I think. Now Mrs. Burns loudly and irritatedly called attention to Eddie's penis. She loudly and irritatedly called attention to what seemed to her the fact that his very abbreviated trunks did not adequately cover him in that region and she said that he must not wear those same trunks again without a jock strap. This sort of behavior must have been terribly destructive and humiliating to the boy although he gave no sign. After supper the following situation developed in the living room. Eddie, who has sort of taken Elvis Presley as an ego ideal, wanted to sing in the living room. Now at about the same time he got the idea of singing his sister put on the record player and he scolded her for putting on the record player just when he started to sing. At this point Mrs. Burns tore into him for trying to get the limelight and yelled at him that he is not boss around here. I had gone into the other room, and later Mrs. Burns commented on this and told me what had transpired. But an almost identical incident developed a few minutes later when he started to sing again and Mrs. Burns scolded him for always trying to be in the limelight. She also scolded him for trying to sing that kind of song instead of other kinds of songs. She scolded him for trying to sing in Elvis Presley's voice instead of his own voice. All this was done in a very loud, irritated, scolding manner. When he started to sing she showed distracted attention. She also interrupted his singing to criticize his singing. He ended up not singing at all. . . . At the table Mrs. Burns soon lost interest in Eddie and began to talk about other things, turning to me. Even in the midst of Eddie's conversation she would change the subject. I'm reminded that at one point when Mrs. Burns was talking to Eddie, possibly scolding him, I heard him sing a bar of one song titled, "Oh, Why Was I Born." The bar he sang was, "Why was I born." All day long Eddie kept singing, if I may use the term, a song . . . a part line of which was, "Are you looking for trouble." . . . Eddie roamed in and out of the rooms of the house, he could not sit still in any one place for as long as five minutes, and I think his mother bawled him out for not sitting still. Somewhere along the line she also bawled him out for being fidgety.

Here the observations speak entirely for themselves. All that is necessary to add, perhaps, is that there was scarcely an area of Eddie's behavior accessible to his mother in which she did not intervene in a disorganizing way. The result was that on the way back to the hospital, where we arrived almost too late because of Mrs. Burns' delaying tactics, Eddie's few shreds of self-confidence had disappeared, his facial tics were severe, he was biting his wrists and singing, "Why was I ever born?"

## CONCLUSIONS

Naturalistic observation of the families of psychotic children is feasible because a scientist can be admitted to their homes and because for a variety of reasons distortions of the usual mode of life of the family are not serious enough to make observation fruitless. Whether we are observing the on-going patterns of life or the return to the home of a psychotic individual, direct observation encounters almost the full drama of family existence. One should bear in mind, meanwhile, that unless direct observation is undertaken, important areas of etiology are concealed from us.

## NOTES

1. I am indebted to Dr. Bettelheim and the Ford Foundation for the opportunity to do the studies on which this paper is based; and I am grateful to the Jewish Children's Bureau for obtaining the cooperation of some families for the study. I am also in the debt of those families that opened their doors to the research, and I regret that in their own interest they must remain anonymous in this paper.
2. See J. Henry, "Common Problems of Research in Anthropology and Psychiatry," *American Journal of Orthopsychiatry*, 18: 698–703, 1948.
3. See, for example, Descartes, *Rules for the Direction of the Mind*.
4. A more extended treatment is contained in J. Henry, "L'observation naturaliste des familles d'enfants psychotiques," *La Psychiatrie de l'Enfant*, 1961.
5. Husserl's general term for excluding the usual world. See *Ideas*, pp. 155 *et seq.*

# 3:
# Some Comments on Method

*Robert D. Hess* and *Gerald Handel*

## BACKGROUND

The central aim of the research was to study families as groups of persons. This objective led us to formulate specific criteria for selecting families. The comments that follow refer not only to the five families presented in this book but also to the total group of thirty-three from which data were collected and from which these were chosen. These are the defining characteristics of the families studied:

1. The unit of study is the nuclear family—parents living with their

Reprinted from *Family Worlds* by Robert D. Hess and Gerald Handel by permission of the University of Chicago Press. © 1959 by the University of Chicago. Robert D. Hess and Gerald Handel are identified in the footnote to Chapter 1.

biological children. Families with adopted children were excluded, since our concern was with ordinary, intact families. Since, further, our interest lay primarily in understanding the interior organization of the unit made up of husband, wife, and children, we did not study the extended family— the unit that includes uncles and aunts, cousins and grandparents, as well as the nuclear family.

2. The children in these families are between the ages of six and eighteen. This criterion is based more on practical grounds than theoretical. Since all of our data-gathering techniques were verbal in nature, six seemed to us the youngest age at which we could obtain adequate data. We were not prepared to get involved with play or other non-verbal techniques because of the added complication these would entail. The upper age limit of eighteen was dictated by our intention of studying whole families. At this age some children leave home, if only to go to college, and are consequently often inaccessible. The basic framework of analysis that we have developed and presented in chapter i is applicable to families with children both younger and older than those of the present study, but its application would almost certainly require modifications in the data-gathering procedures.

The age range adopted is a wide one. The terms of our analytic framework are cast at a level of generality that does not tie them to particular age levels or forms of sibship. For our purposes, it sufficed to have some families with boys, some with girls, and some with boys and girls. The age span adopted had the distinct advantage of enabling us to develop a framework that was general and not age-restricted.

3. The families are northwest European in ancestry. This defining characteristic follows from our aim of studying a group of families relatively homogeneous in ethnic background and of minimal ethnic visibility in American society. Our interest was in understanding something of the differences that exist in that broad band of families who make up the core culture of the United States and who have no sense of tie to or inner conflict over minority group membership and tradition. The families selected are, in a broad sociological sense, not "special" in any way.

One may quarrel with the degree of homogeneity actually represented by the term "northwest European," if one wishes to press the point that only those of English ancestry have no "minority group" characteristics in this society. The objection hardly seems a serious one. There has probably been, in this country, more intermarriage within the northwest European group than between it and central or south Europeans. In addition, persons of Dutch or German or Scandinavian ancestry have on the whole lost their ethnic visibility much more rapidly than persons of, say, Slavic or Mediterranean ancestry.

4. The families are all resident in metropolitan areas, though in

some instances the parents were born and spent their early years in small towns.

5. The families range, along the dimension of social class, from upper lower to upper middle. This variation was deliberate, since we expected that important differences in family life would exist along this dimension. Variation in social class membership was intended to assure a range of differences that might be expected to influence family life. Social class has been a background concept, rather than a focal point, of our analysis. At the same time, this breadth served us in the same way as did that of the children's age span: it facilitated developing concepts for family analysis that are not class-bound, just as they are not age-bound. A wide range of occupations was included, a range generally represented by the families discussed in this book.

6. The families are selected from the community at large and not from a clinic population. The significance of this criterion again derives from our basic objectives. We wished to study the "psychosocial interior" of families, an area that has largely been the province of psychiatrists, psychologists, and social workers treating persons with psycho-clinical disorders. Our study was directed to understanding psychosocial ties in ordinary families.

These, then, are the specifications for the families we set out to study. In the period allotted for field work, we succeeded in collecting data from thirty-three families. In the course of obtaining these, approximately twenty-five families who met our selection criteria and who were approached declined to participate in the study. In addition, one family that had agreed to be studied refused to continue, after half the data had been collected. This was the only dropout.

The names of potential families for study were obtained in two ways. Various people in the community who might be able to furnish names of families were approached. Our aims were explained to them in the same terms as they later were to the families themselves: "Everyone knows the saying 'like father like son,' and we also know that it isn't always true. We would like to know more exactly just how children are like their fathers and mothers, or if they are not, why not. We are interested in studying normal, typical American families. Much research has been done on unusual or abnormal families, but relatively little on the great number of normal families that make up a community. We hope that our work will contribute more information about the important matter of bringing up our children." Preservation of the anonymity of the families to be studied was, of course, stressed. We also indicated something of the range of topics our interviewing would cover and stated that we would not be probing into the most intimately personal aspects of family life but that our interviewing would deal with the ordinary events of daily living.

The great majority of families contacted were obtained from those people in the community who were in a position to refer us to several. The second source of family names was the families actually studied. In response to our request, some referred us to families of their acquaintance. Of the total group of thirty-three, six were referrals from participating families.

The objectives of the study were explained to the husband or wife, or both, of each family contacted. It was also explained that the interviewer would want to talk with each member of the family privately and that what one member of the family said would in no instance be repeated to any other member of the family. The parents were told that all the procedures would require approximately fifteen to twenty hours of the family's time—no more than three or four hours with any one person.

In most instances the explanation of the objectives and time demands of the study were sufficient. In a few cases, families wanted to know what direct benefit they would derive from the study. For some of these, the question meant whether they would receive assistance with their own family problems. For others, the question was vaguer in intent. We explained that we could not offer counseling on family problems and that we would not in any way interpret the family to itself. To have done so would not have been consonant with the principal research condition we established—that each family member would talk about himself and his family in privacy with the interviewer and with assured confidentiality.

We explained that the only reward the family could expect was the satisfaction that, by their participation, they were contributing to scientific knowledge about family life and that, we hoped, this would ultimately be of benefit to other parents in bringing up their children.

The motives for participating in the study were not explicitly or systematically explored. Some of the parents, particularly but not exclusively the less sophisticated ones, voluntarily said that they were pleased and even flattered that they could make a contribution to scientific knowledge in this fashion. Some appeared to use the research as an occasion to express their satisfaction with what they had achieved in family living. Others seemed curious about what such a project could be like or simply welcomed this novel addition to their lives. A few perhaps still hoped, despite our explanation, that they would receive some direct assistance with their immediate problems. We received only one such explicit request from a parent concerning a child; though declining to counsel directly, we did refer the parent to an appropriate agency.

In a few instances a parent attempted to find out how a child had conducted himself with or what he had said to the interviewer. Such probing was quickly discouraged by the interviewer, who made it plain that she would not violate the confidentiality that had been promised all the members of the family. Attempts to find out what a spouse had told the interviewer were even fewer in number and were handled according to the same principle.

## OBTAINING THE DATA

After the family had agreed to participate in the study, the interviewing began with the obtaining of background information on the family. This initial session was most often held with both spouses present, but occasionally only with the wife. The former method was the one we preferred, but it was not always feasible because of the family's schedule. When this was the case, supplementary material was later obtained from the husband. This opening interview, in addition to serving as a warmup and allowing the parents to begin to feel at home with the interviewer, covered two main areas:

A. Face-sheet data
   1. Ages of all family members
   2. Birthplace of each member
   3. Family's residence history
   4. Education of husband and wife
   5. Current and previous occupations of husband and wife
   6. Nationality ancestry
   7. Religious affiliation
B. Data on early life of husband and wife
   1. What kind of people their parents were
   2. Information about brothers and sisters
   3. A characterization of what their home life was like

In retrospect, it seems that a fuller investigation of the early home life of the parents would have been helpful in further illuminating their contemporary motives in the family.

Several types of data were obtained from each family member: an interview, obtained sometimes in one session but often in two and occasionally in three; a TAT; a Sentence Completion; a brief essay from each child on "The Person I Would Like To Be Like"[1] and an essay from each parent on "The Kind of Person I Would Like My Child To Be." The data gathering—all of which was conducted in the family's residence—was concluded with the administration of a set of five TAT-type pictures to the family as a group. These pictures were especially designed for this study. To each picture the family was asked to discuss and develop among themselves an agreed-upon story. The discussions as well as the story were recorded.

Each person was interviewed in privacy for periods of an hour to an hour and a half for children and for two and a half to three hours for parents. The number of sessions devoted to interviewing any one person depended upon individual circumstances. Each member was interviewed on substantially the same topics. The questions were open-ended, designed to encourage the person to comment freely on general topics raised for discussion. Initial responses were followed by more specific probes where indicated. The interview guide covered these areas:

1. Each member's view of his family—what it is like, what the important things about it are.

2. The family's daily life—what they do and how they feel about it. The extent and variety of their activity, inside and outside the home. How the weekends differ from weekdays. The concrete happenings that occur and the kind of interaction among family members that is woven through them.

3. The work and responsibility roles of each member, including not only the earning role of the husband-father and others' feelings about it but also the assignment or assumption of household management responsibilities. Also extra-familial responsibilities in school, church, civic organizations.

4. The course of the family's development, beginning with the parents' own families of origin. What their parents and childhood homes were like. How the parents now see themselves in relation to their backgrounds—what their aims are for themselves and what they want for their children. Their goals, aspirations, regrets, and disappointments.

5. Related to the foregoing, the socialization of the children. Generally, how the parents deal with their children, how they construe the parent-child relationship. What behaviors they consider to be offenses and how these are handled.

6. How the family members perceive and feel about one another. In what ways they feel they resemble or differ from each other.

7. What problems each member feels he has in relation to himself or in relation to other family members. What he particularly likes about each other member. What changes he would like to see in himself and in the others.

The progress of the interview generally followed this order of topics, though the procedure was a flexible one and was adapted to fit individual circumstance.

TAT stories to at least ten pictures were obtained from each person. Two of the pictures were from the specially drawn set mentioned above. The remainder were selected from the Harvard TAT. Parents and children were shown the same pictures. However, some of the pictures used with the first families studied were later dropped as not yielding material sufficiently useful to warrant inclusion. A list of the pictures used is given at the end of this Appendix. The pictures selected were those that seemed to promise useful material for family analysis. Some which we did not include—12BG, for example—might also have proved quite profitable.[2]

Two forms of the Sentence Completion were devised, one for use with younger children, the other administered to older children and parents. These forms are also given at the end of this Appendix.

With the group TAT procedure mentioned above, we sought to obtain concurrent projective and interaction data. We have not yet devised a

c

satisfactory method of analyzing this material, though several have been tried. In the present volume, we have occasionally drawn on the protocols for illustration. In none of the cases here does an interpretation rest primarily on this material.

Supplementing the data obtained directly from the family members is the interviewer's record. The interviewer described the family's residence and each member of the family. She also described their demeanor during the interview and testing sessions.

## ANALYZING THE DATA

The various techniques employed to gather the data for this study are all relatively unstructured. This research strategy was deliberate and was designed to maximize freedom in two directions. It was designed to allow our informants to express themselves as freely as possible about their families and themselves, and it was also intended to allow the investigators a wide area of interpretive freedom. Our aim was clear: to find a way to describe and understand families as units while concomitantly relating the personalities of component members to the unit. This meant that we had to be prepared to work with concepts derived from psychology, anthropology, sociology, and social psychology—but in what combination we did not know in advance. Our task has been one of analysis and interpretation, as it is in any research. In carrying out this task, we have made three fundamental assumptions: (1) The data do not speak for themselves but gain coherence only as they are brought into relation with useful ideas about them. (2) The responses each informant gives us potentially convey much more than his words at face value indicate. He is also informing us about the implicit principles that guide his life and about how he organizes reality. He indicates something of his scope, his energy, his conventionality. Conclusions about such characteristics can be reached by attending not only to what is said but to how it is said. They can confidently be reached only from attending to a great deal of what a person has said, considered together. (3) What each family member says takes part of its meaning from what the other family members say.

These assumptions have guided the way we have handled the data. The essential research procedure can be described as "movement"—of which there are three kinds. We have moved freely back and forth from one type of data to another, evaluating what each person has said on each instrument, utilizing it with whatever skill and understanding we could bring to bear. It was not part of our purpose to compare the various types of data.

We have moved back and forth from one family member's material to another's, looking for meanings in both that connect them to each other. Each member in succession was taken as a point of reference; examining every other member's view of him—as well as his view of himself—we then attempted to follow out the consequences of these congruences and incongruences of image. From any particular congruence, for example, we tried to describe how members were brought together or driven apart; what kinds of overt familial behavior were fostered and what kinds of feeling were discouraged; how each member defined his place in the family and how he was assigned a place by others. In reading across all the material from a family, we asked such questions as these: Is there a clear family image, or is it diffuse? How does the family set its boundaries? To what sources does it turn for stimulation? What experiences and feelings are urged upon the members and which are shunned? How does the family regulate behavior? What opposition is there between implicit and explicit tendencies? How are the distinctions of age, sex, and birth order being treated in this family?

Finally, we moved back and forth from one family to another, considering each as a unit and asking, What distinguishes this family from others? In this procedure, the family as a group is placed in sharper focus, and the characteristics of particular individuals are assimilated to this more inclusive view. At this level of discourse, the various personalities and relationships within the family are expressed in the form of some group tendency. It is then possible to make such statements as: The Lansons provide no overt channels for intensity, which must then be contained in fantasy. The Newbolds demand intensity and assertion, and they react against evidence of its lack. Conclusions such as these are possible only if all the members of the family are studied and only if one family is compared with another.

In setting down the principles according to which the work proceeded, we are nonetheless obliged to say that their utilization cannot be made a matter of precise prescription. On two counts, the application of these principles remains at present beyond the reach of exact method and measurement. First, there is the issue of what the investigator is willing and able to conclude from his data. What he brings to bear and how far he is ready to carry his inference will determine the nature of his conclusions. Second, it is not possible to specify exactly where to look in the data for the answer to any particular question. Scrutiny of our data has taught us that we cannot predict where a person will most clearly and significantly declare himself. Presumably everything that one person says is of a piece, if we knew how to find its shape. In some cases this is easier than in others. But in any case, there is no substitute for sifting and analyzing until the investigator reaches a descriptive interpretation congruent with the data at his disposal.

## NOTES

1. This technique is described in R. J. Havighurst, M. Z. Robinson, and M. Dorr, "The Development of the Ideal Self in Childhood and Adolescence," *Journal of Educational Research,* Vol XL, No. 4 (December, 1946).
2. For a systematic account of the nature of TAT data, see William E. Henry, *The Analysis of Fantasy: The Thematic Apperception Technique in the Study of Personality* (New York: John Wiley and Sons, 1956).

# 4:

# Family Experiments: A New Type of Experimentation[1]

*Jay Haley*

In the search for more satisfying ways of explaining differences between individuals, the emphasis in psychiatry and psychology has been shifting from the study of the processes within an individual to the study of the processes which occur naturally between people. There are increasing attempts to classify and describe the functioning of married couples and families as well as ongoing groups in industry, military organizations, different psychotherapy situations, and other "groups with a history." The study of established relationships offers an opportunity for a new type of experimentation on human behavior; new because the variables to be measured are those which other psychological experiments are designed to eliminate. This paper will present some of the problems in design, sampling, and measurement as well as the results of a pilot experimental program on families containing a diagnosed schizophrenic.

Reprinted by permission from *Family Process,* Vol. 2, No. 1. Copyright 1962 by the Mental Research Institute of the Palo Alto Medical Research Foundation and the Family Institute. Jay Haley is editor of *Family Process* and research associate, Mental Research Institute of the Palo Alto Medical Research Foundation, Palo Alto, California.

## THE PURPOSE OF FAMILY EXPERIMENTS

If there were a satisfactory descriptive system for families, questions like the following might ultimately be answered: Does the delinquent come from a particular kind of family? Is there a similarity between the family of one schizophrenic and the family of another which could be related to the peculiar disorders of the patients? Is the family containing a schizophrenic different in any important way from the family which contains a psychopath or alcoholic? Is there a "normal" family system which could be differentiated from one where psychiatric symptoms exist or are likely to occur? These rather practical questions could be extended to include inquiries about the family as a system of influence, questions of cultural differences between families, the persistence of family patterns over generations, and so on.

Answers to such questions will come only with the development of a descriptive system which will rigorously classify families and differentiate one type from another. The basis for classifying families into groups is only now beginning to be explored. Such a classification cannot be a characterization of individual family members, e.g., what sort of personalities the mothers and fathers have. Similarly, impressionistic descriptions, such as statements that a family exhibits covert resentment or has shared delusions will not lead to rigorous classification. The crucial differences between families would seem to reside in the sorts of transactions which take place between family members; the study of differences becomes a classification of communication patterns in the family.

There are several basic assumptions to family study: (a) family members deal differently with each other than they do with other people, (b) the millions of responses which family members meet over time within a family fall into patterns, (c) these patterns persist within a family for many years and will influence a child's expectations of, and behavior with, other people when he leaves the family, and (d) the child is not a passive recipient of what his parents do with him but an active co-creator of family patterns.

Various research groups, including those of Bateson (1), Bowen (3), Fleck (5), and Wynne (6), have observed families of schizophrenics and are in general agreement that there are similarities among these families other than the schizophrenic behavior of one of the members. The ways the parents deal with each other, as well as the ways they behave with the psychotic child, seem to follow consistent patterns from family to family. All of the researchers seek some way of describing the unique kind of interactive process observed when these family members are brought together. Further, the goal is to phrase such a description in a way which would ultimately permit quantitative validation of descriptive statements.

Clinicians usually are uneasy about quantification, feeling that those variables least relevant to the real problems are always chosen to be counted. Yet it would seem inevitable that study of the family must lead to quantification of some sort. If one suggests that schizophrenia (or any characteristics of an individual) is related to the family, he is implicitly suggesting that there are two types of family system, the schizophrenic and the non-schizophrenic. He is immediately involved in a sampling problem and a problem of measurement. If he suggests that one type of family produces a schizophrenic and another does not, the investigator must support such a hypothesis by observation and description of the two types of family. If his emphasis is upon the *family* rather than upon the indivduals within it, he must bring family members together in some situation where he can observe and record their activity together. Such research inevitably tends toward the arrangement of structured settings in which samples of families can be placed to observe their similarities and differences.

It is becoming more common for families to be brought together and tape recorded or filmed while having a conversation. The investigators attempt to classify the transactions which take place between family members and note which families use which range of transactions. Yet the process of communication between people is extraordinarily complex; they communicate verbally, with vocal inflections, with body movement, and with reference to unique past, familiar incidents. Any classification of this complex of communication will depend upon the skill of the observer— and the skill in observation of those he reports his findings to. Should an investigator note, for example, that a mother has a certain response whenever her child joins with father in some agreement, he would need a way of identifying that "certain response" whether it was a verbal statement, an inflection of voice, or a slight body movement. Other observers might overlook her response or interpret it differently. The ultimate verification of typical family patterns would seem to be possible only if the family is placed in some experimental situation where the responses can be recorded by some other means than the quick eye of an investigator, as necessary as his observations might be before such experimental situations could be devised.

The Bateson project developed a theory and a descriptive system for families, with data drawn from therapy sessions with families of schizophrenics. They placed schizophrenic as well as non-schizophrenic families in a standard interview situation, which included leaving the family alone to talk together, in order to note similarities and differences in the responses to the situation. Finally, the project began to devise explicit experimental settings for measurement of family behavior. When actual experiments were attempted on families, it was found that there was little general theory available to isolate the important variables to be measured, and that the type of experiment and the sampling problems were without precedent.

## UNIQUE PROBLEMS IN EXPERIMENTATION

There is a history of psychological experimentation with animals, with individuals, and with small groups, but experimentation with family systems is a discontinuous change from that history. There is no adequate precedent for this type of experiment; the methodology which has been developed to experiment with individuals and with artificial groups does not apply to the measurement of typical patterns of an ongoing system.

### THE FAMILY VERSUS THE INDIVIDUAL

When one experiments with individuals, it is conventional to eliminate the influence of interpersonal factors. Quite the reverse is the goal of experimenting with an ongoing relationship; the interpersonal factor is to be measured.

Experimentation and testing of individuals classifies different types of individuals or measures some factor which is thought to be generally characteristic of people. These investigations usually emphasize some internal process within the person: his learning ability, his perception, the way he makes decisions, amount of anxiety, and so on. Typically a standard situation is created in which the experimenter exposes a series of individuals to some sort of stimuli and measurement is taken of their responses. It is hoped that the standardization of the situation will mean that the relationship with the experimenter is the same for all subjects so that the only variables will be differences between subjects. When a shift is made from experimenting upon individuals to experimenting upon a relationship, a quite different procedure is necessary. One must create some standard context and place two or more people within it and measure their responses to each other. Then one must place two or more other people, presumably involved in a different type of relatedness, in the same situation and measure their responses. Whereas in individual experiments it is necessary to eliminate as much as possible the subject's response to another person, in experimenting with ongoing systems the typical response of one person to another must be measured.

In general, most psychological experiments could be called Inferential Experiments. Certain inferences are made about an individual, and experiments are designed to test those inferences. For example, an inference is made that individuals will learn more rapidly with reward rather than punishment. An experiment is designed, and the results indicate whether the inference could be said to be accurate or not. What is measured is not the process of learning, but certain behavior which is inferred to have occurred because the process of learning took place. Family experiments could be called Descriptive Experiments. After observation of certain behavioral patterns in a type of family, an experiment is designed to test the behavioral description which has been made. These shifts of emphasis leave the family experimenter unable to use as precedent most of the previous experimentation done in psychology.

### THE FAMILY VERSUS THE SMALL GROUP

Although it might be thought that family experiments would be comparable to small group experiments because the family is a small group, there are marked differences. In the usual small group experiment a situation is arranged and several unrelated people are placed within it. Measurement is then taken of the effect of that context on their behavior. The people are carefully chosen so they are not acquainted, far less related, to eliminate any variable other than the effect of that particular setting on their performance. In the family experiment precisely the opposite is the goal: The problem is to measure how members of a "group with a history" *typically* respond to each other, while attempting to eliminate as much as possible the effect of that particular setting on their performance.

An illustration will clarify the difference. A small group experiment might be designed in which three people, A and B and C, are placed within a communication network where A can communicate with B and B can communicate with C, but A and C cannot communicate with each other. Another network can be set up in which all three people can communicate freely with each other. The two groups are then given a task to perform. Measurement is taken to discover whether the group which can communicate freely has less or more difficulty with the task than the group where individual A and individual C can only communicate with each other through B.

In contrast, suppose an experiment is attempted with the Jones family after preliminary observation indicates that father and mother rarely speak to each other, if at all, but talk to each other "through" their daughter who can communicate with both of them. Instead of merely pointing out this "obvious" communication pattern in this family, we wish to devise an experiment which will show by quantified results that the family follows a typical pattern of speaking through the child.

Although the limited communication network set up for the small group experiment and the limited communication network which this family has developed for itself are similar, the problem of measurement is obviously not the same. Our problem in experimenting with the family is not to show whether with their particular network they have more or less difficulty with a task, but to show what their particular network *is*. We might, for example, place the family in a situation where they could communicate freely or follow their typical restricted communication. Measurement could be taken of how often they chose either method of communication.

The difficulties involved in this type of experimentation are quite different from those in small group experiments. The Jones family in its natural state might consistently follow one pattern, but placed in an experimental setting where they are being observed they might follow another pattern. In this case, for example, father and mother might wish to conceal the fact that they don't usually speak to each other and so during the period of the experiment they might converse.

Although some adaptation of small group experiments might be possible for family experimentation, it would seem that measurement of typical patterns in a particular family, even quite rigid and crude patterns, will differ markedly from measurement of the effect of different contexts on unrelated people who have been placed in them.

## THE SAMPLING PROBLEM

A major purpose of any family experimental program would be to provide some statistical evidence to support points of a hypothesis derived from natural history observations of families. This evidence would presumably be in the form of counting events which did or did not occur or counting units of time in the accomplishment of some task. As a reluctant choice, there might be some use of verbal materials rated by judges along some pre-set scale.

Presuming an experiment were devised where totals could be counted, it would be necessary to run sufficient schizophrenic and non-schizophrenic families to have two sample groups. The average performance of these groups, when contrasted, makes it possible to compare the two types of family. A basis of comparability would be an acceptance or rejection of one or both of two possible hypotheses: (a) we can attempt to accept or reject the hypothesis that there is no difference between the family of the schizophrenic and the non-schizophrenic on the factors being measured, (b) we can set out to accept or reject the hy-

c*

pothesis that there is no more similarity between one schizophrenic family and another on the factors being measured than there is between any schizophrenic family and any non-schizophrenic family.

Whether "statistically significant" differences between types of families imply real differences in the populations sampled must depend upon the sampling procedure. A level of significance which might be adequate with samples selected randomly from well-defined populations could be quite inadequate with the sort of sampling problems involved in family work.

Most sampling designs in psychology are based upon the characteristics of individuals, i.e., the populations to be sampled are defined in terms of the characteristics of individuals. Any individual can be classified according to a pre-existing set of characteristics which can be listed and are considered important, such as sex, age, marital status, religion, education, and so on. If one wishes to take a sample of families, it becomes immediately apparent that the relevant characteristics of families have never been listed.

The rather vague classifications of families which exist are actually based upon the characteristics of individuals in families. For example, the economic level classification of a family is essentially a statement of father's income, the classification "Catholic family" or "Protestant family" is a statement of the religious affiliation of individual family members. A classification of families *as families* would require some statement of the characteristic patterns of responsive behavior in that family. The ways family members deal with each other, if these could be listed, would provide a classification of types of family systems. Any classification of this nature would require statements which describe the interaction of two or more family members. For example, there might be a class of families whose characteristic is an inability to maintain any coalitions between family members, or there might be a class in which the parents maintain coalitions against the children but no child can maintain a coalition with one parent against another, and so on. Such a classification of types of relationship in the family does not exist, and in fact there is not as yet a language to build such a classification. Yet a proper sampling of families should be of types in this sense since the sample should be based upon the characteristics of the system being studied rather than upon the characteristics of an element in that system.

At this time schizophrenic families are identified by the presence of a member diagnosed schizophrenic. To substantiate the hypothesis that schizophrenia is somehow related to the family, one must deal with the definition of a schizophrenic and the definition of a family. The diagnosis of schizophrenia is based in part upon an archaic set of premises dealing largely with unobservable processes occurring within the patient. It is not even generally agreed that there is *a* schizophrenia, but some insist there are multiple types of schizophrenia. It is also not entirely clear that three pychiatrists would make the same diagnosis of schizophrenia in any particular patient except in those cases where the patient has long been hospitalized and is chronic. Recently the question has been raised whether the chronic schizophrenic is actually much more than a person responding to long-term hospitalization in a total institution, and so even that diagnosis might not be useful for doing a family study. Further, there is the question of including under schizophrenia not only different types, such as paranoid, hebephrenic, or catatonic, but borderline diagnoses such as schizo-affective states, schizoid, autistic, and so on. The time interval of a diagnosis also becomes a problem: Is a patient always schizophrenic once that diagnosis has been made, or does he remit and so can no longer be classified as schizophrenic? Is a schizophrenic who has had apparently successful therapy a candidate for experimentation, or is he no longer a schizophrenic? What of spontaneous remission—is a patient who went through a schizophrenic episode but now appears in good shape still to be classed as a schizophrenic? Further, can a patient currently in a psychotic episode be classed with a patient who is no longer manifesting overt symptoms but is still hospitalized?

If we assume that family systems will differ from each other if any one member is *systematically* behaving differently within the family and further assume that the pre-schizophrenic, the overt schizophrenic, the remitted schizophrenic and the schizoid are systematically behaving differently from each other, then it would follow that within the category "schizophrenic family" there would be at least four different types of family system. These types would be in addition to the possibilities of sub-species of families based on the presence of different types of overt schizophrenia.

A further difficulty in definition resides in the question of what is a family. Is it essential to include the extended family, including grandparents and other relatives? Is the family containing a stepfather comparable to a family containing natural parents? Is a patient with a father and older sister but no mother comparable to a patient with a mother and father? If the patient has had little or no contact with his family for some years, can he be classed with the patient living at home? Could a chronic patient's ward doctor and nurse be comparable to a family? Is a family with six children comparable to one where the patient is an only child?

RIGOR IN SAMPLING

To clarify the sampling difficulties, let us suppose an ideal situation. Let us suppose that there exists a population of clearly diagnosed schizophrenics whose parents are alive, available, and involved with the patient. We shall refer to this population as the group of schizophrenic families. Let us further suppose that there exists another population of parents whose children are not schizophrenic. We shall designate this population as the group of non-schizophrenic families.

Since we cannot experiment with all the families in these two groups, we will take a sample of each group. Our samples must be chosen in such a way as to justify some inference about each of the total groups. We must, therefore, take a random sample of each group in such a way that any family has an equal chance of appearing in our sample. Once we have our two sample groups, we place the families in the same experimental situations and quantify the results. We may be then able to make statements about real differences between the two types of families which are inferred at some designated level of significance.

There are two crucial points in such an ideal situation: (a) to determine whether a difference is real or not, our samples must be selected randomly, and (b) the families must be placed in the same experimental context. When we leave the ideal situation and approach the actual situation both criteria are difficult to meet.

THE SELECTION OF A SAMPLE OF FAMILIES

In reality a sample of schizophrenic families is not only doubtfully diagnosed and often shattered with divorces and separations, but also many patients have left home and are more involved with spouses than with their family of origin. However, including only those patients "involved" with their parents, they are identifiable only through an institution or through a psychiatrist in private practice and must "volunteer" to come in and be experimented upon.

In a preliminary attempt to build a sample of families with schizophrenics, it became apparent that a suitable random sample would be difficult to obtain. The reactions of the families indicated that a considerable bias might be apparent in those families who do cooperate. Since the parents assume they are being observed to see what they have to do with the child's illness, they have nothing to gain except embarrassment by coming in, except in those cases where the parents see in such a venture some hope for some help for themselves. The parents' stout defense that they do not have anything to do with the child's illness, which is typical of these families, tends to be a highly selective factor unless the families are required to come in as part of the child's treatment.

The selective problem also is present with a "non-schizophrenic" group. "Non-schizophrenic" families who agree to come in might differ markedly from those who refused. A family having difficulty between members would doubtfully come in to put their difficulties on public display—except in those cases where the difficulty was so extreme they were seeking help. Interviews with "non-schizophrenic" families tend to indicate they are either reasonably amiable with each other or rather desperate, but at any rate they are doubtfully a random sample.

Yet another problem with such a "non-schizophrenic" sample is the fact that the families may not have had contact with a psychiatrist, but a good percentage might well contain a pre-schizophrenic or an undiagnosed schizophrenic. The child brought in for the experiment might be in one of those categories, or the child might be the sibling of a hidden schizophrenic at home. Therefore, our "non-schizophrenic" sample could predictably be expected to include a percentage of families similar to our schizophrenic sample.

Further, it would seem illogical that a "non-schizophrenic" sample would be homogeneous and therefore easily sampled in regard to any aspect of families that we might choose for our purposes. That is, it would be naive to think that there are "schizophrenic" families and "non-schizophrenic" families. Actually, there will be in any normal sample a variety of types of families rather than a single "non-schizophrenic" type, just as there will be a variety of kinds of symptoms in the children in any random sample of the normal population.

### THE SAME EXPERIMENTAL CONTEXT

The second criterion of any experimentation, that the two groups be placed in the same experimental situation, is also difficult to achieve. It would be naive to assume that if two families are given the same verbal instructions for an experiment, they will be in the same experimental context. If a schizophrenic family is brought in feeling accused because something has gone wrong with their child and defensive about what will be shown wrong in their family, they are hardly in the same experimental context as a family coming in with no accusation of anything wrong in the family but merely to be cooperative with some research. Inevitably in a schizophrenic family any request that the parents be brought together with the patient is a suggestion that they have something to do with the patient's illness. A contrast family without a patient cannot approach the experimentation with the same frame of reference. Even if the "non-schizophrenic" family is told that the research centers on family organization and mental health, this is doubtfully accusation enough for the family to be as defensive in proving their mental health as is the schizophrenic family where the patient has been diagnosed and hospitalized. (This problem is quite separate from the question of whether a major characteristic of the schizophrenic family is some form of defensiveness, and therefore something to be measured with experimentation.) It is not possible to separate the performance in any experiment from the context in which the experimentation takes place, nor is it a simple problem to find a way to provide a "schizophrenic" and a "non-schizophrenic" family with the same context. If the context is not the same, performance differences are doubtfully valid.

## THEORY AND METHOD

To choose one family and pluck it from the network of families whose totality make up the culture is to do some violence to the wider influence on the family. Having chosen a family, to select a few family members from it and discard the others means ignoring the complex influence of grandparents, aunts and uncles, and all those related people whose ideas affect the ways individual family members deal with each other. Further, to take a few members of a family and examine only certain species of their interaction together requires an extraordinary simplification of the complicated gestalt of their life together. Yet to build a theoretical conception it would seem necessary to begin with the less complex whenever a relevant formal pattern appears to be present and to proceed from there to additional complexities. An arbitrary decision was made in this research to begin with the central nucleus of the family—mother, father, and one child—and to develop the most elementary types of experiment for this three-person system.

The investigation was preliminary and exploratory; the sampling problem was examined rather than solved, with the emphasis on experimenting with experiments rather than producing conclusive findings about families. The theoretical problems, and an example of a type of experiment which was run on a small sample of families, will be reported here.

### THE SEARCH FOR TESTABLE HYPOTHESES

To classify into groups a number of three-person families, one must be able to label typical patterns of the ways the three people deal with each other. These patterns must be described rigorously enough so that it is conceivable to devise an experimental situation which would prove or disprove a statement about a family. The ingenuity required to devise an experiment which will emphasize rather than obscure a family pattern is one problem; to make a descriptive statement which can be potentially tested is the problem of the moment.

The clue to an approach to this sort of investigation lies in the basic premise on which such a study is based: any one family is a stable system. It is stable in the sense that statements about the family have ongoing truth over time. Such a premise follows from the fact that a family is an organization and so follows a limited range of behavior. This premise is also supported by observations of family members talking together week after week and month after month. Certain sequences occur again and again. Approaching a three-person family as a system which is stable over time, one is led naturally to the kind of theory concerned with the maintenance of stability in any system. If a system is stable, there is a governing process at work which maintains the limits of variability of the system. A family system may break down, and the result is separation and divorce, but if people continue to live together there is a self-corrective process at work which makes their continued association possible, even though this self correction may make continued conflict. If one person goes too far in any direction and exceeds the limits of tolerance of other family members, they will respond in such a way that the extreme behavior is corrected. The system must correct itself or dissolve into separate entities. From this point of view the family is a governed system with each family member one of the governors of that system.[2] The self governing process *within* the family appears particularly important in the family of the schizophrenic. The influence of an external governor is minimized by the ways these family members isolate themselves from other people.

The function of a governor in the usual self-corrective system is supervisory; it takes action when some variable in the system is exceeding a certain range. For example, the household thermostat will turn on a furnace when the room temperature drops below a certain point and turn off the furnace when the temperature exceeds a certain point. The system will regulate itself, fluctuating within a limited range. However, this range is pre-set for the thermostat, usually by a human being who sets the range of temperature he prefers. The thermostat may govern the system, but since the human being sets the thermostat he is the governor of the governor.

If we use the analogy of a self-corrective system for describing a family, we must include as the function of each family member two sorts of supervisory capacity: each person not only responds in an "error activated" way if another family member exceeds a certain range of behavior, but each person also attempts to pre-set the range of behavior for the other people. A mother and child may be in conflict over whether mother takes care of the child properly, but they also may be in conflict over whether a "taking care of" relationship is the type they should have together. What sort of relationship people have together is a matter of pre-setting limits on behavior; whether one or the other is responding appropriately within that sort of relationship is another level of governing process (2, 4). These two levels may be separable for purposes of analysis, but often they occur simultaneously. The message which indicates that certain behavior is inappropriate in that relationship also is questioning, reinforcing, or re-defining, what sort of relationship it is. If mother says

to father, "You treat me like a child," she is indicating that some statement he made is inappropriate to a relationship between two equals and
thereby defining their relationship as one between two equals. However,
she may also be provoking her husband to treat her like a child and then
protesting when he does and so be maintaining a continual confusion as
to their type of relationship.

If we examine parents and child as a stable system with each person
governing the behavior of the other two, it is possible to describe patterns
in the ways they influence each other. These patterns will be abstract in
the sense that they are formal rather than concerned with content. One
way to conceptualize the governing processes in a family is to approach
families as a system of rules established by the ways family members
deal with each other. The members of a particular family will not use the
full range of behavior possible to them; the potential behavior of any one
member will be limited by the responses of the other members. These
limitations are rules for what sort of behavior is to take place in the family.
If father tells daughter to help mother with the dishes, he is establishing,
or reinforcing, a variety of rules. A few can be suggested: he is indicating
that in this family daughter helps mother; he is indicating that in this
family father decides who shall help whom; he is indicating the rule that
he is allowed to comment on what sort of relationship mother and
daughter are to have, and so on. He may also be cooperating in a situation where he is dragged into a conflict between mother and daughter and
so be following a rule that mother require him to join her. Whether the
rules are accepted or not depends not only on father's directions but
daughter's response to those directions as they work out an agreed upon
set of rules. In some other family the mother might ask father to tell
daughter to help her with the dishes and he might say that it is not his
business to do so. By responding in this way, he would be establishing,
or reinforcing, a different set of rules.

Classifying the rules which any one family develops, and the processes whereby they work out these rules, could conceivably lead to a way
of classifying families into groups. However, these rules are not necessarily
explicitly stated by family members or even known to them. They are a
format of regularity imposed upon a complicated process by the investigator. If the investigator is accurate in his observation that a particular
family follows such and such a rule, then it should be possible to place the
family in an experimental context where they would follow such a rule.
The difficulty in such an endeavor rests on the fact that these rules are
not simple but always function at several levels: there are not only rules,
but rules about making rules and rules about how not to follow rules. For
example, one might observe a family and note that whenever the family
is asked to decide something, father announces the decision. One might

say that father is the prime indicator of what is to happen in the family. Yet mother and child might typically not do what he decides. Or mother might consistently say, "You decide, dear," so that the decision may be in his hands, but *who* is to make the decision is in his wife's realm according to the rules. Any statement about a simple rule a family appears to follow may become more complex the more the context of the rule is explored.

### THE FAMILY OF THE SCHIZOPHRENIC

From this general point of view, suppose one imagined a family which was manifesting the following rule: no family member will permit another family member to set rules for his behavior. If a family behaved in this way, there would be a central paradox. The family might be a stable system with each family member governed by the response of other family members, but each would be indicating that the others were not to govern his behavior. If one directed another to do anything, the other would have to indicate that he was not to be governed by that person. This refusal to be directed might be expressed directly, it might be expressed by the person doing what he is told reluctantly, or it might be expressed by the person "taking over" the direction with an indication that he is doing it but for some reason other than the person's direction.

The idea of one person directing another to do something can be enlarged beyond mere requests for specific activity. Actually any message from one person to another must include a "command" or "directive" aspect. The existence of the message, as well as the way the message is given, may compel a certain sort of response from the other person. If one person says to another, "It's a nice day today," he is not explicitly directing the other person how to behave, but he is indicating what sort of behavior the other person should deliver. If a person is "programmed" to refuse to follow any direction from anyone, he must respond in a complicated way even to the most simple sort of message.

The family of the schizophrenic—mother, father, and schizophrenic child—would seem to be following the rule that none of them will permit the other to govern his behavior and so elicit a particular response. The result is a peculiar kind of communication in this sort of family. Whatever one says, the other indicates that he shouldn't have said it or it wasn't said properly or not at the proper time and place. If one says, "Let's do such and such," the others must follow the rule that their behavior is not to be governed by that person, and so they cannot merely reply, "Yes, let's do," and then do it. They may say, "Yes," and then not do it. They may say, "Yes," but qualify it with an indication they really would rather not. They may agree and do it and then later say they hadn't really wanted to. They may say they had that idea earlier themselves and are willing to do it not because they were asked but because they really initiated it.

All of these examples of types of response to direction are formally the same: each example represents an incongruence between what a person says or does and the way he qualifies what he says or does. Just as one can have two levels of governing process when one governor governs another, so one can have two, or many, levels of message when one message qualifies another. When parents and child in this type of family are brought together, they consistently manifest an incongruence between these levels. As a result you rarely hear one affirm what another says, unless at some other time this affirmation is negated. It would naturally follow that if there were a rule in the family that no one was to concede that he was governed or directed by the others, and if every message they exchanged directed a certain sort of response, then they would need to "disqualify" each other's messages consistently.

Since the incongruence between levels of message which these family members consistently show is often subtle as well as crude, such an observation can only be verified if the observer is skillful and then two observers might disagree. At this point experimentation becomes relevant. It is not a simple matter to construct an experimental situation where the family members can communicate with each other at two levels and which involves each directing the others how to respond. Yet from the point of view of this research, it is this sort of patterning of communication which is most relevant to the development of psychopathology in a family and to the classification of families into groups.

A way to create a hypothesis which might be validated by experimentation is to examine one of the results of this peculiar type of communication pattern in the family. It should follow that if the members must "disqualify" what each other says, they would have difficulty forming and maintaining coalitions in the family. Observations of the family of the schizophrenic indicates that this is so. When any one member tries to get together with another, the other responds in a way that disqualifies that invitation. For example, should father and mother join together in an attempt to discipline their child, they typically end in a row with each other with one or the other saying the other is too mild or too severe.

The hypothesis that this type of family has more difficulty forming and maintaining coalitions between two members should be verifiable with an experiment, and a report of such an experiment will be given here. Several versions of an experiment designed to test this hypothesis were attempted. The final version offered family members both the opportunity to form alliances and the opportunity to communicate at two levels. Before describing this particular experiment, a few generalizations can be made about the criteria for this kind of experimentation:

1. The experiments must deal with the responses of family members

to each other rather than their individual responses to stimuli from the experimenter. The measure is of the system rather than the individuals within it, and so the experiment must require family members to interact with each other.

2. At least some of the experiments must be of such a nature that any one family will behave in a consistent way in that experiment over a period of trials. If one family behaves differently each time on the experiment, it is difficult to argue that two families who behave differently are really different.

3. The experiments must be of such a nature that it cannot be argued that intelligence, education, or manual dexterity of the family members was a major determinant of the results, unless one assumes the psychopathology being measured is based upon intelligence, education, or manual dexterity.

4. The experiments must be such that it cannot be argued that because one member is a schizophrenic the results of the experiment inevitably follow. For example, it should not be a task which the schizophrenic could not, or would not, participate in so that it could be said, "No one could do that task with him involved."

5. It must be a type of experiment which a family will participate in, willingly or not. That is, the task must be something everyone in the family can do.

6. The experiment must be of such a nature that it does not impose patterns on the family by forcing them to change under duress their typical patterns, unless measurement is being made of the ability of a family system to change under stress.

7. The experimentation must involve multiple experiments to measure multiple factors in families. There are possibly no single differences between any one type of family and any other type.

8. The experiments must show extreme differences between types of families, granted the sampling problems in this sort of study.

In summary, family experiments must meet some rather complicated criteria, besides providing the usual problems of theoretical conception and problems of measurement, and there is little precedent for the required experimental designs.


## A COALITION EXPERIMENT

Father, mother, and child are placed at a round table with high partitions so they cannot see each other [Figure 1]. In front of each person there is a small box with a window in it. This is a counter, like an automobile speedometer, which runs up a score visible only to the person

Child                                                          Father

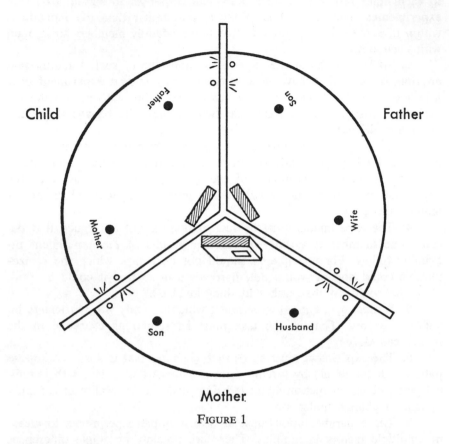

Mother

FIGURE 1

in that area. Also in front of each person there are two buttons which are
labeled for the persons on the left and right. That is, in mother's position
she has a button labeled "husband" and a button labeled "son" (or
"daughter" as the case may be). Besides these two buttons, which we
shall call the coalition buttons, there are two more buttons, one on each
side. These are signal buttons. When pushed, the signal button lights up
a small light in the area of the person on the other side of the partition.
By pushing either of these two buttons, for example, mother can signal
father or child. All of these buttons are connected with pens on an event
recorder in the control room so that all button activity is recorded during
the experiment.

The table is wired so that the counters begin to add up a score
whenever two people choose each other by pressing each other's coalition button. When mother presses the button labeled "husband," nothing

happens until father presses his button labeled for her. When both buttons are pressed at once, then both counters add up a score at the same speed and continue to do so (making an audible sound) as long as both buttons are pressed. Therefore each person can gain a score only if he joins another person, and then he and that person gain exactly the same amount of score. Each person can signal another with the signal button to invite a coalition. The family is asked not to talk together during the experiment so they can only communicate by button pushing.

Father, mother, and child are placed at this table and told this is a game they are to play together. They are instructed that they should each try to win by getting the highest score. They may push buttons one at a time or two at a time or not at all. The only rule is the prohibition against talking during the game.

The "game" consists of three rounds of two minutes each which are begun by the experimenter and ended by him. At the end of each round the family members are asked to read off their scores, and then the next round is begun without setting the counters back to zero so the score is cumulative.

In this situation each person must form a coalition with another to make a score, and yet he can only make the same score as the person he joins. To win, each must shift coalitions and gain score from both of the other two players. That is, if mother only joins father, she will have a high score at the end of the two minute round but father will have the same score if he has only joined her, and neither can win.

The family members are free to signal each other to indicate they want to form a coalition; they are free to signal without following the signal with a push of the coalition button; they can signal one person while forming a coalition with the other; they can form coalitions by getting together without any signalling; and they can form one or two coalitions simultaneously. Therefore the table permits a range of family behavior and all this behavior is recorded.

In addition to the three round game, the family is asked to have a fourth round. Before they begin the fourth round, they are asked to talk together and decide who is to win that round and who is to lose. Then they are to have another two minute round and see if they can make the scores come out the way they planned. This conversation is recorded.

## THE SAMPLE

A total of sixty families was run in this experiment. Thirty normal families were selected on the basis of a random choice of students from a high school directory. The parents of the students were telephoned and the sample consists of those families whose members had never had psychotherapy and who were willing to come in for the experiment. The children ranged in age from 14 through 17, and there were 13 girls and 17 boys in the sample. The educational background of the families can be described in terms of the highest educated member of the family; there were 5 high school graduates, 9 who were high school graduates with some additional training, and 16 college graduates or above.

The group of thirty families containing a schizophrenic child were chosen on the basis of availability. Some families were obtained through a family therapy program, others from the records of state hospitals, and others included children actually hospitalized at the time. The children ranged in age from 11 through 20. The sample included one family with a stepfather who was in the home three years prior to the child's breakdown. In the sample there were 3 girls and 27 boys—a more equal distribution could not be obtained. In education, taking the highest educated member of the family, there were 4 who had completed less than four years of high school, 7 high school graduates, 7 who were high school graduates and had additional training, and there were 12 college graduates or above.

Of the sixty families, twenty normal families and twenty families containing a schizophrenic child were run with the instruction that they could push buttons in any way they pleased and therefore they could form coalitions with one or two people simultaneously. This procedure is called *Experiment One*. Another 10 normal and 10 schizophrenic families were run with the instruction that they could form only one coalition at a time and so could not score with two people at once. This is called *Experiment Two*. On certain measurements the combined totals of the two experiments are reported.

## PREDICTIONS AND RESULTS

Certain predictions were made about the differences between these two groups in the experiment. These predictions will be summarized here along with a brief summary of the actual results.

1. *It was predicted that the family of the schizophrenic would have more difficulty forming and maintaining coalitions. Therefore the schizophrenic group would have a higher percent of time when no member of the family was in coalition with any other member.*

The twenty normal and twenty schizophrenic families which were run in *Experiment One* where the family members could push buttons in any way they pleased differed significantly in the percent of time no member was in coalition with any other member. (The difference was significant at the .05 level.[3])

The ten normal and ten schizophrenic families which were run in *Experiment Two* where the family members could only score with one person at a time also differed significantly in the percent of time no member was in coalition with any other member. (The difference was significant at the .05 level.)

The combined results of *Experiments One* and *Two*, totalling 30 normal and 30 schizophrenic families, differed significantly on this measurement with a level of significance of .01.

2. *It was predicted that the family of the schizophrenic would have longer continuous periods of time when no two family members were in coalition.*

The longest periods of continuous time when there was no coalition in three rounds of the game was significantly greater in the schizophrenic than in the normal group. In *Experiment One,* with twenty families in each group, the difference was significant at the .005 level. In *Experiment Two,* with 10 families in each group, the difference was significant at the .01 level. The results of the two experiments combined showed a significant difference at the .001 level.

3. *It was predicted that the average lengths of time in coalition would be shorter in the schizophrenic group.*

The two groups did not differ significantly on this measurement.

4. *The members of the schizophrenic family would be less consistent with each other than the normals. There would be less consistency in following a signal with a press of the coalition button, and less frequent response by the person signalled.*

The two groups only differed significantly in the consistency of family members in the case of the child. The schizophrenic child followed a signal with a coalition press less often than did the normal child (significant at the .05 level). There was no significant difference between the parents of the normal child and the parents of the schizophrenic child on this measurement.

The child in the schizophrenic family was also less responsive to both parents than the normal child when his parents signalled him and then pressed his coalition button (significant at the .01 level). There was no significant difference between the parents in the two groups on this measurement.

5. *It was predicted that the members of the schizophrenic family would be less "successful" than the normal group, measured by the amount of time pushing the coalition button in proportion to the amount of time they spend scoring with someone.*

The two groups differed significantly in the parent's "success" with the child but not in their "success" with each other. That is, if the amount of time mother and father are actually in coalition with the child is divided by the amount of time they are pressing his coalition button, the resulting percent differs significantly from the results of the parents in the normal group (the difference is significant at the .05 level on the t-test and the Median Test).

Actually the parents of the schizophrenic child tended to be more "successful" with each other on this measurement than the parents of the normal child, although the difference was not significant.

6. *In the planned round, it was predicted that the schizophrenic families would have more difficulty reaching agreement on who was to win and who to lose, and it was predicted that they would have more difficulty making the round come out with the winner and loser they had agreed upon.*

The problems of classifying verbal material were such that it proved too difficult to measure whether the schizophrenic families had more difficulty reaching agreement on who was to win and who to lose than the normal families.

However, there was a striking difference between the two groups in their success at making the winner and loser come out as they agreed.

| | Chosen to win | | | Succeed | |
|---|---|---|---|---|---|
| | Normals | Schizo-phrenic | | Normals | Schizo-phrenic |
| Child | 20 | 20 | Yes | 28 | 15 |
| Father | 6 | 5 | | | |
| Mother | 4 | 5 | No | 2 | 15 |
| | 30 | 30 | | 30 | 30 |

Most of the normal group could make the round come out as they planned, as far as getting the winner right, whereas half the schizophrenic group could not. (The difference was significant at the .001 level on the Chi Square test.)

| | Chosen to lose | | | Succeed | |
|---|---|---|---|---|---|
| | Normals | Schizo-phrenic | | Normals | Schizo-phrenic |
| Child | 7 | 4 | Yes | 29 | 19 |
| Father | 16 | 10 | | | |
| Mother | 7 | 16 | No | 1 | 11 |
| | 30 | 30 | | 30 | 30 |

Most of the normal group could make the loser come out as they planned, and they differed from the schizophrenic group at the .01 level on the Chi Square test.

In summary, out of 30 families in the normal group, 27 succeeded completely in doing what they planned and 3 failed. Out of 30 families in the schizophrenic group, 11 succeeded completely in doing what they planned, and 19 failed.

UNPREDICTED RESULTS

An unexpected result was based upon the simple measurement of who won the first three rounds of the game. The normal family members shared about equally in winning while in the schizophrenic group the father won the majority of games and the child hardly won at all. The difference was significant at the .01 level on the Chi Square test.

| | Won | | | Lost | |
|---|---|---|---|---|---|
| | Normals | Schizo-phrenic | | Normals | Schizo-phrenic |
| Child | 11 | 3 | Child | 9 | 21 |
| Father | 9 | 21 | Father | 7 | 5 |
| Mother | 10 | 6 | Mother | 14 | 4 |
| | 30 | 30 | | 30 | 30 |

This result is similar to the measurement of how the family members divided up the total time in coalition. In the normal group the family members shared about equally in the time they were in coalition. In the schizophrenic group the mother-child coalition was significantly less than the normal (a difference at the .05 level) and the mother-father coalition was significantly greater than the normal (a significant difference at the .01 level).

If one measures the amount of time that family members were not pressing a button at all, the schizophrenic child spends significantly less time pressing buttons than the normal child (significant at the .01 level). The parents of the schizophrenic child also spend significantly less time pressing buttons than the parents of the normal child (a significant difference at the .05 level).

In signalling, the fathers in the schizophrenic group signal the children more frequently than the fathers in the normal group. The mothers signal the fathers more units of time in the normal group than the schizophrenic group. The normal child presses his parents' coalition button more than the schizophrenic child.

SUMMARY

Although it was expected that the schizophrenic group would be more homogeneous than the normal group, the reverse proved to be the case. On almost all measurements the normal families tended to be more like one another while the schizophrenic families showed a considerable range of variability.

The family members in the schizophrenic group press their buttons less than the members of the normal group, and they spend less time scoring with each other and have longer periods of time when no one is scoring. Of the amount of time they spend in coalition together, the normal family members share coalitions about equally, while the parents of the schizophrenic get together with each other more than the normal parents do and they get together with their child less than the normal parents do. The schizophrenic child tends to get together with his father more than he does with his mother. The family members of the two groups signal each other about equally, although the fathers in the schizophrenic group signal the children more, and the mothers in the normal group spend more time signalling their husbands than the schizophrenic mothers do. The child in the schizophrenic group presses his buttons less, is more inconsistent, and is more unresponsive than the normal child.

When asked to plan the winner and loser of a round of the game, the family members in the schizophrenic group tend to predict how the round will come out rather than plan it. That is, the normal family members will say, "Let's have mother win," whereas often the members of the schizophrenic family will say, "Well, father won before so I guess he will win again." They then must be re-instructed that they are to decide who is to win and lose and try to make it come out as they planned. Almost all of the normal families could make the winner of the round come out as they planned, while half the schizophrenic group could not. Since it might be argued that this inability to do what they plan in the schizophrenic group is related to intelligence rather than ability to cooperate, it should be pointed out that the two groups do not particularly differ in education. There are a few with less than high school education in the schizophrenic group, and a few more in the normal group with a college education or above. There seems to be little correlation between education and inability to make the round come out as planned. (Since the question of ability to understand the procedure is at least partially relevant to this result, a group of six families with a mentally retarded child—IQs from 60 to 90— were run in this experiment. All six chose the child to be the winner of the planned round, and all six succeeded in having the child win.)

## THE NEED FOR BASIC RESEARCH

The results of the experiment in this pilot study indicate that on certain measurements there are differences between the group of families which contain a schizophrenic member and the group that does not. Can we then say that families containing a schizophrenic member are actually different from families who do not have such a member? Such a question raises more problems than it answers. It is doubtful whether this experiment differentiates families on the basis of schizophrenia; more than likely it differentiates a "disturbed" family from a non-disturbed family, whatever psychopathology might be present in the family. However, more important questions are raised than the sample, the methodology of this particular experiment, or the question whether the differences in the child's behavior alone accounts for the differences in result. There are more basic questions about the validity of this type of experimentation. We cannot say whether the behavior of a family in an experimental context accurately represents the typical pattern of that family until further research is done upon the possibilities and limitations of family experiments. An immediate task is the exploration of a single family, or a small group of families, with a variety of experiments to test the process of experimentation itself rather than testing a difference between groups. Actually the study which has been done is premature. Before one can experiment with differences between groups of families, basic research on the methodology should be done. There are various questions which need to be answered about the approach itself. Will a family show consistent patterns on the same experiment over a number of runs? In other words, can it be demonstrated that a family is an organized system? Will there be correlations between different experiments which presumably measure the same pattern? How can the factor of the family disguising its typical patterns when on display be minimized? Do the necessary limitations which must be put upon family communication for measurement purposes distort the typical patterns of the family more than they reveal them? Are the statistical methods which have been developed for measurement of individuals and unrelated people appropriate for the study of ongoing systems? What differences are there between single exceptions in the classification of families and the classification of individuals—is the mean or median a significant measurement when dealing with groups of organized systems?

The work done so far in this pilot study has centered largely upon differentiating one type of family from others. The theoretical approach has centered largely upon one dimension—given three people in a room, there is a potential range of communicative behavior possible and any one type of family will habitually confine itself within limits of that range. In that one dimension, the focus ultimately centered upon a single aspect— the measurement of coalition patterns. In the area of coalition patterns, the work was further narrowed down to the patterns involved among only three people in a small sample of families.

The final narrow focus of this study was partly a product of elimination and partly the result of problems in time, personnel, engineering, and availability of families. The process of working out the problem, and the results achieved, indicate to us that the approach is well worth further exploration. This exploration should be of two sorts: (a) the exploration of the process of family experimentation itself, with the emphasis upon experimenting with experiments rather than attempting to test out particular differences between particular types of families, and (b) the development of other dimensions on which to classify families with appropriate experiments.

To select families on the basis of a characteristic of a member would not seem to be the most sensible approach to the problem of family classification. Should one, for example, wish to compare the families of schizophrenics and the families of delinquents, he is immediately involved in the unfortunate problem of defining schizophrenics and delinquents for sampling purposes. Any approach based upon the individual will immerse the research in age old problems of individual psychology.

A proper classification system for families should be based upon types of interaction in families rather than characteristics of individual members. Such a classification problem is formidable, but it would seem the next logical development in the social sciences. Just as the first half of this century has been largely devoted to classifying and describing individuals, it seems probable the second half of the century will be devoted to classifying ongoing systems of two or more people. The dimensions upon which such a classification system will be based have yet to be devised. An exploration of this field must include developing a theory of family organization which can be experimented upon, classifying families on several dimensions, designing and conducting appropriate experiments, and pursuing and entrapping the appropriate families for adequate samples. The theoretical problems are formidable; the problems of experimental design and sampling are exasperating. Yet it would seem that family experimentation is the most appropriate procedure for putting a wedge into the large and important problem of devising a classification system for the human family and other ongoing organizations. These types of experiments would seem to require exquisitely precise theoretical formulations and ingenuity in devising experimental situations; sufficient challenge for any experimentalist.

# NOTES

1. This research was done when the author was a member of the Project for the Study of Schizophrenic Communication, directed by Gregory Bateson. The staff consisted of Jay Haley and John H. Weakland, Research Associates, Don D. Jackson, M.D., Consultant, William F. Fry, M.D., Consultant, Alex Bavelas, Ph.D., Consultant, and Noel Andrews, Research Assistant. The research project was financed by a grant from the Foundations' Fund for Research in Psychiatry administered by the Department of Anthropology, Stanford University, and was indebted to the Veterans Administration Hospital, Palo Alto, California, for office space and other facilities.

2. It is possible that organized relationships follow abstract laws which would not be apparent as long as the focus of interest was upon the individual or the artificial group. If one draws upon cybernetic theory and describes a family, or any ongoing relationship, as a self-corrective system with individuals functioning as governors in their relationships with one another, and if one accepts the idea that it is the function of a governor to diminish change, then one can derive a law of human relations. This First Law of Relationships could be stated in this way: *When an organism indicates a change in relation to another, the other will act upon the first so as to diminish and modify that change.*

Assuming that people follow this law in their relationships, families would be stable systems because each attempt by a family member to initiate a change in relation to another would provoke a response to diminish that change. It would also follow that people in the business of changing people, such as psychotherapists and discontented family members, would find it necessary to avoid straightforward requests for change and would attempt to bring about change in more devious ways, e.g., with a denial that a change is being attempted. This might be why psychotherapists do not say to patients, "I'm going to change you," but rather emphasize self understanding and self help.

3. The statistical test used was the Median Test. In certain cases the t-test was used with the assumption that differences in population variance affected the t-score only very slightly. All P values could legitimately be reduced by half when the results were predicted, but this reduction has not been made on these figures.

# REFERENCES

1. BATESON, G., JACKSON, D. D., HALEY, J., and WEAKLAND, J., "Toward a Theory of Schizophrenia," *Behav. Sci.,* 1 : 4, 251–264, 1956.
2. BATESON, G., "The Biosocial Integration of Behavior in the Schizophrenic Family," in *Exploring the Base for Family Therapy,* papers from the M. Robert Gomberg Memorial Conference. Edited by Nathan W. Ackerman, Frances L. Bateman, and Sanford H. Sherman. Family Service Association of America, New York, 1961. pp. 116–122.
3. BOWEN, M., "Family Psychotherapy," *Am. Jrn. Ortho.,* 31: 1, 40–60, 1961.
4. HALEY, J., "The Family of the Schizophrenic: A Model System," *J. Nerv. & Ment. Dis.,* 129: 4, 357–374, 1959.
5. FLECK, STEPHEN, "Family Dynamics and Origin of Schizophrenia," *Psychosom. Med.,* 22, 333–344, 1960.
6. WYNNE, L. C., RYCKOFF, I. M., DAY, J., and HIRSCH, S. I., "Pseudomutuality in the Family Relations of Schizophrenics," *Psychiatry,* 21, 205–220, 1958.

# 5:
# The Family
# as a Three-Person Group[1]

*Fred L. Strodtbeck*

At different centers and in different disciplines small group research has grown at a rapid rate during the past five years. The limited empirical character of most of these studies has enabled their authors to attain what for students of social behavior is an enviable level of rigor, but a central question remains: How far may we generalize these results? The objective of the present paper is to test the appropriateness of certain propositions concerning ad hoc three-person groups by the use of father, mother and adolescent son subject groups. Insofar as our work is carefully done, our results should contribute to the understanding of the extent to which propositions concerning ad hoc three-person groups may be extended to family groups, and to a more limited degree, to other groups with prior common experience and expectations of continued relations.

Our procedure for obtaining a sample discussion between a father, mother, and adolescent son was, very briefly, as follows: Each family is visited at home. We explain that we are interested in the way a family considers questions which relate to the son's selection of his occupation. To help the family recall specific topics which they may have previously discussed, we ask the father, mother and son to check independently one of two alternatives to 47 items of the following type:[2]

(a) A teen-agers' hobby club plans to enter their models in a state-wide contest. Some of the boys want to put the models up under the club's name and win honor for the club as a whole. Others want to put the models up under each boy's name so that each can gain individual honor. Which plan should they adopt?

(b) Two fathers were discussing their boys, one of whom was a brilliant student and the other an athlete of great promise. In general, some people feel one father was more fortunate and some the other. Do you think the father with the *athletic* son or the father with the *studious* son was most fortunate?

Reprinted by permission from *American Sociological Review*, Vol. 19 (1954), pp. 23–29. Copyright 1954 by the American Sociological Association. Fred L. Strodtbeck is associate professor of social psychology, University of Chicago.

(c) Some people believe that a father should be prepared to speak to a son as a father and direct the son's behavior so long as the son lives, others believe the son should be accepted as completely independent of his father's direction after 18 or 21. Which would you tend to agree to with regard to a boy in his late 20's?

While our introductory remarks are being made in the home, we request permission to set up our portable tape recorder. After the 47 item questionnaire has been checked, we have the family fill out still another similar questionnaire so that we will have time to sort through their responses. We select three items which represent a potential coalition of the type in which the mother and father have taken one alternative and the son another, three with mother-son paired against the father, and three with father-son paired against the mother. We then present the family successively with these nine disagreements rotating the isolate role. They are asked to talk the question over, understand why each person chose the alternative he did, and, if possible, select one alternative which best represents the thinking of the family as a whole. While this discussion takes place, the experimenter withdraws to another room, operates the controls on the sound equipment, and tries to keep any other member of the family from overhearing or interrupting the interaction. During May and June of 1953 we obtained 48 cases in this manner.

Concerning the selection of the 48 cases, three criteria were considered: ethnicity, the families were predominantly second generation (the son, third) divided equally between Jews and Italians; socioeconomic status (SES), equal numbers of high, medium and low; and the son's achievement, half of the boys were underachieving in school and half were overachieving as determined by a comparison of grades and intelligence test performance. By sampling from a frame of more than a thousand 14 to 16 year old boys in New Haven public and parochial schools it was possible to work out a factorial design of the following type:

| SES | Jews | | Italians | |
|---|---|---|---|---|
| | Over | Under | Over | Under |
| High | 4 | 4 | 4 | 4 |
| Medium | 4 | 4 | 4 | 4 |
| Low | 4 | 4 | 4 | 4 |
| | | | Total 48 | |

The recordings averaged about 40 minutes in length. The interaction analysis consisted of breaking the on-going discussion into units, or acts, identifying the originator and target of each act, and assigning each act to one of Bales's 12 categories which are identified in our discussion of the index of supportiveness below.[3]

One primary objective of the present paper is to compare our results with those of Mills who, working with student volunteers, asked them to

create from three pictures a single dramatic story upon which all agreed.[4]
The comparison requires that we utilize jointly the information concerning
the originator and target of each act, as well as the category in which it is
placed, to form an index which reflects the tendency of a particular actor,
number 1, to give positive responses to the attempts at problem solution
by another actor, number 2. The following steps are involved in arriving
at the index of supportiveness:

(a) Sum together the acts in the following categories which have been
originated by person number 1 and directed to number 2:
   1. SHOWS SOLIDARITY, raises other's status, gives help, reward
   2. SHOWS TENSION RELEASE, jokes, laughs, shows satisfaction
   3. AGREES, shows passive acceptance, understands, concurs, complies
(b) Subtract from the above sum the number of acts originated by number 1 and directed to number 2 in these categories to form the
numerator of the index:
   10. DISAGREES, shows passive rejection, formality, withholds help
   11. SHOWS TENSION, asks for help, withdraws "Out of Field"
   12. SHOWS ANTAGONISM, deflates other's status, defends or asserts self
(c) Divide the above numerator by the number of acts originated by
number 2 in the following categories:
   4. GIVES SUGGESTION, direction, implying autonomy for other
   5. GIVES OPINION, evaluation, analysis, expresses feeling, wish
   6. GIVES ORIENTATION, information, repeats, clarifies, confirms
   7. ASKS FOR ORIENTATION, information, repetition, confirmation
   8. ASKS FOR OPINION, evaluation, analysis, expression of feeling
   9. ASKS FOR SUGGESTION, direction, possible ways of action
(d) The result, multiplied by 100, is $I_{12}$, the index of support of person
1 of person 2. Between three persons, six index values are produced.
To simplify our reference to this set of values we organize it in a
matrix, placing the person with the largest number of acts originated
in the first row and column and the person with the least number of
acts originated in the last row and column. To illustrate this convention see Table 1. To form Table 1 we have taken the median of

## TABLE 1.

MEDIAN INDEX OF SUPPORT, FAMILIES COMPARED WITH AD HOC
STUDENT GROUPS*

| Rank of Initiator | Rank of Recipient | | |
|---|---|---|---|
| | 1st | 2nd | 3rd |
| 1st | | −6 (12) | −5 (7) |
| 2nd | −5 (11) | | −5 (4) |
| 3rd | 3 (4) | −2 (2) | |

*Mills's values for ad hoc student groups are given in parentheses.

the corresponding cells for the 48 discussions in each of the six positions. In parenthesis we show the value Mills obtained when he carried out these steps for his 48 groups.

Mills makes the following observation with regard to Simmel's having anticipated the pattern of support which Mills found:[5]

The highest rates of support are those exchanged between the two more active members and the rates are very nearly the same . . . All other distributions of rates are significantly different from these two. This is to say that, as far as exchange of support is concerned, the relationship between these two members is sharply differentiated from the other relationships. The results for this sample confirm Simmel's observation. The two more active members form the pair and the least active member is the relatively isolated third party.

For Mills the 1–2 value is 12 and the 2–1 value is 11, which are higher than the other cell values and similar. In our data the 1–2 value is minus 6 and the 2–1 value is minus 5—these do not differ significantly from the other values. By correlating the sets of medians in particular cells of Table 1, we may compare the relative magnitudes of our values to Mills's without regard for the difference in means. We obtain a rho of —.67. Neither the inspection of the corresponding cells of the two most speaking participants nor the correlation over the whole table can be interpreted as a confirmation of Mills's results on ad hoc groups. Whether the significantly lower mean level of the index of support can be accounted for by the differences in our tasks or by a lesser emphasis on polite behavior on the part of family groups we, of course, can not say.

We are indebted to Mills for the following typology for classifying the individual matrixes. He suggests that we look at the index of support, $I_{12}$ and $I_{21}$. These indices are then compared with the medians for the $I_{12}$ and $I_{21}$ positions, and the experimenter indicates $+$ if the value is above its corresponding median and $-$ if it is below, the following results:

| $I_{12}$ | $I_{21}$ | Support Types |
|---|---|---|
| $+$ | $+$ | solidary |
| $+$ | $-$ | contending |
| $-$ | $+$ | dominant |
| $-$ | $-$ | conflicting |

For our data $I_{12}$ is minus 6 and $I_{21}$ is minus 5.

Mills finds that when the two high ranking participants have a solidary relationship, both the intake and output of support for the low man is lower than in any other circumstances. Our data are not in accord with his finding (see Table 2). The lowest value in any row would have been in the solidary ($++$) column if our data had corresponded to Mills's finding. It may be seen that no one of the four cells involved fulfill this requirement.

D

## TABLE 2.

MEDIAN INDEX OF SUPPORT FOR CELLS INVOLVING THE LOW-RANKING
PARTICIPANT

| Matrix | Support Type | | | |
| Cell | + + (17) | + − (8) | − + (7) | − − (16) |
| --- | --- | --- | --- | --- |
| 1 to 3 | −05 | 12 | 08 | −11 |
| 2 to 3 | 03 | −10 | −08 | −07 |
| 3 to 1 | 03 | −02 | 08 | 01 |
| 3 to 2 | 00 | 02 | −03 | −05 |

Mills goes further to say,

Not only is this determined position of the third party as weak as a power position can be (when the relation between the two principals is solidary), but it is likely that the power interests involved in it are inversely related to the interests of the other member. The stronger the coalition, the weaker the position of the third man, and vice versa.

Unfortunately Mills had no measure of power other than participation. With our data, to form a "power" score, we arbitrarily give two points to each decision. If the isolated person persuades the others he is given two points and they receive none; if he holds them off and no decision is made, he is given one point and the other two get .5 each; if the isolated person is persuaded by the other two, they receive one point each and he receives nothing. Thus, for nine decisions there is a total of 18 points. Under random expectations the mean for each participant would be six.

In our experiment we find that if one attempted to predict power, as measured in this way, from participation he would account for less than three tenths of the variation, though the correlation is significant in the .5 to .6 range. We therefore have attempted to test Mills's statement by comparing the mean power score computed by the system explained above for the first, second and third most speaking participant for each of the four support types. It may be seen from Table 3 that the low man does not appear to be conspicuously worse off in the solidary (+ +) type. There is no significant gap between his power and that of the man in the second position whereas there is such a gap between the low and middle man in the contending (+ −) and dominant (− +) support types.

In three of the four support types the most-speaking person wins the largest share of the decisions and in all cases the least-speaking person wins least. We have found the means for the rank positions within three of the support types to be heterogeneous and the gap between the first and second most-speaking person significant at the .05 level or less.[6] There is

## TABLE 3.

MEAN DECISION-WINNING POWER BY PARTICIPATION RANK AND SUPPORT TYPE

| Rank | Support Type | | | |
|------|:----:|:----:|:----:|:----:|
| | + +<br>(17) | + −<br>(8) | − +<br>(7) | − −<br>(16) |
| 1st | 8.0* | 6.3 | 8.0 | 8.3 |
| | . . . | | . . . | . . . |
| 2nd | 5.2 | 6.6 | 5.5 | 4.9 |
| | | . . . | . . . | |
| 3rd | 4.8 | 5.0 | 4.5 | 4.8 |

* The value 8.0 indicates that the most-speaking participants in solidary (+ +) groups won on the average 8.0 of the 18 possible points. The dots in the columns indicate significant gaps.

a reversal of power scores between the first and second rank position in the contending (+ −) pattern.

One of the observations in Mills's article with broad implications for a theory of group process dealt with the stability of the participation patterns through time. His measure of stability was a comparison of the participation rank in the first third of his sessions with the participation rank in the last third. His conclusions are as follows:

> In summary, there is one pattern where all positions are stable; there is another where all positions are unstable; and in the others, the strongest position is stable while the others fluctuate. The significantly stable pattern is the *solidary* (+ +) one, which, as we have seen, tends to develop into the fully differentiated, interdependent pattern called the *true coalition*. The significantly unstable one is the *conflict* (− −) pattern which is notable for its lack of interdetermination."

From this comment and study of other portions of the text it is our guess that Mills would rank the support types: solidary (+ +), contending (+ −) and dominant (− +) tied, and conflict (− −) lowest regarding their implication for participation stability. For our data we have the relative participation for three decisions each with the father, mother and son as isolate—a total of nine. To parallel Mills's procedure and stratify the incidence of the isolate role, we sum the first three decisions and compare with the sum of the last three decisions. The father, mother, and son are the isolate once in each group. By considering the rank for the first three decisions as the criterion ranking, we can compare the consistency of participation within the four support types by use of Kendall's S (see Table 4).[7] Corresponding values from Mills's study are given in parentheses.

**TABLE 4.**

STABILITY OF RANK BETWEEN FIRST AND THIRD PHASE*

| Required Values | Support Type | | | |
|---|---|---|---|---|
| | $++$ | $+-$ | $-+$ | $--$ |
| S | 344 (278) | 62 (62) | 0 (122) | 96 (62) |
| M | 17 (15) | 8 (9) | 7 (11) | 16 (13) |
| S.05 | 102 (90) | 48 (54) | – (66) | 90 (78) |
| P(S) | <.05 (<.05) | <.05 (<.05) | >.05 (<.05) | <.05 (>.05) |

* Mills's values for ad hoc groups given in parentheses.

In this instance our findings partially correspond to Mills's. Our most stable group is the solidary $(++)$, but our least stable is not the conflicting $(--)$. The dominant $(-+)$ has less stability than the conflicting, but since there are only seven cases this apparent reversal of order must remain in doubt.

Mills includes in his paper certain observations on the temporal shifts of support patterns. He finds that the solidary $(++)$ patterns in the first phase tend to persist into the third whereas other patterns more frequently shift toward solidarity $(++)$ or conflicting $(--)$. Mills refers to these two latter patterns as *terminal* patterns. Unfortunately our data were not tabulated so that this comparison could be made at a modest cost. We do note however that one might infer from Mills's comments that primary groups with a much longer period in which to stabilize their interaction would tend to be more concentrated in the $(++)$ and $(--)$ categories. While our distribution of cases is in line with this expectation,

$$
\begin{array}{ccc}
+ & + & 17 \quad (15) \\
- & - & 16 \quad (13) \\
+ & - & 8 \quad (9) \\
- & + & 7 \quad (11)
\end{array}
$$

the observed differences are not statistically significant.


**DISCUSSION**

Any given hour of face to face interaction can be categorized in many different ways. Even a simple system such as Bales's, which extracts only a small portion of the available information, results in units which can be recombined to form a number of measures or indices. The net effect of this latitude in analysis is to provide a very large set of potential hypotheses which may be tested. Since this is the case, special precautions must be taken against errors of the first kind—the rejection of the null hypothesis when the hypothesis is in fact true.

To avoid errors of the first type some workers only report relationships which they have demonstrated several times and others report, or write as if they are reporting, only those relationships they have deduced, predicted, or anticipated in advance of the experiment. In the present context Mills has used still a third alternative. He reported his basic operations in detail, he carefully specified the particular characteristics of his group, and he was completely candid in noting that his findings arose from what we have come to call "blind analysis" notwithstanding the fact that they had in part been "adumbrated" by Simmel. Mills's treatment invited comparison, and although we had collected our three-person interaction for a different purpose, comparison was easily made.

The subjects we used were related in a particular and pervasive way—they were a family. There was every reason to believe that after the experimental session was over they would pick up their daily relations very much as they had been in the past. Their actions in the experimental session proceeded on a broad basis of common knowledge and their behavior in the experimental situation could very well have consequences in their interpersonal relations at a later time.

The tendency for a three person group to break into a pair and another party, which was the central theme of Mills's analysis, would seem to run counter to certain expectations we associate with a family. Crudely expressed, parents give succorance to children contingent upon the child's conforming to selected rules of behavior. This elemental aspect of the relationship becomes greatly elaborated. By adolescence one is tempted to believe that a son has moved into a position where his censure of parents may be fully as effective a control mechanism as parents' censure of the son. Competition for sexual favors is regulated by incest proscriptions. The action of one family member in the community is not without implications for other family members. In short, three family members may, in many important ways, reward one another and accept responsibility for one another's well being. No member can easily withdraw from the relationship. From considerations of this order one can form a strong common sense basis for the expectation that the division of the trio into two and one will be attenuated in families in contrast with ad hoc groups and in this way account for the disparity between our data and the expectations based on Mills's findings relative to the distribution of support.

An alternative explanation for the disparity can be based upon the task we've set for our subjects. There were nine specific decisions, each person had three isolated and six coupled coalitions and the group was instructed to try to achieve consensus. This shifting of coalitions would strike at the stability of relations which might have grown if only one task were involved, hence the task also might have caused the departure from Mills's distribution of support findings which we report in Table 1.

The effects of our using a task different from Mills's are not entirely negative. We were enabled by virtue of our decision-winning measure to test a proposition concerning the relative power of the low man in the solidary $(+ +)$ group which had not been tested with equal directness by Mills. It is plausible to believe that the members of the major coalition in a solidary $(+ +)$ family would not pool their power against the low man to the same degree as would an ad hoc group. While the evidence we present is in line with such an expectation, the proposition at issue cannot be firmly established until it has been demonstrated, in accordance with Mills's expectations, that the low ranking participant in ad hoc solidarity $(+ +)$ groups is in fact less powerful than the low ranking member in groups with other support characteristics.

A point of correspondence between Mills's study and the present, which encourages one to believe that it is fruitful to think in terms of a common process underlying both primary and ad hoc group interaction, relates to the stability of the participation ranks. In both studies it is demonstrated that the solidary $(+ +)$ pattern results in the most stable participation ranks. In this manner support type takes its place along with previously published discussions of the phase hypothesis,[8] status struggle,[9] and equilibrium problem,[10] as one of a series of more or less cumulative increments in our understanding of factors which influence participation stability.

In conclusion, we have attempted to assess the appropriateness for families of propositions derived from the study of ad hoc three-person groups. We do not find in families the regularities in the distribution of support which Mills reported, nor do we confirm the tendency for solidary high-participating members to dominate the decision-making which Mills anticipated would materialize. We do find in families, like many other groups, decision-making power is associated with high participation.[11] We confirm Mills's finding that when the two most active members are solidary in their relation to one another the stability of their rank participation is high, but we do not find that when the two most active members are in conflict, the stability is as low for families as he found it to be for ad hoc groups.

# NOTES

1. This report was prepared as part of the project, "Cultural Factors in Talent Development" supported by the Social Science Research Council from funds granted to it by the John and Mary R. Markle Foundation for research on the early identification of talented persons.

    Bernard C. Rosen, Florence Sultan, George Psathas, and Leslie L. Clark are appreciatively acknowledged as project members and Ann Dennison, Bob Ellis and William Vosburg for their assistance in the collection and analysis of these data. Yale University, where this work was conducted, actively supported every phase of the project and this assistance is also gratefully acknowledged.

    With regard to this particular paper, the author is indebted to T. M. Mills for a most constructive criticism of the first draft.

2. These items have in large part been adapted from questions originated by the Social Mobility Seminar at Harvard, conducted by Samuel A. Stouffer, Talcott Parsons and Florence R. Kluckhohn.

3. See Robert F. Bales, *Interaction Process Analysis*, 1950.

4. Theodore M. Mills, "Power Relations in Three-Person Groups," *American Sociological Review*, 18 (August, 1953), pp. 351–357.

5. Mills and Simmel's thesis treating of the partition of three into two and one is most effectively stated in von Wiese's, *Systematic Sociology*, translated by H. Becker, 1932, p. 525.

6. For similar findings see A. Paul Hare, "Interaction and Consensus in Different Sized Groups," *American Sociological Review*, 17 (June, 1952), pp. 261–267; same author, "Small Group Discussions with Participatory and Supervisory Leadership," *Journal of Abnormal and Social Psychology*, 48 (1953), pp. 273–275; Fred L. Strodtbeck, "Husband-Wife Interaction Over Revealed Differences," *American Sociological Review*, 16 (August, 1951), p. 16; Robert L. French, "Verbal Output and Leadership Status in Initially Leaderless Discussion Groups," *American Psychologist*, 5 (1950), pp. 310–311; and, if it may be inferred that an instructor has more power than students, F. F. Stephan and E. G. Mishler, "The Distribution of Participation in Small Groups: An Exponential Approximation," *American Sociological Review*, 17 (October, 1952), pp. 598–608.

7. M. G. Kendall, *Rank Correlation Methods*, London, 1948.

8. Robert F. Bales and Fred L. Strodtbeck, "Phases in Group Problem Solving," *Journal of Abnormal and Social Psychology*, 46 (1951), pp. 485–495.

9. Christoph Heinecke and Robert F. Bales, "Developmental Trends in the Structure of Small Groups," *Sociometry* (February, 1953), pp. 7–39.

10. Talcott Parsons, Robert F. Bales and Edward A. Shils. *Working Papers in the Theory of Action*, (1953), pp. 111–163.

11. Other correlates of decision-making power based upon this set of data and related to father, mother, and son roles will be described in later publications.

# 6:

# The Prediction of Family Interaction from a Battery of Projective Tests

*Dorothy Terry Sohler, Jules D. Holzberg, Stephen Fleck, Alice R. Cornelison, Eleanor Kay,* and *Theodore Lidz*

This study represents an attempt to make systematic use of projective techniques in the study of family interaction. It is part of a larger study of the families of schizophrenics which contains, in addition to projective data, detailed family histories from diagnostic and therapeutic interviews with all family members. We shall present material from only one family, which necessarily precludes generalization. It is not our purpose to present the test results of this family as characteristic of other similar families but rather as an illustration of a method.

The data consist of the interpretations and inferences contained in a report of the family based only on psychological test materials with no further information except the age, occupation, and education of each member. The accuracy of this hypothesized picture of the family was then evaluated in terms of information obtained from interviews with the family members, and impressions based on these interviews.

The psychological report on this family was written from the following points of orientation: (1) Our primary interest was in the inter-

Reprinted by permission from *Journal of Projective Techniques,* Vol. 21 (1957), pp. 199–208. Copyright 1957 by the Society for Projective Techniques, Inc. This article also appears in Theodore Lidz, Stephen Fleck, Alice Cornelison, *et al., Schizophrenia and the Family* (New York: International Universities Press, 1965). Dorothy Terry Sohler (now Dorothy Terry Carlson) is grants program specialist, Research Grants Branch, National Institute of Mental Health. At time of writing she was assistant professor of psychiatry, Yale University School of Medicine. Jules D. Holzberg is associate clinical professor of psychiatry, Yale University School of Medicine, and also director of research, Connecticut Valley Hospital, Middletown, Connecticut. Stephen Fleck is professor of psychiatry and public health, Yale University School of Medicine. Alice R. Cornelison is a psychiatric social worker, Pittsfield Mental Health Center, Pittsfield, Massachusetts. At time of writing she was research assistant, Department of Psychiatry, Yale University School of Medicine. Eleanor Kay, at time of writing, was research assistant, Department of Psychiatry, Yale University School of Medicine. Theodore Lidz is professor of psychiatry, Yale University School of Medicine.

action among the family members. (2) We focused on resemblances between children and parents in their patterns of needs and conflicts and the way in which these were manifested. We hoped in doing this to find clues to the developmental reasons for at least gross differences in children of the same family; in particular, the development of mental illness in one child and not in the other. (3) We also were looking for factors which would characterize the family as a whole: relatively unique behavior which established a family climate. (4) Finally, we wondered if study of the test material from an entire family would increase our understanding of the individual members.

This study of one family is not intended as a validation of projective techniques. Nevertheless, this type of approach, if carried out on a sufficient number of subjects, has much to recommend it as a method of validation. It avoids two important limitations found in many validation studies. The first of these has to do with the criterion for evaluating the test results. It does not require, for example, that the tests differentiate among nosological entities nor between successful and unsuccessful employees. One may argue that it is doubtful that interview material and clinical impressions are more nearly accurate as criteria. This may very well be true, but as criteria, they are appropriate and relevant to the purpose for which projective techniques were devised: to describe the individual.

The second difficulty in assessing the validity of projective techniques lies in finding appropriate units of measurement. Formal scoring categories are still of unknown validity, and it is argued that their use violates the significance of the test as a whole. Schafer[1], in discussing this problem, has pointed out the advantage of using the test interpretation as the unit of measurement. By this procedure, it is possible to avoid the problem of losing the significance of the test as a whole. The interpreter is free to base his hypotheses on his total impression of a test or test battery. He also is free to analyze the data without being forced to adhere to any particular scoring procedure. We have adopted this method of evaluating predictions by comparing them with information derived from the interviews. We believe that only by an accumulation of this type of evidence from individual cases can we begin to understand which areas of human behavior can best be described by projective tests.

## SUBJECTS

The Benjamin family consists of the parents, a daughter of 19, and a son, 16, who is a patient at the Yale Psychiatric Institute. The father is a successful businessman, and the mother a housewife. The parents have a high school education. The daughter at the time of testing also had completed high school, and the patient was in his third year of high school when hospitalized.

## PROCEDURE

Each family member was given a series of tests in two sessions. In the first period, 14 Thematic Apperception Test cards[2] and the Rotter Sentence Completion Test were administered. The second period was given over to the Rorschach and the Draw-A-Person. The Rorschach was administered and scored according to Klopfer's method. The Draw-A-Person was administered according to Machover's procedure.

Two psychologists worked independently at first, writing up detailed interpretations of the tests for each individual. One had administered the tests. The other had had no contact with the family. They discussed their individual reports in order to resolve differences in interpretation and then considered each test, card by card and response by response, in order to assess the family as a whole and speculate on their interaction. The tests were considered in the following order: Rorschach, Thematic Apperception Test, Sentence Completion, Draw-A-Person.

After the test productions of the family as a whole were considered a general report was written, based on a previously devised outline. This was made up of 72 items under general headings. Only the general headings will be summarized here.

We described the factors which seemed to characterize the family as a whole. We were especially interested in any suggestion of tendencies to distort reality and the possible effects upon the children of such distortions.

The relationship between the parents was considered next, with regard to factors which drew them together initially and changes in their attitudes toward each in the course of the marriage.

A number of the items referred to parent-child relationships. Did the parents seem to have conflicting roles for the child? Which was the preferred child of each parent? In what way did factors such as the sex of the child influence this preference? How did the child confide in the parents and how important was this to the parents? How did the parents react to the growing independence of the child and his movement away from the family ties?

The question of relationships outside the immediate family was also considered: the parents' strong ties to their parental homes or to individual interests, vocational or avocational.

After the report on the family had been written, it was analyzed into 333 discrete interpretive statements, each of which was intended to represent only one interpretation. Two raters working independently disagreed in 21 instances as to what constituted a statement. The resulting agreement between raters, then, was 93%.

These 333 interpretive statements were then judged for agreement with the interview material. The judgments were made independently by the two psychiatrists in the study. They had taken no part either in the test interpretation or the interviewing of the family, but were thoroughly familiar with the interview material. The amount and richness of this interview material require comment. Both parents were seen once a week for almost two years, for a total of 110 interviews. The patient's sister had a total of 29 interviews, and the patient had 3 or 4 therapeutic hours a week during this time.

The raters judged each interpretive statement to be in agreement with the interview material, in partial agreement, unknown, or in disagreement. The unknown rating was given when there was not enough pertinent information in the interview material to make a judgment.

It was necessary to assess the interjudge reliability. In rating any one statement it was possible for the judges to agree with each other completely or partially, or to disagree.

1. The judges were said to be in partial agreement on a statement when one judge rated it partial agreement and the other rated it either agreement or disagreement.

2. The judges were said to be in disagreement on a statement when (a) one judge rated it agreement and the other rated it disagreement, or (b) one judge rated it unknown and the other rated it either agreement, partial agreement, or disagreement.

The judges agreed with each other on 62% of the statements; they were in partial agreement on 11% and they disagreed on 27%. The percent partial agreement was divided by two and the result (5.5%) was added to the percent complete agreement (62%). In this way an overall rater agreement of 67.5% was obtained.

After both judges had made their ratings independently, they discussed their disagreements and arrived at a joint rating. We were interested to see whether one judge's ratings prevailed over the other's in the joint ratings. This was found not to be the case. One judge had only three more of his original ratings represented in the joint ratings than did the other judge.

CLASSIFICATION OF PREDICTIVE STATEMENTS

The statements were classified in four different ways, independently of the comparison with the interview material. In each instance two raters worked independently. The agreement was then computed and the final ratings were decided after discussion of the disagreements.

*General, Stereotyped, and Idiosyncratic Statements.* An important factor to be considered in the evaluation of the interpretive statements is the extent to which the family and its members are differentiated from families and people in general. Therefore, an attempt was made to determine whether the statements in the writeup which were judged to be in agreement were only safe generalizations which could be made about anyone.

It appeared that there were at least two types of statements which would be relatively undifferentiating. The first concerns behavior which is universally characteristic. Statements of this type, which we call General, differentiate one individual from another only when a rather extreme degree of intensity is specified. Thus "He is seething with hostility" is more specific than "He has feelings of hostility." A statement such as "the mother has a strong need for affection" was called General since everyone needs affection. Even if the interview material gave no evidence of more than average need for affection, the judges might be less likely to rate this statement incorrect than they would an Idiosyncratic statement such as "The parents' sex life may be somewhat bizarre."

A statement was called a Stereotype if it could have been made solely on the basis of group identification of the individual: e.g., socioeconomic status, age or sex, without information from the test material. This is not to say that the tests were ignored when these statements were made. On the contrary, they indicated which of many possible stereotypes might be appropriate. The prediction "They [the family members] are undoubtedly strongly upwardly mobile" might have been made only from the knowledge that the family is upper middle class, that the parents do not have college degrees, and that they are Jewish. However, the father in his Thematic Apperception Test stories made many references to the superiority of people with college degrees and the importance of reading the right books.

We made a larger number of Stereotyped statements than one ordinarily would in a psychological report because we were following an outline which forced us to attempt to answer questions about various activities for which there was often no direct evidence in the test material. These Stereotypes are not necessarily more likely to be in agreement with the interview material than other statements in the writeup, because they are not universally characteristic of the members of the group from which the stereotype is drawn.

Two raters worked independently to classify the statements. Those which were not judged to be General or Stereotyped were called Idiosyncratic. The raters agreed on 238 or 71% of the 333 statements. The final ratings included 32 General statements, 90 Stereotypes, and 211 Idiosyncratic statements.[3]

*Statements about Overt and Covert Behavior.* The problem of predicting overt behavior from projective test material is a difficult one, and we were interested to discover if there were any difference in the judged accuracy of our predictions in this area as opposed to predictions of covert behavior.

The Covert category includes statements about defense mechanisms, other theoretical formulations of personality dynamics, personality traits, needs, feelings, and attitudes toward the self. Statements rated Overt were any which specified behavior, discussion of roles played by the individual, and attitudes toward others. It was difficult to decide how to rate statements about attitudes, since they imply both overt and covert behavior. We decided rather arbitrarily to split in the manner indicated, since attitudes toward others imply a communication between two people, whereas attitudes toward the self may not always be communicated to others.

There was 83% agreement between the raters. A total of 215 Overt and 118 Covert statements was decided on.

*Group and Individual Statements.* The next classification was into Group and Individual statements. Many of the predictions had to do with resemblances in the family, so that the same prediction was made for more than one family member. There was perfect agreement between the raters in this classification.

*Personal and Interpersonal Statements.* The fourth classification was into Personal and Interpersonal statements. The former refer to personality characteristics and the latter to some type of interaction between two or more people. The Interpersonal statements included, in addition to descriptions of behavioral interaction, statements concerning the attitude of one person toward another and reactions or feelings evoked by one person in another. This category also included statements about one person's feelings about the interaction of other members of the family, and descriptions of roles played by the individuals in the family. This classification became difficult when the predictions had to do with one person's attitudes toward other people in general. We became somewhat arbitrary about this. Such a statement as "He is essentially a hostile person" we classified as Personal since the emphasis is more on feeling than on interaction. Statements about a person expressing his feelings to someone else were classified as Interpersonal.

The two raters making the Personal-Interpersonal classifications disagreed on 24% of the statements. There was a misunderstanding on one aspect of the definition of the Interpersonal category which resulted in a consistent error, making it difficult to evaluate the agreement. When the disagreements resulting from the consistent error are removed, the agreement on the remaining items is 257 out of 291, or 88%.

The inter-judge agreement on these four classifications seemed high enough to make it worthwhile to use them in analyzing the data, since they might help clarify differences between the agreements and disagreements with the interview material.

## RESULTS AND DISCUSSION

The results of the comparison with the interview material are summarized in Table I, for the statements as a whole and for the four classifications. Sixty-seven percent of the total number of statements were found to be in agreement; 9% in partial agreement; 8% unknown and 16% in disagreement.

Neither the General nor stereotyped statements differed in accuracy from the Idiosyncratic statements. The Stereotyped statements were the most likely to be judged correct, but the Chi Square comparing them with the rest of the statements fell short of significance at the .05 level of confidence.

There was no overall tendency for the statements about Overt behavior to be any more or less in agreement than the statements about Covert behavior. When they were considered with the other two classifications, Group-Individual and Personal-Interpersonal, one difference appeared: the Overt statements in the Group category have a significantly large number of disagreements. (Chi Square = 3.95, P < .05, df = 1). Most of these are Group-Interpersonal statements about attitudes of family members toward each other.

The Group and Individual statements differ significantly in the proportion of agreements and disagreements. (Chi Square = 7.94, P < .05, df = 3). Sixty-three percent of the Group statements were agreements as opposed to 70% of the Individual statements. Twenty-two percent of the Group statements were disagreements, and only 12% of the Individual statements were disagreements.

The Personal and Interpersonal categories do not differ significantly from each other in terms of agreement with interview material.

The Individual-Personal statements have the smallest proportion of disagreements and the Group-Interpersonal statements the highest. (Chi Square = 4.00, P < .05, df = 1). The Group-Interpersonal statements refer to family interaction, and thus represent a greater departure from the test data than do the Individual-Personal statements about personality makeup usually found in test reports. The tests, apparently, are better sources of information about the individual than about his relations with

## TABLE 1.

DISTRIBUTION OF JUDGMENTS OF AGREEMENT ACCORDING TO FOUR INDEPENDENT CLASSIFICATIONS

| | Total | | General | | Stereo-typed | | Idiosyn-cratic | | Overt | | Covert | | Group | | Indi-vidual | | Personal | | Inter-Personal | |
|---|---|---|---|---|---|---|---|---|---|---|---|---|---|---|---|---|---|---|---|---|
| | No. | % | No. | % | No. | % | No. | % | No. | % | No. | % | No. | % | No. | % | No. | % | No. | % |
| Agreement | 224 | 67 | 21 | 66 | 66 | 73 | 137 | 65 | 145 | 67 | 79 | 67 | 83 | 63 | 141 | 70 | 70 | 71 | 154 | 66 |
| Partial Agreement | 27 | 8 | 6 | 19 | 4 | 4 | 17 | 8 | 14 | 7 | 13 | 11 | 11 | 9 | 16 | 8 | 6 | 6 | 21 | 9 |
| Unknown | 28 | 9 | 2 | 6 | 6 | 7 | 20 | 9 | 19 | 9 | 9 | 8 | 8 | 6 | 20 | 10 | 9 | 9 | 19 | 8 |
| Disagreement | 54 | 16 | 3 | 9 | 14 | 16 | 37 | 18 | 37 | 17 | 17 | 14 | 29 | 22 | 25 | 12 | 14 | 14 | 40 | 17 |
| Total | 333 | 100 | 32 | 100 | 90 | 100 | 211 | 100 | 215 | 100 | 118 | 100 | 131 | 100 | 202 | 100 | 99 | 100 | 234 | 100 |

other specific individuals. Nevertheless, we had some success in describing the family interaction and it is of interest to examine the agreements and disagreements in this area.

## AGREEMENTS

The Interpersonal areas will be summarized here. No attempt will be made to describe all of the agreements in these areas. The Personal categories will be considered later in the section on individual members of the family.

The interview material and the predictive statements both emphasized the intense need of both parents and the patient for closeness with others, approval, and affection. It was manifested primarily in an unusual lack of reticence and sense of personal privacy in the family.

The father's feeling of inadequacy as a man was quite apparent, and a number of predictions were made about the influence this would have on the other members of the family. We thought, for example, that the father would be at least tempted to prove his masculinity by having extramarital affairs, although we were not sure he would actually carry this out. He reported having several. It was predicted that the father would push the patient to prove his masculinity, encouraging and fostering sexual activities and athletic interests. This too was borne out in the interviews.

A basic distortion in the parental roles was hypothesized, on the basis of the father's impulsiveness and immaturity, which would not be likely to be counteracted by the passive mother. The parental attitudes of over-indulgence and lack of dependable authoritative control we felt would lead to acting out in the children.

The father was seen apparently correctly as the focus of jealousy in the family. Destructive quarreling was correctly predicted. The father's need to be close to his children, to know what they were thinking, and the seductive interest of both parents were picked up. The patient had an unusually dependent relationship with his parents. The daughter appeared to be separating herself from the family, but was jealous of the attention her brother was receiving.

### PARTIAL AGREEMENTS

An example of partial agreement was the discussion of the expression of anger. Temper outbursts were correctly predicted for the father. They were also predicted to a lesser degree for the mother and the patient. The patient's therapist pointed out that the patient acted out in a hostile way, but denied angry feelings. When his parents came to visit him he sometimes left them, saying he wanted to watch television instead. Neither he nor his parents could see anything hostile in this. The mother expressed anger indirectly in a masochistic way, by talking so much that she incurred the irritation and anger of her family and outsiders as well. The extreme degree to which the whole family made use of denial was recognized, but it was difficult to predict how it would influence the expression of hostility.

### DISAGREEMENTS

The largest single group of disagreements could be attributed to a particular error in interpretation concerning the relationship between the parents. On the basis of the father's Sentence Completion test, which showed an unusual amount of concern with his wife and family, we hypothesized a relationship where the father took the more nurturant role, to his wife as well as his children. For support we noted a Rorschach response of the patient: "two butlers rolling out a red carpet for the Queen of Sheba," and the mother's intense need for affection and attention. It seems worthwhile to note in some detail the errors stemming from this hypothesis.

We stated that the father probably waited on the mother and paid her a great deal of attention. The actual situation during the patient's life time was one of constant quarreling, extreme lack of consideration by the father for the mother, open contempt, and occasional blows. The father at the time of the patient's hospitalization was painfully guilty about this behavior toward his wife and its effect on the patient. In the two years of weekly individual therapeutic interviews with the parents, there was striking improvement in the marriage. The father came to exhibit the interest in his wife which we had thought to be present at the time of testing, although he was not controlled by her as we had hypothesized. The father was always much involved with his children and his guilt when B. was hospitalized was intense. Both parents were capable of change and their son's illness provided motivation and opportunity.

Because of our assumption that the mother's role was one of demanding dependence, we hypothesized that she would be particularly unable to tolerate dependent behavior in the father, and we stated this as the quality in her husband which Mrs. B. would like least. We had underestimated the degree of explosive temper and irritability in the father, which was, and still is to a lesser degree, the source of the mother's major difficulty with her husband. We also assumed, in discussing ways of disciplining the children, that the parents would insist on consideration for the mother.

One partial agreement is interesting in view of this misinterpretation. We felt that the father would find the mother's demands for attention a burden and that this would constitute the quality which he liked least in his wife. This seemed to be true, but not quite in the sense in which we conceived it: that is, the mother's demandingness was expressed indirectly by a flow of incessant talk, full of irrelevant detail, which Mr. B. found extremely irritating.

### STATEMENTS WHICH COULD NOT BE EVALUATED

The predictions in the unknown category had to do with sexual activities of the family, family activities in the home, attitudes of one member toward another, predictions into the future, and formulations of personality dynamics. Only a few of the formulations of personality dynamics were judged unknown; they appeared in the other categories when there was sufficient evidence to evaluate them.

## INDIVIDUAL FAMILY MEMBERS

When the family members are considered individully, there are some striking differences with respect to the four classifications of data.

The patient received a significantly large and the father a significantly small proportion of General statements. (Chi square $= 16.37$, $P < .001$, df $= 3$). There were no significant individual differences with respect to the Stereotyped items, nor were there any with respect to the Overt-Covert classification.

The individual family members differ significantly with respect to the Group-Individual and Personal-Interpersonal categories. (Chi square $= 41.48$, $P < .001$, df $= 9$). The majority of the items referring to the patient are Individual-Personal (personality description) and Group-Interpersonal (family interaction). There are only two items referring to the patient in the Individual-Interpersonal category (interaction with specific family members.) The significance of this seems to be that the patient was seen not as an individual interacting with other individuals, but as the dependent child of his parents, not yet separated and individuated from them.

The majority of the statements referring to the father fell in the Interpersonal (family interaction) categories. This reflects the degree to which the father was seen as the focus of the family, exerting an important influence on the development of the children.

The daughter was described in a very small number of statements in the Interpersonal (family interaction) categories. This reflects the impression (corroborated by the interviews) that she had separated herself from the family, while the parents and patient were still caught up in an excessively inter-dependent triangle.

The parents were given almost twice as much attention in the report as were the children. This apparently is due to the fact that the report was oriented toward explaining the effect of the parents on the personality makeup of the children.

Seventy percent of the statements about the patient were agreements: a larger (but not significantly so) percentage than for any other family member. However, the qualitative impression is that the patient was the most poorly depicted as an individual. This is explained by the large number of General statements referring to the patient. Of all members of the family, the patient was the most difficult to understand as an individual. This is not surprising in view of the fact that he was psychotic, with a diagnosis of paranoid schizophrenia. His behavior during the tests was fairly well organized, and he managed to hide his more important delusions. The psychologists could only conclude that he was covering over a good deal of material. The degree of disorganization in the patient was undetermined, although it was apparent (particularly from his drawings) that he was in a state of acute turmoil.

The father emerged more clearly as an individual. The degree of compulsive behavior in this man was underestimated, however. More striking in the test material were his aggressiveness, volatile emotionality, and need to prove his masculinity. An implication of this need which perhaps might have been emphasized more was the degree to which he bragged and displayed his wealth in order to prove his competence as a man.

The description of the daughter proved more accurate as time went on and the social worker was able to establish a relationship with her. There had been disagreement between the psychologists as to whether she might have had sexual relations. We learned later that she had been involved in an affair in which she played a sado-masochistic role. There seemed sufficient evidence to corroborate the impression from the test material that she would be likely to act out in a self-destructive way.

## SUMMARY AND CONCLUSIONS

A description of a family, based solely on projective tests given to all family members, has been reported and evaluated. The interpretation of the test material was focused on understanding the interaction between the family members with particular reference to the influence of the parents' personalities on the children, the general themes characterizing the family as a group, and the different developmental problems confronting each child. Similar work has been carried out with several families containing a schizophrenic child, and with three volunteer families in which there was no apparent mental disorder. Although this study was not undertaken as a validation of projective tests, the method could be used for this purpose.

Material from one family was presented to illustrate the procedure. The tests were administered and interpreted with no knowledge of the family except their ages, education, religion, the father's occupation, and the fact that the son was hospitalized at the Yale Psychiatric Institute. The interpretations based on the test material were compared for agreement with extensive material from all members of the family. The parents were seen weekly for almost two years, the daughter was interviewed 29 times, and the patient was undergoing intensive psychotherapy during this time.

The collaboration of two psychologists was an especially valuable aspect of the procedure, since the scope of the predictions was both wider and more specific than is usual in psychological reports. Many implications for family interaction were not realized until the test material had been discussed thoroughly. There also were interpretations in the independent write-ups which were discarded in the combined report because they seemed incorrect and which would have been at variance with the evidence in the interviews. There was little disagreement in the independent interpretations, but a definite tendency for each psychologist to concentrate on different aspects of the material. Thus the joint picture of the family was more comprehensive than either of the individual efforts.

Probably the majority of the hypotheses about family resemblances and partial identifications came from the Rorschach. Clues concerning overt behavior by which important needs were gratified were supplied by the more structured tests such as the Thematic Apperception Test and Sentence Completion. The Thematic Apperception Test seemed to be the best source of information about attitudes toward other members of the family. The Draw-A-Person was used primarily to supply evidence of attitudes toward the self and the opposite sex.

The interpretive statements derived from the tests were classified in four different ways independently of the comparison with the interview material. This was done in order to separate the general statements which could be ascribed to many people from the more specific statements, predictions of overt behavior from covert, and statements about individuals from those about family resemblance and interaction.

The raters did not feel in a position to judge with assurance the degree of congruence between the interpretive statements and interview material until the family had been seen in a semi-therapeutic setting for almost two years. The length and intensity of contact with the family proved very important. A preliminary evaluation of the interpretive statements was made after the patient had been hospitalized for about six months.

The parents had been seen regularly during that time, and the sister had been interviewed five times. In this preliminary evaluation, 31% of the statements were put in the unknown category, whereas only 9% remained in that category in the present evaluation. Furthermore, there were disagreements in the first evaluation which were corroborated in later interviews, and vice versa. It is clear that this kind of evaluation of test material cannot be done on the basis of a few interviews. Certainly many important questions about this family remain unanswered, even after almost two years of contact with them.

In the present evaluation, the agreements constituted two thirds of the total number of statements, 9% were partial agreements, 8% were undetermined, and 16% were disagreements. The individual personality descriptions contained the highest proportion of agreements. The statements most likely to be in disagreement were predictions of attitude of one family member toward another, and statements about family interaction.

In considering the family members separately, it was found that the patient received a significantly large and the father a significantly small number of General (relatively undifferentiating) statements. Other significant differences in the relative number of individual and interactional statements appear to reflect at least gross differences in the roles played by the members of the family. The father was the most active influence in the family, while the mother played a more passive role. The daughter was separating herself, while the patient was the dependent child, not yet individuated from his family.

The B. family does not represent one of the most successful productions of the interpreting psychologists because of the basic error in interpretation which brought a number of other misinterpretations in its wake. This was known before the present study was undertaken. The family was selected because there was extensive information about them, and because elaborate precautions had been taken to conceal the information from the psychologists. Furthermore, it proved important to study the misinterpretations, and to consider how they might have been avoided.

It has not been our customary procedure to make blind interpretations of the tests in the larger study of the families of schizophrenic patients. The test material can be put to better use when the information about the past and present functioning of the family is known. The blind interpretation of several families has helped us understand, however, what can be predicted about family interaction. They have, in fact, given us courage to venture farther in this area than at first seemed possible.

The study of all members of the family has implications for the understanding of the individual. Hypotheses about a person may be confirmed by the attitudes displayed toward him by the other members of his family. Furthermore, the individual's self-concept may differ in important respects from the ways in which the members of his family perceive him. The study of the family as a whole increases understanding not only of the family interaction, but also provides the opportunity to see the individual through the eyes of his family.

## NOTES

1. Schafer, R. Psychological tests in clinical research. *J. consult. Psychol.,* 1949, *13,* 328–334.
2. The cards used were 2, 3BM, 3GF, 5, 6BM, 6GF, 7BM, 7GF, 9GF, 10, 12M, 13MF, 18BM, 18GF. The same series was given to every subject, regardless of sex. This was done because the BM and GF cards, designed as alternates, do not appear to be really equivalent. It was thought too that giving a subject cards designed for the opposite sex might elicit important information about sexual identification.
3. The raters, who in this instance were also the authors of the report, may have been biased in the direction of making too few ratings of General and Stereotyped.

# 7:

# Analysis of Correlative Meaning: The TAT in the Study of Whole Families

*Gerald Handel*

The family is where a person first comes to mean something to himself because that is where he first means something to others. His meaning in the family is fateful because that is his primordial meaning, his prison or his field, the inner world in which he dwells as he moves on beyond the family. What he later offers his peers and teachers is his particular meaningful self, as they offer theirs in particular and selective reciprocities.

Written especially for this volume. Gerald Handel is identified in the footnote to Chapter 1.

Interaction is the offering of selves in a sequence of conjunctions and disjunctions of meaning. Interpersonal relations may be defined briefly as an established pattern of such offerings, conjunctions, and disjunctions. With his primordial meaning to himself, the child proceeds to wider interactions and so on to an accrual of self-meaning that eventuates in his becoming an artist or an accountant, a suicide or a schizophrenic—a particular person developing a particular life course.

The child is born into a group of two or more people who sustain interpersonal relations which are challenged by his birth. His presence (and their anticipation of it) induces alterations in the structure of meaning which must now accommodate the new organism. Parents and older sibs, because of what they are each to himself and to each other, endow the child and his activities with meaning and seek meaning in them.

Fundamentally the nature of family life is the creation of meaning, a process that proceeds unwittingly as well as with intention. A marriage takes place because each partner believes and feels he has found in the other a constellation of qualities that are congruent with what he means to himself. When a child is born, it is insufficient to say that the infant is helpless. More accurately, he *offers* or states his helplessness through his cries (thereby initiating interaction rather than merely receiving it), and his parents offer help according to what they believe the crying means. Crying is undoubtedly very important and perhaps fundamental in early structuring of family meaning since it organizes the child's discomfort into the preexisting framework of expectations, feelings, and activities. The child's cry means, then, not only discomfort to himself but also, to the mother or parents, "noise," "cranky baby," and inconvenience or, alternatively, an urge to give comfort, pleasure that the child is now awake and again available for cuddling, and renewed pride in parenthood. In families where child care is defined as an exclusively female activity, the mother may take the cry in stride or feel resentful at yet another call. Where the father is involved in child care, the cry may summon into play the husband-wife communication system and all its attendant assumptions in such a remark as "Will you see to him, dear?"

Crying provides a useful paradigm for seeing the process of creating family meaning because it is the infant's initial mode of communication.[1] By this means he asserts his uncomfortable self, thereby making it available to others. It calls forth a variety of judgments, feelings, and standards that tend to define the child (as troublesome or pleasure-giving), to establish interpersonal ties (depending, for example, on whether fathers participate in child care), and generally to provide information to all concerned as to what they are and what kind of activity they are engaged in.

We see, then, some of the elements that go into the creation of meaning when crying is the medium of creation. The child declares himself by a means of communication radically different from that used among adults. The parent responds to it not only within the present context of trying to discern what the child wants at the moment but also within a larger context of how he, the parent, feels about extreme dependency, about noise, about being interrupted in some other activity. The response to crying has also been shaped by considerations of parental sex role and how these have entered into the marriage.[2] These diverse predispositions enter into the parental response to crying, so that the child learns what his parents are thinking of him even as he evokes and crystallizes the predispositions that shape their definition of him. It should be clear, then, why we refer to crying as a medium for the creation of meaning. The diverse behavioral components of parents and infant are brought together and connected in the crying: the hunger pangs of the child, let us say, are brought into relation to husband-wife agreements or disagreements about whether fathers should feed infants; to feelings about noise, dependency, interruptions; and all the rest. Thus, in such episodes family members are bound to be shaping their feelings and conceptions of each other in such terms as support and distance, patience and impatience, etc.

Of course, the infant's contribution to the creation of meaning does not occur only through the medium of crying. His gurglings of contentment are also formative, as are his non-vocal gestures. But more than all these is the fact of his presence—and prior to his presence, the anticipation of it. In short, *an infant is evocative,* as are persons throughout their life courses. He calls forth meaning, and in time he both develops a repertoire of evocative techniques and comes to know, however vaguely, the range of meanings he can evoke. From one point of view, the course of a life can be understood as a history of evocation. Fate and fortune, whether in an episode, a phase, or a life career—units of personal time—result from the utilization of evocative power to create conjunctions or disjunctions of meaning.

Psychosocial development is conventionally thought of as a twofold process of socialization and individuation. Both aspects involve the accrual and transformation of meaning. Socialization involves teaching the child the meanings that others share about their common world; individuation is the teaching and learning what his own self means, both to himself and to others.

It is curious that so little effort has been made to understand the relationship between socialization and individuation. Those who are concerned with and study socialization are often not especially interested in individuation and vice versa. Yet we should at least raise the question of whether these two apparently distinct processes are in some way related. Socialization is commonly understood as a process of consciously intended inculcation of social meanings. But we know that even children of the same family do not "turn out alike." To what is this phenomenon attributable? Is it residual, inexplicable in psychosocial terms, the result of sheer biological difference? To conclude thus is to remove prematurely from view a potentially significant problem area. For, given the fact that the human individual grows up complexly involved in his connections to others, it is at least reasonable to suppose that his individuality as well as his social nature are in some way dependent upon his interpersonal ties. To be sure, for some time we have recognized that this is so for the mentally ill; we have reason to believe that their extreme and deviant individuality is at least partly derivative from their interpersonal ties to parents and sibs, but we do not pursue the topic for other kinds of people whose individuality is not a problem to society.

It is clear, however, that it is insufficient to regard what takes place in a family as a process of parents teaching children. That is to say, the creation of meaning in the family is not a one-way process from parents to children; the child contributes actively to the process. Thus, in the paradigm, it makes a difference whether a child cries often or infrequently, whether he is easily soothed or not, and so on. Comparable considerations are relevant in all events that enter into the creation of meaning. When the child becomes capable of independent locomotion, for example, he makes a different impression on his parents if he is an actively exploring child or one who sits quietly much of the time, just as it makes a difference if his parents prefer him the way he is or would rather have him the opposite type in activity.

The child contributes in yet another way to the creation of meaning in the family. As a result of his increasing experiences outside the family in neighborhood play groups and school, he acquires experiences, feelings, and ideas not familial in origin that provide him with an outlook that enters into his family participation.

Thus far, we have been discussing the creation of meaning in the family primarily from the standpoint of individual development. It is easiest to see how the child develops meanings, since that is the most familiar perspective in thinking about development within the family. It is less obvious, because less familiar, that the parents also derive as well as impart meaning. What the child offers them through his activities, his physical appearance, his responsiveness, his presumed resemblances to kin (likely to be unevenly appreciated) all call forth in the parents new experiences of themselves. These are both historical and contextual; that is, the specific situation of the child behaving arouses parental predispositions.

We have been arguing thus far that individual development is a process of the development of meaning; the child means something to himself because he means something to his parents. This family-based self-meaning is the platform on which the child stands as he moves into extrafamilial experiences that provide raw materials for his further development of self-meaning. This line of argument seems to imply that the study of meaning in the family is useful primarily for understanding the development of the child. But if we shift our attention from the development of the individual to the character of the family as a group, we are led to similar conclusions concerning the creation of meaning as the central process of family life.

We may ask: How is family life possible at all? First we must answer that the culture permits it. It allows a man and a woman to formalize their union in a socially prescribed way; they are then socially authorized to have children. Should they in fact have children, they are then responsible, in this society, for rearing them. Proceeding from this requirement, we may then say that society not only permits the formation of family groups but in fact generates considerable pressure toward their formation because it prefers, even though it does not require, that people establish families.

Society is, then, both permissive and persuasive toward the establishment of families. It provides a framework of meaning—a culture—that makes family life possible. However, families are established by people who marry, and society does not ordinarily compel marriage nor is it invariably persuasive. People who marry choose to marry.[3] We may at least hypothesize (since I know of no research on this topic) that people who marry find the society's permissiveness and persuasiveness to marry personally meaningful in ways that nonmarrying persons do not.[4] We may elaborate this hypothesis further and say that the marryer gives a meaning to himself and to the role of others in his life different from those of the nonmarryer. Such meanings are numerous, if not legion. They undoubtedly vary at different moments in the life cycle and certainly change through time. To suggest more fully the nature of the problem, it may therefore be useful to offer a simple paradigm of contrasting meanings for the marriage-oriented and nonmarriage-oriented person.

Table I is not comprised of research results but rather of a series of interconnected hypotheses, some possible outcomes, at a general level, of research on this topic. We would, of course, anticipate many specific variations of the general pattern, depending on age, sex, social class, personality, stage of life, and many other factors. The hypothesis that the marriage-oriented person construes his self as "incomplete" where the nonmarriage-oriented construes his as "complete" is undoubtedly oversimplified; one could, by a different line of thought, reasonably hypothesize exactly the reverse. But these hypotheses, whatever their eventual tenability, serve our present purposes by indicating that family life, is, from its inception, a process of utilization and creation of meaning. To

## TABLE 1

| MEANINGFUL OBJECT | MEANING FOR: | |
| --- | --- | --- |
| | *Marriage-Oriented* | *Nonmarriage-Oriented* |
| Society's permissiveness | (a) A liberating option<br>(b) Welcome conventionality | (a) A deferrable option<br>(b) Invitation to surrender of autonomy |
| Society's persuasiveness | Social support for the wish to marry | A demand to formalize private life |
| Spouse | (a) Support in one's aspirations<br>(b) Close companionship<br>(c) Legitimation of sexuality | (a) Demand upon one's resources<br>(b) Obligatory companionship<br>(c) Constriction of field of sexual objects (or, alternatively, a demand to be sexual) |
| Self | Incomplete | Complete |
| Family life | Congenial domesticity | Restriction of privacy and personal routine |

marry is not merely to do something culturally approved but to do something that is personally meaningful in a particular way. It involves integrating the meaning one has to oneself with the meanings of other objects for oneself. As soon as we say this, of course, we realize that not only is each member of a couple finding his own meaning in entering upon family life but that these two processes within the two individuals also take place in relation to each other. Family life can begin only if two partners each find *some* meaning in the other. These meanings may evolve through time; the ways in which they change and the ways in which they remain the same have not been systematically studied.

The foregoing analysis is, I hope, sufficient to indicate that a family is a group in which each member is engaged in finding meaning both in himself and in the other family members. Further, the collective life of the family generates collective meaning which becomes a reference point for each member, though not necessarily in the same way for each. (The minister's wayward son is a legendary example of how the same reference point—"good behavior"—can be used differently within the same family.) If we wish to understand how families are integrated—that is, how the distinctive personalities that compose a family cohere in an ongoing structure—we shall have to find ways of studying the interrelationships of individual, multi-individual, and collective meaning within a family.[5]

In the remainder of this article I shall try to show that the Thematic Apperception Technique is a suitable instrument for the task, and I shall propose a specific method of analysis of the TAT, the analysis of correlative meaning, as specifically suitable.

The TAT is, of course, a long familiar and well-established instrument for the study of individual personality. It rests on the assumption that when a person tells stories to pictures, the stories have meaning and may be interpreted to yield information about the storyteller. The TAT is not a test in the conventional definition, although some workers do use it much as they would a psychometric instrument. Rather, the TAT is a sample of behavior in which the person, in making up a story to a picture, uses his own imagination and organizes his production in his own way. He is instructed to "make up a story to the picture," which means that he is presented the task of balancing in his own fashion his impulsive tendencies, his tendencies to organization of behavior, and the demands of the picture.[6] While the TAT is a highly flexible instrument, adaptable to many purposes and styles of interpretation, it is perhaps particularly useful when personality is defined in terms of meaning, as Henry suggests:

Following Lawrence K. Frank, we view personality as a dynamic process of organizing and giving meaning to life experiences—a process of giving significance and affective connotations to the environment and of reacting to the environment in terms of these meanings and connotations. In a sense the individual is seen to build for himself a private world of meanings which constitute his interpretation of the world about him and which is unique to that individual. In addition, personality is seen as a process of reacting which develops from the interplay of the needs and feelings of the individual and the demands and sanctions of the culture in which the individual matures. Two important aspects of the developing personality are considered: the process of socialization, involving the development of sufficient conformity in conduct and points of view to permit participation in a common social world, and the process of individuation, involving the developing and establishing of a "private world" of highly idiosyncratic meanings and feelings. These two aspects of the developing personality are seen in constant interaction, the individual personality imposing upon the world its own meanings and feelings and the cultural demands imposing themselves upon the personality.[7]

In the light of this definition we see that interpreting a person's TAT story requires us to work back and forth between two levels of meaning, corresponding to the way in which the story came into being. One level is the meaning in the person; the other is the meaning in the story. The person has experiences and endows them with meaning. In telling a story to a picture, he fashions his story in terms selected and shaped by the meanings he has given to his experiences. Thus, in response to a picture of a boy seated before a violin, his story reflects his feelings and judgments as to what such a picture is likely to be about. The task of interpretation is to discover how the meanings of the person's life are set forth in the stories he tells.

Reexamining Henry's definition of personality, we see that, useful as it is, it is incomplete for some of the problems that we must try to analyze today. It no longer suffices to think of personality as involving only a private world of meanings and a set of socialized meanings for living in a common social world. For the argument which we advance is that *a child is socialized first not into a large common social world but into a particular family,* which only partly and sometimes quite inadequately represents the general society.[8] Indeed, only the recognition of this fact gives us the mandate to explore the relationships between family experience and individual mental illness or social mobility or any other particular kind of significant life outcome, deviant or not. If socialization into a family is simply equivalent to socialization into a larger common social world, we would have no basis for seeking connections between a person's family experience and those aspects of his behavior that mark him as deviant from that larger world. We would instead be obliged to assume that his deviance—whether mental illness, criminality, exceptional social mobility, or whatever—is not at all related to his family experience. No evidence today justifies such a decisive ruling out of family influence upon deviant life course. On the contrary, we are likely to gain greater leverage on these problems (as well as the problem of understanding normal development) if we adopt as a tenable working assumption that socialization into a family is not equivalent to socialization into the larger culture. Perhaps a concept such as "socialization discrepancy" would be useful to describe the difference between socialization into family and into the larger social world. In any case, it seems clear that we must postulate— between the extremes of a private world of meanings and a social world of meanings—a family world of meanings as a crucial component of personality.[9] A certain portion of each person's individuation is not entirely idiosyncratic, in the sense that it is a personal creation entirely distinct from that part of him that is socialized. Rather, it is his individual way of being involved in the general issues engaging his family.

We may approach the problem of analyzing whole families by considering three important tasks facing every family. One is developing an orientation to the world. A family tends to develop certain generalized orientations in terms of which its life is organized or centered. From the multiple possibilities open to it, a family tends to "select" ways of dealing with the world that involve characteristic emotions, motives, and perceptions. These in turn lead to the family's involvement with particular issues or problems that give a general cast to its life. This is not to say that each family member "has the same problem" or that family members "resemble each other," though these are both true in some fashion. Rather, the family's life tends to result in the family's locating significant aspects of their common experience in certain areas of psychosocial space. In one way or another, each family member moves in this space.

While a family is developing general orientations that involve the personalities of all members, it must also provide modalities of separateness for each member. Each member must and does develop a way of being a separate person within the family's world of meaning. I believe we shall enlarge our understanding of personality and of family functioning if we more fully understand how each family member develops his own stance vis-à-vis the family's orientations, which he may accept, resist, or modify. In sum, a second task faced by each family is the development of modalities of separateness.

A third task is building particular patterns of interrelationship among family members. While each family member is both a separate person and involved in the family's general orientations to the world, he also constructs particular modes and bases of interrelationship. Family members are related to each other in particular ways that are based not merely on wider social norms governing behavior and feelings of people who occupy specified kinship roles but also on particular personality patterns of those involved. Each family develops its own pattern of connectedness, but as yet we know very little about this process of internal family structuring.

The analysis of correlative meaning is a procedure that parallels the three tasks just described. A TAT is obtained individually from each family member. The first step in analysis is to consider the stories to Card 1 told by all members of a family as though they constituted a single story, the family's story to that card. This is identical with the procedure Henry calls "horizontal-thematic, in which the whole collection of responses to each individual picture are analyzed as though they were one dynamically interdependent unit."[10] From this analysis we derive the family's orientation to the world. At this point we are not concerned with the individual differences in the stories as indications of personality differences among the members. Instead, no matter how diverse the stories seem, we are concerned with characterizing the family as a group.

The second step is to look at each individual's story to the card, describing his personality as expressed in that story. In doing so, we try to relate this individual description to the family's general orientation. These two levels of analysis together reveal the particular way each family member is involved in his family's orientation. We thus try to be attentive to the interplay between individual and family.

Third, we must regard the stories in terms of patterns of interpersonal relations obtaining either among the family members generally or between particular pairs of persons. On this latter point, initial experience suggests that the stories to a particular card are not equally informative about all the relationships in the family. For example, the stories to a particular card may indicate rather clearly the relationship between a parent and one child, but not the relationship between that parent and another child; the latter may become clear in stories told to another card in the series.

Analysis of the stories to each card thus proceeds in three steps. First, to read all the stories to the card as a collective family product. Second, to look at each story to the card as an individual product of the storyteller. Third, to examine pairs or groupings of stories to discern interpersonal relationships within the family. This three-step procedure is repeated for each card administered. As we do so, we also use vertical analysis, i.e., referring where relevant to material that has appeared in earlier stories. This is done for one person as well as for relationships, since sometimes material from one person's story to a particular card is relevant to another member's story to a different card.

This method of TAT analysis, the analysis of correlative meaning, rests upon the assumption that the meaning of any individual's stories is not exhausted by reference to his own personality or to his own stories. The contrary assumption is, in fact, made: a part of the meaning of any individual's stories is discovered by reference to the stories of the other family members. This assumption, in turn, rests upon two others, one having to do with the properties of TAT pictures and one with the nature of family life. The first involves Henry's concept of latent stimulus demand that refers "to the emotional problem or focus most generally raised by the picture. Latent stimulus demand is thus an emotional matter and will be defined for each card in terms of the analysis and interpretation of subject's responses rather than in terms of inspection of the picture itself. It will vary from group to group somewhat, representing to some extent a definition of the foci of emotional concerns of the group in question."[11] The concept has heretofore been applied to large cultural groups such as American social classes or Indian tribes. It seems no less applicable to families. Henry observes that the TAT is a suitable instrument for any group which has these characteristics:

1. A substructure of dynamically related emotions
2. A persisting and consistent social life-space
3. A consistent pattern of feelings and assumptions toward the elements of the social life-space.[12]

Family relationships and interaction tend to give rise to certain general problems and outlooks involving each family member. Each individual member then develops his own "position" vis-à-vis these problems and outlooks. TAT pictures are stimuli that elicit relevant material from each member. Since each individual's response to the latent stimulus demand of the picture derives in part from his interaction with the other members around the issues tapped by the picture, the responses of the several members are related in meaning. The correlativity of meanings of the members' individually told stories derives from the prolonged inter-relatedness of their experiences. Each member, in telling his own stories, draws on this shared backlog of experience.

To illustrate how these assumptions and procedures can be employed in the interpretation of TAT data, I shall present here the stories told to Card 1 of the standard TAT by the members of two four-person families, followed by my interpretations of them.[13]

## FAMILY H

IDENTIFYING DATA

MR. H. *Age 43.*—Attended college but did not graduate. Occupation: assistant to a business executive.
MRS. H. *Age 42.*—College graduate. Occupation: high school teacher.
HARVEY, *Age 15.*
HOWARD, *Age 9.*

STORIES TO CARD 1

MR. H: I'd say this young chap is a little dejected because something has happened to his violin, something broken [He lays card down as if he had finished with it.] [How does he feel?] . . . Several things enter my head. Perhaps how to break the news to his parents or possibly if he can have it fixed and if he will be able to afford it. He may be feeling dejected because he is scheduled for a concert within a short time so it won't be possible to have the violin fixed in time. . . . [What is going to happen?] I'll say that everything comes out happily. In other words, the violin will be fixed if it is broken.

MRS. H: . . . I would say this little boy has been shown or given this instrument to look at, that he's looking at it, more admiring the wood and strings and the way it's put together. He thinks it's beautiful, but he's not interested in the musical part. He doesn't look like the kind who would be especially anxious to play as far as music is concerned. It's more as if he's trying to think of making violins to sell rather than having too much desire to play it. . . . [Can you tell more about how he feels?] . . . He looks as if he might be critical of the way it's put together. He's thinking of a way to put it together a little more securely and a little more beautifully and make it a better instrument for someone else to play . . . [What is going to happen?] He looks like he might have quite a bit of determination, and I believe he is perhaps capable of sticking with it and really making some very good musical instruments.

HARVEY: I think this boy is just about to play his violin or just finished. He's thinking about how he could become very great at the violin. He's sort of dreaming about how he'll be at Orchestra Hall and how he'll be giving concerts . . . [How does he feel?] It seems he's concentrating very hard on something . . . [What is going to happen?] He'll grow up, I guess, to a great musician.

HOWARD: He's thinking. . . . I don't know what it is on the table. It looks like a gun to me. What he's going to do with his gun. I remember something that reminds me of the picture, "Peter and the Wolf." It reminds me of this, of him and his grandfather . . . [How does the boy feel?] He's happy over the gun . . . [Why?] He just got it and he's looking it over pretty carefully . . . [What is going to happen?] He's going to take it and go out in the forest.

ANALYSIS OF STORIES TO CARD 1

### (1) Orientation to the World

This family has an orientation to the world that is responsible and constructive. (Each member tells a story essentially concerned with the problem of making effective and constructive use of an instrument.) At the same time, it is an orientation rather lacking in assertion or decisiveness. Action does not come easily; it is surrounded, and to some extent replaced, by contemplation, rumination, and fantasy. The motivation to be constructive is stronger than the confidence to be so effectively. The family atmosphere is one of partially blocked effectiveness, accompanied by some self-preoccupation. There is also a sense of being part of a definite and somewhat demanding social structure (manifested in such story details as "scheduled for a concert within a short time," "making violins to sell," "he'll be at Orchestra Hall . . . giving concerts").

### (2) Modalities of Separateness

Mr. H identifies himself primarily as a person who carries on his shoulders the responsibility for seeing to it that social processes, to some extent determined outside himself (the boy is "scheduled" for a concert), are carried out. He wants to meet his responsibility, but he does not feel quite equal to the task. He sees himself as a person who wants and needs solid social support as a condition for effective functioning (the boy not only wants and needs to meet a schedule but also is concerned about parental reaction to the broken violin and may not have enough money—a symbol of social support—to fix it). He is fairly quick to feel burdened by his part in disrupting ongoing activities; he is vulnerable to experiences of mild depression that have the effect of making him feel slightly withdrawn from the smooth social flow he needs. He does not readily find satisfaction and contentment.

Mrs. H is a person who goes at things in her own way. (Her attribution to the boy of a wish to make and sell violins is a highly original idea, when viewed against the background of stories generally told to this card.) Private esthetic experiences are important to her. She identifies herself as a person who maintains high standards; she forms her own judgment as to whether something meets her standards, rather than judging according to received opinions. She regards herself as somewhat of a background figure—but an important one who makes it possible for oth-

E

ers to perform more effectively; she gives social support rather than receiving it. But beneath her principled self-satisfaction she feels less self-approving and less well integrated than she would like. (If we consider the violin as part of her projection of self, the first judgment she renders is that it is beautiful, but, following inquiry, she is critical of the way it is put together.)

Harvey has "dreams of glory"—he wants to achieve in a notable way, and he recognizes that he has to work for it. But his investment in his fantasy is so strong that he has some difficulty accomplishing the task at hand (much more of his story is given over to the wish than to practical details). The intensity of his wish tends to get in his way, yet he does apply himself. (The opening sentence of the story has an immediacy that implies an accustomed "getting down to business.") In addition to distraction by fantasy, he may be impeded by worrisomely overworking a task ("he's concentrating very hard on something" could signify either or both types of distraction).

Howard is concerned with being effectively assertive. He has difficulty integrating his wishes and actions. It is as though he is afraid to tell his own story, so he borrows one that is in the public domain. He seems somewhat confused and inhibited, confined to a fantasy of forceful, even explosive assertion (symbolized by the gun and by adventurous Peter), but trying to integrate the fantasy with social demands (indicated by his making use of a story that has been taught him).

### (3) Pattern of Connectedness

In general, considering all four stories and our analysis of them, we infer that the interrelationships among the family members revolve, to a notable extent, around the presentation of demanding standards and that they involve a good deal of mutual worrisomeness. The data suggest that Mrs. H is the most energetic member and that she supplies push to the family. She tells the family, in effect, to surpass the performance of others, while her husband tells them to perform in a way that meets external requirements. Harvey gives evidence of endeavoring to integrate both parental pressures (the boy will perform or has performed the violin-playing task and he wants to become "great"). He thus appears to be a solid link between the parents.

Howard's position is less clear. He resembles his mother in that they are the only two members to suggest impulses of externally directed aggression, but in his case the aggression is inhibited, somewhat like his father. Thus, rather than integrating pressures from both parents, he is caught between them: impelled to be assertive, as his mother, and inhibited, as his father. We would surmise that he does not feel very comfortable in his relationship with either parent. The relatively poor intellectual organization revealed in this story seems to derive from the fact that he feels both pushed and blocked, a situation that creates some confusion in him. The inference we draw is that Harvey represents both his parents' aspirations and Howard represents his mother's aggressive impulses—which are probably not welcome to his father or to his mother. If these inferences are correct, we would suppose that the parents tend to prefer Harvey over Howard and that Howard does not feel very comfortably anchored in his family.

The second example also comes from a family with two children, both sons, but with quite a different orientation to the world from that discussed above. In describing the latent stimulus demand of Card 1, Henry has stated that "This picture appears to be one dealing with the general issue of impulse versus control, or the question of the relationship of personal demands to those of outside cultural agents."[14] These issues will be apparent in the following stories, as well as in those already presented, but the two sets of stories illustrate how family orientations give idiosyncratic and yet family-wide character to these large issues in human development.

## FAMILY R

### IDENTIFYING DATA

MR. R, *Age 42*.—Education: College graduate with some graduate work in technical field. Occupation: Middle management production executive.

MRS. R, *Age 39*.—Education: College graduate with technical training.

RALPH, *Age 15*.

RUSSELL, *Age 12*.

### STORIES TO CARD 1

MR. R: A child studying violin. Wondering what its mechanism is. Wondering if he will be one of the top impresarios.

MRS. R: You want a story . . . A youngster whose parents feel he should have musical lessons. He's taking them but hating it very much. Hoping the strings would break and he wouldn't have to practice. Ends up with a few squeaky minutes of practice. How well I know. The violin being my favorite instrument, I sort of wished it on Ralph. If that would be Russell's, it would be broken before he got around to practicing.

RALPH: Mind if I study . . . Let's call him Dan. From the looks of the picture, for a long time he wished to play. Every chance he could he would go places to hear men play. He kept begging his mother for a long time and then finally on his eleventh birthday his parents decided to give him a violin. He had a party, and his parents brought out the violin. He was so happy; after his father left he sat for a long time just staring, fascinated by the shiny wood with its long hairs on it, and then after a long time his mother came to him: "Dan, it's your bedtime." He said, "Oh mother, do

I have to go?" and his mother said, "Yes, because it is your first lesson," and so a happy boy went off to bed to dream about his magic instrument.
RUSSELL: This boy, he has to take violin, I guess . . . and . . . he doesn't like to practice or play it, so looks like he gave up. I think he's thinking he's disgusted with it and he's not going to do it any more.

### ANALYSIS OF STORIES TO CARD 1

#### (1) Orientation to the World

This is a family whose members are very much oriented to self-concern and personal states of being. Although the members differ in their cognizance of and responsiveness to other people and external reality generally, they are more concerned with and interested in their own thoughts, wishes, and fantasies than in happenings outside themselves. There is a noticeable tendency toward and expectation of self-indulgence, with a concomitant tendency to minimize the coercive or constraining power of the outer world. This is not to say that they are unaware of that power but simply that they feel that it should not be allowed to become as important as what goes on inside oneself. It is fair to characterize the family as egocentric.

#### (2) Modalities of Separateness

Mr. R appears to be, at bottom, an uncertain man determined not to become bogged down by his uncertainty. (His uncertainty is indicated by the repetition of "wondering." His determination is reflected in the fact that his story is very tightly stated rather than being loosely discursive.) Thus, he is a man who intends to remain firmly in control of his situation. He defines problems for himself rather than accepting conventional problem definitions or seeing himself as responding to demands presented by others. (He introduces no figures into the story, no concept of external demands. All of the activity he reports is that of the child as self-contained. "Wondering what its mechanism is," though not entirely an original idea, is fairly unusual and suggests his interest in going beneath the surface. He does not accept the violin as a conventionally defined social object but wants to probe to a more basic level of reality.) Mr. R thus seems to feel that social definitions of reality are less important than one's personal comprehension of it. On the other hand, he is not content merely with speculation; he wants social recognition of his individuality. He wants to be special, outstanding, make an impression on others ("wondering if he will be one of the top impresarios"). He probably takes some pride in his ability. (His mind works quickly, rapidly establishing relationships among phenomena. He uses the word "studying" to condense two meanings, since each idea that follows refers to a different type of studying. "Studying violin" means both that the child is examining the physical object with a view to understanding it and that he is taking lessons with a view to a hopefully outstanding career.) Mr. R goes at things with an intent concentration on his own goals and does not let himself be distracted by anything he considers irrelevant.

Mrs. R would like to feel free to disregard external demands, but she does not dare to. That she is thus anxious and in conflict leads her to be somewhat exaggeratedly attentive to social demands and to show an eagerness to comply with what she believes is expected of her. (She begins with "You want a story," as if to say to the interviewer that she really does want to know just what is wanted so she can comply. Mrs. R would not have to begin this way if she were, in fact, wholehearted in her desire to meet expectations and if she were not concerned that her unwillingness would be perceived. Her resistance to such demands is further indicated in the projection that the boy is "hating it very much," while her fear of carrying out her resistance directly is indicated by the fact that the boy makes a superficial gesture toward compliance—"a few squeaky minutes of practice.") She regards not only external demands but external reality generally as unpleasant obstacles to her emotional gratification. She relishes her rather full emotionality ("feel . . . hating . . . hoping . . . How well I know . . . my favorite . . . wished"), and she seeks to have her feelings confirmed and reinforced by having others feel as she does. (There are two examples of this in her story. The clearest is her indication that she wanted Ralph to share her positive feeling about the violin. But her comment, "Hoping the strings would break," in this context, can be similarly regarded. It is as though she wishes the violin would share her resentment at practicing and would of its own volition take action that she would like to take.) This seeking for emotional confirmation may perhaps best be interpreted as a form of seeking appreciation. It is as though she were saying, "If you like what I like, then you like me."

If these interpretations are correct, it would be fair to say that, while Mrs. R does not like external demands and the constraints arising from the fact that other people are the way they are, she does want warm emotional ties with others. She wants these ties to develop from expression of her emotionality and to result in consensus (in its original meaning of "feeling together"). While Mrs. R not only does not like to disregard external demands directly and gives somewhat exaggerated attention to them, she does not by any means suppress her feelings. They remain for her the main governing factor in her actions, insofar as possible.

Ralph is a rather self-conscious and self-centered boy. (His opening remarks, "Mind if I study . . . Let's call him Dan," indicate that he is highly conscious of being observed and that he intends to impress the observer by making up a truly impressive story.) He is much wrapped up in his feelings, and he finds pleasure both in dwelling on them in fantasy and in displaying them to others. In both modes, he dramatizes. He enjoys being noticed and singled out for special attention ("on his eleventh birthday his parents decided to give him a violin. He had a party"). He appears motivated by an urgent need to receive gratification from others ("he kept begging"), and, although he seeks such gratification as a precondition for self-motivated activity, he is vulnerable to becoming bogged down in his passive needs. He is struggling with the problem of forming an adequate masculine identity ("Every chance he could, he would go places to hear men play")—and seems quite preoccupied with sexuality and its meaning, a preoccupation that has a marked voyeuristic and auto-erotic quality. He also wants, in a not very determined way, some help in setting limits to his preoccupation. (His whole story gives the impression of being a symbolic expression of fantasies stimulated by puberty. More specifically, the violin, as he describes it, seems a not very well disguised phallic symbol, an interpretation indicated not only by his intent preoccupation with it but also by his reference to the strings as "its long hairs." He introduces the mother as an agent to stir him out of self-absorbed fantasy to a consideration of a reality requirement. This is not effective, since the boy returns to fantasy even while meeting the reality demand.)

Russell seems to be rather willful. He sees himself as being presented with external demands that he does not like. He feels he should not have to do things that he does not want to do. Although he may not assert his opposition as frequently or insistently as he might like, his attitude as expressed in this story suggests that he is not readily accepting of such demands. (His use of qualifying expressions such as "I guess . . . I think," indicates some effort to dampen his oppositional tendencies. At the same time, the general tone and direction of the story express resistance that is relatively unconflicted. There is little evidence of guilt. The qualifying expressions indicate some reality-based caution rather than inner conflict.) Possibly when he cannot be directly defiant, he tries indirect techniques such as pleading inability. (This is suggested by the expression, "looks like he gave up," which is a somewhat different idea from merely saying that the boy quit.) In any case, it would seem that Russell is intent on having his way with as little delay as possible.

### (3) Pattern of Connectedness

One issue or dimension of interpersonal relations in this family is that of finding mutually acceptable limits. With each member rather intent on his own subjectivity, so to speak, the family communicates some sense of unmanageableness. The extent of this should not be exaggerated, but there is a sense of having to struggle with a variety of insistent individual wishes. The clearest expression of this comes from Mrs. R who directly communicates some feeling of resignation. But from our analysis both of her story and of Mr. R's, we would judge that Mrs. R probably feels that she gets insufficient emotional support from her husband. In his drive to master reality in his own way, he seems disinclined to extend himself emotionally and to become involved in other people's problems.

Mrs. R's relationships with her two sons express two different aspects of her personality. Her relationship with Ralph appears quite close and involved. His personality seems to be a symbolic manifestation of her warmer and erotized emotions. (She tells us that she conferred on him her favorite instrument, which we would interpret as expressing her wish that Ralph share in that aspect of herself she especially values. Ralph's story reflects this: he projects an unusually vivid interaction between the boy and the mother. Although Ralph portrays the mother as standing firmly by her request that the boy go to bed, this is not seen as a punitive or even constraining demand but almost as a form of indulgence.) We are also aware that Mrs. R has a rebellious side, which she expresses indirectly. Russell's personality seems to be a manifestation of this side of her nature, and we must assume that in some way she encourages this rebelliousness in him, even though we cannot describe just how this takes place. (Mrs. R tells us directly that Russell is given to expressions of defiance, and his own story confirms what she has told us.) To be sure, Mrs. R consciously deplores Russell's attitude, but it is also clear that, underneath, she has a fair amount of sympathy with it.

Mr. R would seem to relate to his children in a somewhat distant and unsentimental way. In view of his basic uncertainty and his effort to control it tightly, it is reasonable to propose that his sons find him rather arbitrary and not readily approachable, although not punitive either. The evidence suggests that Ralph sees him as interfering with his relationship to his mother. Despite Ralph's eagerness for contact with men, he also seems to want to keep at some distance from his father. (He says of the boy: "He was so happy after his father left . . ." Following this happiness is the interaction with the mother.) Even so, it does not appear that Ralph would stand up to his father very strongly. How Russell feels about his father is less clear from the evidence, but he is likely to be more outspoken than Ralph. We may also suggest that Mr. R might get some gratification from Russell's rebelliousness but that he would consider Russell insufficiently focused and perhaps not thoughtful enough (in the intellectual sense, not the interpersonal).

Certain observations should be made about the data and interpretive procedure. First, I wish to reemphasize what seems to me the value of considering the family's stories together. A set of individually told stories to one picture enables the interpreter—whether research investigator or clinician—to get a view of the whole family in a quite compact array of data. These data have a combination of characteristics that appear to make them especially useful for the complex task of comprehending a whole family: they are compact and systematically obtained, yet complex and personally expressive. This combination of characteristics is highly valuable and not readily found in other types of data. The interpreter, of course, does not limit himself to the stories to one card, as was done here for illustration. Interrelating full sets of stories from the several members becomes a more elaborate task. However, proceeding card by card makes it possible to be systematic, and, as in interpreting the record given by a single individual, the interpretations made of the first story serve as hypotheses to be corrected, discarded, or elaborated as the interpretation proceeds. Although the data lack both the concreteness of interviews or field observation and the precision of scales, inventories, and other metrics, they have virtues of their own.

Are these data valid? Yes, obviously, since they were produced by the persons whose behavior and feelings we wish to understand. The real issue is whether the interpretations are valid. This question does not lend itself to a simple answer. The validity of the interpretations hinges upon a number of considerations. First, is it useful to employ the kind of framework advanced here? Is it correct or incorrect to think of a family as manifesting its character in the individual activities of its members (in this case the individually told stories) in such a way that when those individual activities are examined in conjunction, the collective character of the family is discernible? I have earlier advanced my assumptions for thinking this procedure is justifiable, but they are only working assumptions. Their tenability can only be satisfactorily established with the accumulation of experience. Further, the validity of interpretations depends not only on the assumptions made about behavior and data but also, more mundanely, on the skill of the interpreter. The TAT serves a function analogous to the microscope in biology: it enables one to see things not readily apparent but, as with any such instrument, skill in its use accrues with experience. Only a great deal of experience can teach us how adequately this method of analysis produces information that serves our research and clinical needs.

## NOTES

1. In the strictest sense this is not true. Prenatal movement must probably be reckoned the earliest communication; parents seek meaning in these mov-

ments, attempting to infer from them the probable sex of the child and to use them as premonitory of the pleasures and problems that will accompany his birth. Perhaps we must go back in embryonic development even earlier than these movements to the mother's increased hunger when she first starts to "eat for two"; this may be the child's first significant communication, or at least may be so regarded by the mother if she interprets her hunger as indicative of the growth rate of the fetus.

2. Some alternative possiblities: Do husband and wife agree on what is appropriate to the respective parental sex roles here? If they agree, do they agree that they should take turns responding to the child's cries or that the mother should always be the one to respond? If they disagree, is the mother resentful that the father declines to help; or does the father help in spite of feeling he shouldn't, but feel resentful that he is pressed into this form of service?

3. Such choices vary from determination to marry to reluctant acquiescence in marriage. The full range of choice would be from an extreme of determination to marry to an extreme of determination not to marry. The character of the choice is a reflection of what the person means to himself.

4. It goes without saying that neither marryers nor nonmarryers are presumed to be homogeneous aggregates in this respect. Parenthetically, we may note that in most societies nonmarrying is a form of deviant behavior—not in a moral sense but in the sense that it represents the following of a socially less valued life path, even though permitted and not stigmatized. Yet this topic does not seem to have attracted the attention of students of deviant behavior. Nor do students of human development seem to have studied the meanings of nonmarrying for personal development, except insofar as nonmarrying is incidental to homosexuality. However, since some homosexuals marry and since it is certain that self-chosen nonmarrying occurs on many other bases, studies of homosexuality do not constitute more than a fragmentary approach to an understanding of nonmarrying.

5. One approach to collective meaning is found in the study of ritual. See James H. S. Bossard and Eleanor S. Boll, *Ritual in Family Living* (Philadelphia: University of Pennsylvania Press, 1950). However, this approach does not attempt to take account of the individuality of the family members. The Bossard-Boll approach does have the merit of being sensitive to the fact that integration differs in character from family to family. Such sensitivity is retained by typological or multifactor approaches but is lost in attempts to treat family integration as a matter of degree only. Although the latter may gain in precision of statement, the gain is likely to be very misleading for it is doubtful that any kind of index of integration is adequate to the nature of the phenomenon, at least at the present time.

6. For a useful introduction to the nature of the TAT and the data it yields, see William E. Henry, *The Analysis of Fantasy: The Thematic Apperception Technique in the Study of Personality* (New York: John Wiley and Sons, Inc., 1956)

7. William E. Henry, "The Thematic Apperception Technique in the Study of Culture-Personality Relations," *Genetic Psychology Monographs*, XXXV, No. 1 (1947), p. 7. This definition is compatible with a great body of thinking in sociology; see Edward A. Tiryakian, "Existential Phenomenology and Sociology," American Sociological Review, Vol. 30, No. 5 (1965) pp. 674–88.

8. For an initial statement of this view, see Gerald Handel and Robert D. Hess, "The Family as an Emotional Organization," *Marriage and Family Living,* XVIII, No. 2 (1956), pp. 99–101.

9. Parsons argues, in effect, that this is true for *the* child in *the* family. But where he is discussing family and child as generalized concepts, I am here emphasizing the particularity of each family and child, and of the parents as well. See Talcott Parsons and Robert F. Bales, *Family, Socialization and Interaction Process* (Glencoe: The Free Press, 1955).

E*

10. William E. Henry, "The Thematic Apperception Technique in the Study of Group and Cultural Problems," in Harold H. Anderson and Gladys L. Anderson (eds.), *An Introduction to Projective Techniques* (New York: Prentice-Hall, 1951), p. 239.
11. Henry, *The Analysis of Fantasy,* p. 100.
12. Henry, "The Thematic Apperception Technique in the Study of Group and Cultural Problems," p. 236.
13. Principal support for collection of the data was provided by Research Grant M-543 from the National Institute of Mental Health. This article was prepared after the grant expired, although it develops a line of work supported by the grant. Over a period of years, conversations with Sidney J. Levy and Lee Rainwater have contributed to my thinking, and I am also more specifically indebted to them and to William E. Henry and W. Lloyd Warner for suggestions and encouragement in developing the approach presented here. My earlier collaboration with Robert D. Hess provided my first opportunity to venture upon the study of whole families.
14. Henry, *The Analysis of Fantasy,* p. 240.

# Part III

# THE FAMILY AS MEDIATOR
# OF THE CULTURE

The concept of culture is one of the most fundamental in anthropology. Its influence has spread not only to other social sciences but to many applied fields that increasingly recognize that behavior expresses attitudes and feelings held in common by a large social segment. Kroeber and Kluckhohn, two of the most distinguished American anthropologists, in stressing the importance of the concept of culture, state:

> . . . few intellectuals will challenge the statement that the idea of culture, in the technical anthropological sense, is one of the key notions of contemporary American thought. In explanatory importance and in generality of application it is comparable to such categories as gravity in physics, disease in medicine, evolution in biology. Psychiatrists and psychologists, and, more recently, even some economists and lawyers, have come to tack on the qualifying phrase "in our culture" to their generalizations, even though one suspects it is often done mechanically in the same way that mediaeval men added a precautionary "God Willing" to their utterances. Philosophers are increasingly concerned with the cultural dimension to their studies of logic, values, and esthetics, and indeed with the ontology and epistemology of the concept itself. The notion has become part of the stock in trade of social workers and of all those occupied with the practical problems of minority groups and dependent peoples. Important research in medicine and nutrition is oriented in cultural terms. Literary men are writing essays and little books about culture.[1]

The concept of culture was initially applied to relatively small, homogeneous groups that comprised multiple kinship units, usually a tribe or a village. Each of these groups was considered to have its own culture. When a tribe or a village is the unit characterized as having a culture, the culture is applicable to the entire unit. Although conflict stemming from acculturation—the adoption by some members of ideas, values, and practices learned from members of other societies but not acceptable to all members of the adopting society—may develop within the society, generally the tribal or village society is not thought to harbor more than one culture. Therefore, we have a concept that helps to explain the cohesion of the society. The variation in social activity and attitude that occurs between families is not attributable to culture difference but rather to culturally prescribed differential participation in the culture or to noncultural idiosyncrasy. For example, if one man works harder than his neighbor in the same village, the difference is attributable to noncultural idiosyncrasy rather than to their having two different cultures. If one man in the tribe is a priest while others are farmers, this, too, is not due to their having two different cultures but instead to culturally prescribed differential participation in the same culture.

When the concept of culture is applied to larger units such as the modern nation, a more complex version of the concept must be used. The social differentiation within such a large unit requires us to consider the members of different segments of society as having their own versions of the culture. Margaret Mead writes:

After deciding what larger unit we wish to refer to . . . then smaller observations are considered in terms of the regularities which have been identified for the whole. The term *cultural regularities* includes the way in which the versions of the culture found in different classes, regions, or occupations are systematically related to one another. So a member of the French bourgeoisie who is also a Protestant will manifest behavior which is French, which has certain peculiarities in common with the behavior of French Protestants, which has other peculiarities in common with the French bourgeois, and still others in common with his province, and others in common with his generation, etc., . . . when we are making a cultural analysis, we are interested in identifying those characteristics—including, if not specifying, the possibilities of variation by class, region, religion, period, etc.—which can be attributed to sharing in the tradition of the larger group, whether that group be nation, tribe, province, or some even larger unit with a common tradition, such as the culture of an area like Southeast Asia.[2]

The concept of culture is, then, applicable to social units of varying size and scope. It enables us to discern regularities in the behavior of large classes of people, and also provides tools for understanding how the people within the class (region, tribe, social class, or whatever) govern their relationships with one another in a wide variety of contexts. In this usage of culture, each individual and each family are *carriers* of the culture, enacting the tradition and sustaining it by socializing the young into it.

John Roberts, an anthropologist, presents us with a new wrinkle. Although the concept of culture is applicable to social units of varying range and scope, it has always been applied to units comprising more than one kinship group. This application helps us to understand how a society can be a society rather than a mere aggregate of disconnected individuals and households. Roberts, however, has undertaken to demonstrate that each household constitutes a distinct culture. He studied three neighboring Navaho households in terms of the hypothesis "that every small group, like groups of other sizes, defines an independent and unique culture."[3] Although the three households were selected as being the most similar in the area, Roberts concluded that, despite the cultural similarities he found among them and despite their being "part of a web of interlocking small groups," they did indeed constitute "independent and unique" cultures.

An examination of his data immediately poses problems. For example, in addition to observing the families' religious practices, work patterns, and many other aspects of behavior, Roberts inventoried the material culture of each family. These inventories totaled 578 distinct items. All three families had 154 of these. Each two families had about fifty additional items in common, and each family had about one hundred items not found in the other two households. The question is how do these material inventories constitute evidence of "independent and unique" cultures? The evidence concerning items held in common would seem to be sufficient evidence against any notion that these households constitute independent cultures. If only one family possesses a 1940 New Mexico automobile license plate, two worn-out flashlight batteries, four window blind sticks, etc., does this evidence indicate it is a unique culture? Or if we find that two families own about thirty sheep each while the third owns seventy-two sheep, can we say that this provides evidence of culture difference? Is not the concept of culture being atomized out of existence by this procedure? Culture as a concept for understanding behavior seems most useful when it is thought of in terms of patterns of some kind. Certainly, until now, when the society has been the unit of cultural analysis, the important point has been that one society raises sheep while another does not. Such microscopic differences as that of three neighboring households owning 27, 30, and 72 sheep respectively would seem to be irrelevant to cultural characterization. How is it possible to conduct meaningful scientific work by counting such multiplicities of items in multiple households of every society we wish to study?

The relationship between individual households and utilization of the material culture is not meaningless, but Roberts's painstaking inventory and his comments do not seem to lead in very helpful directions. He does not tell us why the three households have different possessions or different amounts of the same items. Such facts do not in and of themselves justify the conclusion that the three households constitute unique cultures. To use the concept of culture does not require that the carriers of the culture be literally identical in all aspects of their behavior. If households differ in their material possessions, do we then have no basis for analysis? Must we conclude that households in the same society are, for purposes of cultural analysis, identical? Do we have only the two analytical alternatives of every household a unique culture or all households equal representatives of the same culture?

A third alternative is suggested in this comment by Levy: "If we think of a housewife who uses Crosse and Blackwell soups, subscribes to *Gourmet* magazine, flies live lobster in from Maine to Chicago to serve guests, drives a Renault, and doesn't shave under her arms, we sense a value system engaged in choosing things from the market place that add up to a life style that is different from the woman's who uses Campbell's, reads *Family Circle* for ideas on how to furnish a playroom, makes meat loaf twice a week, stretching it with oatmeal, rides in her husband's Bel Air, and scrubs the kitchen floor three times a week."[4] This comment points out something we already know in a common-sense way, namely, that in a large diversified society people can choose how they will make use of the material culture. It emphasizes further that choice is not random but reflects underlying choices in values. However, it does not seem sensible (or correct) to regard these two women as maintaining unique and independent cultures; they are choosing their material objects from an array that is more or less equally known and available to both of them. This being so, and it may be true also for Roberts's Navaho households, we are perhaps justified in saying that a family is not so much a carrier of the culture as the *mediator* of the culture. In some meaningful sense, a family is aware of and cognizes larger portions of the culture than it uses. Some portions it adopts and some it rejects or ignores.

The examples given have been from the material culture. The articles in Part III show that families make choices from the culture in the more intangible realm of values and standards, as well as in behavior. One principal point made by Oscar Lewis is that cultures are much less homogeneous than the traditional reports of anthropologists have seemed to imply, and he advocates the study of representative whole families within a society as a corrective to this oversimplified view. Early in the paper he indicates that a family can be studied *as though* it were a self-contained culture, but he does not take the position that each family is in fact an independent culture. Indeed, he later justifies his advocacy on the ground that it provides a superior method for studying culture patterns of the society. Studying representative whole families provides more extensive information than reliance on a few informants for constructing an account of the society's culture pattern. Lewis here is committed to the anthropologist's traditional task, but offers what he feels is a superior tool for accomplishing it. However, midway between his discussion of families as "societies" and his discussion of them as more informative avenues to a description of the culture of the whole society of which they are a part, he advocates whole family study as the best way to observe the interrelation between the culture and the individual. "One of the advantages of studying a culture through the medium of specific families is that it enables one to get at the meaning of institutions to individuals." This statement is close to the concept of this section's title, the family as mediator of the culture.

Lest misunderstanding arise, it should be pointed out that studying families as selective mediators does not at all invalidate the anthropologist's traditional goal of describing a culture in terms applicable to the whole society sustaining it. That is a different problem from the one concerning us in Part III, not an old-fashioned way of studying the same problem. Studying Mexican culture is one problem. Studying the culture of a Mexican village is another problem, because the unit of analysis is different. Studying how individual families in one Mexican village utilize and interpret the culture of their village is still a third problem; it is more recent in formulation than the preceding two, but it does not render them obsolete. This third problem is important because it focuses on the family as a unit that more or less actively selects from an array of cultural alternatives those that seem most congenial.

Elizabeth Bott's study of families in London discovered that it was necessary to look on families as availing themselves of cultural alternatives rather than merely as idiosyncratically responsive to a common culture. Of course, this was not entirely a novel discovery. Investigators who had studied the family patterns of different social classes or ethnic groups within the same community had often described the different norms, values, and practices governing family life in these different social segments. However, Bott goes beyond this level of knowledge in discriminating family differences within the same social segment.

She began with the idea of studying families from the combined perspectives of anthropology and psychoanalysis. Her goal was to describe the cultural norms of family roles—the ideas commonly held concerning how husbands and wives should act; then, from a psychoanalytic perspective, she hoped to explain that variations in role performance were due to personality differences. Her data compelled her to conclude that this was an unworkable scheme because, as the chapter reprinted from her book indicates, she found that the role norms themselves, as well as role performance, varied.

The third selection, by Cleveland and Longaker, is an account of what happens when a family selects mutually contradictory alternatives from the culture. Their goal was understanding why some families contribute several members as neurotic patients to a small town mental health clinic in Nova Scotia. They examine one family in detail, and, on the basis of their study of this family as well as of others not specifically reported here, they offer some concepts for understanding the pathology in the family. Fundamentally, they say, the family mediates the culture in a way that is damaging to some members, although they do not explain why some members escape the damage. The family adopts conflicting values offered by the culture, and these become internalized in the personalities of the members. Then one set of values is disparaged so that the members engage in self-disparagement.

## NOTES

1. A. L. Kroeber and Clyde Kluckhohn, *Culture; A Critical Review of Concepts and Definitions* (Cambridge, Massachusetts: Harvard University, Papers of the Peabody Museum of American Archaeology and Ethnology), Vol. XLVII, No. I (1952), p. 3.
2. Margaret Mead, in Margaret Mead and Martha Wolfensten, eds., *Childhood in Contemporary Culture* (Chicago: University of Chicago Press, 1955), Chapter 1, p. 10.
3. John M. Roberts, *Three Navaho Households; A Comparative Study in Small Group Culture* (Cambridge, Massachusetts: Harvard University, Papers of the Peabody Museum of American Archaeology and Ethnology), Vol. XL, No. 3 (1951), p. 3.
4. Sidney J. Levy, "Symbolism and Life Style," a paper presented to the 1963 Winter Conference of the American Marketing Association, Boston, December 28, 1963. For what might be called a psycho-anthropological framework for the study of material culture, see Harper W. Boyd, Jr., and Sidney J. Levy, "New Dimension in Consumer Analysis," *Harvard Business Review*, November–December 1963, pp. 129–40.

# 8:

# An Anthropological Approach to Family Studies[1]

*Oscar Lewis*

The field of family studies is one which has become identified with sociologists rather than anthropologists, and even among sociologists it is sometimes viewed as the highly specialized field of practical problems in applied sociology rather than the more general and theoretical treatment of cultural dynamics. One might ask, therefore, just what can anthropology contribute to this field, since anthropologists have, in fact, neglected the field of family studies. However, on the basis of my own experience with family studies in rural areas in Mexico and Cuba, I believe that anthropology can make a distinctive contribution by utilizing the family approach as a technique for the study of culture and personality. In this paper I describe an anthropological approach to family studies and the contribution of such an approach for at least two important methodological problems in anthropology and other social sciences, namely, how to arrive at a more reliable and objective statement of the culture patterns of a given society and obtain a better understanding of the relationship between culture and the individual.

The field work upon which this paper is based was done in the Mexican village of Tepoztlán. It will be recalled that Robert Redfield studied Tepoztlán in 1926. Seventeen years later, in 1943, I returned to the village to do a study of culture and personality. This involved a broad ethnographic study of the community, an analysis of the many changes which had occurred in the village since 1926, a comparison of the total impression of Tepoztlán as revealed by our two studies, and finally, a study of Tepoztecans as individuals and as a people.

At the outset there was the problem of method. Tepoztlán is a large and complex village with a population of approximately 3,500 with seven barrios or locality groupings, generation and wealth differences, and a rapidly changing culture. The traditional anthropological reliance upon a few informants to obtain a picture of the culture and the people,

Reprinted from *American Journal of Sociology,* Vol. 55 (1950), pp. 468–75, by permission of the University of Chicago Press. Copyright 1950 by the University of Chicago. Oscar Lewis is professor of anthropology, University of Illinois.

though perhaps feasible in a small, primitive, tribal society, was inadequate to this situation. The question of sampling and of securing data and informants representative of all the significant differences in the village was just as pertinent here as in a study of a modern urban community. Sampling and quantitative procedures were therefore employed wherever possible, as were census data, local government records and documents, schedules, and questionnaires.

But how could we best study the individual and understand his relationship to the culture? How might we reveal the great variety of practices and the range of individual differences to be found in such a complex village? How might we understand Tepoztecans in all of their individuality? Again, though we came prepared with the traditional anthropological techniques as well as with some of the psychologist's, such as the Rorschach and other projective tests, something more was needed, and we turned to the study of the family. We hoped that the intensive study of representative families, in which the entire family would be studied as a functioning unit, might give us greater insight into both the culture and the people. Family studies therefore became one of the organizing principles in the entire research.

The first problem was how to select the families to be studied. The first few weeks were spent in analyzing a local population census of the village taken a year before our arrival. The census data were reorganized first on a barrio basis. The seven barrios were still, as in 1926, the most important locality groupings. Barrio lists were drawn up and each family and household was assigned a number which thereafter was used to identify the family. In addition alphabetical lists of both sexes were drawn up in each barrio with the corresponding number after each name. In this way we were able to identify all individuals in the village in respect to barrio and family membership.

As a preliminary to selecting families which would be representative of the various socioeconomic groupings in the village for special study, several informants were asked to rank the families in each barrio according to relative wealth and social position. The criteria used in this tentative classification were items which seemed important in this peasant community, namely, the ownership of a house, land, and cattle. Thus we obtained a rough idea of the relative standing of all the families of the village. On this basis three families, representing different socioeconomic levels were tentatively selected for study in each of the seven barrios.

At this point, after I had been in the village for about a month, student assistants from the University of Mexico began to come into the village one at a time. Soon there were six assistants for each of whom arrangements were made to live with a selected family in a different barrio. An effort was made to place these assistants with families representative of the different socioeconomic levels, as well as differences in family size, composition, and degree of acculturation. However, we found that there was a greater willingness among the better-to-do and more acculturated families on our list to have one of the staff live with them. Some of the selected poorer families expressed willingness to accept a student but were unable to do so because of crowded living conditions.

We were now ready to begin to accumulate a great variety of information on every family in the village. Each assistant was made responsible for gathering the data in his barrio. In the three smaller barrios, none of which had over forty families, it was possible to get a few informants who knew of the families there quite intimately. In these smaller barrios practically any male adult knows who does or does not own land or other property. In the larger barrios no single informant was well acquainted with more than a small percentage of the families and we therefore had to use many more informants. In effect we were doing a census in each barrio with the number of items investigated progressively increasing as our rapport improved and as we felt free to ask more questions.

Among the items of information which we eventually obtained by survey for each family were (1) ownership of property, such as house, land, cattle and other animals, fruit trees, and sewing machines; (2) occupation and sources of income; (3) marital status, number of marriages, barrio of origin or other birthplace of each spouse, kinship relations of all persons living on the same house site; (4) social participation and positions of leadership; (5) educational level and whether or not any of the children had attended school outside the village. These items were supplemented by a number of partial surveys on other items; we also utilized and checked much of the information contained in the population census of 1940.

In addition to this survey of the village as a whole, each assistant studied the individual family with which he was living. The family was treated as if it were the society. We learned that most of the categories traditionally used in describing an entire culture could be used effectively in the study of a single family. Thus, we obtained data on the social, economic, religious, and political life of each of the families observed. We studied the division of labor, sources of income, standard of living, literacy, and education. An area of special concentration was the study of interpersonal relations within the family between husband and wife, parents and children, brothers and sisters, as well as relations with the extended family and with nonrelatives. In addition each member of the family was studied individually.

We applied to the single family all the techniques traditionally used by the anthropologist in the study of an entire culture—living with the family, being a participant-observer, interviewing, collecting autobiographies and case histories, and administering Rorschach and other psychological tests. A long and detailed guide was prepared for the observing and recording of behavior. Seven families were studied in this intensive manner.[2] Each family study runs to about 250 typed pages.

How does this approach compare with other approaches? Certainly the family case study is not in itself a new technique.[3] It has been used by social workers, sociologists, psychologists, psychiatrists, and others; but their studies invariably have centered around some special problem: families in trouble, families in the depression, the problem child in the family, family instability, divorce, and a hundred and one other subjects. These might be characterized on the whole as segmented studies in which one particular aspect of family life is considered, and generally the methodology has been of a statistical nature with emphasis upon large numbers of cases supplemented by interviews and questionnaires. Despite all the emphasis in the textbooks on the family as an integrated whole, there is little published material in which the family is studied as that.[4]

If the sociological studies of the family have tended to be of the segmental, specific problem type, the work of the anthropologist has been of the opposite kind, that is, generalized description with little or no sense of problem. In most anthropological community studies the family is presented as a stereotype. We are told not about a particular family but about family life in general under headings such as composition, residence rules, descent rules, kinship obligations, parental authority, marriage forms and regulations, separation, and so on. And always the emphasis is upon the presentation of the structural and formal aspects of the family rather than upon the content and variety of actual family life. Anthropologists have developed no special methodology for family studies and to my knowledge there is not a single published study in the entire anthropological literature of a family as a unit.

Despite all that has been written and the considerable progress which has been made, I believe that it is still a challenge to anthropology and the other social sciences to devise new and better methods for studying the relationship between the individual and his culture. Most monographs on so-called "primitive" or "folk" cultures give an unduly mechanical and static picture of the relationship between the individual and his culture: individuals tend to become insubstantial and passive automatons who carry out expected behavior patterns. For all the pronouncements in theoretical treatises, little of the interaction between culture and the individual emerges in the monographs. Indeed, as theoretical concepts in the study of culture have increased and our level of generalization and abstraction has been raised, we have come to deal more and more with averages and stereotypes rather than with real people in all their individuality. It is a rare monograph which gives the reader the satisfying feeling of knowing the people in the way he knows them after reading a good novel. Malinowski, many years ago in his famous preface to the *Argonauts of the Pacific,* wrote of anthropological monographs as follows: ". . . we are given an excellent skeleton so to speak, of the tribal constitution, but it lacks flesh and blood. We learn much about the framework of their society but within it we cannot conceive or imagine the realities of human life. . . ."[5] More recently Elsie Clews Parsons wrote: "In any systematic town survey such detail is necessarily omitted and life appears more standardized than it really is; there is no place for contradiction or exceptions or minor variations; *the classifications more or less preclude* pictures of people living and functioning together."[6] (Italics mine.) Here we have it. Parsons, in her book on Mitla, has attempted to remedy this situation by writing a chapter on gossip, and in other monographs we sometimes get more insight into what the people are like from scattered field-note references or from chance remarks about the nature of the informants in the foreword than from the remainder of the study. These vivid and dynamic materials are too important to be treated in such a haphazard way.

Anthropologists have made some attempt to salvage the individual through the use of autobiographies and life-histories. Such studies represent a great step forward but they also have their limitations, both practical and theoretical. Autobiographies by their very nature are based upon informants' verbalizations and memory rather than upon direct observation by the trained observer. Furthermore, autobiographies give us a picture of a culture as seen through the eyes of a single person.

Intensive family case studies might help us to bridge the gap between the conceptual extremes of the culture at one pole and the individual at the other. The family would thus become the middle term in the culture-individual equation. It would provide us with another level of description. And because the family unit is small and manageable, it can be described without resort to the abstraction and generalization which one must inevitably use for the culture as a whole. Likewise, in the description of the various family members we see real individuals as they live and work together in their primary group rather than as averages or stereotypes out of context.

It is in the context of the family that the interrelationships between cultural and individual factors in the formation of personality can best be seen. Family case studies can therefore enable us to better distinguish between and give proper weight to those factors which are cultural and those which are situational or the result of individual idiosyncrasies. Even psychological tests become more meaningful when done on a family basis. For example, on the basis of our family Rorschach tests we can study the extent to which personality differences run along family lines and the range within families, as well as what seems to be common among all families and can therefore be attributed to broader cultural conditioning.

One of the advantages of studying a culture through the medium of specific families is that it enables one to get at the meaning of institutions to individuals. It helps us to get beyond form and structure or, to use Malinowski's terms, it puts flesh and blood on the skeleton. The family is the natural unit for the study of the satisfactions, frustrations, and maladjustments of individuals who live under a specific type of family organization; the reactions of individuals to the expected behavior patterns; the effects of conformity or deviation upon the development of the personality. Certainly those problems can also be studied in other contexts. However, I am assuming that the more data we gather on a small group of people who live and work together in the family, the more meaningful does their behavior become. This is a cumulative process, especially important for understanding the covert aspects of culture.

Family case studies can also make a contribution to the study of culture patterns. The concept of culture and culture patterns is certainly one of the proud achievements of anthropology and other social sciences. But here again conceptualization has run far ahead of methodology. Kroeber writes of culture patterns: "In proportion as the expression of such a large pattern tends to be abstract, it becomes arid and lifeless; in proportion as it remains attached to concrete facts, it lacks generalization. Perhaps the most vivid and impressive characterizations have been made by frank intuition deployed on a rich body of knowledge and put into skillful words."[7] This point has been brought home clearly to most sociologists by the recent writings of anthropologists on national character. One of the results of these writings has been to make sociologists and others wonder about the reliability of anthropological reporting even in the case of so-called "primitive" or "folk" societies.

A real methodological weakness in anthropological field work has been too great a reliance upon a few informants to obtain a picture of the culture. The traditional justification of this procedure has been the assumption of the essential homogeneity of primitive or folk societies. But this very presupposition has often affected the methods used and therefore colored the findings. An account of a culture based upon a few informants is bound to appear more uniform than it really is. This became apparent in the restudy of the village of Tepoztlán where we found a much wider range in custom and in individual behavior than we had been led to expect from Redfield's earlier work.

One of the virtues of the intensive study of representative families is that it can give us the range of custom and behavior and can serve as a more adequate basis from which we can derive culture patterns. In doing intensive studies of even two or three families, one must use a larger number of informants than is generally used by anthropologists in monographs on an entire culture. Furthermore, in studying a family, we get a deeper understanding of our informants than is otherwise possible. This intimate knowledge of them is extremely helpful in evaluating what they tell us and in checking the accounts of family members against one another. By the same token such intimate knowledge of informants can be used in checking the usefulness of Rorschach and other projective techniques developed in our own society.

In order to convey some idea of the range in custom and family life which can be found in even a relatively homogeneous peasant society like Tepoztlán, we present a brief summary of findings on two family case studies.

The first family, the Rojas family, consists of the father, mother, four daughters, and one son. The children range in age from thirteen to twenty-six and all are unmarried. The second family, the Martinez family, consists of the father, mother, four sons, and two daughters, the elder of whom is married. The ages of the children range from eight to twenty years.

In terms of size both families are close to the average for Tepoztecan families, which is about five members. In terms of family composition they are the simple biological family living alone on a house site. Over 70 per cent of Tepoztecan families live in this way. Both cases represent families in an advanced stage of development since neither has infants or very young children.

The Rojas family is a better-to-do landowning family in the upper economic group which is made up of about 4 per cent of the families in the village. The Martinez family is one of the poorer, landless families of the lowest economic group, which constitutes about 80 per cent of all families. The latter exemplifies those families which practice hoe culture on communal lands primarily with family labor.[8]

Whereas the Rojas family depends upon the communal lands only for firewood, charcoal, and the grazing of cattle, the Martinez' depend upon the communal lands for their basic food supply. Neither the father nor the son of the Rojas family works as day laborers for others in the village or on nearby haciendas. However, both the father and the older sons of the Martinez family do this as a regular practice to supplement their income. This pattern goes back to the days before the Mexican revolution of 1910, when the head of the Martinez family, as a youth, worked as a peon on the haciendas, while the head of the Rojas family worked only on his father's lands.

These two families have sharply contrasting standards of living. The Rojas family is well housed, well fed and well clothed according to Tepoztecan standards. They can afford some luxuries and their home contains many modern articles such as beds, chairs, tables, a clock, flashlight, and sewing machine. The Martinez family, in contrast, lives close to a bare subsistence level and has but a minimum of clothing and house furnishings and none of the luxuries found in the Rojas family. The latter are reduced to a diet of tortilla, chili, and black coffee during several months of the year. The Rojas family has had more formal schooling than the Martinez' and, as a whole, shows a higher degree of literacy since every member of the family can read and write. Everyone in this family has had some formal education. The father and the two elder daughters have gone through the third grade; the mother through the second grade. In addition, the Rojas family is somewhat unusual in that the three younger children are students preparing for a professional career. However, the father in the Martinez family, though a self-educated man, is much more literate than the father in the Rojas family, and one of the Martinez children has had an advanced education. Like most members of their generation the parents of both families are bilingual and frequently use Nahuatl in speaking with older villagers but rarely with their children. Although the children of both families understand Nahuatl, the Rojas children have more occasion to use it because of their grandmother, who has only a limited Spanish vocabulary.

The question of what the two families represent in regard to social relations is more difficult to answer. In general, the Rojas family is the more respected of the two but this has less effect upon social relations than might be expected. Both families well exemplify the essentially atomistic nature of the social organization of the village, whereby the biological family constitutes the basic economic and social unit. Independence, self-reliance, and a strong sense of privacy, some of the most cherished values of Tepoztecans, clearly emerge in these two families. Both families are characterized by limited relations with the extended family and neighbors, a paucity of intimate friendships, minimal compliance with obligations to *compadres,* reticence in borrowing or calling upon others for help, and, by the same token, reticence in giving help. However, a closer comparison of the two families reveals some differences. The Martinez parents have even less contact with their relatives than does the Rojas family, principally because of the rift over the change of religion. The Martinez', due to the political activity of the father, have much wider contacts among nonrelatives than the Rojas'. However, the Rojas children, because of their greater freedom and higher status, have a more extensive social life among both relatives and nonrelatives than do the Martinez children, whose outside activities are minimal.

Both families are strong, cohesive units and represent relatively close ingroups. Each is held together by traditional bonds of family loyalty and parental authority, by common economic strivings and mutual dependence, by the stability of marriage between the parents, and, finally, by the absence of other social groups to which the family members can turn in time of need. The Rojas family is further bound together by the prospect of inheritance on the part of the children.

These families provide examples of different types of family situations and interpersonal relations, and in some respects represent two extremes of family organization in Tepoztlán. In the Rojas family the wife is the dominating figure, although the husband is the nominal head of the family and maintains some authority. The husband spends much of his time in his fields working tirelessly to support his wife and children and to provide them with their more-than-usual demands. He intrusts household affairs and family finances to his wife, who, in addition to these duties, carries on several gainful activities and substantially contributes to the family economy. Both the wife and children have an unusual amount of freedom and independence. However, interpersonal relations within the family are characterized by considerable conflict, tension, and maladjustment. There is much quarreling on the part of the wife, drunkenness and adultery on the part of the husband, difficulties with in-laws, strong mother-son ties and favoritism on the part of both parents, and competition, hostility, and feelings of rejection among the siblings.

In the Martinez family the husband is a dominating, authoritarian figure who controls his wife and children with an iron hand. The wife is completely submissive and, in contrast to the wife of the Rojas house, inactive and unable to contribute financially to the support of the family. The husband is unusual in the extent to which he supervises expenditures and household affairs. Both the wife and children are extremely restricted in their activities and have little freedom of expression. The older sons work under the direction of their father and frequently work to support the family while the father devotes himself to political activity. The chief conflicts in this household are between the father on the one hand and the mother and children on the other. Under the father's repressions the mother and her sons and daughters have been drawn closer together and often demonstrate mutual loyalty and consideration. There is little of the sibling rivalry to be found in the Rojas home and only occasionally do hostilities between the brothers flare up. In the past the father was extremely indulgent toward his eldest daughter, but he recently has broken off relations with her because of disapproval of her husband.

It can be seen from this summary that any statement of over-all culture patterns would have to be made in terms of the range of differences rather than in the terms of some abstract, hypothetical norm. It should be noted that the difference in the husband-wife relationship in these two families cannot be explained in terms of class or subcultural differences, since they cut across class lines in Tepoztlán.

A practical advantage of this type of approach to the study of culture and personality is that a reasonably complete family case study can be done within a relatively short time, about two or three months, and might be profitably carried on by anthropologists or sociologists who have only their summer vacation in which to do field work. Several intensive family case studies done in as many summers would be in effect a cumulative study of the culture.

The family case study also presents us with an excellent method of introducing anthropology students to field work. The family, small in size but reflecting at the same time almost all aspects of the culture, is a manageable unit of study well within the comprehension and abilities of the student—certainly much more so than an entire community. The traditional training field party too often spends itself in either a confused, pathetic scramble on the part of the students to gather and understand a large amount of data covering all aspects of the culture or in the limited pursuit by each student of a single problem or institution. From my own experience with groups of students in rural Cuba and Mexico, I have found the family approach to field work an invaluable aid. Furthermore, family case studies are very useful as a teaching aid in communicating a feeling for real people.

There is a need for intensive individual family case studies in cultures all over the world. The publication of such studies would give us a literature on comparative family life not now available and would be of use to many social scientists interested in a variety of problems concerning culture and the individual. Moreover, because individual families can be described without recourse to abstractions and stereotypes, the publication of case studies would provide us with some basis for judging the generalizations made by anthropologists and others concerning the total culture patterns of any community. The implication of the family case study for anthropological research is clear. It means that we have to go more slowly, that we have to spend more time doing careful and detailed studies of units smaller than the entire culture before we can be ready to make valid generalizations for the entire culture. These suggestions for individual family studies may seem excessively cautious at this time when some anthropologists are writing with such abandon about the character structure of entire nations. Yet it may be necessary to take a few steps backward if we are to forge ahead on surer ground.

## NOTES

1. This paper was read at the Midwest Sociological Society meetings, April 29, 1949, in Madison, Wisconsin.
2. Two of these family studies will be published in my forthcoming book on Tepoztlán.
3. Professor Thomas D. Eliot comments that Le Play used the family as a unit of research. However, the tradition which he began has not been continued by American sociologists. I understand from Professor Florian Znaniecki that he and his students did family studies in Poland somewhat similar to those described here.
4. Professor Eliot's comment at a meeting of the American Sociological Society in December, 1924, still applies today. He said, "Each feels and interprets only the small part of the problem with which he is in direct contact, and thinks he is describing the whole."
5. Bronislaw Malinowski, *Argonauts of the Pacific* (New York: E. P. Dutton and Co., 1932), p. 17.
6. *Mitla, Town of the Souls* (Chicago: University of Chicago Press, 1936), p. 386.
7. Alfred Kroeber, *Anthropology* (New York: Harcourt Brace & Co., 1948), p. 317.
8. Although about 80 per cent of the families in the village fall in the lower economic group, about 20 per cent of the families regularly work as *tlacololeros*. See Oscar Lewis, "Plow Culture and Hoe Culture—A Study in Contrasts," *Rural Sociology,* XIV, No. 2 (June, 1949), 116–27.

# 9:

# Urban Families: The Norms of Conjugal Roles

*Elizabeth Bott*

The term "social norms" is used in many senses. There are at least two common meanings. First, it is often used to mean statistically average behaviour. Second, it is often used to mean behaviour that is thought to be morally right, or at least expected and customary. When these two meanings coincide, all is well. But often they do not coincide, in which case the double connotation becomes confusing. There is yet another usage to add to the confusion. In this third sense, a norm is a general pattern abstracted by the sociologist from informants' behaviour and from their stated ideals and expectations. In this paper I shall not use the term in the sense of statistically average behaviour, for which I shall substitute the term "behavioural mode." And I shall also exclude the third meaning, the general abstracted pattern, for I find this usage both vague and confusing, since its precise referents are seldom clear. For the purposes of this paper I mean by social norms *people's ideas about what behaviour is customary and what behaviour is right and proper in their social circle.* If expected behaviour is not felt to be ideal, or if ideal behaviour is not expected, I shall make a distinction between ideal norms and norms of expectation. If the expected and the ideal coincide, I shall not use any qualifying adjective.

It is often assumed that there is a large measure of agreement on familial norms in the society as a whole, and that these norms are embodied in the teachings of churches and the rulings of courts. Such a view implies that given individuals will recognize that these agreed-upon external standards exist, and that they will be able to make the norms explicit without difficulty. It seems to me that this view of social norms is much more appropriate to a small-scale homogeneous society than to a large-scale society with a complex division of labour. In a small-scale

Reprinted by permission from Elizabeth Bott, *Family and Social Network,* (London: Tavistock Publications, 1957), Chapter VII. Copyright 1957 by Tavistock Publications, Ltd. Elizabeth Bott (Mrs. James Spillius) earned a Ph.D. in anthropology and then became a psychoanalyst. She practices in London and is a staff member of the London Clinic of Psycho-Analysis. At the time of writing she was on the staff of the Tavistock Institute of Human Relations, London.

society, where many people know one another, where there are few strangers, and most relationships serve many interests, agreement on familial norms develop out of constant interaction, and individuals know what the norms are. Most anthropologists report that their informants have little difficulty in making explicit the approved and customary rules of conduct between members of elementary families and between more distant kinsmen. Behaviour does not always conform to norms, but at least people know what the norms are and when they are deviating from them. If such societies have courts of law, most laymen are familiar with court procedure and know the norms on which the court will draw to make judgments. Similarly, everyone will know what norms of familial conduct are embodied in religion. But recent work shows that even in primitive societies norms should not be regarded as a precise, consistent set of rules. Gluckman (5) points out that the Lozi have some very precise rules ("a husband must not go to his wife's granary") but that others are vague ("a husband should treat his wife properly"). This very vagueness leaves room for flexible adjustment to varying circumstances. Similarly, norms may contradict one another, which permits selection of norms to suit personal and social convenience. Although there is a fairly high degree of consensus on what the norms are, they are rarely made explicit except in times of conflict or crisis, when people use them to justify their own behaviour or to pass judgment on the behaviour of others.

Even in a small-scale society, then, norms are not precise and consistent. But in a large-scale society, the situation is much more complicated, especially where familial norms are concerned. How much agreement on familial norms one would find if one interviewed a representative sample of the general population I cannot say, for I have not been engaged in that kind of study. From an intensive study of twenty urban families,[1] I can report that there was considerable variation in the norms of familial roles. There were some points of agreement; most of these were very vague and general and did not give a precise blueprint for action. On many points there was considerable variation from one research couple to another. Furthermore, not only was there variation among the families interviewed, but several couples also drew attention to the fact that there was variation among the people they knew personally. Two couples also pointed out that there must be variation in the society at large, if one could believe the wireless, television, newspapers, books, and so forth. But most couples did not even mention such sources of information. They discussed only their own little world of the people they knew personally or had known in the past.

Another fact emerged clearly in our interviews: informants found it very difficult to make familial norms explicit at all. There were several reasons for this, which I shall discuss below, but in the present connection the relevant point in that inability to make norms explicit was closely associated with awareness of variation. It was the couples who drew attention to variation who said they could not make generalizations about customary and proper ways of familial behaviour. Their difficulty in generalizing also depended on the context and the situation. They were reluctant to generalize when asked direct questions about norms, although they made many implicit generalizations when talking spontaneously.

In this paper I shall attempt to interpret these two findings: first, that there was less consensus on familial norms than is commonly assumed, and second, that many informants found it difficult to state norms explicitly. Perhaps one should not speak of social norms at all in this situation. If consensus is made essential to the definition of social norms, then the research families had only a few very general social norms concerning familial roles. Most of their views on the subject would have to be described as personal opinions. But the data I shall report below suggest that there is an intermediate stage between complete consensus and random variation. Informants *thought* there was agreement even when there was not. Or, to be more accurate, in some contexts they thought there was agreement and in other contexts they thought there was variation.

Some refinement of terminology is necessary. In ordinary usage the term "social norms" has a double connotation. It means norms that are in fact agreed on by some group or category of persons; it also means norms that individuals think are current in some group or category. I find it necessary to distinguish these two aspects. Throughout this paper I shall use the term *social norms* to refer to the norms people *think* are current in some group or category. I suggest the term *norms of common consent* for norms on which there is *in fact* consensus. I shall use the term *personal norms* for those ideals and expectations that informants think are their own private standards, different from those they attribute to other people.


## DISCUSSION OF FIELD MATERIAL

For the first eight or ten interviews, we did not ask our informants any direct questions about the norms of conjugal roles. Such questions were left until the last two or three interviews. In the course of the earlier interviews it became clear that each family had a fairly consistent set of standards by which they were judging their own and other people's performance as husbands and wives. The field workers picked up these codes very quickly, almost without being aware of doing so. Indeed, I was so convinced that such standards existed that I thought informants had made explicit statements about how husbands and wives should behave. It was only when I went carefully over the field notes again that I realized nothing had been said directly; everything was conveyed by implication, by complimentary or derogatory remarks about friends, neighbors, and relatives. Very few general comments were made until direct questions were asked, and even then many couples were reluctant to make any generalizations.

## 1. VARIATIONS IN CONTENT OF NORMS

On the basis of their spontaneous statements and replies to direct questions, it is possible to summarize the norms the couples adhered to.

There were a few general points of agreement, that is, there were a few norms of common consent. All the couples took it for granted that each elementary family should be financially independent of relatives and friends and should have its own dwelling. All couples took it for granted that there should be a basic division of labour between husband and wife, in which the husband was primarily responsible for supporting the family financially and the wife was primarily responsible for looking after the children and seeing that housework and cooking were done. The world would be upside down if the woman went out to work and the husband stayed home to care for the house and the children, although it was recognized, with varying degrees of disapproval and approval, that husbands sometimes helped with child care and housework and wives sometimes went to work. All couples took it for granted that adultery was a serious offence. It was assumed that parents were obliged to care for their children until they could look after themselves, although the standards of good care differed from one family to another. These norms were not explicitly stated in so many words. They were simply taken for granted. I think one may say that these general points of agreement arise from similarities in familial tasks and *general* similarity of social environment. Most of these norms of common consent were very vague and general so that a considerable variety of behaviour could be encompassed within the bounds of conformity.

There were many norms that varied according to variations in the social environment of the family. In a previous paper, "Urban Families: Conjugal Roles and Social Networks" (3), I have argued that the immediate social environment of urban families consists of a network, not a group. Individual members of families belong to groups, of course, but there is no group that contains families as wholes and regulates all aspects of their activities. Each family has relationships with friends, neighbours, relatives, a place of work, a doctor, a hospital, a school, shops, clubs, and so forth. Some of these external people and institutions are connected with one another independently of the family; others are not. Each of these external people has relationships with other people who are not known to the family. There is no point at which one can draw a boundary and say: "All the people within this boundary form a distinct unit, differing from those outside the boundary." Following John Barnes (1), I use the term *network* to describe this sort of boundary-less social configuration.

But the social networks of the research families differed in what I have called *connectedness*. In some cases many of the people known by a family knew and met one another independently of the family. These I have called *highly connected networks*. In other cases very few of the people known by a family knew and met one another independently of the family. These I have called *dispersed networks*. In between these two extremes were families with intermediate degrees of connectedness, and there were also several families who were in the process of transition from one type of network to another.

In "Conjugal Roles and Social Networks" I have argued that the type of relationship between husband and wife is associated with the connectedness of their network, and I discussed briefly the factors affecting degree of connectedness. In the present paper I shall be concerned with variations in content and expression of norms according to variations in connectedness. Variations in content have been discussed in the previous paper, and need be only briefly summarized here. Couples with highly connected networks expected husbands and wives to have a rigid division of labour. There was little stress on the importance of shared interests and joint recreation. It was expected that wives would have many relationships with their relatives, and husbands with their friends. Both partners could get help from people outside the family, which made the rigid division of labour between husband and wife possible. Successful sexual relations were not considered essential to a happy marriage.

In contrast, families in dispersed networks had a less rigid division of labour, stressed the importance of shared interests and joint recreation, and placed a good deal of emphasis on the importance of successful sexual relations. They were more self-conscious about how to bring up their children than couples in highly connected networks. They were aware that the people they knew had a great variety of opinions on this subject and they were worried about which course they themselves should follow.

In addition to these variations according to connectedness of the family's network, there were many idiosyncratic variations. One couple carried the idea of joint sharing of tasks to a point that almost denied the basic division of labour between husband and wife. They stated their views more strongly on some occasions than others. In the most emphatic statement they said wives and mothers should be able to work if they wished and that it was quite all right for women to work in the same field as their husbands, to be better at their jobs, and to earn more. They implied that this view was generally accepted in their social circle. Another couple with a similar sort of dispersed network had very different norms on the role of the mother. They said that people in their social circle thought mothers of small children should not work, although in some cases they had to. Each couple recognized that the issue of whether mothers should work or not was highly controversial, but each regarded his own solution as the right course of action and indicated that the other people in their social circle held similar views although they did not always adhere to them in practice.

There were other more subtle variations. Couples with dispersed networks, for example, generally stressed the importance of joint decision-making by husband and wife. But one wife implied that men were generally more dominant in fact, although not in theory, whereas another wife implied that men were more dominant in theory, although not in fact. Each was attributing to other people what was in fact the case in her own household. Again, a wife suggested indirectly that women in general were more sensitive than men and better at dealing with children and smoothing over difficulties between people. Here she seems to have been attributing to people in general not what was actually the case in her own family but what she would have liked to have been the case. In our judgment her husband was more skilful at handling interpersonal relations than she was. In another case a wife made a similar statement, but here it seemed that she was in fact generalizing from her own behaviour. In another case a husband maintained, in the face of protests from his wife, that his handling of the family finances was the usual and the right procedure among his friends and among families in general.

In brief, there was a tendency for people to treat their own behaviour and standards as the norm for other people as well as for themselves. In some cases people implied that the exact opposite of their own behaviour was the general norm—a sort of wish-fulfilment about their own behaviour. It seems from these cases that people sometimes treat their personal views as social norms. Ideally, of course, one should interview the people with whom the couple identify themselves to see if they would acknowledge the conjugal standards attributed to them—to see if the social norms of the couple are in fact norms of common consent. In practice this is very difficult when couples live in networks. And in some cases it would be impossible because, as I shall describe below, some couples identify themselves with abstract categories of person. But from statements made by the couples in other contexts, it often appeared that there was a good deal of variation among the members of their networks, not only in behaviour but also in norms, so that in setting up one sort of behaviour as the norm, the couple were making a considerable oversimplification. In consideration of these cases of displacement and projection of one's own norms on to other people, I have come to the conclusion that the usual sharp separation of personal attitudes from social norms does not do justice to the facts of the situation. The research couples assumed they shared certain standards of conjugal behaviour with other people, but some of these social norms were partly things of their own creation. Doubtless they had assimilated norms from experience with other people. But they also seemed to have selected some expectations and ideals rather than others, and they sometimes attributed their own personal version of norms to people in general or to some group or category of their own choosing without being aware of doing so.

### 2. HOW NORMS WERE EXPRESSED

*a. The difficulty experienced by informants in making norms explicit.* I have mentioned above that although informants continually expressed norms indirectly in spontaneous discussion, they made very few explicit generalizing statements. In the last two or three interviews we asked several direct questions that were intended to get people to talk about norms more directly. We found many of these questions difficult to ask, and informants found them difficult to answer, so certain questions were often left out. The questions were these: 1. What do you think the main changes in the family have been in the last fifty years or so? The aim of this question was to find out not only what people thought about social change, but also how they would characterize modern families in general. 2. How would you describe the rights and duties of husband and wife? 3. How would you describe the ideal husband, the ideal wife, the ideal child? 4. How do you feel your own ideas on how to run a family resemble those of people you know, or are different from them? 5. When you got married, did you have a clear idea of what family life would be like? Have your ideas changed? 6. What do you feel are the important things in keeping a family ticking over? What things make it difficult?

Couples found all of these questions, except the first, difficult to answer. Couples with dispersed networks seemed to find the second question particularly difficult. Their usual reaction was either a prolonged uncomfortable silence—two minutes in one case—or an immediate reply to the effect that there was so much variation one could not generalize. Couples with more connected networks found the questions a little easier, although even they often remarked that no two people would agree on how husbands and wives should behave or customarily did behave.

F

I think there are several reasons for the difficulty people experienced in answering these questions. First, since the field workers belonged to the same society, more or less, informants may have felt that we had some ulterior motive for asking the questions. Otherwise why should we ask questions to which we must have answers of our own? We never became very successful in allaying this sort of anxiety or in asking direct questions skilfully. The question about ideal husbands and wives and children was particularly upsetting. Because we interviewed husband and wife together, it was interpreted as an invitation to comment on the other partner's conjugal deficiencies in his and the field worker's presence. This question did not produce much useful information on norms, but we kept asking it because it was useful to compare how people coped with the slight awkwardness of the situation. But although we did not fully realize it at the time, this question upset the atmosphere of the interview so much that people did not give their full attention to the questions that followed it. If I were asking direct questions about norms again, I should omit this question or put it at the end.

But our awkwardness in asking questions about norms cannot be the only factor, because however stupidly we asked about occupational roles, we always got straightforward answers. Occupational roles are specific and easy to describe. Familial roles are diffuse; they cover many different activities, the organization of which is left to the discretion of the individuals concerned. People become so involved emotionally in familial roles that it is very difficult for them to separate themselves from the roles conceptually.

Another factor affecting difficulty in stating norms explicitly may have been the absence of overt crisis in the families. Norms are usually brought forth only in times of crisis and conflict, when they are used to justify one's own behaviour and to pass judgment on that of other people. When nothing much is going wrong, there is no need to state what the norms are.

The fact that couples in highly connected networks found the questions easier to answer suggests another factor. Many of the people they knew were known to one another, so that out of their constant interaction a general measure of consensus had been reached. The family knew, more or less, what the agreed standards were and could make them explicit. Couples in dispersed networks were more aware of variation. Since many of the people they knew were not acquainted with one another, there were fewer norms of common consent. It was impossible for such couples to reply to the questions without making gross oversimplifications. Perhaps some of their discomfort and hesitation when asked direct questions sprang from a realization that they made such generalizations implicitly in spontaneous discussion all the time, but that their generalizations were not very accurate.

*b. References to individuals, groups, and categories.* Most spontaneous expressions of norms took the form of comments on friends, neighbours, and relatives. Very occasionally couples also referred spontaneously to groups or category of person, although these more general references were made much more frequently in replies to direct questions about norms.

No one referred to religious teaching on the family and no one mentioned legal rules. Indeed, although we did not ask enough questions on this point, it was our impression that most of the research couples were almost totally ignorant of their legal rights and obligations as members of a family. Some expressed surprise at the strange rules of familial behaviour enforced by the courts. Unless informants had had direct experience of the law, they thought it was something they did not need to know about, something very far removed from their everyday life. Similarly there were very few references to reports of family life in newspapers and other media of mass communication, and none of the couples expressed the anxiety shown in public statements about divorce, delinquency, the decline of religion, and the moral decay of the family. Of course the fact that there were so few explicit references to religion, law, and the media of mass communication in spontaneous discussion or in reply to our direct questions about norms does not mean that people's conceptions were entirely unaffected by such institutionalized expressions of norms. Our data were not collected to show how public expressions of norms influence people's own views, but it does seem likely that they are highly selective in assimilating such information, taking in what fit in with their own personal experience and ignoring or re-working most of the rest. Similarly it seems very likely that expression of norms varies according to the social situation and the research technique used. The norms expressed in the group discussions we attended were much closer to those of newspapers and the church than to those expressed by the research couples in interviews. If we had used questionnaires or highly structured interviews with the research families, we should probably have been given a rather different view of familial norms. I would suggest that there is no single correct way of getting at the truth about norms. Different techniques will reveal different aspects of it.

In spontaneous discussion all couples made indirect expressions of norms in talking about particular individuals they knew. Of all these specific individuals, references to parents were the most important. Parents provided the basic models of family life that the couples we were interviewing were trying to emulate or improve on. There were also many references, usually negative, to friends, neighbours, and other relatives besides parents. A wife, for example, remarked that her brother-in-law was a good breadwinner but neglected his wife and children so that his was not a happy family. Implicitly she was drawing a contrast with her own husband who was not a great success at his job but did enjoy the company of his wife and children. Or again, a wife remarked that one of the neighbours had ridiculed her own husband in public, with the clear implication that such behaviour was very disloyal and ill-mannered. One husband, in the midst of an argument with his wife, went straight through a list of all his friends to show her that all men were difficult to live with and that she was expecting far too much of him. As we got to know families better, we began to be told their gossip. Gossip is one of the chief ways in which norms are stated and reaffirmed.

Informants referred to groups or categories of person as well as to specific individuals, especially when replying to our direct questions about norms. Many different reference groups were selected.[2] There was no one group or category that everyone chose as a matter of course. This contrasts with a small-scale society, in which the group referent is clear; the norms apply to everyone in the society, or at least to everyone in a clearly defined subgroup within the society. When a family is not contained in an organized group, but only in a network, especially a dispersed network, the referent of the norms becomes much less predictable and more complicated.

When informants were trying to generalize about standards of conjugal behaviour, I believe most of them were thinking primarily of their own personal experience, of their informal social network of friends, neighbours, and relatives. But no one referred to this set of people as such, presumably because it is difficult to conceptualize a network, since it has no beginning and no end. Some couples referred to local areas. Others tended to choose sets of friends or some kind of abstract category such as "people like us" or "our social circle" or "our kind." Such choice depended partly on the connectedness of the family's network. If a couple had a highly connected network, they usually talked about local areas, although they sometimes also referred to the conjugal practices of other generations or social classes. If they had a dispersed network, they referred primarily to sets of friends or to abstract categories. I have pointed out in "Conjugal Roles and Social Networks" (3) that the most highly connected networks were found where most of a family's friends and relatives were living in the same local area as the family itself. It is hardly surprising that such families conceptualized their network as the local area in which most of the members lived. Families with dispersed networks did not choose a local area as a reference group, for their relatives and friends were scattered all over England. The closest they could come to a concrete reference group was a set of friends. When they were trying to generalize more broadly they referred to more abstract categories such as "people like us" and "our social circle." In the cases where we thought to ask who informants were thinking of when they used such phrases, it was clear that the meaning shifted according to context. Sometimes it meant "people of our general class and style of life"; sometimes it meant "people of our age and style of life"; sometimes it meant "our friends" or "potential friends." People who used such words shifted imperceptibly from one meaning to another, and often reference to the category was followed by references to specific individuals who came within it.

People also referred to groups and categories in which they did not place themselves. Families who had had experience of highly connected networks in the past often referred to the local areas in which they had formerly lived. Families with dispersed networks usually referred not to local areas but to other classes and generations. All couples contrasted their own conjugal standards occasionally with those of the older generation and of "Victorian families."

The patterns of selection described above were only general tendencies. Couples varied greatly in choice of reference groups and in feelings towards them. Thus one couple identified themselves with the local area in which they lived and subscribed almost completely to the standard of conjugal behaviour they attributed to the people in it. They contrasted it favourably with conjugal behaviour in other areas. Another couple of similar occupational status and general background (but a more dispersed network) said they liked their local area and would never leave it, although they did not approve of all the local standards of conjugal behaviour. They said it was terrible the way the wives gossiped about their husbands and the way husbands never spent any time at home. They felt they themselves had personal standards that were different and better. At the same time, they condemned the conjugal practices of other areas and other classes.

Many couples used several different reference groups. Thus a plumber and his wife contrasted the confused and variable conjugal standards of their present local area with those of the areas in which they had been brought up. They also contrasted themselves with the households that the husband encountered in the course of his work. Their evaluation of themselves varied according to the context of comparison. Some couples rejected almost completely the norms they attributed to the group with which they identified themselves. Thus one couple acknowledged that they were similar in occupation to their neighbours and relatives but said they had a totally different outlook. They criticized their neighbours and relatives and identified themselves with an abstract category of nice people who had high standards of cleanliness, orderliness, and good manners. At the same time, in the course of spontaneous discussion they revealed that they visited their relatives and neighbours more than this sweeping condemnation implied. Some other couples who rejected the standards they attributed to their local area or friends did not bother to identify themselves positively with some other group or category. They were content to present themselves as deviants above the norms of the category in which they placed themselves. But not all couples selected reference groups in such a way as to make themselves appear in the best light. A few couples went to some trouble to make themselves appear average—that is, they chose categories in which they were placed in the middle when they might easily have chosen categories in which they would have been at the top.

I do not mean to suggest here that the couples we interviewed were deliberately distorting the norms of sets or categories of people. In nearly all cases, we felt their descriptions were consistent and probably reasonably accurate when they were describing concrete individuals with whom they had had direct experience. Of course we cannot be sure of this because we could not interview all their friends, neighbours, and relatives. But when they were asked to generalize about norms, oversimplification and distortion were inevitable. Families with dispersed networks had a particularly difficult time here, since the variation among the members of their networks was greater. In brief, when families live only in networks, when there is no organized group that they must almost inevitably use as a reference group, they must make up their own categories. They must generalize from their varied social experience to reach some simplified description, which is inevitably distorted. If they choose, they can identify themselves or contrast themselves with categories that show off their own behaviour and standards in a favourable light. If they choose, they may select categories that will make them seem average. If they have a highly connected network, they will probably choose categories that are fairly close to their everyday experiences with friends, neighbours, and relatives, although they are not compelled to do so. If they have a dispersed network, their categories are likely to be more abstract and generalized. And the more remote the reference group from their everyday experience, the greater is the opportunity for unfettered exercise of imagination.

Expression of norms thus varied according to the context and the particular individual or group that was being evaluated and compared with the couple's own standards of behaviour. Couples had a considerable range of choice in selecting the group or category with which they identified or compared themselves. This ability to choose one reference group rather than another makes it easy for informants to treat personal norms as social norms, for it is not difficult to find or construct some abstract category of persons who will share one's own views.

### 3. DEVIANCE AND CONFORMITY

Variation and flexibility of norms make it difficult to say what is deviance and what is conformity. In the course of the research I have come to the conclusion that it is impossible to make general, universally applicable assessments of levels of family functioning, which is a major aim of much research on the family. Such an aim assumes that there are many norms of common consent about familial roles. Too often the norms selected as the standard are those that the research worker thinks are current in his own social circle. Even if they are accurate for this category of person, they may be quite inappropriate for other types of family. I am not asserting here that families must never be measured against some standard, only that one should realize that the standard is arbitrary and that many families will not subscribe to it.

I think it is necessary to distinguish between *felt deviance* and *externally defined deviance;* felt deviance being lack of correspondence between the family's behaviour and their own social norms, externally defined deviance being lack of correspondence between their behaviour and some standard chosen by the research worker. It is very difficult to determine felt deviance, partly because people have trouble in conceptualizing norms, partly because they do not like to talk about deviance unless they think they are above their norm rather than below it, partly because they often use several different reference groups, and partly because they may be at or above their norms in some respects and below in others. At the risk of considerable oversimplification, I have tried to infer felt deviance for the research families, with the following results. Seven families conformed in most respects to the norms they attributed to their most frequently used reference group. Seven thought they were better in some respects. Three thought they were worse in some respects. Three thought they were different without being better or worse. There were only two cases in which internal inconsistencies suggested that the couple were seriously misrepresenting their own behaviour and that of the people in their most frequently used reference group. Both these couples placed themselves above their norm.

Felt deviance can be compared with various types of externally defined deviance. If one takes conformity to the very general norms agreed on by all families, the norms of common consent, only two families were below these norms and even these families were below the norms only in some respects, not in all. Both families tacitly acknowledged their deviance in the relevant respects.

If the norms of each set of families with similar degrees of network-connectedness are taken as the standards, there were fourteen cases in which felt deviance (or conformity) and externally defined deviance (or conformity) coincided, and six cases in which they were different. These six cases include the two couples mentioned above who probably misrepresented their own behaviour and the norms of their reference groups. In the other four cases, the social norms of the families were slightly different from those of other families with similar types of network.

If one uses Burgess's "companionship" family as the standard (4), only nine families conformed. Of the eleven deviant ones, the behaviour of two was at their own norm, six were above, one was below, and two were different without being above or below.

In brief, if one uses different standards, one gets different measures of deviance. Perhaps in situations in which there are only a few norms of common consent it would be convenient to determine what might be called *average norms*. These would consist of a quantitatively determined mean of the social norms expressed by the members of some category or set of persons selected by the research worker. Such an average measure would permit comparison of particular informants' social norms against a general standard, admittedly an artificial one, even when there were few norms of common consent. If one must evaluate families, I do not think it matters greatly what standard is used, provided it is relevant for the immediate problem and provided one bears in mind that there is not likely to be consensus on this standard among one's informants. But in almost any evaluative study, I should think it would be instructive to compare felt deviance with externally defined deviance.

### 4. CONFLICTS OF NORMS

Among the research families there were many examples of inconsistencies between norms. A wife should be able to work; a wife should stay home to look after her children. Among the families with comparatively highly connected networks (including here some of those that were classed as intermediate in "Conjugal Roles and Social Networks"), there was a conflict for the wives between obligations to the mother and obligations to the husband. In several cases ideal norms and norms of expectation conflicted with each other. Couples with highly connected networks said that husbands ought to give their wives a liberal housekeeping allowance, but they did not really expect such generosity. One wife complained about her husband's stinginess and another wife constantly stressed how fortunate she was in having a generous husband. The first wife thought most other women suffered as she did, whereas the second thought her husband was most unusual.

It is sometimes assumed that discrepancies and conflicts of norms are a sign of social change—an assertion that assumes the "normal" state of social systems to be one of harmony and consistency. But, as I have stated above, norms are seldom consistent even in small-scale societies that are changing slowly, and it seems likely that certain types of conflict are endemic in a social system. It is difficult to imagine that conflict of norms about loyalty to one's mother and to one's husband could be eliminated from families with highly connected networks. It may disappear if the family moves, but then the whole organization of external and internal relationships is altered.

Conflicts between norms need not, as is sometimes suggested, lead to personal and social conflict. In favourable circumstances people may be able to reconcile the requirements of conflicting norms. Thus one of the wives with a highly connected network was able to fulfil her obligations both to her husband and to her mother, partly because of her own skill and tact, but also because her husband and her mother got along well together. In other cases wives were both working and fulfilling their obligations to their children to their own and their husbands' satisfaction. Individuals may also cope with discrepancies of norms by constructing their own solution as an ideal norm and projecting it on to their social circle or some other reference group of their own choosing. This does not solve the problem on a social level but it does sort things out for the individual.

As I have stated above, people do not usually make norms explicit spontaneously except in situations of conflict, and we were not able to witness many disputes of this kind. The research families knew they were being studied as "ordinary" families, so that it is not surprising that they did not display their conflicts before us. After the first few interviews, when they had lost much of their uneasiness about revealing the fact that they did not always get along well together, they would describe rows they had had in the past or might have in the future. But only one couple had a row in the presence of one of the field workers. In this case each partner asserted that he was behaving correctly and that the other was in the wrong. Each proclaimed different norms and tried to show that his own view was generally accepted in their social circle. It did not happen, as it often does in small-scale societies, that the disputants agreed about the norms in principle but disagreed over whether and how they had conformed to them.


## SUMMARY AND GENERAL DISCUSSION

In this paper I have reported more variation in the norms of familial roles than is commonly assumed, and I have also shown that many of the people we interviewed found great difficulty in making norms explicit. I

F*

have suggested that both facts can be interpreted in terms of the immediate social environment in which the research families lived. The argument may be most clearly summarized by contrasting the position of families that are encapsulated within organized groups with those in highly connected networks and those in dispersed networks.

In an organized group in which members are in constant interaction, one is likely to find a large number of norms of common consent. Constant interaction corrects individual idiosyncracies of ideology. The norms I have defined as social norms, that is, the norms people attribute to the group with which they identify themselves, are likely to be more or less the same as the norms of common consent. In other words, there is little variation in the norms attributed to the group by its various members. Members of the group will find it easy to make norms explicit. Almost inevitably members will use the group itself as a reference group when discussing familial norms. Individual members may of course have discordant personal views, but they will be aware of the discrepancy between their own views and those of other members of the group, just as they will soon find out if their own behaviour is deviant. Opportunities for treating personal norms as social norms are reduced to a minimum. This does not mean, of course, that group norms never change. They may change in response to changed external conditions and through internal upheavals in which the personal views of individual members may play an important part.

In a highly connected network the group situation is approached, but there is more variation in norms, since not all members of the network interact with one another. If one could interview all the members of a highly connected network, I should predict that one would find a fairly large number of norms of common consent: the social norms of the various members would be in fairly close agreement with one another. There would be more variation than in a group, less than in a dispersed network. People in highly connected networks are likely to be intermediate in ability to state norms explicitly; they will have more difficulty than people in organized groups, less difficulty than people in dispersed networks. People in highly connected networks are likely to use their networks as reference groups, although they conceptualize them as local areas. But they are not compelled to make this selection. They may also choose abstract categories or groups of which they have no direct experience. In such a situation, people have some opportunity to treat their personal norms as social norms, but if they are in constant interaction with the members of their network, and if the members of their network are in constant interaction with one another, they are likely to be made aware that their social norms are not norms of common consent.

In a dispersed network fewer members know one another and there is less interaction. More variation in norms is likely to develop. There will be fewer norms of common consent, more variation in social norms from one member of the network to another. Informants find it difficult to make norms explicit, especially when their attention is focused on variation by direct questions. But, at the same time, they do assume implicitly that they share their standards of conjugal behaviour with other people. By my definition they have social norms, although there are few norms of common consent. People in dispersed networks have considerable opportunity to treat personal norms as social norms, to assert that the standards they follow are those that are current in their social circle or in some other similar reference group. The referent of their social norms, although derived from experience with their friends, neighbours, and relatives, is likely to be an abstract category. Because they have so much experience of different standards among the people they know, their reference groups must be generalized and oversimplified, and they have a considerable range of potential reference groups to choose from.

The suggestion that personal norms may unwittingly be treated as social norms raises the question of how norms are acquired by individuals. The psychological mechanisms of this process are very complex, and I shall do no more here than suggest some points that merit further reflection and inquiry.

In the literature of social psychology, much stress is placed on the internalization of norms through interaction with other people (11, 9). This interpretation of the individual as a passive recipient of external norms is too simple for the data I have reported here. When individuals and families live in networks rather than in groups, the process of norm formation becomes more complicated. I would suggest that individuals internalize other people's standards from their experiences with them, but that this is not the end of the matter. If the internalized standards agree with one another, which tends to happen in organized groups and in highly connected networks, there is little necessity for selection and internal rearrangement. If many different and contradictory norms are internalized, individuals select some rather than others and construct their own version in accordance with their personal needs. They may attribute this personal version, or certain aspects of it, to other people besides themselves, and they have a wide range of reference groups or categories from which to choose the recipient of their norms. In brief, projection and displacement play as important a part as internalization in the acquisition of norms.

I would suggest, then, that both psychological mechanisms, introjection (internalization) and projection, are always involved in the acquisition of norms. Indeed, recent findings of psycho-analysis explicitly stress the importance of projection as well as introjection in all learning processes (7, 6). This view is also implicit in the work of George Herbert Mead (8). In the case of couples in dispersed networks, the separate effects of the two mechanisms are comparatively easily distinguished. In highly connected networks or organized groups it is much more difficult to separate the two mechanisms. Errors of projection and of introjection are more rapidly corrected by constant interaction, so that a common standard is reached both internally and externally.

## NOTES

1. This research consisted of an intensive psychological and sociological study of twenty "ordinary" urban families with young children. The families varied considerably in socio-economic status. They lived in various districts of London and did not form a group. The research was sponsored jointly by the Family Welfare Association and the Tavistock Institute of Human Relations. It was financed for three years by the Nuffield Foundation. Previous reports of research techniques and results have been published by J. H. Robb (10) and the author (2, 3).

2. By "reference group" I mean any group or category, real or fictitious, that is thought to have a real existence and is employed for purposes of evaluation or comparison. Within this very general definition, reference groups may be further qualified according to whether the individual belongs to the group or not, whether feelings about the group are positive or negative, and whether the group has a concrete external existence or is an abstract category constructed by the individual. I think this is the best solution to the current chaos in which nearly every social psychologist uses a different definition. I have discussed this problem in a previous paper (2).

## REFERENCES

1. BARNES, J. A. "Class and Committees in a Norwegian Island Parish." *Hum. Relat.,* Vol. VII, No. I, pp. 39–58, 1954.
2. BOTT, ELIZABETH. "The Concept of Class as a Reference Group." *Hum. Relat.,* Vol. VII, No. 3, pp. 259–85, 1954.
3. BOTT, ELIZABETH. "Urban Families: Conjugal Roles and Social Networks." *Hum. Relat.,* Vol. VIII, No. 4, pp. 345–84, 1955.
4. BURGESS, E. W., and LOCKE, H. J. *The Family: From Institution to Companionship.* New York: American Book Co., 1953.
5. GLUCKMAN, MAX. *The Judicial Process among the Barotse of Northern Rhodesia.* Manchester: Manchester University Press, 1955.
6. HEIMANN, P. "Certain Functions of Introjection and Projection in Early Infancy." In Klein, M., Heimann, P., Isaacs, S., and Riviere, J. *Developments in Psycho-Analysis.* London: The Hogarth Press, 1952, pp. 122–68.
7. KLEIN, M. *Contributions to Psycho-Analysis.* London: The Hogarth Press, 1948.
8. MEAD, G. H. *Mind, Self and Society.* Chicago: The University of Chicago Press, 1934.
9. NEWCOMB, T. *Social Psychology.* New York: The Dryden Press, Inc., 1950.
10. ROBB, J. H. "Experiences with Ordinary Families." *Brit. J. med. Psychol.,* Vol. XXVI, Parts 3 and 4, pp. 215–21, 1953.
11. SHERIF, M. *The Psychology of Social Norms.* New York: Harper and Bros., 1936.

# 10:

# Neurotic Patterns in the Family[1]

*E. J. Cleveland* and *W. D. Longaker*

We shall here attempt to examine the impact of sociocultural factors on individual mental health by analyzing the transmission and mediation of values in a family setting. The focus of our effort is the elucidation of neurotic patterns in a single kinship group which contributed several patients to the caseload of a small-town clinic. Basic data were obtained during psychotherapy, and additional information was supplied by the psychologist on the clinic team who gave the results of his testing and the impressions from his own interviews. The data from patients were supplemented by home visits and interviews with various relatives, carried out for the most part by a social worker, though occasionally by a psychiatrist.[2]

It is thought that the occurrence of neurotic patterns in several members of a large family permits us to consider some aspects of etiology in this kind of mental illness, with particular reference to specific social circumstances. The approach complements and supplements an epidemiological research program being carried out in the same community (4).

Within the brief compass of this chapter it will be necessary to simplify the rich complexities of personality structure and the detailed web of valuative influences which affect individual styles of behavior. In describing the transmission of neurotic patterns from one family member to another, we shall inevitably stress psychopathology and neglect the positive attributes which contribute to a rounded assessment of individual functioning. Again, the concentration on values held and expounded by members of the kinship system forces us to slight the many other agents of valuative transmission. Although the tenets of family members

Reprinted by permission from Alexander Leighton *et al.,* eds., *Explorations in Social Psychiatry* (New York: Basic Books, Inc., 1957), pp. 168–95. Copyright 1957 Basic Books, Inc. Eric J. Cleveland is executive director, the Fundy Mental Health Centre, and is also research associate in clinical pastoral training, Acadia University, Wolfville, Nova Scotia, Canada. At the time of writing he was executive director, Stirling County Psychiatric Clinic, and research associate, Cornell University. William D. Longaker practices psychiatry in New York State. At the time of writing he was associate psychiatrist, Stirling County Study, and research associate, Cornell University.

are thus given special prominence, we recognize the host of other value sources impinging on the individual's developing framework of choice and belief; peers, schoolteachers, religious leaders, and the various vehicles of the mass media all modify the family influence on any individual.

In many instances, through this account we shall be developing implications for a general statement of neurotic patterning in families. This tendency to discern the universal in the clinically particular may be as misleading as it is scientifically suggestive. Therefore, we must recognize that the description is really limited to a single family living in a specific cultural milieu. Clinical experience with several other families indicates that the phenomena are recurrent within the culture studied; nevertheless, the qualification of conclusions in terms of the context in which they have been derived should be understood even if it is not constantly reiterated.

The clinic from which the study was made is situated in a small town in a rural county. Both treatment and research are carried out, and the clinic is part of a larger program, the Stirling County Study, concerned with the relationships between mental health and social environment. Coordinated with the clinic for certain aspects of the work is a team of social scientists who have been studying the social and cultural processes in the same county for several years. In the present chapter, we have drawn on the social science team for a characterization of critical elements in the local culture.[3]

The population of Stirling County, which totals about twenty thousand, is divided into two major groups; a little over one half is generally of English-Protestant background, the remainder is French-Acadian-Catholic and speaks French. The economy of the county is based mainly on fishing, lumbering, farming, and a combination of these, and wage work. There are over ninety-three named places in the county—some are rural communities with their own church, school, post office, and general stores, some are mere crossroad settlements or small neighborhoods, others are semi-urban centers with all the utilities found in a small town. The clinic is located in the largest semi-urban center of the county, Bristol, a town with a population of about three thousand.

## FRAME OF REFERENCE AND MAJOR CONCEPTS

As a result of experience with certain cases at the clinic, we became impressed with patterns in the transmission of values from one generation to the next as being significant in the development of neuroses. In approaching this problem we have utilized the concepts of need, role, and value,— and in the cases considered here the data have all been reviewed with reference to these concepts. Each individual was examined in the context of his family of orientation and his family of procreation and also in the context of those sociocultural stresses that seemed to us to be of primary etiologic significance in his disturbed functioning. Our aim was to see how the individual's problems may be related to certain important features of his personality (needs), to behavior expected of him by the society (role), and/or to difficult and conflicting patterns of cultural prescription (value).

The discussion of neurotic patterning in the family will emphasize two chief processes. Although these processes will be more fully defined after the presentation of some specific cases of disorder in a large family system, it may be useful to foreshadow them briefly. The first process is on the level of cultural value configurations and manifests itself most dramatically in the clash of incompatible orientations toward the ends and means of life in this semirural environment.

The second process is on the level of individual development and personality integration. It consists in a culturally recurrent mode of self-devaluation which has roots in the methods of child rearing. Generated in the socialization process, this intense self-devaluation is linked to the failure of individuals to adjust to the incompatible orientations toward the ends and means of life noted above. It will be convenient to term the first process *value conflict,* the second process (a resultant neurotic maladaptation), *disparagement.*

Value conflict is most strikingly observed in the contrast between orientations which stress long-range gratification in individual achievement of material success, as symbolized by money and status, and those which tend to underline the virtues of adjustment to one's environment in a manner emphasizing the pleasurable rhythms of nature and the immediacy of gratifications. The individuals to be discussed in this paper have all been in some sense trapped by the conflicting tenets of these two broad paths of life. It may be supposed that the effort to choose between them, or to resolve them in some workable amalgam, is difficult—but not impossible and not inherently productive of individual disorder. Our hypothesis is that the way in which these value conflicts are mediated within the family setting is critical in the development or nondevelopment of many cases of psychoneurotic disorder.

The pattern of extreme devaluation, which heightens the vulnerability of certain aspects of individual personality, is, we suggest, a learned type of response to particular stresses during the socialization period. Self-disparagement can arise in the developing individual when the socializing agents, primarily the parents, hold out contradictory models of behavior (grounded on conflicting cultural values) or are so suffused with the burden of their own inferiority feelings that some areas of learning become either threatening or coldly nonrewarding to the child. Disparagement can become a fixed tendency in the child to devalue certain facets of his own personality. When an obstacle to learning develops in an area of life relevant to the already vulnerable and devalued segment (for instance, in the sphere of occupational achievement or sexual fulfillment), then the disparaging tendency is activated and may become so acutely negative that it constitutes a neurotic behavior disorder.

Disparagement is quite similar in some respects to Adler's concept of the inferiority complex (1). In both there is the core idea of deep personal unworthiness. Disparagement, however, is conceived to be more closely linked to the cultural context in its etiology, distribution, and consequences. It is tied to group values and is recurrent as a maladaptive pattern in the family. Moreover, the disparagement of self is often not confined to one's own individual capacities but radiates to disparagement of the defined behaviors and value systems of his culture. In short, it touches all that has been internalized by the individual, or with which he identifies.

In the following cases, the phenomena of value conflict and disparagement may be viewed as underlying themes. In each instance, our focus will be on the family as the scene of socialization in which cultural value conflict is translated into interpersonal patterns predisposing to individual illness via the path of disparagement.

## THE DEAN FAMILY—A KINSHIP GROUP

As already noted, we have been able to examine, fairly extensively and intensively, a number of members in several large families or kinship groups. One of those will be presented here and will be called the Dean family. This kind of study makes it possible to cross-check data, since one case frequently corroborates information from another. In addition, the case material is enriched by the diverse viewpoints presented about one member of the family by several other members.

The Deans currently live in several neighboring crossroad settlements a few miles outside Bristol, and, although they consider themselves to be oriented toward the town, they also participate in their own small communities. Except for a few service stations and country grocery stores and small farms, there is little in the immediate neighborhoods to offer work or economic support. The people of the area turn for the most part to the town or the sea for employment. Many of them have small woodlots a few miles away, but these are usually cutover stands from which only a limited number of cords of wood are taken per year for fuel or pulp wood. Each house has a summer garden for vegetables.

The Deans provide services, such as sawyer, garage mechanic, and shopkeeper, which keep them in touch with their neighbors and insure relatively good economic status. They are rather well regarded in the communities, and certain members are recognized for their inventive capacities with machinery, despite modest formal education. As a family they are not extraordinary in matters of religion and morality—they belong nominally to the predominant Baptist sect—and include behavior among different members that ranges from the unconventional to the conventional.

### THREE PATIENTS

Three persons in the Dean family have been selected to serve as points of focus and reference in this presentation. They are Stan Davis, his son Ray Davis, and Stan's first cousin, Alice Mary Seeley. A brief abstract from the case history of each will be presented. Their relationship to other members of the family is shown in Figure 1. The names of those who have been clinic patients are set in capital letters.

STAN DAVIS. Stan is tall and he gives the impression, on casual contact, of being at ease and self-assured. Although he is in his mid-fifties, he looks somewhat younger. Locally he is known as a man of parts, and he has been able to put his marked mechanical abilities to much productive use. He is separated from his wife, yet contributes a small amount toward her support.

Stan was first seen at the clinic some months following an illness which abruptly ended the very active type of life he had been leading. He did not accept bed rest easily, nor the uncertainty and fear engendered by his condition, and it was necessary for his doctor to use morphine and other sedatives in order to keep him at rest. Eventually, during convalescence, overdependency on the drugs became a matter of concern to both the doctor and the patient. It was at this point that he came on his own initiative to the clinic.

His presenting complaints, in addition to concern about the drugs, were that he "felt jittery and trembling," had choking feelings and difficulty in breathing, had no appetite, and had "fluttering in the stomach." He also said that his legs got "trembly and shaky" when things upset him. Along with these complaints, there was a definite tendency to depression and self-blame. He expressed concern over the fact that he had to take things easy and was, therefore, unable to keep up his former standards of hard work. The diagnostic impression was that he suffered from depression and anxiety attacks and that both of these became worse when he tried to relinquish the drugs. There was much to suggest that the patient had anxiety attacks off and on since the age of six.

At the time of Stan's birth the family lived in a woodland area, and it

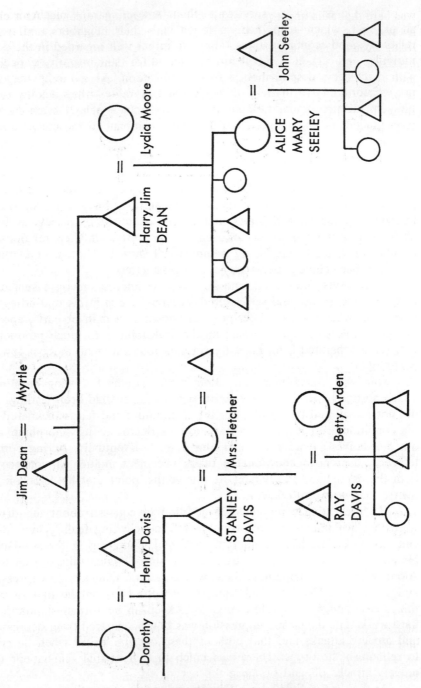

FIGURE 1: The Dean Family

was here that Stan spent most of his childhood and adolescence. As a child he was very close to his father, Henry Davis, who earned an adequate living in lumbering in the winter and farming in the summer, work which he thoroughly enjoyed. Stan describes his father, now deceased, as kind and generous, but with little ambition for getting ahead or for education. They had much mutual enjoyment in working and hunting. In many things they sided against the mother, often playing practical jokes on her. Both liked working at a slow pace and for the pleasure of it. They enjoyed nature and the beauty of the woods and the farm. Personal ambition and a quest for money were kept in the background; sociability was valued. One might sum up this life-way as physically vigorous, independent, lusty, generous, friendly, and geared to the even pace of the changing seasons.

The mother was different. She was a Dean, the sister of Harry Jim Dean, and lived according to a standard of values almost opposite to those of her husband. Stan describes her as not liking the life of the farm and said, "She would much rather be where there was more doing." The whole course of her life had been restless, including a move to the United States and a number of moves within Stirling County. Like many of the women of her generation in this rural district, she was strongly opposed to liquor and rejecting of sexual pleasures. Her values comprised much of the pattern that has been called "Puritan." High standards (often used as a lever on others) and a sense of moral superiority were combined with strong feelings regarding social status, money, material goods, and the importance of getting ahead.

Stan's values seem to be a blend of mother and father. During his close association with his father in early life he readily internalized the "slow pace," enjoyment in working and playing on the farm and in the woods. With this went a thoughtfulness for other people, generosity, fairness, and a verbalized contempt for a money-oriented existence. However, the material values have been apparent too, as for instance in the driving, money-making kind of life he has led, in episodic feelings of guilt with regard to idleness and sexual pleasures, and in the strict kind of woman he selected for his wife.

When Stan was twenty-three he married a woman somewhat older than himself. It seems fairly clear on the basis of clinical evidence that this marriage represented an affiliation with an idealized mother figure. Certainly, there were striking similarities between the two women. We believe he was drawn to his wife because her values were similar to those of his mother and, at a deeper level, by a desire to secure a dependent-submissive relationship to a female who seemed inherently superior. Once he was married, however Stan found that his wife was considerably more strict than his mother had been. Her demands that Stan be a "success" particularly in the area of goods and money led to continual strain between the two. Under this pressure Stan was obliged to work harder and longer hours than before. The couple separated after twenty years of marriage, during which one child, Ray, had been born. The allegiance of the son has always been to the mother.

So far as his current anxiety and depression were concerned, Stan improved in the course of brief psychotherapy as he learned to accept lessened physical activity and a return to a slower pace, the "slow pace" that his wife and mother had decried, the "slow pace" that his father had inculcated in him during his boyhood. Fortunately, he had discovered that he could maintain his financial security while doing this.

RAY DAVIS. Although Ray, who is thirty-two, resembles his father, Stan, in physical appearance, he is unlike him in manner. Ray is always on the go at a fast pace, and there is an evident high level of tension in all his restless movement. On the other hand, he does exhibit his father's inventive and mechanical aptitudes, although his restlessness and shifting goals, and a preoccupation with health, interfere with advancement. He is married and has three children.

Ray came to the clinic after at least a year of contemplating the step. In the meantime, through his advice, he was instrumental in the coming of his father, his mother, and his great-uncle, Harry Jim Dean. The presenting complaints given by Ray were mostly referable to his heart, and the diagnostic impression was of a severe cardiac neurosis which kept him from work six months out of each year. He had been to see many doctors who prescribed medicines and told him not to worry. The chief result of this was a conviction that the doctors knew he had a serious illness but out of mercy would not tell him the diagnosis.

There are indications in his history of severe neurotic disturbance from an early age. From seven to nine years his eyes troubled him, and he wore glasses for "wavy vision." At twelve he was treated by the family physician for "heart trouble," which he described as "pounding of the heart and nervousness." His job history to date has been extremely irregular. He is a perfectionist, restless and never satisfied with a job, seldom remaining in one for as long as a year. Each time he has approached the point of giving up a job there has been an increase in his physiological symptoms. For example, he quit his job as a taxi driver because pains in his heart kept getting worse as each work day wore on. It is noteworthy that his heart pains and palpitations correspond almost exactly to those presented by his mother. These symptoms occur particularly when he exerts himself in an occupation that does not satisfy him; he says, "then I get ugly and disagreeable." Insomnia and frightening dreams were other complaints.

Ray's parents have been sketched in Stan Davis' history. He grew up in an atmosphere of open hostility between his mother and father. As noted earlier, he sided with his mother, and she has dominated him all his life. He has shared her contempt for the father, especially in relation to his father's friends and associates. There has always been, in Ray, compliance toward his mother and an underlying fear that she might "blow up" in anger.

Getting ahead is important to Ray; he is very prejudiced against the local "slow" way of life and dreams of going to the United States. However, he is blocked by his restlessness, his overambitious goals, and his desire to achieve too much too fast. Advancement is also thwarted by his overinvestment in his body. He is afraid, for example, that close work will harm his eyes and that standing on the concrete floor of a garage will injure his health generally.

Ray married a daughter of Tom Arden (also a patient) when he was in his mid-twenties. He had always admired the way Mrs. Arden looked after her husband. Her overprotectiveness and Tom's untroubled acquiescence appealed to Ray and influenced him in choosing their daughter for his wife. She is very much like her mother in that she is a good housekeeper and yet a person of level temperament.

Ray's treatment at the clinic was sporadic and he was not greatly improved.

ALICE MARY SEELEY. A first cousin to Stan Davis, Alice Mary Seeley is, like most of the family, tall and thin. She is also frail looking and appears worn and older than her actual age of thirty. There is an external superficial cheerfulness which acts as a rather thin disguise for an underlying anxiety. When she speaks there is hesitation with frequent blocking. Perhaps this is an indirect expression of a strong undercurrent of resentment which frequently breaks through.

She was referred to the clinic by a physician because of a problem with one of her four children. The referral stated that she was "resentful and hated" this child. This presenting difficulty was, of course, only one expression of more widespread trouble. Most of her complaints centered on her genito-urinary tract, and there was a long history of menstrual difficulties. Several operations had been performed in an attempt to treat his problem. She was seen twelve times at the Clinic and, although she continues to have most of her somatic complaints, she has been able to accept her family problems much better.

Alice Mary's mother, Lydia Dean, was the wife of Stan Davis' uncle, Harry Jim Dean (see Figure 1). She had a hostile orientation toward childbearing and children, especially female children. Moreover, this attitude seems to have reached a high point at the time of Alice Mary's birth. Mrs. Dean thoroughly disliked the rural, slowly paced way of life and showed little interest in her home. She had a fearful, rejecting attitude toward sexual activity, one expression of which was frigidity, and yet she had shown a marked curiosity about the activities of her daughter and was overly suspicious of her relations with boys.

Alice Mary's father is dominated by his wife, but their basic values seem to be about the same. He has rejected the values of such persons as Henry Davis (Stan's father) in that he has no use for farming, hunting, or fishing. He is extremely antagonistic toward the way of life in the "back-woods' farms, and refers to himself sarcastically as coming from "out there with the rabbits and the deer." His major value constellation appears to be found in money and he is known as a miser. He also values independence. This is perhaps the affirmative alternative to hatred of the rural ways of life. He is concerned about his body and worries in a hypochondriacal manner, yet he mistrusts doctors and shops about for medical advice.

## VALUE CONFLICT

In the crossroad neighborhoods where the Deans live there is no clear-cut, obvious prestige hierarchy or power structure. Nevertheless there are prestige values, and two contrasting orientations seem to characterize the persons who have been preeminent at certain times and in certain groups. These orientations are by no means distinct and consistent, nor do they exhaust the range of behavioral variation. Hence, in order to describe them, we offer constructed types which are represented with varying degrees of intensity and coherence in the lives of the Deans and their neighbors.

1. *Striving:* Personal ambition for substantial material success, especially as reflected in occupational striving, acceptance of the rational money economy, the specialization of function and the technological innovations which are so prominent in Western industrial society; emphasis on individual achievement and self-development, on personal responsibility for success and for failure.

2. *Being:* Preference for a rather slowly paced, traditional style of life exemplified by physical labor in a natural environment, such as farming, fishing, timbering, or hunting; absence of intense drives toward occupational or material achievement, yet a strong desire for independence and personal integrity; development of personal satisfactions and warm communal relatedness and of immediate gratifications rather than more abstract rewards of money and position; satisfaction with stable interpersonal relationships and currently meaningful activities.[4]

Older women, who have internalized the "Protestant Ethic" type of scheme marked by striving toward material success and toward the individual grace attested by that success, seem to include the more intensely ambitious persons following the first path. Perhaps even more important, they stake out this pattern of individualistic striving as a model for the men of the family. It involves, for these women, a strong component of felt moral superiority and the use of moral sanctions.

One might say that the first orientation tends to value the individual by his achievements and symbolic rewards of money and status, whereas the second assesses personal worth more nearly in terms of intrinsic features of the personality and expressive interpersonal effectiveness. The first emphasizes triumph over adverse features of the interpersonal or physical environment, the second stresses adjustment to the situation in which one finds himself.

The two types of orientation seem to correspond to a conflict of values in the culture of the group in which the Deans live. Factors in the specific situation of the individual are thought to be of primary influence in turning him to one or the other direction. Undoubtedly the interpersonal relations and socialization patterns of early childhood are of major importance here due to their role in personality development. However, it is probable that the circumstances of later life also play a part. Thus, the low-keyed, communal, accepting orientation is easier to maintain when there is not undue personal hardship and when intimate interpersonal bonds and strong group pressures are present to reinforce it.

Each of the two value orientations is exemplified in quite distinct form by different members of the Dean family. In an effort to explore the patterning and transmission of these values and their bearing on the appearance of psychoneurosis, the orientations of several family members have been examined. It should be noted that our conclusions are apt to be influenced by the fact that our contact with the family is uneven and that we have worked with the material as it came to hand in the clinic or in home visits without endangering therapeutic relationships. Since no attempt was made to achieve either total coverage or a systematic sampling of the extended family, there are important individuals about whom we have very little information. For example, some of the presumably normal members might serve as controls or, at least, points of contrast. On the other hand, the Deans are only one of six families that have been studied in this manner and our impressions are thus based on work with approximately thirty cases. Furthermore, from the studies of the social science team and its anthropological appraisal of the county, it is evident that the patterns of value and communications exemplified by the Deans are widespread in the culture of Stirling.

Although we have assumed the primacy of value conflict in the etiology of neurosis, it is not yet clear how much weight should be attributed to this type of stress as compared with other stresses to which the developing individual is exposed. A number of questions might be asked about the relative potency of variously phrased threats to the personality. Does neurosis sometimes occur with no, or a very slight, background of cultural value conflict? For example, does organ inferiority, bodily illness, or disaster sometimes play the most critical part in the development of neurosis? In our cases, such obstacles seemed of importance only in the precipitation of neurosis—for example, the sudden illness of Stanley Davis which preceded the anxiety state that brought him to the clinic.

In what way are certain *situations* in a given society particularly threatening to the psychological functioning of the individual?[5] For instance, among people who have a striving background and strong upward mobility tendencies, is it particularly stressful to be in an area where the chances of fulfilling such ambitions are slight or where success, if it occurs, produces hostile attitudes and social disarticulation?

Turning now to our approach, we may ask: What are the relationships in problems of need, role, and value in the etiology of neurosis?

## SIGNIFICANCE OF THE CURRENT SOCIAL SITUATION AND ROLE EXPECTATIONS

Modern trends of rapid technological change have had different effects upon persons of various value-orientation and of various age and sex within the same value orientation. These contemporary trends place emphasis on material advancement achieved within a complexly ordered society. The individualistic aspect of the striving pattern has made it easier for some to accept highly ambitious goals of material advancement and the modern means of achieving these goals. Our scientific heritage is also a reinforcing agent in terms of modern educational requirements.

The effect of such trends can be seen, for example, in particular areas emphasized in the value system of Stan's wife. She has impressed Ray Davis, her son, with tremendous upward mobility striving and a restless desire to emigrate to the United States. However, the importance of co-operation in the complicated division of labor characteristic of the modern West has been underestimated or ignored by her. Interpersonal responsiveness is very little compatible with her interpretation of the "striving" orientation. This failure to stress the coordinative aspects of contemporary life is significant in Ray's inability to achieve his ambitions and in his development of neurotic substitute aims, and will be described later in this paper as the process of disparagement.

The situation of Mrs. Seeley is interesting in this connection. As a woman, and because she occurred late in a long line of siblings, she was subjected to somewhat different influences within the same general social situation. Her mother, like Ray's, had very strong upward mobility strivings and restlessness. However, the disadvantages of pregnancy and of children were particularly stressed in her case. Marriage was to be valued as a means to higher social status, but the male should be kept in subservience as an instrument of the female's ambitions. In no case was he to be allowed pleasures.

Mrs. Seeley rebelled and attempted to reverse these values, but she was never able to free herself from disgust with sexual pleasures, presumably acquired from her mother, nor to accept her husband and children on a basis of trust.

Thus her problem, like Ray's, can be traced to inconsistency and disarticulation in the values of the parents, particularly the mother. Later on we shall discuss the relationship of these antecedent events to a basic self-concept of inferiority and the appearance of neurotic symptoms.

## TWO MAIN POSTULATES

In approaching our analysis we have made certain assumptions, or postulates, bearing on the development of concepts regarding the transmission of values through the family. The first is that man is a communicating animal and that communication with other persons is not just a means but is in itself one of his major goals. Man seems to take an active interest in joining in the pursuit of "agreed upon" goals as well as in the simple gratification of what are supposedly bodily instincts.[6] Following Harry Stack Sullivan (7), we conceive of the oral, anal, and genital erogenous zones as serving an important function in communication. In this connection the Freudian principle of unconscious motivation is also assumed—and, in general, the kind of symbolism that is described in such theory. We have focused especially on data that might give a better understanding, however, of the full meaning of such symbolism: for example, being interested in not only the early experiences that may give rise to castration anxiety but also the manifestation of castration symbolism in social living and how this is related to specific modes of role-learning in later life. Thus, the symbolism of Ray Davis, as described by him in his dreams, is suggestive of castration anxiety, and our interest includes the manner in which his mother has played a part in obstructing his learning of occupational roles.[7]

A second postulate is that a framework of common values underlies the process of communication and that these values are passed on by certain modes of behavior and techniques of socialization. Critical elements in this transmission are the mechanisms of reward and punishment, approval and disapproval, which create certain strongly held values and give them the dynamic impress of binding moral force. Such values are reinforced by a social technique, often termed sanctions, which dramatizes them and affords them a substantial potency in the lives of both transmitter and receiver.

The transmission of values and their supporting sanctions may be conceived as occurring at two main levels: they may be passed on without conscious effort, covertly conveyed by symbolic processes of gesture and intonation which elude deliberate recognition by either source or recipient; they may be inculcated by overt manifestations, as precept and example, recognized by both parties to the transaction.

On the basis of general observation it seems obvious that any personality incorporates elements of different value systems and rarely behaves according to a single consistent pattern. As a result, it is necessary to seek some way of formulating the inconsistency and fluctuation which often characterize valuative behavior. One ordering would emphasize that certain values are amenable to conscious selection and activation, whereas others are less susceptible to conscious expression and verbalization: this ordering might be described as the distinction between *manifest-overt* and *latent-covert* values.

Another conceptual distinction is necessary, however, to account for the *hierarchical aspect* of value systems—the fact that values are not all mobilized with equal potency at all times. That is, even within the distinction above between manifest and latent there are subdistinctions conditioned by time, place, situation, and personality state. Among the values amenable to conscious activation, for instance, some will be stressed at one time, some at another. This further refinement might be keyed to the words primary and secondary, or activated and dormant.

The first distinction advanced above is one of *level,* dividing verbalized awareness from the behavioral forces which operate behind the curtain of the unconscious. The second distinction is one of *hierarchy* and *primacy* within levels, distinguishing more active and intensely held values from less active and weakly held values, recognizing that situational variation may condition the hierarchical alignment at any point in time.[8]

In the case of Stanley Davis, we may propose that he incorporated both paternal and maternal values in varying degrees but that their level of conscious realization and their situational order of primacy differed. He acquired his father's values by identification with the attractive paternal figure; and he was engaged in daily practice (and seemingly frequent verbalization) of the paternal orientation toward slowly paced, immediately gratifying activities. On the other hand, his mother's valuative pattern was obviously also impressed on him at a very deep level of personality integration. Had it not been so significant as a point of reference in their lives, Stanley and his father would presumably have had little reason to ridicule it and ally themselves against it. There seems little doubt that Stanley felt guilty about not showing more overt allegiance to the maternal orientation and that he was emotionally convinced of its moral superiority.

This formulation is further corroborated by the fact that he married a woman who expressed his mother's viewpoint and who dominated him in marriage. Although Stanley then exhibited the maternal values for many years and gave them behavioral expression, he has reactivated the paternal orientation in his more recent life. Since being separated from his wife, and especially since his recent illness, he has placed much more emphasis on the *being* pattern of his father. It has required therapy, however, and will undoubtedly require substantial reorganization of his personality for him to overcome the severe guilt generated by his failure to persist in the now covert but latently powerful maternal *striving* values.

Although one might assert that the father's values were more deeply internalized through the process of identification, as indicated by the eventual return to them, it is also apparent that different valuative patterns were mobilized in Stanley under different objective social conditions. One might then account for a large part of Stanley's realistic shifts in values as a functional adaptation to external conditions, partly conscious and cognitive, partly unconscious.

The idea of the Oedipus complex has always been considered crucial to the understanding of psychopathology. Perhaps the concept could well be extended to view the patient as internalizing a whole drama of parental interaction, not confined to sexual alliance but including the parents' total system of values.

## DISPARAGEMENT AS A CONCEPT FOR LINKING SOME ASPECTS OF INDIVIDUAL AND GROUP PHENOMENA

Neurotic patterns contain elements that are largely nonrational and inaccessible to conscious formulation. The very potency of neurosis consists in hyperbolic, disproportionate affect, an emotional overinvestment in some area of life which does not square with a rational strategy of ends and means. Exaggerated emotional valences of a number of different types occur in neuroses, of course, but the one we shall delineate here is thought to be peculiarly enervating since it erodes portions of the individual's system of values, leading to self-defeating behavior. Further, it is damaging to society because not only does neurosis decrease the effectiveness of the disordered person but also this particular pattern weakens certain cohesive group values with resultant societal disability in adjusting to changing circumstances.

The pattern in question, which we term *disparagement,* has not yet been fully elaborated as conceptual orientation, especially with regard to its relation to other elements of personality theory and social theory. This is particularly true with reference to psychoanalytic schemes such as regression; but although the articulation of such different aspects of phenomena and constructs are as yet unclear, we do not feel that there is necessarily any conflict. Sullivan has proposed disparagement as the *sine qua non* of neurosis (7). On the sociological side, Merton speaks of disparagement as *the* characteristic of people in a state of anomie (5). We believe our use of the term has a similar, if not identical, meaning to that of Sullivan and Merton.

In our definition, *disparagement is an habitual choice of extreme devaluation as a pattern for coping with problems of an intrapsychic and interpersonal nature.* As such, it appears to be pervasive as an observed phenomenon in the cases seen at our clinic and to be, within limits, a useful explanatory link in describing the relationships between sociocultural environment and the evolution and perpetuation of neuroses in individuals.

Because man is a communicating animal and because he lives in a framework of values that have hierarchy and primacy, he must constantly make choices and express preferences. In this process, it is patently necessary that he exalt some alternatives over others; the act of choice always implies a relative devaluation of the alternatives not chosen. Devaluation may be a residual category to handle things not especially liked, and it may quite healthily assume the form of a sharp attack on *selected* targets. In the pattern of *disparagement,* however, the process is a global unselective attack on huge areas of both the self-system and the tenets of the social milieu. It is thus a disproportionate, more or less consistent, Stephen Dedalus type of nay-saying, at the extreme end of the arc of devaluative possibility; its corrosive implications stem from both the tendency to deny individual worth, with resultant crippling of selfhood, and the tendency to deny the worth of group values and thus to cripple interaction.

Disparagement as a concept raises a number of as yet unresolved questions. Two that are critical may be stated as follows:

1. How does the extreme devaluative tendency become activated, and what personal needs does it meet?

2. In what conditions does disparagement develop in a way that directs devaluation toward the self or, alternatively, toward others? Perhaps most important—are the depreciation of personal worth and of societal currency dynamically related, so that disparagement always involves elements destructive of both the self-image and certain societal value patterns?

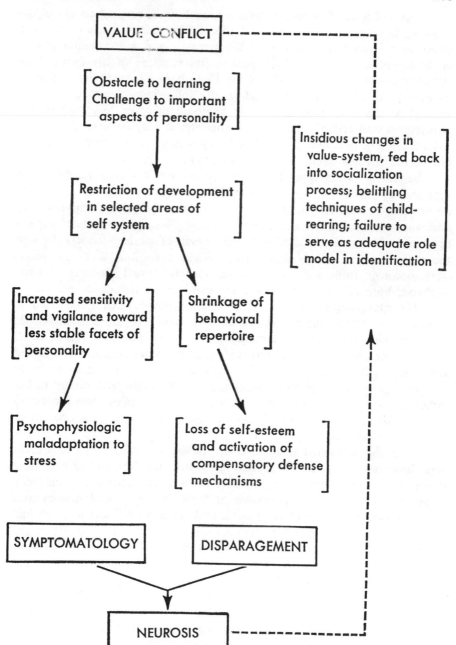

FIGURE 2: Disparagement in the Neurotic Process

Figure 2 is an effort to construct a model of the original course of the disparaging process in the individual. As can be seen, it takes origin in a sociocultural context, mediated by the parents, and is eventually passed on to the next generation if the patient has children of his own. Many elements in our previous account of the Dean family seem to become more meaningful in this framework, and in the following discussion we shall attempt to use that family's neurotic anatomy in order to explicate disparagement and related concepts. To this end it may be helpful to essay a description of one individual, Alice Mary Seeley, as an illustrative example of the process sketched in the diagram.

Beginning at the upper left-hand corner and following the directions indicated by the arrows, we may note that Alice Mary Seeley began life as an unwanted child. Her mother was in rebellion against the feminine role and was vehement in her adherence to striving standards of moral superiority and self-denial combined with the pursuit of worldly success through the acquisition of money and status. These revulsions and aspirations were, however, futile and fruitless, since she had sexual relations with her husband, bore children, and never achieved either money or status.

The child, Alice Mary, grew up in an atmosphere of value conflict, without having available for identification a model of the normal female role. However, rather than internalizing wholly the maternal values in all their conflict and disjunction with reality, Alice Mary rebelled and added something of her own. The rebellion was no doubt in part a response to the mother's rejection. In other circumstances she might have turned to her father as the main figure for identification, but his values were similar to those of the mother and there is no indication that he was ever warm or accepting toward her.

Thus she developed an urge to be "different" from her parents. This urge, however, was from the beginning severely handicapped in two main dimensions. In the first place, she had already internalized her mother's values so that they were pervasive at both conscious and unconscious levels. Secondly, because of geographic and hence social isolation, she had no living model upon which to pattern the way of life toward which she aspired. Hence, she developed a fantasy of a not-too-realistic feminine role that would be sexually responsive, companionable, motherly, and calmly accepting. As is evident, this relates to the *being* pattern rather than the *striving* pattern of her parents. Other aspects of her fantasies so related were a desire for a stable existence close to nature, renunciation of economic and social ambition, together with more enjoyment of love, sharing, and interpersonal vivacity.

To sum up, she disparaged the values of her parents in a blind, all-or-nothing fashion; yet they were already within her and attempts to replace them only added fantasied unachieved contrasts of what life might have been. Thus it came about that, in devaluating her mother's tenets, she devaluated herself.

This picture was well established by the time Alice Mary reached adulthood and has been further compounded by her marriage, since her husband turned out to be one who blocks her effectively from the outdoor existence and sensuous home life of her fantasies.

We find, then, disparagement, first of her mother's values and now of her own worth and role performance, as a critical feature of Alice Mary's psychic structure. This brings us to the box marked "Disparagement" in the lower mid-portion of the diagram. She feels inferior and self-recriminatory; she is hostile toward her child, for he was conceived in the most fiercely rejected (and conflictual) portion of the feminine role—the sexual —and must be raised in an almost equally difficult portion, the maternal. She is beset by physiological complaints which are significantly centered on the genital organs, including postnatal difficulties and menstrual disturbances. These are relevant to the box in the diagram marked "Symptoms." One may see in her case the grim determinism of inadequate socialization and thwarting objective social circumstance. The disparagement of the feminine role, so sedulously practiced by her mother, has continued to flourish; and her isolated social milieu and particular family situation have done little to mitigate this pervading devaluation. The total complex of symptoms and disparagement constitute her neurosis, the lowest box in the diagram; and it appears all too probable that this is exerting an influence on the development of her own children quite comparable to the kind of influence which she experienced at the hands of her mother.

The life stories of Stan and Ray Davis and the evolution of their neuroses show a similar pattern, although with different items of specific content. The same diagram serves equally well to point up the relationships. In this case, however, it is possible to see in Ray the results of the process in a third generation, much as we predict it will be for at least some of Alice Mary's children.

It is impressive in our cases how regularly ideas of disparagement multiply when there is a major obstacle in the (social) learning situation, as for instance when there is a conflict of value systems, a demand to fill difficult roles, or any other inability to meet group expectations or carry out personal ideals.[9] It is as if for the patients any great discrepancy between goal and achievement is registered mentally in terms of absolute and final inferiority. The process seems to be sweeping, irrational, and accompanied by the arousal of powerful affect; the capacity for making finer discriminations seems incapable of functioning. Moreover, the process of disparagement tends to be self-perpetuating; this is due to the antagonizing or unresponsive behavior in relation to people that accompanies it, and it thus acquires a degree of self-fulfilling autonomy in the mentation of the individual which interferes with his reality testing.

One of the social science team has studied the effect of widely shared personality factors on the failure of a trade union, many of whose members lived in the same geographic district from which our cases were drawn (6). The results of analyses of the life histories of several working-men are presented, showing how their rejection of active union participation was related to personal apathy, to self-disparagement and hopelessness. The author traces such feelings to insecure personal relations within the family of origin. His study thus supplements and to some extent confirms the picture we have drawn of a culturally pervasive pattern of self-devaluation. It is perhaps significant that inquiries into phenomena as seemingly diverse as union activity and individual neurosis should lead to similar explanatory patterns in this cultural setting.

Although we have illustrated our thesis in such a manner as to imply that the *striving* values are more noxious and hence more often linked to disparagement and neurosis than are the *being* values, we should like to state explicitly that we feel the crux of the matter to be in the value *conflict* and not in either *striving* or *being* per se. Furthermore, it is possible for a neurotic pattern to have the outer characteristics of either of the two main value systems. "Individualism" is the banner of Stan Davis' wife, but it is neurotic in its nature and context because it constitutes a means of establishing a sweeping, nondiscriminating disparaging relationship to others. On the other hand, it is just as possible to have verbalized attachments to the *being* way of life (as does Alice Mary Seeley) which are neurotically determined, unrealistic, and maladaptive. Unless one looks for the distorting factor of disparagement in stated systems of value, he is easily misled into mistaking a neurotic attachment for a normal adherence to important themes offered by the sociocultural matrix.

Neurotic problems are commonly expressed in terms of an apparently rational conflict of values. In fact, however, if they are neurotic they arise out of a previous state of personal feelings of inferiority and disparaging relationships with others. In such cases, avowed affiliation with a system of values may serve as a vehicle for the disparagement. For example, Ray Davis would say that he prefers modernism and efficiency, but the neurotic indicator in his pattern is the force of the contempt that he feels for "the old ways" of his father. We suspect that the irrational element of disparagement in his attitude is the effect of difficulty in his socialization, the impossible goals set by his mother, and his inability to deal with these factors realistically. He is, apparently, inculcated with ambition by the mother, yet remains emotionally and geographically close to her, so that there is no chance of taking effective steps toward fulfillment. To this must be added that, despite his hostilities toward his father, he has internalized some of the latter's *being* values and thus increased his psychic conflict. He stands disparaged in his own estimation, whether measured by his father's or his mother's standards.

## DISPARAGEMENT AS A VARIABLE IN METHODS OF SOCIALIZATION

Child has reviewed the literature on methods of socialization.[10] The impression emerges that, in any particular area of learning, there is no one-to-one relation between effective socialization and such phenomena as punishment, love, reward, etc.

Adelaide Johnson (3) has pointed out that the regard of the socializing agent tends to become identical with the self-regard of the person socialized. Harry Stack Sullivan has made a similar point with respect to what he calls the development of the self-system. One might conjecture that an essential stimulus to given behavior in an interpersonal situation is the fact of being overtly regarded or estimated by another person. Manifest interest in the person being socialized on the part of the socializing agent may be just as significant as punishment or love, in themselves. If this is so, then a critical factor could be whether the socializing agent regards the person being socialized with esteem or with disparagement. Where there is no regard and no expectation, there is probably little effective socialization.

Numbers of our patients reveal that their parents have used techniques in their upbringing that are relevant to these considerations. Included are excessive rejection, domination by threats, rules, bribes, and verbal or physical punishment. Of particular importance is the impression of the child that the parental example is inconsistent with their own explicit teachings.

It is clear that such techniques of socialization, if excessive, arise out of processes of disparagement and tend to inculcate disparaging tendencies in the person socialized. As Johnson notes, negative techniques of child rearing and of relating to others in general weaken the self-esteem and the capacity of the developing child to meet problems in the particular area in which they are used. In turn, they reflect an anxiety and incapacity on the part of the socializing agent to deal with these areas of interpersonal relations.

It would be interesting and most important to derive valid generalizations regarding relationships in the socialization process. Our cases afford some clues to possible general statements, but they are too few, and their

G

cultural context too singular, to let us do more than pose a series of intriguing questions.

When there is extreme conflict within the value system, or between competing value systems, do certain methods of socialization become more prominent? For example, is there likely to be (due to anxiety on the part of the socializing agent) increased use of extremely repressive measures or even of rejection and withdrawal? How is parental rejection related to children's tendencies to withdrawal? Can we relate certain schizoid trends in the personality to the severity of social stress? Are specific behavior disorders induced by specific methods of child rearing?[11]

Does compulsiveness coupled with rejection provoke a kind of negative learning, so that the rules that are compulsively taught become systematically broken?

The person who forms a dependent relationship is of particular interest in the transmission of values. Stanley Davis, for instance, altered his values significantly when in a dependent relationship with his wife, and again later with a therapist. Perhaps the strength of the trend toward dependency, even though it may be regarded as a pathological way of relating, has the advantage of providing a means of flexibility in the individual that is important in his adjustment to changing circumstances. Its significance in the development of transference and of the reorientation in the early phase of therapy is acknowledged, but perhaps something of the sort that is also useful occurs in everyday life.

### PRECIPITATION OF NEUROSIS

The precipitation of neurosis is very difficult to describe in causal terms. Almost certainly, in a given case, there are multiple determinants at physical, psychological, and social levels. However, it has frequently been observed that the appearance of frank neurotic symptoms—disturbances of affect, disturbance of physiology, obsessions, and other manifestations of pathological mental mechanisms—is intimately related to immediate events in the patient's life situation.

In the case of Stanley Davis, an organic illness was the apparent precipitant. It seems reasonable, however, to consider his physical impairment not only as a threat to life and hence affecting the equilibrium of personality but also in the social context of a disease that renders one inactive and unable to work. His limited scope became a matter of great concern to Stanley Davis, and he continued to be bothered with thoughts of self-blame and obsessive worrying until he had at least partially worked through the problem with a sympathetic listener. This working through involved a trial consideration of possible shifts in role and a reorientation of values. Although the immediate effect of the organic disorder was to increase greatly his anxiety, disparagement, and self-blame, it became a choice-point from which, in the course of a few months, he evolved a new role for himself out of his total past experience.

Many factors seem to enter into the sort of crisis in the learning situation that occurred with the organic illness of Stanley Davis. Some of these might be listed as follows:

1. The role-taking facility that the person has developed throughout his life.

2. Intellectual capacity.

3. The difficulty of the presenting situation, in particular the diverse pressures that are currently being exerted by various family members and acquaintances.

4. The manner of socializing exhibited by significant others—blame, threats, rewards, and other modes.

5. The severity of the person's previously developed tendencies toward disparagement.

The outcome for Stanley Davis might have been quite different if at the time of his illness he had still been living with his wife; she might have scolded him for his dependency on drugs and threatened him with various reprisals. This would probably have led to a perpetuation of his feelings of self-disparagement with further development of overt neurosis, depression, and obsessive thinking. In contrast, he was able to make arrangements that provided nursing attention, sympathy, and acceptance.

In the case of Ray Davis, neurotic symptomatology tended to be chronic. He continued to live near his mother even after his marriage. Whenever there was some slight disappointment in his ambitions, when he failed to make a good business deal or lost a little money, his ordinary worrisomeness would develop to the point of "unreasonable," completely unconstructive obsessional thinking. This would be accompanied by various physiological disturbances such as pain, rapid heartbeat "like my mother," and restlessness, so that he could not stick at his work. Frequently he felt so devalued that he took offense at minor or fancied slights.

Although much has been written about the symbolic significance of such symptoms as vomiting and diarrhea, Ray Davis and others of our cases suggest that psychophysiologic symptoms sometimes appear as a part of the process of identification with a person who has similar disturbances. It may be certain physiologic symptoms have more social than personally symbolic meaning and can be better understood in terms of "transmission" of the same complaints from one person to another as part of identification, internalization, and learning.

In each case described in this chapter, there was a specific vulnerability to certain situations and to certain techniques through which others related themselves to the patient. The reactions of the potentially neurotic may be characterized as erring in the direction of dependency or withdrawal, among other pathological alternatives. In either of these cases any situation where disparagement is implied by others tends to be seen by the patient as either overprotection or rejection, depending to a great extent upon his previously learned patterns of value and perception rather than upon the actual situation.

New situations and new roles impose a particular stress upon the dependent or withdrawn individual who has been nevertheless lodged in a family nucleus. This is because he does not have the outlets for his hostility that are accepted within the family. For example, the neurotic who threatens suicide as a hostile gesture toward his dominating mother will not find this an adequate expression of hostility to a dominating employer.

We now have some clues to the critical questions raised in our earlier discussion of disparagement. The activation of extreme devaluative patterns has been partially located in the socialization process, as seen in segments of the Dean family. Disparagement seems to arise as a protective mechanism when two contrasting patterns of value are presented in incompatible form to the child; since they cannot both be fully incorporated, one may be harshly devalued in the interests of lessened tension and heightened psychic integration. Again, both parents may exhibit sweeping disparagement of broad areas of values (and persons who follow such values), thereby transmitting a habitual devaluing tendency to the child. In this instance, even a firm identification with parental models does not equip the child with a sufficiently flexible valuative repertoire to meet adequately the situations of adult life. Intense feelings of inferiority and self-deprecation appear to follow in two ways or some combination of them: when the parent of the same sex holds values distasteful to the developing individual (as for instance because that parent rejects the child) and the child fails to make a healthy identification with a mature sex role, yet involuntarily slips into the hated model for want of any other; and when the child at the edge of adulthood chooses an ideal role but almost entirely fails to fulfill it, so that an unmanageable gulf exists between aspirations and achievement.

The relation between disparagement of self and disparagement of others is, however, still unclear. Obviously there is an opportunity for the individual who disparages certain value orientations to generalize this negation toward holders of the detested orientation. These holders may in turn be categorized as suitable out-group targets of social prejudice, in conventional clusterings of religion, ethnicity, status, and so on. We suggest that expressed social prejudice is positively linked to neurotic behavior and that both are often based on disparagement. This is a strong clinical impression, but it requires much further exploration, particularly in the light of Adorno's contrasting findings (2).

## SUMMARY

In the most general terms, this chapter has tried to view individual neurosis in its cultural and familial context. Numbers of members of several different large family groups have appeared as patients in a community psychiatric clinic, where a characteristic pattern of their relationships to one another, and to nontreated family members, has been perceived as a vitally predisposing element in neurotic development. Neurotic patterning in the family has been described in part, as a reaction to cultural process through which family members experience their basic introduction to culturally-defined paths of behavior. Evidence from cases not described here, and from other types of study, tends to support the proposition that disparagement is a very widespread maladjustive mode in this culture and that the neurotic patient may represent an exaggeration of a phenomenon recurrent in the larger, nontreated population.

A divergence between two equally sanctioned sets of cultural values has been outlined. Persons growing up in this region are exposed to both orientations in such a way that they have difficulty in assigning clear-cut primacy to either one or in combining them into a satisfying coalescence. Failing such an adjustment, they often reject selected values on a superficial level but continue to deprecate themselves in areas of personality function related to those values. Opportunities for thoroughgoing fulfillment of either "striving" or "being" are seldom utilized, so that one finds a shared ambivalence toward occupational patterns, interpersonal behavior, and general style of life.

Cultural value conflict is most forcefully presented to the individual in early life through the socialization process. The family environment is the most obvious and important link between configurations of group value and the developing alignment of forces within the personality. Ambiguities in socialization, the conflicts, surfeits, and emotional starvations that distort normal functioning, are thought to be the most fertile source of neurosis. The child's parents, the primary agents of socialization, are in this series of cases at odds with one another over incompatible values or internally torn between the prescriptions for behavior generated by different value systems.

The child, then, suffering from difficulties in identification with a mature, consistent role model, and from poorly integrated patterns of value, develops severe vulnerabilities in one or more important phases of life. When these vulnerabilities and restricted facets of the personality are challenged by the need for new learning by the assumption of demanding role responsibilities, the neurotic process of disparagement is likely to be activated. Disparagement seems to be a favored mechanism among our cases and in this culture as a whole. It is really a denial of challenge, in the sense that the individual deprecates himself as unworthy of a serious effort and/or deprecates the values embodied in the challenge as undeserving of his best energies. He is not a failure because he did not try.

Our selected cases of neurotic patterning in one family can, of course, afford only slight evidence of the hypothesized relations between cultural value, family system, and individual disorder. A great deal of systematic research must be performed to substantiate specific correlations among group values, methods of socialization, personality development, and the employment of neurotic mechanisms such as disparagement. It is hoped that this chapter may be helpful as a step in that direction through the formulation presented and the questions raised.

# NOTES

1. This chapter comes from the Stirling County Study which is being conducted by Cornell University in collaboration with the Department of Public Health of the Province of Nova Scotia and with the cooperation of Acadia and Dalhousie Universities. Invaluable help has also been provided by the Faculté des Sciences Sociales, Université Laval. Within Cornell, the Stirling County Study is attached administratively to the Social Science Research Center and is sponsored by the Department of Sociology and Anthropology and the Department of Psychiatry of the New York Hospital and Cornell University Medical College. Financial support is provided by the Carnegie Corporation of New York, the Department of National Health and Welfare of Canada, the Department of Public Health of the Province of Nova Scotia, and the Milbank Memorial Fund.

    The staff of the project at the time the article was written consisted of the following who are listed according to their functions in the study: Alexander H. Leighton, Director, and Allister M. Macmillan, Deputy Director; Eric J. Cleveland, Chief of the Psychiatric Clinic; W. D. Longaker, Associate Psychiatrist; Bruce Dohrenwend, Social Analyst; W. H. D. Vernon, Clinical Psychologist; M. Adelard Tremblay, Chief of the Social Science Unit; Jane M. Hughes, Administrative Assistant; Dorothea C. Leighton, Assistant to the Director. The authors wish to express appreciation for the assistance of Bernard Hebert, clinical psychologist, and Janice Ross, social worker.
3. Grateful acknowledgment is made for extensive and valuable help provided by M. Adelard Tremblay.

    "Stirling" is a code name for the Canadian Maritime region under study.
4. Our categories of "striving" and "being" are extremely close in most essentials to the orientations "doing" and "being-in-becoming" originated by Florence Kluckhohn ("Dominant and Substitute Profiles of Cultural Orientation," *Social Forces*, May 1950). There is also an apparent symmetry between the patterns sketched here and certain features of the many conceptual distinctions of life-style elaborated by Tonnies, Redfield, and others—*e.g.*, "gemeinschaft-gesellschaft," "folk-urban," "sacred-secular." Ours is perhaps a local variation of a theme which runs through much of human culture and history, particularly since the Renaissance.

5. Many investigators have found the seeds of individual neurotic conflict in incompatible cultural prescriptions (cf. the writings of Horney, Fromm, and Frank). Yet the precise juxtaposition of cultural ambiguity and individual disorder remains unclear.

6. The organism's tendency to reach out for meaningful social relationships has been termed by Angyal "The Trend Toward Homonomy," cf. Chap. II.

7. The three cases of Stan, Ray, and Alice Mary exemplified anal-retentive, phallic-aggressive, and oral-incorporative symbolism respectively in their clinical interviews, particularly in their recounting of dreams. Stan has been more concerned with "holding his own," and his dreams included preoccupation with money, fears of being robbed or gypped by a woman. Ray's problem has been to put forth the initiative required to satisfy the maternal ambitions. His dreams reflect his deeper frustration and hostility, his fears of castration and, perhaps by a reversal, his fears that the mother might be killed. Alice Mary, on the other hand, is deeply convinced of the fact of maternal rejection to which she reacts by a rather aimless rebellion that alternates with very marked "oral dependency" that makes her easily influenced by the pressures of others.

8. Cf. A. H. Maslow, *Motivation and Personality* (New York: Harper & Brothers, 1954).

9. The importance of various types of discontinuity and inconsistency in the learning situation has been stressed by Child. See Irvin L. Child, "Socialization," in *Handbook of Social Psychology*, Gardner Lindzey, ed. (Cambridge: Addison Wesley, 1954), Chap. 8, p. 655; also, Jurgen Ruesch, "Social Techniques, Social Status, and Social Change in Illness," in *Personality in Nature, Society and Culture*, Kluckhohn, Murray, and Schneider, eds. (New York, Knopf, 1953), Chap. 9.

10. *Ibid.*

11. Lack of realism in the value system or conflict between contrasting value systems may generate problems in trust, autonomy, and other areas. Different value systems, as Erikson points out (cf. Erik H. Erikson, *Childhood and Society* [New York: Norton, 1950]), are linked to different ways of conceptualizing a situation. Thus a sexual situation may be conceptualized in oral, anal, or phallic terms, and the mode of sanctioning seems to be the primary determinant of whether the problem is to center on dependency, autonomy, etc. For instance, it is perhaps not necessarily the method of bowel-training in itself that produces obsessive neurosis but the parents' treatment of many sorts of situations *as if* they were bowel-training situations.

# REFERENCES

1. Adler, Alfred: *A Study of Organ Inferiority and Its Psychical Compensations.* Trans. Smith Ely Jelliffe. Nerv. and Ment. Dis. Monograph, No. 24, 1917.
2. Adorno, T. W., Frenkel-Brunswik, Else, Levinson, D. J., and Sanford, R. N.: *The Authoritarian Personality.* Harper, 1950.
3. Johnson, Adelaide M.: "Sanctions for Super-ego Lacunae of Adolescence," in K. R. Eissler, ed., *Searchlights on Delinquency.* Inter. Univ. Press, 1945, 1955, p. 225.
4. Leighton, Dorothea C.: The distribution of psychiatric symptoms in a small town. *Am. J. Psychiat.,* 112: 9, 1956.
5. Merton, Robert K.: *Social Theory and Social Structure.* Free Press, 1949.
6. Parker, Seymour: *Union Participation: A Study in Culture and Personality.* Unpublished Ph.D. dissertation, Cornell Univ., 1954.
7. Sullivan, Harry S.: *The Interpersonal Theory of Psychiatry.* Norton, 1953.

# Part IV

## THE MEANINGS OF FAMILY BOUNDARIES

Part III was concerned with ways in which a family unit draws upon the culture and utilizes its selections in shaping its own particular life course. The culture offers a wide array of content from which families may choose.

Part IV considers in several ways how a family establishes boundaries for itself, boundaries that are more or less constraining and more or less permeable to relationships and experiences defined as extra-familial.

The three papers all take the nuclear family as the unit of analysis and study family boundaries from three points of view. Norman W. Bell examines the boundary between the nuclear family and the extended family. Gillian W. Elles studies the boundary between the nuclear family and the larger world of community and institutions. Harold Fallding's article is concerned with how family boundaries encompass the life commitments of family members.

Bell studied two groups of urban working-class families. The families in one group, called disturbed families, each had a functionally disturbed child. The other group, designated well families, had children of whom none suffered from a clinically manifest disturbance. Bell found four aspects of the relationship between the nuclear family and the extended family, and disturbed and well families handle these four aspects differently.

Elles' concept of a family boundary is of a somewhat different order from Bell's. She refers to a system of interlocking fantasies among family members that causes the family to develop a resistance to what they perceive as the "invasion" of outside ideas and feelings. The family also resists, however, by withdrawing from contact with various extra-familial agencies. Elles reports specifically on a highly disorganized family whose members form "a closed circuit" because of a fear of madness and because of criminal behavior that makes them vulnerable to the intervention of police authority. Efforts to help this family failed because the family could not allow itself to be open to any kind of outside power, however benign.

Fallding reports his work with a group of Australian families. He is concerned with how a person integrates the various roles that he plays in society, suggesting that this is accomplished by the development of "a cardinal role." He believes that the adult's family role should be his cardinal role, governing how he participates in the world beyond the family. While many would agree with Fallding, his value preference is arguable, requiring a fuller examination than appears in his article; in any case, however, his values are tangential to the actual study he reports. He shows that families in fact differ in the extent to which the adult familial role is the parent-spouse's cardinal role, or, as he puts it at one point, that families differ in "the spread of their protective cover." He identifies three types of Australian families in which the parents differ in the character and intensity of their commitment to the family. His concern with what families mean to their members recalls Oscar Lewis's point that the anthropologist should study what an institution means to its members. Fallding found that his types cut across social class lines, thereby showing some ways in which families within a class differ.

Fallding insists on being purely sociological in his analysis, but it is evident that the problem to which he addresses himself must also be pursued in psychological terms. His repeated abrupt halting at the boundaries of his discipline is both arbitrary and unnecessary. The reader of this article should have in mind Parsons's observation that one of the two main functions of the family in modern industrial society is the stabilization of adult personality (the other is socialization of children). Perhaps the adaptation-type of family, one type which Fallding found created difficulties for adolescent offspring, is the best way in which the parents in such families can stabilize their own personalities. Whether the spouses in this type of family might have created a different type of family, I would emphasize two points: (1) No one type of commitment to family is necessarily the best for all adults, even if all were capable of making the same kind of commitment to family, which is most improbable. (2) Evaluating the consequences of different types of family commitment requires psychological as well as sociological modes of analysis. Of Fallding's article, as of Burgess's famous article, "The Family as a Unity of Interacting Personalities," one can say with justice that it frames a sociological problem which requires psychological analysis for adequate handling. I would not call this reductionism; I would call it social psychology.

# 11:

# Extended Family Relations of Disturbed and Well Families

*Norman W. Bell*

It has long been recognized that the mental health of individuals is related to the family. However, until recently there has been a failure to conceptualize the family *qua* family; studies of individual pathology have usually reduced the family to individual psychodynamic terms (1). Beginning with Richardson's (2) pioneer attempts to characterize the family as a group with properties in its own right, considerable changes have taken place. Numerous investigators have developed conceptual schemes to describe the subtle and complex processes in families. Such reformulations involve a shift away from the view that mental illness is a characterisic of an individual toward the view that disturbance in one member is a symptom of the functioning of the whole family. Concomitantly, different therapeutic approaches to families as groups (3) or to individuals (4) as family members have been developed.

These reconceptualizations produce a needed corrective to earlier tendencies to overemphasize the significance of an individual's innate tendencies or of isolated segments of relationships in which he may be involved. However, to the family sociologist, there appears a danger that the fallacies of oversimplification and reductionism characteristic of the focus on the individual are being repeated again at the family level. Family psychiatrists seem, by and large, to view the family as a self-contained, invariable unit (5) existing in a social and cultural vacuum. The significance of a grandparent[1] or an extra-family activity of a parent may be recognized as incorporated in one member's pathology in particular instances. But systematic consideration of the interdependence of the nuclear family and related families of orientation, or of the nuclear family and the surrounding society as a universal structural principle have been lacking.[2] Both on theoretical (7) and empirical

Reprinted by permission from *Family Process*, Vol. 1, No. 2 (September 1962), pp. 175–93. Copyright 1962 by the Mental Research Institute of the Palo Alto Medical Research Foundation and the Family Institute. Norman W. Bell is associate in sociology in the Department of Psychiatry, Harvard Medical School, and is chief, Social Science Department, McLean Hospital, Belmont, Massachusetts.

(8, 9) grounds it is difficult to find justification for neglecting the frameworks within which families function.

## PROBLEM

This paper will explore only one segment of the total web of relationships in which families exist, namely relationships with extended kin. Every society recognizes and patterns the relations of successive generations (10). The breaking or changing of old ties and the formation of new ties through marriage are always transition points with potential stresses. As Radcliffe-Brown has expressed it ". . . Marriage is a rearrangement of social structure. . . . A marriage produces a temporary disequilibrium situation. . . . The establishment of a new equilibrium after a marriage requires that in certain types of kinship or family structure there is a need felt for emphasizing the separateness of the two connected families. . . . The principal points of tension created by a marriage are between the wife and the husband's parents and the husband and the wife's parents." (11, pp. 43–58 passim). The thesis of this paper is that disturbed families are ones in which this "disequilibrium created by marriage" has not been resolved but continues to provoke and maintain conflicts and the underlying discrepancies that cause them, and that well families have achieved some resolution of the problems of ties to extended kin so that these kin are neutral or even positive forces in the resolution of family problems.

Before presenting data relevant to this thesis it may be helpful to review briefly the nature of family processes which lead to individual pathology and some features of the American kinship system, two domains not previously related to one another.

In common with various other family researchers I assume that functional disturbances arise from and are maintained by family interaction, including the emotional dynamics associated with overt behavior. Different researchers have focused upon different aspects of the patterns of interaction, some emphasizing the persistent structural features, others the nature of communication processes, still others the discordance between overt behavior and inner feelings. Common to all appears to be some conception that, as a group, the family must try to adapt to the discrepancies within and between individuals and reach some equilibrium. Unless the underlying issues are resolved there will be a strong tendency to act out the problems by involving others in biologically, psychologically or socially inappropriate roles. Such processes lead to disturbances of ego identity. The disturbance, so dysfunctional for the individual, serves positive functions for the family in its efforts to secure or preserve some sort of integration (12). Removal of, or change in, the disturbed individual upsets the "pathological equilibrium" and leads to changes throughout the system. Much less work has been devoted to well families, but conversely it might be formulated that to cope with discrepancies they adopt mechanisms which actually resolve the discrepancies or at least contain them in ways that are not pathogenic for individual members.

The family processes associated with mental illness or health have been described by others in some detail (13) with focus on the operations within nuclear families. But any nuclear family is part of a larger "family field" and must cope with the establishment and structuring of ties to two families of orientation. Some kinship systems stress the continuity of generations by subordinating the younger generation to the authority of the elder and stress the preference of one lineage over the other. The American kinship system (14) emphasizes the structurally isolated nuclear family and is bilateral. The emphasis on the isolated nuclear family means that there is discontinuity and relative independence of adjacent adult generations. The characteristic of bilaterality means that both the husband's and wife's families are potentially of equal importance in reckoning descent, controlling property, giving support and direction and so on. Since neither side of the family receives a culturally prescribed preference, each family must work out its own balance of the ties to, and independence of, two extended families. This task is further complicated by the tendency to define the maintenance of kinship ties as a feminine rather than masculine role.[3]

## DATA

The data which is to be cited here are drawn from a long-term study of disturbed and well families. The broader project, directed by Drs. John Spiegel and Florence Kluckhohn, is concerned with the interrelation of cultural values, family roles and the mental health of individuals.[4] Details of the population studied have been presented elsewhere (1, 15, 16); here it is sufficient to note that intact working-class families with at least three generations available for interviewing were studied intensively for periods ranging from two to five years. The families were of varying ethnic backgrounds. Half of them had a functionally disturbed child (here called "disturbed families"); half had no clinically manifest disturbance (called "well families").

Contact with the "sick" families was mainly in the office setting; the child and both parents, at a minimum, were seen in weekly therapy sessions. Occasionally parents or a parent and child were seen jointly. Family behavior before and after interviews was observed. Eventually all families were visited in their homes on several occasions, and relatives were interviewed where possible or at least were met during visits. With the "well" families there was similarly extended, regular contact by teams of a child psychiatrist, a psychiatric social worker and a sociologist. The bulk of these contacts was in homes. Clearly the meaning of the contact for these well families was different, but we were reasonably satisfied that comparable data were obtained for both groups.

## FINDINGS

Four aspects of how extended kin articulate with nuclear families will be discussed. The first two (extended families as countervailing forces and extended families as continuing stimulators of conflict) deal with the dynamics of intergroup relationships. The second two (extended families as screens for the projection of conflicts and extended families as competing objects of support and indulgence) deal more with the social-psychological qualities of the relationship. Distinguishing these four aspects is, of course, an analytic device; empirically they are intertwined.

### EXTENDED FAMILIES AS COUNTERVAILING FORCES

The ability of the nuclear family to contain its conflicts and control the impact of its discrepancies by means of a child is limited. Adult members in particular may experience guilt about the child, particularly when his condition is defined by outside agencies such as schools, courts and neighbors. But even short of this step, parents are capable of experiencing guilt or anxiety through identification with the child, a necessary but often neglected correlate of the child's identification with the parent.

Mr. Costello, for instance, brought his younger son for medical attention when this son began to stutter seriously. The father had suffered from a speech problem himself in childhood. He "understood" his son's stuttering as something learned from an older brother, although it was more closely related to the chronic stool-retention problems this younger child had, the physical symptom for which medical attention was sought. The older son's stuttering had not affected the father deeply; this symptom in the younger son with whom the father was so closely identified was intolerable.

Aging of the child may shift the child's capacity to absorb family tensions so that he is able to escape parental pressures more and get support for himself from the peer group (17). Maneuvers within the family are not always adequate to restore the pathogenic equilibrium. At such times there may be a resorting to the extended family to shore up crumbling group defenses. Typically this process includes a seeking for support from the natural parents and an attack upon the in-laws. In the full form this becomes reciprocal with the other spouse drawing upon his family for reserves and attacking his in-laws. As the vicious circle progresses, the whole family becomes split. A day in the life of the McGinnis family will illustrate this:

Mr. and Mrs. McGinnis lived in a state of armed truce. Mrs. McGinnis domineered the family in an irrational, active way. Her domination of their oldest son, perceived by herself as maternal devotion, was extreme. Mr. McGinnis had developed set patterns of schizoid withdrawal from the family and persistent needling of the 12-year old son to grow up before he was drafted into the army or was thrown out of the family to go to work. The bane of Mr. McGinnis' life was his old, unreliable car which in its weaker moments he used to kick and curse. For Mrs. McGinnis and her son this car was the proof of the father's stupidity and the family's low status. Mr. McGinnis was continually harassed to get a new car. One day, independently, he did go out and buy a second-hand station wagon. When Mrs. McGinnis was told of this she conjured up an image of a high, homely, small bus. In the telephone conversations with her family, which quickly followed, this distorted image was elaborated. They soon gathered around to "kid" Mr. McGinnis about running a jitney to New York. Their perverse pleasure was short lived when they saw a quite ordinary station wagon. By this time Mr. McGinnis was bitterly attacking his in-laws and soon after paid a rare visit to his aged mother who was nearly indigent and in a nursing home. His visit reawakened Mrs. McGinnis' suspicions that her mother-in-law had money hidden away which should be given to them. When Mrs. McGinnis' spinster sisters came under fire from Mr. McGinnis, she defended them in exaggerated terms and returned with interest comments about Mr. McGinnis' paranoid sister.

For the McGinnises this schismogenic process was not conscious. Mrs. McGinnis called her various family members every day so there was nothing unusual in her telling them of the "bus" her husband had bought. In other families the process is quite conscious and deliberate. The Manzonis, for example, knew that visits to their own families made their partners wildly jealous, and knew just at what point to call or visit a relative.

Even children become sensitive to the familial tensions regarding extended families and disappear to visit grandparents, insult visiting relatives, or engage in other operations to crystallize the parents', and eventually, the whole family's, split feelings about in-laws.

The mechanisms by which extended families are brought into conflict situations may be conscious or, at least apparently, unconscious. Frequently the sequence is initiated by what seems to be a casual and innocent conflict. Until we are able directly to observe the initiation of this spreading of conflict, it is difficult to be specific about the mechanisms involved. I feel fairly sure that the process is a subtle one, that no direct reference to conflicts in the nuclear family or direct request for allies has to be made. Rather both or all parties to the relationship are sufficiently sensitized that the spreading process can begin, or flare up, through minimal cues in tone of voice, timing of contacts and so forth. In all, I believe these mechanisms are not different from those observed in the families of schizophrenics, where therapy teams (18), and hospital staff can become drawn into family conflicts (19).

In the light of Bott's findings (8) regarding the nature of the social network and intrafamilial role allocation, it is important to inquire into the relationships between the extended families. When they are drawn into family conflicts do they themselves echo those conflicts, as Brodey finds that therapy teams do? None of our families had been geographically mobile to any large extent, so most extended families did have superficial acquaintance with each other. The frequency of active relationships was low, being clearly present in only one out of eleven cases. Since the frequency of active relationships in the general population is unknown, it is difficult to be sure of the significance of this. Of course, in our society the respective parental families stand in no particular relationship to each other and there is no term to denote it.[5]

Well families also have conflicts, but they differ in several respects. The open conflicts that occur are incidents on a foundation of basic integration, are self-limiting, and do not compromise a wide range of interaction in the future. In striking contrast to the disturbed families, active engagement in disputes was kept within the family by well families. This does not come about by the kin being unaware of the conflicts. Indeed they often seem quite well-informed about them, but these kin groups are not drawn into the pattern of balancing off one side of the nuclear family against the other.

In some well families there was evidence that the extended families not only did not become drawn into and amplify the conflicts, but even acted in benign ways to reduce conflicts and restore family functioning. An interesting example of this occurred in the DiMaggio family:

One summer Mr. DiMaggio's mother wanted to visit a nephew who had recently migrated to Canada from Italy. Over Mrs. DiMaggio's protests it was decided that the grandparents and four of their five sons, including Mr. DiMaggio, would make the trip; Mrs. DiMaggio would stay at home with her youngest child. During the absence of her in-laws, Mrs. DiMaggio became mildly depressed, and developed fantasies that her husband was having a gay time. Though her own family was living nearby, her contact with them did not increase markedly. The night before arriving home, Mr. DiMaggio phoned his wife. Though she did not complain openly, he sensed her state of mind. He felt guilty and when they arrived home, he managed to arrange it so that the rest of the family entered the apartment before he did. In their first contacts the brothers-in-law and parents-in-law were attentive to Mrs. DiMaggio. One brother-in-law, a priest, took her aside and talked to her about the obligations of marriage and informed her of how unhappy her husband had been while away. When Mr. DiMaggio did come in, his wife put aside her complaints, brightened up and was genuinely glad to see her husband. Mrs. DiMaggio remained aware of her reactions but resumed a normal, close relationship with her in-laws.

### EXTENDED FAMILIES AS STIMULATORS OF CONFLICT

Extended families are not always passive elements in the situation, and in some instances the initiative for provoking conflict seems to rest with them. Extended families may be responding to discrepancies in their family structure in the same ways, thereby inducing conflicts within the nuclear families we have in focus.

The Mozzarellas had for some time had the father's unmarried brother living with them and their three children. At one point this brother took or stole a small amount of money from the Mozzarellas. Mrs. Mozzarella was furious and began to fight with her husband. The conflict grew and the brother moved out. Rather than abating, the conflict between husband and wife widened and deepened. Finally Mr. Mozzarella moved out for a few days, but did not stay with his brother. After a few weeks absence the brother also moved back in with the family.

In all such instances it is likely that the action of the extended family has to fall on prepared grounds in the nuclear family. Often these actions are appropriate—almost uncannily so—to the weak spots in the family organization. In themselves the actions of the extended family may appear innocent enough, but their effects are widespread. Frequently the triggering incident is a gift.[6]

Mrs. McGinnis' mother gave her grandson gifts of money just at the times when Mr. McGinnis was berating his son for his failure to earn his own spending money. The money mitigated the economic problem, but increased the father-son conflict and eventually the whole family was at odds.

In some instances the precipitating incident seems to be more genuinely innocent, with the problem being the inability of the family to develop or employ mechanisms for insulating themselves or for controlling conflicts once they have begun.

Mrs. Manzoni's brother was in an army basic training camp about 40 miles away. He often visited the Manzonis when on leave. His visits were agreeable to the Manzonis who even looked forward to them since their uncontrollable son responded well to direction from this uncle. One weekend, however, he brought a buddy along with him. Mrs. Manzoni tried to be hospitable, but father and son both reacted sharply to this shift. Bitter arguments about the invasions and demands of Mrs. Manzoni's family ensued. Mrs. Manzoni retaliated with accusations that her husband did many favors for his family.

Whether conducted in an innocent or calculated way, extended families frequently do provoke conflicts in the nuclear families. The impact is not always the open conflict described in these examples. Often the impact is at the latent level, exaggerating the discrepancies that already exist.

At the well end of the continuum extended families do not intervene in their married children's lives in ways which set off the trains of reaction described above. The interventions which do occur do not cut to the bone and are not reacted to in a stereotyped way. To illustrate:

Mr. McNally's brother was a heavy drinker and had served time for theft. Occasionally he would come around to the McNally home, presumably looking for food and money. Mrs. McNally would refuse to let him into the house. Mr. McNally, though he had some interest and sympathy for his brother, supported such responses on the part of his wife. At times he sought out his brother and tried to help him, but these approaches were not timed and carried out so as to reflect on his wife or compensate for her rejection of the brother. On her side, Mrs. McNally did not interfere with her husband's attempts to rehabilitate his brother, though she expected little to come of them. Both husband and wife had mixed feelings about this relative but their attitudes toward him appeared to be appropriate.

Rather than acting as *agents provacateurs,* the extended kin of well families are able to remain neutral and respect the boundaries of the nuclear family. For their part, the well families are not hypersensitive to the actions of kin.

Mrs. Flanagan's parents lived nearby. They were old and somewhat infirm. Periodically heavy demands for help were made on Mrs. Flanagan. Even though the whole family was preoccupied with being cared for and had much physical illness, these demands were accepted as a necessary sacrifice, even by the children. Mr. Flanagan accommodated himself to the demands on his wife by being helpful at home and at his parents-in-law.

### EXTENDED FAMILIES AS SCREENS FOR THE PROJECTION OF CONFLICTS

The extended family need not be an active or even potentially active element in the conflict situation. In all cases there was some evidence that the extended family served as a screen onto which a family member could project sentiments which referred more immediately to a spouse, child or parent. This process, which I have labelled the *overgeneralization of affect* is mainly of negative sentiments. Positive sentiments are also involved as a reciprocal tendency, though they are not so conspicuous. The overgeneralization spreads over social space and time. In the extreme cases an impervious dichotomy of good and bad occurs and rationalizes a wide range of avoidance behavior and expression of dislike.

Mrs. Donovan, in her first therapy sessions, painted a picture of the many deficiencies of her oldest son and her husband. She felt that they were no good and were just like her husband's family, all of whom were no good and never had been any good. Her own father, who died in her adolescence, was completely different, having been intelligent, sensitive, liberal, sophisticated and unprejudiced. Her mother, concerning whom she had more mixed feelings, came in for little comment at this time. Mrs. Donovan had had, since her marriage, minimal contact with her husband's family. Contacts which did occur substantiated her view of her in-laws.

The families in which pathology was highly integrated tended to show a pattern of each spouse directing his or her negative sentiments towards the in-laws and directing positive sentiments toward the natural parents. Reality sometimes makes such splitting difficult. However, grandparents who can in calm moments (or in therapy) be evaluated realistically, tend to be defended when they are criticized by the partner, and part of the defense is an attack upon the partner's side of the family. The reverse picture, of one person directing negative sentiments to his own parents and positive ones to his in-laws seems infrequent. In our cases it was noted only in one family and in this case the tendency was mild.

This sort of conflict involves, naturally enough, parents more than children. Still it is not restricted to them. The children are quite likely to assimilate the parental sentiments and to align with one rather than the other or "slide" between the two.

Jackie McGinnis, for example, could echo all of his mother's feelings and suspicions of his paternal grandmother and condemn the paternal grandfather who had died many years before his birth. At such times he was positive about and in close contact with maternal relatives. To a lesser degree he could reverse the roles if he was in conflict with his mother and wanted to get something from his father.

Again, projection of feelings through space and time need not emerge in overt conflict. The projection may be a stable characteristic of an individual's psychological functioning within the family which magnifies the discrepancies which do exist.

Mrs. McGinnis occasionally used her suspicion that her mother-in-law had money secreted in a Canadian bank in her arguments with her husband, insisting it was money which they had a right to. Even when she was not attacking her husband on this account, it was part of her fantasies about giving her son the education her husband was convinced he should not have and was incapable of getting. Buttressed by this projection, she was able to push her son and herself in directions which took them farther and farther from the father.

I hope that it is clear that there is more to this pattern than the pathological functioning of individuals. Individuals, children as well as parents, utilize the structure of the family and the extended family as arenas in which to express their ambivalent feelings. Reciprocally the schisms of the family and the extended family reinforce and perhaps even stimulate complications in their feelings about parent figures. Individuals who may have been able reasonably well to integrate their ambivalent feelings toward their parents may have difficulty in adapting to the existence of parents *and* parents-in-law.[7]

Members of well families, as material cited earlier suggests, do not develop such polarized feelings about kin. There certainly were mixed feelings and, on occasion, strong negative feelings about kin, but these could be handled and even if not fully expressed, the tendency to split feelings and maintain them in a rigid fashion was not present. This lack of overgeneralization of affect was true of positive feelings as well as negative ones. In contrast to Epstein and Westley's (22) normal families, we did not meet the pattern of "adoration" which they observed in the wife-husband relationship. This difference in findings regarding normal families may be a genuine difference in the sample of families studied or may be a function of different methods of investigation used. In our group there was also no "adoration" spreading to the extended families.

### EXTENDED FAMILIES AS COMPETING OBJECTS OF SUPPORT
### AND INDULGENCE

I have chosen to treat separately a theme closely related to all the above. My feeling is that this theme is a central and basic one. It is this: that extended families become competing sources and objects of the support and indulgence for the nuclear family. In American society the norm is for nuclear families to be independent.[8]

The disturbed families we have seen almost universally presented problems of this sort. When the loyalty and commitment of some menbers can no longer be implicitly assumed and is called into question, processes are set in motion to generate and amplify conflicts. In some instances the medium of conflict is money, as with Mr. McGinnis:

He had an ambulatory paranoid sister who journeyed about the country taking skilled clerical jobs. Invariably she would develop suspicions that she was being watched and plotted against and quit her job. In desperate financial straits she would wire Mr. McGinnis for money. Though recognizing her as ill, Mr. McGinnis would usually get money somewhere and send it to her. He maintained that he kept this secret from his wife, though she was well aware of what was going on. (Both, incidentally, silently assumed that all this was kept secret from the children, which was also inaccurate.) For Mrs. McGinnis this

justified her suspicions that her mother-in-law was holding back and in derivative and half-recognized ways complicated the family fights over money.

The diversion of material goods as well as money to the extended
family can be the precipitant of conflicts. For the Manzonis it was the
cost of food which was consumed by Mrs. Manzoni's family. Mr. Manzoni
felt that the food served his in-laws was better than that served *his*
family if they visited, and more of it was consumed.

In other cases the questioned commodity was affection and attention.
Mr. McGinnis was preoccupied with the amount of time his wife spent
talking to her family on the telephone and compared it to the neglect
of his own mother, a neglect of which he himself was guilty. The Manzonis were continually suspicious that the other was seeing his own
family and being influenced by them. Children too were perceived as
liking one side of the family more, paying more heed to one side, and
even of resembling, physically or in personality, one side of the family
rather than the other.

In the Costello family such a pattern was developed to the extreme. Their
first son was a "mother's boy," the second a "father's boy," and they moved
in largely separate interactional spheres. When Mrs. Costello wanted to visit
her parents, which she felt obliged to do weekly, her older son would not tolerate being left behind while her younger son protested strongly about going.
Each visit was thus a struggle for Mrs. Costello and sufficient proof to Mr.
Costello that she should stay at home.

Whatever the resource being contended about, the pattern of real or
perceived favoritism for part of the extended family structure can arise.
The pattern seems to serve multiple functions; it externalizes the internal
conflicts of any given individual and allows him to rationalize his own
shortcomings (as with Mr. McGinnis), for his own shortcomings pale
into insignificance in the light of the others' misdeeds. At the same time
it preserves the conflicts within the family. Being external they are
beyond influence of any one person or combination.

Once again well families stand in contrast. They too have problems
about the allocation of resources but diverting them to one family of
orientation, as the earlier illustration of the Flanagans suggests, does not
stimulate feelings of deprivation and resentment. Correspondingly resources from extended families, even when the differential between the
contributions of the two sides of the family is considerable, do not become
foci of conflict.

To summarize the material presented above, it may be said that disturbed families have difficulties in solving the problems of how to relate to two sets of "parents" and of establishing family boundaries. The
absence of boundaries allows family conflicts to spread to extended kin
and means a deficit of ability of the nuclear family to insulate itself

from the vagueness of the outside world. Thus extended kin are drawn into, or play into the conflicts of the nuclear family so that underlying discrepancies are not resolved but are spread and made more rigid. In this family setting individual members have difficulty in taking roles as representatives of the whole family. *Vis à vis* the outside world of kin they act as individuals; what they give to or receive from kin casts them as competitors with other members rather than as collaborators with the whole family. This interpersonal situation appears to foster the awakening and acting out of ambivalent feelings with a consequent circular effect.

## IMPLICATIONS

The thesis has been advanced here that the extended families are, or become, involved in family pathology and that different patterns of relationship with extended families are set up by disturbed families than by normal or healthy families. In conclusion I should like to explore some of the implications of such findings for theories of the relationship between family processes and mental illness, and for therapeutic efforts at diagnosis and treatment.

Several years ago Ackerman complained of etiological theories in dynamic psychiatry that they ". . . hypothesize a relation between a piece of the child and a piece of the parent." (25, p. 182) His evaluation was that these were inadequate and that we had to evolve theories which related to the integrity of the individual to the family as a whole. A great deal of progress in this direction has been made but the question may be raised again with regard to family-centered theories. The point is not that they are incorrect but that they are only part of the picture. Families are seldom, if ever, isolated from kin. If ties to extended families are present and involved in the family processes must we not at some level include this in our theory? The findings presented, though based upon a small and selected population and derived from studies of neurotic children rather than psychotic adults, seem to me to argue in this direction.

The issue can be posed in a more general form. The systems we deal with are not closed, they are always embedded in and to some degree derive their rationale and patterning from, broader systems. For some purposes we may treat them *as if* they were closed but we must never paint them as the whole truth. In this I have tried to look outward from the family system to its kin. One might equally well take cognizance of the fact that the family is involved in many other networks of relationships and that these too may function to stimulate and maintain conflicts or alternatively to contain and correct them.[9] Ultimately we must refer our finding to the general patterns of values which characterize cultures and subcultures and which have a pervasive influence in shaping personality, family role patterns, and the whole family field extending through space and time, indeed the whole fabric of society. Florence Kluckhohn has devoted her major attention to the analysis of these patterns of value orientations (26). It is, I believe, possible to show that the type of issue which comes up in this process of re-equilibrating the imbalance associated with marriage, the pathological ways of coping with discrepancies, and the available alternatives for resolving the issues can be deduced from the variations in value orientations characteristic of different groups.

Our work is vastly complicated by such a theoretical position but I see no alternative to dealing with reality as it is. If a broader range of variables can be dealt with precisely and adequately, we may develop theories with more specificity than our current conceptions. In an earliei era it was popular to attribute mental disturbances to broken homes I daresay there are 100 papers in the literature reporting such findings It is only part of the problem of these studies that they report incon· sistent findings and that they seldom have adequate control groups. A more serious problem is that broken homes seem to be related to delinquency, neurosis, schizophrenia, and various psychosomatic disorders. An agent so nonspecific is of little help or at best is merely the first step. Most studies of families have also lacked control groups. It is not clear whether the presumably pathogenic processes detected in the families of schizophrenics are really absent in families with less seriously disturbed individuals and perhaps even families without disturbance. Tracing out how pathology is integrated in a broader network than the nuclear family may give some added specificity.

There might also be advantages to paying close attention to the history of families. It is striking that we have not developed models of the developmental processes of families that compare to our models of individual development. For example, in the Donovan family many shifts in group and individual dynamics coincided with changes in the closeness of the nuclear family to the wife's mother.

After their marriage the Donovans lived with the wife's mother, and had a fairly happy marriage. Acute difficulties arose after they moved to their own dwelling; Mrs. Donovan's sentiments about her in-laws became more negative, and Mr. Donovan's contacts with his family, which were more rigidly pursued, became more threatening to the wife. The problems were heightened after Mrs. Donovan's mother remarried. During the course of therapy the two family units jointly purchased a two-family house and lived close to each other again. Many conflicts abated following this move.

If we can learn to listen to the histories patients give, not individual but familial, we can learn much about the dynamics of the group and how the family has got to its present state. Such findings as have been reported may also have implications for our therapeutic endeavors. To the extent that we misplace the causal forces which have led to, and maintain pathology, we may misjudge the potentials for change and how to bring it about. Systematic consideration of patterns of relationships with extended families can give us added leverage in the diagnosis of particular problems with which we are confronted.

Treatment strategies may need rethinking in the light of this view of pathology as a process broader than the individual family. In our research work we saw relatives, not because we had any systematic program or good rationale to intervene therapeutically with them, but in pursuit of our research interests. This was not always readily agreed to by members of the nuclear family but in many cases it had a salutary effect, for the family members, for the relatives, and for their relationships. Relatives were seldom ignorant of the difficulties in the nuclear families or of the involvement with the psychiatric clinic. Nuclear families often preferred to believe that their problems and attempts to get help were unknown to kin, but on close examination, this was another example of "open secrets."

In several cases it was a significant turning point when the person being seen could allow his relatives to be seen by the therapist.

> Mr. Donovan was resistant to therapy in many ways but dead set against his family being seen. After a year with very limited progress (and incidentally some time after the family had moved back into a house shared with Mrs. Donovan's mother), he was unable to discuss his discomfort with authority figures unless he could be on close friendly terms with them. A little later, Mr. Donovan offered to take the therapist to visit the rest of his family. Subsequent to this social visit, there took place meaningful discussions of Mr. Donovan's feelings of loyalty to and sympathy with his own family, and his resentment at his wife's depreciation of them, him, and his son.

While such techniques are regarded by many as unorthodox, dangerous and/or unnecessary, I believe a case can be made that there are instances in which therapy fails unless the therapist can understand and involve himself into the fabric of meanings and the network of relationships the patient knows as natural (4).

As for the relatives, seeing them legitimizes their interest in the nuclear family, but brings this interest under some control. We found they were sometimes able to neutralize their involvement in the nuclear families and get for themselves a broader perspective on the nuclear family. It was also profitable to get, by seeing a relative, a fresh perspective on a case. Just as Brodey sees the advantages of seeing married partners to get a "stereoscopic view" of the relationship, so seeing members of several families offers the advantages of a stereoscopic view of families.

We have not included relatives in therapy on a systematic and regular basis and I can only conjecture about the advantages and problems that "kin group therapy" might bring. There are no logical grounds for stopping at the boundaries of the nuclear family, boundaries which are very permeable and shifting.[10] At one level, movement in therapy consists of changes in the sentiments about and interaction with extended families. To cite the Donovans once more:

> Mrs. Donovan's depreciation of her son, husband and all her husband's family gradually gave way during therapy. In the space of three years, they altered sufficiently to lead her to buy a small Christmas gift for her mother-in-law. Contact of the whole family with her husband's siblings increased. Eventually, she visited her mother-in-law and found that she had good qualities as well as bad, and that it was not unpleasant to visit her. As her sentiments were mitigated, her relationship with her husband expanded and changed and shifts even appeared in the whole family constellation.

It is possible that this central process in the whole family might have been speeded up if both partners could have been influenced simultaneously, as indeed we do in treating mother-child pairs.

### SUMMARY

This paper has taken up the issue of whether our understanding of functional disturbances can afford to stop at the boundaries of the nuclear family. It has been argued, and some evidence has been presented, that disturbed families are distinguishable from well families in terms of their patterns of relationships with extended families. Disturbed families have a deficiency of family boundaries which leads them to involve extended kin in their conflicts and makes them sensitive to influence from extended kin. Directly or indirectly a considerable segment of kindred systems become part of a pathological drama, until pathology is a characteristic of the system, not of individual persons or families. Such findings require replication with larger samples, but do raise questions about the adequacy of our theories of family pathology and our treatment techniques.

### NOTES

1. The first volume of *The Psychoanalytic Review* in 1914 includes abstracts of articles on the "grandfather complex" by Jones, Abraham, and Ferenczi.
2. Ackerman (6) is one of the few who have advanced into this area and he puts the stress mainly on the emotional and attitudinal aspects.

3. I do not mean to imply that the American kinship system presents more, or more intense, problems than other kinship systems. Other systems engender problems too (e.g., the daughter-in-law in traditional China) but the focal problems are different.
4. Sponsored by the Laboratory of Social Relations, Harvard University and the Children's Medical Center, Boston, and supported by grants from the National Institute of Mental Health and the Pauline and Louis G. Cowan Foundation.
5. Other languages do have a term for this relationship, e.g., the Jewish word *Machatenen*.
6. The gift, as Marcel Mauss has shown (20), creates an obligation of the receiver to the donor. Normally this cements the social structure. As I shall discuss presently, for conflicted families the assuming and discharging of obligations is problematic and tends to break down the social structure.
7. Cf. Parsons' (21) proposition that socialization involves the internalization not simply of separate parent figures but also the internalization of the *relationship between* the parents.
8. Legally the situation is confused. Marriage is recognized as a legal union which obligates the husband to support his family, and both parents to support their minor children. Similarly a legal marriage (and even in some circumstances a common-law union) entails the right to pass property onto family members and the right of family members to claim property of a deceased member. At the same time we still have laws, occasionally enforced, that children, even married children, are obligated to support indigent parents (23). This vagueness of our laws and our mores, together with our bilateral kinship system, presents the possibility of conflict. Family resources—whether they be money, goods, affection or services, are not unlimited. There are always alternative directions in which they may be allocated. Even comfortably situated families may have problems in the allocation of wealth and contain "poverty-stricken" members (24).
9. For brief comments on how work associates, neighbors and professionals may be assimilated to pathological family patterns see (4, 12).
10. One wonders what family therapists would do if they attempted to treat matrifocal families such as exist in the south and around the Carribean.

# REFERENCES

1. SPIEGEL, JOHN P. and BELL, NORMAN W., "The Family of the Psychiatric Patient," in Silvano Arieti (Ed.), *American Handbook of Psychiatry*, New York, Basic Books, 1959.
2. RICHARDSON, HENRY B., *Patients Have Families*, New York, Commonwealth Fund, 1945.
3. BELL, JOHN E., *Family Group Therapy*, Pub. Health Mon. No. 64, U. S. Dept. of Health, Educ. and Welfare, 1961.
4. BELL, NORMAN W., TRIESCHMAN, ALBERT and VOGEL, EZRA F., "A Sociocultural Analysis of the Resistances of Working-Class Fathers Treated in a Child Psychiatric Clinic," *Amer. J. Ortho.*, 31, 388–405, 1961.
5. LEICHTER, HOPE, "Boundaries of the Family as an Empirical and Theoretical Unit," in Nathan W. Ackerman, Frances L. Beatman and Sanford N. Sherman (Eds.), *Exploring the Base for Family Therapy*, New York, Family Service Assoc. of America, 1961.
6. ACKERMAN, NATHAN, "Emotional Impact of In-laws and Relatives," in Samuel Liebman (Ed.), *Emotional Forces in the Family*, Philadelphia, Lippincott, 1959.

7. BELL, NORMAN W., and VOGEL, EZRA, F., "Toward a Framework for the Functional Analysis of Family Behavior," in Norman W. Bell and Ezra F. Vogel (Eds.), *A Modern Introduction to the Family*, Glencoe, Free Press, 1960.

8. BOTT, ELIZABETH, *Family and Social Network*, London, Tavistock Publications, 1957.

9. ZIMMERMAN, CARLE and CERVANTES, LUCIUS, *Successful American Families*, New York, Pageant Press, 1960.

10. APPLE, DORRIAN, "The Social Structure of Grandparenthood," *Amer. Anth.*, 58, 656–663, 1958.

11. RADCLIFFE-BROWN, A. R., "Introduction," in A. R. Radcliffe-Brown and Daryll Forde (Eds.), *African Systems of Kinship and Marriage*, London, Oxford Univ. Press, 1950.

12. VOGEL, EZRA F. and BELL, NORMAN W., "The Emotionally Disturbed Child as a Family Scapegoat," *Psychoanalysis and the Psychoanalytic Review*, 47, 21–42, 1960.

13. SANUA, VICTOR D., "Sociocultural Factors in Families of Schizophrenics," *Psychiatry*, 24, 246–265, 1961.

14. PARSONS, TALCOTT, "The Kinship System of the Contemporary United States," in Talcott Parsons, *Essays in Sociological Theory*, Glencoe, Free Press, 1954 (revised edition).

15. KLUCKHOHN, FLORENCE R., "Variations in the Basic Values of Family Systems," *Soc. Cswk.*, 39, 63–72, 1958.

16. SPIEGEL, JOHN P., "Some Cultural Aspects of Transference and Countertransference," in Jules H. Masserman (Ed.), *Individual and Familial Dynamics*, New York, Grune & Stratton, 1959.

17. PITTS, JESSE R., "The Family and Peer Groups," in Norman W. Bell and Ezra F. Vogel (Eds.), *A Modern Introduction to the Family*, Glencoe, Free Press, 1960.

18. BRODEY, W. M. and HAYDEN, M., "The Intrateam Reactions: Their Relation to the Conflicts of the Family in Treatment," *Amer. J. Ortho.*, 27, 349–355, 1957.

19. BOWEN, MURRAY, DYSINGER, R. H., BRODEY, W. M., and BASAMANIA, B., "Study and Treatment of Five Hospitalized Family Groups with a Psychotic Member," paper delivered at the American Orthopsychiatric Association Meetings, Chicago, 1957.

20. MAUSS, MARCEL, "Essai sur le don," in Marcel Mauss *Sociologie et Anthropologie*, Paris, Presses Universitaires de France, 1950.

21. PARSONS, TALCOTT and BALES, R. F., *Family, Socialization and Interaction Process*, Glencoe, Free Press, 1955.

22. EPSTEIN, NATHAN B. and WESTLEY, WILLIAM A., "Grandparents and Parents of Emotionally Healthy Adolescents," in Jules Masserman (Ed.), *Psychoanalysis and Human Values*, New York, Grune & Stratton, 1960.

23. SCHORR, ALVIN L., *Filial Responsibility in the Modern American Family*, Washington, D. C., U. S. Dept. of Health, Educ. and Welfare, 1960.

24. YOUNG, MICHAEL, "The Distribution of Income Within the Family," *Brit. J. Soc.*, 3, 305–321, 1952.

25. ACKERMAN, NATHAN W. and BEHRENS, M. L., "Child and Family Psychopathy: Problems of Correlation," in P. H. Hoch and J. Zubin (Eds.), *Psychopathology of Childhood*, New York, Grune & Stratton, 1955.

26. KLUCKHOHN, FLORENCE R., STRODTBECK, FRED, and others, *Variations in Value Orientations*, Evanston, Ill., Row, Peterson, & Co., 1961.

# 12:

# The Closed Circuit: The Study
# of a Delinquent Family[1]

*G. W. Elles*

The aim of this paper is to show the way unconscious phantasies of various family members interlocked. This enabled the individuals to make use of each other and to exploit each other's compulsive acting out in an attempt to gain relief from their own frightening phantasies. It had the effect of making the family unable to accept therapy, because this was experienced as an overwhelming threat to their own closed circuit.

In earlier research[2] at the Henderson Hospital, a group of psychopaths and their families were followed through their treatment phase and rehabilitation up to five years after discharge. The research established that most of these families had complemental character disorders in the marriage pair. Members of such families broke down easily, and were severely restricted in the relationships they could make. Yet the family organisation could be seen as having a therapeutic function retarding and limiting the nature of the personal breakdown and offering a basis for rehabilitation. From our observations it was possible to work out various patterns of emotional balance in the families. The most important to the present subject was the balance between personal identity and family identity. This family-based identity, in its pathological form, represents the transfer into a central family body of many unacceptable thoughts, feelings and activities of individual adult members. At the same time, persons so shorn of their identity are more likely to be used as an organ or limb of such a family body. Yet survival depends on being surrounded by this family. For, unable to be aware of themselves to any degree, the *family* is then needed as a means of indirect communication, both with themselves and with the world outside. Thus in the small group of families studied, four stages of family imbalance were worked out. At the bottom of the scale stood the family so threatened by disintegration that family

Reprinted by permission from *British Journal of Criminology*, Vol. 2 (1961), pp. 23-39. Copyright 1961 by Stevens and Sons Ltd., Publishers. Gillian W. Elles (now Mrs. Parker) is a psychoanalyst in private practice in London. At the time of writing she was research therapist at Henderson Hospital, Sutton, Surrey, England. She treats both adults and children and is particularly interested in family therapy.

needs took precedence over nearly all personal needs, even the need for individual psychotherapy. The family became a closed circuit, unable to allow any effective help to reach the family members. In this paper such a family is described, the whole family being seen as the "patient," and each individual but a limb of the family.

The Lukes have been married some six years, but the Henderson Hospital has available information going back to 1949, when Mr. Luke was first admitted for treatment. Furthermore, intensive home visiting on two occasions has given cross-sections of the family activities which could be compared to show apparent degenerative personal illness. Both the Lukes have been admitted twice to the Unit—indeed it was at the Unit that they met. Both have been in several other mental hospitals for short periods as a result of suicidal gestures. Here then is a ten-year period covered by the recollections of the Lukes, by clinical notes on them as individual patients, and by observations made within their home at two periods of considerable stress related to Mrs. Luke's pregnancies. Over the years this family has become less and less able to tolerate relationships of a therapeutic nature. At the same time, clinics, mental hospitals, special psychotherapeutic centres have all been unable to devise a treatment approach which can be accepted by the Lukes for long enough to produce a change towards better functioning. Seen as a progressive failure between the Lukes and the Health Services, ten years ago Mr. Luke tolerated an eight-month's stay in hospital. Eight years ago they both stayed about three and a half months, and six months ago the wife stayed three days. One month ago, having sought admission, neither of them could bring themselves to accept treatment, and so simply failed to arrive. Therefore, though the Lukes have been admitted, many times, to many hospitals for observation, there is a pattern of increasing intolerance of *treatment* leading to more precipitate discharge.

Certain points seem important in a family like the Lukes. First, that such a division of family experience into past, present and future really has little meaning. These families feel "futureless" because past memories and phantasies are experienced as action in the present. Family energy is mainly spent on seeing each day through and surviving. Secondly, because of this basic insecurity, such families find it more important to maintain the status quo—however unsatisfactory—than to allow change to take place. Change means insecurity greater than they can bear. Therefore, there is little learning by experience. Finally, the overwhelming fear of these families is that they will be invaded by other people's feelings and ideas, and that they will be defenceless.

In order to discuss the unconscious activity of this family, material has been collected from various sources. The psychiatrist's report gives the family's immediate problem. The report of the research worker adds a picture of the relationships of such a family in its present setting. Information from two other sources is channelled in. There is a distillation from the hospital files on both the Lukes, dovetailed together into a family history of illness. Finally, there is the record of the research worker over six months, during which the family worked with her to show how the family functioned under stress situations.

In collecting all this information together, it is accepted that the various levels of abstraction are not comparable, but that each source of information has something to add to a total picture of a family functioning in difficulty. From it there emerges a picture of the Lukes dealing with three major themes: an oral theme (difficulties of eating, starving, addiction and drunkenness); a theme of violence (fighting, sexual attack); and a theme of death (not being able to stay alive—a passive state—or killing). The themes remain constant, though through the ten years there is both a change in symptomatology and a change of actors. But the drama repeats itself over and over again.

## THE LUKES' PROBLEM
*(As presented by them to the psychiatrist)*

Mrs. Luke had been admitted to the Henderson Hospital for the second time in order that a growing addiction to tranquillisers should be treated. At the initial interview with the psychiatrist, the whole family was present, that is, Mrs. Luke, her husband, and her three-year-old daughter, Mary. Mr. Luke was attentive and gentle with his wife and the child was exceptionally well behaved. Mrs. Luke was thin, anxious and appealing. Mr. Luke, a quietspoken, serious man, looked more robust, and at the time seemed the more mature of the two. The story they told was a tragic one. After their marriage they had an extremely difficult time. In the intervening seven years, Mr. Luke had had only twelve months' employment. Their son, born two years after the marriage, proved a difficult child to feed, apparently passing into a coma-like condition after taking very little milk. He had suffered from colic, and this had kept everyone awake. In desperation one night, they had placed his cot outside their bedroom so as to get some rest, and the next morning they found that he was dead. The post-mortem showed that he had suffered from bronchial pneumonia. At this time Mrs. Luke was again pregnant; she developed eczema first, and after Mary's birth was thought to have developed a gastric ulcer. A similar pattern of feeding difficulties showed up, and the child would not take her feeds, passing into a trance-like state. Mrs. Luke took an overdose of sleeping tablets on two occasions, leading to her admission for short periods into a mental hospital. On the first occasion, it was arranged that Mary should be looked after by fosterparents. During the nine months that she was away from home, there appeared to be no feeding problem. On the other hand, Mrs. Luke became more and more distressed at not having the child, and fought to get her back. Mrs. Luke got Mary back, then aged about eighteen months. By this time Mrs. Luke was three months pregnant. Both the Lukes were thoroughly alarmed about the possible effect a second baby would have on Mrs. Luke, particularly as Mary had redeveloped all her eating difficulties, and now vomited her food easily. Therefore, it was particularly tragic for the couple when the third pregnancy resulted in a still-birth. It confirmed their sense of guilt about not wanting the child, and their feelings of inadequacy. Both felt people were talking about them, or shunning them, and Mr. Luke gave up his job to be with his wife.

This account of themselves was told to the psychiatrist on a Tuesday at the time of Mrs. Luke's admission. Three days later she came in great distress to the sister in charge of the Unit, saying that she must return home immediately as her child was ill, her husband must go out to find work, and the two of them needed her at home.

## RESEARCH WORKER'S REPORT

### THE FAMILY AND ITS ENVIRONMENT

The Lukes live in a road of respectable, solidly built four-storeyed houses, most of which have been divided into flats and maisonettes. In the daytime the road appeared empty, but in the evening groups of neighbours could be seen gardening or tinkering with old cars and motorbikes. At one end of the road is a main thoroughfare and big shops, whilst at the other end there is a small road leading to one-roomed shops.

The Lukes appear very isolated, even though they themselves have lived in the house for seven years, and Mr. Luke's mother had the ground-floor flat until her death. Such relationships as the Lukes have appear to be "tainted," and are felt as likely to lead to trouble. For instance, on the first floor is Mr. Luke's sister and brother-in-law. She is seen by the Lukes as a lewd, jealous woman, very antagonistic to them both, and aggressive towards Mrs. Luke. She is also felt to be dangerously seductive to Mary, who has to be watched to see that she doesn't get up to her aunt's flat. In the basement, which belongs to the Lukes, there is a young coloured couple. They are described by the Lukes as nice people and in themselves friendly. Because they are illegally occupying the flat their presence, though lucrative to the Lukes, is also a threat. Mr. Luke seems to have cut himself off from most of his relatives since his mother's death. Mrs. Luke's kin live in the North of England, and for many years she has been estranged from them until recently. With both there is a story of their parents' marriage breaking up and each parent marrying unhappily again. Neither of the Lukes seem to have any local friends. Indeed, they flinch from speaking to the neighbours. They hear the local gossip through Mr. Luke's sister.

At the level of formal relationships, the same pattern of tainted contacts is to be found. Mr. Luke has a long record of unemployment (seventeen jobs between 1946–49, prison sentence of eight months, and then just over a year's employment in the last ten years). High personal aspirations have all along been linked with inadequate performance. One job appealed to him; he would like to return to it, but it is no longer open to him because he took advantage of the kindness of his employer. With the landlord a similar pattern is developing. This old lady, who has been sympathetically inclined to Mr. Luke because she knew his mother over many years, let the young couple take on Mrs. Luke senior's flat when she died, thus with their basement flat giving them a maisonette. When the landlord visits there is great apprehension in case the tenants' secret is discovered. With the National Assistance Board they again fear discovery, this time the discovery of a false declaration about their income. To mitigate their guilty feelings Mr. Luke has stopped claiming other benefits, either for himself or for the child.

From every side the Lukes fear retribution. Put another way, the Lukes could be described as working with a system of values that has become split and highly conflicting. One half of it, immensely moralistic, rigid and retaliative, leads them to feel that they are forever doing wrong. This brings the expectation that in all their relationships they will never be allowed to keep the good things that they want for themselves. They expect to be forced to give up or offer back the things that have given pleasure. Therefore, in a family defense, they secretly operate by a different value system, one which allows them to steal, defraud and dispose. This system is the exact opposite of all the "oughts and musts" with which their conversation is peppered. The first set of values force them to judge these secret norms as "cheating," but at the same time this first set are felt as an external, coercing set of values, unintegrated into their family life, yet dictating it. It is in the presence of these conflicting sets of norms that gratifying emotional contacts outside the family become destroyed. The resultant isolation makes the Lukes desperately dependent upon each other. Each has come to label themselves as criminal, and also feels an accessory to the other's "bad" deeds. Each has involved the other in more unacceptable behaviour as a way of lessening their own sense of wrong-doing (The "bad" and "wrong" are judged by their first set of values, but at the same time they represent generally accepted social norms too.) Therefore, it becomes even more necessary for them to stay together as a family. Yet because they must be with each other all the while, neither can fulfil adequately the role tasks in the marriage relationship, so that each also despises the other. A vicious circle is established.

### THE ROLE RELATIONSHIP FAILURE, AND ITS EFFECT ON TREATMENT

Mrs. Luke cannot let her husband go out to work, she is too frightened of her responsibility as a mother. On the other hand, she is ashamed of the poverty of her home, feels she can invite no one in, and therefore is very bitter towards Mr. Luke on this account. Mr. Luke cannot allow his wife to accept treatment because he then has to take full responsibility for the child, or else go out to work whilst she is at a nursery. If he goes out to work he feels exposed by his inadequate work skills, and fears that people are laughing and talking about him. In this tangle of failed relationships, there is a further twist. Because each feels a failure in his or her own right, both identify themselves with each other's failure and assume a protective role. Therefore, though Mr. Luke feels that Mrs. Luke needs treatment, he can also feel, on her behalf, the pain she might have to face in discussing her problems in a therapeutic group. Therefore, he finds it extremely difficult to adopt an attitude which might enable her to remain in treatment. Again, though Mrs. Luke feels her husband's work record is despicable, she is so aware of his problems at work that it is easier *for her* to have him unemployed.

It can be seen at this point that Mrs. Luke's reason for leaving treatment is grossly over-determined. At the centre of this family maze is Mary, aged three. Whoever undertakes to feed her then becomes so wrought up that they can scarcely feed themselves. She has to find a way of dealing with her parents' anxiety about her health, her diet, and even her sleep (for they nudge her to see if she is still alive). The child seems loving and obedient, neat and tidy in between not eating or being sick. The parents feel that she is preoccupied with ideas about biting, as she will only take liquid or mashed foods. At least a quarter of the day is spent over her meals. Through her behaviour, Mary exerts an enormous control over her parents, who feel they are being driven to the point of breaking. Most of their day is spent in protecting and cherishing her, but at the same time there is much talk between them about the other two babies, particularly the eldest son, who is idealised. Mary, in her questioning, would seem to feel that this boy was more special and more good than she. Therefore, she has to contend with a rivalry of two dead siblings who are so much in her parents' minds. At the same time she has to deal with her parents' anxiety that she too may suddenly die.

The total family problem can be seen in terms of a recurring unsatisfying parent-child relationship. There is a disbelief in a benign and competent authority who can feel like a good parent. Authority seems to mean

H

forceful control or mad power. Things labelled "good" do not feel good, and therefore pleasant experience has to be secretly found, burdensome responsibilities secretly disposed of. As a result, Mr. and Mrs. Luke, though seeing themselves as essentially upright and law-abiding, find themselves as a family pursued by the furies of their conscience externalized in formal authority figures—officials, employers, doctors in hospitals, landlords, and the police. There are propitiatory acts of self-denial, and these give way, at times, to more cruel acts of self-punishment in suicidal episodes, which, in their turn, inflict more suffering on the other family members. As time goes by, some more formal agencies stand to be involved in the behaviour of this family and, parallel to this, the informal spontaneous and socially gratifying relationships become tainted, disordered and are now practically non-existent.

Basically the Lukes seem to have the capacity to interact with one another in a loving and on-going manner, but inasmuch as the original marriage was a flight from facing what they feared was a "mad" part of themselves, so a large proportion of family energy must be deployed in keeping the marriage alive for purely defensive reasons. The intense care for Mary can stand for a family "acting out" of an inner individual fear that the child within each one of them may become overwhelmed by mad, cruel and driving parental standards.

## THE FAMILY FUNCTIONING

If this report assessed the matter accurately, then a prediction could be made that the Lukes' system of family functioning precluded the possibility of formal psychotherapy. Indeed this was demonstrated in the pattern of family behaviour over the next half-year. The prediction was based on the Lukes' apparent assumption that there was no good powerful enough to help them, and, therefore, they had to do everything for themselves. The unconscious converse of this seemed to the research worker equally important, *i.e.,* that the Lukes had to feel that they could act omnipotently as a way of avoiding their own intense feelings of chaos and failure. To feel that other people could help only highlighted their inadequacy and their guilt.

Shortly after the two visits on which the foregoing report was made, the Luke family engaged in a further drama. Mrs. Luke began to fear that she was again pregnant. In front of the research worker, and in earshot of Mary, the Lukes discussed how they could deal with this. Again both assumed that it would be a disaster for Mrs. Luke to have another baby. Over the weeks, various drugs were procured by Mr. Luke and swallowed by Mrs. Luke to terminate the pregnancy. At the same time, Mary became interested in the baby next door, wanted to know if she could have a baby to play with. During these two months no conclusive evidence came to light that a pregnancy had been established, yet a great deal of family energy was devoted to dealing with the fears relating to it. On two occasions Mrs. Luke made herself rather ill, and on both these occasions had to miss appointments with psychiatrists.

One way of looking at this episode would be to see it as a sort of "family dream." The family is acting out the theme of infanticide and, at the same time, exposing this to the research worker. Mr. and Mrs. Luke become the active people, treating themselves, whilst two psychiatrists and two treatment units are rendered impotent. The Lukes, recognizing that Mrs. Luke left one unit rather than discuss the problem of the death of two babies, now manipulate a situation where they again show their need to have treatment, but only from themselves. They demonstrate their need to be, at one time, patient, doctor and culprit, thereby closing the circuit.

This negative way of using medical services could be shown to the Lukes. It led, in this instance, to some small recognition of how each used the other's problems as ways of dealing with their own. Mr. Luke recognised that, so long as he felt he could not possibly leave his wife, he did not have to face persecutory feelings at work. Mrs. Luke recognised how she could use this situation as a way of avoiding being confronted with her very troubled feelings. For now she saw that some of her problems of feeding Mary represented a mirror image of a similar situation between her and her own mother. Here, for a fleeting instance, there was some slight increase in personal awareness. Both saw in themselves some small fragment of what ordinarily was felt to be a family experience. As a result, it seemed that for twenty-four hours they acted in an "un-family" way. After this, a complex family manoeuvre took place so that the family equilibrium could remain steady. The threatening situation seemed to be one in which *simultaneously* there was an alteration in the balance of defensive projection in both the Lukes. Now Mrs. Luke kept in touch with the research worker, and Mr. Luke did not. Such a balance might have continued longer, but for the fact that Mrs. Luke's father arrived to stay with them.

It so happened that Mrs. Luke's father met the research worker on the day he arrived. Shortly after, Mrs. Luke contacted the Henderson Hospital asking for a home visit to discuss treatment. When seen by herself in the kitchen, Mrs. Luke poured out her despair about her behaviour, and her husband's reaction to it. She felt herself to be a bad mother and a bad wife. She felt her husband often accused her of taking tranquillisers when she hadn't. He did not trust her with any money. Indeed, he continually searched her and her belongings, in case she was hoarding. She painted a picture of herself wanting treatment, but of her *father and husband* making it impossible for her to go to hospital. She felt that their attitude was that she could pull herself together, and that no hospital could help. Yet later, when the father was seen, he tried to get the active co-operation of the research worker to make his daughter go into hospital, saying he was sure she needed help. When the three of them met in the presence of the research worker, the father maintained this attitude, that his daughter needed, and could get, help. Mr. Luke took a neutral position, and Mrs. Luke now took the *opposite* attitude to her previous one in the kitchen two days before. The father had considerable drive and seemed deeply concerned about his daughter and son-in-law. Gradually they both agreed to ask for another interview at a hospital, which had been prepared to see the whole family. The out-patient interview took place, the date of admission was arranged, but this was never kept. It coincided with the father's return to his home. As an indication that this was going to happen, the research worker found, on her last visit, two pointers. First, that Mrs. Luke and her husband now felt that the whole problem "had to do with sex." All they felt was needed was that they should go into this themselves. In other words, the Lukes were going to be both patient and doctor once more. Secondly, Mr. Luke's sister was present for part of the time. Once she had left, the discussion turned on how the Lukes were trying to persuade *her* to get treatment, as they felt sure she needed it. At subsequent visits this tended to be family attitude.

## THE QUESTION OF THEME VARIATIONS

It was suggested earlier that families like the Lukes feel futureless. A sense of future depends, in part, on being able to separate past experiences from present, to become free of enacting, compulsively, massive blocks of such experience. With this family the frightening past had to be projected continually into the relationships around them. Paradoxically, this then tied them even further to those childhood experiences. Furthermore, it led them to become more and more dependent upon each other as a target for these projections, and as a tool in their enactment. By looking at the early history of the Lukes, the central projective themes can be identified, and their modification traced in the family experience.

Mr. Luke had always seen himself as shy, acutely self-conscious and impulsive. His parents were unhappily married, and separated when he was about ten. His mother went to live with another man and Mr. Luke could remember having "murderous" feelings towards him. His mother drank, and he frequently came home to very sordid scenes. He also feared his mother's suicidal tendencies, and on one occasion found her with her head in the gas oven. At one time, he feared that he had wanted to kill her, and it was a great relief when she recovered. His school and early work record were poor, although he enjoyed reading and politics. In company he was afraid that people were laughing and talking about him. His most successful period was whilst serving the R.A.M.C. in a field-ambulance unit. After discharge from the army he had eight months' in-patient treatment as a result of a depressive episode in which he had suicidal ideas. He showed a marked improvement, but on leaving hospital he could not find suitable work. He joined with two brothers-in-law in breaking and entering barges and garages. Eventually he got an eight-months' prison sentence. Again he was admitted to the hospital for treatment, and on this occasion met his future wife and left precipitately after three-and-a-half months' treatment. The reason he gave was that he must get work and find a home so that he could marry. Shortly after this he was admitted to another hospital, having made a suicidal gesture. At this point his mother seems to have found the young couple a flat under hers. The future young Mrs. Luke then left her treatment, and the two of them got married and settled into the flat.

Mrs. Luke, when discussing her early experiences, had none of the hesitancy and understatement of her husband. She talked about it as if it was happening at the moment. Again there was the history of unhappily married parents, who separated and remarried—unhappily—when she was ten. The important things to her were having tonsils and appendix removed by the time she was four. She remembered her father telling her that at the time there was a further worry, a local lad had interfered with her. Later on, there was another occasion when she had been "taken up to the woods" by an older man. When she was five her father lost his job, became morose, and took to drink and going with other women. Her mother went out to work, she went to school and had to find her own mid-day dinner at home. The marriage of her parents finally broke up when her father developed venereal disease. Her mother got a divorce, and then married another man, who was both a drunkard and had V.D. The mother was infected, and Mrs. Luke was subjected to tests. When Mrs. Luke was fourteen, her mother died suddenly. Mrs. Luke was never clear about the cause, whether it was due to her mother's heart, or to pills she had been taking at the time. Therefore, there was a fear that the mother committed suicide. Furthermore, Mrs. Luke became worried about her stepfather's sexual feelings towards her. At this time she had disassociative and hallucinatory experiences, and she also started drinking. After undergoing a short period of treatment, she left her home town and gradually worked her way to London, never holding any job for very long. She liked the work, but became frightened about the boss's feelings towards her. Eventually, she was admitted to the Henderson Hospital after having lost consciousness for eight hours whilst working as a chambermaid in an hotel.

## THE THEMES

The theme of child care has in some measure already been traced in the family history. One child dies at three-and-a-half months, one at birth, and one is just an idea. Mary, in her relationship with her mother, typifies an ill-remembered bad relationship between Mrs. Luke and her own mother—ill-remembered because Mrs. Luke has idealised her mother, who was the one safely loving person in her life. More easily, Mrs. Luke can recall her mother discussing her own childhood. The older woman was brought up by a crazy foster-mother because her own mother had to be put into an asylum. The foster-mother over-fed the children at the beginning of the week and ran out of money at the end. To a certain extent, this also fitted into Mr. Luke's experience of his mother, who at one moment could be warm, protective and giving, and then at another withdrawn into depression or drunkenness. Therefore, in mothering there is a significant theme for the Luke family, that mothers can be overindulgent and at the same time driven mad by their children.

Again, in their experiences connected with drinking, and taking drugs, each of the Lukes has some overwhelming memory that enables him or her to be used by the other as a way of disposing of these haunting experiences. For instance, Mr. Luke's need to save his wife from her excessive use of tranquillisers has this side to it, that to save her is also connected with saving his mother from his own intense anger, the gas oven or the lover, whilst Mrs. Luke enacts both drunken parent and frightened child. The death of the babies (boys) can stand for Mr. Luke's need to find some way of acting out his feared impulses towards his mother's lover, and the fear of retaliation associated with the mother's many pregnancies. On Mrs. Luke's side, her anxiety about having a sexual relationship, and becoming pregnant, is linked to desires for an incestuous relationship, and her reaction to it. So long as she can feel like the small child being interfered with, then she can avoid the responsibility. When the Lukes were single, both at times were suspected of stealing. Mr. Luke's record showed several incidents of breaking and entering. Now the pattern is somewhat altered. Mr. Luke, from time to time, takes all his wife's money, breaking open cupboards, searching her and her belongings. Mrs. Luke counters this by taking from the housekeeping, whilst both of them feel they have defrauded formal agencies. Their sexual relationship has also the features of breaking into a forbidden place.

Furthermore, in all their relationships there is the theme of death, sometimes active death, sometimes just not staying alive. For instance, before marriage, Mr. Luke is twice admitted to a mental hospital following a suicidal gesture; Mrs. Luke's period of unconsciousness is similarly treated by admission. Once Mr. Luke is married, he abandons this form of communication, but his wife makes two suicidal gestures which get her into an observation ward. In all these episodes a gradual condensation of acting out has taken place, as with the other themes. It is suggested that such an act on Mrs. Luke's part represents, not only her own reaction to an intolerable situation, but her unconscious reaction to her husband's need for her to respond in such a way to his expectation. This expectation is one to which Mrs. Luke responds, not only because she has many reasons for feeling suicidal, but also because, in such severely disturbed relationships, one person can make use of an unconscious counter transference in a way that leads to the enactment of their *own* secret impulse, here Mr. Luke's suicidal feelings being enacted by Mrs. Luke.

## DISCUSSION

This paper has set out to describe some small section of the experience of a young married couple in a phase where the family had to remain in a closed circuit. Two pressures forced them to bring this about. The first one represented an unspoken fear of madness. As a family, they combined to defend themselves against this by boosting each other's apparent ego strength, by their own weakness, a defence against psychosis. The steps they then took led them to criminal behaviour, criminal by their own harsh super-ego system, but also, at times, criminal by the social norms surrounding them. This, in turn, became the second pressure necessitating even more drastically closing the circuit. Treatment was felt as a seductive process, which could only lead to *family* disaster, and a return to seeing themselves as isolated individuals, the one with paranoid fears, the other with gross hysterical symptoms. Therefore, as the closing of the circuit became more effective, so the compulsive enactment of certain themes (associated in the first place with childhood traumata) became more determined. The family lived in a perpetual psychodrama, with themselves both as actors and audience. By operating a very complex system of fragmented identification, they could avoid the agony of responsibility. Because they could not accept, at a personal level, the guilt associated with it, they gained no relief of a permanent nature. On the other hand, through the six years of marriage, their use of each other became more "sophisticated," so that gradually a condensation took place. Now in the compulsive acting out, many of the themes originally experienced by both can be assumed by one actor and reacted to by the other. Each of these themes, fortunately, reaches its point of social danger at different times. There has been a movement from action which society might prosecute to one which it could condone, although the basic motivation remains unaltered. As Eissler has pointed out, society is only interested in behaviour—not in motivation. Therefore, though this marriage has brought many grave problems, it also can be seen to have helped in a lop-sided manner these two sick people from becoming chronic state pensioners, either as recidivists or in-patients. Nevertheless, they remain crippled by the limited relationships they are able to make, and this is now being passed on to the next generation.

The fact that families like the Lukes have had appalling childhood experiences that link closely to unconscious phantasy material makes repression an inadequate adult defence against anxieties and leads to the massive use of acting out. With this is associated fears about being invaded by ideas and feelings of others. The currents of projective identification, the waves of sustained acting out drag and toss the family like a small boat on a turbulent ocean, an ocean of the dynamic unconscious of the individuals composing the family. To help these families remains a very big problem. Seen as individuals, they are very sick. As a family, however, they can be seen as developing their own treatment. So long as the movement of this treatment is in the direction of socially accepted behaviour, that is from areas of prosecution to areas of condonement, then it achieves something. However, medical and educational authorities must remain deeply concerned about the health of the children of such marriages, for from birth they are pressed into the service of the family, rather than being felt as individuals in their own right. However, whilst the family circuit remains closed, little direct treatment can reach them.

Finally, it is suggested that with severely disturbed people, usually labelled "character disorders" seen generation after generation, there may be two phases of the illness. The deviant behaviour, drawing down punitive feelings of society, is well known. The second phase, as represented by what is here described as the closed circuit, quiescent from society's point of view, has both destructive and therapeutic factors in it. The balance between these negative and positive elements has to be studied before effective help can be offered to the family.

## SUMMARY

1. This paper describes a family which, in the six years of its existence, gradually became a closed circuit, unable to make use of any psychiatric treatment unless self-administered.

2. The family is described in terms of the relationships that the members could make.

3. Following a diagnosis in terms of family functioning, the family experience of the next half year is described to support this diagnosis.

4. Three aspects of the family are discussed:
   (a) the futureless aspect of the family;
   (b) the need of the family to resist change in family members;
   (c) the family fear of being overwhelmed by the feelings and ideas of others.

5. Three main themes of compulsive behaviour are linked to early childhood experiences, and the modification of these themes, in the family experience, is briefly traced. The changes in the themes are seen in terms of intensity, in social condonement, and also in changes in the actors.

6. The present family experience is seen as a perpetual psychodrama which brings no sense of catharsis. Yet, inasmuch as the compulsive behaviour is moving in the direction of socially condoned behaviour, it is seen as having a limited therapeutic value.

7. Concern for the children within a closed circuit family is mentioned.

## NOTES

1. This study is taken from a pilot research into the after-care needs of patients discharged from the Social Rehabilitation Unit, now Henderson Hospital, Belmont, Surrey. It has been carried out with help from the S. W. Metropolitan Regional Board under Dr. Maxwell Jones and his Deputy, Dr. Fergus Stallard. To them, and to the clinical team, I would like to express my thanks for their interest and support.
2. This study was part of a much larger research project for Belmont Hospital Social Rehabilitation Unit, Director Dr. Maxwell Jones. The research team was directed by Dr. R. N. Rapoport under the auspices of the Nuffield Foundation. Paper read at Psychotherapy and Social Psychiatry Section of Post Hospital Care of the Family, 1957.

## REFERENCES

1. EISSLER, KURT: "Some Problems of Delinquency," *Searchlights on Delinquency,* Int. Univ. Press, 1949.
2. GIOVACCHINI, PETER L.: "Mutual Adaptation in Various Object Relationships," *Int. J. Psych. An.,* Vol. 39, Pt. 4.
3. GLOVER: "On the Relation of the Total Ego to its Environment and the Concept of Adaptation," "Concept of Dissociation," *Int. J. Psych. An.* 1943, Vol. 24.
   GLOVER: "On the Etiology of Drug Addiction," "On the Early Development of the Mind," Vol. I, Imago, 1956.
4. HEIMANN, PAULA: "Dynamics of Transference Interpretations," *Int. J. Psych. An.,* 1956, Vol. 37.
5. JOHNSON, A. M.: "Sanction for Super-Ego Lacunae of Adolescents," *Searchlights on Delinquency,* New York, Int. Univ. Press.
6. MAIN, T. F.: Presidential Address, "The Ailment," *Brit. J. Med. Psychol.,* 1957, Vol. 30, Pt. III, 127–145.
7. MONEY-KYRLE, R. E.: "Normal Counter Transference and Some of its Deviations," *Int. J. Psych. An.,* Vol. 37, 1956.
8. RAPOPORT, R., and ROSOW, I.: "An Approach to Family Relationships and Role Performance," *Human Relations* (1957), Vol. X, No. 3, 209–221.

H*

# 13:
# The Family and the Idea of a Cardinal Role

*Harold Fallding*

## I. THE CARDINAL ROLE

Whether the diverse roles that an individual plays are ever fused into some sort of unity is a question as yet unsettled. Nadel (1957, p. 65) suggested that any appearance of this is due to one role becoming dominant through being the most compelling or consequential in the individual's life. The first case can be illustrated by the schoolteacher who cannot help being an instructor to his friends as well as his pupils. But that would be better represented as role-interference than as role-integration. The other possibility Nadel envisaged resembles what has been called *salient identity*. This is that role which places the individual most decisively in the class structure, by making him acceptable or unacceptable for a conspicuous reason. Broom and Selznick (1958, p. 476) point out that a Negro and a Jehovah's Witness in America would probably find their salient identities in those roles, irrespective of the other roles they played. But this is a matter of role-levelling rather than of role-integration. The individual's other roles are appreciated or devaluated to match the status of the salient one.

George Mead's (1937) treatment of this question is profounder than Nadel's; although in part it is still unclarified. We are scarcely brought further by Mead than to supposing that an individual's many selves are delivered from being a mere mixed assortment by the organization of society itself. According to his capacity for sympathy, the individual's own identity becomes like a drama and his overt behaviour is a reaction to a host of others in himself. There is no difficulty about his playing more than one part, since he becomes the pattern by which *all* the parts dovetail in a social structure. This pattern, in Mead's elusive notion of it, is a *generalized other*.

Reprinted by permission from Harold Fallding, "The Family and the Idea of a Cardinal Role," *Human Relations*, Vol. 14, No. 4 (1961). Copyright 1961 by Harold Fallding. Harold Fallding is professor and chairman, Department of Sociology, University of Waterloo, Ontario, Canada. At the time of writing he was senior lecturer in sociology, University of New South Wales, Australia.

It appears that this *other* is generalized in a gestalt sense of the word; first, in being an organized whole, and second, in being the constant ground against which the individual's separate role enactments loom successively as figures. But this organization itself is of the rational kind since, according to Mead's illustration from the game (Mead, 1937, p. 158–9), the roles articulating in the social structure are seen as means contributing to an end. Subordination of his own efforts to this communal end is the generalized attitude which the individual accepts from the entire community, and it becomes the source of the general principles by which he bends his specific activities away from egoistic gratification to altruistic service, so forming character (Mead, 1937, pp.162–3).[1] It is thus a three-sided generality of social organization, common purpose, and altruistic principle that the individual internalizes in achieving personal unity. The resultant unified self is not in any sense a general role but a general disposition to give comfortable accommodation to many roles. And this requires, of course, that the society shall be well organized if the individual is to be integrated. Linton (1945, pp. 49–53) has acknowledged the same sort of dependence.

It is possible, however, to approach the question of role-integration by examining connections between the actual roles a person plays, and this is the line taken in the present discussion, although it is ultimately linked with Mead's approach.[2] In order to pick out these connections clearly, it will be imperative to bear in mind throughout that roles are not simply things done but are things *expected,* in that sense of the word which carries the force of required or prescribed, and that they only arise where expectations are *shared.*[3]

Barnard (1938, p. 112) has observed that an individual can sometimes effect a 'simultaneous contribution to two organizations by a single act'. He took this to be 'the critical fact in all complex organizations; that is,' he said, 'the complex is made an organic whole by it' (op. cit., p. 112). We can think of examples of this. A farmer, by producing food for the nation, simultaneously earns an income for his family; a small-town retailer, by throwing himself into civic affairs, widens his business contacts; a financier, by advancing development loans, boosts finance company profits. Sometimes bivalent actions like these occur because they are written into the role-expectations arising from the separate organizations. An expectation which yokes the individual because of his accountability to the one is duplicated by an expectation put upon him by the other. This capacity of roles from different groups to duplicate expectations is the basis of the role-integration to be discussed.

If any group duplicates the expectations placed on an individual by another group, the role it confers on him is to some extent integrating; while the integrating power of the role increases as it duplicates expectations from more of the groups in which he moves. The role might even conceivably duplicate the expectations of all the groups in which he plays a part. It would then not be a distortion to say that his role within that group becomes a summation of all his other roles, in that what it expects of him is the sum (at least) of what is expected of him by all the other groups. Such a role would be appropriately named a *cardinal role,* using the word in its most literal sense. For it would be the hinge on which all the individual's other roles would turn. It seems to the writer that it is this kind of global oversight which Cooley (1916) intended by the comprehensiveness he ascribed to the primary group.

Face-to-face interaction is the property most commonly predicated of the primary group (or relationship), but there has been a tendency to make it a sufficient property. Thirty years ago Faris (1932) drew attention to the mistaken tendency of attenuating primary relations in this way. In seeking to restore solidity to the concept, he urged that it should be applied, as Cooley seems to have intended, only to groups that could cradle the essentially human (meaning moral) experiences. He accepted as such those groups which are marked by a free-flowing exchange between members that is the very opposite of institutionalized behaviour.

Faris was right in seeking to re-fasten the notion of primary relationship to its original anchorage, but mistaken, one feels, in opposing it to institutionalized behaviour which would have a describable structure. One has the impression that this mistake is not uncommon even now, and that the primary group's special puissance is supposed to lie in its imponderable properties, in its pervasive affectivity, rather than in the intricate structure of expectations of which affectivity is but the velvet lining. The writer would suggest that the contrary ought to be the case and that the primary group's special importance lies, to a large extent at least, in the structural property of duplicating and so reinforcing a number, and possibly all, of the expectations which govern its members' behaviour in other groups. This power of making its members' external involvements relevant or necessary to itself might even be interpreted as the 'primariness' of the primary group. Primary groups can be distinguished from others by having it, and comparisons can be made between them according to the extent to which this protective cover is spread.

Thus, in one significant sense, the primary group's boundaries reach out to all the activities for which its members are accountable to one another, to the limits of co-accountability rather than co-activity. This is a notion which is especially relevant to analysis of the family, members of which discharge only some of their tasks amongst themselves, separating to perform the remainder by cooperation with outsiders. It is possible for all the activities of either kind to *belong* to the family, if they are carried out within the leash-hold of the family's expectations. In a study of a small sample of urban families made by the writer, differences in the properties under discussion were clearly evident. We could say that the roles conferred on their members by different types of family were cardinal to a very different extent and that, correspondingly, the primary capacity of the families varied.

## II. THREE FAMILY TYPES

Three types of family were distinguished in the sample studied. One need not demur in introducing them through knowing that types are abstractions which real cases only approach, and that the factors which vary so greatly between the types are probably, in a population, normally distributed. In the writer's view types are the sort of abstraction we properly invoke to depict whatever tendency we find for factors to cluster together, and to show in what *emergent* quality variation between clusters occurs.

The research which brought the types into prominence was an exploratory study which did not anticipate them as the result and could not therefore measure them with precision. The door of knowledge flew open, so to speak, only on the last heave, as it so often does. The types as here described were taken as such because certain factors that seemed cognate were found to occur together in fact in a number of cases, although not invariably. But the numbers were too small to test the degree of constancy of their association with one another. Further work would be needed to do that, regarding the types as hypothetical. It would also have to use greater refinement in measuring those factors which now seem to be the important ones.

The research in question was a sociological field study undertaken for the Ph.D. degree at the Australian National University. Between March 1954 and June 1955 the writer made the intimate acquaintance of thirty-eight Sydney families, eighteen of which were tradesmen's families and twenty those of professional workers. It was required of the families chosen that both parents should be still living and together and that there should be two or more children, and it was preferred that one child at least should have entered adolescence. The families were contacted through a variety of channels to ensure that they were diverse in matters for which uniformity was not required. Church affiliation, political position, and residential area, for instance, were highly varied. But families of recent migrants were not included.

Information was collected by interviews with the family as a group, as well as by separate interviews with each member. Usually, a family was visited for a full evening on four to seven separate occasions. By following a schedule, but no fixed interview or questionnaire, the writer attempted to obtain comparable information from all the families regarding the range of activities of members and the relations between members, particularly as those relations were defined by the attitude members took to one another's activities. The scope of the schedule was considerably wider than the subject of this paper. The unpublished thesis (Fallding, 1956) presents the full results of the research undertaken and a summary of certain of the findings has been published (1957). The summary includes a brief reference to the types now to be described, but the fuller account of these types and the examination of their theoretical implications have been reserved for the present paper.

THE ADAPTATION TYPE OF FAMILY

The first type of family is designated the *aaaptation type,* because in it husband and wife sought markedly different satisfactions from life and took measures to adapt to one another in the face of this difference, which they frankly admitted to exist. That was chiefly done by each partner granting the other a charter of independence. Each claimed a large area of personal life for which he did not admit responsibility to the family, and this was agreed to on the understanding of receiving the same consideration.

Four of the thirty-eight families were classed with this type.[4] In one of these the mother's life still revolved around the home of her own parents. She spent a good deal of time with her parents and gave them much service. Her husband, on the other hand, minimized his contact with these in-laws and sought his own satisfactions in separate leisure activities. He spent most of his non-working time following sport, reading, drinking at various hotels, studying form guides, and backing racehorses. This man had married in his late thirties and had been unwilling to modify his former manner of life: he expected to continue unchanged, and encouraged his wife to do the same. In another of these families the father's non-working time was occupied in political activity, in reading political literature, and in drinking. The mother enjoyed a similar reprieve from too great a family commitment and passed her time in a succession of diverting part-time occupations, in women's movements, and in reading novels and political and feminist literature. In a third family it was the mother who was occupied by political activities. She was also a student of socialism, feminism, and political and economic problems, and a supporter of certain educational movements. She was so absorbed in one of these movements as to describe it as her 'way of life.' These activities took her away from the home a great deal during the day and evening and for a number of weekends and longer periods throughout the year. Her husband was in possession of a comparable independence, spending his time in photographic and scientific societies, in cultivating music, in fishing and boat-building. Finally, in the fourth family of this kind, the father's non-working time was devoted to studies in classical language and literature and to music. These studies were pursued partly within the home and sometimes within the circle of the assembled family, but the father's continual withdrawal to a world with which his wife and children were out of contact meant that his independence was no less real than that of the other fathers mentioned above. His wife, similarly, enjoyed a certain independence, though perhaps less willingly than the other mothers mentioned here, as she was considerably more absorbed in her children. She strove for a cultivation of her own in reading modern literature; she followed a theatre movement and gave support to a kindergarten.

The way in which these external activities were regarded by the actors themselves and by other members of their families was peculiar to families of the type. They were thought of as opportunities to slip out of the influence or supervision of the family and responsibility to it and to act, to a large degree at least, without the knowledge or concern of the others. Because their expectation of satisfaction was mainly attached to independent activities of this kind, and because ample opportunity was allowed for such, the parents were generally reasonably well contented with one another and the family. Children and home were regarded as added satisfactions which strongly independent individuals, having other satisfactions to draw upon, might contract to supply, by contributing either an income or domestic service.

These parents were all conscientious in discharging their part of the contract, especially those more public aspects which others would notice, and some were disposed to drawing their relatives' and friends' attention to the fact. Wives would point out, for instance, that they always prepared the meals on time or that they had done everything possible for the children's health and education; husbands that they had always brought in the money and that no member of the family had ever been in want or trouble. But the contract was fulfilled in the spirit of contract; conjugal roles were clipped to a bare minimum. Each was expected to do as much for himself as possible. If the contractual dependence was felt to be a tie, partners comforted themselves with the knowledge that they got something for what they gave.

It was in keeping with the general independence of these spouses that families of this type freely surrendered recreational and religious activities (if they valued religion) to external organizations, not caring to make any provision for them among themselves. Family members, for instance, rarely if ever spent holidays together.

Under these definitely contractual conditions taking decisions for the whole family became an irksome responsibility. In the two trades-men's families of this type, family control was 'left to chance'; in the two professional families there was a faint-hearted assent to a principle of partnership in family management. But what happened in fact in all four was that family management took shape more under the influence of personality than of principle. In the tradesmen's families the father in one case and the mother in the second asserted themselves, these being the less accommodating partners and the quicker to sum up a situation and express their mind about it. In one of the professional families the mother was dominating and took charge. In the other the parents competed to see how much overall family responsibility could be foisted on the partner.

Control measures were also weak in the element of principle in families of the type shortly to be described as false-identification families, but there was a difference. Unprincipled control in the adaptation type of family did not entail the personal frustration which it brought in its train in the other. This is because control measures were usually taken with regard to a tacit agreement on maximum independence for each partner and they were impersonal, directed against the situation. Thus, for example, an assertive mother in an adaptation type of family would decide that no breakfast would be served on Sundays—and everyone could adjust themselves to the fact as they chose. A father would decide to ignore the children's misdemeanours, but the mother was still free to deal with them as she saw fit.

Relationships between parents and children in these families took on something of the same character of distant, calculating adaptation as obtained in the relationship between the parents. There was, for instance, a marked tendency towards segregation of the generations. The children and adolescents did not have a great deal of association with their parents, and the parents did not believe that the children should be allowed to make too great a claim upon them. The children spent much time in their own part of the house, perhaps taking their meals separately from the parents and having their own radio sets. They were encouraged to live a life of their own as far as possible, and both generations in these families sometimes confessed to being wholly unable to fathom the mind of the other. The parents were also prone to excuse themselves from showing affection towards their children, using the plea that they were 'unemotional by nature'.

On the other hand, in spite of this sparing expenditure of attention and affection on the children, the parents were inclined to claim affection *from* them and strove to outmanoeuvre one another to win it. This could be attempted by concentrating indulgence on one child while neglecting another. Indulgence in this context did not mean lavish affection. It meant excusing a child from punishment, being lax about correction or insistence on standards which would be to the child's ultimate benefit, or favouring the child with gifts and privileges. The consequence in the children's attitude to their parents was a shrewd watchfulness, as they waited to see which way the wind would blow; whether the parent's approach would be determined by affection-seeking or the avoidance of bother. They would respond with compliance or disobedience, according to which they thought would best further their own interests and, possibly, put the parent in their power.

### THE IDENTIFICATION TYPE OF FAMILY

The second type of family made a polar opposite to that just described. It will be called the *identification type* of family because in it the parents identified their personal interests with those of the family itself. The term is not mystical, but is used to convey the fact that the satisfactions the parents desired seemed to be largely derivable from the quality of family life, so that was a primary end to which they committed themselves. Any independently derivable satisfactions, such as those to be found in one's occupation or friendships, were incidental to family life and had somehow to be referred to it. These parents had the feeling that their own interest could be so surrendered to the family that if the family itself flourished their own greatest good would be secured. Twenty-three families were judged to be of this type.

Parents regarded the responsibility of the parental roles as a requirement for completing character and personality. Besides, the constant companionship of one another and the children, the charm and grace of childhood and the awakening of adolescence were intrinsically satisfying. They looked for a stable, orderly, sociable existence which their own industry and thrift would ensure, with a gradually improving standard of living to be secured through the father's improvement in his trade or profession. They desired some leisure, to be spent mainly in moderate and simple pleasures which could be shared by the family; and they desired comfort and grace in the home.

A premium was placed on those qualities which were believed necessary for preserving the desired family atmosphere. 'Naturalness' was placed very high, for instance, and family members were expected to be unpretentious and open. If anyone got 'uppish' it was made a joke of till he desisted, and if it looked like developing into a habit he could be pilloried mercilessly. No one was allowed to think that private endeavour and personal achievement could take prior place to the quality of personal relations, and that was what anyone who took himself too seriously was believed to be in danger of doing. Members were made to understand that they should be considerate and unselfish, dropping their task, if necessary, to help another person. One had to learn to be fair, kindly, sympathetic, tactful, courteous, and interested in everyone else. Some of the parents in families of this type had consciously formulated the principle that life was only satisfying if lived for someone else, and said that in the family one always had one's partner and children to live for.

Members of these families, the parents in particular, had a clear notion of what the family depended on each of them for, and most of them took pleasure in measuring up to the expectation and even, for a surprise at times, exceeding it. Thus a mother would do some special cooking, a father go in the car to meet a child after a function, or a child give some additional help in the house.

In some cases parents engaged in a very large amount of outside activity, giving service, for example, in many voluntary associations and keeping up a number of friendships. On the other hand, some of them had voluntarily surrendered practically all such freedom to 'doing things for the family', and experienced no sense of constriction. They would say, 'Well, I don't suppose I do ever have a minute to myself, but I don't notice it. I certainly don't mind, because I've made the family my life.' But whether few or many, their external activities were regarded as arms of the family, appearances in which one represented the others, of which the others were well-informed, and to which one knew they gave support. Parents of these families took great pride and interest in the school life of their children, for example, and the children, reciprocally, took pride in their father's occupation. In the same way, both parents and children were informed and expansive about one another's friends and voluntary and sporting activities. But recreation was something they reserved as much as possible for the family circle. They strove to be together, if at all possible, for outings and holidays. In a small number of cases family worship was observed.

Family management was mainly a matter of giving each parent 'a say', and avoiding undue intrusion on the area of authority which belonged to the partner. The situation was virtually the same whether the parents acknowledged the father to be the family head or regarded themselves as equal partners. A feature of the relationship in which it contrasted with that shortly to be described for the false-identification type of family, was that the parents were not over-dependent on reaching detailed agreements, nor were they over-concerned about doing so. There was a certain robustness in the relationship which seemed to take it for granted that precise agreement on details could rarely be expected between persons of different sex and experience. In many matters it was thought sufficient to make a divergence plain rather than to persist in flogging out agreement. For example, in one family the eldest son had appealed to his father to buy him a car; the mother agreed to his having it but the father opposed it. There was no expectation that agreement would be reached by prolonging discussion, but mother and son were satisfied that their point of view would not be ignored. We would gain a wrong impression if we thought that family consultation necessarily meant decision by agreement. Just as often it was employed to make authority benevolent in matters where no one expected that agreement would be reached, and which it was thought wiser not to labour.

The parents' approach to the children was a fairly sympathetic and understanding one, and marked by loyalty, affection, interest, and respect. They tried to show a sense of responsibility toward the child and to regard him as objectively as they could. He was given scope to develop his own will and judgment. But the parents enforced whatever standards of behaviour they considered to be for the child's good, and did not fear to lose favour by doing so.

In turn, the children's attitude to their parents was one of pride and confidence in them, and respect, affection, and loyalty towards them; and they showed a fair amount of consideration for their wishes and compliance with their directions.

### THE FALSE-IDENTIFICATION TYPE OF FAMILY

It is difficult to delineate the third type of family in a way that sets it apart from the other two, because it has certain elements in common with each of them and yet is distinct. Perhaps its position in relation to the other types could be depicted as a state of indecision between them. It does not develop into the identification type because one partner or both cannot decide what place the family is to take in relation to other interests. On the other hand, it does not develop into the adaptation type because the partners will not allow the intrusion into their common consciousness of certain critical differences of interest, which would almost certainly manifest themselves if they were frank about their deeper promptings. An open and shared admission of these differences is found intolerable, because if they were to be acknowledged the expectation of satisfaction from family life itself might have to be forfeited. This is a crude way of putting the matter and, because it is stated in hypothetical terms of what might be, it is not very sensible; but it helps to show that the type of family now being focused into view is one which is impaled on a dilemma. For this reason, personal dissatisfaction, personal or interpersonal conflict, and tension abound in it and are among its distinguishing characteristics. Since the stratagem used for securing a spurious ease in regulating the family's corporate life is to feign that the parents' interests are identified with the family when that is not really the case, it can be called the *false-identification type* of family. As its analysis demands the unravelling of ambiguities, greater space must be given to it than to the preceding types. Eleven families of the sample were classed with this type.

The conflict of aims in these families need not have been focused as a conflict *between* the partners. The same state of affairs could eventuate if there was a conflict within one partner or both, and the partners might possibly share the same conflict.[5] There was a suggestion in some cases that it was on the basis of their *shared conflict* that the partners felt affinity and had been attracted to one another. In comparison with the more ordinary, pedestrian people with whom they saw themselves surrounded, they felt themselves to be two of a type who could take a broader view of things and manage to eat their cake and have it. They also found in one another the special sympathy needed to keep their conflict shielded from being challenged, as would have occurred had they associated freely with people otherwise minded.

A husband and wife, for instance, were dedicated to religion and church activity on the one hand and, on the other, shared strong passions for sport and the accumulation of property; and they had desired as well, as if it were natural for two people so like-minded on a variety of issues, to marry and acquire a family. Another couple were devoted to religion but in addition they separately exploited their church activities to obtain expressive gratifications which were scarcely of a religious kind at all. They found in marrying one another a welcome refuge from being severely misunderstood by kinsfolk and acquaintances. A third couple desired to pass an aesthetic style of existence, living rather lawlessly but graciously, enjoying literature, drama, and photography, being sentimentally humanitarian and politically radical; and pictured a home as a decorative setting for these shared diversions. A fourth couple desired wealth, conspicuous success, and much stimulating sociability, and a family to give them standing. In these and all similar cases family life was only faintly and always ambiguously invested with value, and its real importance in relation to other interests was deliberately left unclarified.

So far as one was able to reconstruct its development in these cases, a conflict originally shared by both partners was becoming a conflict between them, owing to the fact that one spouse was partially resolving the conflict by giving greater weight to one alternative, while the opposite alternative was being taken by the partner. In the third example above the confusion of aim resolved itself in the following way. The wife, to her husband's surprise, and for the sake presumably of having some simplified identity, reverted to an earlier religious position which she had held before marriage. It was now much moderated and did not include church affiliation, and became the vehicle for expressing her humanitarianism and desire for gracious living. The desire for gracious living entailed social ambition to improve the family's class status. The father, on the other hand, had elected to concentrate on political radicalism. This entailed atheism and opposition to social ambition, both of which caused acute disagreement with his wife. These matters became the subject of many heated, obessional debates which, however, were only epiphenomenal to the real conflict: the question of which direction the corporate life of the family should take. It was characteristic of the false identification of this family, and of all families of its type, that the real conflict was never recognized as such. It was only alluded to under the guise of the much less threatening, abstract topics, argument about which was bravely declared to be something of a game and even an evidence of intellectual tolerance.

Not sure of himself or the other, because of the confusion of aims, each partner in this type of family felt it imperative to have the family entirely his own way. But there were more means of doing this than by overt dominance. The whole of a family's life could be saturated with stratagems for this purpose: unconscious intonations of the voice implying that only agreement with an expressed opinion would be acceptable, compromising situations, *faits accomplis,* threats and insults and shaming. Thus it came about that in families where the parents' fundamental aims were divided and confused there arose a premium on detailed agreements, an urgent anxiety to force likeness, or a feeling of betrayal if the partner diverged. This contrasted with the latitude parents permitted one another in the identification type of family, where there was a broad community of aim centered in the family itself.

This coercion did not only take the form of one partner suppressing some inclination in the other. Just as frequently, and perhaps at the same time, one would suppress some inclination of his own which would have become too difficult to deal with if admitted. Also there was a practice of mutual consent to suppression which carried something of the sanction of taboo. There were parents who were emphatically agreed about what emotionally disturbing disagreements would not be traversed. By silence, perhaps, one partner would give the other to understand that, so far as he or she was concerned, a certain problem or practice had no existence and would never be alluded to; or, if unguardedly raised, would only be played with till it could be gently dropped. Thus, for example, in one family the bad school behaviour of a child appeared to have resulted from lack of unanimity in the child-training practices of the parents, which in turn resulted from disagreement over whether the family should serve the end of better social standing or the educational cultivation of its members. If either partner was so unfortunate as to mention the bad school behaviour of this child, some well-considered remarks would be made about the relative merits of the different schools from which the child had successively been expelled, until both partners could make their escape with dignity.

Whenever communication was opened in these families it was assumed that one's position had to be defended and one's partner repulsed. There was no real expectation that mutual persuasion could effect a convergence of views, and coercion became the object: rarely did communication invite a free reaction from the person addressed. It carried with it rather a presupposition of agreement and implied that the other person must see things the same way—if he was at all a person of taste, judgement, maturity, humanity, or other such virtue. By emphasis, inflection, or other subtlety the person indicated the presupposition which determined the sort of response that would be acceptable to him. The crudest examples of such presuppositional communication are questions of the kind, 'Have you stopped beating your wife?' An actual example was a remark, charmingly delivered, 'Mother's coming for dinner on *Thursday,* John', the stress on Thursday being all that was needed to imply that the only possible doubt which John might legitimately entertain about mother's coming (or even about mother herself) was on what day she would come. Similar communications about mother, habitually repeated, gave John to understand that there was only one possible attitude or view about his mother-in-law which would be acceptable—that of his wife.

Such cold-war tactics were doubly wounding because they left the person who had suffered violence without excuse for retaliation, there being no declared state of war. To take action would be to appear an unprovoked aggressor and most people's self-respecting sentiments inhibited them from being so unflatteringly compromised. Sometimes, however, the tension became intolerable and they were made to behave in ways they were ashamed of. Much apparently uncaused irritability and spitefulness in this type of family arose from situations like these. The situation worsened if such actions were condemned as reprehensible by the partner who had given cause for them; or if that partner's friends and relatives joined the attack on the basis of their superficial knowledge. There was one husband whose wife was given to this presuppositional kind of communication, who took great pleasure in subduing her spirit by devaluing her domestic achievements. He made out that no job of dusting, polishing, or cleaning was up to standard although, in fact, it was perfectly satisfactory. It was displaced aggression on his part, of course, for the point at which he vented it was removed from the point at which he suffered restriction. That was the question of class aspiration; he being given by his wife to understand that, although it would never be discussed, no attitude to the question of social advancement would be acceptable in him except an ambitiousness comparable to her own. Her relatives despised him for his treatment of so capable a wife.

The tensions generated by attempts to control the family by suppressing differences sought their outlet in restless efforts to extend the boundaries of personal independence. The parents were obsessed with a need to 'get out', 'get away', and 'have a complete break' from the family. Their pressed mentality differed both from the relaxed exercise of independence seen in the parents of the adaptation type of family and from the unthinking acceptance of restriction seen in the parents of the identification type. But this need for more personal freedom was aggravated, since each partner kept a close watch to see that the other did not neglect the family for the sake of personal satisfaction. There were disputes about how much personal freedom each one should take.[6]

A common pattern was for the father to escape into his work, using overbusyness as an excuse for being away from the home; while the mother escaped into some sport, perhaps golf, and might engage in this as often as three days a week. Fathers also might spend time in sport or in hotels or withdraw into their workshops. Some mothers were prone to a compulsion to go to town and 'buy something new', irrespective of whether or not it was needed, just for the sheer 'let down' of it. They would let anything go in the home and change their routine for a chance to get out to a tea-party or a charity function. Some confessed to be completely unable to screw themselves down to a systematic programme of work any longer. One mother developed a habit of elusiveness, going away from the home for short strolls with the children or into neighbours' houses, without informing her husband of her movements. Parents of both sexes in some of the families, and even some of the adolescents, felt a need to spend long periods in reverie, 'just sitting' and doing nothing. For taking any of these liberties they had to put up with a certain amount of reviling and usually felt guilty about it anyway, but felt helplessly driven. It hardly needs to be said that these families took very little shared recreation and that holidays together were either positively avoided or anticipated without relish. It is interesting, however, that a few of them did keep up joint religious observances in the home.

As the parents in these families continued to expect satisfaction from the family in spite of the deterioration in their relations, they were liable to be very discontented. Their dissatisfaction with one another expressed itself most commonly as rejection. One blamed the other for the unsatisfactory state of affairs and for having frustrated his expectations, and consequently refused to support the partner's endeavours or give emotional satisfaction. One of the commonest things these parents alluded to in confiding their disappointment was their sense of loneliness in their own homes. Presumably this had something to do with their hankering for detailed agreements and their failure to reach them. They did not have the knack of remaining companionable in the face of differences which was used by parents of identification-type families, of submitting and being agreeable though not agreeing. To do this was something they felt would involve a sacrifice of integrity.

Whereas in the adaptation type of family parents competed for the children's affection, it was power over their wills the parents sought here. They contrived to win this largely by using the presuppositional communication that has been described, thereby exploiting the suggestibility of the young. They imposed fixed attitudes upon their children as being beyond question and the only ones allowable. On the other hand, correction of a child was often delivered as if the parent were having to rebuke something in himself first, being but weakly convinced about standards. Where there were adolescents in this type of family they were in revolt against the parental oppression. It caused them guilt, presumably because under the hypnosis, as it were, of a parent's stifling influence they had at an earlier stage involuntarily internalized things that they now voluntarily opposed. An adolescent's sudden temper, irritation, and intolerance towards his father or mother indicated that there was something of the parent internalized in him which he rejected, but into the power of which he realized he had been given.

It will now be clear from the account given above that the sample contained certain families where the parents included practically all their activities within the family role, in the sense that those activities were expected of them by the family. At the other extreme there were those families in which the parents agreed to exempt each other from responsibility to the family for a definite section of their lives so that a considerable portion of their activities was carried out quite independently of family expectations. There were others, again, that strove for the former kind of life but lacked what appears to be the necessary condition of having parents who are agreed about their fundamental aims and the place of the family in securing them. We could say that the identification type of family was strongly primary, the adaptation type was scarcely so at all and had little pretension of being, while the false-identification type strove for a primary quality but without success.

Of course, any exact demonstration of role-expectation reinforcement would have to show that family expectations coincide precisely with those arising from other sources, and this study has not done that. It has simply inferred this to be more or less the case whenever the family has adopted its members' external activities for itself. This is because the limitations of the field work confined the writer to an inside view on the families. But if this line of inquiry were to be pushed further, it would be imperative to make some effort to view family members in their external connections as well, unwieldy though the task would be. Meanwhile, however, we have gained access to an important part of the data, and the inferences we have drawn from it might not prove unwarranted in the end.

*Psycho - social*

## III. EXTERNAL CONTROLS ON FAMILY CONDUCT

The recent study of twenty London families reported by Bott (1957) takes a turn of thought which is strikingly complementary to that followed here. Our question in the present study is whether expectations arising internally in the family penetrate into the definition of external roles and reinforce them. Bott was preoccupied with the reverse question of how far expectations arising externally penetrate into the definition of conjugal roles and reinforce these. One sympathizes with Bott when she admits that the crucial data for supporting her final hypothesis are sparse, since the hypothesis only crystallized in the course of the work (ibid., p. 133 fn.).

Bott describes conjugal roles as *segregated* when a husband and wife observe a rigid division of tasks and as *joint* when they exchange and share certain activities. She sees any family to be embedded in a network of external relations and calls the network *close-knit* or *connected* when the people who associate with the family also associate with one another independently, and *loose-knit* when this is not the case. Her work led her to the hypothesis that conjugal role segregation is practised in families which occupy *close-knit* networks.[7] She implies that this occurs because the spouses in that situation are controlled by a number of expectations from outside, all of which are fairly uniform with one another. What ultimately bears in upon them is the approval or disapproval of something like a homogenous culture. The homogeneity is accounted for by the exchange of views occurring in the interaction which their associates have with one another. The acknowledged poverty in the data lies just at this vital point of measuring the degree of outside contact between any family's associates.

All this is plausible, but as an explanation it seems to fall short.

Why should uniform external expectations always impose a standard of role segregation on husband and wife? Why should not joint roles be the agreed norm? On the face of it one can see no reason why there should not be close-knit networks which approve and practise joint conjugal roles. If the writer may take the liberty of interpreting Bott's findings in his own way, therefore, he would prefer to view them somewhat differently. It seems that what she is really demonstrating is the existence in certain cases of sex in-groups. These reinforce male and female in a distinctive conception of themselves and their roles, whether they are at home or away from it. The role-segregation of the sexes within the family goes with sexual segregation outside it. Bott gives evidence for this when she points out that husband and wife in this type of family each have their own separate friends and that they do not engage in either joint recreation away from the home or joint entertaining within it (ibid., pp. 65–70). There thus appears to be a *sharp cleavage by sex right across the network,* so that it can hardly be called connected. Bott claims that it is connected finally through kinship and because the men have wives, the women husbands (ibid., pp. 70, 92–3). But the critical linkage is then left to be made precisely at the point of critical segregation and from this we may infer that the people concerned intend to interrupt it in some way. It is pointed out that an exception is made by having joint social participation with kin. But may we not presume that sexual segregation is observed and actively fostered here? It is as though the sexes can only trust themselves to one another in that family and kinship context where segregation is, one might say, actually being manufactured. Beyond this they keep themselves to their own sex fairly rigidly.

Quite apart from the lack of data on the crucial question of network connectedness, which it would be unfair to press, one wonders whether *general* network connectedness has much to do with the case. It does seem to resolve itself very much into kindship solidarity, in which *milieu* sex role segregation is enforced, as against the lack of this solidarity. And it might be of some significance that only this is treated in detail by the author, the friendship element in networks being passed over very briefly.

In Bott's sample of twenty families, five gave friendship ties definite precedence over those with kin, and all of these occupied loose-knit networks (ibid., p. 76). In the writer's sample of thirty-eight families only four did this and in only one did the friendships stabilize, those of the remainder being seeking relationships rather than firmly reciprocated ones. On the other hand, a considerable number of those who were primarily devoted to kin were able to give a second place to stable friendships. But, although some of these friendships were unshakably established, they usually intruded very little into the parents' current lives. Most commonly, parents had very little time to cultivate friends, but some claimed that if they only saw a certain friend at long intervals they could 'take up where they left off'. In many cases these were old friendships which harked back to the days before marriage— to work, university, or school. They seldom involved the mutual help that went with kinship, and opportunities for sociability were sporadic, but they were valued because they shared with kinship the essentially primary function of confirming the continuity of one's identity. Indeed, because these 'old-friend' relationships were so shorn of other functions, this primary quality stood out with exceptional visibility. It is not suggested, therefore, that friendships can play no important part in reinforcing the segregated definition of conjugal roles which Bott has described. But it is suggested that they probably do so rarely and that when this occurs the friends probably take their cue from the standard of the kindred.

Furthermore, the practical benefits of solidarity with the kinsfolk probably play as important a part as the influence of opinion and approval. Bott makes the point that these spouses are actually assisted to perform a segregated role because they can call on practical help from members of their own sex in a way that is not possible for spouses who play joint roles. Indeed, it is almost as if the segregated roles attached to a man and his wife are the *men's role* and *women's role* as distinct from the *man's* and *woman's*. Man and wife are magnets for concentrating all the effort needed to discharge the male and female functions. But would not a large part of the help attracted, perhaps most of it, be expected to come from kinsfolk? The woman's dependence, for instance, on her mother, and on her sisters where she has them, is well known, and Bott acknowledges this (ibid., p. 69). It might be that the kin group's insistence on the segregated role as proper and standard stems from a need to ensure that all will achieve competence in those matters for which they could be called upon for help.

Another family study to lay stress on the dual controlling and assisting function of the kin group in modern society is that made by Young and Willmott (1957). These authors state that a marked falling-off in neighbouring resulted when a set of people moved from an old congested part of London to a housing estate. This is explained as being due very largely to the diminished kinship admixture in the composition of the new neighbourhood. The loss of ascribed status amongst their kin led to a competitive pursuit of achievement status between neighbours who were strangers to one another and who consequently had the appearance of 'giving themselves airs' (ibid., pp. 121–40). The authors also draw attention to the importance of the help which women sometimes received after marriage from their mothers and possibly their sisters as well, and which they could forfeit through moving (ibid., pp.156–62). They consequently urge that housing authorities show some consideration for the wishes of any who might prefer to continue living with the kin around them when they move out (ibid., pp. 165–6).

From the facts reported in these two studies it seems fairly plain that there is a type of family in modern cities which is strongly governed by kinship expectations; although it is part of the burden of their theme that this occurs in certain families only. Bott further claims that voluntary friendships can contribute to this influence. We might also suppose that the expectations reaching back into the family from these outside sources could concern more than the definition of merely conjugal roles. They might well duplicate for all family members the expectations put upon them by the family itself in many or all departments of their life.

One is led to ask, then, whether role expectations ever reach back into the family from sources other than these. The question would have to be answered by research, and it is a good question for keeping research directed to basic processes. But, meanwhile, a few general observations can assist our thinking.

One point that comes to mind is that public prominence does tend to throw a searching beam backwards into the privacy of a person's family. Whereas the ordinary clerk, labourer, tradesman, and professional person may conduct themselves at home more or less as they please, not so the mayor, bishop, professor, judge, cabinet minister, governor, and king. From those who bear these roles, and from many others scarcely less prominent, a stable respectable family life is usually expected. A bachelor is often at a serious disadvantage in competing for prominent office, and a man who is divorced or separated from his wife or known to be an adulterer or a homosexual may be quietly passed over. Sometimes the office itself seems to demand the auxiliary services of a wife, and the monarchy even demands those of children and other close kin. It is not infrequently observed that formerly disreputable individuals become increasingly respectable with their elevation to high office, because they appreciate that the position requires it. On the other hand, those who are discriminated against because of the nature of their private lives can protest in vain that only the qualifications for the job itself should be considered. Societies have an incorrigible habit of reserving their high offices for those they approve in the round, and this often entails approval of the family that stands behind the man.

But apart from this differential control by public opinion over the families of the publicly prominent, the church would appear to be the only other institutional source of expectations of the kind under discussion.[8] A small number of suitably constituted schools seek to do something of this kind. But government schools, which now claim the vast majority of the children, can do little more than instill some generalized notion of citizenship responsibility. They practise discretion, in fact, in regard to those vital sectors of their charges' lives which are affected by their deep-seated differences in religion, politics, class, and privilege. They have too high a pupil-teacher ratio to show any exhaustive concern with their individual charges' life-situations. As is also the case with roles in the economic, governmental, and recreational institutions, roles assumed in the educational institution do not normally include expectations intended to govern the person's whole conduct.

It seemed fitting to place Bott's study and that of the writer in juxtaposition because the conclusions of both are tentative and invite further research. It appeared to the writer that the questions raised in these studies separately could be profitably explored together and, by extending Bott's treatment of conjugal roles to family roles in general, as part of a more comprehensive problem. It seems desirable to study, as a general phenomenon, role-expectation reinforcement, and, in the present connection, to study it as it affects all family members and as it occurs in either direction. The significant question for testing is whether families that confer cardinal roles on their members occupy networks that reinforce those roles, or whether families can confer cardinal roles without such support.

## IV. THE UNITY ATTAINED THROUGH THE CARDINAL ROLE

It remains to notice in precisely what sense a cardinal role makes a unity out of the set of roles which an individual carries, and then to examine whether there is any connection between this integration and that postulated by Mead. It must be fairly obvious that the unity of the cardinal role is basically one of accountability, in that the individual is made accountable to one enduring group for all his actions, whether they be discharged within its presence or in other social contexts. But the converse of this is that it is in some sense a unity of manageability. This small group's circle, with reasonably manageable dimensions, becomes his effectual world. His actual world is much larger and, in a complex urban society, quite transcends both his comprehension and his appreciable influence. If an individual's integration rested solely and simply on internalizing through sympathy the whole order of society in the way Mead depicts, no citizen of a modern nation could experience it, because he cannot know the whole order. But in a primary group the members can telescope in their persons whatever segments of the whole society are selected for each of them to enter, thus creating a microcosmic but comprehensible order for themselves from the untrackable vastness. This much can be known by them, and they can identify sympathetically with those parts of society which thus penetrate into their own group organization. It is probably through the agency of a family with this primary quality that an individual makes the nearest approach possible in modern society to internalizing the whole order of society. But it is essentially schematic and fragmentary and may be quite distorted, even though sufficient to give him some sense of bearings.

This itself causes us to question whether it is the order of the *whole* society that has to be internalized for integration *in any circumstances*. Might it not simply be the order of that primary group to which one admits complete accountability, an order that will be fairly simple, even though the group itself has windows on a thronging world? In the situation where the society is small and homogeneous this primary group can extend well beyond the immediate family; but, even so, there is a well-known tendency in such societies for the family relationship to supply the paradigm for others. Kinship becomes the kernel of the social system and those who do not belong to the kin by birth can be classified with them. Kinship can be understood as a system which simply stretches the family pattern of the seven-pointed star over a bigger area; the star whose centre is ego and whose apices father, mother, sister, brother, spouse, son, and daughter. Every person within it is in a relationship with ego which, however it is named, is father-like, mother-like, sister-like, brother-like, spouse-like, son-like, or daughter-like.

*Moreover, the system thus defined is made for ego, not for the society.* The immense significance of this scarcely dawns on anyone other than the field anthropologist. *Nobody* is one thing and one only in regard to a total scheme; he is, perhaps, father to some, son to others, brother to yet others, uncle to others again. But *everyone* can be one specific thing to ego, according to their distance from him in simple vertical or lateral steps by generation and sex. The kinship network is a scheme made to organize the society around the individual rather than to organize him into it; he is only organized by it, into society at large, by being placed at many different depths by individuals whose depth from him varies. Every individual takes over the same scheme, but applies it to the same set of people from a different point of vantage, for his own need. The individual thus internalizes a simple, highly schematic order.

In the case of complex societies the situation may not be as different, in essentials, as is commonly supposed, so far as the individual's self-placement is concerned. We have seen that the kin group may well be maintained in constant association with the family. In addition, the family may keep up firm friendships, and that such friends can function for moderns as adopted or classificatory kin is at least suggested by practices such as having one's children call a friend 'aunt' or 'uncle' and expressing appreciation in terms of a friend's being 'just like one's own brother.' It is also significant that the role reinforcement of the modern church is made very largely in family terms. One is made a classificatory brother, under the one Father, to all with whom he has to do. The Roman Catholic church uses family titles liberally—father, brother, mother, sister—to define pastoral responsibilities. Thus it would appear that those agencies which are available in modern societies, over and above the family, for reinforcing a person's total-role definition tend to utilize a family schema. No less than in primitive societies the individual internalizes a schematic order. It might be, then, that it is the internalization of this role order of the family which is critical for role-integration rather than the order of society as a whole. Any area of social life which is larger than the actual family is made meaningful by extending a family pattern to it and/or by adopting elements from it into the family itself through the role commitments of its members. And, finally, in its most condensed form, the schema internalized is not even a seven-pointed star, but a two-sided balance: parent and child. To be father or son (alternatively mother or daughter) is to summarize all that one is at that stage of life, while to be bound in the two-generation union is to embrace the known world.

If what we are proposing is true, it might also throw light on the general public interest in the family situation of prominent persons. If the family situation of these persons is satisfactory, it will not only indicate a certain degree of integration and responsibility in them, and readiness to set a standard in family conduct by bearing home whatever transpires with them abroad. It may also be taken as an indication of their preparedness to view their whole social field under a familial paradigm, thus acting towards all with something like a paternal, filial, husbandly, or brotherly responsibility and thereby helping to bind together the public at large and infect them with the same spirit. The kinship systems of simple peoples are not dissimilar to this in their function. For they are not concerned with establishing biological connection so much as with prescribing social responsibilities.

Earlier it was deduced that the role-integration which Mead was describing is a three-sided one of social organization, common purpose, and altruistic principle. Individuals experience role-integration as they devote themselves to and realize a degree of group organization. This they do by opting for a common purpose in preference to individual ones and governing their conduct by consistent principles to achieve it. Although we have rejected the suggestion that an individual's role-integration depends upon his perceived place in the total society, we can still ask whether this triple requirement applies to his place in the family.

By devoting themselves to family membership as a goal, parents in identification-type families thought and acted, in effect, *as if they were the family itself*. Even though they observed a marked division of labour and authority, they were approaching the condition of having *global identities* which were identical with one another. Many differences could be allowed between them when each one's identity included the other's roles. This may explain why status difference between partners, where it was upheld, was acceptable in this type of family. In certain families in the sample the husband was ranked above the wife, on principle and by consent, as the head of the family; and all families with that form of control were of the identification type. (Although it was not the case that all identification-type families used that form of control.) It was rare for any of the wives concerned to show evidence of constriction or resentment because of having a subordinate place.[9]

Identical identity can possibly also explain the occurrence of exchange of roles in these families. Some of the sample families held the outlines of their roles rigidly fixed and sought to make sex differences conspicuous, whereas others allowed elasticity to roles and kept sex differences subdued. This lack of fixity in role differentiation is a different thing from lack of definition in roles, as it is also different again from the joint role to which Bott draws attention. Roles can be quite clearly defined as belonging to husband or wife, but one partner will occasionally take over the other's role without self-consciousness, yet quite without confusion, still realizing that it is the other person's part he is playing. It was only in families of the identification type that this elasticity occurred.

In these families, love, marriage, and the family itself were mainly conceived in terms of a task of embracing others in membership. Some of the members preferred to suffer hurt rather than lose, or allow another to lose, position and support in the family. Besides giving them a cardinal role, this afforded them opportunity for personality unravelling if that were needed; for if in spite of fault one could be held in membership, catharsis could proceed. They could count on the support and permissiveness that are two of its conditions.[10]

The members of these families were scarcely remarkable for their freedom from fault. Some were eccentric or trying or psychologically very ignorant; some had to be handled with great humour and tact. But they were remarkable for their attitude to fault in others in not being offended by it and in making allowance for it. Conceiving of happiness in terms of self-forgetfulness in securely rooted membership, they seemed unwilling that anyone's personal faults should jeopardize the common chance of finding it. They frequently exhibited spontaneity, in a way seldom observed in the members of other families. Perhaps it was because they fastened their attention and devotion to a frame of reference larger than themselves. At any rate, to do that was a *principle* with them; and by it they held themselves to the *common purpose* of *family organization*. Thus the three-sided requirement was fulfilled. The kind of integration Mead has described appears to be realizable, then, through a primary group cardinal role. It was as though these people had chosen a course of action which satisfied individual needs *by virtue of* its social constructiveness.

The neglect in the other types of family of a principled pursuit of membership, of membership values as it might be called, had one fairly consistent result. It led to a revolt in favour of membership values on the part of adolescents in most of those families which included children at that phase. These young people felt dissatisfied with, betrayed by, or contemptuous of their parents' carelessness about membership, and accordingly brought a condemnatory judgement on their standards. A father's exclusive involvement in his work with neglect of his family, or the same kind of result stemming from parents' engrossment in politics, books, sport, property, money, practical matters, or business affairs—all these provoked value reactions towards membership. Accepting infallible guidance, apparently, from nothing more than an inward starvation, these adolescents decided that the authentic gratifications of life were being by-passed at home and they turned elsewhere to find them—in religion, through literature, in the world of imagination, or in intense peer group involvements. To many observers the families concerned would have seemed satisfactory enough, even perhaps distinguished; but to their own sons and daughters they were unspeakably barren. Families which had failed to clothe the parents with a cardinal role had left the children exposed with the same nakedness. They fled for cover. But their problem was to find a refuge that would take to its heart, along with the rest, that considerable part of their lives which belonged to the home they rejected.

## V. A POSTSCRIPT

Critics of this work have accused the writer of 'knowing which of the family types he prefers,' meaning thereby to impugn his scientific integrity. The writer's reply is that he would be perverse if he did not,

I

since he has studied families to clarify some of the standards intrinsic in their operation, the better to measure them. But the writer has not passed any private judgement on the families. It would be out of place to do that—on these or any other sociological data. Not because the stuff of social behaviour is morally indifferent, but simply because it is so morally transparent that it judges itself. The good sociologist is like the good novelist and dramatist. He draws his cases with impartiality, not because there is nothing to choose between them but because, thus drawn, they vindicate or condemn themselves.

In the writer's opinion, the boot is on the other foot in this matter of scientific integrity. It is those who deny that moral discriminations are germane to sociology who err. Their scientific capacity is seriously impaired. The dread of being thought unscientific if caught meddling with values has caused some to shrink from handling that whole area of life which is concerned with value and principle—but that is society itself. The result is a tendency to stop at explanations of social behaviour which are mainly psychological, or even circumstantial or ecological; or at descriptions which are merely formal.

It is scarcely surprising that such accounts are commonly found to be inadequate, and the inevitable rider about hoping for something better from further work is more than usually unconsoling in such contexts. There is the grim possibility that the work may proceed on the same line and bring us no nearer to genuine understanding. Genuine sociological inquiry accepts the challenge of explaining, on its own terms, that department of life which begs to be governed by rule and principle because it takes place *between* people; and it recognizes all the options and dilemmas, successes and failures, that can be encountered there.

# NOTES

1. When Mead says here that the generalized other 'represents the organized responses of all the members of the group,' I wrest from his obscure words the interpretation that it is unanimous responses affirming the subordination of the individual's efforts to the group's purpose that are intended.
2. Erikson's treatment of personality integration is an important one, but it is not conceived in the sociological terms of role organization and therefore lies outside the present discussion. Ego-identity, as Erikson sees it, results from an inner feeling of continuity and sameness which is matched by a sameness and continuity in one's social meaning to others. It is achieved by a growth during which the individual successively masters certain positive attitudes to life in preference to the negative alternative presented at each stage. It begins, for example, with the triumph of trust over mistrust and culminates with the triumph of integrity over disgust and despair: see Erikson (1948, 1950).
3. Compare Parsons's definition of role (Parsons, 1951, pp. 38–40).
4. Since participation in the study was voluntary the sample was virtually self-elected, as is the case in many sociological studies. No importance therefore is attached to the number of cases of each of the types.

5. The conflict to which attention is here drawn is one of aims or values and should be clearly distinguished from the conflict recognized in psycho-analysis, which is one between inclination and principle and one which usually carries implications of repression, in that the inclination tends to be denied conscious recognition because it would be disturbing. Value-conflict, on the other hand, is more like that state commonly characterized as 'trying to serve two masters'. The individual aims simultaneously for incompatible ends. Value-conflict can develop a feature which is analogous to repression, although still distinct. In the state referred to, the individual recognizes the existence of his multiple objectives honestly enough, but deliberately leaves unclarified the question of their compatibility. It should also be recognized that being in a state of value-conflict can entail the psycho-analytical kind of conflict, even though it is a different thing.

6. The isolation of the family types under discussion lends support to Lewin's hypothesis that 'an insufficient space of free movement leads to tension' (Lewin, 1948, p. 93). In the adaptation and identification types of family, respectively, the parents find their space of free movement in external activities and their domains of authority within the family, and tension is low. In the false-identification type opportunity for free movement in both these ways is deficient, and tension is high. But it is also possible to think of the question the other way about, noticing how the need for space of free movement varies. The need is higher in the false-identification type of family, where tension exists owing to the attempt to pursue conflicting values in a state of association; and it is lower in the identification type of family, where like values are being pursued.

7. It is interesting to notice that, although in this study sociological and psychological concepts are said to have been used simultaneously at every stage of the analysis, Bott's important thesis turns in the end on the relationship between these purely sociological factors. Sciences isolate distinct dimensions of reality and seek to explain phenomena by connections within a dimension rather than by connections between one dimension and another. The latter type of reductionist explanation is by no means worthless, but it is not intellectually satisfying or even practically useful in the same way as the former. To rest content with psychological or ecological explanations, for example, of sociological phenomena is virtually to abdicate from sociology. Only confusion can result from allowing oneself to be overwhelmed by the undeniable fact that any single phenomenon has multiple causes on receding planes. Perhaps because the project was designed as interdisciplinary, Bott herself sometimes comes close to being bogged down in this confusion; for example, when she breaks down the influences affecting the relationships of three families with their kin into economic, geographic, sociological, and psychological factors (ibid., pp. 118–58). That complexity is known and could almost have been taken for granted. Interdisciplinary studies seem ill-conceived if they produce merely reductionist explanations. They are well-conceived if they place the insights of different disciplines side by side without loss of distinctiveness.

8. On the point of whether groups with a real primary quality occur more widely, it is of course acknowledged that such groups have been identified in industry, the army, and elsewhere. Groups of this kind in the Services make a special case, since the individual's customary ties are there forcibly severed. But it seems still a question for research whether the other groups referred to commonly meet the requirements postulated here of a primary group. However, it is not implied here, simply because this study is concerned with the family that other agencies than the family cannot supply a cardinal role.

9. This function of sympathy or vicarious identification in making status differences tolerable is something which some psychologists have failed to appreciate. See, e.g., M. Sherif and M. Wilson (1953, p. 174). Faris, in writing

there, even suggests that status differences in primary groups place a strain on the sympathetic basis of relations; but the writer's observations suggest that a reverse influence may obtain, and that a sympathetic basis to relations can be the condition which makes status differences agreeable.

10. Parsons has given support and permission, along with non-reciprocation of distorted expectations and the inducement of sanctions for acceptable behaviour, as the essential elements of psychotherapy; and has argued that these correctives are inherent in social institutions themselves (Parsons, 1951, pp. 297–320). Certain families of the other types failed to supply these conditions because the faults of one or several members had become permanent offences to the others, and were no longer patiently borne.


# REFERENCES

1. BARNARD, C. I. (1938). *The functions of the executive.* Cambridge, Mass.: Harvard University Press.
2. BOTT, ELIZABETH (1957). *Family and social network: roles, norms and external relationships in ordinary urban families.* London: Tavistock Publications.
3. BROOM, L. & SELZNICK, P. (1958). *Sociology.* Evanston, Ill.: Row, Peterson.
4. COOLEY, C. H. (1916). *Social organization: a study of the larger mind.* New York: Charles Scribner's Sons.
5. ERIKSON, E. H. (1948). Childhood and tradition in two American Indian tribes. In C. Kluckhohn and H. A. Murray (Eds.), *Personality in nature, society and culture.* New York: Knopf.
6. ERIKSON, E. H. (1950). *Childhood and society.* New York: Norton; London: Imago Publishing Co.
7. FALLDING, H. (1956). *Aspects of Australian family structure: a field study of a sample of urban families.* Unpublished Doctor of Philosophy thesis, Australian National University, Canberra.
8. FALLDING, H. (1957). Inside the Australian family. In A. P. Elkin (Ed.), *Marriage and the family in Australia.* Sydney: Angus & Robertson.
9. FARIS, E. (1932). The primary group, essence and accident. *Amer. J. Sociol.* 38, No. 1.
10. FARIS, E. (1953). In M. Sherif & M. Wilson (Eds.), *Group relations at the crossroads.* New York: Harper Bros.
11. LEWIN, K. (1948). *Resolving social conflicts: selected papers on group dynamics.* New York: Harper Bros.
12. LINTON, R. (1945). *The cultural background of personality.* New York: Appleton-Century; London: Kegan Paul, Trench, Trubner & Co., 1947.
13. MEAD, G. H. (1937). *Mind, self and society from the standpoint of a social behaviorist.* Chicago: University of Chicago Press.
14. NADEL, S. F. (1957). *The theory of social structure.* Melbourne: Melbourne University Press.
15. PARSONS, T. (1951). *The social system.* Glencoe, Ill.: The Free Press; London: Tavistock Publications, 1952.
16. SHERIF, M. & WILSON, M. (Eds.) (1953). *Group relations at the crossroads.* New York: Harper Bros.
17. YOUNG, M. & WILLMOTT, P. (1957). *Family and kinship in East London.* London: Routledge & Kegan Paul.

# Part V

## THE FAMILY AS A UNIVERSE OF COGNITION AND COMMUNICATION

Cognitive activities—perceiving, attending, knowing, thinking, communicating—are a significant part of man's resources for organizing his life, directing his activities, and solving the problems that confront him. Cognitive activities have interested anthropology, psychology, psychiatry, and sociology, as well as philosophy and linguistics, a field that cuts across anthropology and the humanities.

Anthropology, in an earlier era, was interested in the evolution of thinking processes from what it regarded as the pre-logical thinking of primitive peoples to the higher forms of thinking which supposedly characterize developed societies such as our own. This definition seems now largely discarded as incorrect or at least inadequate. Anthropologists today are more interested in what has come to be known as the Whorfian hypothesis, a view expounded by Benjamin Lee Whorf. He holds that thinking is shaped by language and that a language reveals basic trends in the culture of those who speak it:

". . . the background linguistic system (in other words, the grammar) of each language is not merely a reproducing instrument for voicing ideas but rather is itself the shaper of ideas, the program and guide for the individual's mental activity, for his analysis of impressions, for his synthesis of his mental stock in trade . . . We dissect nature along lines laid down by our native languages. The categories and types that we isolate from the world of phenomena we do not find there because they stare every observer in the face; on the contrary, the world is presented in a kaleidoscopic flux of impressions which has to be organized by our minds—and this means largely by the linguistic systems in our minds. We cut nature up, organize it into concepts, and ascribe significances as we do, largely because we are parties to an agreement to organize it in this way—an agreement that holds throughout our

247

speech community and is codified in the patterns of our language. The agreement is, of course, an implicit and unstated one, BUT ITS TERMS ARE ABSOLUTELY OBLIGATORY; we cannot talk at all except by subscribing to the organization and classification of data which the agreement decrees."[1]

This hypothesis is considered by anthropologists not verified but important and worthy of detailed study. Some idea of the complexities of the task can be gained from a set of papers and discussions devoted to the problems posed by Whorf's hypothesis.[2]

Any given language embodies a set of rules for framing communications. Perhaps also, as Whorf proposes, it shapes thought itself. Yet it is quite clear that, however significant language is in shaping thought, it is not the sole factor. Although a language does change and develop, the ideas prevalent in a community change independently of language. It seems doubtful, for example, that in the last 25 years there has been as much change in the English language as in the ideas current in the English-speaking world. Thus, while a language provides a framework and rules for expressing thoughts, it does not dictate what will be thought, even though it may be influential. The same language can be and is used differently by different individuals and groups. Thinking is, in part, a group process. Experimental social psychology has demonstrated in the laboratory that individual judgments converge through interaction. Even earlier, however, sociology had been proposing a social explanation of thinking. For example, Karl Mannheim wrote:

". . . the sociology of knowledge seeks to comprehend thought in the concrete setting of an historical-social situation out of which individually differentiated thought only very gradually emerges. Thus, it is not men in general who think, or even isolated individuals who do the thinking, but men in certain groups who have developed a particular style of thought in an endless series of responses to certain typical situations characterizing their common position.
". . . The second feature characterizing the method of the sociology of knowledge is that it does not sever the concretely existing modes of thought from the context of collective action . . . Men living in groups do not merely co-exist physically as discrete individuals . . . On the contrary they act with and against one another in diversely organized groups, and while doing so they think with and against one another . . ."[3]

Here, Mannheim views thinking as part of the process of social action. He was writing primarily of political groups, but this viewpoint seems no less applicable to families; in these, too, members act with and against one another and think with and against one another.

Neither language nor social structure nor group dynamics suffice singly or in combination to account for cognitive processes, for these shapers of thought do not affect all persons in the same ways. Psychiatry has long been concerned with individual variations in cognitive functioning. Perhaps the most dramatic variation is found in the patient diagnosed as hebephrenic schizophrenic who does not use language according to any accepted rules but speaks in a way that is termed by the psychiatrist "word salad." Profound disturbances in perceiving, attending, thinking, and communicating are among the defining characteristics of mental illness, and as such have been of concern to psychiatry and psychology.[4]

These various strands of scientific thought are now being brought to bear in the study of whole families. The first article in this section, by Jay Haley, seeks to understand the behavior of the schizophrenic patient as part of a distinctive style of communication characterizing the patient's family. The key concept in Haley's analysis is that communication always occurs on two levels: the level of something said and the level of qualifying what is said. The latter might be called the modality in which something is said, indicating how it should be received (for example, as a joke, as a statement of fact, as a command, etc.). He finds that schizophrenic families develop systematic rules for qualifying what is said. Specifically, they systematically disqualify their own statements and those of the other family members. Haley suggests that "psychotic behavior is a sequence of messages which infringe a set of prohibitions but which are qualified as not infringing them." His observations and analysis point to a subtle system of entanglement in the family of the schizophrenic.

The next article, by Theodore Lidz and his colleagues, is also concerned with how families of schizophrenic patients shape the deviant thought processes that show up in the mental illness. Their presentation focuses on the kinds of ideas and beliefs held by the parents of the patient. Characteristically, these parents maintained very rigid and unrealistic notions about themselves, their children, and their situations. Paranoid suspicions and delusions were common. These parents were often impervious to communications from their children and unable to respond to them except in ways that would sustain their own systems of self-protectiveness. Children who become schizophrenic, according to the hypothesis of the Lidz group, "are prone to withdraw through altering their internal representations of reality because they have been reared amidst irrationality and intrafamilial systems of communication that distort or deny instrumentally valid interpretations of the environment." This type of analysis does not treat communication as a self-contained system of behavior but attempts to view communication in the context of motivation and symbolic processes conceived more broadly. Communication, perception, thinking, and fantasy are considered interrelated components or aspects of experience and behavior. Lidz and his collaborators are interested in content as well as form—in what is in the mind as well as how it is organized and communicated.

For some time, most psychology has not been interested in mental content—what people think as distinguished from how they think.[5] Social psychology provides a partial exception, since one of its tasks has been relating political ideas and beliefs to personality and group membership factors. The third article in this section, by Else Frenkel-Brunswik, while part of this body of work in social psychology, is somewhat atypical in its attention to the whole family as the context for development of social beliefs. The author combines the techniques and interests of clinical psychology and social psychology to understand the relationship between personality and interpersonal relations in the family on one hand and, on the other, various social beliefs such as those relating to minority groups. She describes an authoritarian family and an equalitarian family, and shows that differences between the two are quite pervasive. While she examines attitudes toward a variety of social phenomena, she also notes differences in basic outlook that account in part for some of the more specific differences. The authoritarian family is generally less open to experience than is the equalitarian family, and thus these cases provide another example of the boundary-setting phenomenon in families.

## NOTES

1. Benjamin Lee Whorf, *Language, Thought and Reality*. Selected Writings of Benjamin Lee Whorf, edited and with an Introduction by John B. Carroll (Cambridge: Technology Press of Massachusetts Institute of Technology; New York: John Wiley, 1956), pp. 212–14.
2. Harry Hoijer (ed.), *Language in Culture; Conference on the Interrelations of Language and Other Aspects of Culture* (Chicago: University of Chicago Press, 1954).
3. Karl Mannheim, *Ideology and Utopia; An Introduction to the Sociology of Knowledge*. First published 1936 (New York: Harcourt, Brace and World, Harvest Books, n.d.).
4. A sketch of a theory of thinking from the viewpoint of a clinical psychologist is offered by David Rapoport, "Toward a Theory of Thinking," Part VII of *Organization and Pathology of Thought*, edited by David Rapoport (New York: Columbia University Press, 1951). Various types of neurotic thinking are described in David Shapiro, *Neurotic Styles* (New York: Basic Books, 1965).
5. This disinterest is discussed by David C. McClelland, "The Psychology of Mental Content Reconsidered," *Psychological Review*, Vol. 62, pp. 297–302, 1955, reprinted in E. P. Hollander and Raymond G. Hunt (eds.) *Current Perspectives in Social Psychology* (New York: Oxford University Press, 1963), pp. 48–54. McClelland's article is useful but one-sided, and is balanced by Edmund H. Volkart, "Social Behavior and the Defined Situation," in Edmund H. Volkart (ed.), *Social Behavior and Personality; Contributions of W. I. Thomas to Theory and Social Research* (New York: Social Science Research Council, 1951).

# 14:

# The Family of the Schizophrenic: A Model System[1]

*Jay Haley*

This paper will attempt to show that schizophrenic behavior serves a function within a particular kind of family organization. The emphasis in this description will be on the interactive behavior of the schizophrenic and his parents rather than on their ideas, beliefs, attitudes, or psychodynamic conflicts. This work is largely based on an examination of a small sample of families participating in therapeutic sessions where parents and schizophrenic child, as well as siblings, are seen together and recorded. An excerpt from a recording of a family session will be presented and analyzed in terms of the observable behavior of family members, to illustrate the hypothesis that the family of the schizophrenic is a special kind of system which can be differentiated from other family systems.

The hypothesis that schizophrenia is of family origin has led to a number of investigations of schizophrenic patients and their parents. These studies include both impressions of family members and attempts at statistical measurement of individual traits of parents or the conflict between them. Typically the mother of the schizophrenic is described as dominating, overprotective, manipulative of the child and father, and also overtly rejecting (18). The father is usually described as weak and passive, holding aloof from the patient (15, 17), and occasionally overtly rejecting and cruel (8). Many investigators mention a certain percentage of fathers or mothers who appear "normal."

Besides reporting descriptions of the individuals in the family, investigators report on the relationship between the parents on the assumption that conflict between father and mother could be related to disturbance in the child. Lidz and Lidz (13) reported in 1949 that 20 of 35 schizophrenic patients had parents who were clearly incompatible. Tietze (20) reported in the same year that 13 of 25 mothers of schizophrenic patients reported unhappy marriages and nine marriages which were described as "perfect" were found by the investigator to be otherwise. In

Reprinted by permission from *Journal of Nervous and Mental Disease*, Vol. 129, No. 4, pp. 357–74. Copyright © 1959, The Williams & Wilkins Company, Baltimore, Maryland 21202, U.S.A. Jay Haley is identified in the footnote to Chapter 4.

I*

1950 Gerard and Siegal (7) found strife between 87 per cent of the parents of 71 male schizophrenic patients in contrast to 13 per cent found in the controls. In the same year Reichard and Tillman (17) noted the unhappy marriages of parents of schizophrenics. Frazee (8) in 1953 reported that 14 of 23 parents were in severe conflict with each other and none had only moderate conflict in contrast to 13 control parents who had only moderate conflict. Lidz (16) reported in 1957 that all of 14 families of schizophrenic patients contained marital relationships which were seriously disturbed. Bowen (6) describes the parents in this type of family as experiencing "emotional divorce." Wynne uses the term "pseudo mutuality" to describe the difficulties family members have with each other (23).

These studies provide strong evidence for conflict between the parents of schizophrenics, but do not clarify what strife between parents has to do with schizophrenia in a child. After all, there is conflict between parents who do not have schizophrenic children. Similarly, to show that the mothers of schizophrenic patients are dominating and overprotective and the fathers weak and passive does not clarify how schizophrenia is appropriate in families with such parents. Psychiatric terminology seems particularly unsuited to this problem. The language of psychiatry either describes the processes within an individual, such as his needs, fantasies, anxieties, and so on, or provides static descriptions of two individuals in dominant-submissive or rejecting or dependent relationships. When schizophrenia is described in the traditional psychiatric way, and when other family members are seen with the biased emphasis upon the processes in the individual, it is difficult to relate schizophrenia to a family.

Currently most groups investigating schizophrenia and the family are recognizing that the total family unit is pathogenic, and there are attempts to develop a language which will describe the interaction of three or more people. A transition would seem to have taken place in the study of schizophrenia; from the early idea that the difficulty in these families was caused by the schizophrenic member, to the idea that they contained a pathogenic mother, to the discovery that the father was inadequate, to the current emphasis upon all three family members involved in a pathological system of interaction. Although it would seem impossible at this time to provide a satisfactory language for describing the complex interaction of three or more people, this paper will suggest a rudimentary approach to such a descriptive system. An essential requirement of any such description is that it show the adaptive function of schizophrenic behavior within the family system.

The present paper is a product of the current research conducted by the Bateson project. Historically this project began as a general investigation of the nature of communication and began to focus on the communication of the schizophrenics in 1953. The observation that the schizophrenic consistently mislabels his communication led Bateson to deduce that he must have been raised in a learning situation where he was faced with conflicting levels of message. From this came the "double bind" hypothesis (5) which was put together with Jackson's emphasis on schizophrenia serving a homeostatic function in the family (12). The research project then brought together the families of schizophrenics to observe the actual behavior in the family. Basically the double bind hypothesis was a statement about two-person interaction and it has been extended to areas outside of schizophrenia (9, 11). When the family was seen as an interactive unit, there was an attempt to extend the double bind concept to a three person system (21). Currently the project is attempting to devise a theoretical system for describing the family as a unit and this attempt had led to several papers (2, 3, 4) including this one.

The importance of describing a total system rather than elements within it may explain some of the inconsistencies in the description of individuals in the family and conflict between them. For example, it is possible that a mother could show rejecting traits when her child is ill and dependent upon her, and overprotective traits when he begins to recover and attempt to achieve independence from her. Similarly, parents may not show discord when their child is psychotic and they are drawn together by this burden, but conflict could appear should the child behave more assertively and so threaten to leave them. Alanen (1) studied mothers of schizophrenic patients and found many of them within the limits of the "normal" on the basis of Rorschach tests and individual interview. He mentions, almost in passing, "Some of the cases in which the mother of a schizophrenic patient had been relatively healthy belong to those in which the father was seriously disturbed. The wives of all fathers who had developed chronic psychosis belong, for example, to this category." If the 'normality' or the pathology of a family member depends upon the influence of the behavior of other family members at that time, only a study of the total family system will show consistent findings.

The focus of a family study should be on the total family and on the interaction of parents and children *with each other* rather than on the interaction of family members with interviewers or testers. What a family member reports to an investigator about his relationship with another family member is only hearsay evidence of what actually takes place. To study the system of interaction in the family of the schizophrenic it is necessary to bring family members together over a period of time and directly observe them relating to one another. Inevitably the fact of observing the family introduces a bias into the data for they may behave differently when observed than when not observed. It would seem to be impossible to leave the observer out of this sort of study, and the problem is to include him in the situation in such a way as to maximize the information he can gain. The most appropriate type of observation would seem to be in a therapeutic context. There is serious doubt as to whether this type of family can be brought together without therapeutic support. If the parents are merely asked to be observed interacting with their schizophrenic child, the question is automatically raised whether they have something to do with the illness of the child; accordingly guilts and defenses are aroused and must be dealt with in the situation. Long term observation of the family is also necessary since they may give one impression in a single interview and quite another when they have talked together many times and pretenses are dropping. The presence of a therapist is necessary as sensitive areas in the relationships are touched upon when family members get more intensively involved with one another. Long-term observation also provides an opportunity to verify hypotheses and make predictions as family patterns are observed occurring again and again. Finally, the introduction of a therapist makes possible the observation of a family responding to planned intervention. As ideas are presented to the family, or as therapeutic change is threatened, the family can be observed maintaining their system under stress.

Although the expense of regular filming of therapy sessions is prohibitive, the occasional use of film and the constant use of tape recordings provides data which may be studied at leisure.


## AN ILLUSTRATION OF FAMILY BEHAVIOR

Since few investigators have the opportunity to observe a schizophrenic and his parents interacting with one another, an illustration is offered here. The following excerpt is transcribed verbatim from a recording of an interview where a patient and his parents were seen weekly as an adjunct to his individual therapy, because of his previous inability to see his parents for even a few minutes without an anxiety attack. The patient, a thirty-nine-year-old man, suffered a breakdown in the army and was diagnosed as a schizophrenic. After discharge he returned home and remained with his parents for the following ten years. There were several abortive attempts to leave home and go to work. He was employed for little more than a year during those ten years and was supported by his parents during his temporary absences from home. When he entered the hospital, at the insistence of his parents, he was hallucinating, behaving in a compulsive way, exhibiting bizarre mannerisms, and complaining of anxiety and helplessness.

Earlier in the interview the patient had been saying he felt he was

afraid of his mother, and finally she brought out a Mother's Day Card she
had just received from him. It was a commercial card with the printed
inscription, "For someone who has been like a mother to me." The patient said he could see nothing wrong with the card nor understand why
his mother was disturbed about receiving it.

*Patient:* Uh, read the outside again.

*Mother:* All right, the outside says, "On Mother's Day, with best wishes"—
everything is very fine, it's wonderful, but it's for someone else, not for your
mother, you see? "For someone who's *been* like a mother to me."

*Father:* In other words, this card made mother think. So mother asked
me . . .

*Mother:* (interrupting) When you . . .

*Father:* (continuing) what I think about it. So I said, "Well, don't think
Simon—meant that way, maybe he . . .

*Patient:* (interrupting) Well, I mean you can interpret it, uh—uh, you've
been like a mother is uh supposed to be.

*Father:* No, no.

*Patient:* (continuing) a good—a real good mother.

*Therapist:* Why don't you like the idea that he might have deliberately
sent that?

*Father:* Deliberately? Well . . .

*Mother:* (overlapping and interrupting) Well, that's what I . . .

*Father:* (continuing) well, he says he didn't, he agrees . . .

*Mother:* (continuing) Well, I mean I believe our son would have . . .

*Father:* (overlapping and continuing) that he couldn't get another card.

*Patient:* (interrupting) Well, I meant to sting you just a tiny bit by that
outside phrase.

*Mother:* (overlapping) You see I'm a little bit of a psychiatrist too,
Simon, I happen to be—(laughing) So I felt so—when you talked to (the
therapist) I brought along that card—I wanted to know what's behind your
head. And I wanted to know—or you made it on purposely to hurt me—Well,
if you did, I—I . . .

*Patient:* (interrupting) Not entirely, not entire . . .

*Mother:* (interrupting and overlapping) I'll take all—Simon, believe me,
I'll take all the hurt in the world if it will help you—you see what I mean?

*Therapist:* How can you . . .

*Mother:* (continuing) Because I never meant to hurt you—Huh?

*Therapist:* How can you hurt anybody who is perfectly willing to be hurt?
(short pause)

*Father:* What's that?

*Mother:* I uh—a mother sacrifices—if you would be—maybe a mother
you would know too. Because a mother is just a martyr, she's sacrificing—
like even with Jesus with his mother—she sacrificed too. So that's the way it
goes on, a mother takes over anything what she can help . . .

*Therapist:* (interrupting) What mother?

*Mother:* (continuing) her children.

*Patient:* (interrupting and overlapping) Well, uh, I'll tell you Ma—listen,
Ma, I didn't mean to—to sting you exactly that outside part there.

*Therapist:* Well, you said so.

*Patient:* Oh, all right, but it—it wasn't that exactly. No, I'm not giving ground—uh—it's hard to explain this thing. Uh—uh—What was I going to say. Now I forgot what I was going to say. (short pause) I mean I felt that this—this is what I mean, uh—that I felt that you could have been a better mother to me than you were. See there were things.

*Mother:* Uh . . .

*Father:* Well you said . . .

*Patient:* (interrupting) You could have been better than you were. So that's why—that's that—I felt—it was, uh—uh, was all right to send it that way.

*Mother:* Well, if you meant it that way that's perf—that's what I wanted to know—and that's all I care—you see. But I still say, Simon, that if you would take your father and mother just like they're plain people—you just came here and you went through life like anybody else went through—and—and don't keep on picking on them and picking them to pieces—but just leave them alone—and go along with them the way they are—and don't change them —you'll be able to get along with everybody, I assure you.

*Patient:* (interrupting) I mean after all a card is a card—why I d—it seems to me kind of silly (anguish in his voice and near weeping) to bring that thing in here—they have sold them at the canteen, Ma . . .

*Therapist:* Are you anxious now . . .

*Patient:* Why . . .

*Therapist:* Are you anxious now because she said . . .

*Patient:* I shouldn't be blamed for a thing like that, it's so small . . .

*Mother:* (overlapping) I'm not blaming you.

*Patient:* (continuing) I don't even remember exactly what the thing was.

*Mother:* (overlapping) Well, that's all I wanted to know (laughs)

*Patient:* (continuing) I didn't want to—to—to—to blame you or nothing.

*Therapist:* Will you slow down a minute. Are you anxious now because she said she didn't like to be picked on? And you've sort of been picking on her today. Is that what's making you so—upset?

*Patient:* No, it's now what's making me upset. That they s—after all, mother's got to realize that those people—the people that sell the cards—they sell them and people buy them—the wording isn't exactly right—I've stood for half an hour in a store sometimes picking—picking out a card to send mother or to send to one of the family where I wanted to get the wordings just so—and the picture on the thing just so. I was just too particular, that was before I took sick . . .

*Therapist:* I think you did that this time too—

*Patient:* (continuing) And came back to the hospital. No I wasn't—I bought that thing in five minutes. There was only a choice of four cards—but of course that helped. But I—I—I—uh, I—I do have—I've changed now with those cards, I'm not as particular as I used to be. I mean uh—peop—they sell those cards and, uh—I don't think that they—they got—they don't mean anything by the words. Uh,—they're sold for people to buy, they're sold for people to buy.

*Therapist:* (overlapping) The person who sends them ought to mean something by the words.

*Patient:* No, but I . . .

*Therapist:* And you seem to be denying that you sent . . .

*Patient:* No, I think that can be interpreted in different ways.

*Therapist:* Sure, it's pretty safe, but not quite safe enough apparently.

*Patient:* Is that the way you feel too?

*Therapist:* I feel you tried to say something indirectly so you'd be protected.

*Patient:* (interrupting) No, I wasn't, I just felt that—that—that thing

*Therapist:* Now you're . . .

*Patient:* (continuing) was—was—all right I'm changing a little bit. Uh,— that that mother was a good enough mother. It says "For someone that's been like a mother to me."

*Father:* A *real* mother.

*Patient:* Yeah, a *real* mother—so that's all.[2]

Despite its brevity, this excerpt illustrates a typical kind of interaction in this type of family. From the point of view of psychiatric diagnosis, the patient manifests such symptoms as: 1) blocking and forgetting what he was going to say, 2) showing concretistic thinking when he says "a card is a card," 3) implying that someone else caused the difficulty ("They sell them in the canteen" and later in the interview implying in a rather paranoid way that it was the fault of a post office clerk for mailing it) and 4) claiming amnesia ("I don't even remember what the thing was"). Although less dramatic than symptoms manifested by the full-blown psychotic patient, his behavior could be said to be schizophrenic.

Another family could have responded in this situation rather differently. Should a child in another family send his mother such a card, she might respond to it in any of a variety of ways. And whatever way chosen, her husband and child would also have a range of possible ways to respond to her. This particular family selects these ways, and a description of this family must 1) describe the formal patterns in this type of interaction in such a way as to 2) differentiate the patterns from other possible ones, or those in other families.

## POSSIBILITIES OF A THREE-PERSON SYSTEM

One way to describe a particular family is to present its type of interaction against the background of the potential ways a mother, father, and child might interact with one another. If any set of parents and child are brought together in a room, what sort of communicative behavior is potentially possible between them?

1. Whatever they do together can be seen as communication between them; each will do something and each will respond. Although it seems obvious, it is particularly important to emphasize that family members cannot avoid communicating, or responding, to one another when they are in the same room. If one speaks to another and he does not answer, his not-answering is a response in a real and meaningful sense.

2. Not only must parents and child communicate with each other, but each must communicate on at least two levels. Whatever one says and does will inevitably be qualified by the other things he says and does, and when any piece of communication is *about,* or qualifies, another piece of communication they can be said to be of different levels. Whenever anyone speaks to another person he must qualify what he says because he must speak in a tone of voice, with a body movement, with other verbal statements, and in a particular context. What he says will be qualified with an indication of what sort of statement it is, *i.e.* a joking statement, a sincere one, an unimportant one, a command, a suggestion, and so on. A man can smile and murder as he smiles, and if his behavior is to be described both levels of communication must be included.

If a man says, "I won't stand for that any more!" in a tone of voice which indicates anger and with a gesture of putting a stop to it in a situation where what he says is appropriate, then his statement and qualifications can be said to be congruent, or to "affirm," each other. Messages and their qualifiers can also be incongruent. If a mother makes a punishing statement while labeling what she does as benevolent, she is disqualifying what she says, or manifesting an incongruence between her levels of message. It is important to note that she is not contradicting herself. Contradictory statements are of the same level, such as, "I will do it," and "I won't do it." Incongruent statements are of different levels: "I will do it," said in a tone of voice which indicates, "Don't take what I say seriously." Whether family members qualify their own statements incongruently or congruently, and under what circumstances they do so, can be described as they interact with one another.

3. The three people in the room must also qualify each other's statements. As they respond to one another, they are inevitably commenting upon, or classifying, each other's statements. They may affirm what each other says, or they may disqualify the other's statements by indicating that isn't the sort of thing that should be said. If mother says, "I brought you some candy," and her son says, "You treat me like a child," the son is disqualifying his mother's communication. If he accepts it with a statement of thanks, he is affirming her statement. A description of parents and child must include whether, and under what circumstances, they affirm or disqualify each other's behavior.

4. When three people are in a room, some sort of leadership will take form, even if only in terms of who will speak before the others do. Any one of the three may initiate something, and the other two may go along with him or attempt to take leadership themselves. In some families, father and child may consistently turn to mother for a decision, other families may label father as the final arbiter, while other parents may lean on their child for the initiation of what is to happen.

5. The three people may also form any or all of various possible alliances. It is possible for the three of them to ally against the outside world, for one to ally with someone in the outside world against the other two, or two may ally against the third. In some families father and mother may form a coalition against the child, in others the child may ally with one of his parents against the other, and so on.

6. Finally, when something goes "wrong," there are a variety of possible arrangements for the three people to handle blame. All three may each acknowledge blame, one may never accept blame for anything, two may consistently blame the third, and so on.

This list of some of the possibilities in a three person system is made more complex by the fact that a family member may form an alliance but indicate he isn't forming one, or may take blame but qualify his statement with an indication that he really isn't to blame. The possible range of maneuvers is considerably increased when people are seen to communicate at multiple levels.

## THE RULES IN THE FAMILY OF
## THE SCHIZOPHRENIC

Given a potential range of behavior between three people in a family system, it becomes possible to look at any one type of family as restricted to a certain range of that potential. No one family will interact in all possible ways: limited patterns of interaction will develop. The patterns described here are those in a particular sample and are those which occur when parents and schizophrenic child interact *with each other*. They may behave differently with other people, including psychiatric investigators or siblings of the schizophrenic child. Although siblings are included in our observation of this type of family, the description offered here is of the three person system, partly for simplification in this presentation and partly because parents and schizophrenic child form a special triadic system in the larger family unit.

### THE WAYS FAMILY MEMBERS QUALIFY THEIR OWN STATEMENTS

Consistently in this type of family the individual members manifest an incongruence between what they say and how they qualify what they say. Many people do this under certain circumstances, but when these family members interact they confine themselves almost entirely to disqualifying their own statements.

In this excerpt, the mother confronts her son with the Mother's Day Card because she didn't like it, but she emphasizes what a wonderful card it is. Then she says she wants to know what was behind his head and if he sent it to hurt her, and she laughs. In a context of accusing him of hurting her, she says she wants to be hurt and is willing to take all the hurt in the world to help him. Her description of herself as a special person who will sacrifice all is qualified a few moments later by the statement that she and her husband are just plain people and her son should treat them like anybody else. This "benevolent advice" is offered in a punishing tone of voice and context. When her son says she shouldn't blame him, she qualifies her statements as not being blaming. Consistently what she communicates she qualifies in an incongruent way.

The father is only briefly in this excerpt, but while there he indicates that the son didn't mean to say what the card said, and, besides, the card said she was a real mother.

The son also manifests incongruent behavior. He sends a card to his mother on Mother's Day which indicates she is not really his mother. He further qualifies this message by indicating there was nothing wrong with it and then suggests that it says she is like a mother is supposed to be. Following this, he indicates that it means she could have been a better mother than she was. He then protests that it was silly of her to bring the card in, and qualifies this with the statement that they sell them in the canteen. Besides he doesn't remember what the thing was. After indicating that he bought the card hurriedly, he qualifies this by saying it took him five minutes to choose among four cards. He adds that one should be careful in choosing cards with exact wording, but people sell those cards and they don't mean anything by the words. Finally, he qualifies his greetings by saying that it meant she was not only a good enough mother but a real mother.

The more extreme incongruence between the son's levels of message differs from that of his mother, and this difference will be discussed later. Yet basically a similar pattern of communication is apparent. The mother does not say, "You shouldn't have sent me this card—what do you mean by it?" which is implied by her bringing the card to the session. The son doesn't say, "I sent it to you to sting you, but I'm sorry I did now." The mother is condemning him for sending her the card, but she qualifies her messages in such a way that she indicates she isn't condemning him. The son apologizes for sending the card, but he qualifies his apology in such a way that he isn't apologizing. Father indicates the son didn't mean what he said, and the card didn't say what he didn't mean anyhow. Although these incongruencies between what is said and how it is qualified are apparent in the verbal transcript, they are even more apparent when the vocal inflections on the recording are heard. Mother's tone of voice and laughter are inappropriate and thereby disqualify what she is saying, and father and son similarly do not make a flat statement which is affirmed by the ways they say it.

One can listen to many hours of recordings of conversations between parents and schizophrenic child without hearing one of them make a statement which is affirmed. Usually if one finds an exception, it proves on closer examination to fit the rules. For example, during a filmed session a family was asked to plan to do something together and the father said in a positive way that they were going to do this and do that. He fully affirmed his statements by the ways he said them. However, a few minutes later he said he was only saying these things because they should say something in front of the camera, thus disqualifying his previous statements.

### HOW FAMILY MEMBERS QUALIFY EACH OTHER'S STATEMENTS

Although it is possible for family members to affirm or disqualify each other's statements, in this type of family the members consistently disqualify what each other says. In this excerpt it is difficult to find any statement by one person affirmed by another. The son has actually disqualified his mother's whole past maternal behavior at one stroke by sending her such a card. When she protests, he indicates her protests are not valid. Similarly, the mother disqualifies the greeting she received from her son and also his defenses of it. When he indicates there is nothing wrong with it, she labels this as in error. When he indicates he knew what he was doing and meant to "sting" her a bit, she indicates this was in error. Father joins them to disqualify both the son's message, since he didn't mean it, and his defense of the message. No one affirms what anyone says except 1) when the son says he doesn't remember what the card was, and his mother says that is all she wanted to know; 2) when the father says the card means she is a real mother, and the son agrees. Both of these affirmations involve symptomatic behavior by his son: amnesia and distortion of reality. From this excerpt one might hypothesize that the family members will disqualify what each other says except when a child is behaving in a symptomatic way. Such a hypothesis requires more careful investigation. Apparently even symptomatic behavior by the child is usually disqualified except in certain contexts. When the mother is under attack, the parents may affirm psychotic behavior but not necessarily at other times.

It might be argued that the behavior in this excerpt is exceptional since it deals with a moment of crisis. However, analysis of other interviews suggests that the pattern is typical. In a previous paper (5) the relationship between mother and schizophrenic child was described as a "double bind" situation in that the mother imposed incongruent levels of message upon the child in a situation where the child must respond to conflicting requests, could not comment on the contradictions, and could not leave the field. Further investigation indicates that this kind of communication sequence is a repetitive pattern between all three family members. Not only is each constantly faced with conflicting levels of message, but each finds his response labeled as a wrong one. (Family therapy with this type of family has its unrewarding aspects since almost any comment by the therapist is similarly disqualified.)

Typically, if one family member says something, another indicates it shouldn't have been said or wasn't said properly. If one criticizes the other, he is told that he misunderstands and should behave differently. If one compliments the other, he is told he doesn't do this often enough, or he has some ulterior purpose. Should a family member try to avoid communicating, the others will indicate this "passivity" is demanding and indicate he should initiate more. All family members may report they always feel they are in the wrong. However, they do not necessarily directly oppose each other or openly reject one another's statements. If one suggests going to a particular place, the other may not say "No," but rather he is likely to indicate, "Why must we always go where you suggest?" Or the response may be the sigh of a brave martyr who must put up with this sort of thing. Typically the family members may not object to what one another says, but to their right to say it. Often open disagreements are prevented by an atmosphere of benevolent concern and distress that the other person misunderstands. Family members may also respond in an affirmative way when their response would be appropriate only if the person had made some other statement.

It is important to emphasize that a formal pattern is being described here which may manifest itself in various ways. A mother may be overprotective and thereby disqualify what the child does as insufficient or inadequate. She may also be rejecting and similarly disqualify what he does as unacceptable. She may also withdraw when the child initiates something as a way of disqualifying his offer. Similarly, father may viciously condemn mother or child or merely be passive when they seek a positive response from him, and in both cases he is disqualifying their communication.

Although it is not uncommon for people to disqualify each other's statements, ordinarily one would expect affirmation also to occur. However, when observing these families one does not hear even affectionate or giving behavior appreciated or affirmed. If one person indicates a desire for closeness, another indicates this is done in the wrong way or at the wrong time. (However, if one suggests separation the other will also indicate this is the wrong thing to do. Typically in these families the mother regularly threatens separation but does not leave, and the father does not often threaten separation but spends a good deal of his time away from home or "leaves" by drinking heavily while staying home.) Typically family members behave as if they are involved in what might be called a *compulsory relationship*. For example, a mother in one family indicated with some contempt that her husband was afraid to leave her because he could not stand being alone. She suggested he was cruel to her because he was angry at being tied to her. She also rejected his affectionate overtures because she considered them only a kind of bribery to insure staying with her. She herself was unable to leave him even for a night, though he was drunk several nights a week and beat her regularly. Both felt the association was not voluntary, and so neither could accept as valid any indication from the other about wanting to be together. A compulsory relationship is also typical of the parent and schizophrenic child. Since the child is considered incapable of leaving home and associating with others, his staying at home is taken as involuntary. Therefore should he indicate a desire to be with his parents, they tend to disqualify his overtures as merely a request that they not turn him out, and he finds his affectionate gestures disqualified.

### LEADERSHIP IN THE FAMILY

Since family members tend to negate their own and each other's communication, any clear leadership in the family is impossible. Typically in these families the mother tends to initiate what happens, while indicating either that she isn't, or that someone else should. The father will invite her to initiate what happens while condemning her when she does. Often they suggest the child take the lead, and then disqualify his attempts. These families tend to become incapacitated by necessary decisions because each member will avoid affirming what he does and therefore is unable to acknowledge responsibility for his actions, and each will disqualify the attempts of any other to announce a decision. Both the act of taking leadership and the refusal to take leadership by any one family member is condemned by the others. The family "just happens" to take actions in particular directions with no individual accepting the label as the one responsible for any action.

### ALLIANCES

Similarly, no labeled alliances are permitted in the family. A family coalition against the outside world (represented, say, by an observer), breaks down rather rapidly. Such individuals are also unable to form an alliance of two against one. Often they may appear to have such an alliance, as they tend to speak "through" one another. For example, the mother may ask for something for her child as a way of indicating that her husband deprives her, and so appear in alliance with the child. Or when the parents begin to express anger at each other, they may turn on the child for causing their difficulties and so appear in a coalition against him. Yet should the coalition be labeled, it will break down.

If the child says, "You're both against me," one or the other parent will disqualify this remark and so deny the coalition. If father should say to mother, "Let's stick together on this," she is likely to say, "I'm afraid you'll back down at the last minute," or "It isn't my fault when we don't stick together." The mother and child may appear to form a coalition against the father, but should the child say, "Father treats us badly," mother is likely to say, "He has his troubles too," even though a moment before she may have been complaining to the child about how badly they were both treated by the father. Family members behave as if an alliance between two of them is inevitably a betrayal of the third person. They seem to have difficulty functioning in a two-person relationship, and as a result the separation of any one of the three from the others is a particular threat.

What confines the members so rigidly within their system is the prohibition on intimate alliances of one member with someone outside the family. As a result, the family members are inhibited from learning to relate to people with different behavior and so are confined to their own system of interaction.

### DEFENSE AGAINST BLAME

Characteristically the mothers in these families defend themselves by "transfer of blame." Such a defense follows from the mother's consistent manifestation of incongruent levels: what she does, she qualifies as not having been done or not done in that way. If the child becomes disturbed, it happens "out of the blue." If anything goes wrong, mother indicates it is the fault of someone else. In those rare instances where she does admit she did something wrong, she indicates she did it only because she was told to, or out of duty, so that it wasn't her fault. She may also indicate that something must be wrong with the other person, since he ought not to have been affected by what she did, particularly when she didn't really do it. Even when her behavior affects someone pleasantly, she must deny that it was her fault. Typically she presents herself as helplessly pushed by forces outside her control.

The fathers also follow the family rule of incongruently qualifying their messages, yet they cannot use the same denial of blame and remain with their wives. They tend to use types of defense which complement her defense, and these are of three kinds. 1) Fathers who are withdrawn and passive, accept the blame their wives put upon them, but indicate by their unresponsiveness that they are blamed falsely and do not agree with her. 2) Fathers who have temper tantrums and blame their wives, put the blame on false or exaggerated grounds so the wife can easily point out her innocence. This type of father is easily blamed since he is dominating and tyrannical, yet by going too far he indicates he is an innocent victim driven by forces outside his control. 3) Some fathers do not blame their wives but also do not blame themselves or anyone else. Such fathers make an issue of semantic difference. If asked if they or their wives are at fault, a typical reply is, "Just what do you mean by 'fault'?" By accepting no implicit definition and not defining anything themselves, they obscure everything. Any particular father may manifest these three types of defense, all of which involve both disqualification of one's own statements and a disqualification of the other person's statements.

The child tends to use two types of defense. When "sane" he may blame himself and indicate that everything wrong with the family centers in him, an attitude the parents encourage, while at the same time he gives an impression of being blamed unjustly. When "insane" he negates his own statements and those of others by denying that anything happened. Or, if it did, he wasn't there—besides it wasn't him and it happened in another place at a time when he had no control over himself. The "withdrawal from reality" maneuvers of the schizophrenic make it impossible for him to blame himself or his parents since he defines himself as not of this world.

## THE "DIFFERENT" BEHAVIOR OF
## THE SCHIZOPHRENIC

The inability of the schizophrenic to relate to people and his general withdrawal behavior seems understandable if he was raised in a learning situation where whatever he did was disqualified and if he was not allowed to relate to other people where he could learn to behave differently. Should he be reared in a situation where each attempt he made to gain a response from someone was met with an indication that he should behave in some other way, it would be possible for an individual to learn to avoid trying to relate to people by indicating that whatever he does is not done in relationship to anyone. He would then appear "autistic." However, the peculiar distortions of communication by the schizophrenic are not sufficiently explained by this description of his learning situation. If schizophrenic behavior is adaptive to a particular type of family, it is necessary to suggest the adaptive function involved when a person behaves in a clearly psychotic way.

The recovering schizophrenic patient, and perhaps the pre-psychotic schizophrenic, will qualify what he says in a way similar to that used by his parents. His behavior could be said to be "normal" for that family. However, during a psychotic episode the schizophrenic behaves in a rather unique manner. To suggest how such behavior might serve a function in the family, it is necessary both to describe schizophrenia in terms of behavior and to suggest the conditions under which such behavior might occur. To describe schizophrenic behavior, it is necessary to translate into behavioral terms such diagnostic concepts as delusions, hallucinations, concretistic thinking, and so on.

What appears unique about schizophrenic behavior is the incongruence of all levels of communication. The patient's parents may say something and disqualify it, but they will affirm that disqualification. The schizophrenic will say something, deny saying it, but qualify his denial in an incongruent way. Schizophrenic behavior described in this way has been presented elsewhere (10), but it may be summarized briefly here.

Not only can a person manifest an incongruence between levels of total message, but also between elements of his messages. A message from one person to another can be formalized into the following statement: *I* (*source*) *am communicating* (*message*) *to you* (*receiver*) *in this context*.

By his body movement, vocal inflections, and verbal statements a person must affirm or disqualify each of the elements of this message. The symptoms of a schizophrenic can be summarized in terms of this schema.

1) *Source*. A person may indicate that *he* isn't really the source of a message by indicating that he is only transmitting the idea of someone else. Therefore he says something but qualifies it with a denial that *he* is saying it. The schizophrenic may also qualify the source of the message in this way, but he will qualify his qualifications in an incongruent way. For example, a male schizophrenic patient reported that his name was Margaret Stalin. Thus he indicated that *he* wasn't really speaking, but by making his denial clearly fantastic he disqualified his denial that he was speaking. Similarly a patient may say that "voices" are making the statement. In the excerpt presented, the patient denies that *he* is responsible for the greeting card message by saying "they sell them in the canteen," and yet this denial is by its nature self-disqualifying and so his messages become incongruent at all levels.

2) *Message*. A person may indicate in various ways that his words or action are not really a message. He may indicate, for example, that what he did was accidental if he blurts something out or if he steps on someone's foot. The schizophrenic may indicate that his statement isn't a message but merely a group of words, or he may speak in a random, or word salad, way, thus indicating that he isn't really communicating. Yet at the same time he manages to indicate some pertinent points in his word salad, thus disqualifying his denial that his message is a message. In the excerpt given above, the patient says, "a card is a card," as a way of denying the message communicated. He also says that he doesn't

remember what the thing was, thus denying the message existed for him. However, both these qualifications of the message are also disqualified: the card obviously isn't merely a card, and he can hardly not remember what the thing was when he is looking at it.

3) *Receiver*. A person may deny this element in a message in various ways, for example by indicating he isn't really talking to the particular person he is addressing, but rather to that person's status. The schizophrenic patient is likely to indicate that the doctor he is talking to isn't really a doctor, but, say, an FBI agent. Thereby he not only denies talking to the physician, but by labeling the receiver in a clearly fantastic way he disqualifies his denial. Paranoid delusionary statements of this sort become "obvious" by their self-negating quality.

4) *Context*. A person may disqualify his statement by indicating that it applies to some other context than the one in which it is made. *Context* is defined broadly here as the situation in which people are communicating, including both the physical situation and the stated premises about what sort of situation it is. For example, a woman may be aggressively sexual in a public place where the context disqualifies her overtures. The typical statement that the schizophrenic is "withdrawn from reality" seems to be based to a great extent on the ways he qualifies what he says by mislabeling the context. He may say his hospital conversation is taking place in a palace, or in prison, and thereby disqualify his statements. Since his labels are clearly impossible, his disqualification is disqualified.

These multiple incongruent levels of communication differentiate the schizophrenic from his parents and from other people. If a person says something and then negates his statement we judge him by his other levels of message. When these too are incongruent so that he says something, indicates he didn't, then affirms one or the other, and then disqualifies his affirmation; there is a tendency to call such a person insane.

From the point of view offered here, schizophrenia is an intermittent type of behavior. The patient may be behaving in a schizophrenic way at one moment and in a way that is "normal" for this type of family at another moment. The important question is this: Under what circumstances does he behave in a psychotic way, defined here as qualifying incongruently all his levels of message?

In this excerpt of a family interaction, the patient shows psychotic behavior when he is caught between a therapist pressuring him to affirm his statements and his parents pressuring him to disqualify them. From this point of view, the patient is faced with a situation where he must infringe the rules of his relationship with the therapist or infringe his family rules. His psychotic behavior can be seen as an attempt to adapt to both.[3] By behaving in a psychotic way he could 1) affirm his statement about his mother, thus following the rule in the therapeutic relationship for affirmative statements, 2) disqualify his critical statement of the mother, thus following the family rules that mother is not to be blamed in a way so that she can accept blame and all statements are to be disqualified, and 3) synthesize these two incompatible theses by indicating that the message wasn't his (it wasn't really a message, he couldn't remember it, and he didn't really send it). It can be argued that psychotic behavior is a sequence of messages which infringe a set of prohibitions but which are qualified as not infringing them. The only way an individual can achieve this is by qualifying incongruently all levels of his communication.

The need to behave in a psychotic way would seem to occur when the patient infringes a family prohibition and thereby activates himself and his parents to behave in such a way that he either returns within the previous system of rules or indicates somehow that he is not infringing them. Should he successfully infringe the system of family rules and thereby set new rules, his parents may become "disturbed." This seems to occur rather often when the patient living at home "improves" with therapy. When improving in therapy he is not only infringing the family prohibitions against outside alliances but he may blame the mother in a reasonable way and affirm his statements or those of others. Such behavior on his part would shatter the family system unless the parents are also undergoing therapy. The omnipotent feelings of the schizophrenic patient may have some basis, since his family system is so rigid that he can create considerable repercussions by behaving differently.

A patient is faced with infringing family prohibitions when 1) two family prohibitions conflict with each other and he must respond to both, 2) when forces outside the family, or maturational forces within himself, require him to infringe them, or 3) when prohibitions special to him conflict with prohibitions applying to all family members. If he must infringe such prohibitions and at the same time not infringe them, he can only do so through psychotic behavior.

Conflicting sets of prohibitions may occur when the individual is involved with both mother and therapist, involved with a therapist and administrator in a hospital setting (19), or when some shift within his own family brings prohibitions into conflict. This latter would seem the most likely bind the patient would find himself in when living at home, and an incident is offered here to describe psychotic behavior serving a function in the family.

A 21-year-old schizophrenic daughter arrived home from the hospital for a trial visit and her parents promptly separated. The mother asked the girl to go with her, and when she arrived at their destination, the grandmother's home, the patient telephoned her father. Her mother asked her why she turned against her by calling the father, and the daughter said she called him to say goodby and because she had looked at him with an "odd" look when they left. A typical symptom of this patient when overtly psychotic is her perception of "odd" looks, and the problem is how such a message is adaptive to the family pattern of interaction.

The incident could be described in this way. The mother separated from father but qualified her leaving incongruently by saying it was only temporary and telling him where she was going. The father objected to the mother's leaving, but made no attempt to restrain her or to persuade her to stay. The daughter had to respond to this situation in accord with the prohibitions set by this family system: she had to disqualify whatever she did, she had to disqualify what her mother and father did, she could not ally with either mother or father and acknowledge it, and she could not blame the mother in such a way that the mother would accept the blame.

The girl could not merely do nothing because this would mean remaining with father. However, by going with the mother she in effect formed an alliance and so infringed one of the prohibitions in the family system. The girl solved the problem by going with mother but telephoning her father, thus disqualifying her alliance with mother. However, her mother objected to the call, and the daughter said she only called him to say goodbye, thus disqualifying her alliance with father. Yet to leave it this way would mean allying with mother. She qualified her statement further by saying she called father because she gave him an "odd look" when she left him. By having an odd look, she could succeed in not siding with either parent or blaming mother. She also manifested schizophrenic behavior by qualifying incongruently all levels of message and thereby adapting to incongruent family prohibitions. Previously the girl could withdraw to her room to avoid the alliance problem, but when mother stopped staying home while saying she was going to leave, and left while saying she was not really leaving, the girl was threatened by a possible alliance whether she went with her mother or stayed at home. Her incongruent, schizophrenic behavior would seem necessary to remain within the prohibitions of the family at those times. If one is required to behave in a certain way and simultaneously required not to, he can only solve the problem by indicating that *he* is not behaving at all, or not with this particular person in this situation. The girl might also have solved the problem by disqualifying her identity, indicating the context was really a secret plot, indicating that what she did was what voices told her to do, or speaking in a random or word salad way. In other words, she could both meet the prohibitions in the family and infringe them only by disqualifying the source of her messages, the nature of them, the recipient, or the context, and so behave in a psychotic fashion.

It is important to emphasize that schizophrenic behavior in the family is adaptive to an intricate and complicated family organization which is presented here in crude simplicity. The network of family prohibitions confronts the individual members with almost insoluble problems. This particular incident was later discussed with the parents of this girl, and the mother said her daughter could have solved the problem easily. She could have stayed with father and told him he was wrong in the quarrel which provoked the separation. This would seem to be the mother's usual way of dealing with this kind of situation—she stays with father while telling him he is wrong. However, the mother leaves herself out of this solution by ignoring the fact that she asked her daughter to go with her. This request was even more complicated—the mother asked the daughter to go with her during a period when the mother was saying the daughter must return to the hospital because she could not tolerate associating with her. When the parents reunited later that week, the girl was returned to the hospital because mother said she could not stand daughter in the room watching her, and she could not stand daughter out of the room thinking about her.

The approach offered here differs from the usual psychodynamic explanations. It would be possible to say that the mother's concern about leaving the daughter with the father, even when she could not tolerate the girl's company, might center in the family's concern about incestuous desires between father and daughter. Such a psychodynamic hypothesis could be supported. Later in therapy the father and daughter planned a picnic alone together when they decided they should see more of each other without the mother being present. The evening of the day this was arranged, the therapist received a telephone call from the disturbed mother. She reported that she and her husband had been drinking and arguing all evening and she reported that her husband had told her it was natural for a father to have sexual relations with his daughter. The husband's report was that he had not said this. (He said it was natural for a father to have sexual *feelings* for his daughter, but this did not mean he would do anything about it.) This crisis over suggested possible incest could be explained by saying that the threat of closeness between father and daughter aroused forbidden incestuous desires in them. However, it was the mother who made an issue over the possible incest. From the psychodynamic point of view, hints and discussions of incest would represent unconscious conflicts. From the point of view offered here, this type of discussion is an aspect of family strategy. To label a relationship as possibly incestuous would be one further way of enforcing a prohibition on alliances between father and daughter. Such a maneuver is similar to one where the mother inhibits a relationship between father and daughter by insisting that the father should associate more with the daughter, thus arousing his negative behavior as well as the issue of whether he neglected the daughter. The approach offered here does not deal with supposed motivating forces within the individuals concerned, but with the formal characteristics of their behavior with each other.[4]

## THE FUNCTION OF FAMILY BEHAVIOR

The difficulty for this type of family would seem to lie in the inflexibility of their family system. They often maintain the system despite the sturdy attempts of a family therapist to help them deal with each other more amicably. Apparently family members gain only discord, dissension, and a constant struggle with one another, or periods of withdrawal in a kind of truce, yet they continue so to behave. It would be possible to postulate psychodynamic causes for this type of behavior, or self-destructive drives could be sought, but an attempt is made here to develop an alternative descriptive language centering on the peculiar sensitivity of people to the fact that their behavior is governed by others.

When people respond to one another they inevitably influence how the other person is to respond to them. Whatever one says, or doesn't say, in response to another person is a determinant of the other person's behavior. For example, if one criticizes another, he is indicating that critical statements from him are permissible in the relationship. The other person cannot not respond, and whatever response he makes will govern the critical person's behavior. Whether the criticized one gets angry, or weeps helplessly, or passively accepts the criticism, he must either be accepting the rules or countering with other rules. These rules for relationships which people establish with each other are never permanently set but are in a constant process of reinforcement as the two people interact and govern each other's behavior.

Every human being depends upon other people not only for his survival but for his pleasure and pain. It is of primary importance that he learn to govern the responses of other people so they will provide him satisfaction. Yet a person can only gain satisfaction in a relationship if he permits others to cooperate in setting the rules for the relationship and so influence and govern him. The person who dares not risk such control over him would seem to provoke his own misery by attempting to avoid it. If someone has suffered a series of hurts and frustrations with people he trusted, he tends to try to become independent of people—by not getting involved with them in such a way that they can gain control over his feelings or his behavior. He may literally avoid people; he may interact with them only on his own terms, constantly making an issue of who is going to circumscribe whose behavior; or he may choose the schizophrenic way and indicate that nothing he does is done in relationship to other people. In this fashion he is not governing anyone and no one is governing him.

The family of the schizophrenic would seem to be not only establishing and following a system of rules, as other families do, but also following a prohibition on any acknowledgement that a family member is setting rules. Each refuses to concede that he is circumscribing the behavior of others, and each refuses to concede that any other family member is governing him. Since communication inevitably occurs if people live together, and since whatever one communicates inevitably governs the behavior of others, the family members must each constantly disqualify the communications of one another. Should one affirm what he does or what another does, he risks conceding that he is governed by the other with all the consequences that follow being disappointed again by an untrustworthy person. Schizophrenic behavior can be seen as both a product and a parody of this kind of family system. By labeling everything he communicates as not communicated by him to this person in this place, the schizophrenic indicates that he is not governing anyone's behavior because he is not in a relationship with anyone. This would seem to be a necessary style of behavior at times in this type of family system, and it may become habitual behavior. Yet even psychotic behavior does not free the individual from being governed or from governing others. The person who insists that he does not need anyone at all and is completely independent of them requires people to put him in a hospital and to force feed him. To live at all one must be involved with other people and so deal with the universal problem of who is going to circumscribe whose behavior. The more a person tries to avoid being governed or governing others, the more helpless he becomes and so governs others by forcing them to take care of him.

### A MODEL FOR DIFFERENTIATING TYPES OF FAMILIES

What is lacking in the study of interpersonal relations is a method of describing, by way of some analogy, the process which takes place when two or more people interact with one another. Although there are models for inner activity, e.g., the id-ego-superego metaphor, there is not yet a model for human interaction. Implicit in the approach to the schizophrenic family offered here there is such a model. The essential elements of it are: 1) the proposition that human communication can be classified into levels of message, 2) the cybernetic idea of the self-corrective, governed system. If a family confines itself to repetitive patterns within a certain range of possible behavior, then they are confined to that range by some sort of governing process. No outside governor requires the family members to behave in their habitual patterns, so this governing process must exist within the family. A third essential point is that when people respond to one another they govern, or establish rules, for each other's behavior.

To describe families, the most appropriate analogy would seem to be the self-corrective system governed by family members influencing each other's behavior and thereby establishing rules and prohibitions for that particular family system. Such a system tends to be error-activated. Should one family member break a family rule, the others become activated until he either conforms to the rule again or successfully establishes a new one.

A system of three organisms each governing the range of behavior of the other two, and each communicating at multiple levels, is both a simple idea and a complex model. Yet such an approach offers a general theoretical framework within which the specific rules of any one type of family system can be classified. The rudiments of such a system are suggested here at the most general level. The family of the schizophrenic is a particularly good model for this approach because of the narrow limits of their system. Our few preliminary observations of families containing children without symptoms, children who are delinquent, and children with asthma, lead us to believe that the interaction in the family of the schizophrenic is unique. Members of other types of family sometimes disqualify each other's statements but only under certain circumstances. Mutual affirmation will also occur. We have observed, for example, parents of an asthmatic child finishing each other's sentences and having this approved. Should the father of a schizophrenic finish the mother's sentence, it seems inevitable that she would indicate he provided the wrong ending. In other families leadership will stabilize into a pattern accepted by family members. Certain alliances will be allowed in some types of families, notably the delinquent where the child is capable of forming labeled alliances in gangs outside the family. In the family of the schizophrenic the range of behavior is as limited and inflexible as is the behavior of the schizophrenic in contrast to other people.

The observation of this type of family system inevitably takes place after the child has manifested a schizophrenic episode. Whether the family behaved in a similar way prior to his diagnosis is unknowable. In this sense it is difficult to assert that the interaction in his family "caused" schizophrenia. There are two possibilities. 1) If the family is a self-corrective system and the child behaves intermittently in a schizophrenic way, then schizophrenic behavior is a necessary part of this family system. 2) Alternatively, schizophrenic behavior is a result of a particular family system which has been disrupted by forces outside the system, such as maturation of the child or environmental influence. The family then reorganizes a new system which includes the schizophrenic behavior as an element, and this is what we are presently examining. The evidence leads us to believe that schizophrenic behavior in the child is reinforced by the present family system.

Although psychotic behavior may serve a function in a family system, a risk is also involved. The patient may need to be separated from the family by hospitalization and so break up the system, or he may enter therapy and change and so leave the system. Typically the parents seem to welcome hospitalization only if the patient is still accessible to them, and they welcome therapy for the patient up to the point when he begins to change and infringe the rules of the family system while acknowledging that he is doing so.

## NOTES

1. Project for the Study of Schizophrenic Communication, directed by Gregory Bateson. Staff consists of Jay Haley and John H. Weakland, Research associates, Dr. Don D. Jackson, consultant, Dr. William F. Fry, consultant. The research project is located at the Veterans Administration Hospital, Palo Alto, California, and is financed by grants from the Macy Foundation and the Foundations' Fund for Research in Psychiatry.
2. This excerpt is not offered as an example of family therapy but rather as an example of family behavior. The parents in this case were not considered to be patients and the family as a unit was not officially undergoing treatment.
3. An attempt to synthesize two incompatible situations by a perceptual change is suggested in Weakland and Jackson (22). Describing an incident during a psychotic breakdown, they say, "Psychotic delusions allowed him to free himself of decision making. For example, the cab driver is a hospital attendant in disguise. There is no problem in Home vs. Hospital; it has been resolved."
4. Although statements in the form of family rules deal with observable behavior and are therefore verifiable, the verification depends to some extent upon the skill of the observer. Such statements are more reliably documented by placing the family in a structured experimental situation where the results depend upon whether or not the family functions under certain prohibitions. The Bateson project is now beginning a program of experiments with families similar to the small group experiments of Alex Bavelas.

## REFERENCES

1. ALANEN, Y. The mothers of schizophrenic patients. Acta psychiat. et neurol. scandinav., 33: Suppl. 124, 1958.
2. BATESON, G. Cultural problems posed by a study of schizophrenic process. Presented at the American Psychiatric Association, Conference on Schizophrenia, Honolulu, 1958. In press.

3. BATESON, G. The group dynamics of schizophrenia. Presented at the Institute on Chronic Schizophrenia and Hospital Treatment Programs, Osawatomie State Hospital, Osawatomie, 1958. In press.
4. BATESON, G. The new conceptual frames for behavioral research. Presented at the Sixth Annual Psychiatric Institute Conference at the New Jersey Neuro-Psychiatric Institute, Princeton, New Jersey, 1958. In press.
5. BATESON, G., JACKSON, D. D., HALEY, J. AND WEAKLAND, J. Toward a theory of schizophrenia. Behavioral Sc., 1: 251–264, 1956.
6. BOWEN, M., DYSINGER, R. H. AND BASAMINIA, B. The role of the father in families with a schizophrenic patient. Paper presented at the annual meeting of the American Psychiatric Association, May, 1958.
7. GERARD, D. L., and SIEGEL, J. The family background of schizophrenia. Psychiat. Quart., 24: 47–73, 1950.
8. FRAZEE, H. E. Children who later became schizophrenic. Smith. Coll. Stud. Social Work, 123: 125–149, 1953.
9. HALEY, J. Control in psychoanalytic psychotherapy. Progr. Psychotherapy, 4: 48–65, 1959.
10. HALEY, J. An interactional description of schizophrenia. Psychiatry, to be published.
11. HALEY, J. An interactional explanation of hypnosis. Am. J. Clin. Hypnosis, 1: 41–57, 1958.
12. JACKSON, D. D. The question of family homeostasis. Psychoanalyt. Quart., 31: Suppl.; 79–90, 1957.
13. LIDZ, R. W. AND LIDZ, T. The family environment of schizophrenic patients. Am. J. Psychiat., 106: 332–345, 1949.
14. LIDZ, T., PARKER, B. AND CORNELISON, A. R. The role of the father in the family environment of the schizophrenic patient. Am. J. Psychiat., 113: 126–132, 1956.
15. LIDZ, T., CORNELISON, A. R., FLECK, S. AND TERRY, D. The intrafamilial environment of schizophrenic patients. I. The Father. Psychiatry, 20: 329–342, 1957.
16. LIDZ, T., CORNELISON, A. R., FLECK, S. AND TERRY, D. The intrafamilial environment of schizophrenic patients. II. Marital schism and marital skew. Am. J. Psychiat., 114: 241–248, 1957.
17. REICHARD, S. AND TILLMAN, G. Patterns of parent-child relationships in schizophrenia. Psychiatry, 13: 247–257, 1950.
18. ROSEN, J. N. *Direct Analysis.* Grune & Stratton, New York, 1951.
19. STANTON, A. H. AND SCHWARTZ, M. S. *The Mental Hospital.* Basic Books, New York, 1954.
20. TIETZE, T. A study of the mothers of schizophrenic patients. Psychiatry, 12: 55–65, 1949.
21. WEAKLAND, J. The double bind hypothesis of schizophrenia and three-party interaction. In *The Study of Schizophrenia.* Basic Books, New York. In press.
22. WEAKLAND, J. H. AND JACKSON, D. D. Patient and therapist observations on the circumstances of a schizophrenic episode. A. M. A. Arch. Neurol. & Psychiat., 79: 554–574, 1958.
23. WYNNE, L. D., RYCKOFF, I. M., DAY, J. AND HIRSCH, S. E. Pseudo-mutuality in the family relations of schizophrenics. Psychiatry, 21: 205–220, 1958.

K

# 15:

# Intrafamilial Environment of the Schizophrenic Patient: The Transmission of Irrationality[1]

*Theodore Lidz, Alice Cornelison,*
*Dorothy Terry Carlson,* and *Stephen Fleck*

One of the distinctive features of schizophrenia lies in the disturbed symbolic functioning—in the paralogic quality of the patient's thinking and communicating that alters his internal representation of reality. We are following the hypothesis that the schizophrenic patient escapes from an untenable world in which he is powerless to cope with insoluble conflicts by the device of imaginatively distorting his symbolization of reality. Such internalized maneuvers do not require action, or coming to terms with other persons, or altering their attitudes. The patient can regain the mastery that he once possessed in childhood, before his reality was firmly structured, and it could still give way before the power of his wishes. It can be an alluring way because it is self-contained. It is a bitter way because it is isolating.

The present study will focus on this critical characteristic of schizophrenia, and, therefore, must neglect many other aspects of the developmental forces active during the childhood and adolescence of schizophrenic patients, even though these other aspects can be separated from the forces distorting mentation only artificially.

The distortions of mentation, the core problem of schizophrenia, have been relatively neglected of late because of interest in "borderline cases" and in "pseudoneurotic schizophrenia" and in the similarities of the underlying psychopathology of certain psychosomatic conditions to that of schizophrenia. Patients suffering from these conditions are not clearly schizophrenic, because they remain sufficiently well integrated to permit a consensus between their thinking and that of others, and effective social communication remains possible. Such patients are potentially

Reprinted by permission from *Archives of Neurology and Psychiatry,* Vol. 79, No. 3 (1958), pp. 305–16. Copyright 1958 by the American Medical Association. The authors are identified in the footnote to Chapter 6. This article also appears in Theodore Lidz, Stephen Fleck, Alice Cornelison, *et al., Schizophrenia and the Family* (New York: International Universities Press, 1965).

psychotic, and when their communication breaks down and becomes instrumentally ineffective, they are psychotic. Some never need this solution, but others may be unable to utilize it. It is possible for many persons to break under extreme conditions and achieve flight into irrationality, sacrificing reality to the demands of id impulses or to preserve some semblance of ego structure of self-esteem. A theory of schizophrenia must explain not only the patient's need to abandon reality testing but also his ability to do so. We must seek to understand why some persons can escape through withdrawal into unshared ways of experiencing the world around them more readily than others.

The thinking disorder in schizophrenia has been taken by some, and perhaps classically, to indicate dysfunction of the brain—dysfunction caused by lesions, deficiency, or metabolic disorder. The search for this brain dysfunction has been pursued for over 100 years. Each advance in physiology or neuroanatomy brings new hope, and each new form of physical therapy tantalizingly provokes prospects of leading to definitive knowledge of the malfunctioning of the brain. However, careful studies, and even casual observations, show that the thought disorder in schizophrenia differs markedly from any produced by a known organic deficit or a toxic disturbance of the brain. This is not the place to enter upon the nature of such differences. Although it is true that schizophrenic patients tend to concretize, they are also obviously capable of high degrees of abstraction, and may tend to abstract all too readily. More pertinently, unless a patient is permitted to become dilapidated by social isolation, the irrationality either remains or becomes more or less circumscribed. This girl who writes violently invective letters filled with delusions to her parents will in the next minute write a letter to a friend without a trace of delusional material, and then sits in her room and correctly composes inordinately complex music. No defect of thinking due to dysfunction of the brain permits such highly organized conceptualization.

There have been many approaches to the search for a genetic predisposition to schizophrenia. Our studies do not turn away from such consideration, but consider that a meaningful approach would focus upon a predisposition to symbolic distortion. Although our emphasis leads in another direction for theoretical reasons, which we shall seek to indicate briefly, we wish to point out that neither our theory nor our interpretations of data are of primary concern at present. We are attempting to present data derived from our study which we believe reliable and highly pertinent.

We consider that man is not naturally endowed with an inherent logic of causal relationships, but, rather, that the surroundings in which he is raised influence his ways of perceiving, thinking, and communicating. What makes "sense" at different periods of history and in different cultural settings (and, to a less extent, from one family to another) varies greatly. The Hindu way of regarding life in this world and life after death is irrational to us—and our way is just as meaningless and confused to the Hindu. Still, a trend toward a type of rationality exists in all cultures and in all groups. It is not that any of us has some particular ability to perceive reality as it is, for the actuality of reality—the *Ding an sich*—is never attainable by our senses. There is, however, a pragmatic meaning concerning what is fact—what is reality. It is measurable in terms of how our perceptions lead to effective action: if what we tell ourselves about events in the world around us leads to a degree of mastery over our environment and to workable interaction with the persons with whom we live. The effectiveness of reflective mentation is measured by how it helps the individual master his environment and achieve sufficient consensus with other persons to enable collaborative interaction. Communication, the outward manifestation of symbolic activity, measures the efficacy of mentation by the degree of consensus attained with others concerning what we perceive and what events mean. However, matters are not so simple. A large portion of mental activity is autistic rather than reflective; and autistic reverie is closer to primary process thinking, and to a great extent in the service of the wish of instinctual drives. The permeation of reflective thought, by the autistic processes, provides a major key to the understanding of schizophrenic thinking. Then, too, schizophrenic regression can reintroduce elements of perceptions and thought processes of early childhood that interpenetrate with more mature reflective and autistic mentation. Further, not all shared ideas need be reasonable and effective for purposes of controlling the environment. Man's need for emotional security, while he lives in this world of contingency, leads to systematization of ideas that actually may run counter to experience. Such systems, based upon unproved and untestable axioms, can direct our perceptions and understanding. As they are culturally approved, they are termed "beliefs" rather than "delusions." They result in compartmentalization of experience into segments that are kept from conflicting and challenging one another. Adherence to an axiom into which the perception of experience must be fitted almost requires distortion of perception of the environment. The issue is raised because a similar situation may be found within the family. If a parent must protect his tenuous equilibrium by adhering to a rigidly held need or self-concept, and everything else must be subsidiary to this defense, distortions occur that affect the rest of the family.

The family is the primary teacher of social interaction and emotional reactivity. It teaches by means of its milieu and nonverbal communication more than by formal education. The child's sources of identification and self-esteem derive from the family and markedly influence the developing patterns of symbolic functioning. However, the child is also exposed to the parental interpretation of reality and the parents' ways of communicating. Parental interpretations may have limited instrumental utility when they primarily serve to maintain the parents' own precarious equilibrium. The topic is very complex, and this paper will deal only with some of the more obvious influences of parental instability upon the children's thought processes.

We shall pursue the hypothesis that the schizophrenic patient is more prone to withdraw through distortion of his symbolization of reality than other patients, because his foundation in reality testing is precarious, having been raised amidst irrationality and chronically exposed to intrafamilial communications that distort and deny what should be the obvious interpretation of the environment, including the recognition and understanding of impulses and the affective behavior of members of the family.

The material that we present is derived from an intensive study of the family environment in which fifteen schizophrenic patients grew up, which has now been in progress for over three years (3, 4, 8–11). The selection of cases required that the patient be clearly schizophrenic, be hospitalized in the Yale Psychiatric Institute, and have the mother and at least one sibling available for repeated interviews and observation, as well as for projective testing. It turned out that the father was also available in all but two families. With one or two exceptions, these families were upper-middle or upper class, capable of supporting an offspring in a private psychiatric hospital for prolonged periods. In contrast with many other samples, there is a bias toward intact families with some degree of prestige in the community. The basic means of gaining information has been the repeated interviewing of all members of the family, and the observation of interaction of family members with each other and the hospital staff for periods ranging from six months to three years. Projective tests of all members of each family have been interpreted individually and to yield information concerning family interaction. Diaries, old family friends, former nursemaids, and teachers have been drawn into the study when possible, and home visits made when feasible. The study has been carried out depite obvious difficulties and methodologic shortcomings, because any concept of schizophrenia as a developmental difficulty requires careful scrutiny of the family in which the patient grew up. Any effort to reconstruct a family environment as it existed over a period of 15–25 years will contain grave deficiencies. Still, the effort appears essential, and we believe that it has been highly rewarding, furnishing new leads and perspectives, if not clear-cut answers.

Primarily, we are seeking to describe these families and find common features among them, rather than compare them with other types of families. We are, so to speak, describing the terrain of a country we are exploring, not comparing it with the geography of other countries. We have been skeptical, holding aloof from accepting too readily many current and past theoretical formulations. We have, for example, found many reasons to question hypotheses which seek to focus solely on the mother-child relationship during the early oral phase of development, noting the absence of clear-cut evidence of a type of rejecting or destructive mother-infant relationship which would differentiate the development of schizophrenic patients from persons with certain other psychiatric and psychosomatic conditions. The nature of the psychopathology or the relative health of the patients may well be determined by later events. In general, rather than focusing attention upon one phase of development or any single interpersonal relationship, we have been more interested in studying the forces that interfere with the emergence of a reasonably independent and integrated personality at the end of adolescence—the critical period in the development of schizophrenia, even if the onset is later in life.

We shall discuss in this paper two closely interrelated aspects of the family environment—the rationality of the parents and the nature of the communication within the family.

We shall first consider the rationality of the parents in the grossest terms. The findings are unexpectedly striking, when compared with data from larger statistical studies (5, 12). However, Terry and Rennie found comparable figures, though their data are difficult to evaluate clearly (14). None of the parents of our patients was ever hospitalized in a mental institution and thus probably would not have been indexed as psychotic in any broad epidemiologic survey of psychoses in the parents of schizophrenic patients. Minimally, nine of the fifteen patients had at least one parent who could be called schizophrenic, or ambulatory schizophrenic, or clearly paranoid in behavior and attitudes. The finding is difficult to express explicitly, for the shading between what one terms schizophrenia and what bizarre behavior and ideation is arbitrary, and the line between psychosis and a paranoid outlook is equally fine. Although the proportion of families with more or less schizophrenic parents is very high, minimally 60 per cent of the families, it will become apparent that the cut-off point was quite arbitrary and other families could have been included. The classification is made difficult because of parents who maintain a reasonable degree of social presence and yet display seriously distorted thinking and motivation. Some of the mothers are seriously scattered and confused, particularly when anxious and under pressure. Fathers may be eminently successful but display behavior to their families that is pervaded and dominated by paranoid beliefs. Brief illustrations will clarify these statements.

We shall say little about the two mothers, A and B, who were frankly schizophrenic except to say that despite delusions, hallucinations, and very confused reasoning they had continued to be the parent with the ma-

jor responsibility for raising the children. (For further details and elaboration, see Lidz *et al.,* 10). The husband of one was somewhat grandiose, if
not paranoid, and spent most of his time away from home, while the other
couple was divorced. Although a third mother, Mrs. C, sounded frankly
schizophrenic, she ran the family business after her husband had suffered
a "nervous breakdown" (before the patient was born), after which he had
become passive and subservient to her. She openly expressed beliefs that
her telephone was tapped and that the neighbors might burn down the
home.

There were two mothers, Mrs. D and Mrs. E, who completely dominated the lives of their passive husbands and children. We consider these
women typical "schizophrenigenic" mothers in needing and using their
sons to complete their own frustrated lives. Their sons had to be geniuses,
and any faults in them or anything that went wrong with their lives was
consistently blamed on others—classmates, doctors, teachers, and society
in general. They believed that only they understood their sons. We could
never really understand these mothers, for their incessant talk was driven
and mixed up, displaying unbelievable obtuseness to any ideas not their
own. While we have hesitated to call these women schizophrenic, they are
certainly not reality-oriented and are very close to being psychotic. Brief
descriptions may convey the problem.

Two major private psychiatric hospitals had refused to keep Son E,
not because of his behavior but because they could not stand his mother's
incessant interference. Such behavior had plagued the boy and his teachers throughout his school years. Mrs. E talked incessantly about some fixed
idea of the cause of her son's illness. When her ideas were questioned, she
counterattacked; and if forced to abandon a theme, she would relinquish
it only temporarily, retreating to her next, equally unreasonable idea.
When the family had wished to build a home, she had exhausted four or
five architects, and the house was never built. When the daughter eventually gave up attempting to inform her mother that she intended to get married, and simply announced her engagement, Mrs. E steadfastly ignored
the daughter's intent. While the girl was seeking an apartment, the mother
would only talk about reengaging her college room for the next academic
year. The mother ignored the need to make plans for the wedding until the
father, an unusually passive man, finally intervened shortly before the
date that had been set for the wedding.

Mrs. D's life was dominated by the idea that her twin sons were
geniuses, whose development must not be hindered by setting any limits
except in defense of her own extreme obsessiveness. Delinquent acts of the
twins while still in grade school, such as breaking into and robbing a house
and setting a dock on fire, were ignored and blamed upon other children.
She insistently regarded a move from a suburb to the city, required be-

cause the twins were ostracized, and which disrupted her husband's business and social life, as a move to give her twins the superior education they required. Mrs. D fell into violent rages because of trivia that interrupted her obsessive cleanliness but gave inordinate praise for acts that the twins knew were nonsense. The household under her domination was a crazy place, and description could not be attempted without provoking the charge of gross exaggeration. For example, both twins claim that for many years they thought that constipation meant disagreeing with mother. Whenever one of them would argue with her, she would say they were constipated and needed an enema; both boys were then placed prone on the bathroom floor naked while the mother, in her undergarments, inserted the nozzle in each boy, fostering a contest to see which could hold out longer—the loser having to dash down to the basement lavatory. The projective tests of these last two mothers were judged frankly schizophrenic.

Only one of the four or five fathers who were considered psychotic or paranoid was as disorganized as these mothers. (For further material on fathers see Lidz et al., 8) Mr. F, though a steady provider and a man with an ingenious turn of mind, was constantly engaged in working out one or another of his many inventions, which never materialized. He was vaguely suspicious and paranoid, fostering suspicion in his children; but it was his incessant talk, in which he jumped from one topic and one idea to another in driven fashion, that seemed most disturbing to the family. Like Mrs. E, he would hammer away at a fixed idea, and an hour with Mr. F thoroughly exhausted either of the two interviewers who tried to cope with him. The other fathers were more capable and less disorganized but more fixed in their paranoid ways. Mr. G was also an inventor, but a successful one, for a single ingenious invention had made the family wealthy. He spent much of his time steeped in the mysteries of an esoteric Asiatic cult, believing that he and a friend who shared these beliefs were among the few select who would achieve salvation in reincarnation. Whether he believed in his divinity or it was his wife who deified him is not clear, but this family lived in what we have termed *folie à famille,* which centered about the father and his esoteric beliefs, and according to a social pattern that was widely divergent from the society in which they actually lived. (Fuller details of the family are combined in an article by Fleck et al., 4) Mr. H and Mr. I may be mentioned together as being competent business men who expressed many paranoid beliefs which did not interfere appreciably with their business activities but seriously upset family life. Among other things, Mr. H was paranoidly bitter against all Catholics, not an unusual situation, but here the paranoid bigotry focused upon his wife, who was a devout Catholic. At times he feared going to work because he felt people were against him. His wife, who has not been counted as psychotic, probably as a matter of relativity, was an extremely immature, scattered woman. (See Lidz *et al.,* 11 for further description). Mr. I was so suspicious that people were taking advantage of him that the hospital staff could not establish any relationship with him over a six-month period. His major concern at all interviews was to prove to the staff that his wife, who was actually a seriously obsessive woman, had been a malignant influence and had ruined his daughters, and also to make certain that the hospital was not lying, misrepresenting, or somehow taking advantage of him. Both men were hostile and contemptuous of women, and both had only daughters. The material offered here concerning these parents has been sparse, but we have abundant information which permits us to be certain that all nine have been virtually psychotic or markedly paranoid at least from the time of the patient's birth until the onset of illness. We are more interested in scrutinizing the situations in the remaining six families, in which the parents cannot be labeled so readily.

We can extract some generalizations from the study of these more disturbed parents which seem to apply to most, if not all, of the remaining six families, as well as to parents of many other schizophrenic patients. The struggles of these parents to preserve their own integration led them to limit their environment markedly by rigid preconceptions of the way things must be. The parents' precarious equilibrium will tumble if the environment cannot be delimited or if the parents must shift from the one rigid role they can manage. Mrs. D must see herself as the mother of twin geniuses. We understand something of how this came about. She too, was a twin, but the deformed ugly duckling of the family, who dreamed of the phallus that would turn her into a swan. The birth of twins was her triumph and their accomplishments her means of outshining her dominant twin sister. Mrs. B had written of how she had given birth to a genius, or perhaps a Messiah. She kept a diary of the child's development for fifteen years, presenting an idyllic picture of the home life, which we learned from the sons and husband had little resemblance to reality. In a somewhat different sense, Mrs. H, the rejected Catholic wife, could only raise her daughters as Catholics, for she could not live according to any pattern except the one established for her by the church. Mr. I had to dominate his household and maintain his narcissistic esteem through admiration from all of the females around him—his mother, wife, and two daughters. The slightest challenge to his imperious and unreasonable demands provoked a storm of fury. These people must retain the necessary picture of themselves and their family. Some will fight to retain it; but others adhere to their conceptualization, which reality cannot alter or a new situation modify. They perceive and act in terms of their needed preconceptions, which they relinquish only under extreme pressures, and then with all sorts of maneuvers to explain through projection or ignore through isolation. We should like to take an example from outside the series of fifteen families—

K*

from a case in which the sibling of the schizophrenic patient was in analysis. The father had left home when the children were very young to gain justice and revenge against a rival firm that had ruined his business by publicly accusing him falsely. Nothing mattered to him except to reestablish his power and prestige and gain revenge. He pursued his course for over fifteen years without even visiting his family, though always writing that he would return home the following week. He was markedly grandiose and paranoid, however just his cause. Still, his attitude was scarcely more pathologic than the mother's. All through the years of separation, she insisted that nothing was wrong with the marriage, maintaining a shallow, euphoric attitude and telling her children that their concerns were groundless—the father was just attending to his business and would be back next week. Penelope was finally rewarded, but she could not unravel the fabric she had woven. Her son became schizophrenic, within a month of her husband's return.

The parents' delimitation of the environment, and their perception of events to suit their needs, result in a strange family atmosphere into which the children must fit themselves and suit this dominant need or feel unwanted. Often the children must obliterate their own needs to support the defenses of the parent whom they need. They live in a Procrustean environment, in which events are distorted to fit the mold. The world as the child should come to perceive or feel it is denied. Their conceptualizations of the environment are neither instrumental in affording consistent understanding and mastery of events, feelings, or persons, nor in line with what persons in other families experience. Facts are constantly being altered to suit emotionally determined needs. The acceptance of mutually contradictory experiences requires parological thinking. The environment affords training in irrationality.

The domination of a parent's behavior and attitude by rigid defensive needs clarifies other traits often noted among these parents. "Impervious" is a word we find ourselves using frequently to connote a parent's inability to feel or hear the child's emotional needs. The parent may listen but does not seem to hear and, further, seems oblivious to unspoken communications. These parents cannot consider anything that does not fit in with their own self-protecting systems. Indeed, as Bowen and his co-workers have also noted (2), such parents may respond to the child only in terms of their own needs displaced to the child, thus building up an entire pattern of maladaptive interactions. Bateson et al. have recently studied a related aspect of parent-child interaction (1). The parent conveys the impression of being cold or rejecting, and, of course, may be, but imperviousness is not simply a consequence of rejection of the child, but more a rejection of anything that threatens the parent's equilibrium or self-image.

These parents often talk in clichés conveying a false impression of limited intelligence. Clichés and stereotypes serve to simplify the environment to enable the parents to cope with it in terms of their set needs. Such parents not only label a child as "the selfish one" or "the quiet one" but actually perceive the child only in terms of the stereotype. The fixed notions of an etiology of the illness, which may drive the psychiatrist to the verge of desperation, is a related phenomenon.

"Masking," which also confuses communication, refers to the ability of one or both parents to conceal some very disturbing situation within the family and to act as if it did not exist. "Masking" usually contains a large degree of self-deception as well as an effort to conceal from others; but it involves a conscious negation, as well as unconscious denial. The parent, unable either to accept or to alter the situation, ignores it and acts as though the family were a harmonious and homogeneous body which filled the needs of its members. Although some degree of masking may exist in all families, in some of our families the masking of serious problems dominated the entire family interaction. Problems which family members will not or cannot recognize are unlikely to be resolved. Children who grow up in such homes are aware that something is not right. They may become deeply resentful that the more intact parent takes no action to protect them from the situation. The children are puzzled, but may also learn to mask or ignore the obvious. Their efforts to explain away the situation, or to accept or convey pretense of affection and devotion, which has no resonance or real meaning, distorts their value systems.

The following two cases illustrate rather extreme degrees of imperviousness in which the parents appear severely rejecting.

The J's impressed the hospital and research staff as strange people, but they were one of the few couples in our series who were reasonably happily married. The younger of two daughters was severely hebephrenic. Mrs. J sought to blame the sex talk of the girl's college roommates. However, both parents could convince themselves to an amazing degree that the daughter was not really ill but merely being contrary and refusing to behave normally. This tendency increased as their financial means for retaining the girl in the hospital diminished, bearing little relationship to her condition. However, after some months of intensive therapy, the patient improved considerably. She repeatedly expressed her hopelessness that her parents would ever listen and understand her unhappiness over her school and social problems. As the patient could not be kept in the hospital for a long period and as the psychiatrist who was interviewing the parents found it impossible to get them to focus upon any meaningful problems that might be upsetting, a therapeutic experiment was undertaken, with great trepidation. The patient and the parents would meet together and, with the help of both psychiatrists, would try to speak frankly to one another. The daughter carefully prepared in advance what she wished to convey, and we tried to prepare the parents to listen carefully and to reply meaningfully. The patient, to the surprise of her psychiatrist, freely poured out her feelings to her parents and, in heartrending fashion, told them of her bewilderment and pleaded for their understanding and help. During the height of her daughter's pleas, the mother offhandedly turned to one of the psychiatrists, tugged at the waist of her dress, and blandly remarked: "My dress is getting tight. I suppose I should go on a diet." The mother had fallen back upon her habitual pattern of blocking out anything that would upset her bland equanimity. The next day the patient relapsed into incoherent and silly behavior.

Mrs. K, a cold and highly narcissistic woman, has been the other mother who did not wish to visit her offspring in the hospital. She said: "Wouldn't it upset Billy too much to have his mother see him in a place like this?"; this clearly meant: "I couldn't stand visiting my son in a mental hospital." Mrs. K's intense dependency upon and attachment to her older sister, a very masculine woman, had contributed greatly to ruining her marriage. The sister had developed an intense dislike for the patient when he was still a small boy. After her husband's death, Mrs. K lived with her sister, but her 12-year-old son was not allowed in the house and had to live in a boarding room nearby. One Christmas Eve the mother stood by while the sister turned her son away from the home and from spending the evening with them. Later, when they were all going to visit relatives in a distant city, the sister refused to take the son along, and the mother remained blandly in the car while they passed the boy trying to hitchhike in a snowstorm. Mrs. K's dependency upon her sister took precedence over her son's needs. (Literary and dramatic illustrations of many features of these families which we seek to convey can be found in Eugene O'Neill's *Long Day's Journey into Night,* Tennessee William's *The Glass Menagerie,* and August Strindberg's *Easter* and *The Father.*)

Another type of imperviousness existed in the cases of D and B. The mothers were solicitous enough, but the vision of the genius child who would complete and justify their lives made them oblivious to the actual needs, abilities, and deficiencies of their children. Mrs. C was so caught up in a struggle with her elder, psychopathic son that she scarcely noted anything that occurred in the life of the younger son, who eventually became schizophrenic, even though she was very controlling of much of his life.

"Masking" also distorts the communication within the family severely. Mr. L had been an eminent attorney who supported his family at a lavish level and basked in the light of his legal prestige and his associations with prominent persons. After his partner, the contact man for the firm, committed suicide, his income fell off disastrously. Mr. L was an obsessive brief writer and researcher who could neither gain clients nor plead cases. Gradually, he withdrew into his office, and into his study at home, spending his time making scholarly analyses of legal matters, which earned him almost nothing. The need to consider himself a great legal mind and a prominent person took precedence over the needs of his family. He could not admit his failure to himself or anyone else, and could not alter his ways. His wife, who, fortunately, was a competent woman, went to work and, with the help of her relatives, managed to support the family as well as her husband's law office. For over ten years she helped maintain the pretense to the world and to her children and even managed to keep herself from recognizing the resentment she felt toward a husband who let her shoulder the entire burden of the family. She had to maintain the myth of a successful marriage to a strong father-figure. The children could not help but know that it was all fraudulent. The situation required consistent falsification, and all the communications between members of this household had a high degree of pretense concerning the feelings they felt obligated to express in order to retain the front. The daughter, as a patient, kept protesting the expense of her hospitalization to her father, though she was well aware that he had earned nothing since her early childhood.

Mr. and Mrs. M both strove to mask a situation they could not hide successfully. Mr. M, a successful business man and once an athlete of renown, needed to be the center of considerable adulation. Mr. M could not tolerate the rivalry of his son and required the help of alcohol and numerous affairs to maintain his feeling of masculinity. He pretended that he was not an alcoholic, and that he spent most of his time traveling in order to provide well, rather than to alleviate his anxiety and to prevent open conflict. His wife also tried to maintain the pretense that they were happily married. Unable to consider separation seriously, she strove to blind herself to the seriousness of his alcoholism; his noxious influence on their son, whom he constantly belittled; and his extramarital affairs, which were highly embarrassing to the family.

Mrs. M appeared to accept her husband's obnoxious behavior but sought to establish altogether different standards in her son, in whom she fostered esthetic interests. A son, in such situations, gains confused concepts of what his mother cherishes in a man. The many other problems that beset this family are outside the immediate interests of this paper; but we should note that the highly sensitive mother often became impervious to her son's needs because she had to center her attention on her husband and support his infantile needs.

Habitual masking may then be viewed as an irrational form of communication, but another feature that often affects the child's mental functioning is complete breakdown of communication between parents, especially when the child is caught between different value systems and attitudes which cannot be integrated. Mrs. N resented the daughter who was born after she and her husband had become emotionally estranged, whereas

Mr. N sought from his daughter the affection he could not receive from his wife. The parents had quarreled before the patient's birth over their respective attachments to their families, attachments which took precedence over the marital relationship. Mrs. N's family had accused the husband's oldest brother of ruining their father's business. When Mrs. N had seemed to side with her family, her husband considered her disloyal and never forgave her. Indeed, they never spoke of the matter again, but never became reconciled and were openly hostile, though continuing to live together. Communication between them was largely vengeful and undermining. The father, for example, perhaps partly to punish his wife, and partly to escape her vituperative temper, spent his evenings in his office reading, but, to conceal his own impotence, let his wife and family believe that he had a mistress with whom he spent much of his time. Many of the family quarrels centered on this nonexistent situation. In addition, the father's seductive use of the daughter to bolster his narcissism, while seeking to ignore his wife, further confused communication and meaning in this family.

We could properly place the O's, the remaining family, in the large category of psychotic or borderline parents, even though the parents were not so clearly psychotically disturbed. Mrs. O, particularly when anxious, spoke incessantly and said very little, and even less that was pertinent to the situation. She asked questions endlessly, but constantly interrupted with another question before anyone could answer her. This woman might be termed obsessive, but her obsessiveness was extremely scattered and disorganized when she was anxious. In contrast, her husband's ritualized obsessiveness led to behavior that often seemed highly irrational. He would go into rages if a toothpaste cap was not replaced, throw his wife's entire wardrobe on the floor because it was disorderly, or her fur coat into the bathtub because she left it lying on the bed. Although frequently complaining and worried about money, he could not keep from making unnecessary purchases. When seriously concerned about meeting the cost of his son's hospitalization, he bought a third car and could not understand why his wife was angered by his fine present for her, even though his purchase of a second car had precipitated a violent quarrel just a month before. Mr. O saw nothing hostile in the purchase. We wish to call attention to the irrational atmosphere produced in a family when the parents are obsessive-compulsive, particularly when the two obsessive patterns are in direct conflict. The covert, hostile, and symptomatic behavior of each parent challenges the defensive pattern of the other. Neither makes sense, but both parents find rationalizations for their own behavior which neither the spouse nor the children can really understand. Though Mrs. O, along with Mrs. J, Mrs. K, and Mrs. H could not be considered overtly psychotic, they all were strange, disturbed persons. The defensive structure of all these women led to a type of behavior that created great difficulty in communication within the family, because what they said was more in defense of their fragile equilibrium than a communication pertinent to the given situation.

Before ending this initial survey of the irrationality present in the family environment in which schizophrenic patients grow up, we wish to direct attention to the conscious training of children to a paranoid orientation that takes place in some families. Both Mr. H and Mr. I sought not only to make their daughters distrustful and suspicious toward their mothers but to share their own paranoid suspiciousness of almost everyone. In a different vein, the G parents inculcated a system of religious belief that was aberrant and virtually delusional in the society in which the family lived.

## COMMENT

The study of the irrationality and defective communication in these families presents a complex task. A fairly complete picture of each family would be required to bring out the many frustrating problems involved. Here, we have merely sought to convey an impression of the broad sweep of the distorting influences present in all of the families studied, which have also been apparent in most, if not all, of the families of the many other schizophrenic patients treated in the Yale Psychiatric Institute during the past several years. Other less obvious and subtler influences require attention which we shall consider in subsequent articles.

Although our studies encompass only fifteen families, they form a good random sampling of middle- and upper-class families with schizophrenic offspring. The marked disturbances in instrumental utility of communications that can readily be noted in all of these families cannot be ignored in the search for reasons why these patients may be prone to withdraw from a reality orientation when unable to cope with their serious interpersonal problems.

We are not pointing to such defects in communication and the presence of an irrational milieu as a cause of schizophrenia. We are concerned with multiple factors distorting personality development rather than seeking a "cause." Other papers from this study emphasize the importance of the personalities of both parents, the confused family environments provided the children, and the faulty and conflicting models for identification offered by the parents; and still other facets of the family milieu await scrutiny. Here we simply, but significantly, indicate that our patients were not raised in families that adhered to culturally accepted ideas of causality and meanings, or respected the instrumental utility of their ideas and communications, because one or both parents were forced to abandon rationality to defend their own precarious ego structure. We are, therefore, concerned here with factors that may differentiate the genesis of schizophrenia from the genesis of other psychopathologic syndromes, in that persons who grow up in such families, having had their symbolic roots nourished by irrationality in the family, are less confined by the restrictions of the demands of reality when means of escape and withdrawal are required.

Of course, the presence of poorly organized or disorganized parents can just as well be taken as evidence of a genetic strain that transmits schizophrenia. Indeed, we have probably found more evidence of mental illness among parents and in other relatives than any study of the genetic factors of schizophrenia. At this time we are describing what exists in the family rather than explaining how it came about. According to our concepts of human development, such distortions of reasoning are more explicable through extrabiologic transmission of family characteristics than through genetic endowment. However, we need not seek a solution with an "either-or," for, as with many other conditions, both genetic and environmental factors may well be involved.

## SUMMARY

In an earlier paper we suggested that a theory of schizophrenia must explain not only the patients' needs to withdraw regressively and through abandonment of the restrictions of reality but also their ability to do so. The accumulating data in our intensive study of the intrafamilial environment in which schizophrenic patients grow up suggested the hypothesis that these persons are prone to withdraw through altering their internal representations of reality because they have been reared amidst irrationality and intrafamilial systems of communication that distort or deny instrumentally valid interpretations of the environment. The role of the family in transmitting instrumentally useful perception and mentation is discussed to provide a basis for the study. Markedly aberrant ways of thinking were present in most families; in at least nine of the fifteen families one or both parents were schizophrenic or paranoid, and in all the others less pronounced degrees of irrationality, with seriously disturbed ways of communications, would seriously affect the children's foundation in rational processes. We present these findings, along with an analysis of some of the more obvious difficulties, as but part of our studies of the influence of the family upon the developmental processes in schizophrenic patients.

## NOTES

1. Read in abbreviated form at the 113th Annual Meeting of the American Psychiatric Association, Chicago, May 13–17, 1957. This research is supported by grants from the National Institute of Mental Health and from the Social Research Foundation, Inc.

## REFERENCES

1. Bateson, G.; Jackson, D. D.; Haley, J., and Weakland, J.: Towards a Theory of Schizophrenia, Behavioral Sc. 1:251, 1956.
2. Bowen, M.; Dysinger, R. H.; Brodey, W. M., and Basamanie, G.: Study and Treatment of 5 Hospitalized Family Groups Each with a Psychotic Member, presented at the Annual Meeting of American Orthopsychiatric Association, Chicago, March 8, 1957.
3. Cornelison, A.: Case Work Interviewing as a Research Technique in a Study of Families of Schizophrenic Patients, to be published.
4. Fleck, S.; Freedman, D. X.; Cornelison, A.; Terry, D., and Lidz, T.: The Intrafamilial Environment of the Schizophrenic Patient: V. The Understanding of Symptomatology Through the Study of Family Interaction. Read at the Annual Meeting of the American Psychiatric Association, May, 1957.
5. Kallmann, F. J.: Heredity in Health and Mental Disorder: Principles of Psychiatric Genetics in Light of Comparative Twin Studies, New York, W. W. Norton & Company, 1953, p. 144.
6. Lidz, R. W., and Lidz, T.: The Family Environment of Schizophrenic Patients, Am. J. Psychiatry 106:332–345, 1949.
7. Lidz, R. W., and Lidz, T.: Therapeutic Considerations Arising from the Intense Symbiotic Needs of Schizophrenic Patients, in Psychotherapy with Schizophrenics, edited by E. B. Brody and F. C. Redlich, New York, International Universities Press, 1952, pp. 168–178.
8. Lidz, T.; Parker, B., and Cornelison, A.: The Role of the Father in the Family Environment of the Schizophrenic Patient, Am. J. Psychiat. 113:126–142, 1956.
9. Lidz, T.; Cornelison, A.; Fleck, S., and Terry, D.: The Intrafamilial Environment of the Schizophrenic Patient: I. The Father, Psychiatry, 20:329–342, 1957.
10. Lidz, T.; Cornelison, A. R.; Fleck, S., and Terry, D.: The Intrafamilial Environment of the Schizophrenic Patient: II. Marital Schism and Marital Skew, Am. J. Psychiat. 114:241–248, 1957.
11. Lidz, T.; Cornelison, A.; Fleck, S., and Terry, D.: Parental Personalities and Family Interaction, Am. J. Orthopsychiat., to be published.
12. Pollock, H. M; Malzberg, B., and Fuller, R. G.: Hereditary and Environmental Factors in the Causation of Manic-Depressive Psychoses and Dementia Praecox, Utica, N. Y., State Hospitals Press, 1939, pp. 98–145.
13. Spiegel, J. P.: The Resolution of Role Conflict Within the Family, Psychiatry 20:1–16, 1957.
14. Terry, G. C., and Rennie, T. A. C.: Analysis of Parergasia, Nerv. and Mental Disease Monograph Series No. 64, New York, Nervous and Mental Disease Publishing Company, 1938, pp. 67–70.

## 16:

# Differential Patterns of Social Outlook and Personality in Family and Children

*Else Frenkel-Brunswik*

Most investigators who have written about the American family agree that at present we witness a weakening of the family as an institution and that this change runs parallel to the weakening of many other institutions. It is pointed out by these writers, especially by Ogburn,[1] that the dilemma of the modern family is due to the loss of some of its functions, such as the economic, the educational, or the religious function. But in the interpretation of this loosening of the older, more rigid forms of family organization the writers disagree. Some, such as Zimmerman,[2] see in this change signs of disintegration and point to divorces, delinquency, revolt of youth, and increased individualism as proof of their contention. Others, such as Burgess,[3] find that the increased relaxation of authority and regimentation within the family leads to greater stress on companionship and affection. Instead of regarding it as a sign of disintegration, he sees in the replacement of old-time family structures a phenomenon of growth and increased adaptability, brought about by greater democracy, freedom, and opportunity for self-expression within the family. A cogent analysis of the American family can be found in Mead.[4] In view of such comprehensive collections of the different views on the American family as that by Winch and McGinnis,[5] we need not expand on the subject further.

Although the trend toward democratization of the family is, without doubt, an outstanding development in this country, the old-type authoritarian family with its unquestioned parental rule, even though deviant by modern standards, has not vanished altogether. In the present paper one example each of the two opposite extremes of American families is presented. In each case the presentation is centered about

Reprinted from *Childhood in Contemporary Cultures,* edited by Margaret Mead and Martha Wolfenstein, by permission of the University of Chicago Press. Copyright 1955 by the University of Chicago. All rights reserved. Copyright 1955 under the International Copyright Union. Else Frenkel-Brunswik until her death was lecturer in psychology, University of California, Berkeley.

one of their children. It was the children who were the basis of the selection of the two families; they represent the authoritarian and the democratic attitude and personality structure in their purest form. Neither of them can be considered representative in the statistical sense. To paraphrase a statement of Woodworth, they are so typical that they can be considered to be atypical. They exhibit most of the trends found statistically to be prevalent in their respective groups, to be introduced below, but rarely present in such completeness in a single individual. In accordance with our general findings, existing differences, if any, in sex, intelligence, or size of family may be considered of but secondary importance in the choice of paradigms for our present purpose, which is the concrete demonstration of the authoritarian versus the equalitarian syndrome. As will become evident to the reader, there are rather striking differences in the educational and intellectual levels of the two families. The question as to whether these differences are primary or whether they are secondary effects of the general inaccessibility to experience which is so characteristic of even the more intelligent authoritarian individuals cannot be fully discussed here, although some light will be thrown on this issue by the present material.

The first of the two families belongs to a pattern obviously less frequent in the present American culture than the second. It mirrors the old-fashioned authoritarian type of family structure in its most rigid form. Our second, democratic-minded example, even though by no means free of internal tensions, represents an orientation geared toward the realization of basically equalitarian principles; these are pursued in this family with relentless devotion and without compromise. It must be stressed that neither of the two families presents an ideal from the standpoint of perfect adjustment, as generally both the authoritarian and the nonauthoritarian personality are sometimes associated with their own particular brands of neuroticism.[6]

Since we are describing two individual families, we cannot generalize to the culture as a whole. In fact, our examples stress the variety rather than the uniformity of family life and individuals that can be found within one and the same culture. Furthermore, in the present context we are not primarily interested in social and economic determinants and, therefore, in the origin and structure of such social institutions as the family; rather, our main emphasis is on the influence of such institutions upon the outlook and personality structure of children and adolescents. However, we shall not neglect to point out the ways in which the family patterns described here seem to be rooted in some aspects of the complex institutional structure of our society.

Although our start is from the children and other individuals concerned and our method is a clinical one, with special emphasis on depth interviewing, our eventual concern is with general problems of social psychology. Under this aspect we explored the ways in which parents and children relate themselves to shared norms and values, their feelings of belongingness, their conception of parent-child relationships, of occupational roles and sex roles, and their religious and social outlook in general. Over and above this we tried to probe into the underlying patterns of motivation and emotions.

In a child-family study begun in 1944 and still under way at the Institute of Child Welfare, University of California,[7] approximately fifteen hundred children and adolescents, most of them between the ages of ten and fifteen, were given questionnaire-type tests dealing with attitudes toward minority groups as well as attitudes toward political and economic issues in general. From some of these instruments an over-all ethnic prejudice or "ethnocentrism" score was derived. Among those scoring extremely "high" and extremely "low" on ethnocentrism (that is, scoring within the uppermost or lowermost 25 per cent), one hundred and sixty-one were interviewed and given a specially designed variant of the well-known Thematic Apperception Test.[8] The interviews, conducted in 1946 and 1947, concerned attitudes toward minority groups and the social scene in general, toward school, discipline, work, parents, friends, and the opposite sex, as well as the child's conception of the self. With respect to these procedures, our methods and results are analogous to those of a separate project on "The Authoritarian Personality,"[9] of which this writer was one of the authors and in which the relationship between ethnocentrism and a more generalized authoritarianism was ascertained for the case of adults. Over and above these procedures, one or both of the parents of forty-three of our children were also interviewed concerning their attitudes and child-rearing practices; in addition, the socioeconomic family history was gathered. A further distinguishing phase of our child-family study consisted of an exploration of the children's cognitive mastery of reality by having them perform various experimental tasks in perception, memory, and thinking.[10]

The use of children as subjects in the study of social beliefs offers both advantages and disadvantages. Children are generally more direct and uninhibited; they openly express attitudes and feelings which, though no doubt still alive in adults, are manifested by them with greater reserve and restraint. On the other hand, children's attitudes are less structured and less consistent than those of adults. But even in children we found that the social beliefs held by an individual, though varying in degree of crystallization, tend to fall into a coherent pattern and that this pattern seems to be related to the personal "fate" he had met in his early interpersonal relationships within the family.

1968　ed.　Gerald Handel

A body of data has now been accumulated by various investigators which shows that different socioeconomic classes vary a great deal as to the pattern of child rearing. Since our study was not primarily oriented toward class differences, we tried to select two families which are not too different as far as their economic locus is concerned. In fact, the two families are even matched in the sense that both are objectively moving downward on the economic ladder when compared with the grandparents; yet we find a profound difference in the reaction to the loss of objective status. Although approximately matched economically, the two families differ widely with respect to many other social indices, such as education and prestige. These differences, without doubt, in addition to the differences observed in the personalities of the parents, will explain a good part of the radically different atmospheres prevailing in the respective homes.

## CASE STUDY OF AN AUTHORITARIAN FAMILY AND CHILD

One of the most ethnocentric child subjects is an eleven-year-old boy whom we shall call "Karl."

*Parents and home atmosphere.*—Karl's father comes from an authoritarian family and is a mechanic. Karl's father and paternal grandfather were born in this country, whereas the child's paternal grandmother came from Germany. The paternal grandparents died when Karl's father was four years old, and the father was reared by the great-grandparents, who owned a large farm and a wholesale store and "who were rich but not generous with their money."

Karl's mother was born in this country, and so was her father, while her mother was born in Scotland. Karl's maternal step-grandfather was a notary. Karl's maternal grandmother had divorced her husband shortly after Karl's mother was born. In fact, Karl's mother had a succession of stepfathers, one of whom, a combination of musician and laborer, also played an important role for her. She finished the eighth grade, whereas Karl's father's education stopped even before he had reached this level.

The interviewer describes the home as crowded with overstuffed and dreary oak furniture, with lace doilies on the tables. All this perhaps represents a concerted effort on the part of the parents to stress their middle-class identification and to avoid the possibility of being grouped with the underprivileged. This anxiety stems at least partially from the fact that the socioeconomic history of the family is unstable and that there was some loss of status as compared to the previous generation. There is, however, no evidence of poverty. The family lives in a six-room flat and owns a car and two radios.

The mother's background has much less stability than the father's. "I grew up in big cities and in one hotel after another." Generally, such geographical instability seems relatively common in ethnocentric homes. Both parents, furthermore, report their own parents as foreign-born. This, too, is significantly more often the case with parents of prejudiced than of tolerant children. As a group trend, it may be taken to indicate that the parents still see themselves entangled in the process of assimilation. Apparently as a counterbalance, they stress their "belonging," through both their social aspirations and the rejection of what is considered socially inferior.

Both of Karl's parents had been exposed to strict discipline. The father does not like to talk about his own father, whom he describes as a drunkard and psychopath who deserted his family. He is much more ready to discuss his grandfather, by whom he was raised:

"My grandfather was really strict. He had thirteen children, and even when they were grown up, there wasn't one of them that would talk back to him, and he could handle any of them."

The father of our boy grew up knowing little but work. His grandfather was anxious to see his grandson go to school and even to have his voice trained. Karl's father did not live up to any of his grandfather's ambitions, doing relatively simple work, although he still believes he will one day accomplish a great deal by an invention. He asserts that his occupation is only temporary, since he is likely soon to make a big mechanical invention. This aspiration remains on a fantasy level, since there is little evidence of any concrete work toward the goal.

The idea of achieving fame some day is still alive in the fantasies of Karl's mother as well. Though having worked mainly in factories and being a waitress at the time of the interview, she prides herself on her talents, such as photography, composing, and writing. There is here the same kind of unrealistic fantasy to which attention will be called in discussing Karl himself.

In discussing their children, Karl's parents emphasize that they made rules for them which had to be strictly obeyed. For instance, the children had to be in bed "sharp at six without fail." Asked whether the children ever have tantrums, the mother says:

"I should say not. They had better not. If they got mad, I just sat them on a chair and said to stay there until they could behave. I guess they never really had tantrums."

This is at variance with Karl's own statements, according to which he has outbursts of temper. Either this is mere boasting on his part, or the mother's denial of his ever deviating from what she considers good behavior is a distortion of fact; we are inclined to favor the latter interpretation. Apparently along the same line is the mother's statement about Karl, who is obviously a rather weak child, that "he has a strength but he hides it."

Both parents also report that they have used spanking as a disciplinary measure. To quote the mother: "The boys are more afraid of their father than of me; I guess because he is stronger." She seems not to realize that her children are overtrained and welcome the more severe punishment by their father. The father appears considerably worried about what the interviewer might have guessed about the children's relation to him: "It seems like Karl is afraid of me."

It is the father who represents in the family the rigid dichotomizing of the sex roles, which is, as we shall see, one of the characteristics of the authoritarian milieu: "Boys shouldn't do work in the home, though it's all right for a man to be a chef or a baker. The best of them are men." He apparently feels that it is considered appropriate for a man to be chef and thus to enter the field of women only if there is assurance that he will excel.

The mother, in explaining her children's personality, relies heavily on astrology. She tells us that the personality of Karl's brother, whom we shall call Bill, can be explained by the fact that "he was born under the sign of The Twins." About Karl she says: "He is a dreamer of far places. He will go far and wide. The stars show that." The dependence on fate and the feeling of a mystical connection with supernatural forces has been found typical of the ethnocentric milieu,[11] the exaggerated ideas of self-importance going hand in hand with an underdeveloped self-reliance.

Both parents are ethnically extremely prejudiced. They consider the Negroes America's biggest problem, and the father adds: "Dig up Roosevelt and let him help settle it." He is concerned that the Negroes "want to go everywhere." The mother tells how, at the time she was a waitress, she personally took it on herself to put Negroes in their place. She would give them a glass of water and then ignore them:

"When they went out, we smashed the glass behind the counter good and hard so they were sure to hear it. The Chinese and Japanese should be separate too."

About the Jews the mother says:

"The Bible says they will always be persecuted. You know it wasn't a small thing they did—crucifying Christ—God said they would be punished till the end of time."

This line of argument is the more surprising because in the discussion about religion it is not the mother but the father who stresses the importance of religion, as does Karl himself.

*Karl's social beliefs.*—Karl is an usually fat and passive boy with a history of many illnesses. The parents' ethnocentrism is shared by Karl, who in many other respects mirrors fascistic attitudes. We begin with quotations from that part of his interview record that deals with attitudes toward minority members. Karl says about Negroes:

> "They make trouble, start wars. I wouldn't mind having all the Negroes in Oakland and all the white people in a different state. I would like to have a couple for good fighters. They are good fighters when they fight with a knife. Like somebody starts a fight and you have a gang with some Negroes to fight with you on your side with knives and guns."

Like most of the ethnocentric children, Karl is in favor of segregation of the outgroups, and, like some of them, his statements show implicit envy of characteristics ascribed to minority groups. Karl admires the physical power, strength, and aggressiveness of the Negroes. He rejects them and does not want them to mix with his own group, but he wants them as protectors—we might almost say as bodyguards—in fights against other boys. His passivity and relative immobility also give direction to the stereotype he has about the Jews:

> "They think they are smart and go anywhere they please. They think they are hot. They dress up in all kinds of jewelry. Some just kidnap girls and boys and use them for slaves."

Some characteristics of this image of the Jews, such as their alleged social dominance and their exhibitionism of wealth, are common in ethnocentric children. We find, however, in Karl's statements some emphases and elaborations which, as we shall see, are rooted in his own specific conflicts. Thus the mobility and the enslaving motif is very personal with Karl. We have just heard him express the desire to use Negroes as his fighting slaves. The theme of fighting recurs again and again in Karl's description of minority groups. Although children not uncommonly ascribe aggressiveness to Negroes, it is most unusual for them to mention this quality in descriptions of the Chinese. Karl, however, stresses the point that Chinese are "good fighters"; and about the Filipinos he says: "They are good fighters and definitely good to go through jungles with." As we shall see, the preoccupation with jungles, where one can be lost and subject to deprivation, and the preoccupation with animals dominate Karl's fantasy in general.

Like many of the ethnocentric children, Karl sees general avarice and acquisitiveness as the cause of the last war, while the democratic-minded children specify in greater detail the wants of the different countries. Most of the children in our study think that there will be wars

in the near future, but Karl, along with a great many of the ethnocentric children, takes this fact as natural and inevitable: "I think so
because there's always going to be a war." As do over two-fifths of the
high-scoring and a considerably smaller proportion of the low-scoring
children, he thinks that we won the last war because of the atom bomb,
ascribing a magical quality to its destructive potential. Equalitarian children refer more often in this context to better resources and the better
equipment of America in general.

It is evident that Karl is at least in partial sympathy with Hitler and
that his concern is only about the wrongs Hitler might have done to
Americans. He states: "He was a little bit O.K. Sometimes he got a
little bit too mean and did dirty stuff like putting lighted matches in the
toenails of Americans." This partial sympathy with Hitler does not
prevent Karl from exercising his extreme punitiveness toward the Germans: "We should put all the Germans and Japs on an island and put
an atom bomb to it."

He considers America's biggest problem the fact that "a lot of people
are getting mad because everybody is starting war against each other."
This is the recurrent fighting theme, this time in the form of an assumption of an almost chaotic war of all against all.

In Karl's response to another interview question we find a further
dominant theme—fear of deprivation, especially food deprivation. Karl
is against strikes because "if grocery stores go on a strike, we won't
have no food. Farmers can go on a strike, and there will be no food,
and we will have to grow our own food." Ethnocentric children frequently manifest this particular fear. It is especially exaggerated in Karl
but has, as we have ascertained, no basis in real food deprivation.

Karl's attitude toward the social scene and his role in it is best characterized by the one-sidedness of his answer to the interview question,
"How would you like to change America?":

"I would like to have a filling station every couple of blocks or so and
palm trees and grass along the streets and lawns in front of people's houses
and have the back yards all cleaned up and flowers growing. Every store
should have all kinds of candy and bubble gum. They wouldn't have no fights
in the neighborhood. The cops would take them all in. At Fleishacker's [an
amusement park] have nice warm water [in the swimming pool] and the zoo
cleaned up. Every day there would be hay for the animals that eat hay and
the lions would have lots of meat every day for breakfast and lunch."

As are many of our ethnocentric children, Karl is concerned with cleanliness and external beautification, the removal of aggressive groups, and
with having a constant flow of supplies. The only beings for which he
shows concern are, characteristically, animals rather than people. His
emphasis on rigid order as well as on the regularity in the appearance

of streets and other objects contrasts sharply with his emphasis on, and even open advocacy of, turmoil and chaotic aggression, as noticed above.

Equalitarian children, on the other hand, are better able to remove themselves from the pressure of overanxiety about immediate needs. They are more likely to penetrate to such underlying and more general aspects of human welfare as justice and equality, lower prices and higher wages, and moral and ethical values in general.

Before leaving the topic of Karl's beliefs, we should like to point to the similarity between his statements on this subject and those of his brother Bill, older by one year. These differences exist in spite of the fact that the boys had no opportunity to discuss the subject between the respective interviews. Like Karl, Bill thinks that "we should kick out the colored people from San Francisco" because they get drunk and kill people. He feels that the German war criminals "should all have been hanged and not put in prison." Like his brother, he wants to put "the Japs on an island and throw bombs on them." He considers food to be America's biggest problem, and his main concern in this context is the problem of the rationing of sugar.

*Karl's and his brother's attitudes toward school, family, and sex roles.*—The stereotypical approach to social and ethical challenges, with all its inherent inhibitions, carries over into such related, more specific areas as the conception of teachers, parental roles, sex roles, and so forth. The ambivalent submission to authority, found to be typical of ethnocentric children, is revealed in Karl's statement about teachers. An initial stereotyped denial of criticism, "I like everything about teachers," is followed by the mention of victimization and unjust treatment by teachers: "A lot of them make you go to the principal's office or out of the room for something you didn't do. I had that happen lots of times."

When asked in another context to describe the perfect boy, Karl starts off with a request for obedience to teachers. The craving for a complete surrender to authority is also exhibited in his brother Bill's statement about the kind of teacher he doesn't like: "Those who tell you in a nice way instead of being strict and then don't make you mind." Bill's ideal teacher would be "a man who would be strict," or, as second choice, a woman if "she was very strict." While the emphasis on negative aspects or on strictness seems to be a specific characteristic of ethnocentric children, the tolerant, by contrast, tend more often to emphasize positive traits in the ideal teacher, such as being helpful, laughing at jokes, and the like.

The attitude of ethnocentric children to the teacher appears to be but one of the aspects of a more generalized hierarchical conception of human relations, according to which the weak are expected to exhibit a self-negating surrender to the strong. Karl seems unaware of the fact that he himself succeeds only very partially in fulfilling the strict requirement of submissive obedience. Obviously, he is possessed by destructive and by no means dormant forces which are in part directed toward the very authorities to which he demands allegiance but which are, to an even larger extent, diverted to objects considered by him as underdogs.

In discussing the pupils he likes and dislikes, Karl seems exclusively concerned with the possibility of being attacked by one of the other boys, whereas his brother Bill stresses conventional values, such as politeness and obedience, values also emphasized by Karl in other contexts. Equalitarian children, such as our second major case, Peggy (see below), on the other hand, stress companionship, fun, common interests, and understanding as traits desired in friends.

Both Karl and his brother Bill stress, as do a relatively large proportion of the ethnocentric children, that money helps one to have friends. For Bill, money possesses magical evil attributes:

"It is the root of all evil. It's bad luck to be born with money. If your parents tell you to put it in a bank and you keep it until you are grown up, it's bad luck."

Bill proceeds to describe the disaster which befell several of his acquaintances after they saved their money. This is in line with the general tendency prevalent in the ethnocentric subjects to subscribe to all manner of superstitious statements, to see evil forces at work everywhere, and readily to anticipate doom and catastrophes.

Karl is one of the very few children who would prefer to have a private tutor rather than go to school. He explains that he would like to avoid the effort involved in getting ready to go to school, "to have to pack a lunch and hop a bus." Bill, however, rejects the idea of tutors as "just for rich people, and they are no good." This latter quotation exemplifies the resentment, frequent in ethnocentric subjects, against what they consider oppressors from above, a view which goes along with their fear that those below, such as the minority groups, may rise some day and take over in a fearful revenge.

Both boys have a rigid conception of sex roles, stressing politeness in girls. As Bill points out, "If a boy is talking, they shouldn't butt in." For him the best friend for a boy is a boy, for a girl, a girl. They both reject girls who are discourteous or aggressive toward boys, for example, "If she pulls a boy by the arm and tells him to take her to a show or some place." Although dichotomizing of sex roles is to a certain extent general at this age, children scoring low on ethnocentrism do so to a much lesser degree, stressing more the point that boys and girls should behave naturally with each other. They also do not differentiate their descriptions of a perfect boy from that of a perfect girl as much as do the prejudiced children.

Asked what he would consider a perfect father, Karl, in line with many of the ethnocentric children, speaks mainly of the material benefits this kind of father would provide: "He will let you do anything you like and let you get any kind of food you like and let you take a girl out. Will give you about two dollars every day." Asked how he would like to change his own father, he states emphatically that "my father is good to me" but then goes on immediately to say that he would like to get more money from him to be able "to go to a show or dinner or any place I want." In almost every context he manifests this exploitive-manipulative approach to people.

As is often the case in ethnocentric boys, Karl's hostility is more directly expressed toward the mother than toward the father. When asked how he would like to change his mother, he starts off with "to make her nice," then proceeds to tell what he wants from her, such as "a car." That he is, on the whole, more oriented toward his father is probably related to the fact that the father is more powerful, in a position to provide more goods, and also better able to protect. This kind of dependency is often found to reduce open feelings and expressions of hostility.

While Karl sees people, and especially those in authority, primarily as "deliverers of goods," to use a term of Fenichel's,[12] Bill expects mainly regimentation from them. Thus a perfect father is for him one who, if asked for something, "ought not to give it to you right away." Bill denies that he has any desire to change his parents. There is ample evidence, from his interview and especially from his Thematic Apperception Test stories, of Karl's underlying hostility toward the parents. On a "blind" over-all interview rating of attitudes toward parents, Karl earns the extreme rating of "6" with respect to both parents, representing the rater's impression that he is obsessed by the feeling of being threatened and victimized by their hostility. Bill receives a rating of "5"; this is only one step closer to the opposite extreme, "1," which would indicate an affectionate, secure, companionable relationship as seen by the child.

Both boys are assigned an extreme rating on "externalization of values," a category covering opportunism, conventionality, status-concern, and explicit condemnation of those who do not conform.

Both boys tell of corporal punishment at home, and both of them prefer to have their father rather than their mother punish them. Bill comes out with the explicit explanation that his mother "is a little too soft-hearted." In discussing this topic in general, both boys favor very severe punishment of children for relatively minor misconduct and seem only too ready to advocate intervention of the juvenile court in such cases. According to Karl, children should be punished for "talking back to grownups" and for breaking windows: "You should go to Juvenile one year for that."

In Karl a greater readiness toward explosive fits of aggression is revealed in his descriptions of how he reacts in anger: "I do anything I can—bite, pull hair, kick, tear into them." Bill, however, reports that he tries to control his anger as well as he can, mostly by going out of the field. Both explosive outbursts and frantic efforts of control are typical of our ethnocentric children.

Though both boys have shown some tendency to idealize their parents stereotypically and to stress their goodness, neither of them chooses any of the members of the family as companions on a desert island. Karl, of course, stresses first food and water and also that he would take along a girl. From the dreams that Karl relates, as well as from the Thematic Apperception Test, it is evident that he connects the idea of a girl with feeding her or being fed by her and, furthermore, that a girl means to him safety and absence of possible threats felt in connection with boys or men.

Along the same line are Karl's recurrent dreams, "it's about going with a girl for dinner," and about people getting murdered and hanged. The childhood memories he relates are full of mishaps and catastrophes. He remembers having fallen in a pond, recalls seeing his father kill a chicken that ran about without its head, seeing men killing turkeys, and seeing a crate of eggs broken under a truck.

Among his fears he lists his fear of wild animals, of high buildings, of drunken men, of "death in some dark night." He mentions that usually it is the girls who are especially afraid of the dark. When asked whether he wants to be a girl, he denies it but adds the stock projective answer: "Some guys want to be girls." The feminine identification which can be discerned behind much of the aggressive façade is apparent in the interviews and is especially evident in the Thematic Apperception Test.

*Karl's Thematic Apperception Test stories.*—The rigidification of the child's personality originally induced by the stress on self-negating submission and on the repression of nonacceptable tendencies not only leads to stereotypy; eventually the inherent pattern of conflict may result in a more or less open break between the different layers of personality and in a loss of control of instinctual tendencies by the individual. This contrasts rather sharply with the greater fluidity of transition and intercommunication between the different personality strata which is typical of the child in the more permissive home. The emotional makeup and the rigidity of defense, lack of insight, and narrowness of the ego of the authoritarian personality even carries over into the purely cognitive domain. Here, too, ready-made clichés tend to take the place of realistic spontaneous reactions.

Karl's TAT stories are full of murder and gore, much more so than the usual stories of children of his age. In practically every story a murder is committed under quite extraordinary circumstances. For example, a man who won in a race is "shot in the back five times" while he was "laying in bed, tired from his hard job." Two of the stories, to be further interpreted later, follow:

"It looks like murder. I saw a couple of murder pictures. A girl is down at the dock at night watching them unload freight. There is a man with a cane that is the girl's friend, and he is walking behind her. She had been gambling and won $200. This other man was trying to get the money off her. It was hid somewhere on her. The man with the cane presses on the cane, and a knife comes out. He stabs the man with the gun in the wrist, and the girl calls the cops, and they come and take him away in the patrol wagon to jail. He tries to break away but can't. That night he went to the electric chair, and the girl had the money safe to keep the rest of her life."

"Oh, gads: Sure is murder [cheerfully]. The man was in gambling. He believed the gambling table was crooked. He said it was, and the man behind the gambling table said it wasn't, and he had a whip and started whipping the other in the face. The U.S. Navy guy came in. It was a friend of his. He had a gun, and he shot the bull whip out of the man's hand. The cops came, and the Navy guy told the cops what happened. The guy that owned it was arrested for having a crooked place, and it was turned into a big Safeway store and people went there and bought stuff. And the army guys got $250 for finding out the man had a crooked wheel. The guy in the middle died from bleeding too much."

Usually it is the men who are shot, and only in one story "a lady is hit in the back with a knife." In this case the woman is killed because she betrayed a man. In most of Karl's stories, however, the women manage to be safe and to get food and money.

In almost every one of Karl's stories food is mentioned in a general way or specifically, for example, peanuts, waffles, double-decker cones, etc., and there is reference to specific amounts of money, such as $200, $25, $250, $550,000, $400, 10¢. Usually the person who has the money is in great danger of being deprived of it and of being killed in the process.

Neither the role of the aggressive man nor that of the passive man seems to be workable in these stories. The man who is passive and in possession of some fortune is usually attacked in some surprising way, from behind or while asleep, and is destroyed. The aggressive man, on the other hand, is regularly caught by the police and sentenced at the least to life-imprisonment; more often, he is executed in the electric chair. The earlier story, in which the "crooked place was turned into a big Safeway store," obviously reveals Karl's deep-seated longing that all the dangerous men will be removed and that he will be allowed to be passive and surrounded by food, without fear of aggression and without the ensuing necessity for being aggressive himself. This is also the way he imagines girls to be. Even though the girls are, in the stories, in the more enviable position, not even they are always safe.

Here again we find the preoccupation with animals. In the stories they are being fed, as they were in Karl's projected ideal of America which was quoted earlier. The feminine identification is apparent in the description of the "mother ape that had just laid a baby." Not even the animals and not even the baby ape are safe, since a man tries to "sock the baby ape with his gun."

Of the two types of men, the passive and the aggressive, Karl basically seems to feel closer to the former. In one story he describes in detail how a passive boy who always is being hit by a tough boy "had taken exercises from a guy that helps you make muscles." It is this same passive boy who feeds the animals. We thus have evidence both of insecurity about masculinity and of feminine identification, also manifested in the occurrence of many phallic symbols and castration threats and in an apparent embarrassment about body build and genital organs. In a swimming scene described by Karl he is careful to point out that the boys have swimming suits under their clothes and thus do not have to undress. Karl's stories are not only exaggerated versions of the stories common in ethnocentric boys in general but also have similarities to the stories of overt homosexuals.

Concerning the formal aspects of Karl's stories, the following can be said. They are long and flowing, presenting no necessity for probing on the part of the examiner. In spite of this fluidity, however, the form level of the stories is very low. They are neither coherent nor structured, and what seems like imagination is really a kind of ruminative repetition of the same themes over and over again. Karl is at times aware of this repetitiveness, and he starts one of his stories with the words, "another murder story." One of our foregoing stories begins, "Sure is murder," and the interviewer comments here that Karl makes this introduction with evident cheerfulness. The repetitiveness extends even to such details as numbers: the number $250 occurs in several stories, and other numbers are similar to it. The stories are, furthermore, utterly unrealistic as far as general plausibility is concerned, and they stray away to a marked degree from the content of the picture, which, after the first few sentences, is frequently lost from sight entirely.

The image of the world found in Karl and in most of our ethnocentric subjects—the projection of the hostility they feel toward their parents, and their feeling that the world is a dangerous and hostile place—coincides with the image of the world which Wolfenstein and Leites[13] found in

American movie melodramas. This may represent a common fantasy which in the more "typical" Americans, for whom the powerful father is more imaginary than actual, is present at the most archaic levels only.

Bill's stories contain topics similar to those of Karl, such as quarreling, food, money, ambivalence toward the mother, catastrophes, and unhappy endings. But he is at the same time more constricted, and a great deal of encouragement and probing are necessary to lead him away from a mere description of the picture.

Remembering the evidence from the interviews, it appears that Bill is the more disciplined, not to say regimented, of the two boys and the more cautious, even though perhaps the one who will put his biases more readily into action if the opportunity is offered. On the other hand, social upheavals of a major order may be necessary to bring an individual such as Karl to the fore. Lacking these, he may very well lead an inconspicuous, unsuccessful life, ridiculed and baited by his fellows, and possibly even passing over into a state of slow disintegration.

*Discussion of family influence.*—From this material we gain the impression that the total outlook, just described, seems to a very appreciable extent to have its root in the authoritarian home. Family relationships in such homes are commonly based on roles clearly defined in terms of demands and submission. Execution of obligations rather than affection is the basis of smooth functioning in such homes. Furthermore, there is a stress on stereotyped behavior and on adherence to a set of conventional and rigid rules. The intimidating, punitive, and paralyzing influence of an overdisciplined, totalitarian home atmosphere may well exert a decisive influence upon the thinking and creativity of the growing child. The impoverishment of imagination seems to be analogous to that apparent under totalitarian social and political regimes. At the same time, the consideration of the responses to threats in childhood may reveal much about the ways in which individuals react to threats in adult life.

Intensive experiences in later life are undoubtedly in themselves capable of superseding both earlier influences and the individual predispositions to a certain extent, however, so that no direct or exclusive causal relationship between family structure, attitudes of children, and rise of totalitarianism may be assumed. We must also bear in mind that social conditions and institutions have, in turn, an impact of their own on the family structure.

It is primarily the fact that the home discipline in authoritarian homes is experienced as overwhelming, unintelligible, and arbitrary, demanding at the same time total surrender, which makes for the apparent parallelism with authoritarian political and social organizations. The similarity becomes even more evident if we consider that the child, by virtue of his objective weakness and dependence, is entirely at the mercy of the parental authorities and must find some way to cope with this situation. We found that parents in the authoritarian group frequently feel threatened in their social and economic status and that they try to counteract their feelings of marginality by an archaic and frequently unverbalized need for importance. It is noteworthy that what seems to matter is not so much the actual status on the socioeconomic ladder or the objective marginality within a certain class; what seems decisive in this respect is, rather, the subjective way in which these conditions are experienced and allowed to build up to certain vaguely conceived aspirations. Recent data further suggest that the status concern of individuals susceptible to authoritarianism is quite different from a realistic attempt to improve their position by concerted effort and adequate means-goal instrumentality. An example was given earlier by the rather naïve hope of Karl's father of becoming an "inventor." In addition, we frequently find such aspirations taking the form of an unspecific expectation that help will come from a sudden change in the external situation or from an imaginary person who is strong and powerful.

Authoritarian disciplinary rules seem to have one of their major roots in such vaguely anticipatory, yet inefficient, states of social unrest on the part of the parents rather than in the developmental needs of the child. The parents expect the child to learn quickly certain external, rigid, and superficial rules and social taboos. At the same time they are impatient, demanding a quick execution of commands that leaves no time for finer discriminations and in the end creates an atmosphere comparable to acute physical danger. The rules to be enforced are largely nonfunctional caricatures of our social institutions, based on a misunderstanding of their ultimate intent. In many ways one may even speak of a defiance of culture by external conformity. In any event, the rules are bound to be beyond the scope and understanding of the child. To compel the child into an obedience of the rules which he is thus unable to internalize may be considered one of the major interferences with the development of a clear-cut personal identity.

The authoritarian form of discipline is thus "ego-destructive," in that it prevents the development of self-reliance and independence. The child, being stripped of his individuality, is made to feel weak, helpless, worthless, or even depraved. Parents and parental figures, such as teachers or other authorities, acquire the threatening, distant, and forbidding quality which we have observed in the case of Karl. Disciplining, controlling, and keeping one in line are considered to be their major role. It seems to be largely the resultant fear and dependency which discourage the child in the authoritarian home from conscious criticism and which lead to an unquestioning acceptance of punishment and to an identification with the punishing authority. As we have seen, this identification often goes as far

L

as an ostentatious glorification of the parents. As we have learned from psychoanalysis, however, repressions of hostility cannot be achieved without creating emotional ambivalence, at the least. Thus children who seem most unquestioningly to accept parental authority at the same time tend to harbor an underlying resentment and to feel victimized, without becoming fully aware of this fact. The existing surface conformity that lacks genuine integration expresses itself in a stereotypical approach devoid of genuine affection, so that the description of the parents elicited by interview questions is more often characterized by the use of exaggerated clichés than by expressions of spontaneous feelings. In ethnocentric subjects the range of responses tends to be generally rather narrow and without the variations commonly found in the description of real people. Only the more palpable, crude, and concrete aspects are mentioned.

## CASE STUDY OF AN EQUALITARIAN FAMILY AND CHILD

For contrast, we shall present the case of a twelve-year-old girl, whom we shall call Peggy. She scores extremely low on the ethnocentrism scale and generally exhibits the democratic outlook upon life and society in a particularly clear-cut form. The fact that she is of the opposite sex seemed of little bearing on our comparison; our material shows that boys and girls generally seem to be distributed over the same patterns so far as sociopolitical outlook and its relation to personality and family are concerned. Just as Karl manifested almost all the traits which we find prominent in the highly ethnocentric group as a whole, Peggy exhibits a similar concentration of features characteristic of the low-scoring group, thus highlighting the syndrome under discussion.

*Parents and home atmosphere.*—The socioeconomic backgrounds of the two families show certain similarities. The difference between the present economic situation of Peggy's and of Karl's parents is not too great. And in both cases there is indication of higher social position and greater wealth in the case of the grandparents as compared with the parents. But the two families react very differently to this change. In addition, there is an appreciable difference in the purely social situation of the two families. There is a radical difference between the personalities of Peggy's mother and Karl's mother and certain differences in their social background, including a much greater stability of the family of Peggy's mother.

While Peggy's mother is American born and of American-born parentage, the father was born in Italy, the son of a small-town doctor. At the time of our interview he had just sold a small restaurant which he had come to consider a bad investment. His professional history includes being a salesman, a clerk, and a waiter. He is a college graduate, as is his wife, who is a social worker. Peggy's maternal grandfather was first a small-town lawyer and "a dictator and patriarch to the population. He entered the army . . . and liked the opportunity which it gave him for expressing authority." Peggy's mother apparently received a great deal of warmth from her own mother, but she rebelled against her father.

Although the father's occupational history, especially as compared with that of his parents and that of the parents of his wife, could have led to a feeling of socioeconomic marginality, this family actually does not seem to be dissatisfied with its present status; much of the time of its members is devoted to such pursuits as supporting the causes of the community, participating in discussion groups, and so forth. Both parents are interested in reading, music, and art, and the mother has even written some poetry. Instead of resenting their marginality, the family makes constructive use of the greater freedom given them by their position. They have more time to follow the pursuits in which they are really interested, and they enjoy a great deal of respect among their friends. Although Peggy's parents are divorced, they are on good terms and see each other frequently.

Both parents feel strongly about equality between racial groups, and the father described how shocking the discovery of racial prejudice was to him when he came to this country "after reading Lincoln and Jefferson and men like that." Both parents declare in their interviews that greater tolerance and more education are the direction in which they would like to see America changed. At the same time, they are explicitly opposed to any radical movement.

Affection rather than authority or the execution of obligations dominates the general attitude of Peggy's parents toward the child. The perceptiveness and psychological insightfulness of Peggy's mother are reflected in her answer to the question concerning the positive ideal she holds for her daughter:

"I do hope that she will do something that will make her happy and at the same time be constructive. I hope the girl will have experience early enough that she can integrate it and lead an outgoing, constructive life; that she won't have to spend so long working out her aggression that she finds herself no longer young—not that I wish to spare my daughter the suffering and experience necessary for development, but I hope she may get it early and fast. I feel that I can help by giving a lot of trust and confidence in the girl. I do feel that at times in the past I may have expected too high a performance for the sake of my own gratification, and that may have troubled Peggy. The child has always been given more responsibility than the average, but as a rule it hasn't seemed to be a strain."

This quotation reflects the mother's concern with the inner life of her daughter, with her internal satisfactions, and it reveals how far removed she is from espousing a conventional ideal for her daughter. This absence of stereotyped conventionality becomes even more evident in the mother's response to the question as to what she considers the negative ideal for her daughter. She states that she would hate to see her daughter take a job she didn't like for the sake of money or caring too much for the acquisition of material things so that her ideals would be sacrificed.

Along similar lines are the statements of Peggy's father, in his separate interview. He wants his daughter "to grow up to have an all-around personality in such a way that she can get the best out of herself, be happy with herself and with other people. Whatever work she wants to choose—that is her business. If we can bring her up with self-assurance and not to give up at the first obstacles, we will be doing something."

Both parents stress again and again in varying formulations how much they enjoy the child. The mother considers as the strongest traits of her daughter "her sensitivity and receptivity to artistic things and to people. . . . She has a philosophical interest in people and seems to have a good idea of the interrelationship of people and nations." The father thinks Peggy's strong points are "strength of character and being intelligent and liberal." At the same time, he is aware of some weaknesses in his daughter, such as her insecurity, her exhibitionism, and her interest in boys; the latter he considers as typical of adolescent girls, however.

*The handling of authority in the equalitarian home.*—The idea has been promoted in many homes and in some educational systems and political circles that, in order to avoid authoritarianism, all authority must be forsworn. Against this excessive view it must be held that total permissiveness would verge upon anarchy. Respect for the authority of outstanding individuals and institutions is an essential aspect of a healthy home and society. It does not as such lead to total surrender to, or to an absolutistic glorification of, the given authorities. This is especially true if their leadership is limited to specialized fields or to special functions. Rather than authoritarianism or else anarchy, there must be "guidance," especially when this is combined with acceptance and thus strengthens the moral functions of the child and helps him to overcome the impulses toward selfishness and aggression. By guidance, therefore, we mean the encouragement of the child to work out his instinctual problems rather than repress them, thus avoiding their later break-through; this encouragement, in turn, must be rooted in a frank understanding of the child's particular needs and developmental steps. The child is treated as an individual and is encouraged to develop self-reliance and independence. His weakness is not exploited. He is allowed to express his likes and dislikes without the threat of losing love and the basis of his existence.

The statistical data which we gathered on adults[14] as well as on children[15] suggest that the way of handling discipline is indeed a crucial factor in the laying of the foundation for an authoritarian or a democratic outlook in children. As we have just said, the way in which parents handle discipline reveals the constructive use or misuse of parental authority and the degree to which a genuine socialization of the child and his adoption of cultural values are made possible.

According to Peggy's mother, everything was explained to the child and very little active exercise of discipline was necessary. The mother still feels quite guilty that she spanked the child on a few occasions and thinks now that it was because she herself was angry. The father's independent statement, very similar to that of the mother, is as follows:

"I don't know that we ever tried to discipline her very much. I was guilty of spoiling her when she was a baby sometimes, but I don't remember ever trying to discipline her. Oh, I have given her a few times a spat on the rear when I was mad. I shouldn't do that, I know. I think the girl is a little obstinate, hot-headed, and not disciplined as much as she should be now, but maybe that's because she is an adolescent."

In reading the interview of the mother it becomes quite evident that she has, and always has had, a warm and unconditional acceptance of her child. In fact, she is quite outstanding in this respect as far as our total group is concerned.

However, she confesses that in her eagerness to do the right things she has used many techniques which she now would reject. She feels that she had been "too much influenced by Watson." Thus she thinks that it was wrong to have started toilet training as early as she did. Further inquiry reveals, however, that all she did was to hold the child on a pot after meals when the child was six months old; but no pressure was used, and the child was allowed to regulate her own training, which was complete at two years of age. Furthermore, nursing was discontinued after three months, since the mother's milk failed. When the child was put on the bottle, she began to suck her fingers and continued to do this at bedtime until she was six or seven years old. The child never had tantrums, but she did express her objections and wishes emphatically. This is just the pattern of aggression which has been described as typical of individuals scoring low on ethnocentrism. There was never any evidence of nightmares, and the child called her mother during the night when she needed her. The mother always answered these calls because she remembered so keenly her own childhood fears at night. These details reveal that Peggy's mother, who tends toward intrapunitiveness, has not followed Watson as closely as she thinks she has. Apparently she also remembered well how comforting it was to have her own mother when she called for her.

Concerning the family atmosphere in the childhood home of Peggy's mother, she reports that her own mother had a similar attitude toward her child as the latter has toward Peggy. There seems never to have been any gross punishment. However, the father of Peggy's mother is described by her as a stern and authoritarian person. She thinks that her struggle for independence from her father played an important part in her development. She explains the fact that she, unlike her brothers was able to rebel against her father, by virtue of her being away from her father during the first years of her life. We would add that, as the only girl in the family, Peggy's mother had a better opportunity to identify with her mother than with her father. On the whole, her identification with her mother, whom she describes as "loving and gay when my father was gone," was a positive one. However, in one respect her mother furnished her with a negative example. She considers her mother as "completely cowed by my father, whom she never opposed."

Thus the negative identification of Peggy's mother with her own mother seems to have led to an attempt to have a more independent life which would not imply submission to an authoritarian husband. She realized these aims by attending college, pursuing a profession, which consisted in work with subnormal children, and marrying an utterly unauthoritaran man. As we have said, this marriage did not work out, however, and she blames this at least partially upon the difficulties which she had had with her own father. Peggy's mother needed a long time and the help of a psychoanalyst to work out her problems of feminine identification. In spite of the fact that Peggy's parents are divorced, they and the child do many things together as a family. The parents speak with a great deal of respect about each other, and the father credits the mother with the satisfactory development of their daughter.

*Peggy's social beliefs.*—Concerning minority groups, Peggy emphasizes in her interview that no one race is better than another:

"The Chinese can do really beautiful art work, the Germans have really intelligent and well-known scientists, and things like that. Every race has a certain amount of skill. They are pretty well equal. I go to parties at a Negro girl's house. I wouldn't mind going with a Negro boy to a party, but it would probably be better to go with a white one because the other kids would tease me, and the Negro boy and I would both feel funny."

This opinion is in sharp contrast to what the majority of the children feel along these lines. In the interviews, a staggering 96 per cent of the children scoring high on the ethnic scale, 83 per cent of the middle scorers, and even as many as 22 per cent of the low scorers express ethnocentric attitudes toward Negroes by ascribing negative traits to them and by favoring segregation[16]; about 60 per cent of the high scorers and middle scorers and 18 per cent of the low scorers express similar attitudes toward the Chinese. Peggy, as we have seen, goes all out for an equalitarian view of the various ethnic groups.

While Karl thought that most of the foreign countries are against us, Peggy thinks that America is "really very friendly with many countries," except for Russia, which "doesn't understand our ways and she doesn't understand us." While Karl was at least partially sympathetic toward Hitler, Peggy thinks that "he was crazy with power." Asked what a regular American is, Peggy answers that everyone who has citizenship papers "is an American in his own way. There is some foreign blood in every one of the Americans. The first people were foreigners."

To an interview question, "How would you like to change America?" Peggy responds with the following statement:

"Try to have people be more understanding about the Negro problem. . . . Another thing is to have better schools and teachers; nice schools that kids would really like. Give them a chance to change the subject often so it wouldn't be boring. Also a better department for juvenile delinquents. Not treat them as if they did it on purpose; and a better home for these kids. They really don't want to be bad, but they just don't know what else to do.

Note the contrast with Karl's emphasis on the beautification of streets and on a plentiful supply of food in response to the same question.

Peggy's concern for the welfare of the population is also expressed in her ideal of the President of the United States, whom she considers to be a man who "really thinks of others, not of himself; thinks of them as friends; is always kind and works hard for the people."

*Peggy's attitude toward school, parents, and sex roles.*—In discussing her teachers, Peggy does not show much evidence of an exaggerated submission to authority. She does not demand strictness and supervision from the ideal teacher. Rather, she thinks that the ideal teacher is one who can "understand you, be a friend to you, someone you can confide in, someone you like." The unprejudiced children tend to emphasize positive things in the ideal teacher, whereas the prejudiced children more often offer negative formulations, such as not playing favorites. The teachers whom Peggy doesn't like she describes as "dumb, and scream at the kids and tell them to shut up," and she adds very perceptively: "The kids always answer this kind of teacher back."

In discussing the girls she likes, Peggy stresses companionship and mutual liking. She dislikes girls who are "silly, stupid, giggle all the time and never get their work done but say they do."

The pattern of Peggy's aggression is one which is mild and not repressed, in contrast to that of the prejudiced children, in whom we find suppression of aggression interspersed with violent break-throughs. Thus Peggy confesses that she really tries to like everyone, but she just can't do it. "Nobody can." She seems to have some mild guilt about her occasional hostile feelings that alternates with a readiness to accept them as unavoidable.

These guilt feelings may also be connected with the feeling of acting against her mother's apparent wish to imbue the child with a far-reaching tolerance toward everybody. Peggy reports that the only occasion on which she and her mother disagree is "when I criticize someone who looks stupid and funny. My Mommy and Daddy both think that I shouldn't do this, since people don't know any better, but I think they really do." Her strong identification with the underdog is revealed by the type of occasions on which she reports that she tends to get angry:

"When people pick on someone, even dogs or animals, or when they tease Negroes and call them dirty names."

Peggy thinks of a perfect father as one who "is a good friend to you, understanding and nice. Just a person." We recall here that prejudiced children tend to think of the ideal father mainly in terms of punishment, as either being too little strict or too much so, whereas unprejudiced children tend to stress companionship, as Peggy does. She describes her real father pretty much in the same words as she does the perfect father, and the same holds for her description of her mother. She reports (and this is substantiated in the direct interviews with her parents) that she has never been punished or scolded: "My mother just talks to me. Children should never really be punished, but have things explained to them."

Peggy's flexibility is also carried into her conception of the sex roles. Like the unprejudiced children in general, she does not tend toward a dichotomous conception of sex roles. To the question, "How should girls behave around boys?" she answers: "Not silly but act like herself. Having a boy friend is just like having a good friend." She also thinks that boys "should not try to show off, should not try to show the girls how strong they are so the girls will be impressed." Furthermore, unlike most ethnocentric children, she does not make any marked differentiation between the best profession for a man and the best profession for a woman. Her description of the best profession for a man shows absence of heirarchical thinking in terms of social status: "Whatever he wants to do, whether it is a shoe clerk or a chemist or anything at all. Nobody else should decide for him." Concerning the worst profession for a man, she replies: "To have his life planned, to be what he doesn't want," and to the question about the best or worst profession for a woman she answers: "Same as for a man." Incidentally, Peggy's own professional ambitions are to be "an artist, a poet, a writer, and a dancer."

In spite of Peggy's equalitarian orientation in relation to authority and sex roles, she is far from being uninterested in boys. When asked about her daydreams, she reports that they are concerned with the wish to have a boyfriend and that her real dreams are also mainly concerned with boys. She usually dreams about one special boy and that he takes her to the movies. In fact, in a fond and understanding way, her father calls her "a little boy crazy," and he adds that Peggy occasionally shows exhibitionistic impulses. We have evidence for that in Peggy's childhood memories also. Asked for her earliest memories, she reports one, according to which—at the age of about three—she ran to the top of a near-by hill before her mother had finished dressing her, with only her pants and her shoes on. "The people were shocked by that kind of thing." This may be a projection, since she probably was too small at the time to shock people by her scanty clothes. She also reports that when she was a year and a half or two years old, she "ran out naked to say goodby to Daddy." These slightly erotically tinted early memories are in decided contrast to Karl's early memories, which are preoccupied with death and violence and carry a distinctly sadistic flavor.

*Peggy's Thematic Apperception Test stories.*—Peggy's creativeness and imagination are reflected in her TAT stories. While Karl is obsessed with primitive, archaic themes, as evidenced by his rumination about the topics of food and destruction as if flooded by his unconscious, Peggy seems to be at ease with her unconscious trends, which find expression in stories possessing an artistic flavor. In her case the unconscious problems seem to contribute to imagination in a positive manner. Her stories flow freely and at the same time are cognitively disciplined. While Karl's stories were stereotyped and at the same time chaotic, Peggy's stories show a colorfulness of thought which can come only from ease of communication between the different layers of her personality. Although she is by no means aware of all her problems, she possesses an unrepressed approach to life. Her basic self-acceptance has a disinhibiting effect on her productions, without leading to disintegration.

There are several distinct themes in Peggy's stories. The major motif is the same we encountered in the interviews, that is, a protective feeling toward those who are different or who appear weak. While Karl is contemptuous of the weak and the "sissy," Peggy reveals considerable psychological insight in trying to demonstrate that he who is considered a sissy is often the real hero. She describes, in one of her stories, a nine-year-old boy

L*

"whom all the kids in school used to tease and say he was a sissy. Tommy cried when he went home. Next day the boys dared him to fight the biggest bully of the class. The bully hit Tommy in the face, and it made him mad. Tommy had to fight, and he licked the bully. After that he was liked. There was one boy that was a leader that hadn't liked him before that invited him to have a soda. And after that all the boys liked Tommy."

The picture to which Peggy refers here, and which was specially selected for our study, is that of a cruel-looking white boy hitting a Mexican boy. While Karl has nothing but degratory statements to make about this boy, some children—mainly the equalitarian ones—express some pity for this boy. But it is only Peggy for whom he becomes a hero.

Here are some passages from Peggy's story in response to the picture of a Negro boy who is being maltreated:

"He [the Negro boy] wondered why people could be so ignorant and not know that everybody is created equal, and that people could believe what people say that isn't true. Someone threw something at him and blinded him. Two kids from the army started beating up on him. Yet in the army you are supposed to learn to stand for what is right. . . . He went back to where he came from and thought that someday he would do something about all this."

Another story deals with two young Japanese men, approximately college age:

"Well, there was a Sunday school in San Francisco and, uh, this boy is named Bill. Well, he came here many years ago when he was a little boy. He has grown up here and is proud of it and liked everyone and everyone liked him. Several years later he planned to go to college and get an education as a doctor. When he enrolled for college, people became very prejudiced. They thought he shouldn't go to the same school as white people. Bill felt bad because he liked everyone. So he dropped out of school. A few years later a cousin came from Japan to visit him. The cousin had just started his college education in Japan. He asked Bill why he wasn't going to college. Bill told him why. The cousin wasn't so sensitive as Bill and said the way to lick it was to show people you don't care. And so both of them enrolled for a four years' term, and Bill made friends with several of the professors and some boys and girls, and so did his cousin.

No one knew Bill was a very good pianist. One night at a dance the pianist walked out on them, and Bill offered to play. Everyone was surprised and liked him after that. Finally Bill finished medical school and became an M.D."

This story is quite typical of the way Peggy manages to give a constructive turn to almost every situation. In her reactions to her fellow-men she is generally and genuinely imbued with the spirit of Christian ethics. Thus in still another story she describes a man who was entirely devoted to his success and almost "went to Hell" but was given an opportunity to change his ways, thus being finally saved:

"Well, there was this man named Mr. Benson. He was hard working and very successful, but was not liked by many, because he was an old crab. One day his son got mad at him because he was so mean, and the son told him so. When the man went home, he felt bad and lay down. He fell asleep and dreamed he went down to Hell—to the middle of the world. They go either there or to Heaven. The spirit in charge looked in the book and said he was not registered in either place. Mr. Benson told the spirit what he had done—thinking only of his business. The spirit said, "I think if you go back and change your ways, you can then go to the other place." He woke up on the floor. Next morning he went to his office and did something he never did before. He said a pleasant "Good morning" to everyone in the office. Pretty soon his son came in, expecting the father to be mad when he told him about his plan to marry one of the secretaries. His father surprised him and said, "I hope you will be happy and have many children." He gave his son a present, and the father and son were friends after that, and it all turned out well. When Mr. Benson died, he went to Heaven. Though I don't believe there is any Heaven—we just stay in the earth and turn into little pieces."

Aside from Peggy's consideration for the weak, there is another outstanding theme in her stories, love. Significantly, Peggy often uses a fairytale type of approach in these stories, not losing her grip on the structure of the story, however. Oedipal conflicts are revealed in these stories, although she is obviously not aware of them. In one of her stories she tells about a "giant" who wants to keep a beautiful girl for himself while the girl wishes for a "prince." At the same time the two male figures are mixed in her fantasy:

"A giant found her and took her to his cave and raised her. She grew up to be beautiful. Finally a prince came along and said he would rescue her from the giant. She told the prince that the only way to do that was to go down the river and rescue the giant's heart which he lost there long ago. . . . The prince found the heart and took it to the cave and put it in the giant's supper. When the giant ate his supper, the heart went into his body and he became kind. He let the girl go and the prince married her. And they lived happily ever after."

While most of Karl's stories end in disaster, murder, or death, all of Peggy's stories end well. Every one of them constitutes an attempt to demonstrate positive ways of overcoming external or internal obstacles, including prejudice, selfishness, and possessiveness. It is difficult to say whether Peggy's aggression is merely repressed or whether it is not very strong to begin with. We are inclined to believe the latter. In any event it must be stressed that there is very little discrepancy between the overt level of Peggy's verbalized self-perception and her personality as revealed in the projective stories.

### RELATIONS TO PERCEPTION AND THINKING

Perceptual patterns, especially the mechanism of projection, were brought into the foregoing picture by the Thematic Apperception Test.

But the relationship between social attitudes, personality, and the general cognitive mastery of reality seems to go far beyond that. Experiments in perception, memory, and cognition were thus added in order to investigate more systematically the matter of how far basic personality trends found in the emotional and social sphere may be reflected in this area. Their purpose was to investigate the pervasiveness of ways of functioning within the authoritarian personality. The shift from the social and emotional to the cognitive area has the added advantage of removing us from the controversial social issues under consideration. So long as we remain under the potential spell of certain preconceived notions, the evaluation of what is reality-adequate or reality-inadequate may be difficult. The authoritarian may accuse the equalitarian of distorting reality, and vice versa. Some of the experiments are as yet in a preliminary stage while others have already led to statistically significant results.

In a memory experiment,[17] the children were read a story which described the behavior of pupils in a school toward newcomers to their class. In the fighting that developed, some of the older pupils were described as being friendly and protective of the newcomers, while others were pictured as aggressive. The children were then asked to reproduce the story in writing.

Ethnocentric children tended generally to recall more of the aggressive characters, and the democratic-minded, tolerant children more of the friendly characters. In addition, 43 per cent of the former, as contrasted with only 8 per cent of the latter, recalled the fighting theme exclusively, without mentioning any of the other themes of the story.

It is further to be noted that in the tolerant children the ratio of friendly to aggressive individuals was closer to the ratio occurring in the story as first presented. That is to say, the tolerant children adhered, in this respect at least, more closely to "reality" than did the ethnocentric. A general tendency on the part of the ethnically prejudiced children to stray away from the content of the story is combined with a tendency to reproduce faithfully certain single phrases and single details of the original story. Thus the stimulus is in part rigidly adhered to, while its remaining and perhaps major aspects are altogether neglected in favor of subjective elaboration. This odd combination of accuracy and distortion also characterizes Karl's general cognitive approach as presented earlier in this paper.

Another experiment consisted in presenting the picture of a familiar object, such as that of a dog, and then leading through a number of vague or transitional stages to the picture of, say, a cat. The subjects were asked to identify the object in each picture. If tentative results with small groups are borne out, the stimuli less familiar and lacking in firmness and definiteness would seem to be more disturbing to the ethnocentric than to the unprejudiced children. Ethnocentric children tend to persist in using the name of the familiar object shown in the first picture, ignoring the changes in the successive pictures. Or they seem to fall more often into a spell of guesses, trying to inject known and structured objects into the vague stimulus, again relatively little concerned with reality. It is probably the underlying confusion and anxiety which compel these children to make a desperate effort to avoid uncertainties as much as possible, resulting in "intolerance of ambiguity."[18] The nonethnocentric children, on the other hand, being generally more secure, are apparently better able to afford facing ambiguities openly, even though this often may mean facing, at least temporarily, increased conflicts.

In another preliminary experiment a picture was presented showing four vertically striped zebras standing together and facing a lone, horizontally striped zebra left in a corner by itself. An inquiry as to the cause of the isolation of the horizontally striped zebra brought out interesting material about the attitude of some ethnocentric children to what is "different." Among other things, it appears that any difference setting off a minority from a majority of objects—even though the given difference may not in itself be emotionally tainted—tends to be conceived of by them as automatically establishing a barrier against social contact.

Rokeach[19] has investigated rigidity as related to intolerance of ambiguity. He used a problem in thinking developed by Luchins[20] which involves the manipulation of three water jars. A mental set was first established by presenting the subjects with a series of problems solvable only by a relatively involved method. There followed problems which could be solved either by maintaining the established set or by using more direct and simple techniques. The ethnocentric children tended to persist in using the first, more complex method rather than shift to the more direct approach.

In recent years, experiments of the types described have multipled in number and kind and generally have borne out the earlier findings.

We have already noted that Karl's cognitive makeup can be fitted into some of the categories found typical of ethnocentric children in these experiments. Karl's material further reveals that he tends to alternate in his perceptual and cognitive approach between sticking to the familiar and being overly concretistic, on the one hand, and a chaotic, haphazard approach, on the other. Peggy, by contrast, shows considerable flexibility in her perceptual and cognitive approach, although it must be added that she did exhibit rigidity on the water-jar test just described. Here she used an established set without changing to the more functional, faster method. This may well be due to her general weakness in handling arithmetic problems. We have found that even flexible children may be rigid on tasks in which they show little ego involvement. Such tasks remain peripheral for them, and they do not bring out the best of their ability, so that there is regression to a more mechanized approach. There can be no doubt that everyone has areas of rigidity. In some cases we just find rigidity more pervasive than in others.

## SUMMARY AND CONCLUSION

Out of a sample of children and their families studied by a variety of methods, two cases were selected which represent opposite extremes as to ethnocentric, as contrasted with democratic, outlook, other social beliefs, cognitive organization, personality, and family structure and atmosphere.

In describing the minority groups and the social scene in general, our paradigm of an ethnocentric, authoritarian child, Karl, exhibits rigid dichotomizing, aggressiveness, fear of imaginary dangers or threats of deprivation, and exaggerated adherence to conventional values, such as cleanliness and order. The same themes also occur in his stated attitudes toward parents and friends as well as in the projective material, especially his Thematic Apperception Test stories.

Our example of a democratic-minded, equalitarian child, Peggy, is much less given to dichotomizing and other forms of rigidity and intolerance of ambiguity than is Karl. This is evidenced, among other things, in her attitude toward minority groups and in her view of sex roles. In both cases differences are de-emphasized, quite in contrast with Karl. While at the surface level Karl emphasizes rugged masculinity and is very much concerned with what is masculine and what is feminine, he is covertly engrossed in passivity and dependency; Peggy, with her lesser insistence on the dichotomy of sex roles, is basically much more feminine than Karl is masculine. A similar discontinuity between the manifest and the latent level had been found in Karl's attitude toward his parents; Peggy, on the other hand, reveals a genuine, personalized love for her parents which is not endangered and undermined by occasional eruptions of deep-seated aggression. Karl and his parents had been found to manifest an odd combination of unrest and predilection for chaos and total change with an uncritical, distorted glorification of existing institutions and social conditions; Peggy and her parents, on the other hand, show a certain healthy medium distance to these institutions in the sense of basically identifying with their aim, yet being concerned with seeing them properly executed, as in the case of ethnic equality. They would like to see some improvement and progress, but total upheavals and radical changes of the social scene do not have the same appeal for them that they do for Karl's parents. All these differences are related to the fact that the definition of an American is much more narrowly conceived by Karl and his parents than it is by Peggy and hers and that the former exhibits some preoccupation with what they consider American values which at the same time presents a shrinkage and oversimplification of these values.

Toward parents, teachers, and authorities in general Karl at the surface demands total submission, and he approves of whatever they do; but underlying resentment and hatred against them are only too apparent in the projective material. This discrepancy is but one of the many breaks and discontinuities found in Karl and in ethnocentric children in general. Another discrepancy is evident in Karl's explicit stressing of conventional values, which is combined with an implicit leaning toward destructive and chaotic behavior. In fact, there seems to be vacillation between a total adoption and a total negation of the prevalent values of our society.

Still another conflicting set can be discerned between Karl's strained effort to appear as a masculine boy interested in girls and his underlying identification with the opposite sex. Instead of being oriented toward girls as objects of cathexis, he envies them because he thinks of them as less in danger of being attacked and as being fed and given other material benefits. As becomes apparent especially in the Thematic Apperception Test, to be a boy or a man means to him to be in danger. If a man is passive, he may not get the necessary supplies and is helplessly exposed; if he is aggressive, he is punished. Doom is thus inevitable for him. All through the material produced by our ethnocentric children there is evidence of panic lest food or money run short. In persons possessed by such fears, human relations are liable to become unusually manipulative and exploitive. Other persons, authorities, and even the magic forces of nature will, of necessity, be seen mainly as deliverers of goods. Aggression against those considered strong and powerful must then be repressed; at least in part, this aggression will be diverted toward those who can neither deprive nor retaliate.

While Karl thus shows many discrepancies and discontinuities in his personality makeup, Peggy is obviously more integrated. Karl fails to face some of the important emotional tendencies within himself, such as ambivalence toward the parents, passivity, and fear. His conscious image of himself contradicts the tendencies which are revealed in the projective material and which he projects onto others, such as minority groups. Peggy, on the other hand, accepts hers more fully, although this does not mean that she is not critical of herself. This basic acceptance of herself makes it possible for her to face her own weaknesses; it also leads to a greater acceptance and tolerance of other persons and peoples, although again she is very free in expressing her dislikes. But, on the whole, the world is for her a benevolent one, interesting and challenging, whereas for Karl it is a dangerous and hostile place, to be viewed with distrust, suspicion, and cynicism.

In spite of the ready flow of fantastic ideas about a wide range of topics, Karl's story productions show little evidence of creative imagination. His repetitive rumination in stereotypes, general diffuseness, and distortion of reality are obviously in the service of warding off anxiety.

This rigidity and lack of imagination is in line with results obtained on ethnocentric children in the experiments on perception and other cognitive functions. Ambiguous and unfamiliar stimuli often seem to be disturbing to these children. They tend to respond either with a spell of haphazard guessing, imposing something definite and definitive upon the indefinite, or with a clinging to a response once established. Both these reactions seem to mirror frantic efforts to avoid uncertainty, that is, an "intolerance of ambiguity," even though the price is distortion of reality. In addition, the recall of given stories by ethnocentric children shows distortion in the direction of greater emphasis on aggressive themes.

In analyzing and interpreting our material, extended use has been made of psychoanalytic hypotheses. Depth psychology has challenged the dominance of the phenotype and has sharpened our eyes to the underlying dynamic patterns. Because of this shift, we can discern in Karl the passivity behind his aggressive violence, the feminine identification and latent homosexuality behind the protestation of his heterosexual interests, the chaos behind his rigid conformity. But since the façade is also an essential part of the psychological makeup, we must think of personality in terms of "alternative manifestations."[21] These are quite self-contradictory in Karl, as they are in most prejudiced children. It is the inherent conflict and anxiety concerning the social, sexual, and personal role of the individual which must be seen at the root of the ensuing desperate avoidance of all ambiguity with its dire consequences for the fate of man.

It should be kept in mind that while our chosen paradigms exhibit nearly all the traits which were found statistically prevalent in the respective groups as a whole, such marked personality consistency is not the rule. Furthermore, the over-all immaturity which Karl, our paradigm of an ethnocentric child, has been found to exhibit is to a certain extent shared with younger children, both authoritarian and equalitarian; some of the trends which are connected with ethnic prejudice or authoritarianism must be considered natural states of development, to be overcome if maturity is to be reached. Some of the test items correlated with ethnocentrism are at the same time subscribed to more often by the younger children than by the older ones. The difference is that our ethnocentric children continue to exhibit many trends which in equalitarian children are limited to the younger age levels and are later outgrown. To a notable extent this is independent of the purely intellectual aspects of development. Other factors, such as especially social background, are modifiers of the distinction between ethnocentric and equalitarian children. Important subtypes may thus be identified in both groups. For example, in ethnocentric children coming from distinctly upper-class backgrounds there is more genuine conformity to society, combined perhaps with a certain rigidity in the total outlook, but little of the psychopathic, destructive, and manipulative coloring which characterizes Karl and many other prejudiced children rooted in the lower social strata.

Karl's parents reveal the feelings of "social marginality" which are so common in the ethnocentric family. It is obviously in defense against the possibility of being grouped with the underprivileged that they rigidly identify with the conventional values of the class to which they try to hold on. The strict home discipline they are trying to enforce is in part in the service of these narrow social goals; beyond this, it is perhaps a revengeful repetition of the situation to which they themselves were exposed in the unstable socioeconomic history of the family. We have also seen how much more constructively an objectively similar socioeconomic family history is handled by the parents of Peggy.

Both the families which we have discussed in this paper are American families. At the same time, they are so different that in many ways they appear as opposite ends of a psychological continuum, a continuum which ranges from rigidity and authoritarianism to affectionate guidance and acceptance.

In the context of American culture, Karl and his family are deviants. Fat, fearful Karl is certainly the opposite of the ideal American boy. Most of his and of his family's attitudes are counterpoints to prevailing or consciously espoused American attitudes. Externalization and hostile exclusion are features which they adopt from the wide variety of possibilities, offered within the culture as a whole. Other features contrasting with the major American pattern are their emphasis on hierarchical rather than equalitarian relations, their anxiety about the availability of material goods, and their belief in mystical forces and apprehension about catastrophes as against confidence in one's own efforts and in the collaboration of the environment.

To understand all this, we remember that Karl and his family are caught in an unsuccessful struggle for social status, a status they cannot achieve through their own efforts. Thus they adhere rigidly to some absolute status values which oversimplify the social and cultural realities of our civilization. This renders them helpless and perverts their view of the social scene, making them susceptible to totalitarian propaganda.

It must be specially emphasized that the compulsive type of conformity with its all-or-none character which we have observed in the family of Karl differs in several ways from genuine and constructive conformity. It is excessive, compensating as it does for feelings of marginality and the attendant fear of becoming an outcast and serving the function of covering up the resentment toward the social system as a whole, unconscious as this resentment may be. The lack of a genuine incorporation of the values of society in the authoritarian milieu accounts for the rigidity of the conformity. At the same time it accounts for a certain unreliability, the readiness to shift allegiance altogether to other authorities and other standards. The adherence to the letter rather than to the spirit of the social institutions, which further characterizes the compulsive conformist, issues from his distortion and simplification of the system of norms and commands in the direction of what one may call unidimensional interpretation.

Evidently, Peggy and her family are infinitely closer to the real values of the American civiliation in the ways in which parental authority and child-parent relationships are handled and the democratic outlook is being realized in word and action. They are in search of intrinsic and flexible and at the same time basically more consistent principles. Understanding, emphasis on internalization, thoughtfulness, empathy, compassion, insight, justice, individualism, reason, and scholarship are the values they admire. The core of the human institutions inherent in our culture which must be called upon to explain Peggy and her parents is the democratic tradition, with its protective attitude toward the weak.

## NOTES

1. Ogburn, 1953.
2. Zimmerman, 1948.
3. Burgess, 1948.
4. Mead, 1949.
5. Winch and McGinnis, 1953.
6. Frenkel-Brunswik, 1954.
7. Frenkel-Brunswik, 1949a; Frenkel-Brunswik and Havel, 1953.
8. Murray et al., 1938.
9. Adorno et al., 1950.
10. Frenkel-Brunswik, 1951.
11. Adorno et al., 1950; Frenkel-Brunswik, 1949a.
12. Fenichel, 1945.
13. Wolfenstein and Leites, 1950.
14. Adorno et al., 1950.
15. Frenkel-Brunswik and Havel, 1953; other reports in preparation.
16. Ibid.
17. For details see Frenkel-Brunswik, 1949b.
18. Ibid.
19. Rokeach, 1943.
20. Luchins, 1942.
21. Frenkel-Brunswik, 1949b.

## REFERENCES

1. ADORNO, T. W., FRENKEL-BRUNSWIK, E., LEVINSON, D. J., and SANFORD, R. N. 1950. *The Authoritarian Personality*. New York: Harper & Bros.

2. BURGESS, E. W. 1948. "The Family in a Changing Society," *American Journal of Sociology,* XIII, No. 6, 417–23.
3. FENICHEL, O. 1945. *Psychoanalytic Theory of Neurosis.* New York: W. W. Norton & Co.
4. FRENKEL-BRUNSWIK, E. 1949a. "A Study of Prejudice in Children," *Human Relations,* I, No. 3, 295–306.
5. ——. 1949b. "Intolerance of Ambiguity as an Emotional and Perceptual Personality Variable," *Journal of Personality,* XVIII, No. 1, 108–43.
6. ——. 1951. "Patterns of Social and Cognitive Outlook in Children and Parents," *American Journal of Orthopsychiatry,* XXI, No. 3, 543–58.
7. ——. 1954. "Social Research and the Problem of Values: A Reply," *Journal of Abnormal and Social Psychology,* XLIX, No. 3, 466–71.
8. FRENKEL-BRUNSWIK, E., and HAVEL, J. 1953. "Prejudice in the Interviews of Children: Attitudes toward Minority Groups," *Journal of Genetic Psychology,* LXXXII, No. 1, 91–136.
9. LUCHINS, A. S. 1942. *Mechanization in Problem Solving: The Effect of "Einstellung."* ("Psychological Monographs," Vol. LIV, No. 6.)
10. MEAD, MARGARET. 1949. *Male and Female.* New York: William Morrow Co.
11. MURRAY, H. E., and WORKERS AT THE HARVARD PSYCHOLOGICAL CLINIC. 1938. *Explorations in Personality.* London: Oxford University Press.
12. OGBURN, W. F. 1953. "The Changing Functions of the Family." In *Marriage and the Family,* ed. R. F. WINCH and R. McGINNIS. New York: Henry Holt & Co.
13. ROKEACH, M. 1943. "Generalized Mental Rigidity as a Factor in Ethnocentrism," *Journal of Abnormal and Social Psychology,* XLVIII, No. 2, 259–78.
14. WINCH, R. F., and McGINNIS, R. (eds.). 1953. *Marriage and the Family.* New York: Henry Holt & Co.
15. WOLFENSTEIN, MARTHA, and LEITES, NATHAN. 1950. *Movies: A Psychological Study.* Glencoe, Ill.: Free Press.
16. ZIMMERMAN, C. C. 1948. *Family and Civilization.* New York: Harper & Bros.

# Part VI

---

# PATTERNING SEPARATENESS AND CONNECTEDNESS

This entire book deals with the general topic of interpersonal relations in the family. Part VI, however, focuses more closely on what family members mean to one another and on the consequences of these meanings for the family collectivity and for the individual selves of the members. What people are to one another grows out of what each is to himself, and, reciprocally, what each is to himself grows out of what he is to significant others. Being a particular kind of individual person and being connected to others in the family in a particular pattern of relationships are two aspects of the same phenomenon. Or, to state the matter in terms of traditional subject matter fields, individual personality development and the social psychology of the family are fruitfully regarded as constituting a single subject matter. This standpoint is exemplified elsewhere in the book, for example, in Else Frenkel-Brunswik's article. The articles in Part VI illustrate concretely how certain patterns of separateness-connectedness develop and are sustained.

Part VI is divided into two subsections. The articles in the first subsection discuss the *development* of family relationships, particularly the marriage relationship. The article by Rhona and Robert N. Rapoport treats getting married as a critical role transition, a change of condition that is rather sharply discontinuous from what has gone before in the lives of the marrying couple. Their framework of analysis derives preponderantly from a study of American lower middle-class couples, and they show how this social class provides certain carefully structured rituals—engagement and honeymoon—for pacing and directing young couples into gradations of intimacy. The careful structure within which intimacy is supposed to be accomplished sometimes functions not only to preclude what is felt to be premature intimacy but also to hamper intimacy after marriage that would be acceptable to the wider community. How this structure is utilized depends upon the personalities of the particular individuals who marry.

The middle-classness of the pattern described by the Rapoports is clear when it is compared with Lee Rainwater's account of the formation and maintenance of families in the Negro lower class. In this group, marriage is not nearly so discontinuous with the life course that precedes it. The adult world does not provide Negro lower-class youth with a formalized structure within which they are to develop the interpersonal relationships leading up to and realized in marriage. Marriage is often a somewhat casual undertaking, an episode not radically different in character from the episodic relationships that have preceded it and others that may follow later.

These remarks focus on the most obvious point of comparability between the work of Rainwater and the Rapoports. A close comparative analysis of the three articles would undoubtedly be repaid by insight into differential concepts of male and female vulnerability, commitment to others, the meaning of marriage, and other nodes of affect in white middle-class and Negro lower-class culture.

Different as the Rapoport and Rainwater articles are in aim, they are alike in seeking to characterize how interpersonal relations become structured through the handling of critical transitions that are more or less standardized by particular cultural subgroups. Interpersonal relations in families are shaped not only by cultural expectations but also by idiosyncratic crises. Some studies have been done of how the family as a unit responds to such unanticipated crises.[1] Researches showing how serious and unexpected affliction of the child affects the family can also serve as a reminder that the abnormal is often useful in attempting to understand the normal. It is quite obvious that a mentally retarded or polio-stricken child would have an impact on his family, an impact that is weighty because of family expectations. The two basic conceptual elements of these researches can be abstracted and applied in studies of any kind of family. These are: (1) parents have expectations for their children; (2) children have an impact on their parents (and siblings). Interpersonal relationships between parents and children are generated through the interplay of parental expectations and the child's impact on the parents. To do this, of course, would be to depart from the more usual way of considering what happens in ordinary families. In an extreme version it would mean regarding the child's behavior as a "cause" of the parent's behavior, which we are willing to do if the child is mentally retarded, stricken with polio, or otherwise dramatically afflicted. But perhaps by looking more closely at what happens in ordinary families, we shall also find that children have an impact on parents and that identifiable principles account for the different impacts of children in different families. However, rather than taking a simple cause-effect approach that is turned upside down, we shall probably be most faithful to the phenomena if we can view them in terms of reciprocating effects.

Any interpersonal relationship not only defines on what terms the participants in it are related but also, explicitly or by implication, the ways in which they remain separate from each other. Nonetheless, it is also true that some aspects of separateness and of connectedness are unanticipated consequences of relationships. Both separateness and connectedness can lead in unexpected directions. The working out of the balance between these dual conditions of family life is a continuing task, a central topic in the creation of meaning. The balance takes a great number of forms, and it cannot be said that we are as yet in a position to present a comprehensive summary or analysis of separateness-connectedness patterns. Such an achievement seems a long way off. The articles in the second subsection, Part VI, show some of the ways families struggle with this task of finding gratifying connection while the members also each seek to be his own particular kind of person.

The article by James L. Titchener, Jules Riskin, and Richard Emerson marks a new departure in psychosomatic medicine. Prior research led to the hypothesis that ulcerative colitis tends to be found in persons who feel deeply disturbed by actual, threatened, or imagined loss of a significant relationship, usually with the mother who has made her love conditional upon her control of the relationship. These authors seek to show that the dynamics of the whole family relationship must be considered in the development of ulcerative colitis by one family member, not the mother-child relationship alone. In their analysis of one family, the family's ideal of independence, respectability, and avoidance of selfish desires operated to prevent acknowledgement and expression of dependent needs. The members are expected to keep their distance from one another. The illness of one member is seen as a result of a complex developmental process in which ideal and need conflict, although the conflict is not localized in the member who becomes ill but pervades the family. This article exemplifies one of the growing beliefs in psychiatry: the member of a family who becomes ill (usually in the sense of emotionally disturbed or mentally ill but also, as in this article, psychosomatically ill) is not simply ill in himself but is the representative of his family, the manifest expression of a hidden family process.

How a disturbed family selects a particular member to be its principal symptom carrier must be explained if this whole-family theory of illness is to be tenable. Ezra F. Vogel and Norman W. Bell make this problem the principal subject of their article, which follows that by Titchener and associates. Vogel and Bell view the emotionally disturbed child as a scapegoat for conflicts between the parents and endeavor to explain why some families seem to require scapegoats, how a scapegoat is chosen, and how he is inducted into and sustained in the scapegoat role.

Lyman Wynne, Irving Ryckoff, Juliana Day, and Stanley I. Hirsch advance the concept of mutuality as a general term for healthy or normal separateness-connectedness patterns. Genuine mutuality "not only tolerates divergence of self-interests, but thrives upon the recognition of such natural and inevitable divergence." In contrast, they identify the pattern of pseudo-mutuality which they find in families of schizophrenics. These authors, like Jay Haley, thus seek to understand schizophrenia in terms of its locus in family-wide processes. Where Haley and his colleagues view schizophrenic behavior as part of a disturbed system of cognition and communication, Wynne and his associates analyze it in terms of disturbed relationship patterns. In their analysis, the family member who becomes schizophrenic is not allowed to develop an identity of his own; other family members cannot tolerate the autonomy this would represent. The family endeavors to cover over any indications of divergence, intent on maintaining a sense of fitting together at the expense of individual development. This view of the background of schizophrenia makes schizophrenia a tragic irony, since the intolerance of individual divergence eventuates in a most extreme form of separateness.

The articles in Part VI hardly do justice to the full variety of separateness and connectedness in family life. But they are sufficiently diverse to suggest the variety of ways in which being a separate person and being related to others are structured by families. In addition, the writings also indicate various ways in which body, psyche, and collectivity enter into the formation of separateness-connectedness patterns. Perhaps they are also sufficient to show why a social psychology of marriage and the family based on the concept of needs is ultimately unworkable. People do have needs, but what they experience as needs and what they construe as appropriate ways to satisfy their needs are matters of meaning. Impulses are given meaning and are experienced as needs only after being defined as such. Incestuous behavior by a parent cannot be understood merely as the fusion of a need for nurturance and a need for sex. Rather, the fusion of nurturant and sexual behavior directed toward the child must be understood in terms of what the parent means to himself and to his spouse as well as what the child means to him, to mention only the most immediately relevant meaningful objects. Other forms and aspects of separateness and connectedness in families similarly require analysis in terms of meaning.[2]

## NOTES

1. See, for example, Fred Davis, *Passage Through Crisis; Polio Victims and Their Families* (Indianapolis: Bobbs-Merrill, 1963), particularly Chapters 5 and 6. See also Bernard Farber, "Effects of a Severely Mentally Retarded Child on Family Integration," *Monographs of the Society for Research in Child Development,* Vol. 24, No. 2, 1959, and "Family Organization and Crisis: Maintenance of Integration in Families with a Severely Mentally Retarded Child," *ibid.,* Vol. 25, 1960.

2. Irving Rosow presents a searching analysis of the concept of need complementarity in "Issues in the Concept of Need-Complementarity," *Sociometry,* Vol. 20, No. 3, pp. 216–33, 1957; but he is more sympathetic to this concept than I believe his own analysis warrants. Indeed, he points out: "Some significant variable intervenes between need organization and behavior. This is the person's adjustment to his basic need structure, whether his accomodation is conscious or not. We may call this intervening variable 'self-acceptance' " (p. 220). In other words, the person's view of himself must be taken into account. Rosow attends explicitly to the importance of "subjective meaning" in a later work, "Adjustment of the Normal Aged: Concept and Measurement," in Richard Williams, Clark Tibbitts, and Wilma Donahue, eds., *Processes of Aging* (New York: Prentice-Hall, Atherton Press, 1963), Vol. II, Chapter 38.

# 17:

# New Light on the Honeymoon[1]

*Rhona Rapoport* and *Robert N. Rapoport*

The honeymoon is a custom in Western civilization that seems functionally equivalent to many of the practices thought of as *rites de passage* in the simpler, traditional societies of the world (Van Gennep, 1909). Though it is not in itself a ritual, in the sense of being rooted in the cultural logics and practices relating to the supernatural (Gluckman, 1963), it is a custom that is closely linked to marriage ritual and is an important segment of the cluster of customary practices associated with traversing the role transition of getting married.

Despite the widespread distribution of this custom, its association with the richly documented marriage and family field, and the intrinsic interest in it engendered by the idealization of romantic love in Western society, there is a relative dearth of writings on the honeymoon. In the social science and psychiatric literature serious treatment of the honeymoon is almost entirely lacking.[2] Even in fictional writing there are few works that exploit the potentialities of this human situation.[3]

For the social scientist the reticence may be connected in part with doubts about the ethical aspects of intrusion into this *sanctum sanctorum* of private human experiences. In part it may have had to do with the difficulties in gathering data on the topic. Again, neglect of the subject may reflect a culturally induced blind spot in the social scientist, as in other members of Western culture. The honeymoon has, in characteristic idealized fashion, tended to be seen as a tranquil, trouble-free episode from which one averts one's attention almost as a matter of instinctive human decency.

The viewpoint taken in this paper is that the honeymoon is a potentially fruitful area of scientific investigation. Marriage has long been recog-

Reprinted by permission from *Human Relations*, Vol. 17, No. 1 (1964), pp. 33–56. Copyright 1964 by Tavistock Publications, Ltd. Rhona Rapoport holds a doctorate in sociology and is also a psychoanalyst. Until recently, she was director of the Family Research Unit, Laboratory of Community Psychiatry, Harvard Medical School. She now lives in England where she is affiliated with the London Institute of Psychoanalysis. She continues as associate in sociology, Harvard Medical School. Robert N. Rapoport is senior social scientist, Tavistock Institute of Human Relations and also adviser to the School of Social Sciences, Brunel University, both in London. At the time of writing he was research professor of sociology and anthropology, Northeastern University, Boston.

nized as a major life-cycle transition point, and the rituals associated with it have long been comprehended as helping individuals and society to sever old relationships and make new ones. It is also increasingly apparent that there is a range of variation (sometimes formally,[4] sometimes informally[5] recognized) within any given society as to adherence to any particular cultural pattern, and variants are frequent. Less well understood is the significance of different patterns of meeting such a critical role transition for the subsequent functioning of the individuals and social systems concerned. It is to throw light on this problem that we examine the practice of the honeymoon.

## CULTURAL PERSPECTIVES ON THE HONEYMOON

The literature associated with getting married, everywhere distinguished from mere mating, is voluminous. Accounts of the event bring out the richness of ceremonial symbolism associated with marriage and reflect its essential character as a critical role transition point which proliferates rituals of passage in the classical sense.

From the earliest days of exposure to exotic cultures, anthropologists and others have been impressed with the profusion of symbolic practices immediately following marriage. Reports were plentiful on the widespread distribution of such practices as display of hymeneal blood, ordeals for the bride and groom, ritual defloration, ritual delay of intercourse, seclusion of one or both partners, and so on (Crawley, 1902; Westermarck, 1891; Spencer & Gillen, 1904; Roscoe, 1911; and others).

The common themes that run through the complexes of practices associated with marriage reflect, on the one hand, the fundamental task of *separation* (i.e., in some degree loosening the ties binding the individual to premarital social groups), and, on the other, that of *joining* (i.e., intensifying the ties binding the individuals together in the new social grouping being formed through marriage) (Van Gennep, 1909; Rh. Rapoport, 1962). Many rituals emphasized the fact that marriage is not only an affair between individuals but, and this has been pre-eminently true in the smaller, more folk-like societies, an affair of the larger corporate groups to which they belong.

The separation dynamics were symbolically expressed, for example, by the various forms of mock-struggle between the bridegroom and the family of the bride, from whom he took her. In the struggle the bride's family expressed their ambivalence about letting her go, and at the same time (in many cases) subjected the bridegroom to a symbolic test of strength and commitment. The payment of bridewealth ('progeny price', 'suitor service', etc.) seemed to deal with the economic loss that the bride's family felt they were sustaining. It both compensated to some degree for this loss and provided an element of *joining* pressure in situations where the return of the bride entailed the return of the bridewealth by her family. More directly expressive of the joining dynamics were such rituals as the giving or exchanging of rings, the locking of hands or fingers, the tying together of clothing, and the sharing of food and drink from the same bowl, goblet, leaf, or melon. These smaller ritualized elements were often conducted in the framework of a large public feast in which social participation in and recognition of the changes that were occurring were ensured.

The set of practices with which we are focally concerned here are those involving the newly married persons immediately following the actual wedding ceremony. In general there was a great variety of practices, ranging from a relative absence of ritualized events (including practices associated with a period of withdrawal between the wedding and the establishment of the new family unit) to a relatively great elaboration of rituals following marriage.

Though it is beyond the scope of the present paper to analyse systematically the factors associated with the presence or absence of such rituals, we record some impressions of relevant variables.

First, cultures varied in the *degree to which the pair were physically segregated from their usual social environment* immediately following marriage. This seemed to relate to the degree of discontinuity the individuals experienced in leaving their unmarried roles and entering their married roles. In groups where considerable premarital sexual experimentation was allowed and the couple were publicly known to be intimately involved with one another, the actual marriage tended to be marked with little fanfare and little need for removal of the couple from their usual round of activities. The Eskimo and the Nuer are examples, at different levels of complexity of social structure, of cultures in which there was comparatively little emphasis on a segregated interlude for the newly-weds. Each of these groups allowed relatively free sexual experimentation (within the bounds of incest, adultery, and good form) prior to marriage, and each eased the transition into married life, though in different ways.[6]

Significant role discontinuities seemed to have been associated not only with the presence of a segregated interlude following marriage but with *ritual elaboration*. For example, the Baganda and the Nootka are typical of fairly elaborate post-marital ritualization.[7]

Another variable of interest in understanding the pattern taken by rituals in this period is the *degree to which they emphasize the unity of the couple as an autonomous* unit as against emphasizing their social imbeddedness in other structural units. It should be noted that rituals of various kinds were to be found, expressing different aspects of the feelings of individuals concerned in this complex transition. Thus, even in the American case—which is probably one of the most extreme in its emphasis on the separateness and unity of the couple[8]—practices emphasizing group imbeddedness are found.[9] Perhaps intermediate and most common were such cases as the Nuer and the Baganda, in which expressions of imbeddedness were important, though secondary, accompaniments to the practices emphasizing separation.[10] In extreme cases, like the Nayar (Gough, 1961) and the Menangkabau (Loeb, 1935), the emphasis on imbeddedness was maintained as fundamental, even in the face of the formation of the new marital relationship.[11]

The sheer *length of seclusion of the pair* is another variable worth considering. It seems to be partly a function of economic wealth. In groups close to the bare subsistence level e.g., certain Australian aboriginal groups, even where there was a segregated interlude the seclusion period tended to be confined to the time required for transporting the wife to her new home. In groups with greater surplus, the couple were often supported by relatives for a period of time, undergoing rituals to ensure fertility, to pay ritual respects to family gods, and so on. It is only among societies of relatively great affluence, as in post-industrial European and American society, that the prolonged withdrawal of the marital pair from their usual social obligations has developed.

## THE AMERICAN HONEYMOON

In the context of the range of post-wedding practices known in human cultures, how can we understand the nature and functions of the honeymoon in Western, particularly American, culture?

The honeymoon, as we know it in Western society, is a phase of partial physical and social withdrawal of the newly married couple from the rest of the world, particularly the world of their prior social relationships. Traditionally, too, it reflects the expectation of a major discontinuity in sexual behavior, and it is overtly the occasion for the inauguration of sexual relations, ideally on the wedding night itself. It is relatively long, emphasizes the couple's autonomy to an extreme degree, and has a number of customary practices that are of interest in the context of our present discussion. As the etymology of the term suggests, the period is idealized as one of unparalleled bliss. The molten beauty of the full, 'honey' moon is used, according to this derivation, to characterize the psychological state of the newly wed couple. This psychological state, like the moon, has been characterized as inevitably beginning to wane no sooner than it is full.[12]

Usually in Western civilization the honeymoon involves a trip away from parental families and others one knows well. In the theoretical speculations of early 'evolutionists' it was sometimes seen as a vestigial survival of the practice of marriage by capture, corresponding to the period during which the husband kept his wife in retirement to prevent her from appealing to her relatives for release (Avebury, 1870). Whatever the merits of this dubious theory, it is clear that the honeymoon in contemporary Western society serves none of the functions of the elopement as found still, for example, among some of the Australian aboriginal groups.[13]

Far from struggling against the bride's participation (except where the marriage is considered unsuitable) Western parents are expected to 'give the bride away' happily, and a very frequent form of parental wedding gift is the economic support of the honeymoon itself. The tears that parents are allowed to shed on this occasion are defined as mainly tears of happiness, and the true significance of the separation in a society practicing neo-local residence is blurred by the cliché, 'I do not feel that I am losing a daughter (son) but gaining a son (daughter).' In the period of immediate post-marital seclusion that the honeymoon represents, there is anything but an interdiction of sexuality. Consummation is expected to occur on the first night if possible, and honeymooners are assisted in creating what are considered the ideal conditions for bringing this about.[14]

In the United States several elements seem to contribute to the elaboration of the honeymoon as a social institution. First of all there is the middle-class family life pattern, which is intensely nuclear in residence; this pattern both stimulates the child sexually (by proximity and intensity of living conditions and by the equalitarian, child-centered atmosphere) and simultaneously frustrates it by imposing a strict injunction against pre-marital sexuality, especially for the girl. It therefore makes functional sense to remove the newly wed couple from the intensive supervision of parental figures who have also been prohibited sexual objects. The familiar setting would seem, in this context, to be problematic for developing a good sexual basis for the marriage. Furthermore, the larger cultural setting is one of romantic idealization and commercial exploitation of love as manifested in so many Hollywood films. The honeymoon is both the apical expression of the romantic love complex and a ripe market for commercial promotion in an affluent society.

In the United States the honeymoon takes a variety of forms. There is the *lovers' nest* conception, as exemplified in the convergence of honeymooners in places such as Bermuda, Niagara Falls, and honeymoon camps in the Poconos and Florida. This seems to be a peculiarly North American custom, perhaps reflecting the general culture trait of 'other-directedness', 'groupiness', and the fear of intimacy noted by many observers of the American scene. Europeans tend to be astonished by this custom, noting that they would wish to get away from other people at such a time, certainly from others in the same situation.[15]

Another prominent type of honeymoon in the United States, superficially like that of the European but at a deeper level reflecting some of the same uniquely American traits mentioned above, is the *perpetuum mobile* honeymoon. Here a couple get into the omnipresent automobile and travel, often without predetermined plans, reservations, schedule, or itinerary, but with a budget and a date for return.[16]

The *vacation* type of honeymoon is also characteristic of American life, and here one finds as many sub-types of honeymoon within the category as there are conceptions of what constitutes an enjoyable vacation. Essentially, the honeymoon is defined as a kind of vacation and the criteria for having a good honeymoon get assimilated with those of having a good vacation. Those who like night-life and excitement seek a situation that will provide these diversions for their honeymoon; those who like camping and hiking seek that sort of a setting, and so on.

Within American culture, however, there is the idea that the honeymoon may be a hazard to physical health. It involves an expenditure of sexual energy, presumably under stressful conditions, involving proof of potency, overcoming intimacy fears, and surmounting any guilt that may surround sexuality, especially with a virginal female. It is expected to leave its mark, especially on the male. There is a good deal of teasing about how exhausted the male looks following the honeymoon, and the acquisition of a good tan on the honeymoon is sometimes jokingly remarked on as a way of covering up this condition.

On the other hand, it is also assumed that the period just prior to the wedding is one of great strain and that the honeymoon is necessary for recuperation, preparatory to facing the stresses of life as a married couple. From this point of view the couple are expected to extract from it as much relaxed enjoyment as possible. The general idea prevails that the honeymoon couple should be exempted from the pressures of life. It is considered bad form to ask where a honeymoon couple are going, and the assumption is made for a normal honeymoon that it will be taken by the couple alone, unaccompanied by friends or relatives, in a place segregated from their usual surroundings. It is a period of moratorium on usual stresses and strains, and seems to be characterized by two dominant themes: the first relates to the idyllic quality of the experience and the second surrounds the achievement of intimacy, especially sexual.[17]

Paradoxically, there is a strain entailed in the very pressures toward achieving the idyllic state—the 'honeyed' condition in the lovers' relationship. In American life there is a conspicuous tendency to deny the existence of difficulties in the way of achieving intimacy; and there is little overt recognition that marriage is based on many motives[18] and has many problems associated with it, and that the honeymoon could also be a period in which problems that have to be worked at in order to be solved could be confronted.

Another paradoxical source of strain is to be found in the sheer length of time allowed for the honeymoon by the affluence of our society. In many of the couples in our exploratory study,[19] an eagerness to get back home by the end of the honeymoon was observed. In some cases this was so great that the couple returned earlier than scheduled. This anxiety could be looked at in a number of different ways. To some extent it seems akin to the phenomenon often seen in people at the end of a vacation, of an eagerness to get back to normal routine, the tasks of which may have been piling up. To the extent that the vacation is away from anyone one knows, there may be some anxiety about one's sense of belonging to a particular social group. To the extent that there may be guilt at experiencing pleasure and the absence of hard work, the anxieties may stem from this puritanical source. Personality differences among individuals affect the degree to which these phenomena are manifested (Tomkins, 1962). The majority of the honeymoon couples that we studied were young students just graduating from college; in most cases the individuals were without much prior sexual experience, and we were impressed with the extent to which the desire to return early seemed related to anxiety about the intimacy situation. If there is a lot of anxiety about being involved in an intimate two-person situation, one may expect a corresponding sense of relief or even eagerness at the prospect of returning to a more diffuse pattern of relationships. Getting back to the ordinary context provides, for such people, ways of handling their problems about intense intimacy. On honeymoons, the strain toward getting back to the regular social context is perhaps even more important than on ordinary vacations, because there is the anxiety about getting back to show oneself to one's social group and to test out the new basis for one's relationship with them. In addition to any personal threats that the honeymoon situation itself may hold for the individual, there is a pressure to get back to situations in which other bases for security and identity may simultaneously be felt to be in jeopardy. The extent to which there are career crises occurring in the occupational sphere of the male and/or female may also engender anxieties that aggravate the eagerness to return.

The culturally supported tendency, however, is to play these complexities down, emphasizing that marriage is a matter of free choice based on love between compatible individuals. The cultural tendency towards denying the strains inherent in making the initial adjustments may serve to delay the couple's facing them and dealing with them. Thus, the expression 'the honeymoon is over' may refer not only to the resumption of normal life situations, but also to facing the intimacies of sustained married life without the devices of vacation enjoyment and diversion that may help to avoid them.

## THE HONEYMOON AS A PHASE IN THE CRITICAL TRANSITION OF GETTING MARRIED

Our point of departure is to view the honeymoon as a vital sub-phase of the *critical role transition* of "getting married". The honeymoon as a transitional event between the single state and the assumption of new familial responsibilities is an interlude of varying duration. It epitomizes the joining of the couple as a distinct new social unit in the world. In a way, the honeymoon is a moratorium on regular social participation with the expectation that the couple will use this time partly to prepare themselves for later entering and participating in society in their new social roles. The honeymoon also has a function for society, in that it gives others in the couple's social network time to prepare for the new relationship. Its transitional nature is thus fairly clear. Why do we call it critical?

The concept of *critical role transition* stems from work in social science and psychiatry which is loosely related in a body of writings referred to as 'crisis theory'. Studies stemming from the clinical tradition utilizing aspects of crisis theory have focused on traumatic crises of sudden onset (as with Lindemann's study (1944) of the effects of sudden bereavement), and on crises of an inherently disturbing nature which are negatively valued in our society (as with Janis (1958) on reactions to surgery, Kaplan & Mason (1960) and Caplan (1962) on responses of mothers to the birth of premature babies, Tyhurst (1951) on disaster, Fried (in press) on forced relocation, etc.). An attempt is now being made to apply aspects of crisis theory to normal but significant transitions from one social role to another in the life cycle of the individual in his family and work contexts (Rapoport, 1962).

In the context of the family developmental cycle, the major role transitions include the role changes involved in getting married, having a child, children leaving home, and one's spouse dying. In the more traditional societies these transition points tend to be marked by ceremonial elaboration of ritual activity. These rituals seem to function to ease the transition for all concerned by dealing with the psychic and social implications of the changes entailed (Van Gennep, 1909; Gluckman, 1963). Given the relative diversity of cultural norms, and the secularization of, and the rapidity of social changes in, modern urban life, each of these significant role transitions, however prosaic, involves some degree of uncertainty and tends to be unsupported by traditionally prescribed resolutions. Major transitions are seen as inherently disrupting events, providing for individuals new social environmental contexts within

M

which they relate to one another. As an individual's social role changes, his image of himself is affected, the ways in which he is expected by others to behave are affected, and his legitimate expectations with regard to the behavior of others change. The norms, standards, and groups to which the individual refers his own behavior change as his roles change, and he may grow and develop under the impact of these new stimuli, or he may find them burdensome and distressing.

In short, our framework is one that places a focus on the points at which the evolution of personality systems is linked to social processes, in this case the process of development of the family of procreation. Unlike adolescence, which involves role changes as a consequence of biological growth processes (Blos, 1962; Erikson, 1959), getting married involves changes by virtue of a decision on the part of the individuals to take a step that is marked by an explicit legal transition point. In the case of adolescence, sociocultural transformations are drawn along in the wake of the psychobiological changes; in the case of getting married, the sociocultural change is independent and primary, having a complex relationship to psychobiological changes consequent to it. The two kinds of transition may have in common that the forces set in motion by them lead to deep and enduring consequences, positive or negative. What is certain is the urgency to change. Blos summarizes this viewpoint as present among some psycho-analytic theorists with reference to the topic of adolescence as follows:

'The regressive processes of adolescence permit the remodeling of defective or incomplete earlier developments; new identifications and counter identifications play an important part in this. The profound upheaval associated with the emotional reorganization of adolescence thus harbors a beneficial potential . . . Fenichel hinted at a similar concept: "Experiences in puberty may solve conflicts or shift conflicts into a final direction; moreover, they may give older and oscillating constellations a final and definitive form." Erikson . . . has suggested that we look at adolescence not as an affliction, but as a "normative crisis, i.e. a normal phase of increased conflict characterized by a seeming fluctuation in ego strength, and yet also by a high growth potential" . . . One might add that the definitive settling of conflicts at the end of adolescence means either that they lose their disturbing quality because they have been characterologically stabilized, or they solidify into permanently debilitating symptoms of character disorder' (Blos. 1962, p. 11).

Where adolescence has tended to be viewed by society as entailing more 'illness' and disturbance than appropriate (given this view of the period as one of transitional turbulence with many intrinsically positive potentials), the honeymoon has tended to be viewed by society as entailing more joy and harmony than seem appropriate. This may express a feeling of relief as the termination of a difficult period, or at least at the shifting of responsibilities from parents to spouse.

During the honeymoon, choices are being made as to how to structure the relationship. In modern urban cultures the wide range of latitude allowed may be stressful as well as helpful. Resolutions are made in response to various needs and pressures, often in an atmosphere of uncertainty. What people do at these times is seen as affecting their later behavior in future stages of the life cycle.

In general, we see the critical *role* transition as characterized by a change in the state of both the personal and the relevant social systems of the individuals concerned. Before the new steady state is achieved, role-relational patterns are to some extent fluid and there may be more or less of a sense of personal disorganization. Undergoing a critical role transition carries connotations of significant change. It contrasts with living according to established routines. Once having been traversed, the critical role transition is a point of no return. The previous steady state can never again be attained in exactly the same way. The point in the life cycle once having been crossed, it can never be recrossed. In getting married, for instance, the individuals concerned undergo a change of role relationships from those that held for them as single, never-married individuals (perhaps living in their families of orientation) to those of becoming married individuals, constituting a new family of procreation. In our society this usually entails new living arrangements on a neo-local basis. Despite divorce, remarriage, and so on, the individual can never again be a single person who has never been married. If the girl forever loses her culturally defined status of virginal purity, the boy forever loses his status of a never-married bachelor, though he may once again become 'eligible' if he is divorced. Society redefines individuals who have been through this point, and though they may go through it again there is a sense in which the first transition is unique. The notion of critical role transition does not imply that the individuals concerned cannot accomplish many aspects of the role transition at other points in the life cycle. It does, however, imply that the transition *must* be at this point and that the subsequent state can be favorable or unfavorable, depending on how the work of making the transition has been dealt with. Thus the critical role transition may or may not entail acute emotional disturbance, but it must entail disequilibrium, followed by a restoration of a new steady state. We conceptualize the work of restoring the new steady state as a series of tasks, specific to each of the many critical role transitions that punctuate the flow of life. The fact that an individual performs the tasks of one role transition satisfactorily does not necessarily imply that he can accomplish *all* role-transitional tasks with comparable ease or effectiveness. Each transition has tasks specific to it. The accomplishment of these tasks affects outcome for the particular role transition. The outcome may be better than the previous state of equilibrium in some ways, it may leave things relatively unchanged, or it may be worse. In general, one would expect that favorable outcomes to life-cycle crises increase the chances for favorable outcomes to later crises in the life cycle, but this is not documented empirically and many anomalies are known to exist.

The honeymoon, then, is a culturally patterned event associated with a critical transition point. The transition point, getting married, is inherently disruptive of the steady state that had been established in the lives of the individuals concerned and in the social systems in which they are involved. While marriage differs for different couples according to their premarital relationships and the sort of early marriage they envisage, it is a transition point that must be reckoned with.[20] It is an event that has associated with it specific tasks defined partly by their culture, partly by themselves. The ways in which couples work through and accomplish these tasks hypothetically affect the subsequent stable state of affairs in the social systems of the family and in the personalities of the interacting individuals.

## THE PHASE-SPECIFIC TASKS OF THE HONEYMOON

It is essential to our approach to delineate tasks that are *phase-specific*. Though much of the work—behavioral and intrapsychic—may have been done before the phase in which it becomes crucial to have accomplished the tasks, we postulate that failure to come to grips with them in the period for which they are specific will lead to deleterious consequences for the individuals and/or social systems concerned. For example, many individuals engage in sexual relationships before they marry, and many couples have sexual relations together before their honeymoon. Though a certain amount of work toward task accomplishment may have been entailed for specific persons in this experience, in the context of our culture this is usually not defined as a role rehearsal, but as experimentation with individually meaningful behavior or the seeking of individually gratifying experience. In social psychological terms, the 'temporal gestalts' of individuals having premarital sexual relations differ from those of individuals engaging in similar behavior on their honeymoon in that the former have primarily individual life-cycle referents, perhaps being more backward-facing and parental-family oriented, whereas the latter are primarily forward-facing and oriented to the new social unit into which the individual is bound, his family of procreation.[21]

Four tasks are postulated as specific to the honeymoon. Two of these can be described as essentially intrapsychic or personal in nature, while the other two are interpersonal and focus on the interaction between the marital pair. They all relate directly to what is required for establishing a basis on which the ensuing husband-wife relationship will develop.[22]

Underlying the accomplishment patterns for these tasks are the deeper psychodynamic processes affecting the adjustment of two individuals to intimate living together. Prominent among these are the issues of dependence, interdependence, and independence in relation to one another. What happens in this period of adjustment will affect the course of whatever psychic processes are at work in the individuals at the time, e.g., their dealing with their identity problems. In Western society, much 'in the marriage relationship itself is wrought of the play of these opposite impulses—the regressive search for a "self-less" primary intimacy, and the drive towards individuation and responsible adulthood' (Pincus, 1960, p. 212). During the honeymoon, the individual may be faced for the first time with the conflicts contained in his intrapsychic needs and between his and his partner's needs on these dimensions.

INTRAPERSONAL TASK I: DEVELOPING A COMPETENCE TO
PARTICIPATE IN AN APPROPRIATE[23] SEXUAL RELATIONSHIP
WITH ONE'S MARITAL PARTNER

For persons in our society this task appears to involve a review, conscious or unconscious, of one's feelings about intimate sexual relations in a familial setting and of one's attitudes to various sexual activities; it will involve coping with fears in this area and attempting to resolve them. Our exploratory work shows that young couples are often concerned about their sexual abilities. Women may be afraid of the pain of intercourse, of whether they will get past the initial period, whether they will be able to satisfy their husbands, whether their husbands will be patient and gentle with them, and so on. The men's fears are expressed in terms of their ability or inability to be potent with their wives. For both husband and wife intrapsychic feelings of security are involved, feelings about whether their identity or autonomy will be threatened or enhanced by an intimate sexual relationship with another person in the context of marriage and its overtones of earlier childhood relationships.

During the honeymoon period individuals will be faced with the need to clarify some of their ideas about the place of sex in marriage: their preferences in relation to the character of the sex act; their recognition of the intensity or otherwise of their own sexual feelings, particularly towards their marital partner. For some individuals this task will also involve an initial review of themselves not only as a wife/husband but also as a potential father/mother. For some Catholic couples, for example, this is particularly important, since many begin their sexual life in the honeymoon without attempting to avert or delay conception of offspring. Here intrapsychic feelings associated with dependency, nurturance, and self-esteem are involved. Under this rubric we are concerned with individuals' attitudes and feelings about family planning, spacing of children, use of contraceptives, and so on.

It is felt that this task may also involve an initial clarification, explicit or implicit, of personal goals, values, and desires about a sexual life within marriage and outside it. Each person needs to understand his own ideas and feelings concerning the sexual aspects of marriage: such as the parts to be played by the male and female in the sex act with regard to position, frequency, initiation, and response; and expectations about the desirability for orgasm, its character, and its necessity or otherwise, for a satisfactory sexual life. Within our own culture there is a wide range of individual orientations to sexuality, from the view, on the one hand, that it is an unpleasant obligation, to the view that it is life's most treasured experience. In general, it would seem important for each person to begin to understand what he expects of the total sexual experience and to work out its place in relation to procreation. This latter involves a consideration of family planning goals— or the lack of them—and some review of techniques for controlling conception and of attitudes and feelings towards such techniques.

### INTRAPERSONAL TASK II: DEVELOPING COMPETENCE TO LIVE IN CLOSE ASSOCIATION WITH THE MARITAL PARTNER

For most persons the honeymoon is the first time of living very closely with a person of the other sex. Even the experience of living in the single household with one's family of orientation is not directly transferable. Each person is likely to find that he has some feelings about this new situation, and sometimes these feelings are very strong. Once again a person's needs for autonomy, dependence, unity, and separation will be indicated in his capacity to live closely with another person. If he has a strong need to retain a separate identity he may have great difficulty in developing an ability to live closely with his partner. A person's feelings in this area are likely to show in his preference for a particular kind of honeymoon: where he wants to go, whether he wants to be alone with his spouse a great deal, whether he wants to be on the go much of the time, whether he wants to participate in a honeymooners' camp, and so on. On the actual honeymoon, feelings about sharing the same bed with the spouse, the mode of bathroom usage, feelings about undressing in front of the other person, will all provide clues to this area. The task, in general, involves the development of an understanding of one's own and the spouse's needs with respect to the elements of close day-to-day living; and of an ability to give up some of one's autonomy in favor of an adaptation to living with the spouse, i.e., working to adapt or 'harmonize' one's needs, values, and behavior to those of the spouse. During the honeymoon the range of areas where this is relevant is restricted since the couple are not involved in their usual pattern of activities. However, the honeymoon provides an opportunity for establishing the basis on which the later patterns can be developed. An essential aspect of this personal task is the development of a flexibility to act adaptively to the other person's needs.

### INTERPERSONAL TASK I: DEVELOPING THE BASIS FOR A MUTUALLY SATISFACTORY SEXUAL RELATIONSHIP

It is postulated that some basic sexual relationship must be attained by the end of the honeymoon period, though couples will vary on the degree of intimacy[24] attained in the relationship and on other specific ways of relating in it. From one point of view, the honeymoon can be seen as the time *par excellence* for the couple to get to know each other in a sexual sense; they have the time and the licence to indulge in lovemaking. It is during this period that it may be possible to lay the *basis* for their future sexual relationship. This does not mean that all problems will be ironed out or even that the level of intimacy achieved during this phase will not alter later—there is likely to be further development (or regression) in many couples. It is rather that during this time the couple have unprecedented opportunities for attending to the sexual relationship without other responsibilities of everyday life impinging on them.

In assessing accomplishment on this task we seek data on how each person feels about the sexual situation, on his anxieties and defenses, and on the way the partners relate to each other. Where there is a discrepancy in needs, we inquire into how discrepancies are dealt with and what feelings of satisfaction or otherwise the couple are left with. From this we rate couples on five aspects of their sexual relationship: the degree of mutuality in ideas about satisfaction expected from sexual roles; the degree of understanding of one another's sexual needs; their ability to cope with them; the degree of mutual arousal in sexual relations; and the degree of mutual satisfaction experienced.

### INTERPERSONAL TASK II: HAVING A MUTUALLY SATISFACTORY SHARED EXPERIENCE AS A BASIS FOR DEVELOPING THE LATER HUSBAND–WIFE RELATIONSHIP

From our case material and from the material in popular journals on the subject, it becomes apparent that a 'successful' honeymoon has great symbolic value. It would seem important that the couple have an experience which they both feel has been satisfactory and which provides them with a good start to their married life.

The task of having a 'good' honeymoon can be specified somewhat more dynamically than is implied in visualizing it as a period in which a happy time is cultivated to serve as a shared basis for future life together. The honeymoon couple are, after all, a kind of small group, subject to dynamic processes similar to all two-person groups. The new couple, detached from their former surroundings, with all the connotations of parental authority these contained, seem to have much in common with the kind of groups described by Bion (1961). Emotional drives of obscure origin seem to intrude themselves into the situation, affecting the capacity of individual couples to accomplish the tasks of the honeymoon. The honeymoon period is one in which these forces are rather actively at work, and the structure of the relationship that emerges can be seen partly as a defense against primitive anxieties stimulated in the new situation of intimacy.[25] The form taken by these newly emergent interpersonal structures is not directly predictable from the personalities of the individual members.[26] As Asch (1952) points out, any sort of social interaction, if it is to develop into a relationship, is built on a sense of cooperation. And it is on this basis that family structure develops. In the honeymoon the elements of family structure described by Parsons and Bales (1956) can be seen to develop—with honeymoon couples tentatively establishing the bases for what later becomes their authority structure and their division of labor on the 'instrumental-expressive' axis of family life.

According to our postulate, then, the honeymoon should provide the couple not only with a shared experience of cooperation, but with the sense of an ability to cooperate. The beginning of the new cooperation, arising out of the living together as a marital pair for the first time, should provide the sense of it being possible to work out a structure for meeting subsequent tasks.

Obviously, the specifics of the experience will vary from couple to couple; our postulate is that those who have an experience which they feel was unsatisfactory become part of a population which is at greater risk for poor outcome.[27] The actual assessment of the degree of accomplishment of this task is based on data collected on several aspects of the task, including the managing of the various honeymoon arrangements, the feeling of 'harmony' the couple experience in their activities during the honeymoon, and the degree to which they see the experience as 'idyllic'. What appears to be focal here is the crystallization of some kind of positive emotional toning in relation to whatever pattern the relationship has taken by the end of the honeymoon. This emotional tone (e.g., of interpersonal trust, relaxation, security, admiration or more negative counterparts) may form the basis for a set of stereotypes developing within the interpersonal relationship. The way one perceives one's spouse on one's honeymoon and the concomitant set of experiences seem to set up images and expectations between the couple that are later difficult to alter.[28]

## COPING WITH THE TASKS OF THE HONEYMOON

Different conceptions of the honeymoon exist even within a culture and different couples approach the honeymoon experience with various expectations. What literature there is on the honeymoon tends to emphasize the uniformities of response within given sociocultural settings. In this section we attempt to indicate some of the processes that occur when individuals actualize their sociocultural and personal inclinations together in the new situation of the honeymoon. These coping processes give rise to a new set of factors which, we maintain, intervene significantly between the original inclinations of the individuals concerned and the eventual outcome when the honeymoon is over and the newly wed couple takes up its position as a new family.

Underlying our argument is that what happens on honeymoons tends to have important effects on the development of subsequent marital relationships. This seems particularly to hold for the bride; in our small research series there was a definite tendency for couples to see the honeymoon as something the groom arranges for the bride, whereas the bride and her family were seen as the principal sponsors of the wedding ceremony.

'Coping' and 'task accomplishment' are differentiated concepts in the conceptual scheme we have been using. The former relates to the ways used in confronting and mastering the postulated tasks, whereas the latter relates to the degree to which the task is accomplished. Task accomplishment is regarded as the intervening set of variables between the individual and the collective resources of the couple, and their subsequent structuring of the marital relationship. This concept draws, on the one hand, from the developmental psychology of childhood and, on the other, from the 'crisis theory' of preventive intervention in the community mental health field; it is here extended to social process more generally.

Coping patterns are seen as ways of dealing with the flow of life circumstances. These patterns involve mechanisms of defense (in the psycho-analytic sense) and, more generally, patterns of cognition, motivation, and perception which individuals, in their sociocultural backgrounds, bring to bear on the situation. Coping patterns may thus be described as having contents, styles, approaches, and so on (Murphy, 1962). We are here concerned with coping patterns as *ways* of mastering the tasks specifically confronting the newly wed couple on the honeymoon, rather than with the degree of task accomplishment itself. It is likely that some

M*

coping patterns will be more closely associated with degrees of task accomplishment than others, but our interest in coping patterns is to understand *how* individuals and couples accomplish the specific tasks in hand as well as *how well* they accomplish them (White, 1959; Foote & Cottrell, 1955).

A vignette is presented from our case materials on the honeymoon. The couple were seen immediately before the honeymoon and interviewed again a couple of weeks after their return. The vignette illustrates how the existing elements of culture, social structure, and personality combine in the particular couple to produce patterns of coping with the tasks confronting them.

## THE "A" COUPLE

Richard and Peggy had known one another for many years prior to their marriage, which took place when he was 26 and she was 23. They lived in the same neighborhood, went to the same school, dated each other for a long period, and came from similar religious and socio-economic backgrounds. Peggy, a receptionist in a beauty parlor, lived at home with her family while Richard lived in his own apartment. Richard was early attracted to Peggy with a strong passion; he enjoyed her popularity at school and liked her competence. But marriage was delayed by pressure from their families. By the time they actually came to marry, Richard no longer felt such strong passion but just thought she was the right girl for him. Peggy seems to have been most attracted by what she saw as Richard's knowledgeability and emotional steadiness.

Richard was a senior chemistry student and, though secure in his occupational prospects, he decided just prior to graduation to take an advanced degree. He saw this as a way of making himself more independent occupationally and less subject to non-rational factors in his career advancement.

By the time of the wedding, the young couple had done much of the work usually associated with the tasks of the early marriage stage. They had their apartment all prepared, furniture purchased, decoration well advanced, and a small network of common friends. They had not had sexual relations with each other (or anyone else), and indeed had avoided too much visiting together alone in his apartment ostensibly to prevent neighborhood gossip and to conform with her parents' sense of propriety.

During the engagement period there was a marked division of labor between the pair. The honeymoon was considered to be Richard's sphere of concern while the preparations for the marriage and reception were hers. Richard tended to define the honeymoon as a long-awaited and much-needed vacation. After some perfunctory checking at travel agents about costs he chose Canada and Niagara Falls for their honeymoon. Denying any motives other than economic ones for his choice he stated that he had really wanted a European trip but accepted Niagara as a more economical substitute.

Following the wedding and reception, Richard and Peggy began their drive to Canada. Late the first night they checked into a hotel. After checking in she put on her peignoir, especially bought for the occasion, and went to bed to wait for him while he went out for some cigarettes. When he returned he undressed and put on pajamas. They made what were described as a few half-hearted attempts at lovemaking—kissing and caressing—but without much verbal communication; they both seemed to arrive at the conclusion that it would be best not to press for sexual relations this first night. They were both tired, they wished to start early in the morning, and neither felt like initiating an experience as complex as sexual intercourse appeared to them at this point. After watching TV for a while they went to bed.

Early next morning they started off for Niagara, arriving there just after noon. Whatever Richard's feelings about his choice of honeymoon, it was clear that for Peggy the chosen spot was especially agreeable because of the romantic image it created in conventional middle-class American culture.

At the time of registering at the hotel, they were asked if they preferred to have a table for two or one to share with another couple. They chose the latter, feeling that this would give them someone to talk to. On the second night of their honeymoon, then, they had dinner with their new friends, spent the evening with them, and did not go to their bedroom until late. They undressed with the light out, went to bed, and for a while attempted sexual relations. Peggy found herself in great pain and told her husband so. Richard was reassuring, handling the situation in a matter-of-fact and optimistic way.

Peggy's reaction was one of great disappointment. Initially, this was less related to unsatisfied passion than to failure to live up to her image of the ideal wife, particularly in being unable to satisfy him. He said that there was plenty of time and he could wait; and he put forth anatomical explanations for her difficulties.

On the fourth night they had successful sexual relations in that she experienced less pain and he reached a climax. From this point onward it became apparent that Peggy was probably more capable of affectual arousal than Richard, and the pattern tended to be one in which she wanted sexual relations more frequently than he. He dealt with the problem in his usual orderly, logical way by scheduling relations.

During the honeymoon it was Richard who expressed the more

active need to be with others. He sought out organized activity more than Peggy and, in general, showed signs of avoiding situations that threw them together alone for any extended period of time. She, though having less need to avoid intimate situations than he, went along cheerfully with whatever was being planned.

From the beginning Peggy's conception of the honeymoon was different from Richard's. Whereas he saw it primarily as a vacation, she saw it as a period of adjustment, sexual and otherwise. At some points during the honeymoon she was almost overcome by homesickness and felt a longing to be with her family. Richard reassured her, saying that this was expectable, and gave her quiet support. His affect remained level throughout the entire experience while hers went through various ups and downs: the place was wonderful, she was miserably homesick, she was wretchedly disappointed at first about sex, later rather excited by it; he tended to find everything 'all right' and sex as 'overrated'.

If we look at the way the As coped with the tasks of the honeymoon, we find that to the extent that Richard developed increased competence to live in close association with Peggy, he did so by taking things very slowly, avoiding too much pressure, too many ambiguous or conflictful situations, and too many situations that threw them onto one another in an intimate way. He did this because it was his own characteristic mode of handling feelings.

Peggy dealt with the task of learning to live in close association with Richard by seeking to accommodate to his wishes, being willing, cooperative, cheerful, and appreciative.

As for the sexual aspect of the intrapersonal tasks, Richard dealt with his own sexual needs by scheduling them, regarding them as something that it was normal to have and indulge in, but nothing to get too excited about. Peggy was surprised at how painful and difficult sex was at first, but quickly came to terms with it, transforming her disappointment at herself into a gradual awakening interest in sexuality, so that subsequently she had to deal with her frustrations at the limitations being placed on her own newly awakened sexual feelings.

With regard to the interpersonal tasks, mutually satisfactory arrangements for the honeymoon were arrived at by division of labor and her absolute compliance to his structuring of the situation. He, in characteristic 'debunking of sentimentality' fashion, chose Niagara on economic grounds as a second best to a European trip, but this suited her well because of its conventionally romantic aura.

The sexual relationship that developed was one in which he was more satisfied than she, though she did not allow herself to express (and perhaps not even to realize) her own dissatisfaction. He gave reasonable grounds for limiting and scheduling their sexual relations and she accepted this limitation as inherent in the situation. His approach to sexuality was so matter-of-fact that, even with the opportunities available, she did not often reach climax and showed many indirect signs of sexual tension. This tension could feed into other potential areas of discord and aggravate disagreements and quarrels.

The sense of harmony that was developed in this couple was based on her capacity to idealize the state of marriage itself, on his capacity to deny difficulties that did not fit with his defenses (e.g., spending so much time going around with the other couple that they did not get to bed until late; they short-cut the preliminaries of sexual play, and so on), and on the fact that they were both so well known to one another and so lacking in conflicting elements of personality (except that her 'emotionality' conflicted with his needs), cultural norms, or expectations.

Segregation of activities and diffusion of involvement in other people's presence helped to keep them a little distant from one another emotionally, a state of affairs that was more agreeable for him than for her. To the extent that his orderliness and avoidance of affect can fit well into her idealization of the situation, the state of being married, and so on, they should maintain a sense of harmony. They have several strengths in the situation—his occupational competence, their home, the proximity of her family. However, the fact that their task accomplishment was somewhat low in the area of sexual adjustment, and that there are many areas of rather shallow bases for their sense of harmony, generally makes one feel that there are considerable mental health risks present in the situation. These might be mitigated by the arrival of children if Peggy is successful in conceiving, and she may turn to them for some of the gratifications her relationship with Richard does not provide.

What do we learn of this couple through the use of our particular theoretical orientation that we would not have so easily learned without it? We would probably have predicted a better outcome for the A couple using only the conventional 'closed system' orientation than we are likely to with the task performance framework. On the sociocultural level this is a couple that is well matched; on the personality level they have much that complements one another; situationally they do not have cause for excessive anxieties and insecurities about occupational career, residential location, or any of the other potentially 'stressful' external factors. On the other hand, their performance on the tasks of the honeymoon reveals some of the deficiencies in the way they fit together their individual proclivities into a single system. The harmony achieved on the basis of his denial and her idealization may be a pseudoharmony, for it ignores the extent to which they have not accomplished the work of dealing with her sexual needs, and her greater inclinations toward intimacy. Both, but especially the latter, may be dealt with by the advent of children. Though this may only defer the problems to a later point in the life cycle of the couple's development together, it is probable that they will be factors to be dealt with somehow.

## DISCUSSION

Our concentration on the concept of 'task accomplishment' as the crucial intervening variable in assessing the interplay of forces affecting the outcome of critical transition points in the life cycle has implications for theoretical social science and for the mental health field.

In social science the traditional disciplines divided up the quest for knowledge partly according to the content and partly on the basis of the level on which they made abstractions from the flow of life. Thus, psychologists abstracted information on the psychological level and made predictions or explanations on that level only; similarly for sociologists, social anthropologists, and so on.

We accept the utility of analyzing phenomena both on the socio-cultural level and on the psychological level. Our approach may be seen as having its principal relevance in explaining the emergence of patterns within the setting of complex societies. In the modern urban situation family structure does not follow conventional prescriptions as closely as traditionally, but may vary. The form that family structure ultimately takes is subject to factors that emerge in the interplay of forces among the various systems concerned, personality, cultural, and social structural. The theoretical problem is how to assess the process of 'fitting together' of factors interplaying among the various systems both within the individuals and between them. We suggest that the measurement of 'task accomplishment' provides an approximate assessment. Task accomplishment is itself, of course, a product of the factors antecedent to the situation in which the tasks arise. However, its importance for our purposes is in its emergence as an autonomous predictive variable of consequent outcomes. It thus becomes a definable and measurable set of conditions reflecting the way in which antecedent variables are interacting in a given situation. The measurement of this interaction effect at the time of critical role transitions has special significance in that it is postulated that these are the times in which structure is emerging. Once crystallized, the structure of a family, for example, becomes the effective intimate social environment for individuals. Each couple in the urban setting emerges in these situations of flux with a social structure, in the formation of which they themselves have had an active part.[29]

With reference to implications of this approach for the mental health field, it would seem that the situation with which we are concerned

here is a critical turning point in people's lives and therefore compa.
to other 'crises' that have been studied as points for potential preventi.
intervention (Lindemann, 1944; Caplan, 1961). Assuming that empirical validation of this postulate will be forthcoming in the course of research and ignoring for the moment the problems posed by the special
character of privacy associated with the honeymoon experience, what can
we say about the nature of the honeymoon as a 'crisis' in the context
of community mental health efforts?

First, it is clear from the intensive materials already at hand that
couples in fact go through experiences in the honeymoon that are relevant for their emotional development. The choice of a permanent sexual
partner has clear implications for the self-image of each person, his feelings
of integration (the more so to the extent that there is a strong degree
of intimacy in the relationship), his sense of dependence and independence as an adult person, and his capacity to accept the dependence of
another. Moreover, as each in fact enters the same role as his parents
entered through marriage, there ensues a process of reworking the identifications with the parental figures which have been internalized as integral parts of the personality (Flugel, 1921; Pincus, 1960). The marital
relationship, being closer than any prior relationships apart from that of
the child to his own parents, is also bound to awaken many of the
feelings of love, hate, and other intimate involvements that were characteristic of those felt and observed in the earlier family situation. As the
earlier ones were colored by sexual taboos, the exercise of sexuality in
this new relationship arouses many of the overtones of fear and guilt
which were associated with the earlier ones. Individuals will have freed
themselves of these in different degrees by the time of marriage—or
will have been able in different degrees to dissociate the present relationship symbolically from the old ones.

It would seem, therefore, that getting married, and especially the
honeymoon period, is a situation that is rich with both the potentialities for
growth *and* the potentialities for disturbance. We have postulated a
relationship between the way the couples accomplish the tasks presented
to them in this situation and what sort of outcome ensues from the
point of view of these dual potentialities. In short, the critical role transition of getting married—with its culmination in the honeymoon experience—can be viewed as a hazardous circumstance in which populations
exposed to the experience may be seen as encountering special risks from
a mental health point of view. This is the perspective of the public
health field, and implies the advisability of searching for preventive intervention possibilities.

What sort of preventive intervention is conceivable in such a situation as the honeymoon, with its sacred inviolability, its idealized se-

its sensitivity to the intrusion of outsiders? It must first be
3st the techniques of preventive intervention currently being de-
d by such community mental health programs as that under Caplan's
ction do not intrude directly on the individuals who are the mental
ealth risks—even in circumstances where the risk is more severe, more
clearly demonstrated, and empirically validated, compared with the case
under discussion. The usual approach is to work through intermediaries,
termed 'caregivers'. These are individuals who are, in the normal course
of their work, involved somehow with the populations that are seen to be
at risk. They already have role relationships with the individuals concerned and interact with them in ways that contain similar ingredients
to 'interventions', i.e., they interact with and seek to influence the individuals in ways relevant to task accomplishment. In the case of the
honeymoon these individuals might be ministers (especially where some
counselling is done, as in Pre-Cana conferences), doctors (e.g., where
contraception is medically assisted or where general practitioners play an
educative role in the preparation for sexual relations), and, on the
honeymoon itself, such people as hotel keepers. These last, surprisingly,
often take an interest in honeymooners, not only because of their commercial importance as clients, but out of personal concern. In such cases
we have observed hoteliers arranging activities and relationships for
honeymoon couples whom they perceived as needing some kind of assistance (that affected their task accomplishment) in this period. The community mental health worker seeks to enlist the cooperation of such individuals and to educate them in the perspectives made available through
research and clinical experience. Often these individuals are themselves
eager to gain whatever new knowledge and perspectives they can get,
but they are sometimes not so receptive. The field of mental health
consultation has been developed to work with various caregivers
(Caplan, 1961).

To all this it must be added that our approach stresses the importance
of keeping as alert to the *positive* mental health gains potentially activated by such an experience as the honeymoon as to the hazards to
health. The six major mental health concepts that Jahoda abstracts as
prominent in current usage in the literature are: attitudes toward the
self; growth, development, self-actualization; integration; autonomy; perception of reality; and environmental mastery (Jahoda, 1958). If we
look at task accomplishment on the honeymoon in this context it is apparent that the mental health implications are potentially very great.
For example, as part of the effects on attitudes toward the self, the
major role transition involved and enacted in the honeymoon—of legitimate participation in the adult sex relationship—may have profound
effects on one's sense of personal identity and feelings about oneself.

The joining together of one's fate to that of the other person may profoundly affect one's investment in living and other motivational processes considered essential for growth, development, and self-actualization. To the extent that the couple are able to accomplish the intimate tasks of joining together into a more unified pair, they may find their personal feelings of integration affected—in terms of their feelings of resistance to stresses of living, their general rounding-out of an outlook on life in the context of the couple-perspective, and so on. As each member of the couple enters the more adult role relationship, he may find his sense of autonomy affected through reaching a new balance of inner regulation (e.g., in relation to the sex drive, and in relation to authority), and through gaining a status legitimizing life independent of the parents. The nature of the intimacy relationship may, if the tasks are successfully coped with, enhance perception of reality through providing a trusted partner with whom reality-testing can go on, and the fostering of empathy in this relationship may have a more general effect on other relationships as well. Finally, the ability to love, play, and deal with other of life's problems may be affected by the way the tasks of the honeymoon are dealt with.

Our research task is to ascertain which patterns and levels of task accomplishment on the honeymoon are correlated with such positive outcomes, and which with less desirable outcomes in the ensuing family life. While it is still, of course, an open question as to *how* 'critical' this element of the complex process of getting married is, we are impressed with its importance in the cases we have studied. This exploratory work will have to be supplemented with more extensive studies, in which different types of honeymoon experience can be interpreted in the context of various premarital patterns of experience and various normative patterns of family life following marriage. Whether or not the findings that ultimately emerge are taken to fall within the purview of any particular beneficent agency is not our immediate concern. However, the fact that many representatives of society's help agencies are interested in this phenomenon may lend some utility to our findings, whichever end of the mental health continuum they may turn out to illuminate.

## NOTES

1. This paper is based in part on a research program on family development in the Community Mental Health Program of the Harvard School of Public Health. A project on 'getting married' as a major critical transition is presently under way. The research is supported by a development grant from the United States Public Health Service, NIMH grant #MH-03442; Dr. Gerald

Caplan is the director of the Community Mental Health Program; Dr. Rhona Rapoport of the Family Research. The data on which the present paper draws were gathered in interviews made by Ivor Browne and Beatrice Horvitz in addition to the authors. Peggy Golde, Douglas Hooper, Lawrence Schiff, and Rae Sherwood read an earlier draft of this paper and made helpful comments. The final draft was written while the authors, partly supported by a grant to Robert Rapoport from the Social Science Research Council, were visiting staff members of the Tavistock Institute of Human Relations. Thanks are due to Eric Trist, Fred Emery, and Yonina Talmon for their comments on the later versions of the paper.
2. Exceptions are Brav's 'Note on Honeymoons' (1947), some of the clinical observations of Freud (1953) and Marie Bonaparte (1953), and some of the social-psychological observations of Slater (1963) and Simpson (1960).
3. Some examples are Alberto Moravia's 'Bitter Honeymoon' and Thomas MacIntyre's 'Wedding Hymn', both short stories; Tennessee Williams's play *Period of Adjustment;* and Jules Romain's novel *The Body's Rapture.*
4. For example, among the Hindus the most valued type of marriage is the *Brahma* marriage, arranged on the basis of social considerations by the parents. However, marriage by mutual choice (*Gandharva*), marriage by conquest (*Rakshasa*), by purchase (*Asur*), or by taking advantage of helplessness (*Paishacha*) are all explicitly recognized in Manu, though censured as not reflecting the social will (Tagore, 1927).
5. For example, Spiro (1958) and Talmon (1963) note the informal development of an exogamous marriage pattern in Israeli Kibbutzim, which functions, in part, in response to the quasi-sibling quality of relationship among Kibbutz mates; Howitt (1903) reports the informal development of an elopement pattern among the Kurnai, which seems to have arisen in the face of excessive formal marriage interdictions within the group of potential sexual partners.
6. Among the Eskimos, the newly married couple simply set up a new nuclear household, but shared in the communal resources and enterprises in much the same way as prior to marriage. Among the Nuer, the transition into full married life was accomplished by a series of events, with sexual relations often having been established prior to the actual wedding and regular cohabitation of the couple commencing only after the birth of the first child (Evans-Pritchard, 1951).
7. Among the Baganda the bride, after having been delivered to the compound of the groom by her relatives, remained in seclusion for several days following the marriage with the groom. During this period there were a number of ritualized elements of behavior, including some days' abstention from intercourse, following which the bridegroom sent a blood-stained bark-cloth to her relatives and later the bride performed ritualized demonstrations of tasks associated with her new role in the vicinity of her mother-in-law's house; subsequently she was either invited in or had grounds for dissolving the marriage (Roscoe, 1911). Among the Nootka there was also great ceremonial elaboration during and after the marriage. The Nootka marriage entailed the presentation, as dowry, of some of the bride's father's privileged names, special dances, potlatch seats, territorial rights, and other role elements marking the transition status. In the Baganda case, emphasis on propagation of lineage seemed to underlie the rituals, whereas among the Nootka it was their preoccupation with status and its symbols. Delay of consummation of the marriage is very widespread, giving ritualized recognition to the emotionally charged significance of the event of defloration. Among the Usambara, the bride and groom slept in a friend's house in two beds separated by a fire, and fasted for several days after the marriage. This custom was also found even in Europe, where it was referred to as 'Tobias nights' after the legendary piety of Tobias and Sarah. The 'holy state of matrimony' conception in current Western culture parallels the widespread recognition

of the charged significance of this event—usually associated with premarital taboos on intercourse, supernatural sanctions against intercourse, and, often, ritualized methods of terminating the state of virginity.

8. Philip Wylie (1952), deploring what he views as the malfunctional character of the American honeymoon with reference to the development of a love relationship, also notes the emphasis on couple autonomy. He caricatures this as follows: 'One would indeed presume . . . that the American honeymoon was the modern equivalent of some savage ordeal or tribal initiation ceremony. The newly wed pair is first put under intense financial strain; it is then exhausted physically; it may also be submitted to a trial by alcohol. The pair is exposed to the frustrations of travel by public conveyance; it is thereafter exiled among strangers . . .'

9. Slater (1963) notes that some of the stylized pranks played on honeymooners seem to contravene the explicit emphasis on separation of the couple—e.g., intrusion into their supposedly secret honeymoon retreat.

10. For example, among the Baganda the bride is accompanied by a sister or close friend even after she is actually delivered to the groom's compound for the wedding. This companion stays with her through the rituals of joining and the ordeals of performance in her new role.

11. Among the Nayar the bride's residence, activity patterns, and allegiances remained bound in with her matrilineal kin group's. Among the Menangkabau the bridegroom spent some nights with his wife, but remained closely tied to his own mother's house. After the actual marriage, this latter tie was expressed ritually in the return of the bridegroom to his mother's home, followed by his being ritually fetched back by a deputation of young men representing the bride. Clearly these rituals of imbeddedness related to the strength of corporate groupings within the society. Simpson (1960) notes the custom of the communal Amish, among whom the newly-weds spent the first several weeks visiting those who were guests at their wedding.

12. Another derivation (see *Oxford Dictionary*) places the emphasis on the period of time, the term being a corruption of 'honeymonth', referring to the fixed length of time traditionally set aside for newly-weds to go into retirement: e.g. Johnson, 'The first month after marriage when there is nothing but tenderness and pleasure.' This usage does not preclude the other derivation of the term, mentioned in the text here, but is rather a matter of emphasis.

13. The classical case of marriage by capture, Crawley (1902) was careful to maintain, is one in which there is no proper marriage at all, but rather the taking of a mate from a hostile tribe. This practice has been discussed in various anthropological contexts but it is clearly different from the situation in which there is a ritual tussle expressing the feelings of the bride's relatives at giving up their female group-member to a male from another group (cf. Firth, 1936). The Kurnai practice of elopement, which has been mentioned above, is still another kind of instance in which there is a situation of such inbreeding that no eligible marriage partners exist. In such a situation the killing of totems followed by a free fight and a reshuffling of social alignments makes new marriages possible, with elopement serving to remove the couples for a time from social sanctions pending their reabsorption on a new basis (Howitt, 1903).

14. On the other hand, Slater (1963), viewing the honeymoon as a form of 'dyadic withdrawal', notes that the pranks often played on departing honeymooners— e.g., tampering with their automobile—express the other side of the ambivalence felt at the event. The short story by MacIntyre (1963) brings out some of the problems associated with the expectation of sexual intercourse on the first night, and also some of the impingements on true privacy that commercialization of the honeymoon has made.

15. However, in keeping with the general diffusion of many aspects of American culture, Britain now seems to have developed some honeymoon camps, e.g.,

in the Channel Islands and in some of the Butlin camps, that resemble the American phenomenon.

16. Or, as in the case of Tennessee Williams's example of this in *Period of Adjustment,* a tentative date of arrival.

17. For Slater's observations, see footnotes 9 and 14 above.

18. A cynical appreciation of the complexity of motives underlying the decision to marry is expressed by Wasserman in his novel *Laudin und die Seinen.* He states that the barrister Laudin could have written a treatise on how many marriages were based on 'frivolity and indiscretion, on hasty passion and blind sensuality . . . (on) ambition, vanity, financial gain, good natured weakness or mutual and temporary infatuation, . . . (on) complete indifference or disconsolate resignation. Some obtained their wives by craft (to pay their mistresses with their wives' money) . . .', and so on. This vividly communicates the kind of complexity that is involved in modern mate-selection which many of the more prosaic social science analyses of marital adjustment seek to deal with.

19. The project to which we refer is the one mentioned in the first footnote. Of the dozen couples studied intensively during their engagement and after their marriage, about half were interviewed in detail about their honeymoon experience. One case, suitably disguised, is summarized below.

20. While couples who have had premarital sexual relations or have cohabited on a trial marriage basis or even more extended arrangement would seem to face a less challenging discontinuity at the point of their honeymoon than those who have never had any sort of sexual relations, it must not be taken as an absolute rule. Harmony between the couple may have depended on their not being married, the actual legal tie being felt as a constriction. (The relationship between Sartre and de Beauvoir is one of the more publicly known instances.) However, research is certainly needed on the question of factors that affect the actual pattern of honeymoon chosen, and the patterns of experience to be found on the honeymoon.

21. Cf. Chein's classic paper on the genetic factor in ahistorical psychology for a discussion of the distinction between actual events in a person's life and how such events function in his awareness of his past (and future) at any given time. The task of the genetic psychologist (to which we would add 'and social scientist') is, Chein argues, 'the definition of crucial developmental periods within which, as a framework, the dynamic changes may be comprehended' (Chein, 1947).

22. In our own, or any other, culture, the actual level of accomplishment on the tasks by the end of the honeymoon period, and the particular patterns of accomplishment that correlate with the various patterns of outcome, are as yet unknown. The empirical research from which data described in this paper are taken aims at discovering these correlations in the sample we use. Once these are known, it should be possible to predict mental health outcomes from a knowledge of task accomplishment in samples from similar subcultural backgrounds. These tasks are postulated as inherent in this stage of the marital transition. In cultures where the honeymoon does not exist, we would expect its *functions* to be met in other phases of the transitional process, either before or after the actual wedding. From what has been indicated above in the section on cultural perspectives, it would seem that some reformulation would be required to state the tasks in a universally applicable form. Thus, Intrapersonal Task II, 'Developing competence to live in close association with the marital partner', might be rephrased to indicate that the degree of 'closeness' would be set by cultural prescriptions, with certain matrilineal groups, for example, requiring minimal alteration in this direction.

23. The tasks are stated here in a form geared to conditions of Western society. However, our intention is to aim at isolating tasks that are universally relevant. There is a sense in which the tasks may be universally relevant, though

the *behaviour* that will accomplish them will vary in different cultures. In this context, the qualification 'as appropriate in the particular subculture' is implicit in the statement of each task.

24. We are not at the point where we can postulate whether or not there is an actual degree of intimacy that goes with a good/poor outcome. The critical point is that whatever degree of intimacy is attained in the sexual relations, it must be mutually satisfactory. It seems clear that this issue is one basic to the honeymoon period and that what happens afterward in the marriage will probably be considerably affected by how it has been dealt with during the honeymoon.

25. The involvement of deep levels of personal dynamics in the forging of the honeymoon situation, especially among urban couples, is fostered not only because of the intimacy of the interaction but because of the increasing tendency for the major function of the family prior to the birth of children to be the 'stabilization of the adult personality' (Parsons & Bales, 1956, p. 16). An example of this kind of dynamic process at work in another context is seen in the work of Isabel Menzies (1960) on the socialization of young girls to the nursing role, where an unusually great degree of 'primitive' anxiety is aroused by the nature of the situation confronting the young girls, and the social structure provided by conventional nursing roles tends to be supported more because of its effectiveness in coping with these anxieties than because of its rationality in terms of modern medical care conceptions. The idealization of the honeymoon, and the relative inattention it receives as a topic for systematic concern, may be another form of defense in our culture.

26. Emery, in reviewing the literature on what he terms ABX systems (i.e., two-person relationships, developed in reference to a particular external situation), concludes that in shared psychological fields one can thus detect the emergence of certain system characteristics—'of new possibilities for behaving, believing, and feeling and of determinants that cannot be traced back to the individual actor in isolation but must be referred to the ABX system *per se*' (Emery, 1962, p. 31).

27. It should be remembered that here, as elsewhere in the paper, when we talk of risks for poor outcomes we are referring to statistical chances for populations in the public health sense, not to cases in the clinical sense. Thus, many couples who have an unsatisfactory honeymoon experience may have very good outcomes to their marriage without altering the overall pattern indicating that the chances of poorer outcomes increase when the experience is unsatisfactory.

28. A satirical husband-centered commentary on this aspect is provided in Froy's chapter on the honeymoon (1962). Froy cautions the male to be aware of the fact that the patterns initiated in the honeymoon constitute the 'thin edge of the wedge' by which life-long patterns are established. He cautions: 'All this sightseeing, lolling in gondolas, musing in museums, or cavorting in caves and other aberrations of nature is calculated only to take your mind off the serious campaign ahead. By squandering the little advantage of that well-known first careful rapture, you will make things far too easy for the missus. What, you may wonder, am I suggesting she is up to? . . . SHE IS LAYING THE FOUNDATIONS OF YOUR FUTURE ENSLAVEMENT, that's what the little dear is doing, and on your honeymoon too.'

29. Other theoretical approaches to understanding the dynamics of how personality and the sociocultural system articulate in these situations of complexity and wide latitude may be seen in games theory (Luce & Raiffa, 1957), 'open-systems' theory (Emery and Trist, 1960; Bertalanffy, 1952) exchange theory (Homans, 1961), and the 'dramaturgical' model of Goffman (1959). Though Goffman might not place his studies of 'impression management' in this theoretical sphere, from the point of view of the understandings we seek to bring out here, his work makes a clear contribution in this way. Presented

with new situations, individuals mobilize their personal and sociocultural resources to create a certain impression of themselves in their role situations. If these situations are critical, e.g., placement interviews for an important career-determining job, the effects of the presentation might become crystallized and very enduring.

# REFERENCES

1. Asch, Solomon (1952). *Social psychology,* New York: Prentice Hall.
2. Avebury, John L. (1870). *The origin of civilization and the primitive condition of man.* London: Longmans, Green.
3. Bertalanffy, Ludwig von (1952). General system theory. *General systems,* Vol. I.
4. Bion, W. R. (1961). *Experiences in groups.* London: Tavistock Publications; New York: Basic Books.
5. Blos, Peter (1962). *On adolescence.* New York: The Free Press of Glencoe.
6. Bonaparte, Marie (1953). *Female sexuality.* New York: International Univ. Press.
7. Brav, Stanley, R. (1947). Note on honeymoons. *Marriage and Family Living 9,* 60.
8. Caplan, Gerald (1961). *An approach to community mental health.* London: Tavistock Publications; New York: Grune & Stratton.
9. Caplan, Gerald (1962). Patterns of parental response to the crisis of premature birth. *Psychiatry 5,* 3–15.
10. Chein, Isidor (1947). The genetic factors in ahistorical psychology. *J. gen. Psychol. 36,* 151–72.
11. Crawley, Ernest (1902). *The mystic rose: a study of primitive marriage:* London: Macmillan.
12. Emery, Fred (1962). In search of some principles of persuasion. London: Tavistock Institute Document No. T.10.
13. Emery, Fred & Trist, E. L. (1960). Socio-technical systems. In *Management sciences, models and techniques,* Vol. II. Proceedings of 6th Annual International Meeting of the Institute of Management Sciences. London: Pergamon Press.
14. Erikson, Erik (1959). Identity and the life cycle. *Psychol. Issues 1,* 1–171.
15. Evans-Pritchard, E. E. (1951). *Kinship and marriage among the Nuer.* Oxford: Clarendon Press.
16. Firth, Raymond (1936). *We the Tikopia.* London: Allen & Unwin.
17. Flugel, J. (1921). *The psychoanalytic study of the family.* Vienna: International Psychoanalytic Press.
18. Foote, Nelson & Cottrell, Leonard (1955). *Identity and interpersonal competence.* Chicago: University of Chicago Press.
19. Freud, Sigmund (1953). Contributions to the psychology of love: the taboo of virginity. In E. Jones (Ed.), *Collected papers.* London: Hogarth Press. Vol. 4, p. 234.
20. Fried, Marc. Transitional functions of working-class communities: implications for forced relocation. In M. Kantor (Ed.), *Mobility and mental health.* (In press.)
21. Froy, H. (1962). *How to survive matrimony.* (Second edition.) London: Pan Books.
22. Gennep, Arnold van (1909). *Les rites de passage.* Paris: Emile Nourry.
23. Gluckman, Max (Ed.) (1963). *Essays on the ritual of social relations.* Manchester: Manchester University Press.
24. Goffman, Erving (1959). *The presentation of self in everyday life.* New York: Doubleday Anchor Books.

25. GOUGH, K. (1961). Nayar: Central Kerala. In D. M. Schneider and K. Gough (Eds.), *Matrilineal kinship*. Berkeley and Los Angeles: University of California Press. Pp. 298–384.
26. HOMANS, GEORGE (1961). *Social behavior*. New York: Harcourt Brace & World.
27. HOWITT, A. W. (1903). Native tribes of Southeast Australia. *Amer. antiquarian and oriental J.* 30, 81–95.
28. JAHODA, MARIE (1958). *Current concepts of positive mental health*. New York: Basic Books.
29. JANIS, IRVING (1958). *Psychological stress*. New York: John Wiley.
30. KAPLAN, D. & MASON, E. (1960). Maternal reactions to premature birth viewed as an acute emotional disorder. *Amer. J. Orthopsychiat.* 30, 539–52.
31. LINDEMANN, ERIC (1944). Symptomatology and management of acute grief. *Amer. J. Psychiat.* 101, 141–8.
32. LOEB, E. M. (1935). *Sumatra: its history and people*. Wien.
33. LUCE, R. D. & RAIFFA, H. (1957). *Games and decisions*. New York: John Wiley.
34. MACINTYRE, THOMAS (1963). Wedding hymn. In *Short story international*, November. Pp. 19–30.
35. MENZIES, ISABEL (1960). A case study in the functioning of social systems as a defence against anxiety. *Hum. Relat.* 13, 95–122. Reprinted as Tavistock Pamphlet No. 3, 1961.
36. MORAVIA, ALBERTO (1961). *Bitter honeymoon*. Harmondsworth: Penguin Books.
37. MURPHY, LOIS B. (1962). *The widening world of childhood: paths towards mystery*. New York: Basic Books.
38. PARSONS, TALCOTT & BALES, R. F. (1956). *Family, socialization and interaction process*. London: Routledge & Kegan Paul.
39. PINCUS, LILY (Ed.) (1960). *Marriage: studies in emotional conflict and growth*. London: Methuen.
40. RAPOPORT, RHONA (1962). Normal crises, family structure and mental health. *Family Process* 2, 68–80.
41. ROMAINS, JULES (1939). *The body's rapture*. London: The Bodley Head.
42. ROSCOE, JOHN (1911). *The Baganda*. London: Macmillan.
43. SIMPSON, GEORGE (1960). *People in families*. New York: Thomas Y. Crowell.
44. SLATER, PHILLIP (1963). On social regression. *Amer. J. Sociol.* 28, 339–63.
45. SPENCER, WALTER B. & GILLEN, FRANCIS J. (1904). *The northern tribes of Central Australia*. New York & London: Macmillan.
46. SPIRO, MELFORD E. (1958). With the assistance of Audrey G. Spiro. *Children of the Kibbutz*. Cambridge, Mass.: Harvard University Press.
47. TAGORE, RABINDRANATH (1927). The Indian ideal of marriage. In H. Keyserling (Ed.), *The book of marriage*. London: Jonathan Cape. Pp. 98–122.
48. TALMON, YONINA (1963). Exogamy in collective settlements. Paper read at 8th International Seminar on Family Research, Oslo, August 18–24.
49. TOMKINS, SILVAN (1962). *Affect—imagery—consciousness*, Vol. I. New York: Springer; London: Tavistock Publications, 1964.
50. TYHURST, JAMES (1951). Individual reactions to community disaster. *Amer. J. Psychiat.* 107, 764–9.
51. WASSERMAN, JACOB (1927). Bourgeois marriage. In H. Keyserling (ed.), *The book of marriage*. London: Jonathan Cape.
52. WESTERMARCK, EDWARD (1891). *The history of human marriage*. New York & London: Macmillan.
53. WHITE, ROBERT W. (1959). Motivation reconsidered: the concept of competence. *Psychol. Rev.* 66, 297–333.
54. WILLIAMS, TENNESSEE (1960). *Period of adjustment*. New York: New Directions.
55. WYLIE, PHILIP (1952). Honeymoons are hell. *Redbook Magazine*, October.

# 18:

# Crucible of Identity:
# The Negro Lower-Class Family

*Lee Rainwater*

*But can a people . . . live and develop for over three hundred years by simply reacting? Are American Negroes simply the creation of white men, or have they at least helped create themselves out of what they found around them? Men have made a way of life in caves and upon cliffs, why can not Negroes have made a life upon the horns of the white man's dilemma? . . . American Negro life is, for the Negro who must live it, not only a burden (and not always that) but also a discipline just as any human life which has endured so long is a discipline teaching its own insights into the human conditions, its own strategies of survival. . . .*

*For even as his life toughens the Negro, even as it brutalizes him, sensitizes him, dulls him, goads him to anger, moves him to irony, sometimes fracturing and sometimes affirming his hopes; even as it shapes his attitude towards family, sex, love, religion; even as it modulates his humor, tempers his joy—it conditions him to deal with his life and with himself. Because it is his life and no mere abstraction in someone's head. He must live it and try consciously to grasp its complexity until he can change it; must live it as he changes it. He is no mere product of his socio-political predicament. He is a product of interaction between his racial predicament, his individual will and the broader American cultural freedom in which he finds his ambiguous existence. Thus he, too, in a limited way, is his own creation.*

*—Ralph Ellison*

As long as Negroes have been in America, their marital and family patterns have been subjects of curiosity and amusement, moral indignation and self-congratulation, puzzlement and frustration, concern and guilt, on the part of white Americans.[1] As some Negroes have moved into middle-class status, or acquired standards of American common-man respectability, they too have shared these attitudes toward the private behavior of their fellows, sometimes with a moral punitiveness to rival that of whites, but at other times with a hard-headed interest in causes and remedies rather than moral evaluation. Moralism permeated the

Reprinted by permission from *Dædalus, Journal of the American Academy of Arts and Sciences*, Vol. 95 (1966), pp. 172–216. Copyright © 1966 by the American Academy of Arts and Sciences. Lee Rainwater is professor of sociology and anthropology, Washington University, St. Louis.

subject of Negro sexual, marital, and family behavior in the polemics of slavery apologists and abolitionists as much as in the Northern and Southern civil rights controversies of today. Yet, as long as the dialectic of good or bad, guilty or innocent, overshadows a concern with who, why, and what can be, it is unlikely that realistic and effective social planning to correct the clearly desperate situation of poor Negro families can begin.

This paper is concerned with a description and analysis of slum Negro family patterns as these reflect and sustain Negroes' adaptations to the economic, social, and personal situation into which they are born and in which they must live. As such it deals with facts of lower-class life that are usually forgotten or ignored in polite discussion. We have chosen not to ignore these facts in the belief that to do so can lead only to assumptions which would frustrate efforts at social reconstruction, to strategies that are unrealistic in the light of the actual day-to-day reality of slum Negro life. Further, this analysis will deal with family patterns which interfere with the efforts slum Negroes make to attain a stable way of life as working- or middle-class individuals and with the effects such failure in turn has on family life. To be sure, many Negro families live *in* the slum ghetto, but are not *of* its culture (though even they, and particularly their children, can be deeply affected by what happens there). However, it is the individuals who succumb to the distinctive family life style of the slum who experience the greatest weight of deprivation and who have the greatest difficulty responding to the few self-improvement resources that make their way into the ghetto. In short, we propose to explore in depth the family's role in the "tangle of pathology" which characterizes the ghetto.

The social reality in which Negroes have had to make their lives during the 450 years of their existence in the western hemisphere has been one of victimization "in the sense that a system of social relations operates in such a way as to deprive them of a chance to share in the more desirable material and non-material products of a society which is dependent, in part, upon their labor and loyalty." In making this observation, St. Clair Drake goes on to note that Negroes are victimized also because "they do not have the same degree of access which others have to the attributes needed for rising in the general class system—money, education, 'contacts,' and 'know-how.' "[2] The victimization process started with slavery; for 350 years thereafter Negroes worked out as best they could adaptations to the slave status. After emancipation, the cultural mechanisms which Negroes had developed for living the life of victim continued to be serviceable as the victimization process was maintained first under the myths of white supremacy and black inferiority, later by the doctrines of gradualism which covered the fact of no improvement in position, and finally by the modern Northern system of ghettoization and indifference.

When lower-class Negroes use the expression, "Tell it like it is," they signal their intention to strip away pretense, to describe a situation or its participants as they really are, rather than in a polite or euphemistic way. "Telling it like it is" can be used as a harsh, aggressive device, or it can be a healthy attempt to face reality rather than retreat into fantasy. In any case, as he goes about his field work, the participant observer studying a ghetto community learns to listen carefully to any exchange preceded by such an announcement because he knows the speaker is about to express his understanding of how his world operates, of what motivates its members, of how they actually behave.

The first responsibility of the social scientist can be phrased in much the same way: "Tell it like it is." His second responsibility is to try to understand why "it" is that way, and to explore the implications of what and why for more constructive solutions to human problems. Social research on the situation of the Negro American has been informed by four main goals: (1) to describe the disadvantaged position of Negroes, (2) to disprove the racist ideology which sustains the caste system, (3) to demonstrate that responsibility for the disadvantages Negroes suffer lies squarely upon the white caste which derives economic, prestige, and psychic benefits from the operation of the system, and (4) to suggest that in reality whites would be better rather than worse off if the whole jerry-built caste structure were to be dismantled. The successful accomplishment of these *intellectual* goals has been a towering achievement, in which the social scientists of the 1920's, '30's, and '40's can take great pride; that white society has proved so recalcitrant to utilizing this intellectual accomplishment is one of the great tragedies of our time, and provides the stimulus for further social research on "the white problem."

Yet the implicit paradigm of much of the research on Negro Americans has been an overly simplistic one concentrating on two terms of an argument:

$$\text{White cupidity} \rightarrow \text{Negro suffering.}$$

As an intellectual shorthand, and even more as a civil rights slogan, this simple model is both justified and essential. But, as a guide to greater understanding of the Negro situation as human adaptation to human situations, the paradigm is totally inadequate because it fails to specify fully enough the *process* by which Negroes adapt to their situations as they do, and the limitations one kind of adaptation places on possibilities for subsequent adaptations. A reassessment of previous social research, combined with examination of current social research on Negro ghetto communities, suggests a more complex, but hopefully more veridical, model:

White cupidity

creates

Structural Conditions Highly Inimical to Basic Social Adaptation (low-income availability, poor education, poor services, stigmatization)

to which Negroes adapt

by

Social and Personal Responses which serve to sustain the individual in his punishing world but also generate aggressiveness toward the self and others

which results in

Suffering directly inflicted by Negroes on themselves and on others.

In short, whites, by their greater power, create situations in which Negroes do the dirty work of caste victimization for them.

The white caste maintains a cadre of whites whose special responsibility is to enforce the system in brutal or refined ways (the Klan, the rural sheriff, the metropolitan police, the businessman who specializes in a Negro clientele, the Board of Education). Increasingly, whites recruit to this cadre middle-class Negroes who can soften awareness of victimization by their protective coloration. These special cadres, white and/or Negro, serve the very important function of enforcing caste standards by whatever means seems required, while at the same time concealing from an increasingly "unprejudiced" public the unpleasant facts they would prefer to ignore. The system is quite homologous to the Gestapo and concentration camps of Nazi Germany, though less fatal to its victims.

For their part, Negroes creatively adapt to the system in ways that keep them alive and extract what gratification they can find, but in the process of adaptation they are constrained to behave in ways that inflict a great deal of suffering on those with whom they make their lives, and on themselves. The ghetto Negro is constantly confronted by the immediate necessity to suffer in order to get what he wants of those few things he can have, or to make others suffer, or both—for example, he suffers as exploited student and employee, as drug user, as loser in the competitive game of his peer-group society; he inflicts suffering as disloyal spouse, petty thief, knife- or gun-wielder, petty con man.

It is the central thesis of this paper that the caste-facilitated infliction of suffering by Negroes on other Negroes and on themselves appears most poignantly within the confines of the family, and that the victimization process as it operates in families prepares and toughens its members to function in the ghetto world, at the same time that it seriously interferes with their ability to operate in any other world. This, however, is very different from arguing that "the family is to blame" for the deprived

situation ghetto Negroes suffer; rather we are looking at the logical outcome of the operation of the widely ramified and interconnecting caste
system. In the end we will argue that only palliative results can be expected from attempts to treat directly the disordered family patterns to
be described. Only a change in the original "inputs" of the caste system,
the structural conditions inimical to basic social adaptation, can change
family forms.

Almost thirty years ago, E. Franklin Frazier foresaw that the fate of
the Negro family in the city would be a highly destructive one. His readers
would have little reason to be surprised at observations of slum ghetto
life today:

. . . As long as the bankrupt system of southern agriculture exists, Negro
families will continue to seek a living in the towns and cities. . . . They will
crowd the slum areas of southern cities or make their way to northern cities
where their families will become disrupted and their poverty will force them to
depend upon charity.[3]

## THE AUTONOMY OF THE SLUM GHETTO

Just as the deprivations and depredations practiced by white society
have had their effect on the personalities and social life of Negroes,
so also has the separation from the ongoing social life of the white community had its effect. In a curious way, Negroes have had considerable
freedom to fashion their own adaptations within their separate world.
The larger society provides them with few resources but also with
minimal interference in the Negro community on matters which did not
seem to affect white interests. Because Negroes learned early that there
were a great many things they could not depend upon whites to provide
they developed their own solutions to recurrent human issues. These
solutions can often be seen to combine, along with the predominance of
elements from white culture, elements that are distinctive to the Negro
group. Even more distinctive is the *configuration* which emerges from
those elements Negoes share with whites and those which are different.

It is in this sense that we may speak of a Negro subculture, a distinctive *patterning* of existential perspectives, techniques for coping with
the problems of social life, views about what is desirable and undesirable
in particular situations. This subculture, and particularly that of the lower-
class, the slum, Negro, can be seen as his own creation out of the elements
available to him in response to (1) the conditions of life set by white
society and (2) the selective freedom which that society allows (or must
put up with given the pattern of separateness on which it insists).

Out of this kind of "freedom" slum Negroes have built a culture which has some elements of intrinsic value and many more elements that are highly destructive to the people who must live in it. The elements that whites can value they constantly borrow. Negro arts and language have proved so popular that such commentators on American culture as Norman Mailer and Leslie Fiedler have noted processes of Negroization of white Americans as a minor theme of the past thirty years.[4] A fairly large proportion of Negroes with national reputations are engaged in the occupation of diffusing to the larger culture these elements of intrinsic value.

On the negative side, this freedom has meant, as social scientists who have studied Negro communities have long commented, that many of the protections offered by white institutions stop at the edge of the Negro ghetto: there are poor police protection and enforcement of civil equities, inadequate schooling and medical service, and more informal indulgences which whites allow Negroes as a small price for feeling superior.

For our purposes, however, the most important thing about the freedom which whites have allowed Negroes within their own world is that it has required them to work out their own ways of making it from day to day, from birth to death. The subculture that Negroes have created may be imperfect but it has been viable for centuries; it behooves both white and Negro leaders and intellectuals to seek to understand it even as they hope to change it.[5]

Negroes have created, again particularly within the lower-class slum group, a range of institutions to structure the tasks of living a victimized life and to minimize the pain it inevitably produces. In the slum ghetto these institutions include prominently those of the social network—the extended kinship system and the "street system" of buddies and broads which tie (although tenuously and unpredictably) the "members" to each other—and the institutions of entertainment (music, dance, folk tales) by which they instruct, explain, and accept themselves. Other institutions function to provide escape from the society of the victimized: the church (Hereafter!) and the civil rights movement (Now!).

## THE FUNCTIONAL AUTONOMY OF THE NEGRO FAMILY

At the center of the matrix of Negro institutional life lies the family. It is in the family that individuals are trained for participation in the culture and find personal and group identity and continuity. The "freedom" allowed by white society is greatest here, and this freedom has been used to create an institutional variant more distinctive perhaps to the

Negro subculture than any other. (Much of the content of Negro art and entertainment derives exactly from the distinctive characteristics of Negro family life.) At each stage in the Negro's experience of American life—slavery, segregation, *de facto* ghettoization—whites have found it less necessary to interfere in the relations between the sexes and between parents and children than in other areas of the Negro's existence. His adaptations in this area, therefore, have been less constrained by whites than in many other areas.

Now that the larger society is becoming increasingly committed to integrating Negroes into the main stream of American life, however, we can expect increasing constraint (benevolent as it may be) to be placed on the autonomy of the Negro family system.[6] These constraints will be designed to pull Negroes into meaningful integration with the larger society, to give up ways which are inimical to successful performance in the larger society, and to adopt new ways that are functional in that society. The strategic questions of the civil rights movement and of the war on poverty are ones that have to do with how one provides functional equivalents for the existing subculture before the capacity to make a life within its confines is destroyed.

The history of the Negro family has been ably documented by historians and sociologists.[7] In slavery, conjugal and family ties were reluctantly and ambivalently recognized by the slave holders, were often violated by them, but proved necessary to the slave system. This necessity stemmed both from the profitable offspring of slave sexual unions and the necessity for their nurture, and from the fact that the slaves' efforts to sustain patterns of sexual and parental relations mollified the men and women whose labor could not simply be commanded. From nature's promptings, the thinning memories of African heritage, and the example and guilt-ridden permission of the slave holders, slaves constructed a partial family system and sets of relations that generated conjugal and familial sentiments. The slave holder's recognition in advertisements for runaway slaves of marital and family sentiments as motivations for absconding provides one indication that strong family ties were possible, though perhaps not common, in the slave quarter. The mother-centered family with its emphasis on the primacy of the mother-child relation and only tenuous ties to a man, then, is the legacy of adaptations worked out by Negroes during slavery.

After emancipation this family design often also served well to cope with the social disorganization of Negro life in the late nineteenth century. Matrifocal families, ambivalence about the desirability of marriage, ready acceptance of illegitimacy, all sustained some kind of family life in situations which often made it difficult to maintain a full nuclear family. Yet in the hundred years since emancipation, Negroes in rural areas have been able to maintain full nuclear families almost as well as similarly situated whites. As we will see, it is the move to the city that results in the very high proportion of mother-headed households. In the rural system the man continues to have important functions; it is difficult for a woman to make a crop by herself, or even with the help of other women. In the city, however, the woman can earn wages just as a man can, and she can receive welfare payments more easily than he can. In rural areas, although there may be high illegitimacy rates and high rates of marital disruption, men and women have an interest in getting together; families are headed by a husband-wife pair much more often than in the city. That pair may be much less stable than in the more prosperous segments of Negro and white communities but it is more likely to exist among rural Negroes than among urban ones.

The matrifocal character of the Negro lower-class family in the United States has much in common with Caribbean Negro family patterns; research in both areas has done a great deal to increase our understanding of the Negro situation. However, there are important differences in the family forms of the two areas.[8] The impact of white European family models has been much greater in the United States than in the Caribbean both because of the relative population proportions of white and colored peoples and because equalitarian values in the United States have had a great impact on Negroes even when they have not on whites. The typical Caribbean mating pattern is that women go through several visiting and common-law unions but eventually marry; that is, they marry legally only relatively late in their sexual lives. The Caribbean marriage is the crowning of a sexual and procreative career; it is considered a serious and difficult step.

In the United States, in contrast, Negroes marry at only a slightly lower rate and slightly higher age than whites.[9] Most Negro women marry relatively early in their careers; marriage is not regarded as the same kind of crowning choice and achievement that it is in the Caribbean. For lower-class Negroes in the United States marriage ceremonies are rather informal affairs. In the Caribbean, marriage is regarded as quite costly because of the feasting which goes along with it; ideally it is performed in church.

In the United States, unlike the Caribbean, early marriage confers a kind of permanent respectable status upon a woman which she can use to deny any subsequent accusations of immorality or promiscuity once the marriage is broken and she becomes sexually involved in visiting or common-law relations. The relevant effective status for many Negro women is that of "having been married" rather than "being married"; having the right to be called "Mrs." rather than currently being Mrs. Someone-in-Particular.

For Negro lower-class women, then, first marriage has the same kind of importance as having a first child. Both indicate that the girl has become a woman but neither one that this is the last such activity in which she will engage. It seems very likely that only a minority of Negro women in the urban slum go through their childrearing years with only one man around the house.

Among the Negro urban poor, then, a great many women have the experience of heading a family for part of their mature lives, and a great many children spend some part of their formative years in a household without a father-mother pair. From Table 1 we see that in 1960, forty-seven per cent of the Negro poor urban families with children had a female head. Unfortunately cumulative statistics are hard to come by;

## TABLE 1

PROPORTION OF FEMALE HEADS FOR FAMILIES WITH CHILDREN
BY RACE, INCOME, AND URBAN-RURAL CATEGORIES

|  | Rural | Urban | Total |
|---|---|---|---|
| *Negroes* | | | |
| under $3000 | 18% | 47% | 36% |
| $3000 and over | 5% | 8% | 7% |
| Total | 14% | 23% | 21% |
| *Whites* | | | |
| under $3000 | 12% | 38% | 22% |
| $3000 and over | 2% | 4% | 3% |
| Total | 4% | 7% | 6% |

Source: U. S. Census: 1960, PC (1) D. U. S. Volume, Table 225; State Volume, Table 140.

but, given this very high level for a cross-sectional sample (and taking into account the fact that the median age of the children in these families is about six years), it seems very likely that as many as two-thirds of Negro urban poor children will not live in families headed by a man and a woman throughout the first eighteen years of their lives.

One of the other distinctive characteristics of Negro families, both poor and not so poor, is the fact that Negro households have a much higher proportion of relatives outside the mother-father-children triangle than is the case with whites. For example, in St. Louis Negro families average 0.8 other relatives per household compared to only 0.4 for white families. In the case of the more prosperous Negro families this is likely to mean that an older relative lives in the home providing baby-sitting services while both the husband and wife work and thus further their climb toward stable working- or middle-class status. In the poor Negro families it is much more likely that the household is headed by an older relative who brings under her wings a daughter and that daughter's children. It is important to note that the three-generation household with the grandmother at the head exists only when there is no husband present. Thus, despite the high proportion of female-headed households in this group and despite the high proportion of households that contain other relatives, we find that almost all married couples in the St. Louis Negro slum community have their own household. In other words, when a couple marries it establishes its own household; when that couple breaks up the mother either maintains that household or moves back to her parents or grandparents.

Finally we should note that Negro slum families have more children than do either white slum families or stable working- and middle-class Negro families. Mobile Negro families limit their fertility sharply in the interest of bringing the advantages of mobility more fully to the few children that they do have. Since the Negro slum family is both more likely to have the father absent and more likely to have more children in the family, the mother has a more demanding task with fewer resources at her disposal. When we examine the patterns of life of the stem family we shall see that even the presence of several mothers does not necessarily lighten the work load for the principal mother in charge.

## THE FORMATION AND MAINTENANCE OF FAMILIES

We will outline below the several stages and forms of Negro lower-class family life. At many points these family forms and the interpersonal relations that exist within them will be seen to have characteristics in common with the life styles of white lower-class families.[10] At other points there are differences, or the Negro pattern will be seen to be more sharply divergent from the family life of stable working- and middle-class couples.

It is important to recognize that lower-class Negroes know that their particular family forms are different from those of the rest of the society and that, though they often see these forms as representing the only ways of behaving given their circumstances, they also think of the more stable family forms of the working class as more desirable. That is, lower-class Negroes know what the "normal American family" is supposed to be like, and they consider a stable family-centered way of life superior to the conjugal and familial situations in which they often find themselves. Their conceptions of the good American life include the notion of a father-husband who functions as an adequate provider and interested member of the family, a hard working home-bound mother who is concerned about her children's welfare and her husband's needs, and children who look up to their parents and perform well in school and other outside

N

places to reflect credit on their families. This image of what family life can be like is very real from time to time as lower-class men and women grow up and move through adulthood. Many of them make efforts to establish such families but find it impossible to do so either because of the direct impact of economic disabilities or because they are not able to sustain in their day-to-day lives the ideals which they hold.[11] While these ideals do serve as a meaningful guide to lower-class couples who are mobile out of the group, for a great many others the existence of such ideas about normal family life represents a recurrent source of stress within families as individuals become aware that they are failing to measure up to the ideals, or as others within the family and outside it use the ideals as an aggressive weapon for criticizing each other's performance. It is not at all uncommon for husbands or wives or children to try to hold others in the family to the norms of stable family life while they themselves engage in behaviors which violate these norms. The effect of such criticism in the end is to deepen commitment to the deviant sexual and parental norms of a slum subculture. Unless they are careful, social workers and other professionals exacerbate the tendency to use the norms of "American family life" as weapons by supporting these norms in situations where they are in reality unsupportable, thus aggravating the sense of failing and being failed by others which is chronic for lower-class people.

*Going together.* The initial steps toward mating and family formation in the Negro slum take place in a context of highly developed boys' and girls' peer groups. Adolescents tend to become deeply involved in their peer-group societies beginning as early as the age of twelve or thirteen and continue to be involved after first pregnancies and first marriages. Boys and girls are heavily committed both to their same sex peer groups and to the activities that those groups carry out. While classical gang activity does not necessarily characterize Negro slum communities everywhere, loosely knit peer groups do.

The world of the Negro slum is wide open to exploration by adolescent boys and girls: "Negro communities provide a flow of common experience in which young people and their elders share, and out of which delinquent behavior emerges almost imperceptibly."[12] More than is possible in white slum communities, Negro adolescents have an opportunity to interact with adults in various "high life" activities; their behavior more often represents an identification with the behavior of adults than an attempt to set up group standards and activities that differ from those of adults.

Boys and young men participating in the street system of peer-group activity are much caught up in games of furthering and enhancing their status as significant persons. These games are played out in small and large gatherings through various kinds of verbal contests that go under the names of "sounding," "signifying," and "working game." Very much a part of a boy's or man's status in this group is his ability to win women. The man who has several women "up tight," who is successful in "pimping off" women for sexual favors and material benefits, is much admired. In sharp contrast to white lower-class groups, there is little tendency for males to separate girls into "good" and "bad" categories.[13] Observations of groups of Negro youths suggest that girls and women are much more readily referred to as "that bitch" or "that whore" than they are by their names, and this seems to be a universal tendency carrying no connotation that "that bitch" is morally inferior to or different from other women. Thus, all women are essentially the same, all women are legitimate targets, and no girl or woman is expected to be virginal except for reason of lack of opportunity or immaturity. From their participation in the peer group and according to standards legitimated by the total Negro slum culture, Negro boys and young men are propelled in the direction of girls to test their "strength" as seducers. They are mercilessly rated by both their peers and the opposite sex in their ability to "talk" to girls; a young man will go to great lengths to avoid the reputation of having a "weak" line.[14]

The girls share these definitions of the nature of heterosexual relations; they take for granted that almost any male they deal with will try to seduce them and that given sufficient inducement (social, not monetary) they may wish to go along with his line. Although girls have a great deal of ambivalence about participating in sexual relations, this ambivalence is minimally moral and has much more to do with a desire not to be taken advantage of or get in trouble. Girls develop defenses against the exploitative orientations of men by devaluing the significance of sexual relations ("he really didn't do anything bad to me"), and as time goes on by developing their own appreciation of the intrinsic rewards of sexual intercourse.

The informal social relations of slum Negroes begin in adolescence to be highly sexualized. Although parents have many qualms about boys and, particularly, girls entering into this system, they seldom feel there is much they can do to prevent their children's sexual involvement. They usually confine themselves to counscling somewhat hopelessly against girls becoming pregnant or boys being forced into situations where they might have to marry a girl they do not want to marry.

Girls are propelled toward boys and men in order to demonstrate their maturity and attractiveness; in the process they are constantly exposed to pressures for seduction, to boys "rapping" to them. An active girl will "go with" quite a number of boys, but she will generally try to restrict the number with whom she has intercourse to the few to whom she is attracted or (as happens not infrequently) to those whose threats of physical violence she cannot avoid. For their part, the boys move rapidly from girl to girl seeking to have intercourse with as many as they can and thus build up their "reps." The activity of seduction is itself highly cathected; there is gratification in simply "talking to" a girl as long as the boy can feel that he has acquitted himself well.

At sixteen Joan Bemias enjoys spending time with three or four very close girl friends. She tells us they follow this routine when the girls want to go out and none of the boys they have been seeing lately is available: "Every time we get ready to go someplace we look through all the telephone numbers of boys we'd have and we call them and talk so sweet to them that they'd come on around. All of them had cars you see. (I: What do you do to keep all these fellows interested?) Well nothing. We don't have to make love with all of them. Let's see, Joe, J. B., Albert, and Paul, out of all of them I've been going out with I've only had sex with four boys, that's all." She goes on to say that she and her girl friends resist boys by being unresponsive to their lines and by breaking off relations with them on the ground that they're going out with other girls. It is also clear from her comments that the girl friends support each other in resisting the boys when they are out together in groups.

Joan has had a relationship with a boy which has lasted six months, but she has managed to hold the frequency of intercourse down to four times. Initially she managed to hold this particular boy off for a month but eventually gave in.

*Becoming pregnant.* It is clear that the contest elements in relationships between men and women continue even in relationships that become quite steady. Despite the girls' ambivalence about sexual relations and their manifold efforts to reduce its frequency, the operation of chance often eventuates in their becoming pregnant.[15] This was the case with Joan. With this we reach the second stage in the formation of families, that of premarital pregnancy. (We are outlining an ideal-typical sequence and not, of course, implying that all girls in the Negro slum culture become pregnant before they marry but only that a great many of them do.)

Joan was caught despite the fact that she was considerably more sophisticated about contraception than most girls or young women in the group (her mother had both instructed her in contraceptive techniques and constantly warned her to take precautions). No one was particularly surprised at her pregnancy although she, her boy friend, her mother, and others regarded it as unfortunate. For girls in the Negro slum, pregnancy before marriage is expected in much the same way that parents expect their children to catch mumps or chicken pox; if they are lucky it will not happen but if it happens people are not too surprised and everyone knows what to do about it. It was quickly decided that Joan and the baby would stay at home. It seems clear from the preparations that Joan's mother is making that she expects to have the main responsibility for caring for the infant. Joan seems quite indifferent to the baby; she shows little interest in mothering the child although she is not particularly adverse to the idea so long as the baby does not interfere too much with her continued participation in her peer group.

Establishing who the father is under these circumstances seems to be important and confers a kind of legitimacy on the birth; not to know who one's father is, on the other hand, seems the ultimate in illegitimacy. Actually Joan had a choice in the imputation of fatherhood; she chose J.B. because he is older than she, and because she may marry him if he can get a divorce from his wife. She could have chosen Paul (with whom she had also had intercourse at about the time she became pregnant), but she would have done this reluctantly since Paul is a year younger than she and somehow this does not seem fitting.

In general, when a girl becomes pregnant while still living at home it seems taken for granted that she will continue to live there and that her parents will take a major responsibility for rearing the children. Since there are usually siblings who can help out and even siblings who will be playmates for the child, the addition of a third generation to the household does not seem to place a great stress on relationships within the family. It seems common for the first pregnancy to have a liberating influence on the mother once the child is born in that she becomes socially and sexually more active than she was before. She no longer has to be concerned with preserving her status as a single girl. Since her mother is usually willing to take care of the child for a few years, the unwed mother has an opportunity to go out with girl friends and with men and thus become more deeply involved in the peer-group society of her culture. As she has more children and perhaps marries she will find it necessary to settle down and spend more time around the house fulfilling the functions of a mother herself.

It would seem that for girls pregnancy is the real measure of maturity, the dividing line between adolescence and womanhood. Perhaps because of this, as well as because of the ready resources for child care, girls in the Negro slum community show much less concern about pregnancy than do girls in the white lower-class community and are less motivated to marry the fathers of their children. When a girl becomes pregnant the question of marriage certainly arises and is considered, but the girl often decides that she would rather not marry the man either because she does not want to settle down yet or because she does not think he would make a good husband.

It is in the easy attitudes toward premarital pregnancy that the matrifocal character of the Negro lower-class family appears most clearly. In order to have and raise a family it is simply not necessary, though it may be desirable, to have a man around the house. While the AFDC program may make it easier to maintain such attitudes in the urban situation, this pattern existed long before the program was initiated and continues in families where support comes from other sources.

Finally it should be noted that fathering a child similarly confers maturity on boys and young men although perhaps it is less salient for them. If the boy has any interest in the girl he will tend to feel that the fact that he has impregnated her gives him an additional claim on her. He will be stricter in seeking to enforce his exclusive rights over her (though not exclusive loyalty to her). This exclusive right does not mean that he expects to marry her but only that there is a new and special bond between them. If the girl is not willing to accept such claims she may find it necessary to break off the relationship rather than tolerate the man's jealousy. Since others in the peer group have a vested interest in not allowing a couple to be too loyal to each other they go out of their way to question and challenge each partner about the loyalty of the other, thus contributing to the deterioration of the relationship. This same kind of questioning and challenging continues if the couple marries and represents one source of the instability of the marital relationship.

*Getting married.* As noted earlier, despite the high degree of premarital sexual activity and the rather high proportion of premarital pregnancies, most lower-class Negro men and women eventually do marry and stay together for a shorter or longer period of time. Marriage is an intimidating prospect and is approached ambivalently by both parties. For the girl it means giving up a familiar and comfortable home that, unlike some other lower-class subcultures, places few real restrictions on her behavior. (While marriage can appear to be an escape from interpersonal difficulties at home, these difficulties seldom seem to revolve around effective restrictions placed on her behavior by her parents.) The girl also has good reason to be suspicious of the likelihood that men will be able to perform stably in the role of husband and provider; she is reluctant to be tied down by a man who will not prove to be worth it.

From the man's point of view the fickleness of women makes marriage problematic. It is one thing to have a girl friend step out on you, but it is quite another to have a wife do so. Whereas premarital sexual relations and fatherhood carry almost no connotation of responsibility for the welfare of the partner, marriage is supposed to mean that a man behaves more responsibly, becoming a provider for his wife and children even though he may not be expected to give up all the gratifications of participation in the street system.

For all of these reasons both boys and girls tend to have rather negative views of marriage as well as a low expectation that marriage will prove a stable and gratifying existence. When marriage does take place it tends to represent a tentative commitment on the part of both parties with a strong tendency to seek greater commitment on the part of the partner than on one's own part. Marriage is regarded as a fragile arrangement held together primarily by affectional ties rather than instrumental concerns.

In general, as in white lower-class groups, the decision to marry seems to be taken rather impulsively.[16] Since everyone knows that sooner or later he will get married, in spite of the fact that he may not be sanguine about the prospect, Negro lower-class men and women are alert for clues that the time has arrived. The time may arrive because of a pregnancy in a steady relationship that seems gratifying to both partners, or as a way of getting out of what seems to be an awkward situation, or as a self-indulgence during periods when a boy and a girl are feeling very sorry for themselves. Thus, one girl tells us that when she marries her husband will cook all of her meals for her and she will not have any housework; another girl says that when she marries it will be to a man who has plenty of money and will have to take her out often and really show her a good time.

Boys see in marriage the possibility of regular sexual intercourse without having to fight for it, or a girl safe from venereal disease, or a relationship to a nurturant figure who will fulfill the functions of a mother. For boys, marriage can also be a way of asserting their independence from the peer group if its demands become burdensome. In this case the young man seeks to have the best of both worlds.[17]

Marriage as a way out of an unpleasant situation can be seen in the case of one of our informants, Janet Cowan:

Janet has been going with two men, one of them married and the other single. The married man's wife took exception to their relationship and killed her husband. Within a week Janet and her single boy friend, Howard, were married. One way out of the turmoil the murder of her married boy friend stimulated (they lived in the same building) was to choose marriage as a way of "settling down." However, after marrying the new couple seemed to have little idea how to set themselves up as a family. Janet was reluctant to leave her parents' home because her parents cared for her two illegitimate children. Howard was unemployed and therefore unacceptable in his parents-in-law's home, nor were his own parents willing to have his wife move in with them. Howard was also reluctant to give up another girl friend in another part of town. Although both he and his wife maintained that it was all right for a couple to step out on each other so long as the other partner did not know about it, they were both jealous if they suspected anything of this kind. In the end they gave up on the idea of marriage and went their separate ways.

In general, then, the movement toward marriage is an uncertain and tentative one. Once the couple does settle down together in a household of their own, they have the problem of working out a mutually acceptable organization of rights and duties, expectations and performances, that will meet their needs.

*Husband-wife relations.* Characteristic of both the Negro and white lower class is a high degree of conjugal role segregation.[18] That is, husbands and wives tend to think of themselves as having very separate kinds of functioning in the instrumental organization of family life, and also as pursuing recreational and outside interests separately. The husband is expected to be a provider; he resists assuming functions around the home so long as he feels he is doing his proper job of bringing home a pay check. He feels he has the right to indulge himself in little ways if he is successful at this task. The wife is expected to care for the home and children and make her husband feel welcome and comfortable. Much that is distinctive to Negro family life stems from the fact that husbands often are not stable providers. Even when a particular man is, his wife's conception of men in general is such that she is pessimistic about the likelihood that he will continue to do well in this area. A great many Negro wives work to supplement the family income. When this is so the separate incomes earned by husband and wife tend to be treated not as "family" income but as the individual property of the two persons involved. If their wives work, husbands are likely to feel that they are entitled to retain a larger share of the income they provide; the wives, in turn, feel that the husbands have no right to benefit from the purchases they make out of their own money. There is, then, "my money" and "your money." In this situation the husband may come to feel that the wife should support the children out of her income and that he can retain all of his income for himself.

While white lower-class wives often are very much intimidated by their husbands, Negro lower-class wives come to feel that they have a right to give as good as they get. If the husband indulges himself, they have the right to indulge themselves. If the husband steps out on his wife, she has the right to step out on him. The commitment of husbands and wives to each other seems often a highly instrumental one after the "honeymoon" period. Many wives feel they owe the husband nothing once he fails to perform his provider role. If the husband is unemployed the wife increasingly refuses to perform her usual duties for him. For example one woman, after mentioning that her husband had cooked four eggs for himself, commented, "I cook for him when he's working but right now he's unemployed; he can cook for himself." It is important, however, to understand that the man's status in the home depends not so much on whether he is working as on whether he brings money into the home. Thus, in several of the families we have studied in which the husband receives disability payments his status is as well-recognized as in families in which the husband is working.[19]

Because of the high degree of conjugal role segregation, both white and Negro lower-class families tend to be matrifocal in comparison to middle-class families. They are matrifocal in the sense that the wife makes most of the decisions that keep the family going and has the greatest sense of responsibility to the family. In white as well as in Negro lower-class families women tend to look to their female relatives for support and counsel, and to treat their husbands as essentially uninterested in the day-to-day problems of family living.[20] In the Negro lower-class family these tendencies are all considerably exaggerated so that the matrifocality is much clearer than in white lower-class families.

The fact that both sexes in the Negro slum culture have equal right to the various satisfactions of life (earning an income, sex, drinking, and peer-group activity which conflicts with family responsibilities) means that there is less pretense to patriarchal authority in the Negro than in the white lower class. Since men find the overt debasement of their status very threatening, the Negro family is much more vulnerable to disruption when men are temporarily unable to perform their provider roles. Also, when men are unemployed the temptations for them to engage in street adventures which repercuss on the marital relationship are much greater. This fact is well-recognized by Negro lower-class wives; they often seem as concerned about what their unemployed husbands will do instead of working as they are about the fact that the husband is no longer bringing money into the home.

It is tempting to cope with the likelihood of disloyalty by denying the usual norms of fidelity, by maintaining instead that extra-marital affairs are acceptable as long as they do not interfere with family functioning. Quite a few informants tell us this, but we have yet to observe a situation in which a couple maintains a stable relationship under these circumstances without a great deal of conflict. Thus one woman in her forties who has been married for many years and has four children first outlined this deviant norm and then illustrated how it did not work out:

My husband and I, we go out alone and sometimes stay all night. But when I get back my husband doesn't ask me a thing and I don't ask him anything. . . . A couple of years ago I suspected he was going out on me. One day I came home and my daughter was here. I told her to tell me when he left the house. I went into the bedroom and got into bed and then I heard him come in. He left in about ten minutes and my daughter came in and told me he was gone. I got out of bed and put on my clothes and started following him. Soon I saw him walking with a young girl and I began walking after them. They were just laughing and joking right out loud right on the sidewalk. He was carrying a large package of hers. I walked up behind them until I was about a yard from them. I had a large dirk which I opened and had decided to take one long slash across the both of them. Just when I decided to swing at them I lost my balance—I have a bad hip. Anyway, I didn't cut them be-

N*

cause I lost my balance. Then I called his name and he turned around and stared at me. He didn't move at all. He was shaking all over. That girl just ran away from us. He still had her package so the next day she called on the telephone and said she wanted to come pick it up. My husband washed his face, brushed his teeth, took out his false tooth and started scrubbing it and put on a clean shirt and everything, just for her. We went downstairs together and gave her the package and she left.

So you see my husband does run around on me and it seems like he does it a lot. The thing about it is he's just getting too old to be pulling that kind of stuff. If a young man does it then that's not so bad—but an old man, he just looks foolish. One of these days he'll catch me but I'll just tell him, "Buddy you owe me one," and that'll be all there is to it. He hasn't caught me yet though.

In this case, as in others, the wife is not able to leave well enough alone; her jealousy forces her to a confrontation. Actually seeing her husband with another woman stimulates her to violence.

With couples who have managed to stay married for a good many years, these peccadillos are tolerable although they generate a great deal of conflict in the marital relationship. At earlier ages the partners are likely to be both prouder and less inured to the hopelessness of maintaining stable relationships; outside involvements are therefore much more likely to be disruptive of the marriage.

*Marital breakup.* The precipitating causes of marital disruption seem to fall mainly into economic or sexual categories. As noted, the husband has little credit with his wife to tide him over periods of unemployment. Wives seem very willing to withdraw commitment from husbands who are not bringing money into the house. They take the point of view that he has no right to take up space around the house, to use its facilities, or to demand loyalty from her. Even where the wife is not inclined to press these claims, the husband tends to be touchy because he knows that such definitions are usual in his group, and he may, therefore, prove difficult for even a well-meaning wife to deal with. As noted above, if husbands do not work they tend to play around. Since they continue to maintain some contact with their peer groups, whenever they have time on their hands they move back into the world of the street system and are likely to get involved in activities which pose a threat to their family relationships.

Drink is a great enemy of the lower-class housewife, both white and Negro. Lower-class wives fear their husband's drinking because it costs money, because the husband may become violent and take out his frustrations on his wife, and because drinking may lead to sexual involvements with other women.[21]

The combination of economic problems and sexual difficulties can be seen in the case of the following couple in their early twenties:

When the field worker first came to know them, the Wilsons seemed to be working hard to establish a stable family life. The couple had been married about three years and had a two-year-old son. Their apartment was very sparsely furnished but also very clean. Within six weeks the couple had acquired several rooms of inexpensive furniture and obviously had gone to a great deal of effort to make a liveable home. Husband and wife worked on different shifts so that the husband could take care of the child while the wife worked. They looked forward to saving enough money to move out of the housing project into a more desirable neighborhood. Six weeks later, however, the husband had lost his job. He and his wife were in great conflict. She made him feel unwelcome at home and he strongly suspected her of going out with other men. A short time later they had separated. It is impossible to disentangle the various factors involved in this separation into a sequence of cause and effect, but we can see something of the impact of the total complex.

First Mr. Wilson loses his job: "I went to work one day and the man told me that I would have to work until 1:00. I asked him if there would be any extra pay for working overtime and he said no. I asked him why and he said, 'If you don't like it you can kiss my ass.' He said that to me. I said, 'Why do I have to do all that?' He said, 'Because I said so.' I wanted to jam (fight) him but I said to myself I don't want to be that ignorant, I don't want to be as ignorant as he is, so I just cut out and left. Later his father called me (it was a family firm) and asked why I left and I told him. He said, 'If you don't want to go along with my son then you're fired.' I said O.K. They had another Negro man come in to help me part time before they fired me. I think they were trying to have him work full time because he worked for them before. He has seven kids and he takes their shit."

The field worker observed that things were not as hard as they could be because his wife had a job, to which he replied, "Yeah, I know, that's just where the trouble is. My wife has become independent since she began working. If I don't get a job pretty soon I'll go crazy. We have a lot of little arguments about nothing since she got so independent." He went on to say that his wife had become a completely different person recently; she was hard to talk to because she felt that now that she was working and he was not there was nothing that he could tell her. On her last pay day his wife did not return home for three days; when she did she had only seven cents left from her pay check. He said that he loved his wife very much and had begged her to quit fooling around. He is pretty sure that she is having an affair with the man with whom she rides to work. To make matters worse his wife's sister counsels her that she does not have to stay home with him as long as he is out of work. Finally the wife moved most of their furniture out of the apartment so that he came home to find an empty apartment. He moved back to his parents' home (also in the housing project).

One interesting effect of this experience was the radical change in the husband's attitudes toward race relations. When he and his wife were doing well together and had hopes of moving up in the world he was quite critical of Negroes; "Our people are not ready for integration in many cases because they really don't know how to act. You figure if our people don't want to be bothered with whites then why in hell should the white man want to be bothered with them. There are some of us who are ready; there are others who aren't quite ready yet so I don't see why they're doing all of this hollering."

A scarce eight months later he addressed white people as he spoke for two hours into a tape recorder, "If we're willing to be with you, why aren't you willing to be with us? Do our color make us look dirty and low down and cheap? Or do you know the real meaning of 'nigger'? Anyone can be a nigger, white, colored, orange or any other color. It's something that you labeled us with. You put us away like you put a can away on the shelf with a label on it. The can is marked 'Poison: stay away from it.' You want us to help build your country but you don't want us to live in it. . . . You give me respect; I'll give you respect. If you threaten to take my life, I'll take yours and believe me I know how to take a life. We do believe that man was put here to live together as human beings; not one that's superior and the one that's a dog, but as human beings. And if you don't want to live this way then you become the dog and we'll become the human beings. There's too much corruption, too much hate, too much one individual trying to step on another. If we don't get together in a hurry we will destroy each other." It was clear from what the respondent said that he had been much influenced by Black Muslim philosophy, yet again and again in his comments one can see the displacement into a public, race relations dialogue of the sense of rage, frustration and victimization that he had experienced in his ill-fated marriage.[22]

Finally, it should be noted that migration plays a part in marital disruption. Sometimes marriages do not break up in the dramatic way described above but rather simply become increasingly unsatisfactory to one or both partners. In such a situation the temptation to move to another city, from South to North, or North to West, is great. Several wives told us that their first marriages were broken when they moved with their children to the North and their husbands stayed behind.

"After we couldn't get along I left the farm and came here and stayed away three or four days. I didn't come here to stay. I came to visit but I liked it and so I said, 'I'm gonna leave!' He said, 'I'll be glad if you do.' Well, maybe he didn't mean it but I thought he did. . . . I miss him sometimes, you know. I think about him I guess. But just in a small way. That's what I can't understand about life sometimes; you know—how people can go on like that and still break up and meet somebody else. Why couldn't— oh, I don't know!"

The gains and losses in marriage and in the post-marital state often seem quite comparable. Once they have had the experience of marriage, many women in the Negro slum culture see little to recommend it in the future, important as the first marriage may have been in establishing their maturity and respectability.

*The house of mothers.* As we have seen, perhaps a majority of mothers in the Negro slum community spend at least part of their mature life as mothers heading a family. The Negro mother may be a working mother or she may be an AFDC mother, but in either case she has the problems of maintaining a household, socializing her children, and achieving for herself some sense of membership in relations with other women and with men. As is apparent from the earlier discussion, she often receives her training in how to run such a household by observing her own mother manage without a husband. Similarly she often learns how to run a three-generation household because she herself brought a third generation into her home with her first, premarital, pregnancy.

Because men are not expected to be much help around the house, having to be head of the household is not particularly intimidating to the Negro mother if she can feel some security about income. She knows it is a hard, hopeless, and often thankless task, but she also knows that it is possible. The maternal household in the slum is generally run with a minimum of organization. The children quickly learn to fend for themselves, to go to the store, to make small purchases, to bring change home, to watch after themselves when the mother has to be out of the home, to amuse themselves, to set their own schedules of sleeping, eating, and going to school. Housekeeping practices may be poor, furniture takes a terrific beating from the children, and emergencies constantly arise. The Negro mother in this situation copes by not setting too high standards for herself, by letting things take their course. Life is most difficult when there are babies and preschool children around because then the mother is confined to the home. If she is a grandmother and the children are her daughter's, she is often confined since it is taken as a matter of course that the mother has the right to continue her outside activities and that the grandmother has the duty to be responsible for the child.

In this culture there is little of the sense of the awesome responsibility of caring for children that is characteristic of the working and middle class. There is not the deep psychological involvement with babies which has been observed with the working-class mother.[23] The baby's needs are cared for on a catch-as-catch-can basis. If there are other children around and they happen to like babies, the baby can be over-stimulated; if this is not the case, the baby is left alone a good deal of the time. As quickly as he can move around he learns to fend for himself.

The three-generation maternal household is a busy place. In contrast to working- and middle-class homes it tends to be open to the world, with many non-family members coming in and out at all times as the children are visited by friends, the teenagers by their boy friends and girl friends, the mother by her friends and perhaps an occasional boy friend, and the grandmother by fewer friends but still by an occasional boy friend.

The openness of the household is, among other things, a reflection of the mother's sense of impotence in the face of the street system. Negro lower-class mothers often indicate that they try very hard to keep their young children at home and away from the streets; they often seem to make the children virtual prisoners in the home. As the children grow and go to school they inevitably do become involved in peer-group activities.

The mother gradually gives up, feeling that once the child is lost to this pernicious outside world there is little she can do to continue to control him and direct his development. She will try to limit the types of activities that go on in the home and to restrict the kinds of friends that her children can bring into the home, but even this she must give up as time goes on, as the children become older and less attentive to her direction.

The grandmothers in their late forties, fifties, and sixties tend increasingly to stay at home. The home becomes a kind of court at which other family members gather and to which they bring their friends for sociability, and as a by-product provide amusement and entertainment for the mother. A grandmother may provide a home for her daughters, their children, and sometimes their children's children, and yet receive very little in a material way from them; but one of the things she does receive is a sense of human involvement, a sense that although life may have passed her by she is not completely isolated from it.

The lack of control that mothers have over much that goes on in their households is most dramatically apparent in the fact that their older children seem to have the right to come home at any time once they have moved and to stay in the home without contributing to its maintenance. Though the mother may be resentful about being taken advantage of, she does not feel she can turn her children away. For example, sixty-five-year-old Mrs. Washington plays hostess for weeks or months at a time to her forty-year-old daughter and her small children, and to her twenty-three-year-old granddaughter and her children. When these daughters come home with their families the grandmother is expected to take care of the young children and must argue with her daughter and granddaughter to receive contributions to the daily household ration of food and liquor. Or, a twenty-year-old son comes home from the Air Force and feels he has the right to live at home without working and to run up an eighty-dollar long-distance telephone bill.

Even aged parents living alone in small apartments sometimes acknowledge such obligations to their children or grandchildren. Again, the only clear return they receive for their hospitality is the reduction of isolation that comes from having people around and interesting activity going on. When in the Washington home the daughter and granddaughter and their children move in with the grandmother, or when they come to visit for shorter periods of time, the occasion has a party atmosphere. The women sit around talking and reminiscing. Though boy friends may be present, they take little part; instead they sit passively, enjoying the stories and drinking along with the women. It would seem that in this kind of party activity the women are defined as the stars. Grandmother, daughter, and granddaughter in turn take the center of the stage telling a story from the family's past, talking about a particularly interesting night out on the town or just making some general observation about life. In the course of these events a good deal of liquor is consumed. In such a household as this little attention is paid to the children since the competition by adults for attention is stiff.

*Boy friends, not husbands.* It is with an understanding of the problems of isolation which older mothers have that we can obtain the best insight into the role and function of boy friends in the maternal household. The older mothers, surrounded by their own children and grandchildren, are not able to move freely in the outside world, to participate in the high life which they enjoyed when younger and more foot-loose. They are disillusioned with marriage as providing any more secure economic base than they can achieve on their own. They see marriage as involving just another responsibility without a concomitant reward—"It's the greatest thing in the world to come home in the afternoon and not have some curly headed twot in the house yellin' at me and askin' me where supper is, where I've been, what I've been doin', and who I've been seein'." In this situation the woman is tempted to form relationships with men that are not so demanding as marriage but still provide companionship and an opportunity for occasional sexual gratification.

There seem to be two kinds of boy friends. Some boy friends "pimp" off mothers; they extract payment in food or money for their companionship. This leads to the custom sometimes called "Mother's Day," the tenth of the month when the AFDC checks come.[24] On this day one can observe an influx of men into the neighborhood, and much partying. But there is another kind of boy friend, perhaps more numerous than the first, who instead of being paid for his services pays for the right to be a pseudo family member. He may be the father of one of the woman's children and for this reason makes a steady contribution to the family's support, or he may simply be a man whose company the mother enjoys and who makes reasonable gifts to the family for the time he spends with them (and perhaps implicitly for the sexual favors he receives). While the boy friend does not assume fatherly authority within the family, he often is known and liked by the children. The older children appreciate the meaningfulness of their mother's relationship with him—one girl said of her mother's boy friend:

"We don't none of us [the children] want her to marry again. It's all right if she wants to live by herself and have a boy friend. It's not because we're afraid we're going to have some more sisters and brothers, which it wouldn't make us much difference, but I think she be too old."

Even when the boy friend contributes ten or twenty dollars a month to the family he is in a certain sense getting a bargain. If he is a well-accepted boy friend he spends considerable time around the house, has a chance to relax in an atmosphere less competitive than that of his peer group, is fed and cared for by the woman, yet has no responsibilities which he cannot renounce when he wishes. When women have stable relationships of this kind with boy friends they often consider marrying them but are reluctant to take such a step. Even the well-liked boy friend has some shortcomings—one woman said of her boy friend:

"Well he works; I know that. He seems to be a nice person, kind hearted. He believes in survival for me and my family. He don't much mind sharing with my youngsters. If I ask him for a helping hand he don't seem to mind that. The only part I dislike is his drinking."

The woman in this situation has worked out a reasonably stable adaptation to the problems of her life; she is fearful of upsetting this adaptation by marrying again. It seems easier to take the "sweet" part of the relationship with a man without the complexities that marriage might involve.

It is in the light of this pattern of women living in families and men living by themselves in rooming houses, odd rooms, here and there, that we can understand Daniel Patrick Moynihan's observation that during their mature years men simply disappear; that is, that census data show a very high sex ratio of women to men.[25] In St. Louis, starting at the age range twenty to twenty-four there are only seventy-two men for every one hundred women. This ratio does not climb to ninety until the age range fifty to fifty-four. Men often do not have real homes; they move about from one household where they have kinship or sexual ties to another; they live in flop houses and rooming houses; they spend time in institutions. They are not household members in the only "homes" that they have—the homes of their mothers and of their girl friends.

It is in this kind of world that boys and girls in the Negro slum community learn their sex roles. It is not just, or even mainly, that fathers are often absent but that the male role models around boys are ones which emphasize expressive, affectional techniques for making one's way in the world. The female role models available to girls emphasize an exaggerated self-sufficiency (from the point of view of the middle class) and the danger of allowing oneself to be dependent on men for anything that is crucial. By the time she is mature, the woman learns that she is most secure when she herself manages the family affairs and when she dominates her men. The man learns that he exposes himself to the least risk of failure when he does not assume a husband's and father's responsibilities but instead counts on his ability to court women and to ingratiate himself with them.

## IDENTITY PROCESSES IN THE FAMILY

Up to this point we have been examining the sequential development of family stages in the Negro slum community, paying only incidental attention to the psychological responses family members make to these social forms and not concerning ourselves with the effect the family forms have on the psychosocial development of the children who grow up in them. Now we want to examine the effect that growing up in this kind of a system has in terms of socialization and personality development.

Household groups function for cultures in carrying out the initial phases of socialization and personality formation. It is in the family that the child learns the most primitive categories of existence and experience, and that he develops his most deeply held beliefs about the world and about himself.[26] From the child's point of view, the household *is* the world; his experiences as he moves out of it into the larger world are always interpreted in terms of his particular experience within the home. The painful experiences which a child in the Negro slum culture has are, therefore, interpreted as in some sense a reflection of this family world. The impact of the system of victimization is transmitted through the family; the child cannot be expected to have the sophistication an outside observer has for seeing exactly where the villains are. From the child's point of view, if he is hungry it is his parents' fault; if he experiences frustrations in the streets or in the school it is his parents' fault; if that world seems incomprehensible to him it is his parents' fault; if people are aggressive or destructive toward each other it is his parents' fault, not that of a system of race relations. In another culture this might not be the case; if a subculture could exist which provided comfort and security within its limited world and the individual experienced frustration only when he moved out into the larger society, the family might not be thought so much to blame. The effect of the caste system, however, is to bring home through a chain of cause and effect all of the victimization processes, and to bring them home in such a way that it is often very difficult even for adults in the system to see the connection between the pain they feel at the moment and the structured patterns of the caste system.

Let us take as a central question that of identity formation within the Negro slum family. We are concerned with the question of who the individual believes himself to be and to be becoming. For Erikson, identity means a sense of continuity and social sameness which bridges what the individual *"was* as a child and what he is *about to become* and also reconciles his *conception of himself* and his community's recognition of him." Thus identity is a "self-realization coupled with a mutual recognition."[27] In the early childhood years identity is family-bound since the child's identity is his identity *vis-à-vis* other members of the family. Later he incorporates into his sense of who he is and is becoming his experiences outside the family, but always influenced by the interpretations and evaluations of those experiences that the family gives. As the child tries on identities, *announces* them, the family sits as judge of his pretensions.

Family members are both the most important judges and the most critical ones, since who he is allowed to become affects them in their own identity strivings more crucially than it affects anyone else. The child seeks a sense of valid identity, a sense of being a particular person with a satisfactory degree of congruence between who he feels he is, who he announces himself to be, and where he feels his society places him.[28] He is uncomfortable when he experiences disjunction between his own needs and the kinds of needs legitimated by those around him, or when he feels a disjunction between his sense of himself and the image of himself that others play back to him.[29]

*"Tell it like it is."* When families become involved in important quarrels the psychosocial underpinnings of family life are laid bare. One such quarrel in a family we have been studying brings together in one place many of the themes that seem to dominate identity problems in Negro slum culture. The incident illustrates in a particularly forceful and dramatic way family processes which our field work, and some other contemporary studies of slum family life, suggests unfold more subtly in a great many families at the lower-class level. The family involved, the Johnsons, is certainly not the most disorganized one we have studied; in some respects their way of life represents a realistic adaptation to the hard living of a family nineteen years on AFDC with a monthly income of $202 for nine people. The two oldest daughters, Mary Jane (eighteen years old) and Esther (sixteen) are pregnant; Mary Jane has one illegitimate child. The adolescent sons, Bob and Richard, are much involved in the social and sexual activities of their peer group. The three other children, ranging in age from twelve to fourteen, are apparently also moving into this kind of peer-group society.

When the argument started Bob and Esther were alone in the apartment with Mary Jane's baby. Esther took exception to Bob's playing with the baby because she had been left in charge; the argument quickly progressed to a fight in which Bob cuffed Esther around, and she tried to cut him with a knife. The police were called and subdued Bob with their nightsticks. At this point the rest of the family and the field worker arrived. As the argument continued, these themes relevant to the analysis which follows appeared:

1. The sisters said that Bob was not their brother (he is a half-brother to Esther, and Mary Jane's full brother). Indeed, they said their mother "didn't have no husband. These kids don't even know who their daddies are." The mother defended herself by saying that she had one legal husband, and one common-law husband, no more.

2. The sisters said that their fathers had never done anything for them, nor had their mother. She retorted that she had raised them "to the age of womanhood" and now would care for their babies.

3. Esther continued to threaten to cut Bob if she got a chance (a month later they fought again, and she did cut Bob, who required twenty-one stitches).

4. The sisters accused their mother of favoring their lazy brothers and asked her to put them out of the house. She retorted that the girls were as lazy, that they made no contribution to maintaining the household, could not get their boy friends to marry them or support their children, that all the support came from her AFDC check. Mary Jane retorted that "the baby has a check of her own."

5. The girls threatened to leave the house if their mother refused to put their brothers out. They said they could force their boy friends to support them by taking them to court, and Esther threatened to cut her boy friend's throat if he did not co-operate.

6. Mrs. Johnson said the girls could leave if they wished but that she would keep their babies; "I'll not have it, not knowing who's taking care of them."

7. When her thirteen-year-old sister laughed at all of this, Esther told her not to laugh because she, too, would be pregnant within a year.

8. When Bob laughed, Esther attacked him and his brother by saying that both were not man enough to make babies, as she and her sister had been able to do.

9. As the field worker left, Mrs. Johnson sought his sympathy. "You see, Joe, how hard it is for me to bring up a family. . . . They sit around and talk to me like I'm some kind of a dog and not their mother."

10. Finally, it is important to note for the analysis which follows that the following labels—"black-assed," "black bastard," "bitch," and other profane terms—were liberally used by Esther and Mary Jane, and rather less liberally by their mother, to refer to each other, to the girls' boy friends, to Bob, and to the thirteen-year-old daughter.

Several of the themes outlined previously appear forcefully in the course of this argument. In the last year and a half the mother has become a grandmother and expects shortly to add two more grandchildren to her household. She takes it for granted that it is her responsibility to care for the grandchildren and that she has the right to decide what will be done with the children since her own daughters are not fully responsible. She makes this very clear to them when they threaten to move out, a threat which they do not really wish to make good nor could they if they wished to.

However, only as an act of will is Mrs. Johnson able to make this a family. She must constantly cope with the tendency of her adolescent children to disrupt the family group and to deny that they are in fact a family—"He ain't no brother of mine"; "The baby has a check of her own." Though we do not know exactly what processes communicate these facts to the children it is clear that in growing up they have learned to regard themselves as not fully part of a solidary collectivity. During the quarrel this message was reinforced for the twelve-, thirteen-, and fourteen-year-old daughters by the four-way argument among their older sisters, older brother, and their mother.

The argument represents vicious unmasking of the individual members' pretenses to being competent individuals.[30] The efforts of the two girls to present themselves as masters of their own fate are unmasked by the mother. The girls in turn unmask the pretensions of the mother and of their two brothers. When the thirteen-year-old daughter expresses some amusement they turn on her, telling her that it won't be long before she too becomes pregnant. Each member of the family in turn is told that he can expect to be no more than a victim of his world, but that this is somehow inevitably his own fault.

In this argument masculinity is consistently demeaned. Bob has no right to play with his niece, the boys are not really masculine because at fifteen and sixteen years they have yet to father children, their own fathers were no goods who failed to do anything for their family. These notions probably come originally from the mother, who enjoys recounting the story of having her common-law husband imprisoned for nonsupport, but this comes back to haunt her as her daughters accuse her of being no better than they in ability to force support and nurturance from a man. In contrast, the girls came off somewhat better than the boys, although they must accept the label of stupid girls because they have similarly failed and inconveniently become pregnant in the first place. At least they can and have had children and therefore have some meaningful connection with the ongoing substance of life. There is something important and dramatic in which they participate, while the boys, despite their sexual activity, "can't get no babies."

In most societies, as children grow and are formed by their elders into suitable members of the society they gain increasingly a sense of competence and ability to master the behavioral environment their particular world presents. But in Negro slum culture growing up involves an ever-increasing appreciation of one's shortcomings, of the impossibility of finding a self-sufficient and gratifying way of living.[31] It is in the family first and most devastatingly that one learns these lessons. As the child's sense of frustration builds he too can strike out and unmask the pretensions of others. The result is a peculiar strength and a pervasive weakness. The strength involves the ability to tolerate and defend against degrading verbal and physical aggressions from others and not to give up completely. The weakness involves the inability to embark hopefully on any course of action that might make things better, particularly action which involves cooperating and trusting attitudes toward others. Family members become potential enemies to each other, as the frequency of observing the police being called in to settle family quarrels brings home all too dramatically.

The conceptions parents have of their children are such that they are constantly alert as the child matures to evidence that he is as bad as everyone else. That is, in lower-class culture human nature is conceived of as essentially bad, destructive, immoral.[32] This is the nature of things. Therefore any one child must be inherently bad unless his parents are very lucky indeed. If the mother can keep the child insulated from the outside world, she feels she may be able to prevent his inherent badness from coming out. She feels that once he is let out into the larger world the badness will come to the fore since that is his nature. This means that in the identity development of the child he is constantly exposed to identity labeling by his parents as a bad person. Since as he grows up he does not experience his world as particularly gratifying, it is very easy for him to conclude that this lack of gratification is due to the fact that something is wrong with him. This, in turn, can readily be assimilated to the definitions of being a bad person offered him by those with whom he lives.[33] In this way the Negro slum child learns his culture's conception of being-in-the-world, a conception that emphasizes inherent evil in a chaotic, hostile, destructive world.

*Blackness.* To a certain extent these same processes operate in white lower-class groups, but added for the Negro is the reality of blackness. "Black-assed" is not an empty pejorative adjective. In the Negro slum culture several distinctive appellations are used to refer to oneself and others. One involves the terms, "black" or "nigger." Black is generally a negative way of naming, but nigger can be either negative or positive, depending upon the context. It is important to note that, at least in the urban North, the initial development of racial identity in these terms has very little directly to do with relations with whites. A child experiences these identity placements in the context of the family and in the neighborhood peer group; he probably very seldom hears the same terms used by whites (unlike the situation in the South). In this way, one of the effects of ghettoization is to mask the ultimate enemy so that the understanding of the fact of victimization by a caste system comes as a late acquisition laid over conceptions of self and of other Negroes derived from intimate, and to the child often traumatic, experience within the ghetto community. If, in addition, the child attends a ghetto school where his Negro teachers either overtly or by implication reinforce his community's negative conceptions of what it means to be black, then the child has little opportunity to develop a more realistic image of himself and other Negroes as being damaged by whites and not by themselves. In such a situation, an intelligent man like Mr. Wilson (quoted on pages 381-82) can say with all sincerity that he does not feel most Negroes are ready for integration— only under the experience of certain kinds of intense personal threat coupled with exposure to an ideology that places the responsibility on whites did he begin to see through the direct evidence of his daily experience.

To those living in the heart of a ghetto, black comes to mean not just "stay back," but also membership in a community of persons who think poorly of each other, who attack and manipulate each other, who give each other small comfort in a desperate world. Black comes to stand for a sense of identity as no better than these destructive others. The individual feels that he must embrace an unattractive self in order to function at all.

We can hypothesize that in those families that manage to avoid the destructive identity imputations of "black" and that manage to maintain solidarity against such assaults from the world around, it is possible for children to grow up with a sense of both Negro and personal identity that allows them to socialize themselves in an anticipatory way for participation in the larger society.[34] This broader sense of identity, however, will remain a brittle one as long as the individual is vulnerable to attack from within the Negro community as "nothing but a nigger like everybody else" or from the white community as "just a nigger." We can hypothesize further that the vicious unmasking of essential identity as black described above is least likely to occur within families where the parents have some stable sense of security, and where they therefore have less need to protect themselves by disavowing responsibility for their children's behavior and denying the children their patrimony as products of a particular family rather than of an immoral nature and an evil community.

In sum, we are suggesting that Negro slum children as they grow up in their families and in their neighborhoods are exposed to a set of experiences—and a rhetoric which conceptualizes them—that brings home to the child an understanding of his essence as a weak and debased person who can expect only partial gratification of his needs, and who must seek even this level of gratification by less than straight-forward means.

*Strategies for living.* In every society complex processes of socialization inculcate in their members strategies for gratifying the needs with which they are born and those which the society itself generates. Inextricably linked to these strategies, both cause and effect of them, are the existential propositions which members of a culture entertain about the nature of their world and of effective action within the world as it is defined for them. In most of American society two grand strategies seem to attract the allegiance of its members and guide their day-to-day actions. I have called these strategies those of *the good life* and of *career success.*[35] A good life strategy involves efforts to get along with others and not to rock the boat, a comfortable familism grounded on a stable work career for husbands in which they perform adequately at the modest jobs that enable them to be good providers. The strategy of career success is the choice of ambitious men and women who see life as providing opportunities to move from a lower to a higher status, to "accomplish something," to achieve greater than ordinary material well-being, prestige, and social recognition. Both of these strategies are predicated on the assumption that the world is inherently rewarding if one behaves properly and does his part. The rewards of the world may come easily or only at the cost of great effort, but at least they are there.

In the white and particularly in the Negro slum worlds little in the experience that individuals have as they grow up sustains a belief in a rewarding world. The strategies that seem appropriate are not those of a good, family-based life or of a career, but rather *strategies for survival*.

Much of what has been said above can be summarized as encouraging three kinds of survival strategies. One is the strategy of the *expressive life style* which I have described elsewhere as an effort to make yourself interesting and attractive to others so that you are better able to manipulate their behavior along lines that will provide some immediate gratification.[36] Negro slum culture provides many examples of techniques for seduction, of persuading others to give you what you want in situations where you have very little that is tangible to offer in return. In order to get what you want you learn to "work game," a strategy which requires a high development of a certain kind of verbal facility, a sophisticated manipulation of promise and interim reward. When the expressive strategy fails or when it is unavailable there is, of course, the great temptation to adopt a *violent strategy* in which you force others to give you what you need once you fail to win it by verbal and other symbolic means.[37] Finally, and increasingly as members of the Negro slum culture grow older, there is the *depressive strategy* in which goals are increasingly constricted to the bare necessities for survival (not as a social being but simply as an organism).[38] This is the strategy of "I don't bother anybody and I hope nobody's gonna bother me; I'm simply going through the motions to keep body (but not soul) together." Most lower-class people follow mixed strategies, as Walter Miller has observed, alternating among the excitement of the expressive style, the desperation of the violent style, and the deadness of the depressed style.[39] Some members of the Negro slum world experiment from time to time with mixed strategies that also incorporate the stable working-class model of the good American life, but this latter strategy is exceedingly vulnerable to the threats of unemployment or a less than adequate pay check, on the one hand, and the seduction and violence of the slum world around them, on the other.

*Remedies*. Finally, it is clear that we, no less than the inhabitants of the ghetto, are not masters of their fate because we are not masters of our own total society. Despite the battles with poverty on many fronts we can find little evidence to sustain our hope of winning the war given current programs and strategies.

The question of strategy is particularly crucial when one moves from an examination of destructive cultural and interaction patterns in Negro families to the question of how these families might achieve a more stable and gratifying life. It is tempting to see the family as the main villain of the piece, and to seek to develop programs which attack directly this family pathology. Should we not have extensive programs of family therapy, family counseling, family-life education, and the like? Is this not the prerequisite to enabling slum Negro families to take advantage of other opportunities? Yet, how pale such efforts seem compared to the deep-seated problems of self-image and family process described above. Can an army of social workers undo the damage of three hundred years by talking and listening without massive changes in the social and economic situations of the families with whom they are to deal? And, if such changes take place, will the social-worker army be needed?

If we are right that present Negro family patterns have been created as adaptations to a particular socioeconomic situation, it would make more sense to change that socioeconomic situation and then depend upon the people involved to make new adaptations as time goes on. If Negro providers have steady jobs and decent incomes, if Negro children have some realistic expectation of moving toward such a goal, if slum Negroes come to feel that they have the chance to affect their own futures and to receive respect from those around them, then (and only then) the destructive patterns described are likely to change. The change, though slow and uneven from individual to individual, will in a certain sense be automatic because it will represent an adaptation to changed socioeconomic circumstances which have direct and highly valued implications for the person.

It is possible to think of three kinds of extra-family change that are required if family patterns are to change; these are outlined below as pairs of current deprivations and needed remedies:

| Deprivation effect of caste victimization | Needed remedy |
|---|---|
| I. Poverty | Employment income for men; income maintenance for mothers |
| II. Trained incapacity to function in a bureaucratized and industrialized world | Meaningful education of the next generation |
| III. Powerlessness and stigmatization | Organizational participation for aggressive pursuit of Negroes' self-interest |
| | Strong sanctions against callous or indifferent service to slum Negroes |
| | Pride in group identity, Negro *and* American |

Unless the major effort is to provide these kinds of remedies, there is a very real danger that programs to "better the structure of the Negro family" by direct intervention will serve the unintended functions of distracting the country from the pressing needs for socioeconomic reform and providing an alibi for the failure to embark on the basic institutional changes that are needed to do anything about abolishing both white and Negro poverty. It would be sad, indeed, if, after the Negro revolt brought to national prominence the continuing problem of poverty, our expertise about Negro slum culture served to deflect the national impulse into symptom-treatment rather than basic reform. If that happens, social scientists will have served those they study poorly indeed.

Let us consider each of the needed remedies in terms of its probable impact on the family. First, the problem of poverty: employed men are less likely to leave their families than are unemployed men, and when they do stay they are more likely to have the respect of their wives and children. A program whose sole effect would be to employ at reasonable wages slum men for work using the skills they now have would do more than any other possible program to stabilize slum family life. But the wages must be high enough to enable the man to maintain his self-respect as a provider, and stable enough to make it worthwhile to change the nature of his adaptation to his world (no one-year emergency programs will do). Once men learn that work pays off it would be possible to recruit men for part-time retraining for more highly skilled jobs, but the initial emphasis must be on the provision of full-time, permanent unskilled jobs. Obviously it will be easier to do this in the context of full employment and a tight labor market.[40]

For at least a generation, however, there will continue to be a large number of female-headed households. Given the demands of socializing a new generation for non-slum living, it is probably uneconomical to encourage mothers to work. Rather, income maintenance programs must be increased to realistic levels, and mothers must be recognized as doing socially useful work for which they are paid rather than as "feeding at the public trough." The bureaucratic morass which currently hampers flexible strategies of combining employment income and welfare payments to make ends meet must also be modified if young workers are not to be pushed prematurely out of the home.

Education has the second priority. (It is second only because without stable family income arrangements the school system must work against the tremendous resistance of competing life-style adaptations to poverty and economic insecurity.) As Kenneth Clark has argued so effectively, slum schools now function more to stultify and discourage slum children than to stimulate and train them. The capacity of educators to alibi their lack of commitment to their charges is protean. The making of a different kind of generation must be taken by educators as a stimulating and worthwhile challenge. Once the goal has been accepted they must be given the resources with which to achieve it and the flexibility necessary to experiment with different approaches to accomplish the goal.

Education must be broadly conceived to include much more than class-room work, and probably more than a nine-months schedule.[41]

If slum children can come to see the schools as representing a really likely avenue of escape from their difficult situation (even before adoles-cence they know it is the only *possible* escape) then their commitment to school activities will feed back into their families in a positive way. The parents will feel proud rather than ashamed, and they will feel less need to damn the child as a way to avoid blaming themselves for his failure. The sense of positive family identity will be enriched as the child becomes an attractive object, an ego resource, to his parents. Because he himself feels more competent, he will see them as less depriving and weak. If children's greater commitment to school begins to reduce their involve-ment in destructive or aimless peer-group activities this too will repercuss positively on the family situation since parents will worry less about their children's involvement in an immoral outside world, and be less inclined to deal with them in harsh, rejecting, or indifferent ways.

Cross-cutting the deprivations of poverty and trained incapacity is the fact of powerlessness and stigmatization. Slum people know that they have little ability to protect themselves and to force recognition of their abstract rights. They know that they are looked down on and scape-goated. They are always vulnerable to the slights, insults, and indifference of the white and Negro functionaries with whom they deal—policemen, social workers, school teachers, landlords, employers, retailers, janitors. To come into contact with others carries the constant danger of moral attack and insult.[42] If processes of status degradation within families are to be interrupted, then they must be interrupted on the outside first.

One way out of the situation of impotence and dammed-up in-group aggression is the organization of meaningful protest against the larger society. Such protest can and will take many forms, not always so neat and rational as the outsider might hope. But, coupled with, and support-ing, current programs of economic and educational change, involvement of slum Negroes in organizational activity can do a great deal to build a sense of pride and potency. While only a very small minority of slum Negroes can be expected to participate personally in such movements, the vicarious involvement of the majority can have important effects on their sense of self-respect and worth.

Some of the needed changes probably can be made from the top, by decision in Washington, with minimal effective organization within the slum; but others can come only in response to aggressive pressure on the part of the victims themselves. This is probably particularly true of the entrenched tendency of service personnel to enhance their own sense of self and to indulge their middle-class *ressentiment* by stigmatizing and exploiting those they serve. Only effective protest can change endemic patterns of police harassment and brutality, or teachers' indifference and insults, or butchers' heavy thumbs, or indifferent street cleaning and garbage disposal. And the goal of the protest must be to make this kind of insult to the humanity of the slum-dweller too expensive for the perpetrator to afford; it must cost him election defeats, suspensions without pay, job dismissals, license revocations, fines, and the like.

To the extent that the slum dweller avoids stigmatization in the outside world, he will feel more fully a person within the family and better able to function constructively within it since he will not be tempted to make up deficits in self-esteem in ways that are destructive of family solidarity. The "me" of personal identity and the multiple "we" of family, Negro, and American identity are all inextricably linked; a healthier experience of identity in any one sector will repercuss on all the others.

## NOTES

1. This paper is based in part on research supported by a grant from the National Institute of Mental Health, Grant No. MH-09189, "Social and Community Problems in Public Housing Areas." Many of the ideas presented stem from discussion with the senior members of the Pruitt-Igoe research staff—Alvin W. Gouldner, David J. Pittman, and Jules Henry—and with the research associates and assistants on the project. I have made particular use of ideas developed in discussions with Boone Hammond, Joyce Ladner, Robert Simpson, David Schulz, and William Yancey. I also wish to acknowledge helpful suggestions and criticisms by Catherine Chilman, Gerald Handel, and Marc J. Swartz. Although this paper is not a formal report of the Pruitt-Igoe research, all of the illustrations of family behavior given in the text are drawn from interviews and observations that are part of that study. The study deals with the residents of the Pruitt-Igoe housing projects in St. Louis. Some 10,000 people live in these projects which comprise forty-three eleven-story buildings near the downtown area of St. Louis. Over half of the households have female heads, and for over half of the households the principal income comes from public assistance of one kind or another. The research has been in the field for a little over two years. It is a broad community study which thus far has relied principally on methods of participant observation and open-ended interviewing. Data on families come from repeated interviews and observations with a small group of families. The field workers are identified as graduate students at Washington University who have no connection with the housing authority or other officials, but are simply interested in learning about how families in the project live. This very intensive study of families yields a wealth of information (over 10,000 pages of interview and observation reports) which obviously cannot be analyzed within the limits of one article. In this article I have limited myself to outlining a typical family stage sequence and discussing some of the psychosocial implications of growing up in families characterized by this sequence. In addition, I have tried to limit myself to findings which other literature on Negro family life suggests are not limited to the residents of the housing projects we are studying.
2. St. Clair Drake, "The Social and Economic Status of the Negro in the United States," *Dædalus* (Fall 1965), p. 772.
3. E. Franklin Frazier, *The Negro Family in the United States* (Chicago, 1939), p. 487.

4. Norman Mailer, "The White Negro" (City Light Books, San Francisco, Calif., 1957); and Leslie Fiedler, *Waiting For The End* (New York, 1964), pp. 118–137.

5. See Alvin W. Gouldner, "Reciprocity and Autonomy in Functional Theory," in Llewellyn Gross (ed.), *Symposium of Sociological Theory* (Evanston, Ill., 1958), for a discussion of functional autonomy and dependence of structural elements in social systems. We are suggesting here that lower-class groups have a relatively high degree of functional autonomy *vis à vis* the total social system because that system does little to meet their needs. In general the fewer the rewards a society offers members of a particular group in the society, the more autonomous will that group prove to be with reference to the norms of the society. Only by constructing an elaborate repressive machinery, as in concentration camps, can the effect be otherwise.

6. For example, the lead sentence in a *St. Louis Post Dispatch* article of July 20, 1965, begins "A White House study group is laying the ground work for an attempt to better the structure of the Negro family."

7. See Kenneth Stampp, *The Peculiar Institution* (New York, 1956); John Hope Franklin, *From Slavery to Freedom* (New York, 1956); Frank Tannenbaum, *Slave and Citizen* (New York, 1946); E. Franklin Frazier, *op. cit.;* and Melville J. Herskovits, *The Myth of the Negro Past* (New York, 1941).

8. See Raymond T. Smith, *The Negro Family in British Guiana* (New York, 1956); J. Mayone Stycos and Kurt W. Back, *The Control of Human Fertility in Jamaica* (Ithaca, N. Y., 1964); F. M. Henriques, *Family and Colour in Jamaica* (London, 1953); Judith Blake, *Family Structure in Jamaica* (Glencoe, Ill., 1961); and Raymond T. Smith, "Culture and Social Structure in The Caribbean," *Comparative Studies in Society and History,* Vol. VI (The Hague, The Netherlands, October 1963), pp. 24–46. For a broader comparative discussion of the matrifocal family see Peter Kunstadter, "A Survey of the Consanguine or Matrifocal Family," *American Anthropologist,* Vol. 65, No. 1 (February 1963), pp. 56–66; and Ruth M. Boyer, "The Matrifocal Family Among the Mescalero: Additional Data," *American Anthropologist,* Vol. 66, No. 3 (June 1964), pp. 593–602.

9. Paul C. Glick, *American Families* (New York, 1957), pp. 133 ff.

10. For discussions of white lower-class families, see Lee Rainwater, Richard P. Coleman, and Gerald Handel, *Workingman's Wife* (New York, 1959); Lee Rainwater, *Family Design* (Chicago, 1964); Herbert Gans, *The Urban Villagers* (New York, 1962); Albert K. Cohen and Harold M. Hodges, "Characteristics of the Lower-Blue-Collar-Class," *Social Problems,* Vol. 10, No. 4 (Spring 1963), pp. 303–334; S. M. Miller, "The American Lower Classes: A Typological Approach," in Arthur B. Shostak and William Gomberg, *Blue Collar World* (Englewood Cliffs, N. J., 1964); and Mirra Komarovsky, *Blue Collar Marriage* (New York, 1964). Discussions of Negro slum life can be found in St. Clair Drake and Horace R. Cayton, *Black Metropolis* (New York, 1962), and Kenneth B. Clark, *Dark Ghetto* (New York, 1965); and of Negro community life in small-town and rural settings in Allison Davis, Burleigh B. Gardner, and Mary Gardner, *Deep South* (Chicago, 1944), and Hylan Lewis, *Blackways of Kent* (Chapel Hill, N. C., 1955).

11. For general discussions of the extent to which lower-class people hold the values of the larger society, see Albert K. Cohen, *Delinquent Boys* (New York, 1955); Hyman Rodman, "The Lower Class Value Stretch," *Social Forces,* Vol. 42, No. 2 (December 1963), pp. 205 ff; and William L. Yancey, "The Culture of Poverty: Not So Much Parsimony," unpublished manuscript, Social Science Institute, Washington University.

12. James F. Short, Jr., and Fred L. Strodtbeck, *Group Process and Gang Delinquency* (Chicago, 1965), p. 114. Chapter V (pages 102–115) of this book contains a very useful discussion of differences between white and Negro lower-class communities.

13. Discussions of white lower-class attitudes toward sex may be found in Arnold W. Green, "The Cult of Personality and Sexual Relations," *Psychiatry,* Vol. 4 (1941), pp. 343–348; William F. Whyte, "A Slum Sex Code," *American Journal of Sociology,* Vol. 49, No. 1 (July 1943), pp. 24–31; and Lee Rainwater, "Marital Sexuality in Four Cultures of Poverty," *Journal of Marriage and the Family,* Vol. 26, No. 4 (November 1964), pp. 457–466.

14. See Boone Hammond, "The Contest System: A Survival Technique," Master's Honors paper, Washington University, 1965. See also Ira L. Reiss, "Premarital Sexual Permissiveness Among Negroes and Whites," *American Sociological Review,* Vol. 29, No. 5 (October 1964), pp. 688–698.

15. See the discussion of aleatory processes leading to premarital fatherhood in Short and Strodtbeck, *op. cit.,* pp. 44–45.

16. Rainwater, *And the Poor Get Children, op. cit.,* pp. 61–63. See also, Carlfred B. Broderick, "Social Heterosexual Development Among Urban Negroes and Whites," *Journal of Marriage and the Family,* Vol. 27 (May 1965), pp. 200–212. Broderick finds that although white boys and girls, and Negro girls become more interested in marriage as they get older, Negro boys become *less* interested in late adolescence than they were as preadolescents.

17. Walter Miller, "The Corner Gang Boys Get Married," *Trans-action,* Vol. 1, No. 1 (November 1963), pp. 10–12.

18. Rainwater, *Family Design, op. cit.,* pp. 28–60.

19. Yancey, *op. cit.* The effects of unemployment on the family have been discussed by E. Wright Bakke, *Citizens Without Work* (New Haven, Conn., 1940); Mirra Komarovsky, *The Unemployed Man and His Family* (New York, 1960); and Earl L. Koos, *Families in Trouble* (New York, 1946). What seems distinctive to the Negro slum culture is the short time lapse between the husband's loss of a job and his wife's considering him superfluous.

20. See particularly Komarovsky's discussion of "barriers to marital communications" (Chapter 7) and "confidants outside of marriage" (Chapter 9), in *Blue Collar Marriage, op. cit.*

21. Rainwater, *Family Design, op. cit.,* pp. 305–308.

22. For a discussion of the relationship between Black Nationalist ideology and the Negro struggle to achieve a sense of valid personal identity, see Howard Brotz, *The Black Jews of Harlem* (New York, 1963), and E. U. Essien-Udom, *Black Nationalism: A Search for Identity in America* (Chicago, 1962).

23. Rainwater, Coleman, and Handel, *op. cit.,* pp. 88–102.

24. Cf. Michael Schwartz and George Henderson, "The Culture of Unemployment: Some Notes on Negro Children," in Shostak and Gomberg, *op. cit.*

25. Daniel Patrick Moynihan, "Employment, Income, and the Ordeal of the Negro Family," *Dædalus* (Fall 1965), pp. 760–61.

26. Talcott Parsons concludes his discussion of child socialization, the development of an "internalized family system" and internalized role differentiation by observing, "The internalization of the family collectivity as an object and its values should not be lost sight of. This is crucial with respect to . . . the assumption of representative roles outside the family on behalf of it. Here it is the child's family membership which is decisive, and thus his acting in a role in terms of its values for 'such as he.' " Talcott Parsons and Robert F. Bales, *Family, Socialization and Interaction Process* (Glencoe, Ill., 1955), p. 113.

27. Erik H. Erikson, "Identity and the Life Cycle," *Psychological Issues,* Vol. 1, No. 1 (1959).

28. For discussion of the dynamics of the individual's *announcements* and the society's *placements* in the formation of identity, see Gregory Stone, "Appearance and the Self," in Arnold Rose, *Human Behavior in Social Process* (Boston, 1962), pp. 86–118.

29. The importance of identity for social behavior is discussed in detail in Ward Goodenough, *Cooperation and Change* (New York, 1963), pp. 176–251, and

in Lee Rainwater, "Work and Identity in the Lower Class," in Sam H. Warner, Jr., *Planning for the Quality of Urban Life* (Cambridge, Mass., forthcoming). The images of self and of other family members is a crucial variable in Hess and Handel's psychosocial analysis of family life; see Robert D. Hess and Gerald Handel, *Family Worlds* (Chicago, 1959), especially pp. 6–11.

30. See the discussion of "masking" and "unmasking" in relation to disorganization and re-equilibration in families by John P. Spiegel, "The Resolution of Role Conflict within the Family," in Norman W. Bell and Ezra F. Vogel, *A Modern Introduction to the Family* (Glencoe, Ill., 1960), pp. 375–377.

31. See the discussion of self-identity and self-esteem in Thomas F. Pettigrew, *A Profile of the Negro American* (Princeton, N. J., 1964), pp. 6–11.

32. Rainwater, Coleman, and Handel, *op. cit.*, pp. 44–51. See also the discussion of the greater level of "anomie" and mistrust among lower-class people in Ephraim Mizruchi, *Success and Opportunity* (New York, 1954). Unpublished research by the author indicates that for one urban lower-class sample (Chicago) Negroes scored about 50 per cent higher on Srole's anomie scale than did comparable whites.

33. For a discussion of the child's propensity from a very early age for speculation and developing explanations, see William V. Silverberg, *Childhood Experience and Personal Destiny* (New York, 1953), pp. 81 ff.

34. See Ralph Ellison's autobiographical descriptions of growing up in Oklahoma City in his *Shadow and Act* (New York, 1964). The quotations at the beginning of this article are taken from pages 315 and 112 of this book.

35. Rainwater, "Work and Identity in the Lower Class," *op. cit.*

36. *Ibid.*

37. Short and Strodtbeck see violent behavior in juvenile gangs as a kind of last resort strategy in situations where the actor feels he has no other choice. See Short and Strodtbeck, *op. cit.*, pp. 248–264.

38. Wiltse speaks of a "pseudo depression syndrome" as characteristic of many AFDC mothers. Kermit T. Wiltse, "Orthopsychiatric Programs for Socially Deprived Groups," *American Journal of Orthopsychiatry*, Vol. 33, No. 5 (October 1963), pp. 806–813.

39. Walter B. Miller, "Lower Class Culture as a Generating Milieu of Gang Delinquency," *Journal of Social Issues*, Vol. 14, No. 3 (1958), pp. 5–19.

40. This line of argument concerning the employment problems of Negroes, and poverty war strategy more generally, is developed with great cogency by James Tobin, "On Improving the Economic Status of the Negro," *Dædalus* (Fall 1965), and previously by Gunnar Myrdal, in his *Challenge to Affluence* (New York, 1963), and Orville R. Gursslin and Jack L. Roach, in their "Some Issues in Training the Employed," *Social Problems*, Vol. 12, No. 1 (Summer 1964), pp. 68–77.

41. See Chapter 6 (pages 111–153) of Kenneth Clark, *op. cit.*, for a discussion of the destructive effects of ghetto schools on their students.

42. See the discussion of "moral danger" in Lee Rainwater, "Fear and the House-as-Haven in the Lower Class," *Journal of the American Institute of Planners*, February 1966 (in press).

# 19:

# The Family in Psychosomatic Process[1]

*James L. Titchener, Jules Riskin,* and *Richard Emerson*

This paper is the report of a study of an entire family in which one son developed ulcerative colitis. It has been written to point out a method by which one of the conditions specific to the etiology of psychosomatic processes may be further understood. In setting forth this method we propose an expansion of current hypotheses regarding the object relations factors in the causes of and predisposition to psychosomatic illness.

In his thorough review of the ulcerative colitis syndrome Dr. George Engel writes: "Elucidation of the specific aspects of the object relations constitutes a most important problem for further research."[2] This comment seems appropriate for the whole field of psychosomatic investigation. From his own research and from his extensive review of the work of others, Engel has formulated the recurrent patterns of significant relationships in ulcerative colitis patients and he has pointed out how these rigid and confining patterns predispose these individuals to psychosomatic illness. This formulation is part of a theory of the etiology of ulcerative colitis.

Dr. Engel views ulcerative colitis as a response of the whole organism with a particular locus in the lining of the large bowel. The effective and healthy bowel lining serves as a selective barrier against penetration of organisms and other substances from the "outside," i.e., the lumen of the colon. In ulcerative colitis the physiologic function of the bowel lining quite probably becomes affected in such a way that organisms in the lumen can penetrate and are, thereafter, no longer innocuous, but pathogenic. It is considered likely that a constitutional predisposition is necessary for this situation. Among the other possible factors, some still

Reprinted by permission from *Psychosomatic Medicine*, Vol. 22, No. 2 (1960), pp. 127–42. Copyright 1960 by Hoeber Medical Division, Harper and Row, Publishers. James L. Titchener is associate professor of psychiatry, University of Cincinnati College of Medicine. Jules Riskin is associate director, Mental Research Institute, Palo Alto, California. Richard Emerson is associate professor of social psychology, University of Washington, Seattle. At the time of writing, he was associate professor of sociology, University of Cincinnati.

unknown, is the psychophysiologic factor; there is imposing clinical evidence to support the significance of a psychosomatic relationship.

The reports of Engel and others reviewed by him are persuasive that the essential psychological condition operating with somatic factors towards the onset of ulcerative colitis is an affective state characterized by helplessness and despair arising from a deep disturbance in a key object relation which is lost or threatened, or whose loss is imagined. The ulcerative colitis patient is unable to accomplish the grief work nor any other adjustment to object loss and so suffers a deep disruption of previous adaptation, with consequent development of a state of helplessness. It is probable that this drastic change in psychological systems breaks through to affect the operation of somatic systems, particularly if they are predisposed to dysfunction.

This unfortunate lack of adaptive capacity, combined with incessant need, develops, in Engel's view, from the early, very much prolonged symbiosis between mother and child. In very brief summary, the mother-infant and mother-child relationship are conditional ones in which mother will give love if she can control. The necessary submission of the child lays the groundwork for uninterrupted need for similar relationships throughout life. Such relationships in adolescence and adulthood, when society rules against the maintenance of a symbiosis with mother, are very difficult to find and to maintain with potential substitutes. Usually the patient-to-be manages to find someone who will fill the bill at least partially. But almost always this chosen person, who perhaps unwittingly finds himself or herself a "key" person, cannot stand the strain and the interpersonal needs of the potential patient are frustrated or threatened. Such individuals are so sensitive to the vicissitudes of the mutually controlling relationship that almost any occurrence may upset the tenuous equilibrium.

## THE FAMILY IN A PSYCHOSOMATIC PROCESS

In launching our study we have assumed the conditions for the onset of ulcerative colitis as Engel has hypothesized them. Our contribution toward a new look at this hypothesis is confined to the object relation aspects of the formulation.

Our investigative approach may be likened to the one used by cultural anthropologists who, if interested in the psychodynamics of a relationship in a culture would study not one but both persons involved and, further, would seek any others who could offer intimate observations upon the relationship in question.

Our methods of study of whole families provide us with corroborating and contrasting observations by each family member, including comments upon individual feelings, upon the feelings and behavior of others, and upon their own and other relationships. We are enabled to derive a stereoscopic view of the family as a field and of the individuals' functions in this field. In addition, we can develop concepts of the family's working as a whole system—a social unit with a structure and a dynamic pattern.

We assume that, as with personality, there are patterns of adaptation for a family too. A particular person or a particular relationship—for example, mother and child—are involved continually in mutually influencing transactions with the whole family, as a social system. Let us now return to Engel's hypotheses about the prolonged mother-child symbiosis which becomes a mutually controlling relationship, pathogenic, in some cases, of ulcerative colitis. We would add that this relationship is, from the beginning and during its later vicissitudes, conditioned by the milieu in which it exists—the family. The mother-child axis turns in a social field of which the family constitutes a large and important segment.

To put our case more strongly, our approach would seem to obviate a concept of a colitigenic mother, as it would also the schizophrenogenic mother, for the relationship is not one in which the mother *per se* forces herself in a pathogenic way upon a child, but one made by the mother and conditioned by the dynamics of the family in which she and her child live. The significant element is not simply the mother's persona.ity, but the way she acts in the particular relationship with the particular child in a particular period—all in the context of the *whole* family's psychodynamic patterns.

Let us imagine a study in which personality assessments of 20,000 mothers of ulcerative colitis patients were compared with those of 20,000 mothers of children without colitis. We would surmise that, though there would be a contrast in the groups, the correlation of colitis patients with mothers having certain traits of personality at the time of assessment would *not* be especially high. We are of the opinion that colitigenic mothers are not born nor even made in their own childhood. Their ways of relating to their children come into being *in a family situation* and their special relationships with future ulcerative colitis patients are largely determined by the dynamics of the family environment. The figure of the mother obtained in the anamnestic data from the patient is not reality, nor totally a mythical figment of the patient's psychopathology. Truly, the mother figure, like other figures in the family, is largely *a family legend* created by the relationships of *all* the individuals in the family with a central figure. The patient, then, presents us this image compounded of reality, of his own distortions, and of the family's idea of mother. One

o

thing is probably true, however: Whatever the mother "really" is beneath the figure and the role and the image represented in the family, she is this way most of all with the patient. We can speculate that the deeper, intrapsychic conflicts, emerge most strongly in the relationship with the patient-to-be. This selection of the patient for the focus of family conflict is determined by a number of factors—environmental, individual, and constitutional. For a real understanding of the forces which motivate object choice and which bring about sensitivity to object loss we need to examine early and late object relations from this multidimensional point of view, rather than being concerned only with the binary relationship in a vacuum.

A study correlating mothers' personalities with a psychosomatic illness is in our theory, likely to produce unimpressive results because of the existence of so many other factors crucial in the moulding of the object relations which are the really essential aspects of pathogenesis. More important, studies of this kind fail to provide us with much information about *how* the mother's relations with a patient have influenced him.

In the following case study we wish to demonstrate how object relations can be seen in depth. We shall attempt to illustrate our opinion that the mother's attitudes and behavior alone are not etiologically responsible for the predisposition and onset of the illness. If her characteristics were so responsible, might she not have started a small epidemic of ulcerative colitis in this family? Instead, the theoretically pathogenic object relations are moulded by the whole interlocking set of relations, although the mother is a central figure. We shall further try to demonstrate how the affected member of the family becomes a focus of conflict for the parents and his siblings.

The case report was assembled as part of a larger and more general research on family dynamics,[3] which is related to the expanding interest in the dynamics of the individual and his family. Ackerman,[4] Chance,[5] and Kluckhohn and Spiegel[6] have provided extensive review and bibliography in this area.

The methods of our research included an observed interaction session including all family members, a number of interviews with each member individually, and a family relations inventory designed by our research team. For the purposes of this report we shall include only the individual interviews, although we learned about some aspects of the family inadvertently in some informal sessions with several of the family members. The individual interviews have a sequence which lends them some extra value. One member (J. T.) of the research team does all of the interviewing with a family, seeing its members in sequence. Then, when a series has been completed, it is repeated. In the family studied, the series was repeated four times with the exception of the patient's brother who could be interviewed only once for somewhat more than an hour. In this case we also have notes from a course of psychotherapy undergone by the patient. The interlocking or revolving sequence of interviewing tends to bring out some aspects of a family's characteristic transactions. The interviewer's ear soon becomes very sensitively tuned to the communication of the family group he is seeing, and the material covered in the associative anamnesis interviewing is directed somewhat by what the interviewer hears from all the family members. For example, in this family there was a surprising tendency for all to comment upon some early memories first reported by the patient. This tendency was encouraged by the interviewer. The fact that several people involved in a fairly intimate situation comment upon the same current issues is also extremely helpful in seeing, almost *in vivo,* what characteristically transpires in a family.

## CASE HISTORY

Our acquaintance with the Neal family (pseudonym) began in early 1957 when Bob, Jr., was admitted to our psychosomatic study service upon the urgent recommendation of an internist and a psychiatric consultant. By that time Bob had lived through more than 12 months of discouraging battle with his ulcerative colitis. The anniversary of onset had passed just before Christmas without signs of improvement and, in fact, it had seemed to be marked by a moderate relapse. His self-respect had suffered with the suggestion of psychiatric treatment and his reluctant agreement to the hospital admission had carried some degree of last-resort submission on his part.

As far as we know, the illness began about the middle of December 1955 with twelve watery and bloody stools per day, diffuse abdominal pain, and nausea. Through December and January 1955–6 the diagnosis of ulcerative colitis was confirmed by proctosigmoidoscope and x-ray. He improved slowly with antibiotics and supportive care although there was a gradual decline in weight from his original 170 lb., and an anemia that stabilized at medium-low levels. A psychiatrist had one brief contact in February 1956, but his interview and the suggestion of hospitalization in a Veterans Administration psychiatric service resulted only in a petulant change of physicians. After Bob left the hospital, his condition improved a little, then relapsed a little, each setback shaking further his hope of final relief. By the fall of 1956 the relapses were more severe and enduring than the remissions, while home medical care became less effective and less resourceful.

When we first met him, Bob was a long, thin young man of 24, usually huddled and curled in his bed with a stool-chair close by. He weighed about 115 lb. Any conversation of more than 10 minutes had to be interrupted by a rush from the bed and a burst of diarrhea. He had long, dark-blond hair falling over a pale, strained, and thin face. Talking with others was painful for him, not so much because it was fatiguing and he was ill, but more because it was emotionally difficult. Medically he was toxic and psychiatrically he was helpless and hopeless. The alternate sides of Bob's character can, even at this point, be illustrated by the contrasting picture of him 12 months later, after treatment, surgery, and steroids. Then we see him standing, emerged from the cocoon of bedclothes and psychic withdrawal, with a full, heavy face and an air of complacent, assured stiffness.

Mrs. Neal was seen the day of admission. She is a moderately obese woman of slightly more than average height. She seemed relaxed, accessible, and poised. She talked easily, gave quick assurance of understanding our methods, and promised cooperation. She appeared to be empathic towards her son's recent ordeal, although first impressions could have been mistaken. She never showed much tension in response to the course of Bob's illness. Nevertheless, even a researcher oriented to the subtleties of family dynamics was surprised by the occurrence that took place immediately after this first interview, when the mother went from the office to her son's room and burst in saying, "Your father is in an agony of stomach pain from worrying about you." This drastic double-bind[7] and conflictful expression of common family problems, which will be explained more completely below, expresses the divided pity of the mother and forces Bob, in a loving way, to accept the responsibility for the father's illness. It would be impossible to say whether the occurrence had a physiological effect, since the bowel was already operating at near maximum speed of contraction, secretion, and hemorrhage. Soon thereafter, Bob was seen in his room. He was tightly huddled, sometimes trembling and almost unable to talk except to emit short bursts of anger at his father for not taking care of himself and his stomach. The conversation was strategically directed towards introductory small-talk. A little anxious himself, the interviewer strayed to the window and there spoke aimlessly of promises to bring magazines and of the hospital's need for new buildings to replace the old, dreary ones. While the interviewer was looking away, the patient hurried from his bed and had a torrential bowel movement. With the decision, then, that the patient needed a nurse more than a doctor, the interviewer ended the first contact.

Mr. Neal (Bob, Sr.) is a stout, full-faced man of about 50, with silver hair and moustache. He leaned back in his chair in a posture of confidence, but sometimes would tilt forward on his elbows to make a point. With a few exceptions his manner was that of a man of straightforward half sincerity. He exuded a confidential and friendly air which is useful in business and was usual in his interviews, although he spoke meaningfully of personal feelings and of his observations of others in the family. Several brief times in each interview the impact of events would change his voice a little to an imploring tone.

There were three other children: Doris, 29, and Dottie, 22, were not available, although we know something of them. Ken, 27, is a trim air force officer with a quiet, friendly, but noncommittal manner.

### PRECIPITATION OF THE ILLNESS

The precipitating events of a serious illness seem to gather in one period linking and joining forces to upset a psychosomatic equilibrium. Bob Neal's difficulties were preceded by a set of associated occurrences, some of which were probably not truly separate precipitating factors, but rather representations or subordinates of the more significant ones.

By the fall of 1955 Bob was out of the Navy 2 years and in a business college, where his work was deteriorating. He seemed distracted, while his parents were urging him on and demanding to know why he could not do better. He partially supported himself, feeling a little angry that he had to, but, at the same time, ashamed and guilty that he was being helped by his parents. It was impossible for him to know whether it was proper to be dependent upon his father while attending college, since it was never decided whether he appreciated the financial strain on his parents. His younger sister was being sent to the same college at the same time; was this reason to pay his own way or justification for expecting more?

These circumstances further affected object relations. The mother, by her own report and from those of others, had entered menopause in early 1955. She seemed less attracted by previous interests, was more likely to be irritated, and withdrew from her previous maternal attitudes. She was subject to crying spells, manifesting less energy, more complaints, and increased expectations of others.

About the same time (and also related to the uncertainties regarding college) Bob became puritanically angry at his younger sister, although they had previously had a close and sympathetic relationship. He felt she was "running with the wrong crowd," that she had involved herself with the "wrong" man and, worst of all, was behaving in a disrespectful, irresponsible, and impudent manner. He knew, and said, that he could not have escaped censure had he acted that way. But, most important, his criticism and bitterness, openly expressed, brought about resentful quarrels and a subsequent break with his sister. Coincident with Bob's near failure in college and the financial complications arising from his attendance, his father began to show, in the form of gastrointestinal symptoms, the effects of strain. However, these symptoms did not deter him from his exhausting work, but rather forced an even more frenzied and hard-driving application to business interests. The father's response to the mother's emotional change was that of strenuous work over long hours while, as an executive, he took on complex tasks that promised one crisis after another. Mother and son shared the worry over the father's alleged foolhardiness; in Bob's case it turned to exasperation. Perhaps realistically, he wondered how necessary it was for his father to exert and punish himself so much when the return of a peptic ulcer threatened. The father's ways of dealing with his illness affected Bob's relations with both parents, adding to his problems of self-respect and feelings of inadequacy. While the father strove mightily and while he obviously had pain, he urged his son as he always had, to fear not and to perform better—At what price? the son might ask. Bob must have known the frustrations his father suffered in his self-incurred struggles. Perhaps as a parable of his attitudes to his father, Bob reported an incident that occurred in the fall of 1955 and involved his relations with a part-time employer. As assistant to a bartender, he was caused anguish by the demands of the latter that he have the courage to throw out unruly customers. Bob knew that at the same time this same man was stealing from the cash drawer.

For several years Bob had been courting a girl, with whom there was an informal understanding about marriage. This girl, named Dottie, as was his younger sister, we know little about, except that the state of his relationship with her heavily affected our patient's equilibrium. In very gross summary it seems to be true that by the fall of 1955 the courtship had gotten to the point where he felt pressed to commit himself, yet he did not feel secure enough to set a date for marriage. In early 1955, he thought he was involved in a pregnancy case as a result of a presumed interval of dalliance with another girl. The latter had married by that time out of malice toward Bob, but claimed to be pregnant by him. This episode threatened scandal, but proved a false alarm and taught him a stern lesson in fidelity. Bob thought he wanted to marry late in 1955, while his father, particularly, thought it a good idea that Bob become a "family man" and show his independence. The couple tacitly agreed upon the spring of 1956. In the midst of this excitement and during some celebrating at college, where he had very recently acquired the habit of taking some alcohol every night, he found himself on edge about the coming holidays and the trip home. He vaguely remembers having some diarrhea before the vacation, but this symptom dims in importance relative to the acute onset of his illness soon after coming home for Christmas.

From this account three main currents stand out, yet even these cannot be clearly disentangled.

First, there is evidence concerning the change in Bob's mother in the direction of withdrawal, depression, irritability, and less maternal dependability.

Secondly, perhaps as consequence of the change in Mrs. Neal, the father began to manifest a recurrence of his gastrointestinal illness and, at the same time, an increase in the over-compensating drive expressed through the search for business crises. He doubted more the advantages of supporting his son in college, urging better performance and more independence upon him, and advising incessantly that fear of the future should be shunned. Meanwhile, Bob did poorly in school and became dreadfully uncertain that he would have the funds to finish.

Thirdly, there was the commitment to marry, which seemed something thrust upon him rather than being sought and desired. He wondered whether he had dealt with another girl cruelly, and was partially relieved to find that he had not. In spite of insecurity about marriage, he felt that he was obliged to marry and hoped that he would find someone dependable. His troubles with his sister seem to represent the conflicts involving his fiancee and his mother, as well as the malice of an old rivalry that added to his guilt and shame. He felt an ambivalence involving anger and a wish to break from all three of these women, but this wish was opposed by his continuing needs. We know from both Bob and his mother that very shortly after the onset of the disease the older brother and sister petitioned the mother by letter (since Bob was then home and ill) that she not "baby" him as she always had.

The force of these trends in the year that preceded the onset of the illness is made more evident from what we learned about the patient's life history and from his reactions during the months of psychotherapy that followed admission.

### FAMILY HISTORY

The Neal family had two children by 1932. The father tells us that he left home early in his life and fought hard to protect his family during the depression. Though the Neals always had an income, the father's early experience warned him that he must be industrious if poverty were not to overtake him. The arrival of Bob, Jr., in the depth of the depression in 1932 undoubtedly posed some threat to the family security, although we have no way of really knowing how much. The Neals tell a story about Bob's birth that may reflect upon the significance to them of his arrival in the family. Mr. Neal tells it most dramatically: "But Bob was a little bit different than the rest of them. Did she tell you the way he was born? Well the children had the mumps when she was carrying Bob—or the whooping cough, that's what it was. So I took them up to my folks and left them and I went up to see them one night a week. When I got back, my gosh, the police was swarming all over the place. I went in there thinking, 'What in the world is wrong!' Well, her and this woman were sitting out on the front porch and my wife got up to go in the house to do something and a nigger came running out of the bedroom around the bed and jumped out the window. It liked to scare her to death. So she run out—we didn't have a telephone—she ran out the front door and started over to the neighbors and the neighbor's dog jumped off the porch and scared her. She was a nervous wreck! Well, the next morning Bob was born. That was on a Friday night 'cause Saturday I had to get the payroll out. I don't know whether that could affect a child or whether it would have made her feel any different towards him, but he was a good child, he slept good, and had very little sickness or anything else."

We have little doubt of the truth of this story with respect to the essentials of its plot. We have interpreted the story for its current significance as a kind of family legend to explain to the rest of the family why Bob is "different." The way that the parents tell the tale and the portentous meaning they attach to it make this episode a family legend with symbolic significance. They seem to speak of the anxiety Bob's birth signified. Each parent attributes the main fright to the other. Most evident is the indication of an intruder entering the home. Several times we have been asked for our opinion on the effect of this incident upon Bob's later development. In other words, they ask what effect their feelings had upon the intruder.

We know from the comments of everyone in the family that this child, with his father's name, was given extra care and protection by the mother. The mother admits to some of it, but denies that the term baby is descriptive of her attitudes. She claims to have sensed that this boy needed more, particularly in rivalrous situations with his siblings.

Some of Bob's memories constitute comments upon the effects of early childhood. He recalls the financial strain of buying a new house shortly after the birth of his younger sister, and that this house was endangered by the flooding river. The mother comments that actually the new house had been a step forward for the family, and that this same house was one of those most safe from the floods threatening their community. This memory at once depreciates the father and adopts his feeling of threat and insecurity. Bob relates another memory of childhood as though it were an episode of childish rebellion. He recalls collecting

Christmas trees from the neighborhood and piling them in the driveway to the extent that they blocked the father's entrance to the garage. Mother tells of the incident as though it was a bit of sportive behavior on the part of her son. Bob also tells—with some of the original terror—of being cornered in the back yard by rats and of being rescued by his mother. No one else remembers this incident, but there is little wonder that his mother felt he needed help in relations with his siblings. We know little of his later childhood, except that after the age of five or six, Bob was an appealing and outgoing boy according to the reports of both parents. By the time he entered high school he had acquired a severe form of examination anxiety, although he did his best to conceal his fear. This hiding was reinforced by his father's incessant and particular advice to stifle all recognition and expression of anxiety. "When it came to butting his head against a wall, when he *had* to do something, he had a psychological fear of it," his father said.

Nevertheless, Bob became a reasonably successful athlete as a high school varsity football and basketball player. This activity had his mother's enthusiastic sponsorship, an attitude she had acquired from her brothers. She was a spectator at all of his games, although the father never could find the time to attend even one of them. Although he had been more successful in these activities than in anything else in his life, Bob never talked of his athletic experience with any pride or pleasure.

He finished high school at the start of the Korean conflict and, managing to overcome his mother's stout resistance, entered the Navy, as had his brother before him. His recollection of the service career is characterized by a feeling of isolation and loneliness in relation to his fellow sailors. He recoiled from the language commonly used by the others, but he felt ashamed when he found himself speaking it. His ship was hit off the Korean coast by shore batteries. When his mother read the news, she became distraught, expecting to receive the announcement of his death. Bob was disgusted when he heard of his mother's reaction. This event had none of the terror for him that he felt when caught with a soiled uniform during an admiral's inspection.

## THERAPY

It can be appreciated that the doctor (J. R.) responsible for the psychotherapeutic part of the total treatment faced some difficult tasks. However, anyone experienced in such matters will know that the coordination and balance of the three methods of treatment (psychiatric, medical, and surgical) in a complicated case is difficult to maintain. Try as the psychotherapist may to coordinate the efforts of the internist and the surgeon with

o*

his own work, at times the collaboration becomes imperfect. Occasionally the psychiatrist will find himself making surgical and medical decisions certain to influence his relationship with the patient; at other times he will find that a decision has been made without his consultation and with which he would not have agreed. His treatment goals, his comprehension, his therapeutic anxieties, and his countertransference are all complicated by the delicate imbalances inevitably occurring in a three-way collaborative treatment. Although these were factors influencing the treatment of Bob Neal, they never completely upset his progress. Over the approximately 16 months of Bob's treatment on our service, his principal therapies consisted of steroids, two operations (an ileostomy and a colectomy, 10 and 13 months after hospital admission), and his work with the psychotherapist. To describe the nuances of the interactions between these approaches would require another study. In fact, it will be necessary to be cautious in interpreting the occurrences of relapse and remission as responses to psychotherapy. In this study we can hope only to learn more about the patient's conflicts and defenses, leaving aside the question of the absolute value of psychotherapy for ulcerative colitis.

Analysis of the purely verbal interaction of the first month of psychotherapy is of little use. In the interviews there was a halting and stereotyped expression of thought and feeling. He really doubted the value of this work, but tried to conform. Certainly, the acute phase of his physical illness affected his participation, and he slowly made some adjustment to the ward, the nurses, and other patients. Rorschach tests done shortly after admission and then repeated a month later show some change. In the beginning he was seen as an outwardly adjusted and conforming person with underlying detached and depreciative attitudes toward others. At a still deeper level there was evidence of angry frustration—of an individual who wanted much but expected only husks of things or token gratifications. He seemed regressed to an infantile level, but even there he was depressed. A month later, after improvement on steroids, Rorschach tests found him much the same, although there were increased indications of hostility and other signs of an enhanced willingness for emotional expression.

After this very halting, difficult beginning, Bob began to express some material relevant to his suspicion of the frightening power of his needs and feelings. He noted that he was worse when home on pass or when the psychotherapist was away. A struggle for power and control began to emerge as a feature of his relationship with his fiancee: "She is the one who can relax me." However, it was necessary that she be there at the right time and do the right things or she would disturb him more than anyone else. Meanwhile, he worried about the drain of the hospital expenses upon his father. Following one interview in which these problems with father and fiancee became associated, he suddenly acquired a sensitivity to one of his medicines and developed a distressing and massive urticaria. "Amazingly," the observer's notes state, the diarrhea and cramps disappeared for the duration of his skin disorder. Prior to this anxiety occurrence the therapist had decided to facilitate the relationship through a bit of role playing in which he became the "good doctor," on the patient's side, against the "bad doctors" who unfeelingly prescribed things to make him uncomfortable. We cannot say whether this maneuver was necessary, but it appeared to raise the question of the trust the patient could have in the relationship. He first doubted the therapist's reliability, then relaxed with him and hinted, shamefully, that he found himself at the apex of a triangle involving his doctor and the head nurse. However, at the same time, the therapist's role of siding with the patient led to expressions indicating that the doctor would bend to the patient's will, which produced tension in both Bob and the therapist. Bob could not find the relationship really gratifying and the doctor found Bob "demanding" and "oral-aggressive"—both irritating qualities. But then, for reasons no longer manifest, the psychotherapist began to take control enough to balance some of the patient's drives and, at that point, Bob seemed more a master of his own feelings and less fearful of abandonment. The therapy could by no means settle on this plateau, for there were other forces to contend with: problems with the family and fiancee, and difficult issues concerning the ulcerative colitis. However, Bob tried to hold the relationship at this mutually controlled level. He feared the anger that might break it and he resented the therapist when a decrease in his defensiveness was urged. He wondered how much was demanded of him in terms of psychiatric performance in therapy. The latter has a realistic basis, since it appeared that with physiological improvement the expectations of everyone—therapist, family, fiancee, and nurses—increased.

These trends in therapy brought from him memories of submission to his mother's urging during the year of illness before admission to our hospital. She would cheerfully suggest that he "go out" and enjoy himself to prove his strength, and that he widen his shrinking perspective. Although he had no enthusiasm at all for such activity, he would be afraid not to humor her. He also submitted, despite his own opinions, to her repeated suggestion that he ignore the doctor's advice and eat foods not on his prescribed diet. In fact, he was not tempted by these foods, but his mother thought he should be. Her urging seemed to say: "I am offering you signs of love, but you won't accept them." He felt guilty about resisting the foods that he thought it wrong to eat. These memories were associated with a description of the tenseness that had been present in the relationship with the mother since his return from the service. The "change of life" previously noted required more energy and more appeasement from the patient in order to maintain the old equilibrium. His father had warned that the mother had changed while Bob was away. He recalled ruefully in the same interview the closeness with his mother when he had been a successful athlete. It is possible that he longed for the days when the mother-son relationship had been mutually most gratifying.

Meanwhile, there seemed to be little chance for relaxation in the psychotherapy. This was never a relationship which permitted some quiet and rewarding reflection upon thoughts and feelings. There was a tautness, difficult to analyze at the time, which represented a push and pull in the interaction between doctor and patient. There could be no sharing, no peaceful discussion. Remarks had to be expressed or shamefully withheld while the patient expected to be pushed and pulled in the same manner. He tested repeatedly to see what would be required from him and what he could safely resist without the danger of severing the relationship. It was difficult as a therapist to see beyond the patient's stubbornness and his tendency to deal with every event in strictly literal terms. Although we see now that he wanted a dependent relation with the therapist, he wanted it to be without intrusion into emotions on the verbal level and without danger of anything unexpected. He said once, "You're just like my mother: you asked me if I wanted another appointment; I said, 'No,' and you came anyway." He went on to say that he could not understand why the therapy had to concern itself with such irritating matters as his worry over finances (father), dreams, and the idea "that I'm trying to hang on to some feelings." He could talk somewhat about his irritation towards his mother, since he felt at fault for that.

Thereafter, the more open hostility towards the therapist increased until headaches replaced bowel symptoms. This phase, in which the therapist was becoming pessimistic and shifting to the viewpoint that the patient needed surgery, seemed to be preparation for the next phase in the treatment. A more frankly dependent move occurred in which, in Bob's mind, the therapist became a clearly reliable person who made decisions, commiserated with the patient over his need for surgery and, in general, had taken or had been given the control of the relationship. Most likely this mutually controlled relationship repeated in an assuring way the early mother-child relationship. With very little trouble Bob provoked his fiancee to defy him and thus to give him reason for breaking the engagement. His reaction to this break was not intense. It seemed to have meaning only in the context of his new and more reliable symbiosis. He could afford to give up the fiancee at this point.

However, by this time surgery did seem indicated. The patient had had steroids so long and in such doses that it did not seem that he could soon relinquish them. Hence, rather than serving as a start for a long process of psychiatric treatment, the relationship was instead an aid in helping the patient through surgery.

For the purposes of this study the events in psychotherapy demonstrate for us the type of object relations our patient tends to form. We can see the push and pull, arduous for both Bob and his therapist, and how the interaction finally settled to some form of equilibrium in which the stronger member of the symbiosis has control but is also controlled.

In the following section, the causes of Bob's need for this kind of situation are sought in the milieu in which such habits were made necessary, the network of relationships within which Bob's personality developed—his family.

## THE NEAL FAMILY

Throughout the worst of Bob's illness, Mrs. Neal had been his faithful, though often insistent, nurse. During some of the most difficult times at home Bob was close to morphine addiction, and the prevention of this was arduous for mother and son. His sleep pattern reversed, and his mother sat with Bob through the hours from midnight to day talking endlessly of his childhood days. She commented: "I think it's been rough on me, since on top of it I'm going through the change of life. I said to a friend that maybe it's been a blessing in disguise, since maybe I would have given up to my own feelings had I not had him to worry about this year." In discussing this remark she explains at length that she "swallowed my own feelings." Anger, her disappointment regarding the lack of financial and social success, and depression were diverted into maternal care, pity, and worry over the adversities of another. Bob's illness revived, in many of its essentials, the guilt-appeasing, controlling, emotionally expensive symbiotic relationship of earlier days—but not quite!

In talking of herself Mrs. Neal was the most guarded of all. Although immensely voluble and indirect in telling of her life, she dealt with her own feelings and her personal history on a chatty and bland level. She was an only girl with three brothers, one of whom—the youngest—died when she was about seven. She had no memory of feelings about his death. She recalls a tiny and sickly mother, some kindly brothers, and a strong, authoritarian, and distant father. Family solidarity and respectability, without sign of emotional disturbance, was her ideal and a treasured memory of her childhood experience. She revealed slightly the feelings of insecurity imparted by her husband and reinforced by the realities of the economic depression, but these emotions were not nearly as intense as her perception of others' needs, particularly those of her husband and her third child, Bob. As mentioned above, she has no doubt that Bob required her special attention during childhood; she also knows that her husband has always disagreed and even resented this tendency. She said that the rest of the family thought she "favored" the third child, but she knows that it was simply that he needed her more.

Mr. Neal (Bob, Sr.) was far more open in talking of himself, at least in so far as he reveals his character. We see more clearly in him the nature of the equilibrium between needs and reactions to them, and between conflicts and adaptive techniques to quiet the anxiety arising from them.

In addition, Mr. Neal's personality stands out in his relations with Bob, Jr. He spoke first, and with affect, of his perception of an inability to speak effectively and comfortably to his children and particularly to the one who bore his name. He could see that his lifelong absorption in his work, and his consistently long hours had deprived him of the feelings of closeness and other gratifications his family might have afforded him. But, more self-righteously, he repeatedly told of how he had tried to convey a belief in fearlessness and independent strength. He felt he had demonstrated to his son what hard work could do for a man, and he emphasized hard work because he had known poverty in a large family as a boy, because it had been necessary that he support himself when he was 16, and because his mother had died shortly before he left home. The evidence is clear that the hard driving suited his angry fight against material insecurity, that it helped withdraw him from his need for love, that it reassured him that he could overcome his difficulties—in a word, overcompensation. In later years when economic adversity was not so threatening, Mr. Neal sought out and obtained executive positions which were not so financially rewarding as they were filled with unending crises and laced with complicated troubles. He is known in his business circles as one whom employers have given the thankless, troublesome tasks that require much worry and a 70-hour week. Mr. Neal enjoyed voicing his unconvincing complaints and he was genuinely proud that he had almost never had a vacation except for sick leaves.

The woman he left at home through all this—Mrs. Neal—was allowed to respond to his wishes for loving care only when he was troubled by his ulcer. He knew that he was usually too tired, too headachy, and too preoccupied to ask from her or give to her. When he wanted to yield a bit to his needs he had to "shove off" his wife's sympathy and affection. Currently he sometimes feels that even when he is ill his wife has lost her ways of approaching him, presumably because she had been held off so often.

There are indications that Mr. Neal permitted some warmth between himself and his older son and two daughters; but he was alienated from Bob somehow. He thinks that perhaps it was because of the protectiveness Mrs. Neal lavished on the boy, making it necessary for him to strengthen the child by the opposite treatment; it also seems that the special attitude of the mother towards Bob may further have shut out the father. The latter idea neatly rationalizes the father's own participation in frustration of his own needs.

He explains his conviction that his son needed to cultivate independence and fearlessness with an incident from Bob's boyhood: One evening, Bob was out when supper was served. His father went to fetch him and, finding him, called his name. The boy retreated further into the shadows. The father called again and walked towards him, but Bob ran again. Ignominiously he called and called into the silence, but had to go back without his son. He was deeply hurt and the question he never could face was, had he, the father, caused fear in his son? From that time he sought often to extinguish signs of anxiety in Bob and, in doing so, warned him repeatedly of the things feared by himself. His rivalry with his namesake could not help but emerge. When the mother was overprotective, father was "rough." It was this offspring who had to do the most to get his college education. It was Bob who, by implication, was the greatest drain on finances even before his illness. When young Bob was home long his father forcefully suggested marriage and a job elsewhere. When the mother worried about the son's illness, the father reassured her that death too could be tolerated; for after all, he had known the death of both parents and two siblings.

Mr. Neal had a recurrence of his ulcer just before Bob's admission to our hospital. Then, when the events in the hospital were most acute, Mr. Neal decided that, for the first time in more than 10 years, a vacation and rest were in order. Mrs. Neal agreed that her husband needed this trip with her; for once he seemed to be submitting to her wish to care for him. Near the end of Bob's hospitalization, when plans were being made, Mr. Neal again put forth his idea that his son would be better alone in a distant city. As we reflect on the problem the father, of course, seems to be wrong—but he was also right.

Ken Neal, 27 and Bob's older brother, is, in many respects, a model of his father. He has the self-assurance and complacent ease, but his exterior is not quite so brittle. He has rather successfully adopted the themes of independence and strength and he does not find it necessary to struggle quite so much to compensate for his need for some emotional attachment. He is a successful career officer in the Air Force, risen from the ranks. He moved from post to post, always seeking another technical school and cheerfully taking the distant assignment, claiming he needed no place to "light." In his relationships he was outwardly noncommittal and nonchalant. He was matter-of-fact about his mother's forceful attitudes. He recognized her needs and put distance between himself and her. He was sympathetic, but not especially worried or stirred emotionally by his brother's illness. In fact, he seemed not at all surprised that an illness would bind his mother and brother. He agreed with the father's idea that

Bob should depart from his parents' home. In our contacts with Ken he revealed the conflictful side of himself in only two ways: one of these was characteristic, the other a surprise. First, he told us with little affect that he had been twice engaged. He had drifted rather easily from the first relationship and the second was near a break at the time of our interviews. About a week before, he had planned a marriage after his fiancee had proposed it; a law suit involving the girl had then intervened. He rather dispassionately accepted the interruption and seemed little concerned whether the marriage would ever take place.

Near the end of our last talk, Ken was asked if he had any questions. Without change in facial expression he said, "Well, I get lonely sometimes." Then he halted and floundered a little before adding, "I have one thing that bothers me. I can't express any emotion. I have a terrible time with it. I want to stay just as far away from emotion as I can. I hate to get emotionally involved, even with my family. It hurts me . . . it hurts them sometimes, I know." This sudden expression is surprising from a taciturn young man who joins the rest of his family in the unity of dampening feeling, and in upholding the family ideal that emotional quiet and a respectable calm must be maintained in family life.

We are not at all certain of our data concerning the two sisters, since we have not seen them. However, from the corroborating comments of the others we have strong hints that Doris, 29, the oldest, is a slightly more rigid and imperious version of her mother. Dottie, 22, must have been— in the view of this family—"spoiled," since she is more truly independent and boisterous than the rest. She was obviously a rugged competitor with her brother.

## AN ATTEMPT AT FAMILY ANALYSIS

Remaining is the goal of demonstrating from the above account that, in Bob's case, the rigid and confining patterns of object relations were not only formed in the binary mother-child symbiosis, but were conditioned by the multidimensional matrix of object relations constituting the field in which his personality developed. When we attempt, in studies of human behavior, to analyze events occurring in multidimensional fields rather than in simple binary systems, we compound our difficulties. However it is the argument of this paper that the ways of forming and selecting object relations are shaped in a complex system such as the family.

We have chosen to simplify this task for ourselves and the reader in the following paragraphs by describing a number of interpersonal cycles which, in time, fixed the type of interpersonal relations Bob would have to make in adolescence and maturity. These cycles are conceptually designed to depict the flow of feelings and conflicts among family members. It is possible to construct an almost endless number of these cycles. Their schematic nature allows only a summary of the complexity of incessantly interacting systems. We hypothesize that most of these cycles operate simultaneously, and that the one on which we concentrate at any moment is determined by our point of view at the time. However, one or more may predominate in particular aspects of the family transactions and also at one time in the family's history. It is our thesis that the whole field—that is, all the individuals—is involved and influenced by each of the cycles. For the sake of convenience and simplicity in this paper the field will be limited to the mother, father, and patient—a system complex enough for a first attempt. The others, nevertheless, influence this three-person system in many ways. [Lindemann[8] has used a similar conceptual scheme in the explanation of his hypotheses concerning the key object relation in the pathogenesis of ulcerative colitis.]

The basic cycle operating in the relationship of these three began before Bob was born. It had its overt impact briefly and then was deeply buried, although it made the succeeding family adaptations necessary. Figure 1 is a graphic representation of the cycle. In this and subsequent representations, *M, F,* and *S* signify mother, father, and son, respectively.

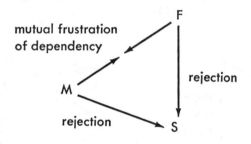

FIGURE 1

The mutual frustration of dependency needs in a mother who needed more than she seemed and a father who, for a long time, greatly feared poverty, led to the unconscious wish that they could exclude an additional burden from their family and home. Maintenance of equilibrium in a system functioning like this cycle is impossible. It is potentially explosive, and each of the three family members must be driven off.

Hence, two more cycles come into almost immediate operation (Fig. 2).

In the first of these two cycles the mother compensates partially for her dependency needs and counteracts her guilt by maternalizing

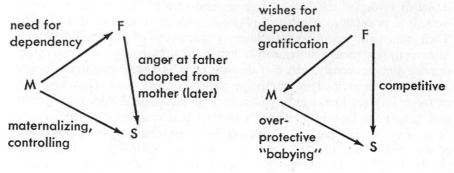

FIGURE 2

the new son. In a sense, the mother obtains an opportunity for expression of her own needs, but the father gets only a rival. Later, the son adopts the style of his mother's angry feelings toward the husband and father. In the second cycle the mother's "babying" of her son intensifies the father's competitive feelings.

The father's defensiveness is the main impetus for another set of cycles in which we can use the almost identical terms given us by father and son for their feelings towards the mother: shoving her off when they perceive any need for her (Fig. 3).

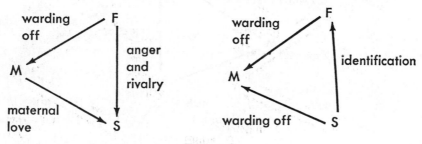

FIGURE 3

Father has to ward off mother as part of his overcompensation, but still feels the rivalry towards his son as the mother is pushed into expressing maternal love to him. However, to help balance the system, the son identifies with the father, and does his own warding off.

The situation which most probably was significant in the precipitation of Bob's illness is shown in Figure 4.

Essentially the above cycle is initiated by the mother's withdrawal

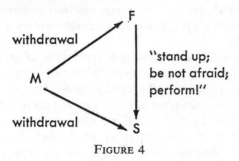

FIGURE 4

from both father and son as a result of a menopausal depression. The father reacts in his usual manner (with overcompensation) and competitively demands that his son show the same alleged courage. But Bob's defenses are not so well developed, and thus his father's attitudes towards him only intensify the reactions to the relative loss of the mother. An attempt at renewal of the old symbiosis leads to a cycle which involves the whole family (Fig. 5).

The siblings' and father's feelings in response to the mother's withdrawal stimulates rivalry toward the one who has supposedly enjoyed the most maternalizing in this family. There are not many possibilities for achieving an equilibrium in this cycle unless the illness causes a major shift in the total family adaptation. An escape was needed, and it was most likely that this would involve sickness.

Several other reconstructions are possible to conceptualize the dynamics of this family as a history and as a factor in the precipitation of our patient's ulcerative colitis. Our motive is primarily illustrative: to

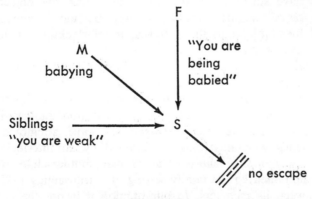

FIGURE 5

show that reconstructions can be made—by our schematic cycles or by some other evaluative system which attempts to span the entire field of family relations.

The family's adaptation involved resolution of a conflict between frustrated needs for dependency and the family ideal of independence, respectability, and avoidance of allegedly selfish desires. To do this, the members of the family must remain, for as long as possible, deeply committed to each other. In the process of this devotion to common needs there must be no overt demonstration of individual needs, since such an eruption would compromise the family ideals. There can not be the slightest hint of the emotions which arise from frustration of needs. Our methods of study of this family revealed that, to accomplish this resolution, a definite organization of family life is required. Essentially, the organization in the Neal family consists of the maintenance of a rigid system from which the unexpected and the uncertain are eliminated. Roles within this organization are carefully prescribed and rigidly adhered to. For the maintenance of emotional tranquillity this family requires that communication be confined largely to the matter-of-fact; vagueness, excitement, or disturbance are shunned. Nevertheless, there must be some break-through and when this occurs it can be extreme. The stereotyped form of communication cannot permit much perception of another's inner feelings. In our summarizing phrase—anxious cohesion—for a family of this kind, we refer to a quality of family life in which the individuals maintain almost desperately their cohesion as a group at the high cost of *underlying* anxiety.

## SUMMARY

1. We have suggested in this case study that the object relations aspects of psychosomatic hypotheses may be more comprehensively investigated by inquiry into the patterns of interlocking relationships in the family. Use of the field study method of the anthropologist in observing the whole family provides a view in depth of important relationships, instead of reports from the individual patient.

2. We have proposed an expansion of current hypotheses concerning the object relations aspects of predisposition and etiology in psychosomatic research. In the case discussed we have attempted to show that the patient's adaptation was conditioned by an interlocking set of relationships within the family. The crucial mother-child relationship was itself conditioned by the family setting as a transacting field of object relations between its members. In our opinion it is not the *mother* who affects the child, but the *family's mother,* whose relationship with the

child is a product of the dynamics operating within the family as a social system.

# NOTES

1. Research reported in this paper was supported by research grants M999 and M2534 from the National Institute for Mental Health, U. S. Public Health Service, Bethesda, Md.
2. ENGEL, G. L. Studies of ulcerative colitis III. The nature of the psychological processes. *Am. J. Med. 19:*231, 1955.
3. TITCHENER, J., and EMERSON, R. Some methods for the study of family interaction in personality development. *Psychiat. Res. Rep. 10:*72, 1958.
4. ACKERMAN, N. W. *The Psychodynamics of Family Life.* New York, Basic Books, 1958.
5. CHANCE, E. *Families in Treatment.* New York, Basic Books, 1959.
6. KLUCKHOHN, F., and SPIEGEL, J. (Eds.) Integration and conflict in family behavior; a report of the Committee of the Group for the Advancement of Psychiatry. Report #27, 1954.
7. BATESON, G., JACKSON, D., HALEY, D., and WEAKLAND, J. Toward a theory of schizophrenia. *Behavioral Science 1:*4, 1956.
8. LINDEMANN, E. Modifications in the course of ulcerative colitis in relationship to changes in life situations and reaction patterns. Life stress and bodily disease. *Proc. A. Res. Nerv. & Ment. Dis. 29:*706, 1950.

# 20:

# The Emotionally Disturbed Child
# as the Family Scapegoat

*Ezra F. Vogel* and *Norman W. Bell*

The phenomenon of scapegoating is as old as human society. Sir James Frazer records, in *The Golden Bough,*[1] numerous instances, reaching back to antiquity, of public scapegoats, human and other. He views the process of scapegoating as one in which ". . . the evil influences are embodied in a visible form or are at least supposed to be loaded upon a material medium, which acts as a vehicle to draw them off from the people, village, or town."[2] The scapegoat's function ". . . is simply to effect a total clearance of all the ills that have been infesting a people."[3] Frazer was dealing with the phenomenon at the level of a society, tribe, village, or town. It is the purpose of this paper to examine the same phenomenon within families, by viewing an emotionally disturbed child as an embodiment of certain types of conflicts between parents. This pattern is a special case of a common phenomenon, the achievement of group unity through the scapegoating of a particular member. It is, perhaps, more widely known that a group may achieve unity through projection of hostilities to the outside,[4] but there are also a large number of cases where members of a particular group are able to achieve unity through scapegoating a particular member of that group. Thus, the deviant within the group may perform a valuable function for the group, by channeling group tensions and providing a basis for solidarity.

The notion that the family is in large part responsible for the emotional health of the child is a compelling one in contemporary behavioral science. By and large, however, the research has focused largely on the mother-child relationship, and the independent variable by which the mother-child relationship and the child-rearing practices are usually ex-

Reprinted with permission of the Free Press from *A Modern Introduction to the Family,* edited by Norman W. Bell and Ezra F. Vogel. Copyright © 1960 by The Free Press, a Corporation. Ezra F. Vogel is research associate, Center for East Asian Studies, Harvard University. His research interests have migrated from the study of mental health in the family to the study of the Japanese family to the study of larger aspects of Japanese and Chinese society. Norman W. Bell is identified in the footnote to Chapter 16.

plained is the personality and developmental history of the mother. Recently, an attempt has also been made to treat the father-child relationship, again largely in terms of the personality and developmental history of the father. While in clinical practice there is some awareness of family dynamics, in the literature the family has largely been treated simply as a collection of personalities, and the child's personality development has been seen almost exclusively as a direct result of the separate personalities of his parents.[5] Rarely is the interaction of parents treated as a significant independent variable influencing childhood development. Even when broader cultural patterns have been considered, childhood development has been related to child-rearing practices and socialization into the culture, with little consideration of the family as the mediating unit.

Data for this paper are derived from the intensive study[6] of a small group of "disturbed" families, each with an emotionally disturbed child, and a matched group of "well" families without clinically manifest disturbance in any child. Of the nine families in each group, three were Irish-American, three Italian-American, and three old-American. The families were seen by a team including psychiatrists, social workers, psychologists, and social scientists. The disturbed families, on which this paper is based, were seen weekly in the offices of a psychiatric clinic and in their homes over periods ranging from one to four years. Detailed information was gathered about the members' developmental histories and character structure, but even more specific data were obtained about current processes.

The present paper is concerned with how a child in the family, the emotionally disturbed child, was used as a scapegoat for the conflicts between parents and what the functions and dysfunctions of this scapegoating are for the family.

In all the disturbed families it was found that a particular child had become involved in tensions existing between the parents.[7] In the "well" families used for control purposes, either the tensions between the parents were not so severe or else the tensions were handled in such a way that the children did not become pathologically involved. In general, both parents of the emotionally disturbed child had many of the same underlying conflicts, but in relationship to each other, they felt themselves to be at opposite poles, so that one spouse would act out one side of the conflict and the other would act out the other side of the conflict. They had developed an equilibrium in which they minimized contact with each other and minimized expressions of affect, particularly hostility, which they strongly felt for each other, and this made it possible for them to live with each other.[8] But this equilibrium had many difficulties, the most serious of which was the scapegoating of a child.

## 1. SOURCES OF TENSION THAT LEAD
## TO SCAPEGOATING

It is our contention that scapegoating is produced by the existence of tensions between parents which have not been satisfactorily resolved in other ways. The spouses in the disturbed families had deep fears about their marital relationship and about the partner's behavior. They did not feel they could predict accurately how the other would respond to their own behavior. Yet, the other's response was of very great importance and was thought to be potentially very damaging. The partners did not feel they could deal with the situation by direct communication, because this might be too dangerous, and they resorted to manipulations of masking, evading, and the like. This atmosphere of tension has several sources. One of the sources was the personality problems of each spouse, but in the present analysis the focus will be on the group sources of the tension. These tensions usually have several sources. At a very general level, one of the main sources of tension was conflict in cultural value orientations.[9] Value orientations are abstract, general conceptions of the nature of human nature and man's relationship to it, of man's relation to man, of the most significant time dimension, and of the most valued type of activity. All societies have preferences and alternative preferences to these basic dimensions; these preferences are expressed within a wide range of phenomena. In complex ways, they are related to personality and social structure and to more specific values. When people are in the process of acculturation, as was the case with the families of Irish and Italian backgrounds, many possibilities for value-orientation conflict arise. Any one individual may have been socialized into conflicting or confused patterns, and be unsuccessful in bridging the gap. Marriage partners may have been socialized into different patterns and be working on different assumptions. All our disturbed families had problems of these sorts. Some were trying to shift quickly to a set of orientations they had not thoroughly internalized, and without having neutralized previous orientations. Others were trying to live by conflicting orientations.[10]

A common example of the cultural value conflicts was the conflict centered around the problems of individual performance. There were considerable pulls toward the American middle-class achievement patterns. In families which had partially internalized both sets of value orientations, it was impossible to live up to both sets of values, and whichever the family chose, this meant that certain conflicts would result.

Another source of tension was the relations of the family and the larger community. Disturbed families usually had problems in this area, rejecting and/or being rejected by the community. In some cases, a family had very severe disapproval of a very close-knit ethnic neighborhood directed at them. In other cases, families had moved from ethnic neighborhoods to more fashionable suburbs and suffered in their own eyes by comparison to their new neighbors. Consequently, their social relationships with these neighbors were often minimal; when they did exist, they were usually strained or else one spouse had fairly good relationships with some friends and the partner had poor relationships with these friends. All families, to a greater or lesser extent, had problems in their relationships with families of orientation. Typically, the wife was strongly attached to her parents and antagonistic towards her husband's family, while the husband was attached to his parents and antagonistic to his wife's family. If either spouse was critical of his in-laws, the partner typically defended his own parents and became more critical of his in-laws. If one spouse was critical of his own parents, the partner was often friendly to them. The unbalanced attachments to parents and parents-in-law was not resolved. Changes usually produced more tension, but the basic sources of strain remained unchanged.[11]

## 2. THE SELECTION OF THE SCAPEGOAT

The tensions produced by unresolved conflicts were so severe that they could not be contained without some discharge. It is not surprising that some appropriate object was chosen to symbolize the conflicts and draw off the tension. Conceivably, some person or group outside the family could serve in this capacity. However, in these disturbed families, the parents had by and large internalized the standards of the surrounding community sufficiently so that they had great difficulty in finding a legitimate basis for scapegoating outsiders. In addition, most of these families had very tenuous ties with the community, and since they were very concerned about being accepted, they could not afford to antagonize their associates. While some of the families did, at times, have strong feelings of antagonism toward various members of the community in which they lived, they could rarely express this antagonism directly. Even if at times they were able to manifest their antagonism, this usually led to many additional complications, and the family preferred to scapegoat its own child.[12]

Channeling the tensions within the family did not lead to difficulties with the outside, but usually the latent hostilities between the husband and wife made it very difficult to deal with problems openly between them. There was always danger the partner might become too angry, which would lead to severe and immediate difficulties. A number of factors made a child the most appropriate object through which to deal with family tensions. First of all, the child was in a relatively powerless position compared to the parents. While he was dependent on the parents and could not leave the family, he was not able effectively to counter the parents superior power. Although the parents' defenses were fairly brittle in comparison with those of well parents, still their defenses were much stronger than those of their children. Because the child's personality is still very flexible, he can be molded to adopt the particular role which the family assigns to him. When the child does take on many of the characteristics which the parents dislike in themselves and each other, he becomes a symbolically appropriate object on which to focus their own anxieties. Since the person scapegoated often develops such severe tensions that he is unable to perform his usual task roles, it is important that those family members performing essential, irreplaceable functions for the family not be scapegoated. The child has relatively few tasks to perform in the family, compared to the parents or other elders, and his disturbance does not ordinarily interfere with the successful performance of the necessary family tasks. The "cost" in dysfunction of the child is low relative to the functional gains for the whole family.

In all cases, with partial exception of one family, a particular child was chosen as the scapegoat, while other children were relatively free of pathology. The selecting of a particular child is not a random matter; one child is the best symbol. Just as a dream condenses a variety of past and present experiences and a variety of emotional feelings, the scapegoat condenses a variety of social and psychological problems impinging on the family.

Who is selected as the scapegoat is intimately related to the sources of tension. Where value-orientation conflicts existed, the child chosen was the one who best symbolized these conflicts. For example, if the conflicts revolved about achievement, a child who failed to achieve according to expectations could become the symbol of failure. Alternatively, a child might be an appropriate object because he was achieving independently and thus violating norms of loyalty to the group.

The position of the child in the sibling group frequently became a focus for the unresolved childhood problems of the parents. If the parents' most serious unresolved problems were with male figures, the child chosen to represent the family conflict was usually a male child. Similarly, sibling order could be a strong factor. If one or both parents had difficulties with older brothers, an older boy in the family might become the scapegoat.

In two cases, the sex or sibling position of the child seemed to be particularly important in the selection of a particular child as the family scapegoat. In one of these cases, the mother was the oldest of three siblings and had considerable feelings of rivalry with her next younger sister which had never been effectively resolved. Although the father had two older siblings, they were so much older that to him they were a separate family.

In his effective family environment, he was the older of two children and had considerable feelings of rivalry toward a younger brother who displaced him and for whom he subsequently had to care. This couple has three children, and there was an unusual amount of rivalry between the oldest and the second sibling. Both the parents sided very strongly with the oldest child. They were continuously conscious of the middle child bothering the older, for which they severely criticized this middle child. There are many striking parallels, even to small details, in the relationship between the parents and their next younger siblings and the relationship between their oldest child and the next younger sibling.

Another pattern revolved about the identification of a child with a parent whom he resembled. This was found in all families, sick and well, in one form or another; but in the disturbed families, the child was seen as possessing very undesirable traits, and although the parent actually possessed the same traits, the focus of attention was the child and not the parent. In one family, in particular, this pattern was striking. The father and the eldest son had very similar physical characteristics; not only did they have the same first name but both were called by the same diminutive name by the mother. At times, the social worker seeing the mother was not certain whether the mother was talking about her husband or her son. The wife's concerns about the husband's occupational adequacy were not dealt with directly, but the focus for her affect was the child and his school performance. In fact, the son was criticized by his mother for all the characteristics which she disliked in her husband, but she was unable to criticize her husband directly for these characteristics. She channeled all her feelings, especially anxiety and hostility, to the child, although her husband had similar problems. Furthermore, in order to control her feelings toward her husband, she remained very aloof and distant and was not able to express to him her positive or negative feelings. While she channeled many criticisms and anxieties through the child, she also expressed many of her positive feelings to the child, thereby leading to severe Oedipal conflicts. The husband was not happy about his wife being so aloof from him, but on the other hand he found that by co-operating with his wife in criticizing the child, he was able to keep the burden of problems away from himself. He thus joined with the wife in projecting his own difficulties and problems onto the child and in dealing with them as the child's problems rather than as his own.

In three of the families, the scapegoat had considerably lower intelligence than did the other children in the family. In all these families, there were serious conflicts about the value of achievement, and the parents had great difficulty themselves in living up to their own achievement aspirations. In all these three cases, the parents were unable to accept the fact that their children had limited abilities, and they continually held up impossible standards for these children. Although all three children had I.Q.'s in the 80's or below and had failed one grade or more, all three mothers stated that they intended that their children should go to college. At the beginning of therapy, one of the mothers hoped her son would attend medical school and become a doctor; another had begun to put away a small amount of money from a very tight budget for her daughter's college education, even though the daughter's intelligence was that of a moron. At the beginning of therapy, none of the parents was able to deal directly with his own difficulties in achievement. In contrast, in one of the families, there were two children in the family who had very low intelligence, one of whom had failed a grade in school, but the family scapegoat was a boy who had normal intelligence. In this case, the parents, who had average intelligence, had resolved their conflicts about achievement by denying that they were interested in achievement and accepting their social position. This child of slightly higher intelligence and greater physical activity was seen by them as a very aggressive child who was always doing too much, and the parents were continually worried that he was "too smart."[12]

In a number of cases, the disturbed child either had a serious physical disease when he was young or a striking physical abnormality such as a hare lip, bald spots in the hair, or unusually unattractive facial features. The mere existence of some such abnormality seemed to draw attention to one particular child, so that if there were some sorts of anxieties or problems in the family at all, the child with the physical peculiarities seemed to become the focus of the family problems. Here again, however, it was not the mere existence of a physical defect but its meaning[14] in the life of the family which gave it its significance. For example, in some families there was a feeling that they had committed certain sins by not living up to their ideals, for instance by using contraceptives. This was a very common problem, since many families could not possibly live up to the two opposing sets of ideals which they had at least partially internalized. The child's physical abnormality became a symbol of the family's sin of not having lived up to some partially internalized values, and the malformed child was seen as a sinful child who was not living up to the standards of the group. Since the family's relationship with the community was often tenuous, the fact that one of their children had physical abnormalities that made the child the focus of neighborhood ridicule served to make the parents increasingly ashamed of the child's physical characteristics and to focus increasingly more attention on this child. For example, one of the main concerns of the family with the unusually ugly child was that other children were continually teasing her about her appearance. However, the concern was less for the child herself, and more for the whole family. Her problems symbolized the parents' past and present problems with the neighborhood; rather than sympathize with the child, they abused her all the more. In another case in which a female child's physical illness became a focus of the family's problems, the parents were extremely concerned about her safety, which was again related in part to the potential dangers in social relationships with the outside world. As a result of the girl's illness, the family became much more cautious than was necessary, and on some occasions they were even reluctant to accept medical advice that she could participate in certain activities without danger to her health. The continual contacts that the child had with middle-class professional personnel through hospitalization and clinic visits led her to accept certain middle-class American values more than did the rest of the family, and the family was continually expressing the feeling that she had different attitudes after hospitalization and contact with hospital personnel. The disliked attitudes ascribed to the child were in general those of middle-class American culture.[15] Not only abnormalities but general body type could become the symbol to call forth scapegoating. In two families, the spouses had many problems in their sexual life. Rather than face these maladjustments directly, the problems were expressed through concern about the masculinity and normality of a slender, graceful son.

While the general process of symbolization of a scapegoat is very similar to the dream symbolization, there is one problem in the family selection of a scapegoat which is not met in the selection of a dream symbol, and that is the problem of availability. While in dreams, any symbolic representation is open to the dreamer, in the family only a very small number of children are available as the potential scapegoats. Hence, when there is a serious family problem and no child is an appropriate symbol of the problem, there must be considerable cognitive distortion in order to permit the most appropriate one available to be used as a scapegoat. For example, in one family which was very concerned about the problems of achievement, the focus of the family's problems was the eldest son. Although he was receiving passing grades in school, whereas the parents had had very poor school records, the parents were very critical of his school performance. Because of this pressure, the child worked hard and was able to get somewhat better marks on his next report card. However, the mother stoutly maintained that her son didn't deserve those grades, that he must have cheated, and she continued to criticize him for his school performance.

The other aspect of the problem of availability resulted from the fact that the parents apparently have had tensions since early in marriage. As nearly as it was possible to reconstruct the marital history, it appeared that the spouses had selected each other partly on the basis of the fact that they shared many of the same conflicts and understood each other quite well. Not long after marriage, however, they seemed to have become polarized in their conflicts, so that one parent represented one side of the conflict and the other represented the other side. This seems to have given each of the spouses a way of handling his own conflicts and allowed each to remain fairly consistent and well integrated by projecting difficulties onto the partner. However, it also led to very severe difficulties in the marital relationship and created many tensions which were quickly displaced onto the first available and appropriate object, very often the first child. Since the eldest child was the first one available for scapegoating, he often seems to have been assigned this role and, once assigned, has continued in it. Perhaps because of his prior availability and his closer involvement in the adult world, he is a more appropriate object for the scapegoating.[16] In the one case in which a child was able to escape the scapegoat role by decreasing his attachment to the home, the next most appropriate child was used in the scapegoat role.

### 3. INDUCTION OF THE CHILD INTO THE SCAPEGOAT ROLE

If the child is to be a "satisfactory" scapegoat, he must carry out his role as a "problem child." The problem behavior must be reinforced strongly enough so that it will continue in spite of the hostility and anxiety it produces in the child. This delicate balance is possible only because the parents have superior sanction power over the child, can define what he should or should not do, and control what he does or does not do. This balance necessarily requires a large amount of inconsistency in the ways parents handle the child.

The most common inconsistency was between the implicit (or unconscious) and the explicit role induction.[17] In all cases, certain behavior of the child violated recognized social norms. In some instances stealing, fire-setting, expressions of hostility, or unco-operativeness affected the child's relationships with people outside the family. In other instances, bed-wetting, resistance to parental orders, or expression of aggression to siblings affected relationships in the family. But in all instances, while the parents explicitly criticized the child and at times even punished him, they supported in some way, usually implicitly, the persistence of the very behavior which they criticized. This permission took various forms: failure to follow through on threats, delayed punishment, indifference to and acceptance of the symptom, unusual interest in the child's symptom, or considerable secondary gratification offered to the child because of his symptom. The secondary gratification usually took the form of special attention and exemption from certain responsibilities. While the parents had internalized social norms sufficiently to refrain from violating the norms themselves, they had not sufficiently internalized them to prevent giving encouragement to their children for acting out their own repressed wishes. The wish to violate these norms was transferred to the child, but the defenses against this wish were never as strong in the child.[18]

Another type of inconsistency seen was that one parent would encourage one type of behavior, but the other parent would encourage an opposing type of behavior. The result again was that the child was caught in the conflict. This also permitted one spouse to express annoyance to the other indirectly without endangering the marital relationship. For example, in one case, the father objected to the son's leaving toys lying around and would violently explode at the child for such behavior, implying that the mother was wrong in permitting him to do this. The mother realized that the father exploded at such behavior and did not stop the father since she "knew he was right." Nevertheless, she often indicated that the child need not bother picking up the toys, since she felt that he was too young to have to do such things by himself and that the father was too strict. If the mother's encouragement of the behavior annoying to the father was explicit, there would be danger that the father's hostility would be directed at the mother rather than the child. By keeping the encouragement implicit the mother was able to deny that she had encouraged the child. The father was usually willing to accept this denial, even if he did not believe it, rather than risk an explosion with his wife. In some instances, however, the other spouse was angered or felt compelled to criticize the other for not handling the child properly. Then the encouragement of the child to behave in a certain way would have to become more subtle to avoid criticism of the other spouse, another delicate balance to maintain. A parent had to give sufficient encouragement to the child to perform the act, without making it so obvious that his spouse felt obliged to criticize him.

In addition to the inconsistent pressures resulting from the difference between explicit and implicit expectations and from the differences between the expectations of the two parents, the child also had to deal with changes in each parent's expectations. From the parent's conscious point of view, this inconsistency resulted from an attempt to reconcile two conflicting desires: teaching the child to behave properly and not being "too hard on the child." When a parent was consciously attempting to teach the child proper behavior, he was extremely aggressive and critical.[19] At other times, the parent felt he had been too critical of the child and permitted him to behave in the same way without punishment, and would be extremely affectionate and supportive. While the explanation given for this inconsistency was that he wanted to teach the desired behavior without being "too hard on the child," its latent function was to prevent the child from consistently living up to the ostensibly desired behavior and to preserve the disliked behavior. The period of not being "too hard on the child" served to reinforce the disapproved behavior and the period of "being firm" permitted the parents to express their anxieties and hostility. This balance was also very delicate since it was always possible that negative sanctions would become so severe that the child would refuse to behave in such a way that parents felt he could legitimately be punished.

The delicacy of this balance was perhaps best exemplified by the problem of bed-wetting. Parents complained about bed-wetting, but at the same time they could not bring themselves to do anything to alter the child's behavior. If the therapists could get both parents to be firm at the same time, the child would usually stop bed-wetting. Very soon, however, by putting a rubber sheet on the bed, or buying special night clothes "just in case he wets," the child was encouraged again to wet. One mother succeeded several times in finding methods to stop her son's wetting, but immediately stopped using them "since he's stopped now." In several cases, the parents would alternate in being concerned and trying to be firm and being unconcerned and implicitly encouraging the behavior, at all times remaining inconsistent, one with the other. It seemed clear that whether or not the child wet his bed was a relatively sensitive index of just where the balance of rewards from the parents lay. In general, however, the implicit demands carried the greater sanction power and the child continued with the behavior of which the parents unconsciously approved and consciously disapproved. Presumably, the sanctions of the parents against bed-wetting would increase as the child grew older, and the balance would become delicate only at that later time.

Since these conflicting expectations existed over a long period of time, it is not surprising that the child internalized these conflicts. Once a child was selected as a deviant, there was a circular reaction which tended to perpetuate this role assignment. Once he had responded to his parents' implicit wishes and acted in a somewhat disturbed manner, the parents could treat him as if he really were a problem. The child would respond to these expectations and the vicious cycle was set in motion. Both the child and the parents, then, had complementary expectations. The particular role assigned to the child was appropriately rewarded. It is difficult, if not impossible, to distinguish just at what point the parents began treating the child as if he were a problem and at what point the child actually did have internalized problems. There does not seem to be any sudden development of the child's problems; rather, it is a process occurring over a period of time. By the time the family was seen in the clinic, the vicious cycle was well established, and the child had internalized his disturbed role to such an extent that it was difficult to effect change only by removing external pressures. This was, of course, particularly true for older and more disturbed children. The fact that the child becomes disturbed adds stability to the role system, so that once set in motion, scapegoating did not easily pass from one child to another. In the well families, when scapegoating did take place, it was less severe and did not become stabilized with one child as a continual scapegoat.

## 4. THE RATIONALIZATION OF SCAPEGOATING

When a scapegoating situation was established, a relatively stable equilibrium of the family was achieved. However, there were difficulties in maintaining the equilibrium. Parents had considerable guilt about the way they treated the child, and when the child was identified as disturbed by neighbors, teachers, doctors, or other outside agencies, pressure was brought to bear for some action to be taken. When called upon to explain, parents did not have much difficulty in explaining why they were so concerned about the child, but they did have great difficulty in rationalizing their aggressive and libidinal expressions to the children.

One way in which the parents rationalized their behavior was to define themselves, rather than the children, as victims. They stressed how much difficulty there was coping with all the problems posed by their child. For example, mothers of bed-wetters complained about the problems of keeping sheets clean and the impossibility of the child staying overnight at friends' or relatives' homes. Such rationalizations seemed to relieve some of the guilt for victimizing the children and served as a justification for continued expressions of annoyance toward the children.

Another way was to emphasize how fortunate their children really were. For most of these parents, the standard of living provided for their children was much higher than the standard of living they enjoyed when they were children. One of the central complaints of these parents, particularly the fathers, was that the children wanted too much and got much more than the parents ever got when they were children. This was seen by the parents as a legitimate excuse for depriving their children of the toys, privileges, and other things they wanted, and for refusing to recognize the children's complaints that they were not getting things. A closely related type of rationalization stems from the change of child-rearing practices over the past generation. The parents felt that their parents were much stricter than they were with their children and that children nowadays "get away with murder." Many of the parents had acute conflicts about how strict to be with children, and when the parents did express aggression to the children, they often defined it as beneficial strictness and "giving the child a

P

lesson." Since their own parents were much more severe with them, their own children don't realize "how good they have it."

The parents also used various specific norms to justify their behavior. Even though the parents may be giving implicit encouragement to break these norms, the fact that these social norms are explicitly recognized gives the parents a legitimate basis for punishing the children. As long as the permission for disobeying the sanctions is implicit, it is always possible for the parents to deny that they are really giving it. In general, these parents were reluctant to admit that their child had an emotional disturbance or that he was behaving the way he was because of certain inner problems. They generally interpreted the disturbed child's behavior as willful badness. They felt that the child could behave differently if he really wanted to. Hence, what was needed, in their view, was not consideration, advice, and help, but a "lesson" in how to behave, i.e., severe reprimands and punishment; but even this they could not give. At times, the parents attempted to deny completely that they were scapegoating this particular child. They insisted very rigidly that "we treat all the children just the same." At other times, the parents insisted that this one particular child was just different from all others, implying that this child deserved punishment and that they were good parents since their other children have turned out so well.

Frequently, the mothers expressed, although inconsistently, unusually strong affection for a son. They justified this almost invariably in the same way: the child had problems and difficulties and thus needed more help and care than the other children. However, what they considered care and protection far exceeded the usual limits. This can be seen for example, in the mother who carried her twelve-year-old son from the bed to the bathroom so that he could avoid bed-wetting, in the mother who continually fondled her adolescent son and called him "lovie," and in the frequent slips of the tongues by a variety of family members which identified the mother and son as spouses. Fathers, on the other hand, often had special attachments to, and fondness for, daughters.

All these attempts of the parents to rationalize their behavior had a very defensive quality and showed the difficulty these parents had in reconciling their own behavior with general social norms about child-rearing. In the more severely disturbed families, the pressing nature of their problems required serious distortion of social norms, but in the mildly disturbed families, more attention was given to the social norms, and attempts were made to express emotions in more acceptable ways. In any event, much energy was required to keep the balance stable, a state which required coordination of many subtle and inconsistent feelings and behaviors. It was, in effect, an "armed truce," and the danger of an explosion was constantly present.

## 5. FUNCTIONS AND DYSFUNCTIONS OF SCAPEGOATING

*a) Functions.*—Although the present paper has been concerned with the dynamics of the family as a group in relation to an emotionally disturbed child, some comments should be made on the functions that scapegoating serves for the parents individually and for external social systems. For the parents, scapegoating served as a personality-stablizing process. While the parents of these children did have serious internal conflicts, the projection of these difficulties onto the children served to minimize and control them. Thus, in spite of their personality difficulties, the parents were able to live up to their commitments to the wider society, expressing a minimum of their difficulties in the external economic and political systems. Most of the parents were able to maintain positions as steady workers and relatively respectable community members.

While the scapegoating of the child helped the parents live up to their obligations to the community, often they did not live up to their obligations as adequately as other families, and the whole family became a scapegoat for the community. Then the same mechanisms existed between the outer community and the family as between parents and child. The families, like their children, seldom fought back effectively; instead they channeled their additional frustrations and tensions through the child. Once established, many forces may play into the scapegoating situation. Though the child suffered additional burdens, through the medium of the family, he helped drain off the tension of the broader community in relation to a particular family.

From the point of view of the family, the primary function of scapegoating is that it permits the family to maintain its solidarity. In all the disturbed families, there were very severe strains which continually threatened to disrupt the family.[20] In all the disturbed families, very serious dissatisfactions between spouses came to light during the course of therapy, which were much more severe than those found in the well families. In the two families with the most severely disturbed children, when the scapegoating of the child eased up during therapy, the explosions between parents became so severe that there was serious fear that the family might break up. In the one case in which the problems between spouses remained relatively latent throughout therapy, marital problems emerged more clearly after the termination of therapy, and this led to serious anxiety attacks of the father. Yet, considering these internal strains, all of these families have shown surprising stability. Only in one family had there been a brief period of voluntary separation between the parents, and it had occurred before their first child was born. By focusing on one particular child, the families were able to encapsulate problems and anxieties which could potentially disrupt various family processes. There seemed to be an added solidarity between the parents who stood united against the problem child. The fact that it is a child who is disturbed permits the parents to continue to perform the tasks necessary for household maintenance with relative stability. Since the child is in a dependent position and contributes relatively little to family task activities, his malfunctioning does not seriously interfere with family stability.

b) *Dysfunctions.*—While the scapegoating of a child is effective in controlling major sources of tensions within the family, when a child becomes emotionally disturbed, this leads to disturbing secondary complications which are, however, generally less severe than the original tensions. One dysfunction is that certain realistic problems and extra tasks are created for the family. The child does require special care and attention. If, for example, the child is a bed-wetter, then the family must either wake him up regularly, or wash many sheets and take other precautions. This becomes particularly acute when traveling, visiting, or attending camp. Often the child cannot be left alone, and someone must continually look after him. If the child is to receive treatment, then the parents must expend time and money in providing this.

In addition, while the child is responsive to the implicit sanctions of his parents, he, too, may develop mechanisms of fighting back and punishing his parents for the way they treat him. Often the child becomes very skilled in arousing his parents' anxieties or in consciously bungling something his parents want him to do. Of course, the mother, being present during most of the day, experiences more of this counteraggression, and this in part accounts for her readiness to bring the child in for treatment. In most of these families it was the mother who took the initiative in seeking treatment. It would appear that as long as she can carefully control the amount of hostility the child expresses to her, she can tolerate this dysfunction, but when hostility rises above a certain point she is willing to seek outside help.

While the functions of the scapegoat within the nuclear family clearly outweigh his dysfunctions, this is typically not the case with the child's relationship outside the nuclear family. While the family gives the child sufficient support to maintain his role in the family, the use of him as a scapegoat is often incompatible with equipping him to maintain an adjustment outside the nuclear family. This problem becomes particularly acute when the child begins important associations outside the nuclear family in relationship with peers and his teachers at school.[21] It is at this time that many referrals to psychiatric clinics are made.[22] While the child's behavior was perfectly tolerable to the parents before, his behavior suddenly becomes intolerable. While he may still be performing the role the family wants him to play in order to be a scapegoat, this comes into conflict with his role as a representative of the family. The family is thus in conflict between using the child as a scapegoat and identifying with the child because of his role as family representative to the outside. Both sides of this conflict are revealed most clearly in the one family which carried on a feud with the outside and alternated between punishing the daughter for her poor school behavior and criticizing the teachers and children in school for causing problems for their daughter. In nearly all of these disturbed families, school difficulty was a crucial factor in the decision to refer the child for psychiatric treatment. While the child's behavior was rewarded at home, it was not rewarded at school, and while the family could tolerate the child's maladaptive behavior at home, when the school took special note of the child's behavior, this proved embarrassing and troubling to the parents.

This problem in relation to the outside world is perhaps most striking in the case of the school, but it is also true, for example, in relationships with neighbors and relatives. Neighbors and relatives are likely to be very critical of the family for the child's disturbed behavior, and it is often at such times that the family makes the greatest effort to get rid of the child's maladaptive behavior. In those families which alternated between punishing and rewarding the child's behavior, difficulty with the outside was often a cue to the family to move into the stage of punishing and criticizing the child's behavior.

While, as a whole, the child's disturbance served to relieve family tensions, it often led to further family tensions. To the extent that outside norms or standards, by which the child does not abide, are considered legitimate, inevitable frustrations arise. While the parents made strenuous efforts to interpret this as a result of the child's behavior and not of their own behavior, this effort was never completely successful. In accordance with modern child rearing theory to which they are at least exposed, they consider themselves at least partly responsible for the disturbance of the child, and this seems to have been particularly true at the time of therapy. Thus the child's disturbance feeds back into the problems which must be faced by the parents, and the marital pair often project the responsibility for the child's disturbance onto each other. The mother will say, for example, that the father doesn't spend enough time with the children, and the father will say that the mother doesn't manage the children properly. While this was thus dysfunctional to the marital relationship, it never became so prominent that the parents ceased using the child as a scapegoat. The predominant direction of aggression was still toward the badly behaved child rather than toward the other spouse.

While the disturbed behavior leads to some dysfunctions for the family, it is the personality of the child which suffers most as a result of the scapegoating. Any deviant or scapegoat within a group feels strong group pressure which creates considerable conflicts for him.[23] While other groups may also maintain their integration at the expense of the deviant, in the nuclear family this can be stabilized for a long period of time and result in far more serious personality impairment of the child assigned to the deviant role. The development of the emotional disturbance is simply part of the process of internalizing the conflicting demands placed upon him by his parents. While in the short run the child receives more rewards from the family for playing this role than for not playing this role, in the long run this leads to serious personality impairment. In short, the scapegoating mechanism is functional for the family as a group but dysfunctional for the emotional health of the child and for his adjustment outside the family of orientation.

# NOTES

1. Sir James Frazer, *The Golden Bough* (abridged ed.; New York: Macmillan, 1927).
2. *Ibid.*, p. 562.
3. *Ibid.*, p. 575.
4. In addition to Frazer, *op. cit.*, see also Emile Durkheim, "Deux lois de l'évolution pénale," *L'Année Sociologique*, IV (1899), 55–95; Henri Hubert and Marcel Mauss, "Essai sur la nature et la fonction du sacrifice," *L'Année Sociologique*, II (1897), 29–138; William Robertson Smith, *The Religion of the Semites* (London: A. and C. Black, Ltd., 1927); Roger Money-Kyrle, *The Meaning of Sacrifice* (London: Hogarth Press, 1930); George Herbert Mead, "The Psychology of Punitive Justice," *American Journal of Sociology*, XXIII (1918), 577–620; Ruth S. Eissler, "Scapegoats of Society," in Kurt R. Eissler (ed.), *Searchlights on Delinquency* (New York: International Universities Press, 1949), 288–305; and Clyde Kluckhohn, "Navaho Witchcraft, *Papers of the Peabody Museum of American Archaeology and Ethnology*, Harvard University, Vol. XXII (1944).
5. This is not to deny relevance of psychological aspects. The same facts can be related to a number of different theoretical systems, but here focus is on the group dynamics.
6. For other reports of this research, see John P. Spiegel, "The Resolution of Role Conflict Within the Family, *Psychiatry*, XX (1957), 1–16; Florence Rockwood Kluckhohn, "Family Diagnosis: Variations in the Basic Values of Family Systems, *Social Casework*, XXXIX (1958), 1–11; and John P. Spiegel, "Some Cultural Aspects of Transference and Countertransference," in Jules H. Massermann (ed.), *Individual and Family Dynamics* (New York: Grune and Stratton, Inc., 1959). A more inclusive statement of the conceptual framework will be published in the near future as, John P. Spiegel, "The Structure and Function of Social Roles in the Doctor-Patient Relationship." Lectures delivered at Tulane University, 1958.
7. It should be noted that only families which had never been separated or divorced were included in the present sample. Of course, there are also cases of emotionally disturbed children where only one parent is living with the children and cases in which one parent is living with other relatives. Hence,

tensions between parents cannot be the universal cause of emotional disturbance. A more general hypothesis would be that the emotionally disturbed child is always the focus of primary-group tension.

8. This is spelled out in more detail in Ezra F. Vogel, "The Marital Relationship of Parents and the Emotionally Disturbed Child" (Unpublished Ph.D. thesis, Harvard University, 1958).

9. See Florence R. Kluckhohn, *loc. cit.;* and F. Kluckhohn, Fred L. Strodtbeck and others, *Variations in Value Orientations* (Evanston, Ill.: Row, Peterson & Co., forthcoming).

10. Well families, by contrast, had bridged the gap between the orientations of different ethnic or class groups. They had succeeded in neutralizing old orientations before taking on new ones. Usually such families were changing in a slower and more orderly fashion.

11. Discussed at length in Norman W. Bell, "The Impact of Psychotherapy Upon Family Relationships" (Unpublished Ph.D. thesis, Harvard University, 1959).

12. The one family which did occasionally express antagonism directly to outsiders was the most disturbed family in the sample. The expression of hostility to neighbors was filled with such conflicts and added complications that it inevitably proved inadequate and the family returned to the scapegoating of their child.

   While many members of these families did express prejudice towards minority groups, this prejudice did little to drain the severe tensions within the family. Perhaps the minority group was not symbolically appropriate for the handling of any of the family conflicts, or perhaps they were not sufficiently available to serve as a continual focus of family tensions.

13. While in virtually all these families, there were considerable problems about achievement, another family seen by one of the authors as part of another investigation was very closely tied to the traditional ethnic patterns and had not yet seriously begun to incorporate American achievement values. In this family, there was one child, seriously substandard in intelligence, with very ugly physical features, who had epileptic seizures. There were also some children who were above average in intelligence. This family had no serious conflicts about achievement, and none of the children were scapegoated.

14. Alfred Adler, *Understanding Human Nature* (New York: Greenberg, 1927), and Alfred Adler, "The Cause and Prevention of Neurosis," *Journal of Abnormal and Social Psychology,* XXIII (1928), 4–11.

15. In the well families, there were cases of comparable physical illness which did not result in the same type of anxieties in the family.

16. No adequate large-scale studies are available to provide an estimate of the proportion of emotional disturbances found in the eldest child. Many small-scale studies have been made, but they are inconsistent and contradictory. See John P. Spiegel and Norman W. Bell. "The Family of the Psychiatric Patient," in Silvano Arieti (ed.), *American Handbook of Psychiatry* (New York: Basic Books, Inc., 1959). In the present study, slightly more than half were eldest children, a finding similar to that in another small sample of emotionally disturbed children: Sydney Croog, "The Social Backgrounds of Emotionally Disturbed Children and their Siblings" (Unpublished Ph.D. thesis, Yale University, 1954). It has also been noted that eldest sons are more likely to be involved in problems of inheritance and rivalry, and are more likely to be adult-oriented. See such diverse studies as George Peter Murdock, *Social Structure* (New York: Macmillan, 1949); Sigmund Freud, *Moses and Monotheism* (New York: Alfred A. Knopf, 1939); and Charles McArthur, "Personalities of First and Second Children," *Psychiatry,* XIX (1956), 47–54.

17. The way the parent gives the child implicit approval to act out his own unconscious wishes has already been well described for the relationship between a single parent and a single child. Adelaide M. Johnson, "Sanctions for

Superego Lacunae of Adolescents," in Kurt R. Eissler (ed.), *Searchlights on Delinquency* (New York: International Universities Press, 1949); Melitta Sperling, "The Neurotic Child and his Mother: A Psychoanalytic Study," *American Journal of Orthopsychiatry,* XXI 1951), 351–64. For a more detailed account of family role-induction methods, see Spiegel, "The Resolution of Role Conflict within the Family."

18. Here again, the analogy to the individual personality system is instructive. Just as Freud's hysteric patients expressed a *belle indifference* to their symptoms and a surprising reluctance to change them, so did these parents have a *belle indifference* to the symptoms of their children. Just as the individual's symptom represents an expression of his own unconscious wish, so does the child's symptom represent an expression of his parents' unconscious wishes.

19. While the control imposed by parents in well families sometimes appeared to be extremely aggressive and punitive, this aggression was not such a massive critical attack on the child and did not carry the threat of such severe sanctions as did the aggression by the disturbed parents. In the well families, the punishment of the child was not regarded by the child as so damaging, and there was ordinarily the possibility of escaping further punishment by behaving in a different, desired way. There were few possibilities for the child to escape this hostility in the disturbed family.

20. In one well family, when there was considerable marital tension it was handled in a very overt fashion, and marital problems were not dealt with through the child.

21. At adolescence, the time when more demands for independent existence are made, a large number of acute disturbances appear. Many who were adequately adjusted to the roles they were assigned within the family, were unable to meet the new adjustment outside the family. See, for example, Nicholas J. Demerath, "Adolescent Status and the Individual" (Unpublished Ph.D. thesis, Harvard University, 1942). A large number of acute psychoses also occur as soon as the army recruit leaves home and enters military service. Under ordinary circumstances, the socialization of the child prepares him for the social demands of external society. See, for example, Talcott Parsons, "The Incest Taboo in Relation to Social Structure and the Socialization of the Child," *British Journal of Sociology,* V (1954), 101–17; and David Aberle and Kaspar Naegele, "Middle-Class Fathers' Occupational Roles and Attitudes toward Children," *American Journal of Orthopsychiatry,* XXII (1952), 566–78.

22. The importance of difficulties with the associations outside the nuclear family in directing the family for psychiatric treatment has long been recognized by clinicians. See, for example, Anna Freud, "Indications for Child Analysis," in *The Psychoanalytic Study of the Child,* Vol. I (New York: International Universities Press, 1945).

23. See, for example, the analysis of the case of Long John's nightmares in William F. Whyte, *Street Corner Society* (Chicago: University of Chicago Press, 1943); and a report of Asch's experiments in Solomon E. Asch, *Social Psychology* (New York: Prentice-Hall, 1952).

# 21:

# Pseudo-Mutuality in the Family Relations of Schizophrenics[1]

*Lyman C. Wynne, Irving M. Ryckoff,*
*Juliana Day,* and *Stanley I. Hirsch*

The purpose of this paper is to develop a psychodynamic interpretation of schizophrenia that takes into conceptual account the social organization of the family as a whole. We shall formulate a series of concepts and hypotheses applicable to various phases of schizophrenic processes—prepsychotic, acute, and chronic—in which we shall focus particularly upon the relevance of family relations to these processes.

In a sense, this has become a preliminary statement of a theory of schizophrenia, not by any means a theory attempting to account systematically for all schizophrenic phenomena, but, rather, a search for a coherent viewpoint about certain features of schizophrenia. We assume that other factors not included in this formulation may well combine on several levels of organization at various stages in the pathogenesis of schizophrenia, or the group of schizophrenias. In the present formulation we are content to hypothesize that those considerations which we do specify can make a significant contribution to the form taken by schizophrenic illness.

The work reported here is part of a long-range research program on the family setting of schizophrenic patients, begun in 1954 at the National Institute of Mental Health. In this program a case is regarded as consisting of an entire family unit, including both parents and offspring. During the first phase of the program the schizophrenic patient received intensive psychotherapy in the hospital, parents were seen twice weekly on an outpatient basis by different psychiatrists or a psychiatric social

Reprinted by special permission of the William Alanson White Psychiatric Foundation, Inc. from *Psychiatry,* Vol. 21 (1958), pp. 205–20. Copyright 1958 by the William Alanson White Psychiatric Foundation, Inc. Lyman C. Wynne is chief, Adult Psychiatry Branch, Clinical Investigations, National Institute of Mental Health. Irving M. Ryckoff practices psychiatry in Washington, D.C. At the time of writing he was special consultant, National Institute of Mental Health. Juliana Day is a psychiatrist in Clinical Investigations, National Institute of Mental Health. Stanley I. Hirsch is program supervisor, Social Service, Clinical Center, National Institute of Mental Health.

worker, and data from other family members, as well as from the nursing staff and the ward administrator, were included in the reconstruction of family patterns.

We have used this kind of psychotherapeutic and observational study of the first group of families to generate the working hypotheses of this paper. Most of the clinical examples which we shall cite are drawn from work with four families, but some of the observations have been obtained from other families studied less thoroughly.

Our thinking thus far has mainly centered on schizophrenic illness in which the onset of psychosis occurred acutely in late adolescence or young adulthood, not on simple schizophrenia or "process" schizophrenia. The specification of the range of cases to which the present hypotheses apply is a problem of current and future research. Thus, our clinical examples are included for illustration and clarification, not for statistical verification.

## THE CONCEPT OF PSEUDO-MUTUALITY

Let us first try to make explicit certain of our basic assumptions or postulates. We assume that movement into relation with other human beings is a fundamental principle or 'need' of human existence. To restate this in psychoanalytic terminology, man is inherently object-related. For our present purposes, the striving for relatedness to other human beings may be regarded either as a primary,[2] or as an early and essential, although perhaps secondary, feature of the human situation.

Another key postulate for the formulation which follows is that every human being strives consciously and unconsciously, in a lifelong process, to develop a sense of personal identity. The sense of identity consists of those self-representations, explicit and implicit, which give continuity and coherence to experience despite a constant flux of inner and outer stimuli. Identity processes can be regarded as those ego functions through which the self is perceptually differentiated from objects. As Erikson points out, processes initially taking the form of what has been conceptualized as introjection and projection pave the way for multiple identifications, which are selectively repudiated, assimilated, and synthesized into the new configuration of identity[3]

We consider that the universal necessity for dealing with both the problems of relation and identity[4] leads to three main 'solutions.' These three resultant forms of relatedness, or complementarity, are mutuality, nonmutuality, and pseudo-mutuality. Pseudo-mutuality is a miscarried 'solution' of widespread occurrence. We shall hypothesize that this kind of relatedness, in an especially intense and enduring form, contributes significantly to the family experience of people who later, if other factors are also present, develop acute schizophrenic episodes.

Pseudo-mutuality refers to a quality of relatedness with several ingredients. Each person brings into the relation a primary investment in maintaining a *sense* of relation.[5] His need and wish for this particular relation is especially strong for one or more of a variety of possible reasons, such as, in adults, isolation from, or failure in, other relations because of personality or situational difficulties; or in children, painful earlier experiences of separation-anxiety. The past experience of each person and the current circumstances of the relation lead to an effort to maintain the idea or feeling, even though this may be illusory, that one's own behavior and expectations mesh with the behavior and expectations of the other persons in the relation.

Clearly, all interpersonal relations that persist are structured in terms of *some* kind of complementarity or fitting together. However, in describing pseudo-mutuality, we are emphasizing a predominant absorption in fitting together, at the expense of the differentiation of the identities of the persons in the relation. In contrast, each person brings to relations of genuine mutuality a sense of his own meaningful, positively valued identity, and, out of experience or participation together, mutual recognition of identity develops, including a growing recognition of each other's potentialities and capacities.

With growth and situational changes, altered expectations inevitably come into any relation. Then, at least transient nonfulfillment of expectations—that is, noncomplementarity—necessarily occurs. In pseudomutuality the subjective tension aroused by divergence or independence of expectations, including the open affirmation of a sense of personal identity, is experienced as not merely disrupting that particular transaction but as possibly demolishing the entire relation.

The alternative outcome is overlooked or cannot be awaited: that the recognition and exploration of difference may lead to an expanded or deepened, although altered, basis for the relation. Genuine mutuality, unlike pseudo-mutuality, not only tolerates divergence of self-interests, but thrives upon the recognition of such natural and inevitable divergence. In terms of role theory, a relation of mutuality is experienced as having a larger context than a particular role so that particular items of role noncomplementarity can occur as a stimulus rather than as a disruption to the relation as a whole.

In pseudo-mutuality emotional investment is directed more toward maintaining the *sense* of reciprocal fulfillment of expectations than toward accurately perceiving changing expectations. Thus, the new expectations are left unexplored, and the old expectations and roles, even though outgrown and inappropriate in one sense, continue to serve as the structure for the relation.

The relation which persists can then neither be given up, except under very special or dire circumstances, nor be allowed to develop or expand. It is highly invested, often intensely charged emotionally, but at the same time constricts growth and impoverishes any sort of freshness of interpersonal experience. Ambivalence is inevitable in such relations that have the appearance of offering much on one level that is not confirmed on other levels. Without mutual perception and recognition of the identity of each person appropriate to the current life situation, the continuing relation increasingly becomes subjectively empty, barren, and stifling. Positive aspects of the relation cannot be explored and expanded; what outside observers might regard as coercive or manipulative negative aspects are interpreted *within* the relation as simply part of the effort to dovetail more fully with one another.

In short, the pseudo-mutual relation involves a characteristic dilemma: divergence is perceived as leading to disruption of the relation and therefore must be avoided; but if divergence is avoided, growth of the relation is impossible.

### NONMUTUAL COMPLEMENTARITY

Clearly, many interpersonal relations are not characterized by either mutuality or pseudo-mutuality. The interchange of customer and sales clerk, for example, does not ordinarily involve, beyond the purchase of merchandise, a strong investment in excluding noncomplementarity or in exploring what the relation has to offer either person. Such transactions, statistically frequent and generally quite highly institutionalized in form, do have an integration of reciprocal or complementary expectations, but this is *nonmutual* complementarity.[6] Nonmutuality is usually role-limited it is, applying Parsons' terms, functionally specific for a particular role rather than functionally diffuse for the relation.[7]

Nonmutual complementarity often evolves, especially if a relation persists in duration or heightens in significance to the participants, in the direction of either mutuality or pseudo-mutuality. For example, a customer and clerk who linger on, anxious about noncomplementarity and hesitant to admit openly to each other that no sale is in prospect, become engaged in a mild form of pseudo-mutuality. Finally, some lame excuse about "coming back later" may be offered, but here the social context is strikingly different from the usual family setting. In family relations the persisting or recurrent necessity of dealing with the relations in some way or other may bring either richer possibilities of mutuality or more complex mechanisms for maintaining pseudo-mutuality.[8]

Let us now state more explicitly our first main hypothesis about the family relations of potential schizophrenics:

*Hypothesis 1. Within the families of persons who later develop acute schizophrenic episodes, those relations which are openly acknowledged as acceptable have a quality of intense and enduring pseudo-mutuality.*

As we have already implied, pseudo-mutuality is not unique to the relations of schizophrenics but provides one kind of continuum between schizophrenic and other modes of relating. Hence, we do not mean to imply in this first hypothesis that pseudo-mutuality *in itself* is productive of schizophrenia, but we do hypothesize that it is a major feature of the kind of setting in which reactive schizophrenia develops when other factors are also present.

A further immediate qualification should be noted: In specifying that the pseudo-mutuality applies only to that part of the family social organization which is openly acknowledged, we are implying that this part of the family structure may be very sharply split off from other parts of the family organization which are not so acknowledged. The splitting off of these persons or roles that are not involved in the pseudo-mutuality may, as we shall indicate in discussing shared familial mechanisms, be highly functional for the family organization as a whole, even though these persons or roles may be consciously depreciated or ostracized.

We are, let us emphasize, still speaking of the family social organization before acute schizophrenic episodes have occurred. In these families the predominant prepsychotic picture is a fixed organization of a limited number of engulfing roles. While the roles existing in the overall family social organization tend to remain fixed, the particular persons who enact these roles may vary. Thus, there may be considerable competition and fluidity about who takes the role of the most dependent and helpless family member, the role structure may remain unchanged as child, mother, and father successively take this role.

For example, in one family we have studied, the mother and one daughter maintained the pseudo-mutuality that the whole family *overtly* agreed was proper and desirable. The mother maintained a highly controlled, placid exterior, making a well-mannered social presentation to the outside world, and one of the daughters, from birth, was a model of "goodness" and of placid, quiet, completely conforming behavior that "never needed correction." In contrast, the father and the other daughter took roles which they themselves overtly deplored and which they felt did not represent the pseudo-mutual standards they too desired for the family.

The father was expected by everyone in the family to take a domineering of the daughters was accepted as "wild," rebellious, and insolent since early role punctuated with marked irritability and fiery temper outbursts, and one childhood. During the course of psychotherapy with the mother it became apparent that she was struggling to keep very similar "wild" impulses in herself in check; these impulses had been disturbingly displayed during her own adolescence. In late adolescence the "wild" daughter became passive, quiet, and dutiful, and, in a sense, exchanged roles with her "good" sister who erupted with violently hostile rebellion in an acute schizophrenic episode. The family role structure as a whole thus remained essentially unchanged.

Such a family role structure may be already forming in the fantasy life of the parents before the birth of a child, who sometimes is expected to fill some kind of void in a parent's life. Lewis B. Hill has noted a number of instances in which the expected role of the child in the family was symbolically represented in the choice of name for the child. In later life the child never seemed to emerge from this early role assignment.[9]

While early expectations and role assignments occur in nonschizophrenic families, we feel that there is a difference in the rigidity of the family role structure. Normally, this structure both affects the personality development of the offspring and is reworked and modified, more or less continually, in accord with the changing needs and expectations of the family members toward each other. With pseudo-mutuality, however, expressions of the changing or emerging needs of family members are not reflected in changes in the role structure of the family. In schizophrenic family organization the role structure may not be reshaped even in the face of such major characteristics as the sex, age, and degree of passivity or aggressiveness of the person. Depending upon the fit between native characteristics and the rigid family structure, the psychological experiences of the family members will vary.

From the observational standpoint, family pseudo-mutuality shows certain characteristics which can be readily noted: (1) A persistent sameness of the role structure of the family, despite physical and situational alterations in the life circumstances of the family members, and despite changes in what is going on and being experienced in family life. (2) An insistence on the desirability and appropriateness of this role structure. (3) Evidence of intense concern over possible divergence or independence from this role structure. (4) An absence of spontaneity, novelty, humor, and zest in participation together.

We are hypothesizing that noncomplementarity is a *more intense and enduring* threat in the families of schizophrenics than it is in other families in which pseudo-mutuality may also appear. The threat to the established family role structure from independent or aggressive behavior is experienced as an impending disaster, often crystallized into specific anxieties. In one family with whom we have worked, open aggression between the family members was expected to produce a cerebral hemorrhage in the mother and a heart attack in the father. In instances where serious depression in a family member has previously occurred, a recurrence may be expected if one member makes moves toward psychological independence.

The ever-present menace of noncomplementarity within these families leads to pseudo-mutuality as a way of life. Only a major crisis, such as an acute schizophrenic episode, is then experienced within the family as truly altering the meaning of family relations, and even then, as we shall note later, reinterpretation can quickly alter the meaning of the episode.

The concept of degrees of intensity and persistence of pseudo-mutuality suggests a dimension common to both schizophrenic and non-schizophrenic relations. The common element in this dimension is the presence of some degree of pseudo-mutuality. However, we feel that the differences in intensity and persistence are significant and considerable. Even more important are the differences in the kind and quality of shared mechanisms by which the pseudo-mutuality is maintained.[10]

## SHARED MECHANISMS FOR MAINTAINING PSEUDO-MUTUALITY

*Hypothesis 2. In the families of potential schizophrenics, the intensity and duration of pseudo-mutuality has led to the development of a particular variety of shared family mechanisms by which deviations from the family role structure are excluded from recognition or are delusionally reinterpreted. These shared mechanisms act at a primitive level in preventing the articulation and selection of any meanings that might enable the individual family member to differentiate his personal identity either within or outside of the family role structure. Those dawning perceptions and incipient communications which might lead to an articulation of divergent expectations, interests, or individuality are, instead, diffused, doubled, blurred, or distorted.*

Here we wish to make clear that we are *not* simply referring to the concealment or masking of information or to direct efforts to coerce or elicit an attitude of a particular kind. These are characteristic 'normal' and neurotic mechanisms for maintaining or restoring pseudo-mutuality, which of course, are likely to occur in the families of schizophrenics *in addition* to the more specifically schizophrenic mechanisms. The willfulness and temper tantrums of the hysteric can be regarded as ways of forcibly inducing and defending an illusion of relation. Similarly, the substitutive, undoing, and isolating defenses of the obsessional dissociate and ward off the experience of noncomplementarity. However, in characteristic schizophrenic relations perceptual and communicative capacity is involved in an earlier and more primitive way. The problem is a more primary failure of the ego in articulating the meaning of experience and participation, not so much a defense by the ego against the conscious recognition of particular meanings.

In ordinary relations, contradictory or variant expectations are frequently communicated, often by differences between the content of verbalization and the setting or style of communication. Normally, however, shared cultural mechanisms and codes facilitate the selection of those aspects of the over-all communication to which attention will be paid. In contrast, in characteristically schizophrenic relations, when both of a pair of contradictory expectations are communicated, the shared mechanisms facilitate a *failure* in selection of meaning.[11] In the family relations of potential schizophrenics, it is not simply that divergence is kept out of awareness but rather that the discriminative perception of those events which might specifically constitute divergence is aborted and blurred. Jointly recognized divergence is, thus, never openly risked, but neither is the pervasive and diffuse danger of being divergent ever absent.

### THE RUBBER FENCE

In the prepsychotic life of acute schizophrenics, we are hypothesizing that these shared family mechanisms serve to mitigate the full impact of chaotic, empty, and frightening experience by providing a role structure in which the person can pseudo-mutually exist without having developed a valued and meaningful sense of identity or its age-appropriate precursors. However, these shared mechanisms at the same time contribute to a failure by the potential schizophrenic in learning to discriminate or value who he is or where he is except in terms of a blurred place in the family role structure. This difficulty of the potential schizophrenic in articulating a differentiation of himself from the family role structure means that *the family role structure is experienced as all-encompassing.*

Normally, in this culture, the child's experiences are with persons who themselves participate in roles and relations outside as well as within the nuclear family. Certain of the needs and expectations of family members cannot normally be fulfilled within the nuclear family, necessitating a meaningful participation in the larger society, and parents normally anticipate and facilitate such expansion of the growing child's experiences beyond the nuclear family. The normal pattern or organization of family roles and relations therefore constitutes a differentiated subsystem of a society rather than a self-sufficient, complete social system.[12]

In contrast, when there is a continual effort in family relations to maintain pseudo-mutuality, the family members try to act as if the family could be a truly self-sufficient social system with a completely encircling boundary. Schizophrenic family members, in failing to articulate a differentiation of family member from family role structure, tend to shift and obscure the idea of the family boundaries. The unstable but continuous boundary, with no recognizable openings, surrounding the schizophrenic family system, stretches to include that which can be interpreted as complementary and contracts to extrude that which is interpreted as noncomplementary. This continuous but elastic boundary we have called the rubber fence. This metaphor is a way of summarizing the effects of family pseudo-mutuality and the reinforcing shared family mechanisms in establishing a situation in which the person feels that he cannot trust his own perceptions and from which there seems no escape. We hasten to stress that we do *not* regard the potential schizophrenic as simply a passive victim of his family environment; in a subsequent section we shall bring up the active investment of the potential schizophrenic in helping to create and maintain this family structure.

CLINICAL EXAMPLES

While we shall not attempt to make a complete inventory of the mechanisms used in varying degrees to maintain this omnipresent pseudo-mutuality, some of them are illustrated by the following clinical examples. A very general kind of mechanism, subsuming some of the others to be described, is the creation of a pervasive familial subculture of myths, legends, and ideology which stress the catastrophic consequences of openly recognized divergence from the fixed family role structure. We have already mentioned that even minor divergence may be experienced as threatening to precipitate, for example, a heart attack. Family legends about fury and violence may be pervasive reminders of the supposed consequences of divergence.

Sometimes the subcultural ideology involves a desperate preoccupation with harmony in all relations within the family. As one mother again and again insisted, and the father echoed:

We are all peaceful. I like peace even if I have to kill someone to get it. . . . A more normal, happy kid would be hard to find. I was pleased with my child! I was pleased with my husband! I was pleased with my life. I have *always* been pleased! We have had 25 years of the happiest married life and of being a father and mother.

Among the simplest of the family mechanisms we have studied is a bland, indiscriminate, but determined approval of the person's activities and interests, without differentiating whether they are actually incompatible with the family code of values. In some cases, the sweeping parental approval of any of the child's behavior is verbalized as respect for self-determination, "freedom," and family "democracy," and is typified by the oft-repeated response of one set of parents, "We only want you to do what you want to do." The open recognition of differences then becomes literally impossible, except by a truly violent, disruptive move, which the schizophrenic break seems to represent.

Often *all* of the behavior of the preschizophrenic child is perceived and approved by the parents as "good," in the sense of fulfilling the parental expectations. For example, one mother said about the prepsychotic relation with her daughter: "There were never any problems because she always know what was right without being told." A father said about his daughter's childhood: "We didn't need to build a fence around our lot. It was as if there was an invisible line beyond which she knew she should not go."

Indiscriminate approval can be regarded as a mechanism by which a role important in the family can be maintained in the face of real and changing characteristics of the person assigned the role. Of course, when a child's 'innate' characteristics initially happen to be attuned to a particular family role, it seems likely that the role will be more often taken by this child than by another sibling or a parent. Hence, when a child has been regarded as invariably "good" or docile, this parental report may represent a combination of actual 'innate' docility, a stereotyped role assignment, and the child's learned skill in filling this stereotyped role assignment.

In one instance we had the opportunity, by comparing the parental report with the son's letters, to realize how undiscriminating was the evaluation of the son that continued right up to the time of his hospitalization for catatonic mutism. In order to document for us that "nothing had changed," the parents showed us the correspondence from him during the four months prior to hospitalization. These letters actually portrayed extremely vividly the marked changes in the son, which the parents were unable to recognize even when the letters were discussed with them directly.

At the beginning of his army experience, the son actively expressed in his letters many GI gripes and even made a "big fuss up the rank" to the lieutenant over being issued badly fitting shoes. Increasingly, however, he repetitively described a marked withdrawal to his bunk. The following are representative excerpts from his letters during the fourth month:

Another weekend shot. Got off about seven yesterday threw my stuff from bag into footlocker made the bed and then called you. Afterwards came back and went to bed.

Many of these guys hop out for town or move first thing but would rather sleep.

Haven't even dressed today [Sunday, 7 P.M.]. Got up smoked one ate some apricots and just got some out now. Went back till 2:00 then took shower and washed my boots and spent rest time rolling socks and arranging footlocker. Have still to read part of the papers and polish my boots. Spent some time rubbing crap off locker and shelves.

Had today off as its Holiday [Monday, February 22] and have been loafing since Saturday. Had a parade, then got off at 9:30 A.M. Went to bed and slept right through till Sunday morning. Skipped Sat. lunch and dinner and Sun. breakfast and lunch. Did make supper though Sunday. Haven't written as just go to bed when get off.

Been laying in bed all day and thats a good weekend. . . . Have yet to take a shower and shave but seems quite an effort could soak in for another day or three anyway. Not much to write as have been doing nothing but sleeping. Read the papers and ate a can of sardines and that's about it. After talked to you came back and also slept. Really can't think of anything to write just went and got some water but that doesn't seem to make much more to write. Was going to call tonight but decided to wait until later in the week. Lots of Love.

Yet the following is how the mother perceived her son's participation and experience before the parents were notified he had been hospitalized:

Eddie always had a good time. He was always very active and was always a very happy and normal boy as far as we could see, and there was no suggestion of anything like this happening. That was why it was so difficult for us to understand his illness. If he had been the kind of kid who wasn't friendly or active we might have been able to understand. There wasn't a thing he missed out on.

Although indiscriminate approval can keep much behavior from being recognized as being disturbingly deviant, the intensity of anxiety about divergence may lead to contradictory scrutiny, judgment, and disapproval of the same behavior that has ostensibly been approved. Then, in order to maintain pseudo-mutuality, the contradiction itself, however blatant, may be reinterpreted or simply be blandly ignored.

In one family, the parents of an adolescent only son, later to become schizophrenic, emphasized his right to decide privately, at 16, whether to get married or not. The parents, however, anxiously contacted his fiancée and filled her with questions and doubts until she became so perplexed and upset that she broke off the engagement. The parents remind the interviewer, as they state they did the boy, that they had left him entirely free to make his own decision. The boy seems to have made no complaint in the face of these two contradicting, mutually obscuring levels of communication, but, nine years later, he had never gone this far again in considering marriage.

A corollary to indiscriminate approval is secrecy, which results in the formula, That which cannot be approved will remain unknown. Both mechanisms keep divergence from having a recognized and meaningful impact upon the family ideology and role structure. Each family member may be expected to conceal large areas of his experience and not open to communication with the others. Sometimes the expectations of secrecy are expressed in an exaggerated deference for what is labeled as privacy—that is, the invariable right of each family member to share only what he wishes.

Secrecy seems to be especially marked in schizophrenic family social organization for those roles which move in extrafamilial directions. Usually such roles and the personal attitudes and characteristics associated with them are kept dissociated from the rest of the family social organization. As an example, we have been impressed in these families with how unknown and foreign to the family are the personal characteristics which the father shows in his occupational role, even when he has been occupationally successful. Typically, the father collaborates with the other family members in acting as if the personal characteristics revealed by his occupational proficiencies do not exist.

Secrecy, however, like indiscriminate approval, may be simultaneously contradicted by its opposite. Driven by an anxious concern about the possible disruptive nature of concealed thoughts and interests, the family members may desperately attempt to anticipate, guess, or secretly investigate that which they simultaneously insist is inviolably private. The child is thus confronted—and the child comes to confront the parent—with simultaneous, contradictory expectations: to conceal large areas of his experience as private; to allow the intensive investigation of this same 'private' experience. In addition, the contradiction itself, however obvious it may seem to be to an outside observer, is not recognized within the family.

While emphasizing, vehemently, the right of their son to keep private his plans, wishes, and activities, the mother [of the same patient reported on above] engaged in an intensive encompassment of her son's experiences in the form of minute record-keeping, by means of which she was able to create a detailed, month-by-month report of her son's activities for his entire life. She spoke of her "files," in which she had all the original documents, and offered prepared duplicates of his school records, employment records, social security receipts, letters, and so on. It is perhaps not surprising, then, that this boy, two years prior to his overt psychotic breakdown, had transient paranoid ideas that he was being followed by detectives hired by his mother and that his best friend was spying on him at the mother's instigation.

The father of another patient had major private objections to his daughter's interest in a foreign hospital attendant, but, unable to express his concern to her openly, he checked the mileage she used on the car and then calculated on a map whether she could have gone to his residence.

Such combinations of secrecy and investigation guard against any open recognition of differences or noncomplementarity and also block any real clarification in the mind of either patient or parents as to when the family member is acceptably outside or independent of the family system.

As part of the exaggerated deference to "democracy" and "self-determination," there may be a tendency to formalize experiences that in less pathological families would be part of a free-flowing way of life. In one family, the parents instituted "Little-Boy Day" for their son during his younger years—a special day when he could choose the family's activity, such as going to the zoo or the movies. This was in response to his complaint that the grown-ups always did the deciding. However, this formalized mechanism for dealing with the complaint blocked any spontaneity in family participation, and pseudo-mutuality was heightened. In this family and in another, highly self-conscious "discussions," usually of such impersonal subjects as religion, sports, politics, and so on, were established as a carefully limited area for arguments. However heated they might become, such experiences were labeled in advance as not involving personal differences. Giving such a form to the experience helps eliminate possible areas of divergence and noncomplementarity, while informality would leave room for the unexpected.

A common operation of these family systems is the use of intermediaries between the family members. Pseudo-mutuality may be more easily maintained and difference avoided if reciprocal expectations are communicated via the intermediaries. For example, whenever the parents of a hospitalized patient took their son out on pass, they wanted him to have a fresh shave beforehand. But, they said, he might refuse to go out if they took a stand on the shaving, and this would be too much of a risk. Hence, they asked the ward administrator to tell the attendant to tell their son to shave. When intermediaries participate in this way, the direct expectations within the family can be more easily blurred and the possible noncomplementarity remain untested. In effect, intermediaries who fill such a role are incorporated into the family system temporarily; for a specific purpose the elastic boundaries have been stretched to include such persons, who are then not related to as separate identities.

When the same patient was destroying a clock, radio, magazines, and food parcels that his parents brought to him, they felt that this behavior had nothing to do with them because they had left these objects with the nursing personnel to give to the patient. The nurses, feeling uncomfortable in this role and wishing to be free to deal with the patient in their own right, suggested that the parents deliver the parcels in person, even though they came at other than visiting hours. Immediately following this change in policy, the mother's anxiety increased, and, coincidence or not, her blood pressure suddenly rose so alarmingly that her family doctor forbade her from visiting.

Just as these nurse intermediaries who did not collaborate in helping to maintain the family pseudo-mutuality were extruded from the family system and were treated as outsiders thenceforth, so may members of the biological family be outside the rubber fence. In one family the father was held responsible for a time for some of the patient's symptoms and felt ostracized in his own house. The threat of being cut off from family relations because of divergence was literally carried out.

Quite often, the family member labeled as schizophrenic is the one who is extruded from his family system. In some instances, prior to the onset of frank psychosis, the patient had been considered "peculiar" or the "black sheep" of the family, while in other cases, he was extruded from the overt family role structure only after hospitalization. In the conscious perceptions of the family members all of the family noncomplementarity is then localized in the one person who is overtly regarded as not fitting in. This person, unless he has achieved a sense of identity in his own right, shares with the rest of the family a negative valuation of himself and his role in the family, but everyone in the family will become very anxious if he disturbs the role structure by trying to abandon this role. From the observer's standpoint, the ostracized or scapegoated person thus takes an important covert family role in maintaining the pseudo-mutuality or surface complementarity of the rest of the family.

The problems within the family system can also be by-passed by focusing upon physical ailments or the schizophrenia itself as being responsible for upsetting "smooth" family relations. In effect, the schizophrenia is regarded as an intruder which is held accountable for interpersonal difficulties. It is then possible within the family to say that the pati .t "really means" to be agreeable, and his desperate efforts to be more direct, even though noncomplementary, can be interpreted as not representing his intent.

In one family, for example, the fact that the hospitalized son did not wear his glasses—he had smashed several pairs—was repeatedly interpreted by the parents as explanatory of the patient's negativism. He had begun voluntarily going to the recreation area until his parents heard about this change and took over his initiative by urging him to go. He stopped going immediately. His parents were puzzled, but concluded, even though he read newspapers in their presence, that he must be afraid of falling when walking without his glasses.

At about the same time, the patient was returning his parents' letters to them unopened. His girl friend, who had become very much a part of the family system, also began writing to him, and he also forwarded these letters unopened to his mother. The mother was perplexed until she decided that he had not been able to read the address without his glasses. Thus, any interpersonal meaning of the son's action could remain unacknowledged.

Family pseudo-mutuality, as we have described it, does not require the physical presence of all members, since role expectations can be maintained at a distance. Thus geographical or situational changes, emphasized in the usual psychiatric social history, may not always be associated with significant changes in the underlying expectations or meanings of the person's family relations. Going away to college, for example, may be experienced as the continuation of an established role by a son who pleases his family by a particular kind of school achievement. In the case of one of our patients, the correspondence and telephone calls between her, when she was away at college, and her family provided very much the same degree and quality of communication for over a year as had occurred when she lived at home. Similarly, going into the army, moving to another city, even getting married and having children of one's own, may in some cases mean going through the motions of following social conventions as part of familial expectations, without a genuine sense of identity apart from the family system. In the hallucinations of one patient, she was still actively involved in establishing and warding off relations with her family members, all dead, in actuality, for many years.

## INTERNALIZATION OF FAMILY ROLE STRUCTURE

We take the view that, in the normal process of internalization, the over-all family role structure, together with the quality of relations and the shared subcultural mechanisms maintaining this system, is taken over into the child's personality structure. In psychoanalytic theory the identifications with the parents and the internalization of parental codes are essential contributions to the quality of the child's ego and supergo. This paper extends the more traditional view by emphasizing the significance of the internalization of the over-all family role structure.

We are using the term internalization to refer in a generalized way to the organized pattern of the *meanings* which external objects, events, and relations have acquired.[13] Thus, internalization includes the meanings a person finds attached to his position in the social structure of family and wider community. Also internalized are the ways of thinking and of deriving meaning, the points of anxiety, and the irrationality, confusion, and ambiguity that were expressed in the shared mechanisms of the family social organization.

*Hypothesis 3. The fragmentation of experience, the identity diffusion, the disturbed modes of perception and communication, and certain other characteristics of the acute reactive schizophrenic's personality structure are to a significant extent derived, by processes of internalization, from characteristics of the family social organization.*

We have described how roles and role behavior in intense pseudomutual relations come to be largely dissociated from subjective experience. Such roles are not integrated into the functioning of an actively perceiving ego, but come to govern the person's behavior in an automatic, 'reflex' fashion, having the quality of "going through the motions." These patterns of role behavior have been learned, are carried into new situations, and in a general sense are internalized into the personality, although they are not under the jurisdiction of an actively discriminating ego. In certain schizophrenics, *the internalized family role structure and associated family subculture serve as a kind of primitive superego,* which tends to determine behavior directly, without negotiation with an actively perceiving and discriminating ego.

The meaning of the self or of personal identity is buried in such a superego. It is only through experiencing the impact of noncomplementarity and articulating its meaning that a perceiving ego begins to be differentiated with an identity of its own. However, the shared mechanisms operating in these families specifically interfere with the articulation of meanings that hint at noncomplementarity. For a child who grows up and develops his perceptual capacities in a setting in which obvious contradictions are regarded as nonexistent, it seems reasonable to suppose that he may well come to regard his senses and emotional responses as a tenuous and unreliable guide to understanding the expectations he has of himself and others. Thus, modes of thinking, perceiving, and communicating built up in such a way render unavailable to the person the capacity to attach clear meanings to his own intrapsychic states, such as anger at the mother or disappointment. Instead, he may have a vague uneasiness, sometimes merging into panic. Under these conditions, the person becomes flooded with anxiety at precisely those moments when he is starting to articulate a meaningful indication of his individuality, in the same way that pseudo-mutual family relations became flooded with anxiety when noncomplementarity threatened to emerge into shared recognition.

Individualized impulses, which are typically perceived as necessarily noncomplementary in these family relations, are split off or dissociated from acknowledged family life by shared secrecy mechanisms. As we have noted, however, the same activity which, it is agreed, will be secret is simultaneously subject, by tacit agreement, to secret family investigation. We tentatively and metaphorically suggest that familial secrecy mechanisms have an internalized counterpart in the mechanisms of repression and dissociation and that the familial investigative mechanisms have a counterpart in anxious superego surveillance of that which has been dissociated. The result is a chronic, vague uneasiness about autistic experience that is constantly but obscurely re-exposed to awareness. The impulses and ideas of such autistic experience thus are neither clearly and fully dissociated nor sufficiently in the open to be directly confronted.[14] This situation, we feel, is the individual counterpart of the family patterns we have been describing.

Such processes, of course, can be expected to contribute to a marked constriction and impoverishment in ego functioning and development.[15] The potential schizophrenic, like other family members, tends to pick out in his perceptions that which can be seen as complementary and to exclude from his perceptions that which is seen as noncomplementary. In the acute schizophrenic episode the dissociation of noncomplementarity breaks down and he becomes anxiously sensitive to the slightest hint of possible noncomplementarity. This heightened sensitivity to a particular variety of expectations which are ferreted out in any and all situations cannot be regarded as genuine perceptiveness and imaginative capacity in any general sense. Imaginative capacity—the flexibility to discriminate, evaluate, and select meaning in a widely and freely ranging fashion—is closely related to what has been excessively condensed in the term "reality-testing."

Imaginative capacity of this sort is, clearly, not possible if there has been an internalization of a rubber fence beyond which one's experience may not wander without disaster. Instead, the characteristics of perception and thinking, whether stereotyped or amorphous, which occurred within the internalized rubber fence will be brought into all tasks and relations. The potential schizophrenic thus is particularly unprepared in ego skills and perceptions that would make possible the assumption of those roles, such as occupational and marital roles, which might be an expression of his personal identity, outside the family system of expectations, yet respected and valued by the family.

The formulation that we have been developing implies that as internalization takes place the child develops a reciprocal, active investment in maintaining the equilibrium of those family patterns which have contributed to the characteristics of his personality equilibrium. With various reinforcements or weakenings of his motivation arising from individual 'constitutional' sources and from the effects of extra-familial experience, the potential schizophrenic typically develops considerable skill and an immense positive investment in fulfilling family complementarity and in saving the family as well as himself from the panic of dissolution. Indeed, the schizophrenic's ego identity often seems to consist of himself viewed as someone who takes care of the needs and expectations of his family or family-substitute. One preschizophrenic, even after a number of years of marriage, was frequently called at 11 or 12 o'clock at night by his parents to drive 15 miles to straighten out their quarrels. Later, he felt himself needed in a similar way by his wife, and, as he became overtly schizophrenic, he was filled with panic and suspicions that his usefulness to his wife had disappeared.

## ACUTE SCHIZOPHRENIC EPISODES AND THEIR TRANSITION INTO CHRONIC STATES

The brittle and limited ego identity of the preschizophrenic, based upon an inner representation of the family system, is sorely strained in this culture as he approaches chronological adulthood. Through his own growth, the shift or loss of family figures, and the exposure to new outside relations which are more seductive or coercive than earlier ones, there comes a time when he can no longer superimpose the family identity upon his ego identity. Erikson has described the resultant disorganization in terms of acute identity diffusion.[16] Acute schizophrenic panic and disorganization seem to represent an identity crisis in the face of overwhelming guilt and anxiety attendant upon moving out of a particular kind of family role structure. In the transition from the acute episode to a chronic state, pseudo-mutuality is re-established, usually at a greater psychological distance from family members, with an increase in guilt and anxiety over subsequent moves toward differentiation, and with heightened autism, loneliness, and emptiness of experience.

A more detailed example of such a sequence, in which an acute schizophrenic episode passed into a chronic catatonic state, may further show how some of these devices for maintaining family pseudo-mutuality operate.

The patient, a single man of 25, diagnosed as catatonic schizophrenic, was admitted to the hospital in a slowed-down state. He was largely mute with hospital personnel, but still somewhat responsive to visits from his parents and girl friend. During the first visit, the patient took his girl friend off to an empty recreation room and left his parents alone in his room. Later that day, the girl friend requested and was granted permission to visit the patient at a separate time from the parents. The parents, however, began intensive communication with the girl friend and induced her to visit the patient with them. During the next visit, the parents gave their encouragement to the patient and his girl friend's petting together in the patient's bedroom; the parents sat in the room with them, thumbing through magazines. When the necking became so heavy that the nursing staff intervened, the girl friend remarked to the nurse that she had wondered about it and had wanted to talk to the doctor about its advisability but had been told by the mother not to speak to the doctors about it.

The following is an excerpt from the transcript of a recorded interview with the mother about a parental visit a week later.

He had put the bolster up in front of him so he didn't see Jean at all, and all she saw of him was his feet, and I leaned over to him and said very quietly, "Eddie, have you thought of what you would like to have us get for you to give to Jean for Christmas?" Quietly, so she couldn't hear us. And he said, "I don't want to get her anything." And I said, "She'd feel very badly if you didn't." And he said loudly enough so you could hear him across the hall—I mean he wasn't hollering or anything, but he spoke right out and he said, "Unless I can buy my own Christmas presents and do my own Christmas shopping it's not Christmas as far as I'm concerned." He said, "This business of having everything done for you. You can't do anything for yourself." And then he was vulgar—it's the first time I've ever heard him talk like that—he said "You can't even—" he said, "as far as I'm concerned I can't even shit for myself." It was shocking for me—I mean I wasn't—I mean I was shocked at the fact that he felt the need to express himself that way, and I said, "Well, it's perfectly all right if you don't want me to. We won't do it. It's entirely up to you." . . . And a little while later I said to him, "Eddie," I said, "I believe the doctors out here—I just want to say that I can appreciate—we can all appreciate what you are going through and that it's a pretty tough time, and the doctors say that sometimes these things become pretty painful—not physically, but pretty painful to you mentally, and we do understand and appreciate that, and everybody around here does too." And he said, "Well, what do they want me to do?" And I said, "Well, I don't know what anybody wants you to do, Eddie, but everybody, regardless of what you think, they want you to do what you want to do. But I said that there are so many times that you don't express yourself, and if you don't tell us and if you don't tell the doctors here what you want, all we can do is kind of guess about what it is you want, unless you say definitely that you do or you don't. There isn't any way of anybody knowing what you want unless you let us know." And he said, "Well, what do they want me to do? What do I have to do to get well?" I said, "Well, the only thing that I could suggest that might help is to talk to them just like you are talking to me now. Tell them how you feel about things." And he said, "Why do I have to talk to them?" He said "Are they God? Did they make me? Am I required to tell them my innermost feelings?" I started to say something and forgot what it was. Anyway, before I could say anything he said in a very controlled, and restrained, and courteous voice, as you would speak to an utter stranger on the streetcar, he said, "Would you please leave now." I said to him, "What did you say?" I couldn't believe my ears. He said, "I said, would you please leave now." And I said, "Eddie, you don't want me to go now. We've been looking forward to this visit all week, and I know that you have too." And he stood up and said, "Well, if you won't leave I will have to." He left the room and walked all the way down the corridor as far as he could possibly go . . . the very last door down there. So then we went outside.

This interchange signalled the onset of complete muteness and catatonia that continued for 13 months. It illustrates a serious disruption of the pseudo-mutuality which characterized the familial relations. The earlier background included an episode of violence on the part of the patient involving escaping from a hospital by scaling a ten-foot wall, threatening people in the vicinity with a knife, stealing a car, and finally being apprehended by the police in another city. The parents have never seen in this dramatic incident any expression of rage, but have attributed it solely to post electroshock confusion, specifically disclaiming this behavior as indicating a potential for rage within him. Thus the incident reported here occurs against a background of disruption and violence followed by withdrawal, passivity, and seeming submission to parental encompassment as an attempted restoration of earlier family relations.

In the incident cited, the parents clearly have taken over one of the few remaining areas of private experience and self-determination of the patient—his relation with his girl friend. This parental taking-over included being present during the sexual activity of the couple. The mother's whispered question, in front of the girl, about getting a present for him to give to her, was apparently the last straw, leading to an outburst of forcefully expressed resentment. The mother, although shocked, said this was "perfectly all right" and entirely up to him. Then, in a confusing denial of his explosive efforts to be direct in expressing his resentment, she suggests that his difficulty is in *not* expressing himself and, lastly, that the doctors would be the appropriate people to be the recipients of his feelings. This referral to the doctors is an attempt by the mother to heal the family breach by introducing outside persons into the picture. The patient is offended at this attempted deflection of his feeling to people who are unrelated to the immediate situation and asks, "Why do I have to talk to them?" It is additionally incredible and offensive since it violates the family code of keeping everything within the family. The patient seems to feel that his unprecedented effort to get his feelings across directly to his parents are hopeless, and he withdraws physically and psychologically.

However, his "polite" withdrawal is also his contribution to a restoration of pseudo-mutuality at a safer psychological distance. His own anxiety is thus reduced at the same time that he protects his parents from the intense anxiety which his continued open divergence would provoke in them. All three of the family members have demonstrated repeatedly in the past that they become anxious over any hint of disruption in their emotional attachment to each other; and both parents have frequently emphasized their vulnerability to cardiovascular disaster if they should become upset. In contrast to open divergence, the patient's subsequent muteness lends itself readily to a variety of interpretations, either disturbing or comforting, and hence this is a particularly appropriate vehicle for the expression of ambivalence.

During the following weeks and months the whole family set up a highly stable form of pseudo-mutuality. The incident described is reinterpreted by the parents: They developed the retrospective thesis that his withdrawal was out of anger at the nursing staff for intervening with the necking during the visit of the week before and that the whole incident had nothing whatsoever to do with them. They thus could quite comfortably resume visiting him as he lay silent, unresponsive, immobile, and certainly not openly aggressive toward them. Through his 'collaboration' by appearing as a passively helpless object of parental concern, the parents were able to become 'good parents' again. The new pseudo-mutuality with the son as a chronic schizophrenic was thus only quantitatively different from that which prevailed in the prepsychotic state.

So far, we have been considering the incident as illustrative of the cycle of breakdown of pseudo-mutuality followed by attempted restitution to a new version of the old pattern of relatedness. But the psychotic episode as a whole, including this present incident, also represents a miscarried attempt at attaining individuation. The initial breakdown in the pseudo-mutuality was motivated by the patient's drive toward individuation, and his behavior in this incident illustrates his wish for independence which he succeeds in attaining, in some ways, only by withdrawal. Thus, what may be considered a breakdown of relations within the family is simultaneously the attainment of some individuation, albeit of a seriously distorted kind.

However, in families in which strivings toward a separate personal identity are regarded as a nonintegrated, crazy, or chaotic experience, *each* member of the family—not only the patient—experiences frustration of his needs for achieving a sense of identity. The overt psychosis, then, may have a covert function of giving expression to the family's collective, although dissociated, desires for individuality. One of the covert family roles the patient takes in becoming overtly schizophrenic thus may be to allow other family members to achieve vicariously some measure of individuation.[17]

In contrasting pseudo-mutual complementarity with mutual and non-mutual forms of complementarity, we have attempted a new extension of role theory which takes into account the quality of subjective experience of the person taking a role. In mutuality, the complementarity has a larger context; individuation and noncomplementarity of particular expectations give rise to perceptual exploration and participation together, which expands and deepens the basis for the relation. Imaginative flexibility and perceptual accuracy are essential in mutuality, especially in the perception of noncomplementary expectations that may create for a time an element of alienation within the relation. In pseudo-mutuality, the full impact of alienation and loneliness is avoided, but a sense of relation unsupported by accurate perception of the realities of participation becomes a hollow and empty experience. In nonmutual complementarity, there is neither a strenuous effort to save the relation by warding off the perception of non-complementarity, nor is there any great interest in exploration of the meanings each person may have to offer the other.

In the families of certain schizophrenics we hypothesize that pseudo-mutuality takes an especially intense and enduring form, in which the family members strive for a sense of relation by trying to fit into the family role structure. The social organization in these families is shaped by a pervasive familial subculture of myths, legends, and ideology which stress the dire consequences of openly recognized divergence from a relatively limited number of fixed, engulfing family roles.

The shared, familial efforts to exclude from open recognition any evidences of noncomplementarity within the pseudo-mutual relation become group mechanisms that help perpetuate the pseudo-mutuality. In the families of schizophrenics these mechanisms act at a primitive level in preventing the articulation and selection of any meanings that might enable the individual family member to differentiate himself either within or outside of the family role structure. Family boundaries thus obscured are continuous but unstable, stretching, like a rubber fence, to include that which can be interpreted as complementary and contracting to extrude that which is interpreted as noncomplementary.

Role-taking in these families has not been modified by the events of actual participation or personal experience, and thus the roles cannot be integrated into the functions of a discriminating ego or become a valued part of a synthesizing ego identity. Rather, we hypothesize, the family role structure is taken into the personality functioning of these persons as an archaic superego which determines behavior directly, without negotiation with an actively perceiving ego.

In the acute schizophrenic episode can be found representations of the breakdown of pseudo-mutuality, its attempted restoration, the attainment of a distorted kind of individuation, and the vicarious expression of the need of the other family members for individuation. The chronic state that follows can be regarded as a return to pseudo-mutuality at a greater distance, with symptoms that represent a more stable compromise between an expression of individuation and a failure at individuation, between acceptance of a particular family role and nonacceptance, between achievement of relation and disruption of relation.

## NOTES

1. This is an expanded and modified version of a paper presented at the annual meeting of the American Psychiatric Association in Chicago, May, 1956, under the title, "Family Relationships of Schizophrenics: A 'Rubber-Fence' Hypothesis." Selected portions of the present version were presented in a symposium on the Family Milieu of Schizophrenics (Jean Delay, Chairman), at the Second International Congress for Psychiatry, Zurich, Switzerland, September, 1957, and at a meeting of the Harry Stack Sullivan Society, New York, April, 1958.
2. For example, see W.R.D. Fairbairn, *Psychoanalytic Studies of the Personality;* London, Tavistock Publ., 1952; Michael Balint, *Primary Love and Psychoanalytic Technique;* London, Hogarth Press, 1952.
3. Erik Homburger Erikson, "The Problem of Ego Identity," *J. Amer. Psychoanal. Assn.* (1956) 4:56–121.
4. See Martin Buber, "Distance and Relation," PSYCHIATRY (1957) 20:97–104, for a philosophical study of the issues involved in this necessity.
5. In the version of this paper presented at the annual meeting of the American Psychiatric Association in May, 1956, the phrase, *sense of complementarity,* was used throughout, instead of pseudo-mutuality. Because we attach so much importance to the difference between a sense or illusion of complementarity and genuine mutuality, we felt a more distinct difference in terms was warranted, since the qualifying words, *sense of,* were easily overlooked.
6. We are indebted to Dr. Herbert Kelman for calling to our attention the desirability of making explicit this third variety of complementarity.
7. See, in this connection, *Toward a General Theory of Action,* edited by Talcott Parsons and Edward A. Shils; Cambridge, Harvard Univ. Press, 1951.

8. John P. Spiegel has been a valuable and helpful stimulus to our thinking about role theory. See John P. Spiegel, "The Social Roles of Doctor and Patient in Psychoanalysis and Psychotherapy," *Psychiatry* (1954) 17:369–376; "The Resolution of Role Conflict Within the Family," *Psychiatry* (1957) 20:1–16. However, in distinguishing three varieties of complementarity—mutuality, pseudo-mutuality, and nonmutuality, we extend attention to the quality of subjective experience and personality functioning that occurs during role performance. When Spiegel speaks of role reciprocity as conferring spontaneity upon behavior by sparing a person "the necessity of coming to decisions about most of the acts he performs" (*Psychiatry*, 1957, p. 4), we feel that he is referring only to the reciprocity of basically nonmutual relations. In pseudo-mutuality, decisions are spared a person but at the price of *blocking* spontaneity. In genuine mutuality decision-making and spontaneity are interwoven; spontaneity in the service of imaginative capacity is from the beginning an integral part of the relationship system. We question whether the physiological model of homeostasis can be transposed to human relations and still leave room for the imaginative, selective, nonautomatic details of fully mutual complementarity. It is only in the simpler situation of nonmutuality and in the pathological situation of pseudo-mutuality that the automaticity of homeostatic equilibration seems an appropriate analogy.

9. Personal communication.

10. The dimension along which some degree of pseudo-mutuality may be found includes the psychoneuroses and character disorders but also certain phases of normal development. For example, romantic infatuations in normal adolescent development in American culture can be regarded as a relatively transitory pseudo-mutual attempt to deal with the identity diffusion that occurs with the prospect of assuming new, adult roles. 'Normally,' in time, there is perceptual correction and recognition of dissatisfaction with these illusory romantic relations.

11. Our views on the importance of this aspect of schizophrenic relations were developed independently but seem to concur with those of Bateson and his co-authors, who have recently referred to this as a "double bind" situation. Gregory Bateson, Don D. Jackson, Jay Haley, and John Weakland, "Toward a Theory of Schizophrenia," *Behavioral Sci.* (1956) 1:251–264.

12. Talcott Parsons and Robert F. Bales, *Family, Socialization and Interaction Process;* Glencoe, Ill., Free Press, 1955.

13. Talcott Parsons, "The Theory of Symbolism in Relation to Action," Chapter 2 in *Working Papers in the Theory of Action;* Glencoe, Ill., Free Press, 1953.

14. Compare Harry Stack Sullivan, *Clinical Studies in Psychiatry,* edited by Helen Swick Perry, Mary Ladd Gawel, and Martha Gibbon; New York, Norton, 1956. "The schizophrenic change, I believe, is quite generally due to an inability to maintain dissociation. . . . Thus the schizophrenic has an unsure mental state in which he is clearly aware of the activity of the dissociative system but unable to get the thing into clear personal focus" (p. 187).

15. Our emphasis on familial experience, for purposes of exposition, does not, of course, exclude effects on ego development from other sources, such as hereditary and constitutional factors. On the contrary, we consider the interaction of multiple factors as very likely of crucial significance. We have indicated that the kind of fit between native characteristics and family structure will affect the kind of psychological experience any given person may have. As a simple and obvious example, a girl who is assigned a 'feminine' role in a family will have a kind of experience different from that of a boy who is cast in the same feminine role.

16. See reference footnote 3.

17. We are indebted to Harold F. Searles for bringing this point to our attention.

# Part VII

---

# RETROSPECT AND PROSPECT

This book begins with a quotation in which Robert Oppenheimer tells us how work must and does proceed in "the necessarily early stages of sorting out an immensely vast experience." He makes clear that these early stages cannot be bypassed and that development of a field requires careful attention to its phenomena. Borrowing more sophisticated techniques from more highly developed sciences cannot *in itself* advance a new field if the phenomena of the field are not carefully and thoughtfully observed and conceptualized.[1]

It is clear that the study of the psychosocial interior of the family unit is in its early stages. Concentrated work in this field can be said to have begun in the early 1950's, although one can identify earlier forerunners.[2] A growing band of workers in psychiatry, psychology, sociology, anthropology, social work, and human development have been actively making observations and attempting to order their observations in a meaningful way. Enough work has been done from these various viewpoints to try some more systematic ordering, such as this book. The two articles in Part VII, bringing the book to a close, attempt more focused syntheses.

Possibly more intensive attention has been given to the problem of understanding the families of schizophrenic patients than to any other category of family. Elliot G. Mishler and Nancy E. Waxler are themselves now engaged in experimental studies of such families; here they systematically and intensively review the main observations and ideas that have been offered to understand the relationships between family interaction and schizophrenia. Their article is invaluable as a guide to and thoughtful critique of this work.

The concluding article, by the editor, attempts a broad overview of the field of whole family study. It seeks to sum up the work that has been done in terms of angle of approach, concepts, findings, and methods.

It is my hope that Part VII provides sufficient clarification and integration of the work accomplished to date so that future work may proceed with a clearer sense of direction than has been possible heretofore.

## NOTES

1. A fuller analysis of the nature of scientific development is presented by Thomas Kuhn in his illuminating, not to say dazzling, essay, *The Structure of Scientific Revolutions* (Chicago: University of Chicago Press, 1962).
2. One work that had made research workers and clinical practitioners sensitive to the potentials of the field is Henry B. Richardson's *Patients Have Families* (New York: Commonwealth Fund, 1945). However, the most important single guide undoubtedly has been psychoanalytic theory, which is not only a forerunner but also a continuing source of contributions.

# 22:

# Family Interaction Processes and Schizophrenia: A Review of Current Theories[1]

*Elliot G. Mishler* and *Nancy E. Waxler*

Many investigators have been concerned with whether specific features of family life are associated with the etiology and development of schizophrenia. Both personality characteristics and social attributes of parents have been objects of considerable research and speculation since the pre-World War II period; the well-known notion of the schizophrenogenic mother was one of the products of this early line of inquiry. (Reviews of much of this work may be found in Sanua, 1961, and Spiegel and Bell, 1959.) During the past decade there has been a noticeable shift in the focus of attention among students of this problem. Interest is now centered on the whole family as a unit for study and conceptualization and, in particular, on the patterns of interaction and communication among the members of the family.

This has been an exciting development accompanied by an array of new concepts and hypotheses about schizophrenia, suggestive of new techniques of treatment and productive of a growing body of research. It seemed to us both appropriate and timely to attempt a review and comparative analysis of current theories relating family processes and schizophrenia.[2] While many investigators have contributed to this development, three groups of investigators have had a major influence on the shape and direction of current thought and research; these are the research groups led by Gregory Bateson, Theodore Lidz, and Lyman Wynne. We shall place particular emphasis on their formulations.

Reprinted by permission from *Merrill-Palmer Quarterly of Behavior and Development,* Vol. 11, No. 4 (October 1965), pp. 269–315. Elliot G. Mishler is director of psychological research, Massachusetts Mental Health Center, and clinical associate in psychology, Department of Psychiatry, Harvard Medical School. Nancy E. Waxler is research associate in psychology, Massachusetts Mental Health Center and Department of Psychiatry, Harvard Medical School.

Our intent is both expository and analytic. We wish to clarify each theory's basic concepts, and compare their respective foci and levels of conceptualization. We have a special interest in how well the theories might serve as guides for research and will therefore be concerned with the degree of precision and testability of the various hypotheses. Experimental approaches to the study of family interaction have seemed to us to have a special relevance for these new formulations, and we shall refer at a number of points to the methods and findings of experimental studies of patient families. We hope that this review of these theories and methods will permit a specification of particularly critical areas for further work.

It will be seen below that the several theories differ from each other in a number of important ways—from their descriptive terms to their assumptions about schizophrenia; in whether they focus on difficulties in communication or affective relationships; in the degree of their concern with social roles or personality dynamics. While we have tried to preserve the flavor and the essential conceptual concerns of each theory, our primary interest has been in comparing them with each other. This has been done by contrasting the answers that each gives to a minimum set of basic questions with which any serious and systematic theory of family process and schizophrenia must be concerned. Taken together, answers to these questions would permit a relatively complete account of the specific conditions under which schizophrenia develops. This paper is organized around this set of questions.[3]

1. What are the patterns of family interaction that are related to the development of schizophrenia?

2. What is schizophrenia, and what are the psychological mechanisms through which family patterns of interaction enter into the development of the schizophrenic process?

3. How do these interaction patterns persist over time, that is, what individual and family functions are served that help to maintain the schizogenic forms of interaction?

4. What are the preconditions for these patterns of interaction? That is, what are the social and personal attributes of family members that are associated with the development of these processes?

Only the theories associated with Bateson, Lidz, and Wynne will be examined in detail. However, other formulations will be referred to at points in the discussion where they may provide further understanding of the various issues.

Before presenting detailed analyses in terms of the outline of critical questions listed above, it may be useful to the reader unfamiliar with one or another of the theories to have brief resumes of each of them in which the major concepts and special emphases may be seen in overall view.

## RESUMES OF THEORIES

### BATESON GROUP

The general theory of this group of investigators is often identified with the idea of the *double bind*. While this one concept does not do full justice to the complexity of the theory, it nevertheless mirrors in microcosm many of the latter's important aspects. The *double bind* is defined as a special type of learning context from which the growing child cannot escape; a context where he is subjected to incongruent messages that require him to deny important aspects of his self or his experience. The necessary ingredients are: repeated experience between two or more persons where one of them, i.e., the victim, is confronted with two incongruent negative injunctions, for example, "I order you to disobey me." Negative injunctions could be expressed in the affective quality of statements or be implicit in the situation of interaction as well as being expressed directly in verbal content. Punishment is expected to follow either choice in this conflict situation; a third negative injunction is present that prohibits the child from attempting to escape from the situation. Repeated exposure to such situations results in the individual's stripping his own messages of meaning since punishment can be avoided only by preventing the other person from understanding his response. Eventually, he behaves as if he had lost the ability to discriminate the true meanings of his own and others' messages, that is, he manifests schizophrenic behavior.

It is important to note that these hypotheses about schizophrenia derive from a proposed general model about human behavior where communication is viewed as equivalent to human behavior rather than as only one aspect among others. Further, there is a special focus in this theory on the equilibrium of the family state, that is, on the ways family members maintain stability in their communication with each other by developing rules governing who says what to whom in what contexts.

Originally, the theory was arrived at deductively, that is, by considering the nature of schizophrenic communication and "deducing" a set of requirements in the family that would lead to this form of pathological communication. Since that beginning, the formulation has developed through observations and analyses of family therapy sessions and, more recently, experimental studies of family behavior.

### LIDZ GROUP

While an explicit focus on the family as the unit of theoretical and empirical interest distinguishes this group's formulation, there is, nevertheless, a close resemblance to familiar psychodynamic traditions of theorizing about personality development and psychopathology. In many ways, this theory is a direct extension and application of orthodox psycho-analytic concepts to the family triad. There is a central concern with age-sex structure of the family. A critical etiological feature for schizophrenia lies for these theorists in the blurring of age and generation boundaries; parents behave inappropriately for their sex and age with respect both to each other and to their child and the child therefore learns inappropriate behavior. The consequence is that identity development for the child is distorted, and it is in the distortion of adequate identity development that the theory locates the psychological basis for schizophrenia. Empirically two types of schizogenic families are distinguished—one, organized around a central, dominating, pathological figure, usually the mother, and referred to as "skewed"; a second pattern of "schism" where the relationship is characterized by chronic hostility and mutual withdrawal. Different proc-esses in the development of schizophrenia for males and females are postu-lated and related to the different problems of identity development in each of these types of families. The entire family is seen as pathological, and patterns of irrational thinking and unrealistic views of the outside world are taught to the developing child. Finally, the dramatic quality of family relationships is described more explicitly here than in the other theories; both murderous and incestuous wishes, reciprocated by parents, threaten to break out of control during adolescence and are seen to play an important part in the schizophrenic breakdown.

Empirical work of the Lidz group has centered on an extensive in-vestigation of a small sample of hospitalized schizophrenic patients and their families; information has been gathered largely through diagnostic and therapeutic interviews.

### WYNNE GROUP

This theory is closer to that tradition in social psychological theory about socialization and personality development that gives prominence to the concept of an individual's identity as the link between the person and his culture. Within this general orientation, special attention is given to the impairment of ego functioning and its associated thought disorders in schizophrenia. In Wynne's formulation, an adequate identity and a healthy, well functioning ego require not only a stable and coherently meaningful environment but an opportunity to test out and to select as part of one's own individual identity a variety of roles during the course of development. The families of schizophrenics do not provide such a stable environment—in role structure they are either too rigid or too loosely and ambiguously structured, a lack of true complementarity is concealed under a facade of "pseudo-mutuality," communication and interaction are disjointed and fragmented, irrational shifts in the focus of attention prevent real continuity of interaction. Pressures to maintain this facade and to deny or to avoid the recognition of the basic meaninglessness of the relationships force the child to conform to the family system; the imposition of sanctions isolates him effectively from other sources of socialization. There is a general guiding hypothesis that the thought disorder in schizophrenia derives from the disordered patterns of interaction in the family.

Observation of families in family therapy situations were the major source of early formulations. More recently, emphasis has shifted to the systematic analysis of both psychological test protocols and family interactions within a "predictive" research strategy, that is, an attempt to predict from parental characteristics to presence and type of schizophrenia in the child.

## INTERACTION PATTERNS IN SCHIZOGENIC FAMILIES

If social interaction is defined broadly to include consistent ways in which persons act toward and respond to each other, then each theory under review gives a central place to the influence of certain types of intrafamilial interaction on the development of schizophrenia. However, the theories also differ markedly from each other, at the general level of the aspect or dimension of interaction with which each is concerned, and specifically in the particular types of distortion of normal interaction that are seen as critical and distinctive in schizophrenogenic families. Their similarities and differences in these respects will be explored in this section.

The Bateson group's felicitous phrase, *the double bind,* has gained wide currency although its precise intended meaning seems not to be as well understood as its general usage would suggest. (See the comments by Watzlawick, 1963). In part, its success as a term may reflect its surface relationship to the popular notion of a "bind" as a troubled and self-defeating interpersonal relationship. The difficulty is that a "bind" is a term with a vague referent rather than a precise definition of a particular type of relationship. If it is assimilated to this familiar and unclear concept, the new concept of the *double bind* loses both the formal precision that entered into its original formulation as well as its specific properties.

In their first comprehensive statement of a "communicational theory of the origin and nature of schizophrenia"—that is, a theory that centers the etiology of schizophrenia in parental communication to the child—Bateson and his co-workers (1956, pp. 253–254) specified the following necessary ingredients of a double bind situation: "1. Two or more persons. . . . 2. Repeated experience. . . . 3. A primary negative injunction. . . . 4. A secondary injunction conflicting with the first at a more abstract level, and like the first enforced by punishments or signals which threaten survival. . . . 5. A tertiary negative injunction prohibiting the victim from escaping from the field. . . ." These five elements exemplify in concrete form one of the ways in which the abstract idea of the double bind becomes manifest as a system of interaction.

In addition to this general formulation of a communication pattern consisting of conflicting injunctions, there is specification of three other features of the double bind that in this theory are necessary conditions for the development of schizophrenic reactions. In a sense, these are different types of "tertiary negative injunctions"—first, the fact of conflicting injunctions is denied; second, the child cannot escape from the situation; third, he is not permitted to "metacommunicate," that is, he can neither comment upon nor point to the contradictory nature of the communication. Of these "other features of the context" also to be mentioned, Bateson (1959, p. 133) states: ". . . there is, or appears to be, an absolute prohibition upon calling attention to the parents' incongruity in any overt way. . . . Neither the parents nor the patient is able to act as if fully aware of the incongruities. There is also a prohibition upon escaping from the field and, in addition, an insistence on the part of the parents that the patient respond. There shall be no non-responding and no not-caring and all these prohibitions are linked together. After all, to leave the field or to express 'not caring' would be to point the finger at the incongruities."

In the earlier paper (Bateson et al., 1956, p. 259), he and his co-workers provide a good example of a double bind in describing a situation involving a schizophrenic patient and his mother:

A young man who had fairly well recovered from an acute schizophrenic episode was visited in the hospital by his mother. He was glad to see her and impulsively put his arm around her shoulders, whereupon she stiffened. He withdrew his arm, and she asked, "Don't you love me any more?" He then blushed, and she said, "Dear, you must not be so easily embarrassed and afraid of your feelings."

The mother's communication includes conflicting sets of messages, putting her son in an impossible dilemma: "If I am to keep my tie to mother I must not show her that I love her, but if I do not show her that I love her, then I will lose her."

This is a "dammed if you do and dammed if you don't" situation for the child, who is trapped by the incongruent demands and forbidden to call attention to his predicament. Such a patient is, to apply here a statement made elsewhere by Bateson (1960, p. 477f), "faced with the dilemma either of being wrong in the primary context or of being right for the wrong reasons or in the wrong way. This is the so-called double bind. We are investigating the hypothesis that schizophrenic communication is learned and becomes habitual as a result of continual traumata of this kind."

The idea of incongruity is pervasive in the writings of members of this group of investigators. It is defined by example and implication and refers essentially to the lack of consistency between different aspects, levels, or elements of a message. Incongruity in communication may take any of a variety of forms. For example, the affect conveyed by tone of voice may differ from the literal meaning of the words, as in sarcasm or in joking hostility; the message may be inappropriate to its context, as in gallows humor; or the gestures may contradict the verbal content, as in the previous example of a double-bind situation between a patient and his mother; incongruity may result from denying or negating any of the elements of a message.

Such incongruities are involved in many forms of human discourse including humor and poetic metaphor. The problem lies with those special types of incongruity, i.e., double binds, where the individual is threatened with punishment whichever aspect of the incongruent message he chooses to respond to and where there is the underlying "prohibition upon comment." Bateson and his group generalize their views by referring them to Russell's theory of logical types where basic paradoxes are explored that result from the proposition that a class cannot be a member of itself.[4] If we understand them correctly, they are suggesting that the analogue to resolving logical paradoxes, by recognizing that two different levels of abstraction are involved, is the act of metacommunicating or commenting upon the incongruity between parts of a message. Where this last is forbidden, the incongruency cannot be resolved and the person receiving the messages remains trapped.

As a formal statement of relationships among levels of meaning, the double-bind hypothesis and its associated ideas is viewed as applicable to all types of social and cultural systems. (See, for example, the comments on cultures caught in double binds in Bateson, 1959.) However, within the narrow frame of family interaction the hypothesis as originally stated focused attention primarily on dyadic interaction, particularly between mother and child, in the etiology of schizophrenia—with the emphasis placed on the problems faced by the growing child "caught" in the double bind. More recently, there has been increased emphasis on the active role of the "victim" in maintaining this system.

While he uses the same basic paradigm of the double bind and its insoluble paradoxes, Haley (1963), in further developing the original formulation, gives more emphasis to the whole family unit as an interacting system. In so doing he suggests some of the parameters of a social system within which double binds may be adaptive responses. He points to the importance of the struggle for power and control in these families

Q*

and suggests that a primary issue in all human relationships has to do with "who" is going to set the rules for the relationship. He defines the family as a self-corrective social system in which behavior is governed, regulated, and patterned by internal processes where family members set limits to each other's behavior. Haley (1963, p. 160) stresses the need for complex models of such systems, since ". . . two levels of governing processes must be included: (a) the error-activated response by a member if any member exceeds a certain range of behavior, and (b) the attempt by family members to be the metagovernor, i.e., the one who sets the limits of that range."

As in all families, members of schizogenic families govern each other's behavior by imposing sanctions and other correctives when their rules and prohibitions are violated. The difference in these families, according to Haley, lies in the collective denial that anyone is setting the rules, that is, that anyone is the metagovernor. In this respect he notes:

> Typically in these families the mother tends to initiate what happens, while indicating either that she isn't, or that someone else should. The father will invite her to initiate what happens while condemning her when she does. Often they suggest the child take the lead, and then disqualify his attempts. . . . The family "just happens" to take actions in particular directions with no individual accepting the label as the one responsible for any action (p. 366). . . . The family of the schizophrenic would seem to be not only establishing and following a system of rules, as other families do, but also following a prohibition on any acknowledgment that a family member is setting rules. Each refuses to concede that he is circumscribing the behavior of others, and each refuses to concede that any other family member is governing him (Haley, 1959a, p. 372).

Haley points out that the act of communicating inherently involves defining one's relationship with the other person; that is, to communicate is to set rules at some level with regard to the nature of the behavior that is to take place in the relationship. Within schizogenic families, the members attempt to avoid defining their relationships to each other by negating or disqualifying any or all elements of their messages. These elements are listed as: "(1) I (2) am saying something (3) to you (4) in this situation" (Haley, 1959b, p. 325). A person may deny that he is the person speaking, may contradict one message with another, may refuse to acknowledge whom he is addressing. For example, Haley describes the husband whose wife asks him to do the dishes, responding with: "I would like to do the dishes, but I can't. I have a headache." By this response, the husband indicates that *he* is not defining the relationship by this refusal; after all it was the headache which prevented the dishwashing, not he. In a sense, these different ways of denying elements of a message appear to be varieties of double binds. Haley seems to be suggesting that the double bind is an adaptive response in a family whose members refuse to acknowledge that they are setting rules for each other's behavior, and as a consequence interaction is oriented toward denying any responsibility for the nature of their relationships.

Among other theorists concerned with the etiological role of family interaction processes in the development of schizophrenia, both Searles and Laing have described mechanisms that emphasize types of incongruity similar to those described in the Bateson-Haley formulations. Searles (1959a) outlines six "modes of driving the other person crazy," each of which tends to activate various areas of the person's personality in opposition to each other. These modes are: pointing out areas of the other's personality, of which he may be unaware, that are inconsistent with his ideal or actual self-image; stimulating the person sexually in settings where attempts at gratification would be disastrous; simultaneous or rapidly alternating stimulation and frustration; relating to the other simultaneously on two unrelated levels, for example, sexual advances during an intellectual-political discussion; switching erratically from one emotional wave length to the other while discussing the same topic; switching topics while maintaining the same emotional wave length, for example, discussing life and death issues in the same manner as trivial happenings.

While each of these is a concrete example of a pair of conflicting messages and therefore stands as an instance of that one ingredient of the double bind, Searles' treatment of the "binding" nature of these interactions focuses on the mutual satisfaction of needs rather than on the formal structure of the interaction.

Laing discusses "confirmation" of the self as a process through which individuals are recognized, acknowledged, "endorsed" by others—"the crux seems to be that it is a response by the other that is *relevant* to the evocative action, . . . a direct response, in the sense at least of being 'to the point,' or 'on the same beam' or 'wave-length' as the first person's initiatory or evocatory action" (Laing, 1961, p. 89). His discussion of the lack of true confirmation in the families of schizophrenics bears obvious similarities to the general idea of the double bind, but differs in the stress Laing places on the experiencing self as the object of the incongruous act. Thus, ". . . there is minimal genuine confirmation of the parents by each other and of the child by each parent, separately or together, but there may not be obvious disconfirmation. One finds, rather, interactions marked by pseudo-confirmation, by acts which masquerade as confirming actions but are counterfeit. . . . the schizogenic potential of the situation seems to reside largely in the fact that it is not recognized by anyone; or, . . . this knowledge is not brought out into the open" (Laing, 1961, p. 91). This tangential failure to "endorse" the other's experience is evident in the incident reported by Laing (1961, p. 93) where a litle boy runs to his mother with a worm in his hand and says,

"Mummy, look what a big fat worm I have got." To which the mother responds, "You are filthy. Away and clean yourself immediately."

There are several problems that deserve brief mention in concluding this summary of the Bateson group's formulation of critical interaction processes in the families of schizophrenics. First, there is a lack of precision and clarity in their writings that presents serious difficulties for an accurate understanding of the types of interaction sequences that do and do not fall within the definition of the double bind. From the way the concept is used, it sometimes appears that all communication sequences may be interpretable, at some level of analysis, as double binds, and, if this be so, the concept loses all usefulness. This ambiguity regarding the generality of the concept also obscures its specific relationship to related formulations. For example, the relations between the original double-bind hypothesis and Haley's later analyses of family rules has not been made explicit and remains unclear.

Two important problems do not receive attention in the writings of this group. One is that, in emphasizing the structure of communicative acts, the possibility is ignored that the critical influence of the double bind may reflect the substantive nature of the conflict presented. For example, if the conflict embodies deep and important intra-psychic conflicts (perhaps love vs. hate, or dependence vs. autonomy) or centers around significant family norms, then this may be more important than if the conflict concerns more trivial issues. Laing (1961, p. 90) makes the same point: "It may be that there are some areas of a person's being for which there is a more crying need for confirmation than others. It may be that there are some forms of disconfirmation which may be more actively destructive of the person's developing sense of himself than others, and which could therefore be schizogenic." However, this view is not shared by the Bateson group. Jackson writes that they "have not been impressed" by the need to include content in their analysis since they find a particular style of interaction manifesting itself irrespective of the content discussed. "The act itself alerts the participants that there is conflict and in itself constitutes a kind of psychological trauma, whatever the substantive issue."[5]

Second, there is the question of whose perspective is being used in determining the presence of incongruency or of disqualification. While the theory appears to refer to the perspectives of participants in the interaction, case materials and interpretations tend to reflect observers' viewpoints as to what are considered congruent or incongruent messages. This is a difficult problem for research and analysis, since messages an observer judges to be incongruent with reference to general external standards may carry with them implicit meanings, developed in the culture of that particular family, that make the messages congruent to the family members. While either the internal or external perspective could provide useful bases for interpretation, the differences between them are of critical importance and criteria for making the appropriate judgment require a more explicit statement than they have so far received.

There are many contrasts between the Bateson group's formulation and that of Lidz and his co-workers to whom we now turn. One of the most noticeable differences is the less formal and less abstract quality of the latter's statements; there is marked emphasis on the content of the pressures and conflicts as well as on their structure. Also, the point of reference of the theory shifts away from the level of communicative acts to the level of interpersonal role relationships.

The age and sex axes of role differentiation have a critical place in the Lidz analyses of different types of schizogenic families, and specific distortions in what they consider to be normal parent-child role relationships play a key role in their interpretations of the development of schizophrenia. The influence of Talcott Parsons' sociological formulation of family role structure is explicitly acknowledged. Thus, Lidz (1963, p. 53) writes that there are certain "requisites" for a marital relationship if it is to provide for the harmonious development of its offspring: "What appears to be essential can be stated simply. . . . The spouses need to form a coalition as members of the parental generation maintaining their respective gender-linked roles, and be capable of transmitting instrumentally useful ways of adaptation suited to the society in which they live."

This ideal model of a normal family, implied in the above quotation, pervades much of the work of these investigators. They find two deviant types of marital relationships in the family backgrounds of schizophrenic patients, one of which appears empirically to be associated with schizophrenia in female children and the other in male children. In the first pattern, designated as *marital schism,* there is a "state of severe chronic disequilibrium and discord . . . [and] recurrent threats of separation. . . . Communication consists primarily of coercive efforts and defiance or of efforts to mask the defiance to avoid fighting. There is little or no sharing of problems or satisfactions. . . . [There is] chronic 'undercutting' of the worth of one partner to the children by the other. The tendency to compete for the children's loyalty and affection is prominent. . . . Absence of any positive satisfaction from the marital relationship (excluding the children) is striking. . . . Mutual distrust of motivations is the rule . . ." (Lidz *et al.,* 1957b, p. 244). In the second pattern, called *marital skew,* the couples achieve a state of relative equilibrium in which the continuation of the marriage is not constantly threatened. However, ". . . family life was distorted by a skew in the marital relationship. . . . the rather serious psychopathology of one marital partner dominated the home" (Lidz *et al.,* 1957b, p. 246).

Their emphasis on the concrete substance of underlying conflicts, and on the strength of both the hostile and seductive elements in the situation, has led this group to explore the different implications for the development of schizophrenia of these two types of pathogenic marital relationships. They find that schizophrenic girls are more likely to have had a "schismatic" background; each parent in this open conflict situation seeks the support of the daughter. The boys with schizophrenia, on the other hand, are more likely to come from "skewed" situations which tend to have dominant mothers and passive fathers.

In neither of these types of marital relationship is there true "role reciprocity" which Lidz and his group see as one of the requisites for a successful marriage. They note (Lidz *et al.*, 1957b, p. 243) that ". . . role reciprocity requires common understanding and acceptance of each other's roles, goals, and motivation, and a reasonable sharing of cultural value orientations." This lack of role reciprocity is associated with distortions in role-appropriate behaviors for the different age-sex groups within the family. Thus, distinctions between the generations are not observed, the normal parental coalition is not maintained, and children become involved in the parental conflicts, with each parent competing for the child's support.

A schismatic family that includes many of these elements is thus described by Lidz:

> Mr. Nussbaum remained away from home as much as possible, and turned to his daughter [the patient] for the affection and admiration he could not gain from his wife. At times, he seemed to be spiting his wife by the alliance with the girl. He became very seductive toward the daughter, sleeping with her when she became anxious at night, and cuddling her to sleep until she began, during adolescence, to express fears of becoming pregnant. The child's problems became a major concern to both parents, but also a source of mutual recrimination. The mother sought to devote herself to her daughter's care when she became increasingly difficult during adolescence, but would lose patience and go into rages in which she would tell the girl that she wished she were dead. The mother, fairly typically, lacked empathy for her daughter, and because of her inconsistent behavior and the father's devaluation of her formed an unacceptable model, while the father seductively substituted the daughter for his wife. Thus the patient was at times a scapegoat and at other times a divisive influence (Lidz *et al.*, 1963, p. 10).

Lidz attaches much significance to the notion of role reciprocity, but it is not given a more precise definition than that implied in the quotation in the preceding paragraph. While Spiegel's (1957) analysis of family equilibrium and disequilibrium in terms of complementary role expectations is referred to as an explicit source, there are some differences in Lidz's use of the concept and some special problems associated with these differences. First, his idea of role-appropriate behavior involves the use of an assumed model of normatively correct family role behavior. Spiegel's original formulation leaves room for much inter-familial as well as sub-cultural variation in role expectations; Lidz, on the other hand, tends to neglect these variant patterns. Spiegel also provides for the possibility that strain and tendencies toward disequilibrium may exist with complementary role expectations, whereas equilibrium and role reciprocity appear to be viewed as synonymous in Lidz's formulation.

Associated with the general blurring of sex-generation roles in the families of schizophrenics is a preoccupation with and anxiety about incestuous feelings and behavior. "In our studies, we have noted the central moment of incestuous impulses, and our studies of their families revealed that these were not simply regressive symptoms of the patient, but that one or both parents was also caught in incestuous ties to the patient. . . . There is a reciprocity to these impulses of the patient that provokes panic lest loss of their own self control might lead to actual incest" (Lidz, 1963, p. 72).

These types of interpersonal relationships are viewed as "abnormal" family environments in which it is difficult for children to learn and behave in ways appropriate to their age and sex during the course of development. As a further consequence, these relationships predispose toward irrationality and distortions in thinking. Lidz (1963, p. 96) has described it as ". . . a strange family milieu filled with inconsistencies, contradictory meanings, and denial of what should be obvious. Facts are constantly being altered to suit emotionally determined needs. The children . . . learn that meanings are not primarily in the service of reality testing. . . . The acceptance of mutually contradictory experiences requires paralogical thinking. Such environments provide training in irrationality." Lidz (1963, p. 101) also points to a tendency for these families to be isolated from their social and cultural environments, noting for example, ". . . that the patients were habitually exposed to conflicts and meanings deviant from the shared communicative meanings of the culture. . . . " Opportunities for reality testing that would be provided by more contact with the normal world outside the family are restricted, and internal irrational patterns in the family are further reinforced.

Generally speaking, this formulation has both the flavor and vocabulary of traditional psychoanalytic theory—but as applied to the family rather than the individual as the unit of description and analysis. For example, as we shall see below, incestuous and hostile wishes, as well as difficulties in the successful resolution of the Oedipal situation figure prominently in their analyses of why these particular family patterns appear to be conducive to schizophrenia. This psychoanalytic toning of the theory is also evident in their treatment of social roles. While there is frequent reference to the concept of social role and to the notion of the family as a social system, the real dynamic sources of interaction in this theory lie in the personality structures of the individuals. Thus, the difficulties in establishing a harmonious marital relationship with true role reciprocity are attributed to the psychological problems brought to the marriage by husband and wife. Further, while pathogenic family backgrounds are described by such system terms as schism and skew, these family types appear empirically to be related to different types of parental personalities—a cold, punitive mother with a seductive father in the former; a dominant, seductive mother and a passive father in the latter. In attempting to predict the likelihood of a schizophrenic outcome, it appears that we have to depend on an understanding of the psychodynamics of the parents; to the extent that this is necessary, the analysis of the family as a social system is superfluous.

Unfortunately, there is much vagueness and ambiguity in Lidz's use of the social role concept. Sometimes, particularly in the early papers, it refers simply to stable ways of interacting that reflect personality, such as the "dominant mother" role. At other times, roles are normatively defined modes of "appropriate" behavior, that is, differentially appropriate for specified age and sex categories. In general, the complicated relationships between personality, role, and interaction are not specified; at times they appear to be used as different names for the same thing.

In general, Lidz's formulations are weakest when considered critically from the point of view of evaluating his theory as a set of coherent and rigorously defined concepts and abstract propositions. Concepts are borrowed from sociology, psychoanalysis, and theories of language development; these concepts have not yet been welded together into a unified system. On the other hand, the strength of this group's approach lies in their emphasis on those powerful concrete parameters of family life, namely, the differentiating axes of age and sex. This has been associated with their discovery of different types of family structures in the developmental histories of male and female schizophrenics; such distinctions are not made systematically by other investigators.

The theory of schizophrenic development proposed by Bowen and Brodey deserves mention at this point, since it has marked similarity to that of Lidz as well as an important difference in the conception of family roles. The similarity is evident in such things as the description by Bowen and Brodey of their study families as having marked conflict, "emotional divorce" between the parents, an overadequate mother with a peripherally attached father (Bowen, 1959; Bowen, 1960)—a pattern closely resembling Lidz's schismatic group. There is also an emphasis on the psychodynamic sources of the marital role relationships. The difference lies in the etiological significance attributed by Bowen and Brodey to the structure of the role relationships rather than to its content. The important factor for them is the extremity and rigidity of the role structure. The tendency in these families as they describe them is for the roles to become polarized, for example, for an omnipotent-helpless polarity to develop (Brodey, 1959). Behavior is then molded into conformity with these extreme and stereotyped role definitions. While a high degree of rigidity in role structure is evident in the case descriptions given by Lidz, this feature does not enter into their formulations as a significant variable. As with Lidz, there is some difficulty with the Bowen-Brodey formulations in separating personality pathology in the parents from the pattern of role polarization as etiological influences in the development of schizophrenia.

Wynne and his co-investigators at the National Institute of Mental Health are also concerned primarily with the quality and structure of role relationships within the family, rather than with the particular content of these relationships. Their emphasis is on the family system as the unit of conceptualization rather than on dyadic or triadic relationships within the family. Thus, their objective is to develop an interpretation of schizophrenia "that takes into conceptual account the social organization of the family as a whole" (Wynne et al., 1958, p. 205). The rationale for this approach, stated in an early paper, is made explicit in the general hypothesis underlying their work: "The fragmentation of experience, the identity diffusion, the disturbed modes of perception and communication, and certain other characteristics of the acute reactive schizophrenic personality structure are to a significant extent derived, by processes of internalization, from characteristics of the family social organization, . . . also internalized are the ways of thinking and of deriving meaning, the points of anxiety, and the irrationality, confusion, and ambiguities that were expressed in the shared mechanism of the family social organization" (Wynne et al., 1958, p. 215).

The definition of schizophrenia and the psychological mechanisms involved, that are implicit in the above statement of rationale, will be examined in later sections of this paper. At this point we wish to review the specific properties of family social organization that are thought to be significant by the NIMH group.

In a number of papers dealing with the relationships between schizophrenic thinking disorders and family transactions, Wynne and Singer have described what they believe to be the main features differentiating the families of young adult schizophrenics from other families. They note that these are the features that "work" empirically in the sense that they permit predictions to whether and what type of schizophrenia is present in the offspring on the basis of information about parental patterns of behavior and cognition. A recent statement refers to the four main features of these families as follows:

. . . first and foremost, *patterns of handling attention and meaning* [that interfere with the child's capacity for selective attention and purposive behavior]; second, styles of relating, *especially erratic and inappropriate kinds of distance and closeness;* third, *underlying feelings of pervasive meaninglessness, pointlessness and emptiness;* and fourth, an *over-all structure of the family* in which members have collusively joined together in shared maneuvers which deny or re-interpret the reality or existence of anxiety-provoking feelings and events. These shared maneuvers, including what has been called pseudo-mutuality and pseudo-hostility, tend to encompass the experience of the growing child and cut off or render anxiety-laden, experiences with peers and the broader culture. This kind of family structuring, previously described as the "rubber fence" phenomenon, reduces or negates the corrective influence which extra-familial contacts could otherwise have and heightens the impact of the disturbed intra-familial environment. (Wynne and Singer, 1964, p. 10).

Major attention has been given in their recent work to the first of the four features—patterns of handling attention and meaning in the family. The "transactional thought disorders" in schizophrenic families are evident in communications that are fragmented, blurred, poorly integrated and disjunctive. The assumption here is that these "familial transactions and maneuvers would be especially likely to disrupt and impair the development of an offspring's capacity to focus attention and to think sequentially and adaptively" (Singer and Wynne, 1963b, p. 14).

Transactional thought disorders, represented in the communication and the interaction of the whole family, are classified along the same amorphous-fragmented continuum as are individual thought disorders. Amorphous patterns of interaction in these families are exemplified by vague drifting of a discussion through shifts in the object of attention, blurring of meaning by using uncertain referents, and irrelevant meanings. Singer and Wynne (1963b, p. 20) describe an amorphous response to a TAT story given by the parent of a schizophrenic that might be considered an example of how this parent interacts with his child: "A father began a story about a young boy wanting to go out with his friends instead of practicing his violin. He was reminded of a movie about an older fellow who went joy-riding with his friends. After a lengthy, aimless story, he concluded: 'And so, into the sunset'." Fragmented patterns of interaction and communication consist of such characteristics as intrusion of primary process, using odd vantage points for communications such as peculiar spatial or temporal positions, and crypticness; each of these modes of communication results in poorly integrated messages. For example, one parent's complete response to a Rorschach card was, "If you read stories of Cossacks, that's self-explanatory."

These styles of communicating meaning are assumed to be characteristic of the family as a whole, not simply the thought patterns of one parent. Further, it is hypothesized that these ". . . styles of attending, perceiving, thinking, communicating and relating used in family transactions are likely to have promoted the cognitive development of the offspring in certain directions, either by serving as models for identification or by eliciting complementary behaviors" (Singer and Wynne, 1963b, p. 9).

The second general feature of the schizophrenic family included in the summary listing given above has to do with styles of relating, especially with erratic and inappropriate kinds of distance and closeness. Here the maintenance of proper distance refers both to cognitive and affective functions, both to distance from people and distance from ideas or objects. Schizophrenic family patterns seem to be characterized by "fluctuating and variable cognitive sets and relational distances. . . . The distance taken is often inappropriately close or remote and when an alteration in 'foca distance' is made, which in normals occurs smoothly and unnoticed, it is disjunctive and awkward" (Singer and Wynne, 1963b, pp. 27–28). For example, the mother of a schizophrenic child, related to the psychologist in much the same way she probably related to her child. "[She] limited herself to describing the Rorschach cards as symmetrical, and as 'reproductions,' [and] seemed remote both from the card and the tester. Suddenly she asked the tester what brand of lipstick she was wearing" (Singer and Wynne, 1963b, p. 27). These shifts in affect and style of relating make for confused expectations in the child and provide odd and fragmented models for identification.

These modes for handling meaning and the styles of relating, in Wynne's theory, seem to serve as defenses against underlying feelings of pervasive meaninglessness, pointlessness and emptiness. Feelings of meaninglessness are defined as subjective states, "in which purposes, wishes, aspirations, interpersonal relationships, work, and other activity are felt by the person himself to be without point, without direction, without leading to decisive satisfaction or dissatisfaction, to clear success or defeat, to genuine mutuality or total alienation or separation."[6] These feelings are not continuously present and manifest to family members but rather are similar to repressed or unconscious material in the sense that family members attempt to defend themselves against their recognition.

Finally, the overall structure of the schizophrenic family is characterized by shared maneuvers that serve to deny or reinterpret the reality of anxiety-provoking feelings, and apparently, of the underlying meaninglessness of the relationships. Wynne uses the concepts of pseudo-mutuality and pseudo-hostility to describe these structural patterns. Pseudo-mutuality is defined by contrasting it both with mutuality or a relationship of true complementarity, and with nonmutuality or a situation without reciprocal obligations. Complementarity is lacking in pseudo-mutual relationship, but the facade of mutuality is maintained energetically: ". . . in describing pseudo-mutuality, we are emphasizing a predominant absorption in fitting together, at the expense of the differentiation of the identities of the persons in the relation. . . . In pseudo-mutuality emotional investment is directed more toward maintaining the *sense* of reciprocal fulfillment of expectations than toward accurately perceiving changing expectations" (Wynne *et al.*, 1958, p. 207).

In illustration, Wynne quotes one mother whose desperate preoccupation with harmony at all costs is obvious. "We are all peaceful. I like peace even if I have to kill someone to get it. . . . A more normal, happy kid would be hard to find. I was pleased with my child! I was pleased with my husband! I was pleased with my life. I have *always* been pleased. We have had twenty-five years of the happiest married life and of being a father and mother" (Wynne *et al.*, 1958, p. 211).

The negative counterpart of pseudo-mutuality is pseudo-hostility. It differs from the former in defining a state of chronic conflict and alienation among family members, but this difference is seen as unimportant and superficial. What is important is that both states are fixed, rigid, and "pseudo." Both are viewed as collective defenses, permitting family members to maintain some semblance of a life together without having to confront directly the essential and pervasive "meaninglessness" of their life as well as their underlying fears of separation, hostility, tenderness or intimacy.

These qualities of family relationship are associated with family role structures that are either rigid and stereotyped or loosely and ambiguously structured. The specific type of structure, whether rigid or ambiguous, may be associated with the specific sub-type of schizophrenia developed (a point to which we shall return), but either structure creates difficulties for the development of appropriate personality-role and role-role relationships. The sources of these difficulties are as follows: Deviation is not permitted from prescribed and simple "formulas" for behaving; distinctions are not made between the person and his role. This "blurring" of boundaries between individual and role results in the family's being experienced by the developing child as all-encompassing of the self; there is no identity separate from one's role within the family.

A number of mechanisms are described through which deviations from the family's rigid role structure are either excluded from recognition or reinterpreted, thus preserving the illusion of harmony and mutuality. Among these are family myths and legends that stress the catastrophic consequences of divergence from the rigidly-defined roles; a bland and indiscriminate approval of each other's actions preserving a facade of harmony and peace; the denial of contradictions in one's own or others' behavior; a stress on secrecy and a concomitant concern with prying into other persons' private experiences; and, a formalization or ritualization of normal family experiences. Reinforcing these processes is the lack of adequate articulation between the family and the larger social system—so that ". . . family members try to act as if the family could be a truly self-sufficient social system with a completely encircling boundary" (Wynne *et al.,* 1958, p. 211). This "continuous but elastic" boundary is referred to as a "rubber fence."

In his attempt to characterize the patterns of interaction in these families, Wynne employs concepts at several different levels of analysis. Thus, the structure of role relationships is described as falling along a continuum from rigidity to amorphousness, the affective quality of relationships varies from pseudo-mutual to pseudo-hostile or fluctuates from close to distant, and interpersonal communication shows degrees of fragmentation or amorphousness. Further, the structure of role relationships is seen as a collective defense against recognizing the underlying "meaninglessness" of the relationship. The strategy of research and theory formation seems to be to view each of these as independent dimensions and to determine whether and how they are empirically associated with each other. Thus, no *a priori* claim is made that pseudo-mutuality is theoretically required by rigid roles, or that fragmentation is a function of pseudo-mutuality. Rather than deriving the connections among these different levels from systematic theory, the aim is to accumulate relevant data and work toward empirical generalizations of the conditions under which these different patterns are found together.

The preceding review of how these different theories approach the problem of schizophrenia suggests some of the difficulties of comparing them to each other in a systematic way. While they share an emphasis on family interaction, the conceptual foci vary markedly as do the particular dimensions of interaction they isolate as significant. It is tempting—but we believe deceptive and not particularly useful—to consider double binds as illustrative of fragmented communication, or pseudo-mutuality as the affective quality of a skewed marital relationship. The formulations differ from each other in more serious and significant ways than in the labels they apply to phenomena. They point to different phenomena, and these differences merit clarification before an attempt is made to reduce them to one comprehensive theory.

Some of these differences will become more evident in the following sections, but a few may be noted here. First there is the question of conceptual focus—of how "sociological," "psychological," or "interactional" the different theories are. It seems to us that Wynne and Haley in focusing on family roles and norms are most sociological in their analysis. Lidz's use of role terms, as we have noted before, is not systematic and his primary emphasis on personality and motive places him at the psychological pole of theorizing. Bateson is concerned neither with roles nor motives but with a different unit of analysis entirely, namely, the communicative act. Both Haley and Wynne, of course, are also interested in communication but always within its context of the role structure. These varied conceptual foci permit the different theories to avoid direct confrontation at a theoretical level. Empirical comparison of the theories with each other is, for this reason, an extremely difficult and complex problem.

A further point of difference refers to the concrete relationship that the theories tend to focus upon. Bateson's use of the double bind in its specific application to schizophrenia is dyadic in emphasis; for example, one of the stated essential ingredients is two persons. One consequence is that the family tends to be viewed as consisting of a set of dyadic relationships. In Lidz, the stress is also on the dyad, in this instance the marital relationship; however, it is a dyadic relationship that has an effect on a third person, that is, the developing child. Finally, in Wynne and Haley, the concepts refer to the whole family as the unit for analysis and theory without concern for any specific role player or players.

Both of these points on the different emphases of the several theories must be qualified by noting that over time each theory has tended to become more comprehensive and more eclectic. Wynne's view has already been referred to regarding the independence of the different levels—role, interaction, and psychological functioning. Lidz, for whom ". . . every area of interaction in these families was found to be faulty in some respect . . ." (Lidz and Fleck, 1964, p. 4) views each separate area of deficiency or failure—parental nurturance, appropriate role structure, and the transmission of culturally instrumental techniques—as related to a specific problem in development. And he suggests that the severity of the illness may be related to how extreme and generalized the deficiences are. In Bateson's formulation, the distinctions between levels are erased through the use of the highly abstract model of communicative behavior as a general framework for describing all behavior.

Since each of the theories is concerned with the same basic phenomena, this "strain toward comprehensiveness" gives recent statements of the Wynne, Lidz, and Bateson groups a stronger appearance of similarity than was evident in early statements. However, it has seemed to us that the differences in emphasis outlined in this section, and detailed further in the following ones, remain and are important determinants of both the research and theoretical directions still being pursued by the different groups.

## THE SCHIZOPHRENIC PROCESS

The distinctive feature of the theories we have been discussing lies in their emphasis on the critical role in the development of schizophrenia played by particular interaction patterns and family role relationships. In this section we shall be concerned with the accounts given by each of the theories about the ways in which this family environment leads to schizophrenia in the child. Several different questions are involved, and the theories vary in the degree of explicitness and detail with which they attempt to answer them. How is schizophrenia defined? What are the psychological mechanisms through which a person becomes schizophrenic? What distinguishes the pre-psychotic schizophrenic personality structure from the psychotic schizophrenic? What are the precipitating events for a psychotic breakdown?

In discussing "overt" schizophrenia or the "identified" schizophrenic in the family (thus distinguishing this from the endemic "covert" schizophrenia in these families), Bateson (1960a, p. 487) states:

> The more serious and conspicuous degree of symptomatology is what is conventionally called schizophrenic. . . . [They] behave in ways which are grossly deviant from the cultural environment . . . characterized by conspicuous or exaggerated errors and distortions regarding the nature and typing of their own messages (internal and external) and the messages which they receive from others. . . . In general, these distortions boil down to this: that the patient behaves in such a way that he shall be responsible for no metacommunicative aspects of his messages. He does this, moreover, in a manner which makes his behavior conspicuous.

Elsewhere (Bateson, 1959, pp. 133–134) the typical schizophrenic message is described as a "stripping of all explicit or implicit metacommunicative material . . ." and the "boundary of sanity is, however, crossed when the subject uses these tricks of communication in situations which the common man—one hesitates to say the 'normal'—would not perceive as the schizophrenic seems to perceive them."

For Bateson, distinguishing between "overt" and "covert" schizophrenia is an explicit problem, because the ways in which schizophrenic patients communicate appear (in terms of his theory) to be only exaggerations of forms of communication that are pervasive in their families. On the whole, while he is not clear on this matter, Bateson would appear to make the distinction between overt and covert schizophrenia a function of the severity and extent of these forms of communication. The identified schizophrenic behaves this way "conspicuously" and in "normal" situations; the other members of his family are more selective and restrained.

Bateson's views about schizophrenia as an "illness" are outlined in his introduction to an autobiographical account of a schizophrenic psychosis, *Perceval's Narrative* (1961). In a sense, he turns the whole question of illness on its head—by proposing that the symptoms of schizophrenia are adaptive responses of an individual to an underlying illness, in much the same way that fevers and other somatic symptoms are recognized in medicine today as the body's response to primary pathology. While he does not explicitly connect these observations with his other views on the role of the overt schizophrenic within the family, it appears as if the "pathology" to which the psychosis is a response refers to the distorted patterns of family relationships. In this context, the schizophrenic psychosis is conceived to have a potentially curative function and a normal course that may end with the remission of symptoms, a course that may be aided or hindered by the forms of therapeutic intervention attempted. As he has stated in the introduction referred to (Perceval, (1961):

[This is] . . . one of the most interesting characteristics of the strange condition known as schizophrenia: that the disease, if it be one, seems sometimes to have curative properties. . . . we are today familiar with the fact that many of the so-called symptoms of organic disease are the efforts that the body makes to correct some deeper pathology. . . . The dynamics of the curative nightmare are, however, quite obscure. It is one thing to see the symptom as a part of a defense mechanism; it is quite another to conceive that the body or the mind contains, in some form, such wisdom that it can create that *attack* upon itself that will lead to a later resolution of the pathology (pp. xi–xii). . . . Once precipitated into psychosis the patient has a course to run. . . . Once begun, a schizophrenic episode would appear to have as definite a course as an initiation ceremony—a death and rebirth—into which the novice may have been precipitated by his family or by adventitious circumstances, but which in its course is largely steered by endogenous process (p. xiv).

Haley approaches the problem of defining the nature of schizophrenia within the context of an attempt to develop an interactional description of schizophrenia, in contrast to either the classic psychiatric or psychodynamic approaches. Expanding upon a basic theme that persons cannot avoid dealing with the problems of the definition and control of their relationships with others (since all communication presupposes rules about "who" is permitted to say "what" to "whom", "when" and "where"), Haley proposes that there is, however, one way by which a person can avoid defining a relationship and that way is by negating or disqualifying his communications. It is not easy to "strip" one's messages of their metacommunicative meanings; Haley suggests that it requires various types of denial and distortion of one's responsibility for messages. He notes:

When everything a person says to another person defines the relationship with that person, he can avoid indicating what sort of relationship he is in only by denying that he is speaking, denying that anything is said, denying that it is said to the other person, or denying that the interchange is occurring in this place at this time. . . . It seems apparent that the list of ways to avoid defining a relationship is a list of schizophrenic symptoms. . . . The various and seemingly unconnected and bizarre symptoms of schizophrenia can be seen to have a central and rather simple nucleus. If one is determined to avoid defining his relationship, he can do so only by behaving in those ways which are describable as symptoms of schizophrenia. . . . The differences from the normal lie in the consistency of the schizophrenic's behavior and the extremes to which he goes (Haley, 1959b, pp. 326–327).

Thus, schizophrenic behavior is viewed both as purposeful, in that the individual is attempting through his behavior to avoid committing himself to a particular definition of his relationships with others, and as unavoidable, since the only solution open to someone caught in a double bind is to respond in kind. In the end he gives up the attempt to discriminate meanings in the messages of others and attempts only to ensure that others will not find "meaning" in his own messages. It is not clear whether Bateson, Haley, and others in this group view the schizophrenic patient as having lost the capacity to discriminate or whether it is simply that he ceases to respond in terms of normally discriminated meanings. Their descriptions focus on his behavior rather than on his internal states. His behavior is "learned" in the sense that all human communicative behavior is learned. The learning context, however, is the rather special one where he is punished by withdrawal of love, abandonment, or hostility for alternative and more adequate responses to the double bind.

Haley considers the overt psychotic phase of schizophrenia "an intermittent type of behavior" occurring in situations of a particular kind of stress: ". . . when the patient is staying within the rules of his family system, he is behaving 'normally.' However, when he is required to infringe the rules, and at the same time remain within them, he adapts by schizophrenic behavior" (Haley, 1960, pp. 466–467). By "normal", Haley means normal for the patient's family in the sense that he is qualifying his statements in ways that are similar to that of his parents. Faced with the possibility of having to infringe a family prohibition, "[as] when (1) two family prohibitions conflict with each other and he must respond to both, (2) when forces outside the family, or maturational forces within himself, require him to infringe them, or (3) when prohibitions special to him conflict with prohibitions applying to all family members" (Haley, 1959a, p. 369), the schizophrenic behaves in a unique and actively psychotic way; that is, he displays incongruence at all levels of communication. These conflicting prohibitions may occur when the patient is in treatment and involved with both his mother and therapist, or they may occur with greater frequency at certain times, such as in adolescence.

In the formulations of Bateson, Haley and their co-workers, schizophrenia as an active psychosis is intermittent and specific to the "identified" patient in the family. The schizophrenic process as a form of communication, however, is continuous and generalized to all family members. Thus, any member of the family might become an "overt" schizophrenic if faced with the conflict of infringing and staying within the family prohibitions. In another aspect of his analysis, which we shall discuss in the next section, Bateson also hypothesizes that these families require only one "overt" schizophrenic and that his existence serves to stabilize the family.

There are many contrasts between the views outlined above and those of Wynne and his collaborators regarding the nature of and basic processes involved in schizophrenia. In overview, the Wynne group sees schizophrenia as the result of an individual's failure to develop a clear and stable ego identity—a failure reflecting a faulty family environment that prevents the individual from developing the necessary ego capacities and strengths for normal personality development. Within this general approach, they have centered their specific research and conceptual analyses on the thought disorder aspects of schizophrenia. "We have stressed the desirability of focusing research upon those aspects of schizophrenia which have seemed central and primary, rather than peripheral and secondary, that is, upon *structural* features, particularly the formal thinking disorders, rather than the content of the disturbance" (Wynne and Singer, 1963b, p. 200).

In their general formulation, the process of schizophrenic development is contrasted explicitly with a model of normal personality development. An assumed basic requisite for normal development is the establishment of an adequate ego-identity. This, in turn, is viewed as dependent upon a family environment with a clear and organized role structure where the focus of attention in interaction is consistent and unambiguous. In other words, the family system must be a learning environment that permits both appropriate identification and reality testing. With explicit acknowledgment to Erikson's formulations, Wynne conceives of an adequate and healthy identity as consisting not only in the sum of different role components, but as involving the selective integration of various role components into a unique personal identity.

The learning environment constituted by the role structure and interaction processes in families of schizophrenic patients, described in the previous section of this paper, permits neither adequate reality testing nor opportunities for the flexible integration of roles into the developing self. For example, the rigid role structure combined with the norm of pseudomutuality force the child to act out the form of a role but not to grasp its substance. The role cannot be adequately integrated as a part of his self since the required actions do not correspond to inner feelings and needs. Thus, in describing the process of internalization of the family role structure, Wynne *et al.* (1958, pp. 215–216) state: ". . . roles and role behavior in intense pseudo-mutual relations come to be largely dissociated from subjective experience. Such roles are not integrated into the functioning of an actively perceiving ego, but come to govern the person's behavior in an automatic 'reflex' fashion, having the quality of 'going through the motions.' These patterns of role behavior . . . in a general sense are internalized into the personality, although they are not under the jurisdiction of an actively discriminating ego."

Further, because the patterns of interaction are either amorphous or fragmented, in ways described previously, a stable and coherent "focus of attention" is lacking that would permit adequate reality testing and the development of rational and ordered thought. In formulating the link between the type of thought disorder present in schizophrenia and patterns of family interaction, the concept of "focal attention" (borrowed from Schachtel) is given a prominent place. "In schizophrenia, as we are formulating it, there is an impairment or defect of those ego structures which involve the various aspects of focal attention . . . the failure of the capacity to focus and maintain a major set in the face of intrusiveness from both external and internal stimuli" (Wynne and Singer, 1964, p. 7). The family patterns of handling attention and meaning, described above as lying along the continuum from amorphous through fragmented styles of interaction, are seen as "directly related to the development of capacities for focal attention in offspring."

While these distorted modes of thinking and patterns of rigid role performance are inadequate and inappropriate from the point of view of the general culture, they nevertheless permit the individual to function adequately within his family until adolescence. At this point in his life, both his inner drives and the expectations of society require an independent and secure ego identity if the individual is to participate fully on the wider social scene. Acute schizophrenia, in this theory, occurs in the context of an identity crisis. This crisis derives from the societal requirement that the individual move out of the rigid family role structure and behave as an independent and flexible person. This is an insoluble problem for the child since he can no longer remain completely within the family but cannot meet adequately the new demands. The schizophrenic reaction is his solution.

Wynne and Singer also distinguish between types of schizophrenics— those with primarily amorphous and those with primarily fragmented thought disorders. Although mentioned occasionally, such distinctions are not used systematically by other theorists. They suggest (Wynne and Singer, 1963b, p. 18) that these differences may be rooted in different family structures: "In using this differentiation-integration formulation for classifying schizophrenia, we shall group global, predominantly undifferentiated forms of functioning under the heading of '*amorphousness.*' Failures of hierarchic integration, after some degree of clear differentiation has been achieved, we shall call '*fragmentation.*' Along a continuum these represent, in our formulation, different varieties of cognitive disorganization or thought disorder." They also suggest (Wynne and Singer, 1962, p. 71) that these types of schizophrenic thought disorders may be associ-

ated respectively with different family types whose interaction characteristics correspond to the amorphous-fragmented patterns of cognitive disorganization: ". . . One of the implications of the work is that patterns
of the families of schizophrenics need to be considered as heterogeneous
in order to link them successfully with the heterogeneity of schizophrenic
offspring."

Given the pervasiveness of thought disorder within these families,
should all members be viewed as schizophrenic—perhaps covert schizophrenics as in Bateson's formulation? Wynne does not deal explicitly with
this question and does not distinguish between thought disorder as part of
the active psychosis and thought disorder as part of a more general
schizophrenic-type process. It appears as if he starts with the schizophrenic
patient as a "given" and then attempts to define and describe his characteristic ways of thinking. Thus, in a sense, the patient has been diagnosed as
schizophrenic on other grounds and features of his cognitive styles are
then examined to determine if there are consistencies in this area of his
behavior. In this connection we find the following view expressed:

> . . . it should be clear that we do *not* regard the patterning of attentional
> and thinking disorders as basically transitory states which come and go in
> response to temporary stresses whether induced by psychological disturbance,
> drugs, fatigue, etc., but as underlying enduring forms or styles of functioning.
> To be sure, psychological or physiological stresses may facilitate the emer-
> gence into view of the disorders, but more fundamentally they are the rela-
> tively stable, built-in pattern in which an individual functions in a considerable
> variety of circumstances, experimental and clinical (Wynne and Singer, 1964,
> p. 9).

Wynne's formulations have been developed on the basis of data derived from family therapy, experimental studies, and the use of a predictive method. The latter has been particularly prominent in the recent
work (Wynne and Singer 1963a). Essentially, in this method an attempt
has been made to predict whether and what type of schizophrenic illness
is present in an offspring (typed in terms of style of thinking) on the basis
of an analysis of data from other members of the patient's family; this
data has usually been projective test material, but excerpts of parental interaction have also been used. They believe that the systematic use of this
method has moved them toward ". . . greater precision in differentiating
and defining concepts and greater attention to the processes and methods
by which data are assessed" (Wynne and Singer, 1964, p. 3). Associated
with the increased use of this method in their work has been increased attention to psychological processes in the development of schizophrenia,
and less emphasis than there was in the early papers on the patterning of
roles within these families.

The view of schizophrenia presented by Lidz and his co-investigators is similar in many respects to that of Wynne and his NIMH group. Thought disorder is paramount in the definition of the illness: ". . . the critical characteristics that distinguish this category of mental illness concern the disturbed symbolic processes without degradation of the intelligence potential. The core problem . . . : disordered concept formation, concretistic thinking, mislabelled metaphor, impaired categorical thinking, intrusions of primary process material, derailment of association, etc." (Lidz, 1963, p. 91). Further similarities with Wynne lie in Lidz's view of schizophrenia as primarily a disease of adolescence and in the emphasis placed both on the lack of an adequate identity and on the learning of paralogic and distorted ways of thinking as major components of the schizophrenic developmental process.

However, the problems of identity formation in adolescence and the consequences for the child are specified very differently. Rather than locating the source of identity problems in either a poorly or rigidly articulated role structure, as Wynne does, Lidz sees the basic problem as consisting in a lack of adequate identity models within the family. He distinguishes between concrete problems in development for boys and girls. However, he notes that in both cases the essential difficulty is the same, that is, how to form a sex-appropriate identity in the presence of the faulty identity model provided by the parent of the same sex. For the girl, the mother is cold, aloof, and hostile; for the boy, the father is passive and inadequate. In both cases the opposite sex parent is engaged in undercutting his or her spouse and in making seductive overtures to the child. This blurring of generation boundaries and the lack of proper adult models, results in an inadequate, weak ego identity: ". . . these parents fail to provide a satisfactory family milieu because they cannot form a coalition as members of the parental generation maintaining their appropriate sex-linked roles, or transmit instrumentally valid ways of thinking, feeling, and communicating suited to the society into which the child must emerge. The child who grows up in a family lacking in these fundamentals has confused and confusing models for identification, has difficulty in achieving a sex-linked identity, in overcoming his incestuous attachments, and in finding meaningful and consistent guides for relating to others . . ." (Lidz *et al.*, 1963, p. 3).

At adolescence, rather than an identity crisis of the kind described by Wynne, the acute onset of a schizophrenic psychosis is precipitated by the fear of loss of control over either incestuous or hostile impulses. The threat of being overwhelmed by these drives, of being unable to control them, forces the child to adopt a schizophrenic response where either the perception of his own needs is altered radically or he abandons rational ways of behaving. Or as outlined by Lidz (1963):

[The] progression of the erotically toned child-parent attraction to an incestuous bond threatens the existence of the nuclear family, prevents the child from investing energy into extra-familial socializing channels, and blocks his emergence as an adult. . . . His conscious avoidance of incest becomes necessary because of defective family structure and role confusion, the personalities of family members become further distorted because spontaneous interaction becomes impossible, role conflict inevitable, and crippling defenses necessary (p. 73). . . . Confronted by an untenable conflict and unable to find a path into the future, the schizophrenic patient withdraws from the demands of society and reality by breaking the confines imposed by the meanings and logic of his culture which, in turn further isolates the patient. The condition tends to become self-perpetuating, because the patient ceases to test the instrumental utility of his concepts and no longer seeks the consensus of meanings required for living cooperatively with others (Lidz, 1963, p. 92).

Essentially this is a description of a psychosis that develops when a weak ego can no longer manage its inner drives. Contributing to the choice of a schizophrenic pattern in this conflict is the fact that the child's background has been deficient in rational problem solving. His learning environment was one where irrationality and denial were pervasive. He thus has little in the way of either internal or external resources that can be drawn upon at the time of acute crisis.

The problems of development outlined above are linked by Lidz to general deficiencies in parental nurturance patterns and the failure of the familial environment to provide an adequate socialization context for normal personality development. In recent papers, equal attention has been directed to "defects in transmitting the communicative and other basic instrumental techniques of the culture to the child" (Lidz and Fleck, 1964, p. 5). The acquisition of language is seen as primary to the acquisition of other adaptive skills for participation in the culture:

The foundations of language are established within the family. Whether the child gains trust in the utility and validity of verbal communication as a means of understanding and collaborating with others, or learns that words are in the service of fantasy rather than of problem solving, or are a means of avoiding recognition of the obvious, or are used to blur or obfuscate, depends upon the nature of the intrafamilial communications. The topic is crucial to the study of schizophrenia and extremely complex. Here, we can only assert that these families in which schizophrenic patients grew up fail to inculcate consistent or instrumentally valid meanings (Lidz and Fleck, 1964, p. 20).

The critical role in the onset of schizophrenia assigned by Bateson, Wynne, and Lidz to the stressful period of adolescence is in agreement both with epidemiological findings on age differentials in rates of schizophrenia (see, for example, Locke, Kramer et al., 1958, p. 175; and Mishler and Scotch, 1963, p. 318) and with the views of many other investigators of family relationships in schizophrenia. There are some differences, however, in the nature of the particular stresses that are judged to be important. For example, the conflict between dependence and independence is stressed by such workers as Lu (1961, 1962), Bowen (1959, 1960) and Brodey (1959). They suggest that the groundwork for the particularly intense conflict experienced by the individual who becomes schizophrenic is prepared by parents who overtly stress independence and achievement in one context, but foster dependence in another context sometimes at a covert and sometimes at an overt level. At adolescence there is either a sudden demand for adult responsible behavior, failure to meet this demand, and consequent schizophrenic withdrawal; or the individual is faced with insoluble and conflicting demands to be both dependent and independent and resolves his dilemma by a schizophrenic breakdown.

From this discussion, certain contrasting emphases are evident among these theorists in how they define schizophrenia and see its development. Wynne sees schizophrenia as essentially a problem in identity development with associated cognitive difficulty; the psychosis is an exaggerated form of a relatively enduring cognitive style. Bateson, on the other hand, views schizophrenia as an inability to label and respond accurately to messages, which inability has developed from particular types of learning situations. While the manifestations of the psychosis in distorted patterns of communication are exaggerations of previous patterns, the psychosis is for Bateson a symptom of the individual's struggle for psychological health. Lidz seems to combine problems of sex-role identification with the learning of distorted and maladaptive ways of thinking in his characterization of the nature of the illness; schizophrenia is seen as a "deficiency" disease, i.e., the end result of a long family history of failures in adequate enculturation.

These different formulations of the schizophrenic process correspond in many ways to the theorists' different descriptions of patterns of family structure and interaction that were presented in an earlier section. Thus, in seeing schizophrenia as a problem in identity development, Wynne tends to describe the socializing environment in terms of inadequate role relationships, i.e., a rigid or ambiguous family role structure. These relationships prevent healthy role identifications and at the same time provide a confusing learning environment that interferes with the development of a stable identity. If, on the other hand schizophrenia is seen as a problem of distortions in communication, as Bateson sees it, then the developmental context tends to be described in terms of situations where one is punished for responding to messages as if they contained clear and definite meaning. There are both gains and losses from a degree of internal consistency of point of view within each theory. Obviously, there must be some form of correspondence between the descriptions of interaction patterns and the schizophrenic process if the former are to be etiologically related to the latter. However, it is also obvious that if the theories are to provide comprehensive accounts of the etiology of schizophrenia, then additional concepts must be introduced which may stretch this fabric of consistency. Lidz and Wynne have been moving toward more comprehensive statements. For example, both are concerned with cognitive and affective aspects of personality, and with developmental sequences and processes, as well as with family interaction processes. The relationships between the different types and levels of concepts is not always clear in their work and the gaps between levels tend to be bridged by implicit assumptions rather than by empirical findings. We shall return to this general problem in the concluding section of this paper.

## THE PERSISTENCE OF INTERACTION PATTERNS

The previous two sections were devoted to the central questions with which these theories are concerned, namely, what are the special characteristics of interaction in the families of schizophrenics, and how do they lead to schizophrenia. While answers to these two questions constitute the core of each of the theories with respect to the etiology of schizophrenia, there are two other questions that are of interest in their own right and also throw additional light on the similarities and differences among the several approaches that we have been comparing. These are: first, what accounts for the persistence in these family patterns? Second, what are the predisposing background factors for the development of these interaction patterns and the schizophrenic solution? We will discuss the first question in this section and the second in the following one.

While the level and focus of description vary among the several theories under review, there appears to be general consensus about characterizing these families as in states of chronic distress. This does not imply that there is continual and manifest dissatisfaction and unhappiness. In Wynne's analysis, as one example, a family may avoid the overt expression of underlying and pervasive tension by a retreat behind a facade of harmony. However, if such a solution were adopted it would be considered in all of these formulations as inherently unstable and unsatisfying in the same sense that neurotic defenses are considered unsatisfying in analyses of personality dynamics. That is, the defenses may be necessary to avoid overwhelming anxiety and further disintegration, but serious costs are involved. Thus, the presumed cost for the family of a retreat behind a harmonious facade to the posture of Wynne's pseudo-mutuality in role relationships is the denial of reality and the loss of personal identities for all family members.

Nevertheless, despite the distress and lack of mutual satisfaction, it appears that these families persist and their members persist in dealing with each other over and over again in the same ways. Bateson (1961, p. 104) points explicitly to the stability of the system despite its pathogenicity, in that "these families, in a gross sense, continue as families. The statement, 'this is a closely intercommunicating system,' continues to be true in spite of the very considerable unhappiness of the members. . . ."

Given this paradox—of relationships that persist despite the distress they occasion—it is important to ask how the system maintains itself. Or, more precisely it is important to ask how each of the theories attempts to answer this question. What functions are presumed to be served by these patterns of interaction, at both an individual and group level, that might account for their persistence?

In the approach of Bateson and his co-workers, functions served for the family as a social unit receive attention. In his analysis of the "steady state" of these families, Bateson (1959, p. 128) writes that, "first and foremost that which is characteristic is a very tough stability . . . homeostasis. . . . When the identified patient begins to get well, we observe all sorts of subtle pressure being exerted to perpetuate his illness . . . It is not that at all costs the identified patient must be kept confused; rather it seems as if the patient himself is an accessory—even a willing sacrifice—to the family homeostasis."

How does the theory attempt to account for this "tough stability"? We could not find an explicit attempt to provide an explanation. However, in general discussions of this problem of homeostasis, two broad hypotheses are proposed that would seem to be relevant to this question of why the patterns persist—one at the level of group and the other of individual dynamics. At the level of group dynamics, Bateson suggests that these are families that do not permit stable coalitions. He views coalitions as requisites for viable solutions to the recurrent problems faced by such social units as families. In the absence of viable solutions, family members cannot achieve stable and adequate self-identities; they are "continually undergoing the experience of negation of self." This hypothesis at the level of the family as a social group is connected with a hypothesis at the individual level to account for the persistence of unsatisfactory interaction patterns. This is the belief on the part of family members, presumably derived from the self-negating experience, that the self can actually be destroyed: "In fact, the double-binding interaction is a sort of battle around the question of whose self shall be destroyed and the basic characteristic of the family, which is shared by all the relevant members, is the premise that the self is destroyed or can be destroyed in this battle—and *therefore* the fight must go on" (Bateson, 1959, p. 136). In outline, this proposes that in families, stable coalitions are necessary for successful problem-solving and successful problem-solving is necessary for the development of

R

adequate self-identities. In the absence of this pattern, the double bind becomes persistent and pervasive as a mode of communication, apparently because it permits individuals to avoid the complete destruction of the self that they believe would follow an unambiguous expression of real feelings and beliefs.

Haley attempts to account for these persistent patterns of mutually destructive activity by proposing a conceptual model that he believes has particular appropriateness for the analysis of interaction processes. His point of departure is the ". . . peculiar sensitivity of people to the fact that their behavior is governed by others" (Haley, 1959a, p. 371). Central to his approach are the two ideas that human communication can be classified into several message levels and that social groups are self-corrective, governed systems. "If a family confines itself to repetitive patterns within a certain range of possible behavior then they are confined to that range by some sort of governing process. No outside governor requires the family members to behave in their habitual patterns, so this governing process must exist within the family. . . . When people respond to one another they govern, or establish rules, for each other's behavior. . . . Such a system tends to be error-activated. Should one family member break a family rule, the others become activated until he either conforms to the rule again or successfully establishes a new one" (Haley, 1959a, p. 373). This analogy of an error-activated system is proposed as a model for describing all families. The special characteristic of the family of the schizophrenic is that it is "not only establishing and following a system of rules, as other families do, but also following a prohibition on any acknowledgement that a family member is setting rules. Each refuses to concede that any other family member is governing him" (Haley, 1959a, p. 372). Haley's model has obvious similarities to traditional sociological conceptualizations of social systems where behavior is mutually regulated by shared norms (i.e., rules) and where social control is exercised through the imposition of sanctions when deviant behavior occurs (i.e., error-activated responses to rule breaking).

The view that the double-bind interaction pattern may persist because it serves a defensive psychological function is noted though not stressed by Bateson. For example, a child may have a special significance for the mother such that her anxiety and hostility are aroused when she is in danger of intimate contact with the child. In order to control her anxiety, she tries to control her distance from the child by giving incongruent messages, that is, messages that reject but simultaneously deny the rejection. Haley also points to the potential psychological function of the double bind but formulates its general aim as the maintenance of a fluid and undefined relationship; the basic anxiety in this instance would seem to be that in entering into a defined relationship one must acknowledge that one is setting rules for governing the relationship.

Whether the specific defensive function is to allay anxiety about intimacy or the fact of a relationship itself, the Bateson-Haley formulation gives the child an active role in the maintenance of the pathological interaction. This results from the specific reward-punishment schedule in this type of learning context. The child is led to respond to incongruent messages with incongruencies of his own; only this type of response is rewarded since it serves to maintain the mother's denial, while other behaviors of the child are met by punishment and the threat of abandonment or the withdrawal of love.

The views set forth by Searles (1958, 1959a) are relevant here, since he also sees the child as actively involved in the maintenance of the special forms of interaction in these families and relates this to the child's perception of the mother's intra-psychic conflicts and needs. However, he ascribes this involvement to different sources than Bateson. Starting from the perspective that there are "positive feelings in the relationship between the schizophrenic and his mother," he suggests that the child stays within the relationship out of compassion and love for the mother, with the related concern that were he to leave her or to change the mother would be "annhilated" or "go crazy." Thus, he argues that the child is not kept in the relationship by "hateful" double binds, but remains in it so that he will not hurt the mother.

The problem of why these unsatisfying interaction patterns persist receives less explicit stress in the work of Lidz and his co-workers, although at the same time they seem to give more attention in their descriptive accounts to states of disturbance and conflict in these families. In their model of family social organization the marital role relationship serves the function of maintaining each partner's emotional equilibrium; different types of marital roles are seen as deriving from individual differences in intra-psychic needs and conflicts. As we understand the implications of this view, however distorted or abnormal the role relationship in a schizogenic family may appear to an observer, it persists because it serves tension-reducing functions for both partners. There is an obvious relationship between this formulation and their general psychodynamic approach noted earlier.

The child appears to be "recruited" into the system, that is, taught appropriate but pathological behavior, in order to help stabilize the system. In other words, he is not permitted to work out a role for himself that would threaten the existing parental role pattern, whether it be a relationship of marital schism or marital skew, since that would threaten the emotional equilibrium of one or both parents. He is permitted to take any of a number of positions within the structure—as a mediator, as a scapegoat, as an ally of one or the other parent—but any role must be consistent with the ongoing relationship and in this way his actions serve to maintain the system.

We have noted previously two other characteristics of these families that are reported by Lidz which would seem to be of further help in maintaining their basic relationship patterns. These are the pervasive atmosphere of irrationality within the family and the associated isolation of family members from the common culture. The effects of this atmosphere on the child are to restrict drastically his ability to perceive and communicate appropriately in the world outside the family. The distortions of perception and communication on the part of the parents, in the service of their own rigid defense systems, are transmitted to the child who finds these forms of perceiving and behaving necessary if he is to maintain his position within the family. He is forced into a more complete dependence on the family and into patterns of behavior that are consistent with the emotional requirements of the parents.

One problem in interpreting Lidz's position on this general question is that he sometimes discusses the social organization of the family as if only the normal family had a stable organized form, defined by a condition of effective role reciprocity, while the pathology of the schizogenic family is treated as if in itself it constituted a state of disorganization. (For example, see Lidz, 1963, pp. 39–76.) However, at other times the characteristic patterns found in the schizogenic family, such as schism and skew, are clearly recognized as stable and persistent; they are simply less harmonious and more conflictful forms of family organization than that of full role reciprocity. This lack of consistency in his conceptual analysis of the idea of the family as a social organization has resulted in a lack of attention to the problem of the persistence of pathological patterns. In particular, the functional analysis has been restricted to the individual level and there has been no analysis of the functions served for the family as a social unit.

As we noted in an earlier section, Wynne and his team of NIMH investigators view pseudo-mutuality as a collective defense against a recognition of the underlying and pervasive meaninglessness of family members' experience and of their relationships with each other. The interaction patterns associated with the pseudo-relationships appear to persist for the same reason that personality defenses persist, namely, they are effective in reducing overwhelming anxiety. As a result, considerable energy and affect is invested in the denfensive pattern, and other alternatives are excluded.

In this theory, there seems to be a general but implicit assumption that social systems like families maintain themselves through complementary role expectations. Sanctions are imposed if behavior is not consistent with the normative definitions of the group; the imposition of the sanctions serves to perpetuate accepted behaviors. The pseudo-relationships in the schizogenic family are like this, only more so. The respective roles are stereotyped and rigid; deviations or failures in role performance are either denied or reinterpreted. The similarity between this and Haley's formulation of the family as an error-activated system is evident. However, while Haley separates rule-setting activity from the rules themselves and proposes that it is the rule-setting activity that is denied, Wynne has emphasized the denial of violations of the rules.

In addition to this mutually regulative process of complementary role expectations, Wynne suggests that one consequence of the rigid role structure is that each family member develops a strong personal investment in maintaining things as they are. This comes about because the system does not permit a separation of their personal identities from their family roles. This is clearest in the case of the child. Wynne argues that the development of an adequate ego identity requires a socializing environment where the individual is free to step back from and reflect upon his role, to try out different ways of carrying out his role, to select and reintegrate aspects of his several different roles into his own distinctive identity. Where there is little tolerance for not fitting completely into a role and where emphasis is placed on the rigid maintenance of a facade of relationships, there is neither the proper atmosphere nor appropriate opportunities to engage in the type of role-playing experience through which the identity can be separated from the family role system. Since there is no self as distinct from the role, the role must be carried out in an exact way, or there would be no self. The same general function is served for the parents, whose identity problems derive from their own backgrounds. In order to retain any sense of self, each parent must invest great energy in maintaining the set of rigid family roles since underneath these "identities" there is only a frightening "meaninglessness."

Among these theorists, Wynne is closest to the tradition of social psychology that is equally concerned with group and personality dynamics. His formulations, therefore, share with Lidz an interest in the personality dynamics underlying an individual's behavior in his social roles and with Haley a sociological emphasis on norms and sanctions as group regulatory mechanisms. The inclusion of both levels of analysis leads, we believe, to a somewhat different orientation to the problem of persistence. Whereas for both Lidz and Haley, the fact of persistence has a passive or responsive quality—the patterns serve personality needs or continue through the operation of an error-activation mechanism—for Wynne, persistence is an active state. Family members struggle to maintain their existing relationship patterns and resist pressures to change. It should be noted that Bateson's views are also "dynamic" with reference to this problem and this may be related to his focus here on issues of personality development similar to Wynne's focus on identity, namely, the issue of the self and the possibilities of its destruction.

The general answer given by the several theories to the question of why particular patterns of social relationships and interaction persist is that they serve defensive functions at both an individual and group level. In attributing persistence to the functional significance of the behaviors and relationships, the theories are consistent with traditional conceptual models in the social and behavioral sciences that attempt to account for the repetitive "ongoingness" of both social and personality systems. One of the problems with such functional explanations, however, is that they lead us to infer the motives or needs in whose service the resultant behaviors are presumed to function. In Bateson, Lidz, and Searles the line of inference leads to the personality structures of the parents and, in particular, to a pathological level of anxiety when faced with problems of intimacy and control in normal parent-child relationships. In Haley and Wynne, emphasis is given to inferred group processes for maintaining or restoring stable relationships. It is important to point out that these individual and group processes are inferred from the observed patterns of interaction, and, while they are used as hypothetical explanations, as presently stated they are not useful for purposes of prediction.

## PREDISPOSING FACTORS IN THE DEVELOPMENT OF SCHIZOPHRENIA

What personal and social characteristics of the parents are associated with the types of interaction patterns that are postulated as schizogenic? Are these specific attributes that make involvement in these interaction patterns more likely for one child rather than another in the family? Do certain combinations of parent-child traits increase the likelihood that these patterns will develop around a particular child? Each of the theories proposes answers to these questions by specifying predisposing factors, or "sorting" variables, that serve to make certain families and children more vulnerable than others to the postulated schizogenic processes.

There is general reference in each of the theories to the pre-existing personality pathology of one or both parents or the existence of a "difficult" interpersonal relationship between them (or a combination of these). For example, Lidz notes that a distorted marital role pattern, either "schismatic" or "skewed," is the family environment into which the child is born. He also points to their findings (Lidz *et al.,* 1963, pp. 2–3) that half of the fathers and half of the mothers have serious personality disturbances: "All of the families were seriously disturbed. The difficulties pervaded the entire family interaction. . . . We have noted the severe psychopathology of the fathers as well as the mothers, and we have found that these families were either schismatic . . . or were 'skewed' in that the serious personality disturbance of one parent set the pattern of family interaction." The emphasis in this theory is on the distortion of the "normal" role patterns resulting from and associated with personality pathology in one or both parents—"the fathers, as are so many of the mothers, are so caught up in their own problems that they can rarely satisfactorily fill the essentials of a parental role" (Lidz *et al.*, 1957a, p. 342).

Wynne gives little attention to the problem of predisposing background factors. While in general he seems to locate the determinants of interaction patterns in the parental role relationship, he also views the personality characteristics of the parents as among the determinants of role patterns. Bateson's discussion of these factors is also sketchy. Nevertheless, he appears to give more weight to the personality of the mother than to the parental role relationship in the initiation of the double bind; once it begins, however, other factors maintain it. For example, the mother's anxiety may be aroused when she is threatened by the possibility of a close interpersonal relationship. She tries, therefore, to develop a particular style of interaction—that is, the double bind— that will protect her from a "close" relationship with the child. The specific role of the father and his relationship to the mother in the development of the family's interaction pattern is left unstated. It is further suggested by Bateson (1960a, p. 485 f) that the pathological interaction patterns develop over time through a process of mutual reinforcement among family members: ". . . It seems that in schizophrenia the environmental factors themselves are likely to be modified by the subject's behavior whenever behavior related to schizophrenia starts to appear. . . . The symptomatic behavior of the identified patient fits with this environment and, indeed, promotes in the other members those characteristics which evoke the schizophrenic behavior." In other word, while the process may start with the mother's attempts through double binds to defend herself against anxiety, the factors involved in its origin are considered less important than the process through which in time the child and other family members come to behave toward each other in similar ways.

The question of the increased or special vulnerability of a particular child comes down in large part to the question of why not all of the children in these families are schizophrenic. One solution to this problem is to propose that all the children "really" are schizophrenic but only one of them shows manifest symptomatology, usually because of the particular patterning of stressful circumstances in some situation or at some point in time. As we pointed out earlier in discussing Bateson's distinction between covert and overt schizophrenia, he tends to adopt this position. "If the family is schizophrenogenic, how does it happen that all of the siblings are not diagnosable as schizophrenic patients. . . . In the schizophrenic family there may be room for only one schizophrenic" (Bateson, 1960a, p. 486). This last point is related to the more general equilibrium theme we have found in this theory; the particular type of homeostasis in these families is achieved by one and only one of its members being overtly schizophrenic. In other contexts, it is suggested that while genetics may play a role in deciding which of several siblings shall be the schizophrenic, the particular attributes of the child "selected" to be the overt schizophrenic may be less important determinants than the nature of the mother's emotional conflicts; the latter determine which child will be focused upon as "special" and threatening to her defenses. For example, in some instances male children may be special in this sense and thus be more vulnerable; in other instances it may be female children.

While Wynne is more specific in mentioning the types of biological characteristics that may be important—such as the sex of the child, place in the birth order, activity pattern at birth, or physical features—his general view is that the significance of the characteristic depends upon the psychological situation of the parents rather than upon what the concrete characteristic may be. Variations in significance reflect some "fit" between the parents' intra-psychic makeups and the attributes of the child. In their discussion of etiology, Wynne and Singer propose a "transactional and epigenetic view of development" where interactions between parents and offspring depend at each phase on the outcome of previous phases. In this context, they stress the necessity of considering the kinds of transactions the parents will make together as a team and the ways in which their "role fit and emotional meshing" give different meaning to such concrete characteristics of the child as sex, or place in the sibling order (Wynne and Singer, 1964, pp. 13–20).

Lidz and his co-workers have focused more directly than other theorists on the problem of specific predisposing factors. In their work the most significant attribute for the selection of one rather than another sibling for schizophrenia appears to be the sex of the child. This follows from two general assumptions in the theory: (a) the developmental tasks of male and female children differ from each other, and (b) schizophrenia occurs in a context of familial role relationships that do not permit the child to complete his or her normal cycle of development. Specifically, the male child is particularly vulnerable in the "skewed" type of family where there tends to be a passive, weak father and a seductive, engulfing mother. Thus, the male child's opportunity for normal identity development will be markedly impaired. In "schismatic" families on the other hand, it is the female child who is most vulnerable. Here, the marital role relationship typically reflects an aloof and devalued mother with a grandiose and narcissistic father. In these families, the developmental tasks for the female child are most difficult and the chances of developing a normal and adequate identity are reduced. (It should be noted that the association described between marital role type and the pathology of the particular parents is reported as a trend; there are instances where mothers are dominant and grandiose in the schismatic families and fathers are dominant in the skewed types.)

Among other theorists, Lu has been specifically concerned with differences between schizophrenics and their non-schizophrenic siblings in the relative intensity both of the contradictory demands made by the parents and the attempts by the child to fulfill the demands. She notes (Lu, 1962, p. 229) that the ". . . process of such parents—pre-schizophrenic interaction and emotional entanglement seems to begin as early as the patient's birth and infancy." Two sets of unusual circumstances are described which may lead mothers to pay more attention to or give more protection to the pre-schizophrenic child; the child has special characteristics or the birth occurs at a time of particular frustration and tension within the family. Bowen and Brodey's formulation is similar to Wynne's in stressing that the pre-schizophrenic child in some sense "matches" an area of personality conflict. For example, a sickly child or one who may need extra help and nurturance has a mother with strong unresolved conflicts around dependency needs; the non-schizophrenic child does not "match" these needs and therefore can remain somewhat outside of the entangling involvement (Brodey, 1959).

In focusing on the differences among the theories in the predisposing factors they specify, we have given insufficient stress to certain general themes that are common to all of them. For example, in each of the theories the parents of schizophrenics are seen as immature people, anxious and conflicted, and tending to use primitive mechanisms of defense. The marital relationship is unsatisfying and distorted; role relationships are rigid; ways of meeting each other's needs are disturbed and pathological; there is a state of chronic disequilibrium in the family. The child who becomes schizophrenic is "weak" to begin with; he may have a physical handicap, be ill in infancy, have severe eating problems, or in some way be defined quite early as needing special attention. There is also reference to, although not systematic examination of, the possibility of exceptional stress at the time of the child's birth or early infancy such as extreme financial pressure, illness in the family, or sudden shifts in place of residence.

Both Bateson and Wynne are explicit about the transactional nature of the process and point out that the selected child comes to act as required and in turn elicits special types of response from others. Wynne and Singer (1962, p. 61) point out how this approach differs from certain traditional points of view: "Each offspring clearly has an impact upon the rest of the family, including the parents, so that the offspring alter and help shape the family system from which they in turn derive some of the

R*

personality characteristics and forms of functioning. Our viewpoint thus differs from those psychodynamic theories which have sometimes implied that particular kinds of psychological trauma have a unidirectional effect upon a passively receptive child or that 'schizophrenogenic' mothers or parents have one-way victimizing effects upon their offspring."

Associated with this transactional approach is a general recognition that none of the specific or general predisposing factors is *the* cause of schizophrenia. Rather, the several factors are viewed as setting the stage for schizophrenia by increasing the vulnerability both of the family and of the selected child to the development of the schizogenic process.

## DISCUSSION

It would be relatively easy, as anyone could confirm who has read papers by Bateson, Lidz, Wynne and their co-investigators, to detail a long list of criticisms of these theories. Some specific criticisms have been noted explicitly at appropriate points in preceding sections. Other critcisms have been implicit but presumably evident; for example, our persistent concern with whether we had fully understood the meaning of one or another concept is obviously related to what we feel to be an unnecessarily high level of ambiguity and imprecision in their writings. The basic aim of this review, however, is not to score points but to clarify as best we can the meanings of these theories so as to achieve a fuller understanding of the implications of their work for research and theory on the role of family interaction processes in personality development. In this last section, therefore, rather than reviewing previous criticisms or listing new ones, we wish to draw attention to some of the important new directions in theory and research that are suggested by the body of work summarized in this paper. Our emphasis will be on shared characteristics of the different theories, rather than upon the differences stressed in previous sections. Thus, we shall be treating the theories as different expressions of a general approach to the study of family interaction.

Taken collectively, there are two major contributions that these theories may make to our general understanding of personality and social processes. First, their serious and sustained effort to focus on the family group as the unit of observation and conceptualization marks an important advance over traditional approaches to both normal and pathological personality development. Second, through specific concepts like the *double bind, fragmentation,* and *pseudo-mutuality* they have alerted us to important phenomena in family life and other interpersonal relationships that have heretofore been neglected by other investigators.

The potential significance of this focus on the total family unit cannot be overstressed. It would be inaccurate to draw the implication that information should now be collected about the husband of the schizophrenogenic mother; this would miss the point. The more accurate implication is that information must now be collected about relationships and transactions among family members; the latter, as we know from a long history of work in small group studies, cannot simply be reconstructed on the basis of knowledge of the personal attributes of the several family members. The introduction of this new level of conceptualization leads toward more complex models of causation, as, for example, in Wynne's "epigenetic transactional" approach. At the same time, it points to simple mechanisms at a concrete behavioral level through which personality is shaped by intrafamilial social processes. Because these mechanisms are specified in terms of observable behavior, they are more open to empirical study than the abstract propositions that have heretofore constituted much of social interaction theory as it has been applied to problems of socialization.

The implications of these theories are not restricted to the area of personality development but extend to our understanding of processes at work in other types of groups. Analyses of problem-solving, training, therapy, and work groups could benefit from attention to the forms of interaction isolated in these family studies. At the level of individual behavior, some of the persistent styles of interaction might transfer from the family to other group settings and the conditions under which such transfer did or did not take place would be an interesting area of investigation. At the level of group dynamics, since all groups face the same types of problems that are described as facing families—the development and reinforcement of norms, the control of affect, the differentiation of roles—the mechanisms observed in these family studies can serve as hypotheses in studies of other groups.

There is no need to multiply examples of how these theories alert and sensitize us to important aspects of interpersonal relationships. We have implied throughout that these phenomena are open to systematic investigation because they have been formulated in behavioral terms. This will permit the introduction of rigorous methods of study that have been developed in experimental studies of *ad hoc* groups. This latter complex of methods—including experimental procedures and techniques of quantitative coding of interaction—would seem to be particularly appropriate to the further study of the processes reported by clinical observers of these families. Several investigators have already recognized the potential value of linking these two traditions of experimental social psychology and the clinical study of the schizogenic family. An overview of these recent developments will help to underscore our general point that we may be approaching a confluence of these two traditions and that such an event would be of value for both of them.

We have selected five studies for brief comment to serve as examples of this direction in research. In these studies, the focus of analysis is the difference between families with diagnosed schizophrenic members and other types of families. This is clearly only a first step in assessing the hypothesized etiological function of these patterns of interaction.[7] Farina's (1960) experiment is the first reported of this type. He compared interaction between parents of male schizophrenics and parents of male tuberculosis patients in order to investigate patterns of dominance and conflict. Using the "revealed difference" technique to generate parental interaction (Strodtbeck, 1954), he scored tape recordings on certain aspects of the structure of interaction (who speaks first, number of interruptions, etc.). He found a higher degree of conflict between the parents of schizophrenics than between parents in his tuberculosis control group. He also found systematic differences between parents of patients with good premorbid histories ("reactive" schizophrenics) and those with poor premorbid histories ("process" schizophrenics). For example, mothers of poor premorbid patients showed high dominance, but in good premorbid families fathers tended to be dominant. Caputo's (1963) study of interaction between parents of chronic schizophrenics was concerned with similar questions. He used parents of "normal" sons as a control group, and tested the hypothesis of role reversal in schizogenic families, that is, that mothers would play a dominant role and fathers an expressive role. He also predicted unilateral patterns of hostility, from wife to husband, in these families. Using the "revealed difference" procedure and a modified Interaction Process Analysis category system (Bales, 1950) to code tape recordings, he found that none of these hypotheses was supported by the data.

It is less important at this stage of research and knowledge that the results of these two studies are somewhat inconsistent with each other than that together they suggest modifications in theory and method regarding interaction in these families. For example, Farina's findings point to the need for careful discrimination in theory and research between types of schizophrenia. Findings from both studies indicate the need for several coding systems at different levels to measure important concepts such as power and conflict that appear repeatedly in the clinical and theoretical literature. Perhaps consistent conflict patterns in these families are manifested in their styles of interaction and would be evident in an "interruptions" code such as Farina's, but not manifested in verbal content and would not be found in a verbal content code such as that used by Caputo.

Frances Cheek's (1964) experiment takes into account some of the previously mentioned design problems and her results raise the question of consistency between parental values and parental behavior. This is the first reported experimental study of schizophrenic family interaction in which the patient was actually present in the discussion and the first to compare families of male and female patients. Cheek's hypotheses center on the distribution of affect and power; she used a modified Bales system to code tape recordings. Examples of her findings are: in interaction with husband and child, mothers of male schizophrenic children show greater hostility and greater tension than mothers of females; in contrast with mothers of normal children, schizogenic mothers are more withdrawn and cold. A comparison of expressed values with observed behavior showed that mothers of schizophrenics who report high values on support and permissiveness in child training do not show this behavior in their interaction; in contrast mothers of normals report that they value giving support and being permissive to children and actually behave this way in family discussions.

In these experiments indexes of types of interaction are based on an average rate of participation over some period of time. However, the theories previously discussed, particularly Bateson's and Wynne's, stress the transactional nature of relationships and thus are more concerned with sequences of interaction. Haley's (1964) experiment is focused on the kind of ordered pattern of communication that may be characteristic of schizophrenic families. Comparing interaction in a set of "disturbed" families with normal families, Haley showed that when "who follows whom" patterns are compared with random sequences, the "disturbed" families tended to show a more rigid sequential pattern than the normal families. He interprets this difference as reflecting the normal family's ability to be more flexible and to change patterns in accord with the requirements of the situation.

In an experimental study now in process, the present authors have attempted to take into account some of the design and measurement problems present in earlier investigations (Mishler and Waxler, 1964). The design includes families of male and female patients with good and poor premorbid histories as well as comparable normal control families. As an important additional control, parents are observed in interaction with a well sibling of the patient as well as with the patient himself. Family discussions are generated through the "revealed difference" procedure and typescripts of the discussions are multiple-coded with the use of a number of independent coding systems. This study will permit the analysis of sequences as well as average scores and will allow for a determination of whether parental interaction patterns are child- or family-specific.

We believe that the general approach illustrated by the several studies reviewed above holds great promise. It opens up to systematic investigation the range of interpersonal relationships in natural groups which has until now been studied almost exclusively either through self-report questionnaires or qualitative case study procedures. Of equal importance, in constructing general theories about personality and group process, we will no longer be limited to findings from studies of artificial *ad hoc* groups but will be able to draw upon well-controlled studies of natural groups.

One aim of this review when we began was to derive crucial hypotheses through comparison of the several theories that would permit an empirical assessment of their relative validity. As we learned more about the theories, our conviction was reinforced that they each contained hypotheses and concepts that led easily into empirical study. We have emphasized particularly the appropriateness of experimental methods for this. However, it also became clear, as we have suggested at a number of points in the body of the paper, that the theories cannot be compared directly with each other in ways that would permit a critical empirical test of differential hypotheses. It is always evident that the theories refer to the same general phenomena, viz., schizophrenic patients and their parents. However, this is a level of similarity equivalent to asserting the similarity of Van Gogh, Monet, and Andrew Wyeth because they have all painted landscapes.

The analogy to artists is helpful in understanding a major source of the difficulty in achieving a systematic comparison of the different theories. They are less like scientific theories than artful constructions or coherent accounts arrived at independently through different perspectives and methods of conceptualization. Their value for other investigators, like that of art, lies in giving us a new way of looking at the world. Techniques and methods are available for systematic empirical study of the processes they have observed and reported. There is some likelihood that guided by this new view of the phenomenon, such studies will result in an increased understanding not only of schizophrenia but of normal human behavior as well.

## NOTES

1. This is a report from a project entitled, "An Experimental Study of Families with Schizophrenics, which is supported in part by NIMH Grant No. MH-06276. The authors wish to acknowledge the detailed and serious response to an earlier draft of this paper by several of the investigators whose works are reviewed here—Gregory Bateson, Jay Haley, Don D. Jackson, Theodore Lidz, Yi-chuang Lu, and Lyman Wynne. The paper has benefited greatly from their suggestions and criticisms, although responsibility for the use made of those comments of course rests solely with the authors. Extended discussions with Alan Blum, Loren Mosher, and Rhona Rapoport of a number of issues raised in the paper were also most valuable in preparing the final revision.
2. A recent paper by Meissner (1964) also attempts a review and critique of these and other theories of family relationships. The two papers overlap in the territory covered but differ considerably in point of view and in the framework used for the comparative analysis of these theories.
3. Response to an earlier draft of the paper has called our attention to a special problem of comparative analysis of theories that are still in process of development. In brief, the theorists felt that we did not emphasize sufficiently the

fact that their formulations were presented over a period of time and that their theories are not finished statements but theories "in process." We do not believe that there is a completely satisfactory solution to this problem since any attempt at analysis involves the use of standard dimensions for comparison and requires an assumption that a theory at any point in time is to be taken seriously as it is stated at that point in time. We have tried, however, to remain sensitive to what we see as the basic thrust and direction of each theory and to give primacy to the most current statements in our interpretations of their work. The reader is asked to bear in mind this historical and developmental aspect of the theories discussed.

4. Historically, interest in Russell's theory of logical types preceded work on schizophrenia; the schizophrenic was seen as a person who manifested special difficulties in the classification of messages. The original article on the theory of schizophrenia was ". . . a product of deduction more than of observation, for we had hardly looked at the families of schizophrenics. It was hypothesized that given a learning organism which communicates like this then this sort of learning context [i.e., one involving conflicts in levels of communication] would have led to his communicating like this." (Jay Haley, personal communication.)

5. Don D. Jackson, personal communication.

6. Lyman Wynne, personal communication.

7. It is recognized by many observers of the characteristics of schizogenic families that they bear a close resemblance to characteristics reported of other "disturbed" families, such as families of homosexuals, autistic children, children with school phobias, etc. Clearly one of the tasks of future research is to specify in detail the relationship between family structure and particular disturbances in the child. Meissner's review (1964) includes references to studies of these varied types of families.

# REFERENCES

The references for each of the three theories reviewed in this paper are grouped together—i.e., Bateson, Lidz and Wynne groups, in that order. Other references cited will be found under "General References."

BATESON GROUP

BATESON, G. Cultural problems posed by a study of schizophrenic process. In A. Auerback (Ed.), *Schizophrenia: an integrated approach,* A.P.A. symposium 1958. New York: Ronald Press, 1959.

BATESON, G. Minimal requirements for a theory of schizophrenia. *Arch. gen. Psychiat.,* 1960, 2, 477–491. (a)

BATESON, G. The group dynamics of schizophrenia. In L. Appleby (ed.), *Chronic schizophrenia.* Glencoe, Ill.: Free Press, 1960. Pp. 90–105. (b)

BATESON, G. The biosocial integration of behavior in the schizophrenic family. In N. Ackerman, *et al.* (Eds.), *Exploring the base for family therapy.* New York: Fam. Serv. Assn. Amer., 1961. Pp. 116–122.

BATESON, G., JACKSON, D., HALEY, J., & WEAKLAND, J. Toward a theory of schizophrenia. *Behav., Sci.,* 1956, 1, 251–264.

BATESON, G., JACKSON, D., HALEY, J. & WEAKLAND, J. A note on the double bind—1962. *Fam. Process,* 1963, 2, 34–51.

HALEY, J. The family of the schizophrenic: a model system. *J. nerv. ment. Dis.,* 1959, 129, 357–374. (a)

HALEY, J. An interactional description of schizophrenia. *Psychiat.,* 1959, 22, 321–332. (b)

HALEY, J. Observation of the family of the schizophrenic. *Amer. J. Orthopsychiat.*, 1960, 30, 460–467.

HALEY, J. Family experiments: a new type of experimentation. *Fam. Process*, 1962, 1, 265–293.

HALEY, J. *Strategies of psychotherapy*. New York: Grune & Stratton, 1963.

HALEY, J. Research on family patterns: an instrumental measurement. *Fam. Process*, 1964, 3, 41–65.

JACKSON, D. Introduction. In D. Jackson (ed.), *The etiology of schizophrenia*. New York: Basic Books, 1960. Pp. 3–20.

JACKSON, D., & WEAKLAND, J. Schizophrenic symptoms and family interaction. *Arch. gen. Psychiat.*, 1959, 1, 618–339.

JACKSON, D., RISKIN, J., & SATIR, VIRGINIA. A method of analysis of a family interview. *Arch. gen. Psychiat.*, 1961, 5, 321–339.

PERCEVAL, JOHN. *Perceval's narrative*, edited by Gregory Bateson. Stanford, Calif.: Stanford Univer. Press, 1961.

WATZLAWICK, P. A review of the double-bind theory. *Fam. Process*, 1963, 2, 132–153.

WEAKLAND, J. The double-bind hypothesis of schizophrenia and three-party interaction. In D. Jackson (Ed.), *The etiology of schizophrenia*. New York: Basic Books, 1960. Ch. 13, pp. 373–388.

WEAKLAND, J., & FRY, W. F. Letters of mothers of schizophrenics. *Amer. J. Orthopsychiat.*, 1962, 32, 604–623.


LIDZ GROUP

FLECK, S. Family dynamics and origin of schizophrenia. *Psychosom. Med.*, 1960, 22, 333–344.

FLECK, S. Comparison of parent-child relationships of male and female schizophrenic patients. *Arch. gen. Psychiat.*, 1963, 8, 17–23.

FLECK, S., CORNELISON, ALICE, NORTON, NEA, & LIDZ, T. The intrafamilial environment of the schizophrenic patient: II. Interaction between hospital staff and families. *Psychiat.*, 1957, 20, 343–350.

FLECK, S., CORNELISON, ALICE, SCHAFER, SARAH, & LIDZ, T. Incestuous and homosexual problems in schizophrenia. In J. Masserman (Ed.), *Individual and familial dynamics*. New York: Grune & Stratton, 1959. Pp. 142–159.

LIDZ, T. Schizophrenia and the family. *Psychiat.*, 1958, 21, 21–27.

LIDZ, T. The relevance of family studies to psychoanalytic theory. *J. nerv. ment. Dis.*, 1962, 135, 105–112.

LIDZ, T. *The family and human adaptation*. New York: Internat. Univer. Press, 1963.

LIDZ, RUTH, & LIDZ, T. The family environment of schizophrenic patients. *Amer. J. Psychiat.*, 1949, 106, 332–345.

LIDZ, T., PARKER, BEULAH, & CORNELISON, ALICE. The role of the father in the family environment of the schizophrenic patient. *Amer. J. Psychiat.*, 1956, 113, 126–132.

LIDZ, T., CORNELISON, ALICE, FLECK, S., & TERRY, DOROTHY. The intrafamilial environment of the schizophrenic patient: I. The father. *Psychiat.*, 1957, 20, 329–342. (a)

LIDZ, T., CORNELISON, ALICE, FLECK, S., & TERRY, DOROTHY. The intrafamilial environment of schizophrenic patients: II. Marital schism and marital skew. *Amer. J. Psychiat.*, 1957, 114, 241–248. (b)

LIDZ, T., CORNELISON, ALICE, TERRY, DOROTHY, & FLECK, S. The intrafamilial environment of the schizophrenic patient: VI. The transmission of irrationality. *Arch. Neurol. Psychol.*, 1958, 79, 305–316.

LIDZ, T., FLECK, S., CORNELISON, ALICE, & TERRY, DOROTHY. The intrafamilial environment of the schizophrenic patient: IV. Parental personalities and family interaction. *Amer. J. Orthopsychiat.*, 1958, 28, 764–776.

LIDZ, T., & FLECK, S. Schizophrenia, human interaction, and the role of the family. In D. Jackson (Ed.), *The etiology of schizophrenia*. New York; Basic Books, 1960.

LIDZ, T., FLECK, S., ALANEN, YRJÖ, & CORNELISON, ALICE. Schizophrenic patients and their siblings. *Psychiat.*, 1963, 26, 1–18.

LIDZ, T., & FLECK, S. Family studies and a theory of schizophrenia. Unpublished mimeograph, authors, 1964.


WYNNE GROUP

LOVELAND, NATHENE, WYNNE, L., & SINGER, MARGARET. The family Rorschach: a new method for studying family interaction. *Fam. Process*, 1963, 2, 187–215.

RYCKOFF, I., DAY, JULIANA, & WYNNE, L. Maintenance of stereotyped roles in the families of schizophrenics. *A.M.A. Arch. Psychiat.*, 1959, 1, 93–98.

SCHAFFER, L., WYNNE, L., DAY, JULIANA, RYCKOFF, I., & HALPERIN, A. On the nature and sources of the psychiatrist's experience with the family of the schizophrenic. *Psychiat.*, 1962, 25, 32–45.

SINGER, MARGARET, & WYNNE, L. Differentiating characteristics of the parents of childhood schizophrenics, childhood neurotics and young adult schizophrenics. *Amer. J. Psychiat.*, 1963, 120, 234–243. (a)

SINGER, MARGARET, & WYNNE, L. Thought disorder and the family relations of schizophrenics: III. Methodology using projective techniques. Ditto copy, authors, 1963. (b)

WYNNE, L. The study of intrafamilial alignments and splits in exploratory family therapy. In N. Ackerman, *et al.* (Eds.), *Exploring the base for family therapy*. New York; Fam. Serv. Assn. Amer., 1961. Pp. 95–115.

WYNNE, L., RYCKOFF, I., DAY, JULIANA, & HIRSCH, S. Pseudo-mutuality in the family relations of schizophrenics. *Psychiat.*, 1958, 21, 205–220.

WYNNE, L., & SINGER, MARGARET. Thought disorder and the family relations of schizophrenics. Ditto copy, authors, 1962.

WYNNE, L., & SINGER, MARGARET. Thought disorder and the family relations of schizophrenics: I. A research strategy. *Arch. gen. Psychiat.*, 1963, 9, 191–198. (a)

WYNNE, L., & SINGER, MARGARET. Thought disorders and family relations of schizophrenics: II. A classification of forms of thinking. *Arch. gen. Psychiat.*, 1963, 9, 199–206. (b)

WYNNE, L., & SINGER, MARGARET. Thinking disorders and family transactions. Paper presented at the Amer. Psychiat. Assn., May 1964.


GENERAL REFERENCES

ACKERMAN, N., BEATMAN, FRANCES, & SHERMAN, S. (Eds.) *Exploring the base for family therapy*. New York: Fam. Serv. Assn. Amer., 1961.

BALES, R. F. *Interaction process analysis*. Cambridge: Addison-Wesley, 1950.

BOWEN, M. Family relationships in schizophrenia. In A. Auerback (Ed.), *Schizophrenia: an integrated approach*. New York: Ronald Press, 1959. Pp. 147–178.

BOWEN, M. A family concept of schizophrenia. In D. Jackson (Ed.), *The etiology of schizophrenia*. New York: Basic Books, 1960. Pp. 364–372.

BOWEN, M., DYSINGER, R., & BASAMANIA, BETTY. Role of the father in families with a schizophrenic patient. *Amer. J. Psychiat.*, 1959, 115, 1017–1020.

BRODEY, W. Some family operations and schizophrenia. *Arch. gen. Psychiat.*, 1959, 1, 379–402.

CAPUTO, D. The parents of the schizophrenic. *Fam. Process*, 1963, 2, 339–356.

CHEEK, FRANCES. The schizophrenogenic mother in word and deed. *Fam. Process*, 1964, 3, 155–177. (a)

CHEEK, FRANCES. A serendipitous finding: sex roles and schizophrenia. *J. abnorm. soc. Psychol.,* 1964, 69, 392–400. (b)

FARINA, A. Patterns of role dominance and conflict in parents of schizophrenic patients. *J. abnorm. soc. Phychol.,* 1960, 61, 31–38.

JACKSON, D. (Ed.) *The etiology of schizophrenia.* New York: Basic Books, 1960.

LAING, R. *The divided self: an existential study in sanity and madness.* Chicago: Quadrangle Books, 1960.

LAING, R. *The self and others: further studies in sanity and madness.* Chicago: Quadrangle Books, 1961.

LOCKE, B. Z., KRAMER, M., TIMBERLAKE, C. E., PASAMANICK, B., & SMELTZER, D. Problems in interpretation of patterns of first admissions to Ohio state public hospitals for patients with schizophrenic reactions. *Psychiat. Res. Rep.,* 1958, No. 10, 172–196.

LU, YI-CHUANG. Mother-child role relations in schizophrenia: a comparison of schizophrenic patients with non-schizophrenic siblings. *Psychiat.,* 1961, 24, 133–142.

LU, YI-CHUANG. Contradictory parental expectations in schizophrenia. *Arch. gen. Psychiat.,* 1962, 6, 219–234.

MEISSNER, W. W. Thinking about the family—psychiatric aspects. *Fam. Process,* 1964, 3, 1–40.

MISHLER, E. G., & SCOTCH, N. Sociocultural factors in the epidemiology of schizophrenia. *Psychiat.,* 1963, 26, 315–351.

MISHLER, E. G., & WAXLER, NANCY E. Interaction in families of schizophrenics: an experimental study. Paper presented at Amer. Sociol. Assn., Sept. 1964.

SANUA, V. Sociocultural factors in families of schizophrenics: a review of the literature. *Psychiat.,* 1961, 24, 246–265.

SEARLES, H. Positive feelings in the relationship between the schizophrenic and his mother. *Internat. J. Psycho-Anal.,* Part 6, 1958, 39, 569–586.

SEARLES, H. The effort to drive the other person crazy—an element in the aetiology and psychotherapy of schizophrenia. *Brit. J. med. Psychol.,* Part 1, 1959, 32, 1–18. (a)

SEARLES, H. Integration and differentiation in schizophrenia: an over-all view. *Brit. J. med. Psychol.,* Part 3, 1959, 32, 261–281. (b)

SPIEGEL, J., & BELL, N. The family of the psychiatric patient. In Silvano Arieti (Ed.), *American handbook of psychiatry,* Vol. 1. New York: Basic Books, 1959. Pp. 114–149.

STRODTBECK, F. Husband-wife interaction over revealed differences. *Amer. sociol. Rev.,* 1951, 16, 468–473.

STRODTBECK, F. The family as a three-person group. *Amer. sociol. Rev.,* 1954, 19, 23–29.

# 23:

# Psychological Study of Whole Families

*Gerald Handel*

In his article, "Abnormalities of Behavior," White (1959) introduces a group of references on schizophrenia with this comment: "It is reassuring to find that several workers are using the concept of interaction patterns in families rather than the questionable cause-effect model of parent influencing child [p. 279]." The implied rarity of this concept in the psychological literature is indicated by the fact that four of the five publications White mentions are of psychiatric origin, while only one is psychological; the rarity is underscored by the fact that Hoffman and Lippitt's (1960) entire presentation of family research methods in child psychology is cast explicitly within the cause-effect framework of parent influencing child.

There is an ambiguity in White's term "interaction patterns in families." On the one hand, it may be taken to mean interaction between some but not all members of a family, such as interaction between husband and wife (Tharp, 1963), mother and child, father and child, or child and child. Hoffman and Lippitt report that studies of parent-child interaction are increasing and they suggest that this is partly because of the failure of the simple parent-child cause-effect model.

White's term may, on the other hand, be taken to refer to interaction of all the family members, whether the whole family be defined as the nuclear or conjugal family whose members share a common household or the extended family residing in one or more households. The concept of family interaction in this broader sense has scarcely gained notice in psychology, although psychiatry (Group for the Advancement of Psychiatry, 1954), anthropology (Lewis, 1950, 1959, 1961), sociology (Hill, 1949; Parsons and Bales, 1955), and social work (Voiland, 1962) are giving it increasing attention. Psychology has been concerned with events within the family but has made little effort to conceptualize and study the family as a unit.

This paper reports the progress made thus far in studying whole fam-

Reprinted by permission from *Psychological Bulletin*, Vol. 63 (January 1965), pp. 19–41. Copyright 1965 by American Psychological Association. Gerald Handel is identified in the footnote to Chapter 1.

ttention is given to work by investigators and thinkers in psychology related fields. The paper does not deal with two-person interaction, rtly because discussions of work in this area are already available (Eisenstein, 1956; Hoffman & Lippitt, 1960; Tharp, 1963), but mainly because moving beyond the two-person framework has proved to be an especially difficult problem. The discussion is not restricted, however, to interaction in the sense of studies of face-to-face behavior. The problem focus is the psychological study of the family as a whole, and observation of face-to-face interaction is only one of the procedures that have been used. If the parent-child, cause-effect model has been only slightly successful, there are grounds for believing that studies of two-person, parent-child interaction, which omit observation of other family members, will also prove of limited value for understanding child personality. But quite apart from evaluations of the merit of two-person interaction studies in child psychology, the psychological study of whole families is of interest in its own right.

The adequacy, though not the utility, of the interaction concept—regardless of whether the data be obtained by direct observation of face-to-face behavior or by subject reports—is itself problematic, even for the study of whole families. One of the many reasons the burgeoning field of small group study has scarcely concerned itself with the family is perhaps the recognition that the ahistoric framework appropriate for ad hoc laboratory groups is not well suited to the family, which is constituted by enduring interpersonal relationships. Strodtbeck (1954), in one of the few small-group studies using families as subjects, tested propositions derived from ad hoc groups and found important differences which he explained on the basis of these enduring relationships (pp. 28–29). Later work by Strodtbeck (1958) seems clearly to indicate that family interaction can only be understood in conjunction with the family's prevailing interpersonal relationships. The question may be put, then, whether interaction or interpersonal relationship will prove the more fruitful concept in understanding families or, indeed, whether adequate investigation will not require data on both kinds of phenomena as reciprocally determining. (To use both concepts interchangeably as though they were equivalent, as is sometimes done, can only lead to obscuring important problems.)

Thus far, we have been using the term whole family as a means of differentiating a field of study that lies beyond the traditional study of subfamily pairs such as the mother-child pair. For our purposes the term serves adequately, but notice must be taken that its referent is not precise. An issue centers on whether it is fruitful to select the nuclear family as a unit of study or whether adequate understanding requires study of the extended family. Some investigators (Handel & Hess, 1956; Hess & Handel, 1959) have argued that, regardless of the ties that link a nuclear family to kin and wider social groups, there is a sense in which the nuclear family is a bounded universe. The nuclear family is a meaningful unit of study because, typically, its members inhabit a common household which is not shared with relatives; within these boundaries—the home—the family members develop long-sustained, relatively more intense and meaningful relationships among each other than with outsiders, including kin residing in other households. Spiegel and Bell (1959), on philosophical and anthropological grounds, consider this viewpoint too narrow for understanding psychopathology. They consider it essential to view the nuclear family as a component of the extended family and the entire family network as embedded in a larger social and cultural network, if the emotional disturbance of a particular family member is to be adequately understood. The problem of defining the unit of study is discussed briefly by Leichter (1961) who concludes that "the family unit may shift according to the purpose of analysis [p. 143]."

In passing, it may be noted that Spiegel and Bell make common cause with White, Hoffman and Lippitt, Ackerman (1958), and others in questioning the adequacy of the cause-effect model of parent influencing child. Most of the work reviewed in this article has similar import. Some studies focus on the extended family (e.g., Cleveland & Longaker, 1957; Fisher & Mendell, 1956; Mendell & Fisher, 1956) while others focus on the nuclear family (e.g., Ackerman & Sobel, 1950; Frenkel-Brunswik, 1955; Hess & Handel, 1959).

## EMERGENCE OF THE PROBLEM

Any discussion of the problem of conceptualizing and investigating whole families must begin with Burgess's (1926) formulation: "The Family as a Unity of Interacting Personalities."[1] From the perspective of contemporary psychology this is a remarkable phrase, as far reaching in its implications as it is compact in expression. It provides a basic orientation that can guide many research programs, regardless of how the unit of study be defined.

First, we may note that the formulation calls attention to the fact that a family is made up of persons, each with an individuality of his own, a personality. By implication, it seems to call in question the cause-effect model which locates independent variables exclusively in the parents and dependent variables exclusively in the children. At the very least, it suggests an alternative perspective in which each family member is regarded as a source of some relatively autonomous action. A child, as well as a parent, is construed as having individuality. Sufficient ground for this assumption is provided by the fact that each child in a family has a unique ordinal position. (The question of whether children in a particular ordinal position differ systematically from children in other ordinal positions is irrelevant here. The point is that within any given family, the first-, second-, and thirdborn, etc., can be expected to be different from each other in significant ways.) Other grounds for the assumption can be adduced, though one would also like to have studies of such dimensions as perceptual sensitivity and activity level of infants (Bergman and Escalona, 1949; Escalona and Heider, 1959; Escalona and Leitch, 1952; Fries and Woolf, 1954) conducted on infants in the same family. However, it is apposite to point out that one of the research problems immediately suggested by the Burgess (1926) formulation is the problem of how different children in the same family develop different identities. The problem is implicit in any effort to understand why one child develops a mental illness while other children in the same family do not. Uniqueness of ordinal position provides a basis for expecting that the personalities of children in the same family will differ from each other in some way, but what those differences will turn out to be and the processes by which they come about require research on whole families. One process is indicated in Harris's (1959) study, where he reports that:

Both the mothers and the fathers in our study invariably showed evidence of using their parenthood to continue or to resolve, through their children, some aspects of their own growing up, and therefore each of their several children might represent a somewhat different aspect of their past [p. 39].

The same child can, of course, represent different things to the two parents.

By characterizing the family as a unity of interacting personalities, Burgess points to the problem of understanding interaction and interpersonal relationships in terms of the personalities of the participating members. A recent attempt by Miller (1961) to present an organized framework for dealing with the problem is a valuable contribution and perhaps the most explicit statement yet available. It is, however, framed in terms of two-person relationships, and modifications would undoubtedly be required in order for it to be applicable to family groups.

It should be noted that the central research problem raised by Burgess is not that of socialization, child training, or transmission of personality characteristics from parent to child but a problem that is in a sense anterior to these, while also having social psychological interest in its own right. The problem may be phrased: *How do the several personalities in a family cohere in an ongoing structure that is both sustained and altered through interaction?* Regarded in this way, Burgess' formulation may be seen as, in effect, a charter for the study of whole families. As such, it demands research which (*a*) is directed to conceptualizing the family as a unit; (*b*) studies the personalities of the several members and the interrelationships among them; (*c*) obtains data from each member of the family. The Burgess formulation thus points to a unified psychological approach in which the intrapsychic processes and personality structures of family members are considered in conjunction with the interrelations among the members. This is a tall order, and it cannot be said that the nature of such a psychology is now at all clear. Nonetheless, some definite steps in this direction have been taken, as this article hopes to indicate. The problems are formidable, and the writings of workers in this field often contain confessions of burdensome difficulty. It seems clear that the application of widely accepted concepts of methodological rigor in psychology must, in this field, be adapted and perhaps deferred pending the development of both a minimally adequate conceptual framework and hypotheses that seem fruitful enough to warrant rigorous testing. Due recognition must be made of the recency of effort in this field. It is hoped that the survey presented here contributes a sufficient sharpening of focus to make possible a more concentrated and rigorous research.

Burgess's (1926) concept has received great veneration and reiteration in family sociology, but for about a quarter of a century little effort seems to have been made to pursue its implications. In his study of family adjustment to the stresses of war separation and reunion, Hill (1949) referred to thinking at the family level as third-dimensional in contradistinction to thinking at the level of the individual and the pair—one- and two-dimensional, respectively. He noted that third-dimensional thinking had only recently been attempted.

A beginning of psychoanalytic attention to the whole family is evident in the 1930s. The International Congress of Psychoanalysis in 1936 was devoted to the topic "The Family Neurosis and the Neurotic Family" (Grotjahn, 1959). Ackerman's (1938) first paper on family unity came soon after. Oberndorf (1938) and Mittelman (1944, 1948) broke with the orthodox psychoanalytic rule that the analyst should treat only one person in a family and avoid contact with the relatives; each was analyzing concurrently both partners to a marriage.

Psychiatric attention is now beginning to move from two-person relationships in the family to the whole family. Several considerations prompt this shift. One is that the disordered behavior of the patient is coming to be viewed as involving a certain stabilization of relationships with other family members so that changes in the patient's behavior resulting from therapy disrupt these relationships, often with untoward consequences for other family members. Improvement in the patient is sometimes accompanied by the development of symptoms in other family members; the symptoms are transitive, but the therapeutic effects often are not (Jackson, 1957; Jackson and Weakland, 1959, 1961). However, Fisher and Mendell (1958) report instances of a spread of therapeutic effect from patient to family members not in therapy. One of the tasks of family study is to discover the conditions that favor the spread of symptoms and those that favor the spread of therapeutic effects.

Another consideration is that improved behavior in family relationships is seen as a criterion of therapeutic progress, but such progress cannot always be effected if other parties to the relationship are not engaged in the therapy. Ackerman (1956) states that he finds it increasingly difficult to carry therapy to successful completion without dealing directly with other family members so as to restore healthy family relationships (p. 140).

It is evident that in the thinking of Ackerman (1954) and others the concepts of mental health and illness are changing. These workers view the family, and not the individual, as the primary locus of mental health or illness. Bowen (1960), reporting research on a treatment program in which the families of schizophrenic patients lived with the patients in the hospital, states his view that "The schizophrenic psychosis of the patient is, in my opinion, a symptom manifestiation of an active process that involves the entire family [p. 346]." Similar views are found in the work of Jackson and his colleagues and Lidz and his colleagues, which will be discussed below.

These newer psychiatric concepts have led to various innovations in therapy. The newer techniques include: (a) outpatient treatment of the whole family as a group by one therapist, which Jackson (1961) calls conjoint family therapy; (b) diagnostic evaluation of the whole family in order to select one member as the most suitable candidate for therapy in order to induce change in the whole family; (c) residence of the immediate family of the schizophrenic patient in the hospital with him, with individual therapy of the patient and group therapy of the family proceeding concurrently; (d) family group counseling (Freeman, Klein, Riehman, Lukoff, and Heisey, 1963). In addition, concurrent but individual therapy of husband and wife or parent and child by two therapists who compare notes increases in prevalence. Although clinical reports of this work grow in frequency as therapists report their efforts to devise more effective therapies, no systematic evaluations are yet available, so far as this writer is aware. Discussions of the various family therapies and their rationales are presented by Ackerman (1958, 1961) and Grotjahn (1960). Grotjahn's book includes a historical overview of developing psychoanalytic interest in family therapy, while Ackerman's (1958) book contains a discussion of changing concepts of personality which underlie this trend.

## CONCEPTUAL VANTAGE POINTS

In recent years, several workers have addressed themselves to the psychological problem raised by the Burgess (1926) formulation, the problem of family unity. They have approached it in several ways; a review of them will form the subject of this section. First, however, a conceptual and terminological clarification is necessary. The term family unity is not in vogue these days, having been replaced by several terms which distribute its meaning: family homeostasis (Jackson, 1957), equilibrium (Parsons and Bales, 1955), integration, and solidarity. All of these terms involve viewing the family as a system, and there is overlap among them, but the first two seem more appropriate for describing interaction and its short-range shifts, while the latter two seem more appropriate for describing interpersonal relations in their more enduring aspect. One further distinction needs to be made. Bossard and Boll (1950) state: "We use the term 'family integration' to mean the welding or unification of its diverse elements into a complex whole or harmonious relationship [p. 199]." It is evident that this definition commingles two elements which are not only analytically distinct but the relationships between which pose empirical problems. Harmonious relationships refer to feelings of well-being or absence of deep conflicts, whereas the welding of diverse elements into a complex whole carries no such connotation. In fact, the work on families of psychiatric patients reveals that such families are often tightly integrated in such a way as to preclude harmony. One of the tasks of psychological research on families can well be to discover which kinds of integration lead to harmony and feelings of well-being among the members and which do not. It is clearly useful to distinguish integration, a construct that can deal with family systems in a non-evaluative way, from harmony, a term that refers to a widely valued family goal. Instead of harmony, however, it seems better to adopt the term solidarity which, as defined by Cousins (1960), can be operational. Integration and solidarity refer to somewhat different aspects of family life; the relationships between them constitute a subject worthy of research. Further, studies can be designed to show how various kinds of interaction (such as, e.g., in conjoint family therapy) affect both integration and solidarity.

We consider now the various conceptual vantage points that have been used in studying whole families.

### FAMILY AND CULTURE

Psychologists have become increasingly familiar with the anthropological concept of culture. The importance of the anthropological perspective in understanding personality development was dramatized by Margaret Mead's (1928) pioneering study of adolescence in Samoa and received increased recognition with the publication of Kluckhohn and Murray's (1948) collection of papers in personality and culture. Kaplan's (1961) recent collection indicates that this approach has developed greatly in sophistication.

Until recently, it has been customary to regard the culture or some particular general feature of it—notably the child-rearing practices typical in the culture—as an independent variable and personality as a directly dependent variable. Attention is beginning to shift—very slightly —toward consideration of the individual family as mediating agent of the culture. Cleveland and Longaker (1957) examined the impact of cultural factors on individual mental health by analyzing the transmission and mediation of values in a family setting. In a report deriving from the Stirling County study directed by Alexander Leighton, they studied one kinship group which contributed several patients to the caseload of a small-town clinic in Nova Scotia. On the basis of data derived from psychotherapy, psychological tests, and home visits with relatives, they conlude that the neurotic patterning found in the family is a function of two processes: (a) value conflict within the culture; (b) a culturally recurrent mode of self-disparagement, with roots in the child-rearing methods, linked to the failure of individuals to adjust to incompatible value orientations. The value clash was between a striving orientation, involving personal ambition, acceptance of a rational money economy, and emphasis on personal responsibility for success and failure, and, on the other hand, a traditional being orientation, emphasizing physical labor in an outdoor setting, strong desires for personal independence and integrity, and currently meaningful activities as opposed to longer-range goals. According to the authors' analysis, self-disparagement develops when: (a) the parents, oscillating between the conflicting value orientations, present contradictory models of behavior to their children, (b) the child devalues one of the orientations which he has incorporated in his personality; (c) an obstacle to learning develops in a life area relevant to the already vulnerable and devalued personality segment. In terms of this process, they report a case in which a father, his son, and the father's first cousin developed neurotic behavior disorders.

From the standpoint developed in the present paper, the study just described is incomplete since it does not explore the reasons why other family members did not become neurotic. Presumably some family process is operating selectively. The study is useful, however, because it explicitly interposes the family, as an element of analysis, between the culture and the individual. It suggests the necessity of more microscopic studies of socialization, raising new questions. Instead of the broad question—How are children socialized in this culture?—it suggests that we must ask the more specific question of how a child is socialized into a particular family or—hopefully—type of family. Relevant to this point is a study under way directed by Spiegel and F. Kluckhohn, described by Spiegel and Bell (1959) but not yet reported in detail. Their study closely parallels the Cleveland-Longaker study (1957)—the approach to value analysis used by both pairs of investigators was in fact developed by Kluckhohn (1950)—but Spiegel and Kluckhohn seem to be pushing their clinical analysis further than did Cleveland and Longaker.

Spiegel and Kluckhohn, though moving in a new direction by comparing families with and without an emotionally disturbed child in three subcultural groups, work with the prevailing framework that locates values in the culture (or ethnic and social class subculture). They then analyze family behavior as a response to these external standards. There are, however, signs of a more radical view which is stated by J. Henry (1951), an anthropologist interested in personality development and clinical problems: "every family is almost a different culture [p. 800]." Roberts (1951) studied three neighboring Navaho households and judged that they constituted discrete local cultures, though interlocking. Bott (1957), in her study of family roles and norms in London, states that she started out with the idea of first determining cultural definitions of family roles and then seeing how the members' personalities governed their role performances. But she found so much variation not only in role performance but in role definition, because the environment permits wide latitude of choice, that she was obliged to adopt a more psychological and family-centered view.

These anthropologists thus espouse the view that each family, as a small group, develops its own norms, values, and role definitions. The general case for such a viewpoint has been familiar to psychologists since the early work of Sherif (1936), but its application to families is relatively recent. It is not a widely disseminated view among anthropologists, nor has it received much attention in social psychology as practiced by both psychologists and sociologists, although Frenkel-Brunswik (1955) adopted and exemplified it in her comparison of the social outlooks of an authoritarian and an equalitarian family. Whether it is useful to consider each individual family as having a culture of its own in any strict sense is open to question. But the effort to do so is nonetheless worthwhile in sensitizing us to the fact that analyses of values and norms that are useful at a macrosocial level need refinement when applied at the microsocial level. In the series of midwestern American families reported by Hess and Handel (1959) and Handel (1962), there are four upper-middle-class families all of whom can be regarded as manifesting the striving orientation defined by Kluckhohn. This orientation takes different forms in the four families: one emphasizes responsibility; one, independence; one, competition; and one reveals marked conflict between independence and responsibility. It is useful to consider them as similar when comparing them with families from a nonstriving society, but these four families have different consequences for the personalities of their respective component members.

### FAMILY STRUCTURE AS PERSONALITY COMPONENT

It is customary to regard identification as a process in which the developing child models his behavior on that of his parents, particularly on that of the same-sex parent. This view implicitly assumes either that the child has no cognizance of the interpersonal relationships prevailing between the parents and between them and their other children, or that such cognizance constitutes no more than a condition which affects the identification of the child with the parent who serves as model.

Exemplifying some of the newer thinking in psychoanalysis is the view of Josselyn (1953) who states that:

an analysis of the interpersonal relationships between child and mother, child and father, and child and siblings only partially reveals the significance of the family. The intermeshing of these multiple relationships creates a structure that has meaning over and above the meaning of its parts [p. 337].

Josselyn stops just short of saying that the structure of interpersonal relationships in the family is internalized by the child to constitute a part of his ego. This next step is taken by Parsons and Bales (1955) who present a theory of socialization in which personality development is construed as a process of inner differentiation brought about by the child's participation in and identification with a system of intrafamilial social relationships that are, from his point of view, also becoming progressively differentiated. Initially, the child does not differentiate himself from his mother; the mother-child identity is the first system the child internalizes. Next, when the child differentiates himself from his mother, a 2-role system has been formed from the previously undifferentiated system. Corresponding to this process in the external, interactive world, the simple object internalized in the child's personality during the primary identification also becomes differentiated into an object whose complexity matches that of the 2-role system. Next, according to the theory, the 2-role system is succeeded by one of 4 roles: father, mother, son, and daughter. The authors propose that the 4-role system is succeeded by an 8-role system and then a 16-role system, accomplished by each role being divided into functional role components so that each person performs multiple roles. They term this division process binary fission and aver that the same process occurs concurrently within the child's personality in terms of need-dispositions. The child's first need-disposition is that of dependency. By binary fission, this primary need-disposition becomes differentiated into dependency and autonomy need-dispositions. As the child becomes involved in the 4-role system, dependency divides into a nurturance need and a conformity need, while autonomy divides into a security need and an adequacy need.

The account just given is a great oversimplification of an uncommonly abstruse theory which attempts to account for some familiar phenomena and some never yet observed through a series of deductions that are alternately logical, rigid, and arbitrary. The concept of binary fission strains credulity, though the same can be said for some earlier concepts that later proved influential as well as for some that did not. To the present writer, the theory makes a suggestive contribution in its proposal that personality differentiation is, to an important degree, a function of involvement in a progressively complex series of systems of social interaction and that the child internalizes not only a parental model but also systems of family behavior. Important also is the emphasis on studying the meanings which family members have for one another; studies which pursue this direction can cast light not only on how self-concepts and identities are formed but also on how the personalities in a family form an interlocking structure.

### FAMILY INTERACTION, INTERPERSONAL RELATIONSHIPS, AND PERSONALITY

Burgess, in the article referred to, says that he was tempted to call the family a superpersonality. Although this term has since been carefully avoided, some of the work devoted to the study of whole families in fact involves an attempt to characterize them in personality terms. These characterizations are arrived at either through an analysis of family interaction or through an analysis of the personalities of the several family members or through a combination of these approaches. The idea that groups, including families, each have a distinctive psychological character is implicit in earlier work. Lewin, Lippitt, and White's (1939) concept of social climate is an important forerunner. Their categorization of groups as authoritarian, democratic, and laissez-faire has found its way into discussions of the effects of the family on children's behavior. In the latter context, however, these categories are categories of parent behavior rather than of families.

Recent work frequently shows several features which differentiate it from previous practice: (*a*) Instead of using predetermined categories such as authoritarian and democratic, no assumption is made in advance as to which dimensions are likely to prove most significant for a particular family. A meaningful system or set of family categories is seen as lying in the future, present efforts being exploratory steps toward that goal. Although the importance of categories referring to how power is exercised in the family is indisputable, the familiar dimensions such as power and warmth quite obviously do not exhaust the range of significant family phenomena, and to focus on the effects of these dimensions at the expense of searching out and formulating others can only result in premature closure. (b) Instead of using the cause-effect model of parent influencing child, the family is conceptualized as a group. (c) The personalities of the component members and/or the interplay between intrapsychic and group processes constitute the data matrix from which the concepts are built. This conceptual procedure does not usually take the route of analyzing the personality of each family member in detail before proceeding to the group characterization. Rather, personality materials are examined in order to move directly to characterization of group processes. Family interaction is thus conceived as occurring at the personality level.

A pioneering study exemplifying this viewpoint is that of J. Henry (1951) who proposed that a neurosis can be considered a rigid intrafamilial interaction pattern that is pathogenic in quality. The transmission of the neurosis in the family is the transmission of this pathogenic interaction pattern. Henry studied records of a psychiatric social worker's interviews with the mother of a boy referred to a child guidance clinic. He recognized the limitations imposed by using data obtained only from one member of the family, but at the time of his study these were the best data available for the task he set himself. Using ad hoc categories, he coded every intrafamilial interaction reported by the mother in interviews extending over a period of about 2 years, including interactions between the mother and her own mother and brother, as well as within the nuclear family. The coding procedure enabled him to summarize the interaction pattern of each pair and triad of family members. On the basis of this analysis of family interaction episodes reported by the patient's mother, Henry diagnosed the family as one in which tendencies to dominance, provocation, and clinging are worked out. This family is contrasted with one reported earlier the same year by Henry and Warson (1951) and diagnosed as narcissistic. Henry makes an observation that is important in any attempt to conceptualize families in psychological terms. He points out that family traits are scattered unevenly among family members and may not occur at all in some members. Each family member may embody the pathology in a different way, and some may be free from it. This scatter phenomenon is found repeatedly in the studies reported in this paper and it can safely be assumed that all families will manifest psychologically significant intermember diversity. If there is to be any successful psychological classification of families, it cannot rest upon any simple search for personality similarity among members but will have to be founded upon some conception of dynamic interplay among members, a conclusion which is clearly implied also by Hoffman and Lippitt (1960).

Interaction is a diffuse concept, as yet insufficiently analyzed. It is used to refer to a variety of phenomena which may be regarded as not yet codified components or levels of interaction. Among these are: *physical contacts* such as those of mothering; *cognitive interchanges* in which information is exchanged and which proceed toward a definition of reality (as in Sherif's autokinetic experiments) or toward decision making (as in Bales's interaction-process analysis); behavior in which *norms* and *roles* are created and validated, or in which *selves* are discovered and created (predominantly a sociological usage but also exemplified in such diverse psychological writers as Piaget, Rogers, and Sullivan); *affective behavior,* in which feelings and emotions are transmitted or exchanged (as in much psychiatric writing, perhaps most explicitly in that of Sullivan). There are various concepts of interaction which cross-cut or are at a higher level of abstraction than the categories just named, such as G. H. Mead's theory of symbolic interaction (Rose, 1962) or other theories of communication, of which that advanced by Bateson, Jackson, and their colleagues will be discussed below.

Although in no way attempting to codify interaction phenomena, Hess and Handel (1959) offered some rudiments of a framework for analyzing family interaction and interpersonal relationships, a framework which is psychologically relevant, which seems capable of fruitful development, and which is capable of encompassing a number of other studies already published. On the basis of their study of nonclinical midwestern American families, they advanced a number of concepts which simultaneously refer to the personalities of the individual family members and the character of the family as a group. First, they postulate that *separateness and connectedness are the underlying conditions of a family's life* and that *a basic family process is the effort to achieve a satisfactory pattern of separateness and connectedness.* As each member of a family develops his own personality, adapts to changes through the life cycle, seeks gratification and, generally, creates an individual life space, he also is involved in more or less binding ties with other family members, ties which he endeavors to create and ties which the other members endeavor to create with him. These ties are likewise expressions of the several personalities involved, as well as of many other kinds of factors.

In the course of establishing patterns of separateness and connectedness each member of a family develops an image of each other member. That is, each family member comes to invest each other member with particular cognitive and affective meaning and significance. These images have certain stable aspects but they also change as the family members move through the life cycle. A second process which these authors identify is that *behavior in a family may be viewed as the family's effort to attain a satisfactory congruence of images through the exchange of suitable testi-*

*mony.* This family interaction comes to be centered around a particular theme in each family. Themes found in the families reported include: flight from insecurity, equanimity and its vicissitudes, dynamics of disconnectedness, demonstration of constructive independence, and comforts and crises of companionship. A family's theme does not, of course, find identical expression in the personalities of each member; this is implied by the two processes previously described. The theme describes the centering of the family's interaction. Although the concept of theme was developed from qualitative data, the concept has a logical foundation analogous to concepts of central tendency used for quantitative data. By implication and further analogy, therefore, a family's interaction may be considered to have a dispersion. Eventually, it may be possible to compare families both qualitatively and quantitatively in terms of dispersion as well as the centering of their interactions.

Hess and Handel (1959) identify another family process which is, in a sense, a qualitative formulation of dispersion: *establishing boundaries of the family's world of experience.* As each family maps its domain of acceptable and desirable experience it raises signposts for goals and signals for danger. But these boundaries, which lie within persons as well as among them, are continually tested as new experiences occur, new feelings arise, and new actions are taken. Limits to experience are established in a variety of ways and along several dimensions. Four particularly important dimensions are: the differentiation of individual personality, the intensity of experience, the extensity of experience, and the tendency to evaluate experience.

The last process which these writers identify is: *dealing with significant given biosocial issues of family life,* particularly sex, generation, and birth order. These issues include not only sexuality and authority but, more broadly, how each generation and each sex is defined in terms of feelings, rewards, and restraints.

Interaction gives rise to interpersonal relationships within the family. These relationships do not merely follow the intrinsic lines of sex and age but derive from the interlocking meanings which the members have for one another. Hess and Handel propose the term pattern of alignment to refer to the distribution of ties among members of a family. This concept is broader than that of coalition as it is used in small-group research. Whereas coalition refers to the phenomenon of teaming up to exercise power, pattern of alignment includes any basis on which family members line up with each other, unconsciously as well as consciously, in fantasy as well as in action, for reasons of comfort or affection as well as those of power, to enhance each other as well as to defeat each other. From a psychological point of view, the intrapsychic bases of affiliation are as important as the fact of it, both for the persons affiliating and for the group as a whole. Redl's (1942) study of group emotion in school classrooms has useful implications for the study of families. Clearly the phenomena included under pattern of alignment require differentiation and codification just as do those subsumed under interaction. Just as clearly, the concept points to needed areas of research. To name but one, we require research on sibling support (including identification of siblings with one another) that will balance our research into sibling rivalry. It is not unreasonable to suppose that the relative primacy of sibling support as against sibling rivalry is a factor affecting mental health, and personality formation generally. But sibling relationships are part of the total pattern of alignment in a family and they will be adequately understood only if studied in that context. It is evident from everything that has been said thus far in this paper that the personalities of the parents and the motives and meanings they bring to bear in their interaction with their children contribute to the kind of sibling relationships their children will develop.

Hess and Handel (1959) developed their concepts in the course of studying nonclinical families. Several reports of clinical research suggest that these concepts are potentially fruitful for understanding behavior disturbances of various kinds. Distortions in the separateness-connectedness pattern are seen as contributing to clinical behavior pathology. Wynne, Ryckoff, Day, and Hirsch (1958) take as their basic assumption that every human being strives both to form relationships with others and to develop a sense of personal identity. They conceive that the effort to solve this dual problem leads to two main kinds of solutions, mutuality and pseudomutuality. (They also recognize a third category, nonmutual complementarity, which is not relevant in the present context.) Mutuality entails recognition and appreciation of divergence of self-interests. Pseudomutuality is characterized by preoccupation with fitting together at the expense of the identities of the people in the relationship. Drawing on their work with families of late adolescents and young adults who have suffered acute schizophrenia, the authors develop the hypothesis that the relationships in these families that are acceptable and may be openly acknowledged are intensely and enduringly pseudomutual. Although they do not claim either that pseudomutuality in itself produces schizophrenia or that it is unique to the relations of schizophrenics, they do find that it is a significant feature of the setting in which reactive schizophrenia develops. Pseudomutuality is sustained by various mechanisms all of which make it difficult for the potential schizophrenic to differentiate himself as an individual with his own identity. Following Parsons and Bales, the authors propose that the potential schizophrenic internalizes the system of family relationships that keeps him from differentiating himself and that he thereby collaborates in maintaining the family pattern in which he is caught. Pseudomutuality requires concealment at the expense of openness,

S

so that communication is distorted and perception blurred. A further result is that the roles enacted by the family members vis-à-vis each other are dissociated from subjective experience.

Bowen (1960) and Lidz, Cornelison, Fleck, and Terry (1957) also found that disturbed separateness-connectedness patterns play a part in the genesis of schizophrenia. Bowen found a relationship much like pseudo-mutuality in some of the schizophrenic families he studied intensively. These families are characterized by conventionalized and controlled relationships without sharing of personal feelings, thoughts, and experiences. This, however, is only one of the two types of emotional divorce that he found. The other type is hostile and argumentative. He also discovered an interesting pattern of alignment. At the outset of his work, he believed that all the family members were involved in the processes which led to schizophrenia in one member. As time went on, however, he concluded that father, mother, and patient constitute an interdependent triad from which normal siblings withdraw. This is a challenging finding which points to the need to understand more fully how alignments are formed and how some members manage to escape from pathological involvements. Clausen and Kohn (1960) pointed out that systematic data on the siblings of schizophrenics had not been presented in any of the intensive family studies reported to date. However, subsequent to their survey of the literature on social relationships in schizophrenia, Lu (1961) reported a study directed to just this problem. On the basis of participant observation and interviews with 50 schizophrenics in a state hospital and with their siblings and parents she found certain differences between the schizophrenics and their siblings: (a) From early childhood the mother-patient relationship was far more intense than the mother-sibling relationship. (b) Although the mother attempted to dominate all the children, the eventual patient was highly submissive and dependent whereas the patient's siblings rebelled at the domination; the patient thus reciprocated the mother's demands while the siblings did not. (c) The greater inner freedom of the siblings allowed them to develop a wider range of social relationships than was true of the eventual schizophrenics; the schizophrenic grows up in a more constricted world than do his siblings. Lu announces her intention of publishing further, more detailed reports from this project and we may anticipate further specification and elucidation.

Somewhat akin to Bowen's concept of emotional divorce is the Lidz group's finding of marital schism and marital skew. In families characterized by marital schism, coercion, threat, provocation, and distrust are pronounced; satisfaction in marriage is lacking; and both parents compete for the children's affection. Marital skew is a situation in which the psychopathology of one parent is the focus around which family relationships are organized.

Pseudomutuality is a pathologically exaggerated form of connectedness which is established at the cost of the schizophrenic's failure to achieve a distinctive identity (Ryckoff, Day, & Wynne, 1959). Vogel and Bell (1960) described a pathological form of separateness in which a child is pushed into the role of family scapegoat and becomes emotionally disturbed (diagnosis unspecified). Their paper is an interim report from the Spiegel-Kluckhohn study described earlier. On the basis of intensive data from nine families—three Irish-American, three Italian-American, and three old American, all working class—they concluded that a characteristic pattern of events leads to emotional disturbance in a child. The elements of the pattern are as follows: (*a*) Between the parents major unresolved tensions exist, based on deep fears about their marital relationship. (*b*) The tensions are so severe that some discharge is necessary, but for various reasons the parents dare not seek a scapegoat outside the family. The powerlessness of the children invites selection of one of them as a scapegoat. (*c*) One particular child in the sibship most readily symbolizes the variety of social and psychological problems impinging on the family. He is "selected" as the scapegoat, and his subsequent behavior provides suitable testimony to the appropriateness of the initial selection. Selection of the particular child is governed by such factors as his sex, position in the birth order, intelligence, physical characteristics, and other factors which have a particular emotional meaning to the parents. The other children remain free of emotional disturbance. (*d*) The child is inducted into and sustained in the scapegoat role by the application of inconsistent parental expectations. Behavior which is explicitly criticized is implicitly encouraged. Or behavior discouraged by one parent is encouraged by the other. Or the parental expectations are inconsistent in their severity. (*e*) The scapegoat role is further sustained by several mechanisms. These include parental denial that the child is emotionally disturbed and parental definition of themselves as victims rather than the child. Further, preoccupation with the child serves the function of enabling the parents to avoid directly confronting their own problems.

Vogel and Bell's (1960) paper is an important one. If their analysis of the scapegoat process be regarded as a particular instance of a general process, we are provided with a new avenue to understanding personality formation. Their model invites us to look at the ways in which the child's own characteristics and behavior are processed in the family by having meanings attached to them by others, meanings which the child variously resists, modifies, or cooperates in sustaining. In the process of growing up, the child endeavors to create new meanings for himself which the other family members are more or less willing to share with him. His perceptual, cognitive, affective, and motivational capacities and propensities mesh with or collide with the corresponding capacities and propensities of the other members in such a way that the child is encouraged or induced to grow into the particular kind of person he is to become. Murphy's (1962) concept of coping is relevant in this context because from birth the child is faced with the task of coping with the meanings which his parents and sibs impute to him and his behavior, while he works at imputing meanings to them and their behavior. Vogel and Bell do not present as full a description as we would like of how the scapegoat copes with the meanings his parents assign to him, but Wynne and his collaborators present some vivid examples of how the young schizophrenic resists the meanings assigned by the members of his family. Lidz, Fleck, Cornelison, and Terry (1958) illustrate how the parental personalities influence the meanings they assign to the behavior of children who become schizophrenic.

Wynne (1961), following Hess and Handel (1959), adopted the concept of alignment pattern in his study of schizophrenics. One of his main findings is that, in the families of schizophrenics, alignments are highly unstable; this finding is at variance with that reported by Bowen (1960). Neither writer reports sufficient data to enable the reader to discern what might account for the difference. Another finding by Wynne indicates a situation in families of schizophrenics which seems to be rather different from that in the families studies by Vogel and Bell. He found it a great oversimplification to consider the schizophrenic child a victim of schizophrenogenic parents. Rather, all family members are engaged in reciprocally victimizing—and rescuing—processes. The difference between this conclusion and that of Vogel and Bell may be more apparent than real, for the tension between the parents that they discuss suggests that the scapegoat child is not the only victim in the families they studied. Further, Vogel and Bell's analysis reveals the reciprocating effects which the scapegoat child has upon his parents, effects which sustain their own personality and marital difficulties.

Cumulatively, the foregoing discussion strongly suggests that the processes of personality formation and the processes of family integration are, to an important extent, the same phenomena. While Parsons has made the point that personality, culture, and social system are three different conceptualizations of the same basic data, the point being made here is that when the family is the focus of study it is necessary and possible for some purposes to have a unified conceptualization which encompasses both the individual and the group. As the child copes with the meanings attributed to his behavior by the other family members, he both shapes his own personality and contributes to defining the pattern of separateness and connectedness in the family. The meanings assigned set limits, perhaps, to the coping behavior he will be able to attempt, and in the course of accepting, modifying, or resisting these limits the child both works toward his own identity and builds particular kinds of ties to other members. His ways of coping are at the same time an important part of his contribution to his ties to other members. The child's perceptual and cognitive adjustments, his cathexes, identifications, fantasies, acting out, and all other emotional and behavioral manifestations are at one and the same time constitutive of his own personality, constitutive of his ties to other members in a proactive sense (to use Murray's term), and constitutive of the meaning he has as an object for the other members.

Analysis of interpersonal relationships in the family is bound to raise questions about the usefulness of the concept of role. This is a vast topic in itself, and space limitations preclude an adequate discussion. Suffice it to say in the present context that, if the concept is to prove useful for psychological study of families, we require more highly refined analyses than are yet available. Categories such as male and female roles or parent and child roles are, though necessary as a starting point, simply too gross for adequate understanding. One dimension of the problem is suggested by the Vogel and Bell study. The emotionally disturbed child may be said to occupy a scapegoat role. But do all emotionally disturbed children have comparable roles in their families? If so, how are we to distinguish in role terms between different kinds of emotionally disturbed children, or do these differences have nothing to do with role? An answer to this question does not seem to be available at the present time. Also, since a role is fully understandable only as part of a role system, we need to know what parental and sibling roles complete the system of which the scapegoat (or other roles of emotionally disturbed children) is a part. Further, we have yet to develop an adequate analysis of the various kinds of family roles of normal children—and, for that matter, of mother-wives and husband-fathers. Much greater effort has been made to codify the phenomena of role (see, e.g., Goffman, 1961; Neiman & Hughes, 1951; Sarbin, 1954; Sargent, 1951) than the phenomena of interaction, but much remains to be done. Ackerman (1951, 1958) presents some ideas about role that are particularly useful for psychology, but neither he nor anyone else has yet given us systematic studies of whole families, making use of these ideas.

The detailed study of personalities of the several members of a family and the interrelationships built up among them is important for a great many purposes. In addition, however, we would also like to have ways of classifying, on a psychological basis, families as groups. A useful classification should eventually enable us to understand the psychological properties of various kinds of families. This task is not altogether distinct from those discussed so far, but it does involve a somewhat different level of analysis. As noted earlier, Hess and Handel (1959) have proposed that the identification of family themes may be a useful procedure for understanding some of the binding forces in families. Search for themes may also serve the purpose of directing attention to relationships in many different behavioral modalities (e.g., thinking, perception, motivation, etc.) among the family members.

Paralleling Hess and Handel's finding of themes in nonclinical families, Fisher and Mendell (1956) and Mendell and Fisher (1956, 1958) have detected themes in neurotic families, 6 of them consisting of 3 generations and 14 of 2 generations. On the basis of Rorschach and TAT data they found in 1 family, for example, that all 7 members, spanning 3 generations, were preoccupied with exhibitionism and self-display. Another family was concerned with death or destructive loss of self-control. The projective responses are often strikingly similar. The Rorschach protocols from the members of the self-display family, for example, included the following responses: a boy referred for treatment for exposing himself to young girls saw a "peacock" and a "medallion" in the cards; his mother's most clear-cut human response was that of a "dandy"; his father perceived exposed genitals of women; his maternal grandmother perceived a "man coming out from between clouds or curtains, stepping out nicely on a stage, [Fisher & Mendell, 1956, p. 43]." These investigators also report thematic congruence between projective and interview data. Their work leads them to a conclusion completely in keeping with that reached by Ackerman, Bowen, Vogel and Bell, and others, namely, that the central problems of the patient must be understood in terms of how they are embedded in the total family process. The projective data cited by these investigators are intriguing and point to the need to understand how such striking thematic similarity of response comes about.

Elles (1961) presented a case study of a delinquent family, utilizing psychiatric, medical, and extensive field data. She found a central theme which she characterized as the family's feeling of being futureless. The family's overt behavior and fantasy revealed three subthemes which exemplified the larger one: an oral theme involving difficulties of eating, starving, addiction, and drunkenness; a violence theme focused on fighting and sexual attack; and a theme of death involving both killing and a fear of not being able to stay alive. Her study also provides a particularly good illustration of how a family contracts the boundaries of its experience as a defensive maneuver. In contrast, Bell (1962) finds that disturbed families (by which he means families with an emotionally disturbed child) are distinguished from well families by the fact that the former have a deficiency of family boundaries that leads them to become highly embroiled with extended kin.

In a detailed case analysis of a family in which one son developed ulcerative colitis, Titchener, Riskin, and Emerson (1960) present a new approach to psychosomatic research. As their starting point, the accept a view proposed by some leading investigators in this field that the main psychological factor in the etiology of ulcerative colitis is helplessness and despair arising from actual, threatened, or imagined loss of a key object relationship. This view further holds that this affective state is the result of the patient's fruitless efforts to reinstate the kind of intensely symbiotic relationship he had in early childhood with a controlling mother who gave love conditionally. This research team's innovation consists in showing that the patient's emotional state derives not merely from his relationship with his mother but is a product of the whole family's effort to deal with a conflict between frustrated dependency needs and the family ideal of independence, respectability, and avoidance of selfishness. They conclude that the family was integrated in a fashion they term anxious cohesion which required each member to give suitable testimony of his adherence to the ideal while vigorously suppressing his needs for emotional contact.

Fleck, Lidz, Cornelison, Schafer, and Terry (1959) and Fleck (1960) report that incestuous and homosexual themes are quite pronounced in the families of schizophrenic patients that they studied. The patient's intrapsychic conflicts over these kinds of sexual impulses reflect flagrantly seductive behavior by the parents.

The concept of family theme seems a useful one for a number of reasons. It provides a way of briefly summarizing the central psychological processes in a family group. Perhaps even more important, it is a stimulus to, and an avenue for, breaking out of the constraint of seeing families only in terms of power (authoritarian-democratic; dominant-submissive) and affection (strict-permissive; warm-cold). Power and affection as concepts constitute entirely too narrow a base for comprehending the rich psychological diversity of family life. Searching for themes prompts the investigator to gather a richer variety of data and to be more open to what the data reveal. At the same time, it must be recognized that the search for themes entails the potential (but as yet undemonstrated) disadvantage of endlessly idiosyncratic findings. Consequently, while some such summarizing concept seems useful for many purposes, it also appears necessary to develop some basis on which families may be systematically compared. A solution to this problem proposed by Handel (1962) and influenced by Kluckhohn's mode-of-value analysis involves moving down one level of abstraction to focus on certain core dimensions which may be regarded as constituent elements of themes. Analyzing individually obtained TATs from each member of five four-person families, Handel found that the family themes obtained could be dissected to yield five orientation categories, so-called because they refer to the family's orientation

537

ie world. These were: nature of the external world, nature
: source of goals, nature of action, and nature of heterosexu-
st is not considered exhaustive.

important attempt to characterize whole families grows out
vork context and is reported by Voiland (1962); the project
began .... Paul and was later extended to six other cities. A survey of
social agency services in St. Paul showed that there was a small group of
multiproblem families that made unusually heavy demands on the resources of many agencies. Initially, these disturbed families were classified in terms of marital axes—interaction patterns of the marital partners.
Efforts to correlate other family problems with these axes were not
successful.

The study then moved to a broader framework utilizing four main
dimensions: (a) types of disorder in the family, including personality disorders of any member, financial disorders such as irregular income production, and family dissolution disorders due to desertion, divorce, separation,
placement of children; (b) family social functioning, including marital,
child rearing, child development, and financial; (c) individual characteristics of each member—personality, intellectual, and physical; (d) development of each parent in his family of origin.

On the basis of this framework, four types of disordered family were
identified: perfectionistic, inadequate, egocentric, and unsocial. The types
are presented as being supported by statistical analysis of systematically
coded, case data. These data are not presented in the book but are said to
be available from the organization which sponsored the research.

Each family type is characterized by its own syndrome of disorders.
For example the perfectionistic family tends to involve parental concern
about habit-training practices and concern about guiding self-reliance in
the child; anxiety and guilt-ridden behavior in the child; problems of emotional give and take between the spouses and problems of maintaining
mutual self-esteem; anxiety-dominated behavior patterns in one or both parents. These disorders are described as distorting realistic handling of problems without interfering with good social conduct. In contrast, the unsocial
family's disorders tend to be child neglect and fostering of disrespect for
social authority; delinquency, truancy, psychosis, or other serious personality disturbances of the child; multiple symptoms and rapidly changing attitudes in the marital relationship which often bring the parents into court
or evoke complaints to police; divorce often followed by remarriage of the
partners to each other; hospitalization for mental illness; crime; addictions;
sexual deviations common in adult members.

Although the framework for analysis is heterogeneous, this study is
notable in two respects. First, it is the only study known to the writer
which attempts a psychosocial typology of whole families oriented to total

family functioning rather than to some specific life area. Secondly, the study explicitly rejects interaction as a basis for family classification in favor of interpersonal relationships as the basis.

### FAMILY COMMUNICATION AND SCHIZOPHRENIA

Interaction and communication are sometimes loosely used as equivalent concepts. Although, as noted earlier, it does not seem possible at the present time to formulate a definition of interaction that is at once both rigorous and comprehensive, it seems clear that interaction is a term of broader scope than communication. The referents of the latter term are not easily delimited, but generally communication may be said to refer to the process of organizing and transmitting messages. Bateson, Jackson, and their associates consider this process to play a significant part in the development of schizophrenia.

The central concept of their approach is that all communication takes place on at least two levels, and often on more than two. One level is that of the content itself—what is said. The second level in some way qualifies what is said: affirms it, denies it, indicates that what is said is serious or a joke, is a suggestion or a command, etc. The first level of communication is ordinarily the level of words; the second is ordinarily the level of vocal intonation and bodily gesture. The schizophrenic is a person who grows up in a family in which what is said is typically qualified in such a way as to be utterly incongruent. To take a simple example, the mother may characteristically address her child as "Dear" but in a tone of voice which conveys hostility. If the child attempts to note and comment upon the incongruence between these two levels, the mother may resort to a third level of communication, namely, deny that there was any incongruence in her mode of address (Weakland, 1960). The child, because of his dependency and need for love, cannot leave the field and escape from the extreme pain of having to cope continually with these incongruent messages, but neither do his parents allow him to comment on their communication behavior in a way that would induce them toward greater level-congruence. The child is caught in a double bind (Bateson, Jackson, Haley, & Weakland, 1956). As a result of growing up in this prevailing double-bind situation, the child who later becomes schizophrenic suffers an impaired capacity to discriminate correctly communication modes within himself and between self and others.

The concept of multiple levels of communication has been pushed several steps further. The concept that every message necessarily involves some form of qualification is expanded to encompass the idea that families develop implicit rules for qualifying messages (Haley, 1959b). Such rules arise from the fact that all communications are necessarily efforts to define a relationship.

s*

Haley proposes that families govern their behavior by establishing rules for communication and that it would be fruitful to develop a typology of families based on the nature of these rules. On the basis of his research group's extensive study of families of schizophrenics and preliminary observations of families containing children without symptoms, children with asthma and children who are delinquent, he concludes that the family with a schizophrenic is a unique type of family. Briefly, he finds that: The members in a family with a schizophrenic consistently manifest an incongruence between what they say and how they qualify what they say, the members consistently disqualify what each other says, and the consistent disqualification prevents the development both of clear leadership in the family and of stable alliances either between family members or between any family member and someone outside the family. The inability of the schizophrenic to relate to other people, as well as his general withdrawal, is understandable in terms of his being raised in a learning situation where his actions were always disqualified and where he was not permitted to relate to other people so that he could learn to behave differently (Haley, 1959a).

Finally, we should note that this theory proposes an explanation of the schizophrenic break with reality in terms of family communication rules.

This approach to analysis of communication within the family is intriguing. It focuses attention on observable behavior, and the analysis of this behavior reveals something of the complexity of family interaction. Among other merits of this approach is the demonstration of the way in which absence of family arguments can be a pathologic sign (Jackson, 1959), and this is surely a needed corrective to oversimplified notions regarding the nature of family integration. Jackson also, however, states that one of the merits of communication theory as an approach to family interaction is that it avoids the necessity of attributing affects to the subjects. In fact, it does no such thing. In a later report which demonstrates how to analyze a taped family interview, not only is attention paid to the communication pattern but inferences about affect and motivation are also made; the two modes of analysis are said to be complementary (Jackson, Riskin, & Satir, 1961). And, in fact, the ways in which communications of hostility and affection are qualified are staple illustrations in many of the writings of this research group.

COGNITIVE PROCESSES

A comprehensive view of how a family functions would seem to require that we direct attention not only to the structure of communication but as well to the cognitive structures of the senders and receivers. If, for example, one parent is highly given to thinking in generalities (overproduction of $W$s, in Rorschach terminology) and the other is very practical (perceiving the world in terms of $D$ and with a high $F\%$ and $F+\%$) what problems does this pose for their children and how do the children solve them? What style of thinking do they develop? Do different children in the same family develop different styles of thinking? If so, why? Do factual fathers have problems with imaginative daughters, or is the contrast in styles of thought mutually gratifying and growth promoting—or does it depend upon the presence of suitably factual sons or the nature of the mother's input? In short, how are families integrated at a cognitive level? What part do cognitive processes play in family integration? The range of meaningful questions that can be asked is enormous, but the writer is not aware of any systematic effort to develop a social-personological psychology of cognitive processes in the family. Here and there one finds occasional papers that touch upon this problem area. Flavell (1957), for example, in a speculative paper suggests that an adequate explanation of the etiology of schizophrenic thinking must show specifically how cognitive development becomes affected by pathogenic early interpersonal relations. He refers to a suggestion by Powdermaker (1952) to the effect that one factor may be the parents' intolerance for the child's presocialized autistic ideas so that the child is forced to think realistically rather than being allowed to grow more slowly into socialized thinking. The child's loss of self-esteem thereby incurred is suggested as a predisposing factor for a later abandonment of reality in a psychotic episode. A very similar point of view is taken by Lidz, Cornelison, Terry, and Fleck (1958) who argue that a theory of schizophrenia must explain the patient's ability to abandon reality testing as well as his need to do so. The basic point that emerges from their study of the families of 15 upper-middle and upper-class schizophrenics is that these patients had been in various ways trained in irrationality in their families. Working on quite a different problem, Frenkel-Brunswik (1955) found various kinds of systematic constriction of thought processes in all members of the family of an extremely ethnocentric boy.

Getzels and Jackson (1962) suggest that creative children come from families that differ in important ways from the families of high IQ, noncreative children. Whatever be the limitations of their study, they have surely raised a significant question which merits social psychological attention: How do family processes affect cognitive structure and cognitive freedom? In one aspect, the problem is similar to that tackled by Vogel and Bell: Do families select one child as creative innovator much as they might select one to be an emotionally disturbed scapegoat?

## RESEARCH METHODS

There are as yet no established methods for studying whole families. Nonetheless it is worthwhile calling attention, however briefly, to some of the most common procedures and some issues that are raised. The discussion can be no more than suggestive.

### THERAPY

Psychiatrists have increasingly been using family therapy as a research method. Various clinical research teams are filming and tape recording family therapy sessions and analyzing these in a search for significant relationships. As noted earlier, there are also attempts to study whole families on an inpatient basis (Bowen, 1960). In terms of volume, family therapy is probably the largest single source of data for whole family study at the present time. Should this situation continue, the psychological study of whole families may well repeat the history of personality study; conceptions of abnormal functioning will be dominant for a long time until, belatedly, studies of nonclinical families will be undertaken in an effort to achieve a more rounded view of how families function. The value of obtaining data from family therapy not only to develop more effective therapies but also to increase general understanding of the psychosocial dynamics of family life is not in dispute. The issue is whether studies of families in therapy should be the major source of knowledge in this field, to the relative neglect of other kinds of research. There can be little doubt that psychiatry now leads the way (although admittedly sometimes in collaboration with psychologists and other social scientists) in attempting to understand the family from a psychosocial point of view. If psychology as a discipline does not soon address itself more vigorously to this problem, the result may be that a generation hence psychologists will be devoting their time to trying to verify propositions originating in family psychiatry, just as in the field of personality study they have been significantly preoccupied with the merits of propositions originating in psychoanalysis.

### FIELD METHODS

As here used, this is an omnibus term which includes any procedure for obtaining data in the home of the subjects. Thus, interviewing, psychological testing, and observation of family interaction are field methods which have been used. These are, to be sure, diverse procedures, but the point of grouping them under this rubric is to call attention to the fact that the task of studying whole families that are normal or nonclinical poses a challenge for psychology, accustomed to dealing with easily accessible subjects in laboratories, clinics, nursery schools, and other captive or controlled environments. Useful discussions of some fieldwork problems and procedures in studies of whole nonclinical families will be found in Robb (1953), Bott (1957), and Hess and Handel (1959).

PROJECTIVE METHODS

Rosenzweig appears to have been the first psychologist to propose that close relatives of psychiatric patients, as well as the patients themselves, be given projective tests so that the diagnostician can understand the full psychodynamic setting of the patient's life (see Rosenzweig & Cass, 1954; Rosenzweig & Isham, 1947). Although projective techniques have been used before and since for the purpose of studying personality similarities, Rosenzweig and Isham's proposal is the first recognition that these techniques, particularly the TAT, can provide an avenue to understanding the psychic life of the family as a functioning unit. As noted earlier, Fisher and Mendell also used projective techniques in studying whole families, as did Hess and Handel.

Sohler, Holzberg, Fleck, Cornelison, Kay, and Lidz (1957) attempted to predict family interaction from analysis of a battery of projective tests, which included the TAT, Rorschach, Draw-A-Person, and Rotter Sentence Completion, individually administered to each member of a four-person family in which the son was hospitalized for schizophrenia. Over a 2-year period, the patient had been seen for 3 or 4 therapeutic hours per week; both his parents had been seen once a week; and his sister had been interviewed 29 times. All of this psychiatric-interview material constituted the criterion against which the psychological test interpretations were judged. The psychological report was dissected into 333 discrete interpretive statements about each family member and about family interaction. Although, overall, two thirds of these statements were found to agree with the psychiatric material, the individual personality descriptions contained the highest proportion of agreements, while predictions of attitude of one family member toward another and statements about family interaction were the most likely source of disagreements. Even so, some measure of success in this area is reported. Considering the novelty of the attempt, the results seem encouraging.

The interpretive approaches used by Rosenzweig and his associates. Fisher and Mendell, and Sohler *et al.* entail certain limitations which seem neither necessary nor desirable. First, all of these workers conceive of the family as a group of interrelated individuals but they do not also conceive of the family as having psychological properties of its own that are not explicitly attached to a specific member or pair of members. This restriction means that interpretations about family behavior are always from one person to another (e.g., how patient and mother relate to each other) and never from person to group or group to person. This latter type of conceptualization would seem to be necessary if, for example, one hoped to be able to use TAT data to make a diagnosis such as family scapegoat. Assessments of this order require thinking in group dynamic terms and not simply from person to person in point-to-point fashion, however necessary this way of thinking also is. In addition, of course, conceptualizing at the group level is also necessary if one wishes to use projective data to diagnose families in such terms as Voiland uses or Handel's orientation categories. Conceivably, although this remains to be determined, one might discover from the protocols obtained individually from each family member the family's communication rules as delineated by Haley— or other kinds of rules that might be thought of such as affective rules, defensive rules, rules for dealing with esteem-lowering events, etc.

A second limitation, found in the work of Fisher and Mendell, is the emphasis on responses which are unusual and yet are also similar among members, as in the example cited earlier. Focusing only on highly similar responses among family members leads one to ignore useful, perhaps necessary, data. Further, striking similarities of response among members are not always to be found; neither are highly unusual responses. It is necessary to have a procedure that is free of such limitations.

Handel (1962) proposed a method of TAT analysis for family study, called analysis of correlative meaning, which is not dependent upon the occurrence either of unusual responses or of similarity of members' responses, and which also makes possible analysis of psychological characteristics of a family as a group. The method, which makes use of W. E. Henry's (1951) horizontal-thematic analysis, rests upon three interlocking assumptions: (a) Each card of the TAT has a latent stimulus demand which is "the emotional problem or focus most generally raised by the picture. . . . It will vary from group to group somewhat [W. E. Henry, 1956, p. 100]. (b) The meaning of any individual's stories is not exhausted by reference to his own personality; on the contrary, a part of the meaning of any individual's stories is discovered by reference to the stories of the other family members. (c) Family interaction gives rise to certain general problems and outlooks which involve each family member, each individual's response to a TAT picture in part derives from his interaction with the other family members around the issues tapped by the picture, and the correlativity of meanings of the members' individually told stories derives from the prolonged interrelations of their experiences.[2] The orientation categories mentioned earlier were obtained by use of this method of interpretation. Its validity remains to be established, but the assumptions underlying it seem reasonable working assumptions.

Hess and Handel attempted a procedure in which a family as a group told stories to a set of specially designed, TAT-type pictures, an idea borrowed from W. E. Henry and Guetzkow (1951) who had successfully used this technique with nonfamily groups. In addition, the interaction of the families as they made up the joint stories was recorded with the aim of relating the overt interaction to the story material. Although some of this material is cited illustratively in Hess and Handel (1959), the technical and interpretive problems of relating the two kinds of data were not solved by the time their project was concluded. The potentiality of this method remains undetermined.

### CONTROLLED EXPERIMENT

Few controlled experiments using family groups are known to the writer. Certainly one of the few adequately reported ones, and perhaps the first, is that of Strodtbeck (1954). A unique aspect of this experiment is that it was carried out in the homes of the families rather than in a laboratory. Employing as subjects family groups consisting of father, mother, and adolescent son, Strodtbeck devised a procedure termed the revealed difference technique. Each family member was individually presented a list of 47 described situations and for each situation was asked to pick one of two alternatives. One such situation, for example, described two fathers discussing their sons: one a brilliant student and the other an outstanding athlete. The respondent was asked to decide which father was the more fortunate. After each family member had made his 47 choices, the investigator selected three items on which mother and father took one alternative and the son the other; three items on which mother and son had agreed but not the father; and three items on which father and son had agreed but not the mother. The family was then set to discussing these nine issues and urged to reach an agreement on each one. Their discussion was recorded and subsequently scored using the categories of Bales's interaction-process analysis. The interaction data were then analyzed in terms of the relationship between amount of activity in the discussion and number of decisions won. The experiment provides material for another form of analysis not pursued, namely, the symbolic meanings of agreement between each pair of members on different types of item. What, for example, is the difference between a family in which the mother and father but not the son agree that the father with the athletic son is the more fortunate and a family in which one parent and the son but not the other parent agree on this? Do we have any sound reason for believing that this type of analysis would be less illuminating than the interaction-process analysis? What is revealed by revealed differences? Would not the two types of analysis together be more informative than either alone?

Haley (1962) makes a strong plea for experiments with families and discusses some of the special problems involved in experimenting upon groups whose members have a long history of relationship. He argues that the goal of family experiments must be different from the goal of experimenting with ad hoc groups. Whereas the aim of experiments in social psychology is usually to demonstrate the effect of a particular set of conditions upon group performance, the goal of family experiments, as he sees it, is to describe and measure the way family members typically respond to each other, that is, outside the experimental situation. Although experiments with families do present certain difficulties, many discussed by Haley, it is questionable whether the logic underlying such experiments differs from the logic underlying other types of group experiment as radically as Haley believes it does. In this same paper he reports two experiments in which, all told, 30 families with a schizophrenic member were compared with 30 normal families. The experiments showed that families with a schizophrenic member had a harder time forming coalitions within the family than did normal families. However, he himself questions whether the results can be taken as demonstrating the typical behavior of these families outside the experimental situation. He suggests, however, that this latter problem can be solved by running the same families several times in the same experiment and by running them through different types of experiment designed to test the same basic processes. More generally, Haley sees experimentation as the procedure that will yield a suitable classification of families, and he suggests that whereas the first half of this century has been largely devoted to classifying and describing individuals, the second half of the century will likely be devoted to classifying families and other ongoing organizations. Needless to say, he, like every worker studying whole families, does not underestimate the magnitude of the task, but neither does he overestimate its importance.

## NOTES

1. Most of the studies cited in this paper descend from the seminal thinking of Freud, G. H. Mead, Cooley, and others. Since a full genealogy of ideas is not attempted here, Burgess's formulation is the most appropriate starting point. Further, no effort is made to show the relevance of the work of such significant investigators as Lewin, Sullivan, Erikson, and others; attention is restricted to writers who addressed themselves fairly explicitly to the study of whole families.
2. I thank William E. Henry for suggestions which improved upon my initial concatenation of these assumptions. If the linkage remains unclear, or is proved untenable, the responsibility is mine alone. I express also my appreciation to Sidney J. Levy and Lee Rainwater for their lively and helpful interest in my efforts to use these assumptions in the interpretation of data.

## REFERENCES

1. ACKERMAN, N. W. The unity of the family. *Archives of Pediatrics,* 1938, 55, 51–62.
2. ACKERMAN, N. W. Social role and total personality. *American Journal of Orthopsychiatry,* 1951, 21, 1–17.

3. ACKERMAN, N. W. Interpersonal disturbances in the family: Some unsolved problems in psychotherapy. *Psychiatry*, 1954, 17, 359–368.
4. ACKERMAN, N. W. Interlocking pathology in family relationships. In S. Rado & G. E. Daniels (Eds.), *Changing conceptions of psychoanalytic medicine*. New York: Grune & Stratton, 1956. Pp. 135–150.
5. ACKERMAN, N. W. *The psychodynamics of family life*. Basic Books, 1958.
6. ACKERMAN, N. W. Emergence of family psychotherapy on the present scene. In M. I. Stein (Ed.), *Contemporary psychotherapies*. New York: Free Press of Glencoe, 1961. Pp. 228–244.
7. ACKERMAN, N. W., & SOBEL, R. Family diagnosis: An approach to the preschool child. *American Journal of Orthopsychiatry*, 1950, 20, 744–753.
8. BATESON, G., JACKSON, D. D., HALEY, J., & WEAKLAND, J. Toward a theory of schizophrenia. *Behavioral Science*, 1956, 1, 251–264.
9. BELL, N. W. Extended family relations of disturbed and well families. *Family Process*, 1962, 1, 175–193.
10. BERGMAN, P., & ESCALONA SIBYLLE. Unusual sensitivities in very young children. *Psychoanalytic Study of the Child*, 1949, 4, 333–352.
11. BOSSARD, J. H. S., & BOLL, ELEANOR. *Ritual in family living*. Philadelphia: Univer. Pennsylvania Press, 1950.
12. BOTT, ELIZABETH. *Family and social network: Roles, norms and external relationships in ordinary urban families*. London: Tavistock, 1957.
13. BOWEN, M. A family concept of schizophrenia. In D. D. Jackson (Ed.), *The etiology of schizophrenia*. Basic Books, 1960. Pp. 346–372.
14. BURGESS, E. W. The family as a unity of interacting personalities. *Family*, 1926, 7, 3–9.
15. CLAUSEN, J. A., & KOHN, M. L. Social relations and schizophrenia: A research report and a perspective. In D. D. Jackson (Ed.), *The etiology of schizophrenia*. Basic Books, 1960. Pp. 295–320.
16. CLEVELAND, E. J. & LONGAKER, W. D. Neurotic patterns in the family. In A. Leighton, J. A. Clausen, & R. N. Wilson (Eds.), *Explorations in social psychiatry*. New York: Basic Books, 1957. Pp. 167–200.
17. COUSINS, A. N. The failure of solidarity. In N. W. Bell & E. F. Vogel (Eds.), *A modern introduction to the family*. Glencoe, Ill.: Free Press, 1960. Pp. 403–416.
18. EISENSTEIN, V. W. (Ed.) *Neurotic interaction in marriage*. New York: Basic Books, 1956.
19. ELLES, G. W. The closed circuit: The study of a delinquent family. *British Journal of Criminology*, 1961, 2, 23–39.
20. ESCALONA, SIBYLLE, & HEIDER, GRACE. *Prediction and outcome: A study in child development*. Hogarth Press, 1960.
21. ESCALONA, SIBYLLE, & LEITCH, MARY. Early phases of personality development. *Monographs of the Society for Research in Child Development*, 1952, 17 (1, Whole No. 54).
22. FISHER, S., & MENDELL, D. The communication of neurotic patterns over two and three generations. *Psychiatry*, 1956, 10, 41–46.
23. FISHER, S., & MENDELL, D. The spread of psychotherapeutic effects from the patient to his family group. *Psychiatry*, 1958, 21, 133–140.
24. FLAVELL, J. H. Some observations on schizophrenic thinking: Observation and onset. *Canadian Journal of Psychology*, 1957, 11, 128–132.
25. FLECK, S. Family dynamics and origin of schizophrenia. *Psychosomatic Medicine*, 1960, 22, 333–344.
26. FLECK, S., LIDZ, T., CORNELISON, ALICE, SCHAFER, SARAH, & TERRY, DOROTHY. The intrafamilial environment of the schizophrenic patient: Incestuous and homosexual dynamics. In J. H. Masserman (Ed.), *Individual and familial dynamics*. New York: Grune & Stratton, 1959. Pp. 142–159.
27. FREEMAN, V. J., KLEIN, A. F., RIEHMAN, LYNNE, LUKOFF, I. F., & HEISEY, VIRGINIA. "Family group counseling" as differentiated from other family therapies. *International Journal of Group Psychotherapy*, 1963, 13, 167–175.

28. FRENKEL-BRUNSWIK, ELSE. Differential patterns of social outlook and personality in family and children. In Margaret Mead & Martha Wolfenstein (Eds.), *Childhood in contemporary cultures.* Chicago: Univer. Chicago Press, 1955. Pp. 369–402.

29. FRIES, MARGARET, & WOOLF, P. J. Some hypotheses on the role of the congenital activity type in personality development. *Psychoanalytic Study of the Child,* 1954, 8, 48–62.

30. GETZELS, J. W., & JACKSON, P. *Creativity and intelligence.* Wiley, 1962.

31. GOFFMAN, E. *Encounters: Two studies in the sociology of interaction.* Indianapolis, Ind.: Bobbs-Merrill, 1961.

32. GROTJAHN, M. Analytic family therapy: A survey of trends in research and practice. In J. Masserman (Ed.), Individual and familial dynamics. New York: Grune & Stratton, 1959. Pp. 90–104.

33. GROTJAHN, M. *Psychoanalysis and the family neurosis.* New York: Norton, 1960.

34. GROUP FOR THE ADVANCEMENT OF PSYCHIATRY. *Integration and conflict in family relations.* (Report No. 27) Topeka, Kans.: GAP, 1954.

35. HALEY, J. The family of the schizophrenic: A model system. *Journal of Nervous and Mental Disease,* 1959, 129, 357–374. (a)

36. HALEY, J. An interactional description of schizophrenia. *Psychiatry,* 1959, 22, 321–332. (b)

37. HALEY, J. Family experiments: A new type of experimentation. *Family Process,* 1962, 1, 265–293.

38. HANDEL, G. A study of family and personality. Unpublished doctoral dissertation, University of Chicago, 1962.

39. HANDEL, G., & HESS, R. D. The family as an emotional organization. *Marriage and Family Living,* 1956, 18, 99–101.

40. HARRIS, I. *Normal children and mothers.* Glencoe, Ill.: Free Press, 1959.

41. HENRY, J. Family structure and the transmission of neurotic behavior. *American Journal of Orthopsychiatry,* 1951, 21, 800–818.

42. HENRY, J., & WARSON, S. Family structure and psychic development. *American Journal of Orthopsychiatry,* 1951, 21, 59–73.

43. HENRY, W. E. The thematic apperception technique in the study of group and cultural problems. In H. H. Anderson & Gladys L. Anderson (Eds.), *An introduction to projective techniques.* New York: Prentice-Hall, 1951. Pp. 230–278.

44. HENRY, W. E. *The analysis of fantasy.* Wiley, 1956.

45. HENRY, W. E., & GUETZKOW, H. Group projection sketches for the study of small groups. *Journal of Social Psychology,* 1951, 33, 77–102.

46. HESS, R. D., & HANDEL, G. *Family worlds: A psychosocial approach to family life.* Chicago: Univer. Chicago Press, 1959.

47. HILL, R. *Families under stress: Adjustment to the crises of war separation and reunion.* New York: Harper, 1949.

48. HOFFMAN, LOIS, & LIPPITT, R. The measurement of family life variables. In P. H. Mussen (Ed.), *Handbook of research methods in child development.* New York: Wiley, 1960. Pp. 945–1013.

49. JACKSON, D. D. The question of family homeostasis. Part 1. *Psychiatric Quarterly Supplement,* 1957, 31, 79–90.

50. JACKSON, D. D. Family interaction, family homeostasis and some implications for conjoint family therapy. In J. H. Masserman (Ed.), *Individual and familial dynamics.* New York: Grune & Stratton, 1959. Pp. 122–141.

51. JACKSON, D. D. Family therapy in the family of the schizophrenic. In M. I. Stein (Ed.), *Contemporary psychotherapies.* New York: Free Press of Glencoe, 1961. Pp. 272–287.

52. JACKSON, D. D., RISKIN, J., & SATIR, VIRGINIA. A method of analysis of a family interview. *Archives of General Psychiatry,* 1961, 5, 321–339.

53. JACKSON, D. D., & WEAKLAND, J. Schizophrenic symptoms and family interaction. *Archives of General Psychiatry,* 1959, 1, 618–621.

54. JACKSON, D. D., & WEAKLAND, J. Conjoint family therapy: Some considerations on theory, technique and results. *Psychiatry*, 1961, 24(2, Suppl.), 30–45.
55. JOSSLYN, IRENE. The family as a psychological unit. *Social Casework*, 1953, 34, 336–343.
56. KAPLAN, B. *Studying personality cross-culturally*. Evanston, Ill.: Row, Peterson, 1961.
57. KLUCKHOHN, C., & MURRAY, H. A. *Personality in nature, society and culture*. New York: Knopf, 1948.
58. KLUCKHOHN, FLORENCE. Dominant and substitute profiles of cultural orientations: Their significance for the analysis of social stratification. *Social Forces*, 1950, 28, 276–293.
59. LEICHTER, HOPE J. Boundaries of the family as an empirical and theoretical unit. In N. W. Ackerman, Frances L. Beatman, & S. N. Sherman (Eds.), *Exploring the base for family therapy*. New York: Family Service Association, 1961. Pp. 140–144.
60. LEWIN, K., LIPPITT, R., & WHITE, R. K. Patterns of aggressive behavior in experimentally created "social climates." *Journal of Social Psychology*, 1939, 10, 271–299.
61. LEWIS, O. An anthropological approach to family studies. *American Journal of Sociology*, 1950, 55, 468–475.
62. LEWIS, O. *Five families: Mexican case studies in the culture of poverty*. Basic Books, 1959.
63. LEWIS, O. *The children of Sanchez*. Secker & Warburg, 1962.
64. LIDZ, T., CORNELISON, ALICE, FLECK, S., & TERRY, DOROTHY. The intrafamilial environment of the schizophrenic patient: II. Marital schism and marital skew. *American Journal of Psychiatry*, 1957, 114, 241–248.
65. LIDZ, T., CORNELISON, ALICE, TERRY, DOROTHY, & FLECK, S. Intrafamilial environment of the schizophrenic patient: VI. The transmission of irrationality. *Archives of Neurology and Psychiatry*, 1958, 79, 305–316.
66. LIDZ, T., FLECK, S., CORNELISON, ALICE, & TERRY, DOROTHY. Intrafamilial environment of the schizophrenic patient: IV. Parental personalities and family interaction. *American Journal of Orthopsychiatry*, 1958, 28, 764–776.
67. LU, YI-CHUANG. Mother-child role relationships in schizophrenia: A comparison of schizophrenic patients with non-schizophrenic siblings. *Psychiatry*, 1961, 24, 133–142.
68. MEAD, MARGARET. *Coming of age in Samoa*. Penguin.
69. MENDELL, D., & FISHER, S. An approach to neurotic behavior in terms of a three-generation family model. *Journal of Nervous and Mental Disease*, 1956, 123, 171–180.
70. MENDELL, D., & FISHER, S. A multi-generation approach to treatment of psychopathology. *Journal of Nervous and Mental Disease*, 1958, 126, 523–529.
71. MILLER, D. Personality and social interaction. In B. Kaplan (Ed.), *Studying personality cross-culturally*. Evanston, Ill.: Row, Peterson, 1961. Pp. 271–298.
72. MITTELMAN, B. Complementary neurotic reactions in intimate relationships. *Psychoanalytic Quarterly*, 1944, 13, 479–491.
73. MITTELMAN, B. The concurrent analysis of married couples. *Psychoanalytic Quarterly*, 1948, 17, 182–197.
74. MURPHY, LOIS. *The widening world of childhood*. New York: Basic Books, 1962.
75. NEIMAN, L. J., & HUGHES, J. W. The problem of the concept of role: A re-survey of the literature. *Social Forces*, 1951, 30, 141–149.
76. OBERNDORF, C. P. Psychoanalysis of married couples. *Psychoanalytic Review*, 1938, 25, 453–465.
77. PARSONS, T., & BALES, R. F. *Family, socialization and interaction process*. Routledge & Kegan Paul, 1956.
78. POWDERMAKER, FLORENCE. Concepts found useful in the treatment of schizoid and ambulatory schizophrenic patients. *Psychiatry*, 1952, 15, 61–71.
79. REDL, F. Group emotion and leadership. *Psychiatry*, 1942, 5, 573–596.

80. ROBB, J. H. Experiences with ordinary families. *British Journal of Medical Psychology*, 1953, 26, 215–221.

81. ROBERTS, J. M. Three Navaho households: A comparative study in small group culture. *Papers of the Peabody Museum of American Archaeology and Ethnology, Harvard University*, 1951, 40(3).

82. ROSE, A. A systematic summary of symbolic interaction theory. In A. Rose (ed.), *Human behavior and social processes*. Boston, Mass.: Houghton Mifflin, 1962. Pp. 3–19.

83. ROSENZWEIG, S., & CASS, LORETTA K. The extension of psychodiagnosis to parents in the child guidance setting. *American Journal of Orthopsychiatry*, 1954, 24, 715–722.

84. ROSENZWEIG, S., & ISHAM, A. C. Complementary Thematic Apperception Test patterns in close kin. *American Journal of Orthopsychiatry*, 1947, 17, 129–142.

85. RYCKOFF, I., DAY, JULIANA, & WYNNE, L. C. Maintenance of stereotyped roles in the families of schizophrenics. *Archives of General Psychiatry*, 1959, 1, 109–114.

86. SARBIN, T. R. Role theory. In G. Lindzey (Ed.), *Handbook of social psychology*. Vol. 1. Cambridge, Mass.: Addison-Wesley, 1954. Pp. 223–258.

87. SARGENT, S. S. Conceptions of role and ego in contemporary psychology. In J. H. Rohrer & M. Sherif (Eds.), *Social psychology at the crossroads*. New York: Harper, 1951.

88. SHERIF, M. *The psychology of social norms*. New York: Harper, 1936.

89. SOHLER, DOROTHY TERRY, HOLZBERG, J. D., FLECK, S., CORNELISON, ALICE, KAY, ELEANOR, & LIDZ, T. The prediction of family interaction from a battery of projective tests. *Journal of Projective Techniques*, 1957, 21, 199–208.

90. SPIEGEL, J., & BELL, N. W. The family of the psychiatric patient. In S. Arieti (Ed.), *American handbook of psychiatry*. New York: Basic Books, 1959. Pp. 114–149.

91. STRODTBECK, F. L. The family as a three-person group. *American Sociological Review*, 1954, 19, 23–29.

92. STRODTBECK, F. L. Family interaction, values and achievement. In D. McClelland, A. Baldwin, U. Bronfenbrenner, & F. L. Strodtbeck, *Talent and society*. Princeton, N. J.: Van Nostrand, 1958. Pp. 135–194.

93. THARP, R. Psychological patterning in marriage. *Psychological Bulletin*, 1963, 60, 97–117.

94. TITCHENER, J., RISKIN, J., & EMERSON, R. The family in psychosomatic process: A case report illustrating a method of psychosomatic research. *Psychosomatic Medicine*, 1960, 22, 127–142.

95. VOGEL, E. F., & BELL, N. W. The emotionally disturbed child as the family scapegoat. In N. W. Bell & E. F. Vogel (Eds.), *A modern introduction to the family*. Routledge & Kegan Paul, 1961.

96. VOILAND, ALICE L. *Family casework diagnosis*. New York: Columbia Univer. Press, 1962.

97. WEAKLAND, J. H. The "double-bind" hypothesis of schizophrenia and three-party interaction. In D. D. Jackson (Ed.), *The etiology of schizophrenia*. New York: Basic Books, 1960. Pp. 373–388.

98. WHITE, R. Abnormalities of behavior. *Annual Review of Psychology*, 1959, 10, 265–286.

99. WYNNE, L. C. The study of intrafamilial alignments and splits in exploratory family therapy. In N. W. Ackerman, Frances L. Beatman, & S. N. Sherman (eds.), *Exploring the base for family therapy*. New York: Family Service Association, 1961. Pp. 95–115.

100. WYNNE, L. C., RYCKOFF, I. M., DAY, JULIANA, & HIRSCH, S. I. Pseudo-mutuality in the family relations of schizophrenics. *Psychiatry*, 1958, 21, 205–220.

# INDEX

# Index

Acculturation, 426
Ackerman, Nathan W., 200, 203 n., 404, 519, 521–522, 535–536
Activity, unconscious, 207
  symbolic, 278
Adler, Alfred, 162, 441 n.
Adolescent peer groups, 372
Adorno, T. W., 182
Adultery, 144, 238
Age-sex structure, 472
Alanen, Y., 253
Alignment, pattern of, 23, 530
Alliances; see Coalition
Anomie, 174
Asch, Solomon, 346
Atmosphere, emotional, 12
Attitudes, personal, 147
Authoritarian family, 292, 295
Authority, 67
  parental, 22–23, 228, 308, 310
  patriarchal, 379
  structure, 346
Autistic processes, 278
Autonomy of couple, 334, 357 n.
  in the Negro family system, 368
  and sexual relations, 343
Avebury, John L., 336

Bachelor, 238
  See also Decision, to marry
Bales, Robert F., 89 n., 123 n., 346, 359 n., 465 n., 510–511, 517, 523, 526, 529, 531, 545
Barnard, C. I., 221
Barnes, John A., 145
Bateson, Gregory, 55–56, 78 n., 252–253, 274 n., 284, 465 n., 469–471, 473–475, 477–479, 487, 494, 496–497, 499–501, 503–508, 511–513, 529, 539
Bell, Norman W., 187, 329–330, 441 n., 469, 519, 525, 533–536, 541
Bergman, P., 520
Bettelheim, Bruno, 30, 46 n.
Bion, W. R., 346
Biosocial issues, 21, 530

Birth, 10, 105
Blos, Peter, 340
Body, meanings and functions, 2, 282, 305, 337, 344, 374–376, 391–392
Boll, Eleanor, 523
Bossard, J. H. S., 523
Bott, Elizabeth, 129, 194, 235–239, 242, 245 n., 525, 542
Bowen, M., 55, 252, 284, 482–483, 497, 507, 522, 532, 534, 536, 542
Boy friends, 385
Brain, dysfunction of, 277
Brodey, W., 194, 202, 482–483, 497, 507
Broom, L., 220
Burgess, E. W., 154, 188, 292, 519–521, 523, 527, 546 n.

Caplan, Gerald, 339, 353–356
Caputo, D., 510
Caribbean mating pattern, 369
Carlson, Dorothy Terry, 29, 276, 280, 532, 534, 537, 541, 543
Cass, Loretta K., 543
Castration anxiety, 171
  symbolism, 171
Chance, E., 404
Cheek, Frances, 510–511
Child-rearing practices, 424, 435
Christensen, Harold T., 4, 8 n.
Clark, Kenneth, 395
Clausen, J. A., 532
Cleveland, Eric J., 129, 184 n., 519, 524–525
Coalition, 28, 60, 72–73, 75–76, 81, 259, 263–264
  See also Alignment, pattern of
Cognition, 540–541
  See also Thinking; Thought disorders
Communication, 67–68, 106, 232, 249, 257–258, 422, 471, 473, 539
  and erogenous zones, 171
  patterns, 28
  system, 105
  and values, 171
Community mental health, 353–354

Conflict, 91, 148, 230, 252
    family, 193–196
    of norms, 154–155
    resolution of, 422
    symbolization of, 427–432
    value conflict, 161, 168–169, 178,
        183, 245 n.
Conformity, 153, 308
Conjugal roles; *see* Roles, conjugal
Connectedness; *see* Separateness-
        Connectedness patterns
Consultation, mental health, 354
Cooley, C. H., 222, 546 n.
Cooperation, 346
Coping processes, 347, 366
Cornelison, Alice, 532, 534, 537, 541,
        543
Cottrell, Leonard, 348
Counselling, 354
Cousins, A. N., 523
Crawley, Ernest, 333
Crisis, 148, 328
*Critical role transition; see* Marriage, as
        critical role transition
Critical transition points, 352
Crying, 105–106
Cultural alternatives, 129
Culture, 11, 31–32, 108, 125–131, 523–
        526
    covert aspects of, 136
    patterns, 136, 139
Cycles, interpersonal, 418


Day, Juliana, 330, 531, 533
Decision, 66–67, 88, 226
    to marry, 377, 408–409
Defense, 264–265, 284
Dependent relationship, and transmis-
        sion of values, 180
Development, psychosocial, 106, 111
    *See also* Identification; Internaliza-
        tion; Personality, development;
        Role, expectation reinforcement;
        Socialization
Deviance, 111, 153
Diagnosis, 60–62
    *See also* Methodology, classification
Discipline, 306–307, 311
Disparagement, 161–162, 174–179, 182
Displacement, 157
Divorce, 238
    *See also* Marital disruption
"Double bind" hypothesis, 253, 261,
        471, 473–479, 487–488, 491,
        499–501, 505
Drake, St. Clair, 363, 397 n.

Eisenstein, V. W., 518
Eissler, Kurt R., 218, 441 n.
Elles, Gillian W., 187, 536
Ellison, Ralph, 362
Emerson, Richard, 329, 536
Energy, family, 207
    sexual, 337
Engel, George L., 401–403
Epstein, Nathan B., 198
Equalitarian family, 308 ff.
Equilibrium, 190–191, 283, 425, 435,
        471, 479–480, 499, 523
Erikson, Erik H., 13, 185 n., 244 n., 340,
        399 n., 444, 460, 464 n., 492,
        546 n.
Escalona, Sibylle, 520
Ethnocentrism, 294
Extended families, 6, 518–519


Fallding, Harold, 187–188
Families, authoritarian, 292, 295
    classification of, 546
    and culture, 523–526
    middle class, 336, 371
    normal, 72–76, 479
    "ordinary," 155
    of orientation, 427
    schizogenic, 472–488
    schizophrenic, 55, 60, 72–76
    working class, 187, 191
Family and community, 426–427, 437–
        439
Family, corporate character of, 3, 64–
        65
    boundaries, 2, 10, 19, 187, 203, 519,
        530
        in schizophrenic family, 450
    conflict, 192–198
    correlative meaning, 29, 544
    creation of meaning, 29, 104 ff.
    culture, 126–129
    energy, 207
    pattern of alignment, 23, 530
    regulatory processes, 65–68, 231, 249,
        271, 273, 476, 499–504
    themes, 17, 208, 214, 216, 258, 530,
        536–537
    *See also* Authority; Coalition; Com-
        munication; Interaction; Inter-
        personal relations; Separateness-
        Connectedness patterns
Family legend, 403, 410, 451
Family planning, 344
Fantasy, 10, 218, 249, 448
    interlocking, 187, 206
Farina, A., 510
Faris, E., 222, 245 n.

Fenichel, O., 302, 340
Fidelity, 379
Fiedler, Leslie, 367
Fisher, S., 519, 522, 536, 543–544
Flavell, J. H., 541
Fleck, Stephen, 55, 282, 488, 496, 532, 534, 537, 541, 543
Flugel, J., 353
Focal attention, 493
*Folie à famille,* 282
Foote, Nelson, 348
Frank, Lawrence K., 110
Frazee, H. E., 252
Frazer, Sir James, 424
Frazier, E. Franklin, 366
Freedom, personal, 224–226, 233
    *See also* Privacy
Freeman, V. J., 522
Frenkel-Brunswik, Else, 250, 327, 519, 525, 541
Freud, Sigmund, 441 n., 442 n., 546 n.
Fried, Marc, 339
Friendship, 236, 238
Fries, Margaret, 520

Generalized other, 220
Gerard, D. L., 252
Getzels, J. W., 541
Gillen, Francis J., 333
Gough, K., 335
Gluckman, Max, 142, 332, 339
Goffman, E., 359 n., 535
Grandmothers, 384
Grotjahn, M., 521–522
Group, household, 387
    primary, 222
    small, 346
Guetzkow, H., 544

Haley, Jay, 27–28, 78 n., 249, 274 n., 330, 465 n., 475–478, 487–488, 490–491, 500–501, 503–504, 511–513, 539–540, 544–546
Handel, Gerald, 27, 29, 123 n., 397–400 n., 518–519, 525, 529–531, 534–537, 542–545
Harris, I., 520
Heider, Grace, 520
Heisey, Virginia, 522
Henry, Jules, 26, 29 n., 46 n., 297 n., 525, 528
Henry, William E., 54 n., 110, 117, 123–124 n., 544, 546 n.
Hess, Robert D., 27, 123 n., 400 n., 518–519, 525, 529–531, 534–536, 542–545

Hill, Lewis B., 448
Hill, R., 517, 521
Hirsch, Stanley I., 330, 531
Hoffman, Lois, 517–519, 528
Holzberg, J. D., 543
Homeostasis, 499
    *See also* Equilibrium
Homosexuality, 123 n., 238
Hotel keepers, 354
Household groups, 387
    Negro, 370
    openness of, 383
Housework, 144
Hughes, J. W., 535
Husband-wife relationship, 36, 42, 105, 145, 378–380

Identification, fragmented, 217
    of child with parent, 182–183, 429
    of parent with child, 192
Identity, 330, 343–344, 367, 444, 459, 472
    crisis, 460
    formation, 495
    salient, 220
Images, 14–17
    of family life, 372
Imagination, 306, 315, 322
    *See also* Fantasy
Incest, 330, 481
Individuality, 1, 6, 11
Individuation; *see* Development, psychosocial; Separateness-Connectedness
Inferiority complex; *see* Disparagement
Institutions, 292
    meaning of, 129, 136
Instrumental-expressive axis, 346
Integration, family, 3
    role, 220–221, 241
Interaction, 10, 22, 32, 105, 156–158, 190, 346, 527
    analysis, 81
    parental, 173, 425
    patterns in schizogenic families, 473–488, 498–504, 517–518
Interests, shared, 145, 227–232
Internalization of family role structure, 432–435, 457–459
Interpersonal bonds, 12, 14
    cycles, 418
    relations, 105
    relationship, 346, 518, 527
Intimacy, 327–328, 337, 343, 345–346
Introjection, 157–158
Isham, A. C., 543

Jackson, Don D., 253, 274 n., 465 n.,
    478, 512–513 n., 522–523, 529,
    539–540
Jackson, P., 541
Jahoda, Marie, 354
Janis, Irving, 339
Jealousy, 98
Johnson, Adelaide M., 179, 441 n.
Joining dynamics, 334
Josselyn, Irene, 526


Kaplan, B., 524
Kaplan, D., 339
Kay, Eleanor, 543
Kendall, M. G., 85, 89 n.
Kinship, 240
    extended system, 367
    solidarity, 236
    systems, 191
Klein, A. F., 522
Klopfer, Bruno, 92
Kluckhohn, Clyde, 125, 130 n., 440 n.,
    524
Kluckhohn, Florence R., 89 n., 184 n.,
    191, 201, 404, 440–441 n., 525,
    533, 537
Kohn, M. L., 532
Kramer, M., 496
Kroeber, Alfred L., 125, 130 n., 136


Labor, division of, 144–145
Laing, R., 477–478
Language, 247–249
    acquisition of, 496
Leadership, 258, 263
Learning, 161–162, 177, 207
    environment, 492
    situation, 265
Leichter, Hope J., 519
Leighton, Alexander, 524
Leitch, Mary, 520
Leites, Nathan, 305
Levy, Sidney J., 124 n., 128, 546 n.
Lewin, K., 245 n., 527, 546 n.
Lewis, Oscar, 128, 140 n., 188, 517
Lidz, Ruth W., 251
Lidz, Theodore, 249, 251, 281–283,
    469–472, 479–483, 487–488,
    495–498, 501–506, 508, 512 n.,
    513, 522, 532, 534, 537, 541, 543
Life style, 5
Lindemann, Eric, 339, 353, 419
Linton, R., 221
Lippitt, R., 517–519, 527–528
Locke, B. Z., 496

Loeb, E. M., 335
Loneliness, 234
Longaker, William D., 129, 184 n., 519,
    524–525
Love, romantic, 332, 336
Lower class, 328
Lu, Yi-chuang, 497, 507, 512 n., 532
Luchins, A. S., 319
Lukoff, I. F., 522


McGinnis, R., 292
Machover, Karen, 92
Mailer, Norman, 367
Malinowski, Bronislaw, 135–136, 140 n.
Mannheim, Karl, 248
Marital disruption, 380–382
Marital schism, 479
Marital skew, 479–480, 482, 504, 506,
    532
Marriage, 105, 108–109, 190, 204 n.,
    225, 328
    as critical role transition, 339–342
    and culture, 332–338
    free choice in, 338
    rituals, 332–335
Masculinity, 98, 390
Masking, 285
Mason, E., 339
Mass media, 149
Matrifocality, 379
Mead, George Herbert, 158, 220–221,
    239, 241, 243–244 n., 529, 546 n.
Mead, Margaret, 126, 130 n., 292, 524
Meaning, 484–485
    and context, 151
    correlative, 104
    creation of, 105–107, 157, 329
    individual, 327
    interpersonal, 327, 330
    levels of, 475
    of physical defect, 430
    of the self, 458
Medicine, psychosomatic, 1, 329
Mendell, D., 519, 522, 536, 543–544
Mental content, 249–250
Mental health, 159, 189, 352–354, 522,
    531
    consultation, 354
Mental illness, 5, 91, 111, 159, 189,
    191, 200
Merton, Robert K., 174
Methodology, v., 4, 7, 8 n., 9
    assumptions, 171, 470
    cause-effect model, 517, 519
    classification, 27, 54–55, 60, 78, 223 ff.,
        272–274, 280, 535, 538, 539, 540,
        546

conceptualization, 8 n., 9, 512, 521, 523 ff.
experiment, 7, 509–511, 545–546
  validity of, 26, 77
generalization, 90, 135, 160
hypothesis, 68, 87, 91, 104, 444, 471, 512
interpretation, validity of, 122
observation, 3, 8 n., 31–35, 56, 66, 68, 102–103, 253, 467
paradigms, 293
prediction, 93–96
qualitative, 7, 8 n.
quantification, v., 7, 8 n., 56, 154
sampling, 56, 59–63, 71–72, 132
theory, 470 ff.
types, 223 ff., 272–274, 538, 540
validity, of experiment, 26, 77
  of interpretation, 122
  of projective techniques, 91
See also Research methods
Middle class, 327–328, 336, 426, 431
  Negro, 362–363, 365, 371
Miller, D., 520
Miller, Walter B., 393, 399–400 n.
Mills, Theodore M., 83–89
Mishler, Elliot G., 467, 496, 511
Mittelman, B., 521
Models, parental, 149, 182
  role, 386
Mother-child relationship, 280, 329, 402, 422, 424
  role of, 146
Moynihan, Daniel Patrick, 386
Murphy, Lois B., 347, 534
Murray, H. A., 524, 535
Mussen, Paul H., 4, 8 n.
Mutuality, 330
  pseudo, 330, 345, 445

Nadel, S. F., 220
Need complementarity, 331 n.
Needs, 91, 98, 160, 330
Neiman, L. J., 535
Neurosis, precipitation of, 180 ff.
Norms, 129, 141–144, 146–148, 428, 433, 436
  conflicts of, 154–155
  internalization of, 157

Oberndorf, C. P., 521
Object loss, 402
Object relations, 404, 422
Oedipus complex, 173
Ogburn, W. F., 292

O'Neill, Eugene, 286
Oppenheimer, Robert, v., 7, 8 n., 467
Oral phase, 280
Ordinal position, 519–520
Orientation, 111
  families of, 427
  value, 426
  to the world, 115, 118

Parent-child relationships, 92, 226, 424–425
Parsons, Elsie Clews, 135
Parsons, Talcott, 89 n., 123 n., 188, 204 n., 244 n., 246 n., 346, 359 n., 399 n., 442 n., 446, 464–465 n., 479, 517, 523, 526, 531, 534
Participation, stability of, 85, 88
Peer groups, adolescent, 372
Perception, 249, 317–320
Perceval, John, 489–490
Personal time, 106
Personality, 110, 131, 188, 321, 425–426, 527 ff.
  development, 135, 327
Phantasy; see Fantasy
Piaget, Jean, 529
Pincus, Lily, 343, 353
Powdermaker, Florence, 541
Power, 84, 88, 427–428, 432, 475
  See also Authority
Pregnancy, premarital, 374–376
Preventive intervention, 353
Primary group, 222, 239
Privacy, 23, 98, 109, 453–454
  See also Secrecy
Projection, 157–158
Psychoanalysis, 157, 481
Psychology, social, 327, 330
Psychopathology, 159
  See also Mental illness
Psychosomatic medicine, 329
Psychotic episode, 265

Radcliffe-Brown, A. R., 190
Rainwater, Lee, 124 n., 328, 398–400 n., 546 n.
Rapoport, Rhona, 327–328, 333, 356 n., 512 n.
Rapoport, Robert N., 219 n., 327–328, 339, 356 n.
Reality testing, 277, 279
Redfield, Robert, 4, 8 n., 131, 136
Redl, F., 531
Reference groups, 150–152, 157, 158 n.

Regulatory process; *see* Family, corporate character of
Reichard, S., 252
Relationships, father-child, 425
  husband-wife, 144, 378
  interpersonal, 105, 346, 518
  intrafamilial, 6
  mother-child, 280, 329, 402, 422, 424
  parent-child, 92, 226
  sexual, 334, 342–343, 373
Religious teaching, 149
Rennie, Thomas A. C., 280
Research methods, 25–29, 541–546
  autobiography, 135
  case study, 11, 135–136, 139–140
  Draw-A-Person Test, 92, 102, 543
  field work, 26, 136, 139, 143, 542
  interviewing, 134, 147 ff., 404–405
  participant observation, 134
  projective techniques, 28, 132, 135, 137, 190–191, 543
  psychometric method, 25
  Rorschach Test, 92, 99, 102, 132, 134, 543
  Sentence Completion Test, 92, 99, 102, 543
  TAT, 29, 92, 102, 104, 109–110, 315, 484, 537, 543–544
  tests, psychological, 132, 134–135
Richardson, Henry B., 189
Riehman, Lynne, 522
Riskin, Jules, 329, 536, 540
*Rites de passage,* 332
Rituals, of marriage, 333–335, 339
Robb, J. H., 542
Roberts, John M., 126–128, 130 n., 525
Rogers, Carl, 529
Rokeach, M., 319
Role, 535
  expectation reinforcement, 235, 239
  models, 386
  reciprocity, 480
  in schizophrenic family system, 447–451
  segregation, 236
  structure, 479, 482, 486
  and subjective experience, 463
  transition, 332, 339–342
Role induction, 432–435
  *See also* Internalization of family role structure
Roles, 160
  cardinal, 188
  for the child, 92
  conjugal, 141, 144–145, 225, 235, 379
  familial, occupational, 148
  -integration, 220–221, 241

intrafamilial allocation, 194
  of the mother, 146
  relationship, 211
  sex, 106, 320
Roman Catholic Church, 241
Roscoe, John, 333
Rose, A. A., 529
Rosenzweig, S., 543
Rubber fence, 450
Rules; *see* Family, corporate character of
Russell, Bertrand, 475
Ryckoff, Irving M., 330, 531, 533

Salient identity, 220
Sanua, V., 469
Sarbin, T. R., 535
Sargent, S. S., 535
Satir, Virginia, 540
Schachtel, Ernest, 493
Schafer, Sarah, 537
Schizophrenia, 55, 60–61, 72–76, 276–290, 330, 488–498, 539
  age-sex structure, 472
  behavior, 266–267
  definitions of, 497
  predisposing factors in the development of, 504–508
  role in family system, 447–451
Schizophrenics, siblings of, 532
Scotch, N., 496
Searles, Harold F., 465 n., 477, 501, 504
Secrecy, 453–454, 458, 486
  *See also* Privacy
Seduction, 373–374
Segregation, sexual, 236
  role-segregation, 236, 379
Self, 104 ff.
  confirmation of, 477
  devaluation, 174, 178
  disparagement, 161, 182
  -image, 174
  meaning of, 458
Self-corrective system, 273
  *See also* Family, corporate character of
Selznick, P., 220
Separateness-Connectedness patterns, 10–12, 115–116, 118, 120, 145, 444, 455–456, 462–463, 529
  and clinical behavior pathology, 531, 534
Separation dynamics, 333
Sex, age-sex structure, 472
  and autonomy, 343
  energy, 337

experimentation, 334
in-groups, 236
relations, 342–343, 373
relationships, 335
role, 106, 320
segregation, 236
Sexuality, 2, 109
orientations to, 344
premarital, 336, 342
Sherif, M., 158 n., 245 n., 525, 529
Shils, Edward A., 89 n., 464 n.
Sibling position, 428
Sibling relationships, 4, 105, 328
rivalry, 139, 531
of schizophrenics, 532
support, 531
Siegel, J., 252, 275 n.
Simmel, Georg, 87, 89 n.
Singer, Margaret, 483–485, 492–494, 506–507
Sobel, R., 519
Social change, 154
Social class, 11, 327–328
Social interaction, 346
Social mobility, 111
Social networks, 144–148, 150, 152, 194, 235
Social psychology, 327, 330
Socialization, 106, 178–179
process, 183
techniques of, 179
See also Development, psychosocial
Socialization discrepancy, 111
Society, 108–109, 141–142, 150, 173, 190, 218, 238–240
Sohler, Dorothy Terry; see Carlson, Dorothy Terry
Solidarity, 236, 424, 437–438, 523
Spencer, Walter B., 333
Spiegel, John P., 191, 400 n., 404, 440–442 n., 465 n., 469, 480–481, 519, 525, 533
Street system, 367, 372
Strindberg, August, 286
Strodtbeck, Fred L., 28, 89 n., 398 n., 400 n., 441 n., 510, 518, 545
Sullivan, Harry Stack, 171, 174, 179, 465 n., 529, 546 n.
Support, 82–84, 87–88, 193, 198
Survival strategies, 393
Symbolic processes, 172, 276, 278–279
Symbolism, castration, 171
ceremonial, 333
of names, 448
oral-incorporative, 185 n.
Symbolization, of conflict, 427–432
of reality, 279

Symptoms, physiologic, 181
presenting, 5
System; see Family, corporate character of

Task accomplishment, 347, 352, 354
Terry, Dorothy; see Carlson, Dorothy Terry
Tharp, R., 517–518
Therapy, 522, 542
Thinking, 247–249, 317 ff.
Thought disorders, 493–495
Tillman, G., 252
Time, personal, 106
Titchener, James L., 329–330, 536
Tomkins, Silvan, 338
Treatment, 207, 211, 217–218
strategies of, 202
Tyhurst, James, 339

Unconscious activity, 207 ff.

Value conflict, 161, 168–169, 178, 183, 245 n.
orientation, 426, 525–526
sources, 160
systems, 32, 128, 130, 172–173, 201
Values, 130
mediation of, 159
transmission of, 160, 172
Van Gennep, Arnold, 332–333, 339
Victimization process, of Negro, 363, 387
Vogel, Ezra F., 329–330, 400 n., 441 n., 533–536, 541
Voiland, Alice L., 517, 538, 544

Warson, S., 528
Watzlawick, P. A., 473
Waxler, Nancy E., 467, 511
Weakland, John H., 78–79 n., 274 n., 465 n., 522, 539
Westermarck, Edward, 333
Westley, William A., 198
White, R. K., 527
White, Robert W., 348, 517, 519
Whorf, Benjamin Lee, 247–248
Williams, Tennessee, 286, 358 n.
Willmott, P., 237
Wilson, M., 245 n.
Winch, R. F., 292
Wolfenstein, Martha, 305
Woodworth, Robert S., 293

Woolf, P. J., 520
Wynne, Lyman C., 55, 252, 330, 469–
       470,   472,   483–488,   492–498,
       502–509,  511–513,  531,  533–534

Young, M., 237

Zimmerman, C. C., 292

*Auckland: P.O. Box 36013, Northcote Central, N.4*
*Barbados: P.O. Box 222, Bridgetown*
*Beirut: Deeb Building, Jeanne d'Arc Street*
*Bombay: 15 Graham Road, Ballard Estate, Bombay 1*
*Buenos Aires: Escritorio 454–459, Florida 165*
*Calcutta: 17 Chittaranjan Avenue, Calcutta 13*
*Cape Town: 68 Shortmarket Street*
*Hong Kong: 105 Wing On Mansion, 26 Hancow Road, Kowloon*
*Ibadan: P.O. Box 62*
*Karachi: Karachi Chambers, McLeod Road*
*Madras: Mohan Mansions, 38c Mount Road, Madras 6*
*Mexico: Villalongin 32, Mexico 5, D.F.*
*Nairobi: P.O. Box 30583*
*New Delhi: 13–14 Asaf Ali Road, New Delhi 1*
*Ontario: 81 Curlew Drive, Don Mills*
*Philippines: P.O. Box 4322, Manilla*
*Rio de Janeiro: Caixa Postal 2537-Zc-00*
*Singapore: 36c Prinsep Street, Singapore 7*
*Sydney, N.S.W.: Bradbury House, 55 York Street*
*Tokyo: P.O. Box 26, Kamata*

NATIONAL INSTITUTE FOR SOCIAL WORK TRAINING SERIES


READINGS IN SOCIAL WORK   VOL. I
# SOCIAL WORK WITH FAMILIES

This book gathers together some outstanding contributions to various aspects of social work with families. This subject is now more than ever of concern to social workers as fresh knowledge adds to their understanding of the dynamics of family life and interaction. The papers which compose this book are by well-known authors on both sides of the Atlantic. They are arranged in three sections, dealing with normal and less normal families as a group, with particular crisis situations for children, and with some more theoretical concepts contributing to an understanding of family types.


# ADOPTION POLICY AND PRACTICE
Iris Goodacre

How are adoptions arranged? How far do the present adoption services really meet the needs of the adoptive family? These are the questions examined in this searching investigation—one of the few to be undertaken since legal adoption was introduced in this country in 1926.

The scope of the survey is comprehensive for every type of adoption is included: those arranged by societies, by local authorities, by relatives and private individuals. Each step in the process is described and appraised both from the angle of the agencies and of the adopters.

The careful analysis of agency policy and practice and the compelling accounts of the adopters' experiences and attitudes makes this report of particular interest to anyone concerned with the development of this branch of the social services.

The writer has had extensive and varied social work experience, both in the statutory and voluntary field, and has herself arranged adoptions.


# LONDON: GEORGE ALLEN & UNWIN LTD